CHESHIRE
Its Traditions & History

Including
A RECORD OF THE
RISE AND PROGRESS OF FREEMASONRY
IN THIS ANCIENT PROVINCE

By
ALFRED INGHAM
Fellow of the Royal Historical Society

Author of "The History of Altrincham and Bowdon"; Annals of "The Caledonian Lodge, No. 204"; "A Cheshire Patriot"; Historical Drama, &c., &c.

TO THE READER:

" Peruse with heede, then friendlie judge,
And blaming rashe refraine ;
So maist thou rede unto thy goode,
And shall requite my paine."

Whitney's Emblems, A.D. 1586.

Copyright © 2018 Read Books Ltd.
This book is copyright and may not be
reproduced or copied in any way without
the express permission of the publisher in writing

British Library Cataloguing-in-Publication Data
A catalogue record for this book is available from
the British Library

INTRODUCTORY CHAPTER

BY

JUDGE JAMES BARKER.

EARLY SETTLEMENT OF CHESHIRE.

CAUSES LEADING TO THE INCORPORATION OF A TOWN. FIRST SALES OF LAND. NICHOLAS COOK AND JOSEPH BENNET. NEW PROVIDENCE. CAPT. JOAB STAFFORD. THE NOTCH BURYING GROUND. JOHN WELLS. SCENERY. LAND GIVEN FOR THE SUPPORT OF THE GOSPEL. CAPT. SAMUEL LOW HOLDS SLAVES. EPITAPH OF ELDER PETER WERDEN.

THE town of Cheshire was incorporated on the 14th of March, 1793. The title of the Act indicated that its territory was made up of parts of the towns of Lanesborough, Windsor, Adams and of the District of New Ashford, the inhabitants of New Ashford not having been incorporated as a town until May 1st, 1836.

On the 6th of February, 1798, so much of the farm of Jacob Cole, of New Ashford, as lay in that district was, "together with the said Jacob and his personal estate, set off from the said district, and annexed to the town of Cheshire, there to do duty and receive privileges." This annexation added three more to the twenty corners made by its boundary lines, and established its pre-eminence in this respect over all the towns in the Commonwealth on a so much firmer footing. Whether this predilection for corners came from the same cause which has made the population, and business and social life of the place desert its once thickly settled hill-tops, and congregate in that locality of the town known as Cheshire Corners, is a question which may at some future day be settled by the scientific branch of our Association. But it is reasonably certain that the bounds given in the Act of Incorporation, were not the result of an attempt to follow physical boundaries, but to bring into a community people of like tastes and religious feelings as far as possible. The attempt seems to have been remarkably successful, and the people of Cheshire to have been so remarkably unanimous even in political sentiment as to make current the familiar tradition that when the first lone opposition ballot was put in the box by a citizen opposed in politics to all his neighbors, it was thrown out by the selectmen as having evidently been cast by mistake. It is among the earlier settlers of this territory that we must look for the leaven which was powerful enough to work throughout a township, creating the town in the first instance, and continuing its power until substantially all its citizens seem to have been united in sentiment, and vigorous and earnest in its expression.

These earlier settlers came more largely than the settlers of any other considerable portion of Berkshire from the Colony of Rhode Island and Providence Plantations. They were descendants, some of them of the very men who were the first to follow Roger Williams to Rhode Island, and generally they were men who had inherited and imbibed the spirit of her free institutions, and were educated in the religious beliefs prevalent in that colony rather than in the orthodoxy of the Massachusetts Colony.

The present paper will not be able to give the story of their emigration from Rhode Island, and their settlement in Berkshire in any connected form, or with a claim to that accuracy which ought to be attained in the documents prepared for an historical society. At most it will only gather the names and some facts in the lives of these early settlers, and call your attention to a village once flourishing and beautiful, but which has now utterly disappeared. A Berkshire hill-top once crowned with a church, and hillsides once dotted with farm houses and tenanted by a vigorous, an intelligent and a thriving population, but from which the buildings have disappeared, and whose only tenants now are the inmates of those narrow homes on which no signs of "To Let" or "For Sale" are exhibited, and in another portion of Cheshire we find later, but still early settlers who followed the first from Rhode Island, and took up their abode in that part of the town which is included in or is near to the present village of Cheshire, and was then within the limits of Lanesborough.

The story of the men who made the New Providence Purchase, and in 1767 removed their families and goods from Rhode Island to the splendid eminence which they christened New Providence Hill in affectionate remembrance of the hill in Providence, and there essayed to found and did found a new community, is worthy to be told. We will try to name some of the actors in it, and to open the field for further research.

* * * * * * *

The portion of Cheshire to which we have already referred by its more ancient name of the New Providence Purchase and the crown of which was named by its early settlers New Providence Hill is now known as Stafford's Hill, a name derived from the Col. Joab Stafford who was one of the prime movers in the emigration from Rhode Island to Berkshire, and one of the most prominent men in the settlement which they established. It appears certain that the territory embraced in the purchase was sold by the province in 1762 and was originally included in the township known as No. 6, the larger portion of which is now in the town of Savoy. An examination of the Province records in the office of the Secretary of the Commonwealth at Boston, discloses a full statement of the action of the General Assembly and Council in ordering and making the sale of several townships of province land in the western part of the province in 1762, most of them in Berkshire which sale included those parts of Cheshire which were formed from Windsor and Adams. That part which was formerly Lanesborough had been sold at an earlier date, and was then known as New Framingham. The records of these sales which included the old town of Adams then known as East Hoosuck, and the territory now included in Hinsdale, Peru, Windsor, Savoy and other towns may be found in the archives of the Historical Society, Pittsfield.

Of the townships there sold parts of two are within the limits of the present town of Cheshire, namely the northwestern portion of No. 4 and the west end of No. 6. Of these No. 4 seems to have been earliest settled. From deeds appearing on record it is evident that it had proprietors among whom there had been a division of common lands before the sale by order of the General Court in 1762.

There on the twelfth of June, 1762, James Burchard of a place called No. 4, in Berkshire County, conveys to his grandson, Matthew Wolf Jr., son of Matthew Wolf of the same town, house lot No. 66, on the southerly side of the same township butted and bounded according to the original survey as by the proprietors' book of records may appear, and as early as 1764, they were enjoying the luxury of selling lands for taxes in No. 4.

This township seems to have been as rich in names as Cheshire has been in corners, since it has borne successively the following in addition to No. 4; Dewey's Town, Bigot's Town, Williamsburg, Gageborough and Windsor.

The Noah Nash to whom it was sold in 1762 was a resident of Hatfield, and he continues to make deeds of lands in the township to 1784. Among these are deeds to David Parsons and many other names given in Barker's early history, page 24.

An examination of the latest county map shows that the New Providence Hill was directly north of the part of Windsor which was incorporated in the new town of Cheshire, and almost adjoining it the meeting of the five roads at the school house, one of which leads over the hill to Adams, and is on the line between No. 6, and No. 4.

In the vicinity of this portion of Windsor to the hill we find the moving force which brought it into the new town. Here too, lies one of the old burying grounds, to be noted further on, opposite the residence of W. P. Bennet.

It is not so easy to trace the history of the township known as No. 6. The present town of Savoy comprises the greater portion of the territory which was included within its bounds, as given in the order of sale of Feb. 17, 1762, and merely states that it was originally No. 6.

The Rev. David D. Field, in his history of Berkshire county, published in 1829, gave Bullock's grant as the foundation of the town, some other lands being incorporated with it. He states that Col. William Bullock of Rehoboth, as agent for the heirs of Capt. Samuel Gallop, received from the General Court of 1770 and 1771, a township of six miles square, in consideration of their services and sufferings in an expedition into Canada about the year 1690, in what was called King William's war, the township to be located in any unappropriated land belonging to Massachusetts, and that Col. Bullock located the grant to the southeast and north of Bernardston grant comprising the western and greater part of Florida, and which had been previously located. Recalling the bounds of No. 6, as given in the General Court's order of sale, the report of the committee, and the plan, it is certain that most, if not all, of this territory is included in No. 6, and also that the part of Cheshire which comprises the New Providence Purchase, or Stafford's Hill is in the same township of No. 6. This township was sold June 3d, 1762, by the committee to Abel Lawrence for £1,350, and his bond taken, with Charles Prescott, Esq., surety, for £1,330 of the purchase money.

Who this Abel Lawrence was does not appear, nor has the writer been able to ascertain in what manner the title conferred upon him by this sale was divested.

There is no deed of record from him in the Pittsfield Registry, and the whole township seems to have been traded after the sale, and a part of it within the term of five years, during which he was allowed to settle it according to the vote, as unappropriated land of the Province.

This break in the chain of title has been very provoking in the search for a record of the history of a settlement of Stafford's Hill, causing it at one time to be given up in despair. But information gained by sitting down to examine page by page, in course, the early volumes of records in the Registry of Deeds, enables us to give a probable account or theory.

For some unknown reason Abel Lawrence surrendered to the Province his right to the township soon after his purchase. The town of Hatfield, portions of whose lands had been included in the new townships Nos. 5 and

7, which were sold by the same committee in June 1762, made claim for compensations for the land thus taken, and the General Court in the same year seems to have awarded to them an equivalent located in part, at least, on the west end of the township which had been sold as No. 6 to Abel Lawrence. This land the town of Hatfield placed in the market and we find a conveyance of it made in 1765 by Israel and William Williams of Hatfield, and Israel Stoddard of Pittsfield. This tract was of 1,176 acres in one rectangular parcel, 432 rods east and west, by 435 rods and 14 links north and south and bounded southerly by the line of New Framingham, afterward Lanesborough.

Another and larger parcel of No. 6, seems,—upon evidence similarly found—to have been granted to Aaron Willard, Jr. Esq., and his associates purchasers of the new township No. 3, now Worthington, as an equivalent for a deficiency of land taken off from No. 3, and in 1766, we find "John Worthington and Josiah Dwight both of Springfield, Timothy Dwight of Northampton, Salah Barnard of Deerfield, and Aaron Willard Jr., of Lancaster in the County of Worcester, Esq's.," conveying three thousand seven hundred and forty acres and fourteen perch of land lying north of, and adjoining to Lanesborough, incorporated from New Framingham in 1765, and encircling on three sides the former parcel granted to Hatfield. These two parcels undoubtedly cover all that part of the original No. 6 which is now within the limits of Cheshire, and together they constitute the New Providence Purchase, and it was on them that the definite settlement to which Cheshire is traceable was made. The deeds run to "Nicholas Cook of Providence, in the County of Providence in the Colony of Rhode Island, Esq., and to Joseph Bennet, in Coventry, in the County of Kent in the Colony of Rhode Island, Esq.," making them equal tenants in common of both trades. The copies of these deeds are on page 31 of Barker's History.

This Nicholas Cook of Providence and Joseph Bennet of Coventry are the prime movers in the settlement of Cheshire, and of the early emigration from Rhode Island to Berkshire. Prior to their purchase there is mention in the Registry of Deeds only of one conveyance to an inhabitant of Rhode Island so described, of lands in the county. On the 28th of June, 1763, one Moses Warren of Hopkinton, Rhode Island, Clothier, buys of Joseph Warren of Tyringham, lot No. 137, in Tyringham, 70 acres "whereof," says Joseph Warren, "I was the original proprietor." Whether Joseph Warren also came from Rhode Island and afterwards induced a brother to follow him does not appear; but with this exception the first ten books in the Registry of Deeds disclose only purchasers in New Providence, Gageborough, Lanesborough and East Hoosuck by residents of Rhode

Island, save only that the Rev. Samuel Hopkins, who removed from Great Barrington to Newport in 1770, on the 27th of March, 1772, conveys lands in Great Barrington to his son David, who is also described as of Newport, Rhode Island. Of the two original proprietors of the New Providence purchase Nicholas Cook, the more prominent, seems to have been engaged in it merely as a speculation. He remained in Rhode Island. He was a member of the Court of Assistants of that Colony from 1752 to 1761, and Deputy Governor in 1768 and 1769. Joseph Bennet seems to have been admitted a freeman of the Rhode Island Colony from Coventry, in May, 1758. A Mr. Joseph Bennett of Newport, possibly an ancestor, was made High Sheriff on the 1st of May, 1700. The only other mention of Joseph, of Coventry, is under date of 23d of February, 1761, when he was made one of a committee, consisting of Nicholas Cook, Esq., Messrs. John Brown, Knight Dexter, Joseph Bennet, Joseph Bucklin and George Jackson, to apply to paving the streets of Providence, a lottery of three classes for raising the sum of £6,000 granted by the General Assembly upon the petition of the citizens of Providence. We might speculate whether Nicholas Cook, Esq., the chairman of this committee, found Mr. Joseph Bennet, his colleague, so efficient in the management of the lottery, or the work of paving that he selected him as his partner in the subsequent operation in wild lands, and, also, whether both of them realized, out of the lottery or the contracts for paving, the money which they paid for their Berkshire purchase. But in whatever way they became acquainted they were able to induce their neighbors to share in their enterprise and to remove with Bennett to the new country or to follow him. Captain, afterward Colonel Joab Stafford was employed by them to lay out and map their purchase, and the map which was filed in the Registry of Deeds, shows that the gallant captain was a master of the pen and rule as well as of the sword. This map was found by the process of examination above referred to, looking through the book page by page, after all hope of seeing it had been lost. Captain Stafford, a townsman in Coventry, of Joseph Bennet himself, made the first purchase of lands from Cook and Bennet, on the 5th of November, 1766, 396 acres in 3 lots, and on the next day Cook and Bennet, by a deed acknowledged in Providence and witnessed by Joab Stafford and Silas Downer, made partition between themselves of their remaining lands. It is surmised that Nicholas Cook, Esq., was a lawyer and drafted his own deeds, and if so he was a good one, for this indenture of partition is a model, delighting a lawyer's heart.

This partition having been made, sales were made to others, and the settlement advanced. The earliest to remove from Rhode Island seem to have settled on the New Providence Hill as it was called, and to have belonged to the Baptist denomination. Following them came other inhabitants of Rhode Island, many of them settling farther to the north in what was then East Hoosuck, or No. 1, now Adams, and of these very many were Quakers. To this difference in religion is probably due the fact that the New Providence settlement was not incorporated with East Hoosuck into the town of Adams in 1778, in which contingency probably there would have been no Cheshire; for, according to the Rev. John W. Yeomans in Field's History of Berkshire, it was the wish of the New Providence settlers to be incorporated with Adams, and during 1778 the inhabitants of East Hoosuck were twice called on to vote on the question of extending the charter so as to embrace New Providence, but each time rejected the proposition. New Providence Purchase must, however, have been subsequently annexed (by an Act of which we fail to find mention,) to the town of Adams. For, for some years prior to 1793, we find the people residing upon it, dating their letters from Adams, and the church established on the hill calling itself the Baptist Church in Adams. The present south line of Adams is evidently the old south line of East Hoosuck, so that it seems reasonably certain that the part of Adams which at the incorporation of Cheshire in 1793 went into the new town, was just the New Providence Purchase, and that it had been annexed to Adams after the incorporation of that town. The list given in appendix shows the conveyance recorded in the first ten books of the Pittsfield Registry of Deeds running to persons named as residents of Rhode Island. It included all the surnames given by Dr. Field in his history of early and prominent settlers of Cheshire and many more, and there is reason to suppose that most of the persons named in it became residents on the land conveyed to them.

To return to the first settlers—we find that Capt. Joab Stafford attended the general assembly at Newport in May, 1762, as a deputy from Coventry. In 1778 we find him empowered as Colonel Joab Stafford, to issue his warrant to some principal inhabitant to the newly incorporated town of Adams, requiring him to warn the inhabitants thereof to assemble for their first Town Meeting, and on the 21st of August 1801, we find him describing himself as Joab Stafford of Cheshire, Gentleman, quit-claiming to Allen Briggs of Adams, Gentleman, Daniel Reid, Yeoman, and Timothy Mason, Gentleman, both of Cheshire, for $400 all the remnant of his land in the New Providence Purchase, including 14 acres, "on which an execution was sometime since extended in favor of Ruloff White against me." Doubtless the court records would disclose the cause of action; but it is better not to peer too curiously into the gallant Colonel's embarrassments.

One of the witnesses to the deed is Richard Stafford, perhaps his son, and it is acknowledged before Ezra Barker, as a justice, a son of one of his

Rhode Island compatriots. Richard Stafford seems to have married Susannah, daughter of Elisha Brown, another of the Rhode Island people, and in 1823 they were living at Canajoharie, N. Y.

Tradition preserves a pleasant account of his introduction of Mrs. Stafford to her new home on the summit of New Providence Hill. While he was mapping out the purchase, and erecting a house on the Lots, to which he took title, his wife remained in Rhode Island. When the new building was ready for occupancy he returned for his family. As they journeyed on the good woman wished to know, and sought for an exact description of the new house she was to occupy and of its surroundings. But the Captain did not see fit to gratify her curiosity, and as they approached their destination, sought her opinion of the different dwellings, and locations which they found upon the way. At last Mrs. Stafford found one which delighted her exceedingly, and after the Captain had stopped to allow her to examine and admire it she exclaimed, "Oh! if I could only live there I would be perfectly satisfied." Whereupon the Captain turned into the inclosure and informed her that they were at home.

It was from this home—whence he could see the summits of the Graylock range apparently on a level with him at the west, and the valley of the Hoosuck nestling beneath them at the north, with glimpses of the vales at the south where rises the Housatonic—that Colonel Stafford went with the Berkshire men to the battle of Bennington, where he fought and was wounded. Let us hope that it was from this home that in the golden autumn days of 1801, three months after he had parted with his last acre of land—his neighbors and the old pastor, whom he had helped to bring from Rhode Island, at their head, carried the departed Colonel down the southern slope of the hill to the peaceful burying ground where his remains now repose.

At the southernmost foot of the hill, on a gentle eminence, around which curves a babbling, crystal-watered brook is one of the ancient burial places in Cheshire where sleeps this man, who according to the inscription on his tombstone, (a stone almost bowed to the earth as though it sought to keep closer company with the dust of him whom it commemorates, so that he who reads it must perforce kneel):

"Fought and bled in his country's cause at the battle of Bennington, and descended to his tomb with an unsullied reputation."

In front of him curves a splendid amphitheater of wooded hills, their forest covering almost unbroken, extending from Whitford's rocks on the east, to the high pinnacle of quartz which glistens like a jewel in the sun above the present village of Cheshire. Behind him rise the slopes of the hill which he surveyed and helped to clear and settle, great fields of pasturage from which now almost every dwelling has disappeared; but rarely vexed with the plough, and trodden but seldom by any feet save those of lowing kine and bleating sheep.

A great beech tree on the edge of the bank above the brook shades him from the morning sun, and so sequestered is the spot that at this moment a golden-winged woodpecker has her nest in a decayed portion of the tree, her notes the only sound but that of the rippling brook to break the absolute silence of his long home. A peaceful and an appropriate resting place for the patriot and the pioneer; but one which might well receive some care from those who are enjoying the fruit of the labors and sacrifices of him and his associates.

In the lot of the Bennet family in this old graveyard we find many Quakers, and the quaint simplicity of the Quaker thought is shown in the inscriptions.

About the John Wells who died the 17th of the seventh month 1813, in the 69th year of his age, and Frances his widow who survived him, living to the advanced age of 98, there is this tradition:

Frances was a sister of Daniel Brown. These Browns were well to do people. John Wells had nothing but an honest heart, a clear head, and a strong arm with which to make his way. They were married against the wishes of her father and family. So distasteful was the match that she was refused even the smallest setting out. So with nothing but themselves and their love the newly wedded pair, mounted upon one horse and with no other worldly goods, made the journey from Rhode Island to New Providence. Another sister married Caleb Tibbets, who was accounted well off and who also removed to New Providence, but remained only a short time, returning to the older settlements where he could enjoy more of the luxuries of life. He took back the opinion that probably Mr. and Mrs. Wells would get along, as Wells had made a clearing, put up a log house, and had one cow. The years passed by; John Wells worked his farm by daylight and made shoes by fire light. Frances Wells managed the house and the dairy, and earned money as a tailoress. They added farm to farm, and accumulated money until, when John died, his estate was one of the most considerable in Berkshire county, and with all this, both Frances and himself had gained the respect of all. Meantime, poor Caleb Tibbets had wasted his substance, and it was found that the daughter who had ridden portionless away behind her lover had made the better match.

Leaving this quiet burial place, let us retrace our steps to the old Bennet house, one of the few original ones yet remaining, and follow the road leading from it to the north along the western side of the hill. We shall not pursue it a great distance before we shall cross the line which marks the southern boundary of the New Providence Purchase, the old north line of No. 4, or Windsor, and a continuation easterly of the old north line of New Framingham, or Lanesborough. It can be traced on the ground at present for miles to the westward until it disappears at the summit of the hill lying to the west of Cheshire. On our right rise the grassy slopes of Stafford's Hill, a few apple trees on the summit being all that from this point is visible to indicate that it has been the site of a village. On the left rises Mount Amos, wooded on its northern slope, but clear and smooth on its southern, where, among the maple trees, the early settlers used to keep the sugar boiling while the wolves howled around the fires in the night. Far below, at the north, is the Adams valley and, perhaps, a mile in advance of you, if your eyes are keen, you can see rows of white stones by the roadside, another resting place of these first settlers of New Providence. It occupies a little plateau with but a gentle slope toward the west, the road sweeping around it down the hill with a dark, solemn spruce tree standing in the background.

It was here that these Rhode Islanders of the Baptist denomination planted their first church and set up the public worship of God. No trace remains upon the spot of the ancient building, nor any mark by which to fix its location, but tradition says that it was next to the road and that its site is now occupied by graves.

The building, however, is now standing on the northern slope of the hill to which it was removed, and where, as a two-story red farm house, it still does duty in the cause for which it was framed and raised. It has changed its uniform, but still does service in sustaining the preaching of the word in the New Providence Purchase.

Before we enter this village of the dead, let us gather something of the work which they who rest there did in the foundation and maintenance of a church which has been the thing that, more than anything else, must have educated the men and women of Cheshire and moulded the life of the town. The New Providence Purchase, not having been constituted as a district, or to worship by itself, or included in the limits of any such community, was not under the obligation ordinarily imposed, of devoting a portion of its land to the support of the ministry, or of maintaining public worship. Whatever its inhabitants did in the cause of religion was, therefore, a free gift, and was done because of the moving of the Spirit. As before stated, many of the more prominent of the early settlers were Baptists. They had no thought of escaping the burden of supporting public worship, and the story of the church that they founded is best told by its records. These records are in the possession of Mr. Shubael W. Lincoln, whose house, in the extreme easternmost part of Cheshire, on the mountain side opposite the north slope of the Stafford Hill, looks across to Graylock. * * * Mr.

Lincoln has gathered together many documents and relics of this early church and its members, and many a tradition of its early history.

Elder Peter Werden continued to be the pastor of this flock for nearly 40 years, until his death, on the 21st of February, 1808. He was a remarkable man; somewhat unlettered, perhaps, but full of grace and zeal, and actuated by love of God and man. His epitaph is said to have been composed by himself before he left Coventry. The discipline of his church was strict, and it cannot be doubted that its work was of the utmost importance to the well being of the community. An unbroken service, that spanned a century, was devoted to religious uses by a modest donation, a fact from which the charitably inclined may take courage.

As we have seen, the proprietors of the purchase were not obliged to devote a part of it to the support of the gospel; but Nicholas Cook and Joseph Bennet learning that a church had been thus founded at New Providence, gave by deed* on the 17th of January 1770, 50 acres of their best land on the northern slope of the hill to Joab Stafford, in trust as a ministerial lot or glebe land for the support of a preacher of the Anabaptist denomination.

Upon this land lived Elder Peter Werden, and from it he obtained his subsistence. He was succeeded in the ministry by Elder Braman, and he by Elder Bross, described as a stirring practical man, under whose administration the old church building was removed to the glebe land, a new church having been erected sometime before on the top of the hill where was a flourishing and beautiful village—the village of Cheshire. It had besides its church its post office and its masonic lodge. Of all the buildings which then crowned the summit of the hill not one remains. The new church decayed and fell, and most of the farm houses were removed to Adams, and after a time the church organization became moribund. Elder John Leland supplied the pulpit for some time, but was never settled as pastor of the church. Elder Sweet also preached for them after the destruction of the new church building. However, a claim was made by the heirs of the donors of the glebe that the condition of the deed of trust had been broken, and the land forfeited. This claim was successfully resisted in the courts, and Shubael W. Lincoln appointed trustee. He now holds the trust, and applies the income of the fifty acres to the support of preaching in the school house hard by, looking hopefully for the time when he may see a tasteful chapel again crowning the old hill.

Let us enter the sacred ground and spend a few minutes with the pastor and his flock. But we must first record an episode of their work and discipline which throws light upon the manner of men they were and the views they held. Col. Samuel Low was one of the most wealthy and prominent of those who founded the settlement and its church. His residence was nearest its site. In 1763 he was entrusted with the duty of organizing a lottery to raise and grade the streets of Providence, Rhode Island. In New Providence he owned slaves—four at least—William Dimon, Molly Dimon and their two children, one of whom was Antony. About 1790, he removed to Palatine, New York, having freed old William and Molly, but taking Antony and the girl with him. He afterward applied to the church for dismissal, but it was refused unless he would free the two slaves. A long correspondence between him and Elder Werden ensued of which this is a sample:

"DEAR BROTHER—We received your letter and the brethren hath heard it red. That part that concerneth Antony and it doth not serve our minds. Our minds is that your duty was to have set him at liberty at the age of twenty-one which was about a year ago. And as to the bills of cost that you speak of you and he must settle that yourselves. We look upon it that we have nothing to do in that matter. We wish you, very dear brother, to attend to the proposition that you mentioned— all men are born free. Therefore our request and desire is that you liberate him emmediately to ease our sister and ourselves of our pain, as we think it will dishonor our profession if it is not dun. * * *"

ADAMS, MARCH 2d, 1792.

It may be well here to refer to a brief account of Elder Peter Werden, given by Elder John Leland in his works:

"Here lies the body of Peter Werden, late pastor of the Church of Christ in Cheshire. He was born June 6th, 1728. Converted by the mighty power of God in the Lord Jesus Christ May 9th, 1748. In the month of May 1751 he was ordained to the work of the ministry in Warwick, and continued measurably faithful in his pastoral charge to the close of his life, which was February 21, 1808.

>His soul to God he used to send,
>To cry for grace for friend and foe,
>But blessed be the God of love,
>His soul is now with Christ above.
>
>This crumbling sculpture keeps the clay
>That used to house the noble mind,
>But at the resurrection day,
>A nobler body he shall find.

Descending from the village of the dead toward the southwest the road passes around Mount Amos, and overlooks the valley in which is the present flourishing village of Cheshire. This village lies in the valley of the Hoosuck, and is in that part of the town formerly called Lanesborough. There was very early a road following the stream and leading from the center of the county to East Hoosuck. Crossing this is a road over the foothills of Graylock, from Lanesborough, and the present village has grown up at the four corners made by the intersection of these roads. When New Providence Hill was popular and flourishing it is said that there was not a single house where the present village stands. It is difficult to trace the early settlement of this portion of the town, at least without more time than the present writer has been able to devote to the task.

The early settlers were citizens of a large town, the social and political center of which was over the hill to the west. They differed from the most of their fellow citizens in religious belief, and in the early records of the Six Principle and the Second Baptist churches would probably be the richest field for investigation as to their names and acts. .

PREFACE

THIS work is intended to embrace a popular and concise summary of the History of the County Palatine of Chester from the earliest ages to the present time. It is not a mere stringing together of other men's views and opinions: it is the outcome of patient research among State Papers, documents, newspapers, and books, as also the result of inside observation of county affairs garnered during long experience of an active journalistic and literary career. A perusal of the chapter headings will show the scope of the work—as also its multifarious features, many of which have never hitherto been published—far more than any dry display of facts and figures.

The Author recalls with deep feelings of pleasure the reception given to the "History of Altrincham and Bowdon" in 1879, amplified to include Sale and the surrounding townships in a second work some twenty years ago. Both editions are now out of print. They have since brought a premium on published prices and are looked upon as heirlooms in local families. Special stress may be laid on chapters relating to Parliamentary and Local Government, including description of the first election and meeting of the Cheshire County Council. They are the most complete ever published. The life and times of Henry, Lord Delamere, first Earl of Warrington, the Cheshire patriot *par excellence*, are set forth at length, including the famous trial for High Treason before Judge Jeffreys. Especially interesting also will be found the doings of Cheshire men in wars, ancient and modern, Cheshire characteristics, proverbs, ballads, legends, quaint sayings, Cheshire in the days of bluff King Hal, etc.

The record of the rise and progress of Freemasonry in the Province of Cheshire (the oldest in the world), will, it is hoped, find acceptance amongst the members of that noble order. This is the first time it has been put in a readable and popular form, and, like the secular part of the work, is the result of personal observation of half a century.

The Appendix at the end of the work will be found of great service for reference.

The illustrations, like the text, have followed original lines. Included is a facsimile page of the speech by His Grace the Duke of Westminster on the presentation of a portrait of Mr Duncan Graham, first Chairman to the Cheshire County Council. Extremely interesting also will be found the portraits of the first Earl of Warrington and Sir Peter Leycester.

Photo] Chester Cathedral—Exterior. [Phillipson & Golde

Photo] Chester Cathedral—Interior. [Phillipson & Golde

CONTENTS

			PAGE
CHAPTER	I.	Prehistoric Salt Mines—Poets and Geological Science	1
,,	II.	The Genesis of Cheshire History—Sir Peter Leycester's Illustrious Work	12
,,	III.	Feudalism and the Divine Right of Kings	24
,,	IV.	Whence came Christianity to Cheshire?—Cheshire Saints	33
,,	V.	Foundation of Nonconformity in England	45
,,	VI.	Martial Cheshire—The Crusaders—Civil Wars	68
,,	VII.	The splendid Traditions and Services of the Militia	77
,,	VIII.	The Cheshire Regiment—Its Work on "India's Coral Strand"	86
,,	IX.	Cheshire Minstrels—Whitsun Plays and their Players	106
,,	X.	Cheshire Sports and Pastimes—Wakes Revelry and May Day Festivals	118
,,	XI.	Cheshire in the Days of Bluff King Hal—Murders, Abductions, and Affrays	131
,,	XII.	Cheshire and Parliamentary Representation at Westminster	145
,,	XIII.	Parliamentary Cheshire (continued)	155
,,	XIV.	Local Government—Court Leets—Cheshire County Council	170
,,	XV.	The House of Dunham—The Foundation of the Family	185
,,	XVI.	Lord Delamere's Eventful Life—The Stewart Period Reviewed	200
,,	XVII.	Lord Delamere's Efforts in the Revolution	213
,,	XVIII.	Plague, Pestilence, and Famine—Sandbach Crosses	221
,,	XIX.	Lord Chancellor Egerton and other Notable Cheshire Men	237
,,	XX.	Cheshire Characteristics, Proverbs, and Sayings	259
,,	XXI.	Ballads, Traditions, and legends of Cheshire	270
,,	XXII.	King and Parliament	280
,,	XXIII.	Early History of the Provincial Grand Lodge	289
,,	XXIV.	Cheshire and the Grand Lodge of England	308
,,	XXV.	Provincial Grand Lodge History (continued)	320
,,	XXVI.	Installation of Hon. Alan de Tatton Egerton, M.P.	329
APPENDIX		Cheshire Magistrates—Cheshire County Council—Population of the County	352
INDEX			365

LIST OF ILLUSTRATIONS

Chester Cathedral, Exterior } Interior }	*Frontispiece*
A Modern Northwich Subsidence	*facing* 8
Northwich Shop Property Damaged by Subsidence	*facing* 9
Sir Peter Leycester	*facing* 12
Earl Egerton of Tatton	*facing* 13
Sword and Crest of Hugh Lupus	28-29
Earl Beatty	*facing* 96
Countess Beatty and Son, Viscount Borodale	*facing* 97
The Bravest Street in Cheshire	*facing* 104
Bull-Baiting	*facing* 105
Courtyard, Chester Castle (*Circa* 1215)	106
A Heated Discussion	107
Rags and Tatters to the Rescue	108
The Welsh Routed	109
Gamecocks ready for Battle	115
Cockpit at Lymm Hall	*facing* 120
Arley Green	*facing* 120
Morris Dance	*facing* 121
Lymm Stocks	*facing* 121
Leading in Chester Cup Winner, 1919	*facing* 128
Knutsford May-day Festival—Crowning of the May-Queen	*facing* 129
Facsimile, Duke of Westminster's Speech	179
Henry, Lord Delamere, first Earl of Warrington	*facing* 200
Wythenshawe Hall	*facing* 201
Lymm Dell	*facing* 201
Burying Lane, Bowdon	*facing* 220
Warburton Old Church	*facing* 220
View of Railway Accident at Chester Viaduct	*facing* 221
View of Stockport	*facing* 252

viii   *List of Illustrations*

		PAGE
Tatton Hall	. *facing*	253
Moated Grange, High Legh	. *facing*	288
A Cheshire Farmer outwits Pitt	. *facing*	288
Eaton Hall	. *facing*	289
Provincial Grand Lodge Meeting at Chester	.	290
An Old-Time Tyler	. *facing*	292
Ancient Warrant, Unanimity, No. 89	. *facing*	293
Lord Leverhulme, P.J.G.W. (Eng.)	. *facing*	300
Brother T. H. Annett, Treasurer, Fund of Benevolence	. *facing*	301
Lodge of Unanimity, Stockport, Centenary	.	302
Royal Masonic School for Boys	. *facing*	320
Brother Wm. Booth	. *facing*	321
Alderman D. L. Hewitt, P.A.G.D.C. (Eng.)	. *facing*	328
Lord Egerton of Tatton, P.P.G.M., Cheshire	. *facing*	329
Centenary Souvenir, Unity Lodge, No. 321	. *facing*	332
Lieut.-Col. Cornwall-Legh, Prov. Grand Master of Cheshire	. *facing*	333
Brother Eustace G. Parker	.	334
Brother Joseph Clarke, Provincial Secretary	. *facing*	338
Brother Alfred Ingham, P.M., etc.	. *facing*	339

Cheshire: Its Traditions and History

CHAPTER I.

Origin of the Earth, the Nebular Theory—Early geological history—The periods of rock formation—An imaginary voyage over an early developed surface—Prehistoric Cheshire; its characteristics, rock formation, salt mines—The fate of Northwich prophesied—Typical subsidences—The legend of Rostherne Mere—Poets and geological science—Conclusion.

ASTRONOMY and Geology twin sisters of Science, have made us acquainted with the story of the origin and formation of the globe, which was once enwrapped in the mysterious regions of superstitious speculation. Whether it had a nebular origin, or that our earth was once a mass of fiery substance, from which was detached a huge mass known to us as the moon, cannot be determined.

In the earth's crust various processes have modified the primeval rocks, which were first solidified from its original molten condition and composed entirely of igneous rocks, formed by the action of heat, and from aerial deposits produced by the action of atmospheric agencies. Early geologists thought this beneficent change from volcanic rocks and the fire-smitten deserts of the early world to the fertile fields which now grow ripe to harvest and the kindly soil on which man lives, must have been due to some correspondingly extraordinary change in the order of Nature. They were always ready to invoke the aid of some gigantic cataclysm to explain its geological history.

Hence we are driven to further exploration in the solar system and to seek for an explanation of these terrestrial changes to " the glorious firmament on high," for the proclamation of their great Original and Architect. Sea and land have changed places again and again in the history of the earth. The sea has not changed so much as the land, but we do not measure these changes geologically by thousands of years but by eternities. In the earth's existence we find processes which modified the primeval rocks, which were first solidified from its original molten condition and entirely composed of crystalline rocks.

In beautiful language Tennyson has expressed a far-reaching geological fact when he says—

>There rolls the deep where stood the tree ;
>O Earth, what changes hast thou seen ;
>There where the long street roars hath been
>The stillness of the central sea.
>
>. : . . . .
>
>The hills are shadows, and they flow
>From form to form, and nothing stands ;
>They melt like mists, the solid lands ;
>Like clouds they shape themselves and go.

A

Hugh Miller says:—"There are no sermons that seem stronger or more impressive to one who has acquired just a little of the language in which they are preached, than those which, according to the poet, are to be found in stones. . . . The eternity that hath passed is an ocean without a further shore, and a finite conception may in vain attempt to span it over. . . . We see on towards the cloudy horizon many a dim islet and many a pinnacled rock, the sepulchre of successive eras—the monuments of consecutive creations; the entire prospect is studded over with these landmarks of a hoar antiquity, which, measuring out space from space, constitute the vast whole a province of time; nor can the eye reach to the open shoreless infinitude beyond, in which only God existed," and "we borrow a larger, not a smaller idea of the distant eternity, from the vastness of the measured periods that occur between."

He adds a charming picture of the earth's appearance in its early stages of development. He points out that there existed dry land in the coniferous lignite of the lower (middle) Old Red Sandstone, and that land wore, as at after periods, its soft mantle of green, and he takes us for an imaginary voyage on some prehistoric ship.

We proceed, he writes, upwards into the high geological zones, passing from ancient and still more ancient scenes of being, and, as we voyage along, find ever in the surrounding prospect a graceful intermixture of land and water, continent, river and sea.

We first coast along the land of the Tertiary, inhabited by the strange quadrupeds of Cuvier, and waving with the reeds and palms of the Paris Basin; the land of the Wealdon with its gigantic iguanodon rustling amid its tree ferns and its cycadaec comes next; then comes the green band of the oolite, with its little pouched insectiverous quadrupeds, its flying reptiles, its vast jungles of the brora equisetum, and its forests of the Helmsdale pine; and then dimly, as through a haze, we mark, as we speed on the thinly scattered islands of the Red Sandstone, and pick up in our course a large floating leaf veined like that of a cabbage, with not a little that puzzles the botanists of the expedition.

And now we near the vast Carboniferous continent, and see along undulating outlines, between us and the sky, the strange forms of vegetation, compared with which that of every previously seen land seems stunted and poor. We speed along endless forests, in which gigantic club mosses wave in the air a hundred feet overhead, and skirt interminable marshes, in which thickets of leaves overtop a masthead.

And where mighty rivers come rolling to the sea, we mark, through long, retiring vistas which open into the interior, the higher grounds of the country covered with coniferous trees, and see doddered trunks of vast size reclining under the banks in deep muddy reaches, with their decaying tops turned adown the current.

At length the furthermost promontory of this long range of coast comes into full view. We come abreast of it and see the shells of the mountain limestone glittering white along the further shore and the green depths under our keel lightened by the flush of innumerable corals; and then, bidding farewell to the land for ever, we launch into the unmeasured ocean of the Old Red, with its three consecutive zones of animal life. Not a single patch of land more do those early geologic charts exhibit.

The zones of the Silurian and Cambrian succeed the zones of the Old Red darkly fringed by an obscure bank of cloud ranged along the last zone in the series: a night that never dissipates settles down upon the deep. And it is in the middle of this vast ocean, just where the last zone of the Old Red leans against the first zone of the Silurian, that we have succeeded in discovering a solitary island, unseen before, a shrub-bearing land, much enveloped in fog, but with the hills that, at least, look green in the distance. There are patches of floating seaweed much comminuted by the surf all around it, and on one projecting headland we see a cone-bearing tree.

These coniferous trees are held to have preceded our true forest trees, such as the oak and elm, that in like manner the fish preceded the reptiles, that the reptile preceded the bird, that the bird preceded the mammiferous quadruped and the quadrumans, and that these preceded Man.

It is to the post glacial period that the appearance of man on the earth is assigned. This period is supposed to have originated in the Arctic regions and to have covered an incredible space, literally denuding vast areas, and leaving behind marks of its gigantic power in the shape of huge boulders, many of them hundreds of tons in weight, brought, it is estimated, far beyond what are now the Highlands of Scotland, and depositing them in various parts farther south. One of these boulders is in the Manchester Museum, and the student could not do better than pay a visit to that institution if only to view the remains of prehistoric gigantic lizards or crocodiles found in the Midland counties and other places.

As to the exact time of Man's appearance on the earth all authorities on geological research are silent. The gap is too wide to be bridged, notwithstanding many discoveries of remains which point to a common ancestry. Darwin, who wrote several treatises bearing on the subject, in his latest volume, " The Descent of Man," comes to the main conclusion which is now held, he says, by many naturalists who are competent to form a sound judgment, that man is descended from some less highly organised form. " The great principle of Evolution," he says, " stands up clear and firm. It is incredible that all these facts (including geological distribution) in past and present times, and their geological succession should speak falsely. All point in the plainest manner that man is the co-descendant with other mammals of a common progenitor. Nevertheless, all the races appear in so many unimportant details of structure and in so many mental peculiarities, that these can be accounted for only by inheritance from a common progenitor; and a progenitor thus characterised would probably deserve to rank as a man. . . . By considering the embryological structure of man—the homologies which he presented with the lower animals—the induments which he retains and the reversions to which he is liable, we can partly recall in imagination the former conditions of our early progenitors, and can approximately place them in their proper place in the zoological series. We thus learn that man is descended from a hairy tailed quadruped, probably arboreal in its habits, and an inhabitant." There you get some idea of the Darwinian doctrine, pure and unadulterated. The reader who wishes to pursue this interesting, but argumentative, subject further, can have his views widened quickly and economically by applying for the various works now happily obtainable at any Public Reference Library.

It is now universally admitted that the East was the cradle of the human race. It is thence we get the first glimpses of a religion founded on the worship of God's power exhibited in the forces of Nature. Lands, houses, flocks, herds, men, and animals were more frequently at the mercy of the wind, fire, and water than in Western climates, and the sun's rays appear to be gifted with a potency quite beyond the experience of any European country. Honour and worship were accorded to the air, the rain, the storm, the sun, and to fire. For twelve or thirteen centuries before Christ the sky and air were deified by the Indo-Aryans, and there was evolved a belief in a divine power or powers regulating the universe. The belief in a personal God became the Pantheistic creed of India, and the ancient Vedic hymns deify the sky as Heavenly Father (the Zeus or Jupiter of the Greeks and Romans), until a more spiritual conception resulted which led to a worship which rose to the nature of a belief in the Great-Our-Father-which-art-in-heaven. A perusal of some of the Vedic hymns addressed to deified forces is most interesting. We have there pictured the various deities regarded as the union of the progeny of earth with heaven, and it is thought that these deified forces were not represented by idols in the Vedic period, though doubtless the early worshippers clothed their gods with human form in their own imaginations. Thus we have hymns in praise of Varuna, the investing sky, the sun, the dawn, the one God, death, etc. One of them conveys a remarkable setting forth of the mystery of creation, such as is found in the Bible when we are told that " In the beginning, there was neither naught nor ought, neither day or light, nor darkness. Only the Existent One breathed calmly, self-contained. . . . Who knows, who can declare how and from what has sprung this universe; the gods themselves are subsequent to its development. Who can penetrate the secret of its rise ? whether 'twas framed or not, made. He only, who in the highest sits, the omniscient Lord assuredly knows all, or haply knows he not."

Having suggested this train of thought without desire to introduce

CHESHIRE: ITS TRADITIONS AND HISTORY

anything controversial or theological, we now proceed to deal with the subject from a local standpoint.

Cheshire does not seem to have presented "a happy hunting ground" for geologists, such as is to be found in other parts of the kingdom, especially the extreme north and south. The geological survey of the United Kingdom, with its maps, sections, and memoirs, together with the information to be found in the proceedings of the various Geological Societies of the country, is characterised by simplicity and uniformity. Nine-tenths of the area of Cheshire is composed of rocks belonging to one geological formation only—the Trias or New Red Sandstone. The remainder is composed of the Carboniferous Age, which forms the hilly region of the east and north-east.

Cheshire has been humorously described as roughly resembling a bird's wing in shape, an axe head, and a shoulder of mutton: again, as a chicken with its head in featherbed moss; Macclesfield in its crop; and the tail formed by the Wirral Peninsula. It has also been likened to a broad, earth-tipped shield, of the College of Arms type, divided palewise by a central line of hills, of which the isolated rocks of Halton and Beeston occupy the chief point and the fesse point of the shield respectively. Geologically, the county really forms an exception to the fact that in England the oldest rocks occur, as a rule, in the north-west part of any district. In Cheshire the first formed and oldest rocks occur in the east and north-east, where the boundary line extends up to the Yorkshire moors. The cause of this is to be found in the upheaval of the Pennine Chain, so that the rocks of the lower Carboniferous Age have been brought to the surface and exposed by subsequent denudation. These lower carboniferous beds we find in their correct place on the west side of the River Dee, where a fine ridge of rocks of the age of the carboniferous limestone and millstone grit runs north and south for a distance of twenty-one miles, the town of Mold being the central point. Looking from these hills eastward we have before us an extensive plain of red rock of Triassic Age, thickly overlaid with boulder clay, and composing, as before noted, nine-tenths of the county. The plain is over forty miles in width, and its eastern boundary is formed by a repetition of the identical strata—the carboniferous limestone, millstone grit, and lower coal measures, upon which we have taken an imaginary stand in Flintshire. In the mountainous country to the eastward, with its fine and varied scenery, pastoral in parts and dotted at wide intervals usually, except occasionally, a little village nestles away on its sometimes sunlit slopes, we come across the mountain limestone, which is so prominent and profitable a feature in Derbyshire, and especially round Buxton, with its peculiar and rather weird "shivering mountain" in the distance. It peeps up in Cheshire only at one point, Astbury, near Congleton. This was said to have been the discovery of a Derbyshire servant girl a couple of hundred years or so ago. She noticed that the rock in the brook was the same she had seen burnt in her county. The Astbury lime works have been carried on for a long period, and not only is the lime produced used for agricultural purposes, but it is a splendid hydraulic lime which is used for foundations of bridges, and building purposes of a like character.

The majestic chain of hills in the Macclesfield district are around 4000 feet thick, consisting in the lower part of black shales, alternating with thick, black, earthy limestone, superimposed with hard, fine grained sandstone, surmounted in turn by alternations of dark shales and sandstone. Fossils are rare, but specimens have been found in the neighbourhood of Congleton.

The Cheshire coalfield is a prolongation of the coalfield of South Lancashire, and the middle coal measures contain the principal workable seams at Poynton, some coal being of excellent quality; but coal has been mined at Neston, on the other side of the county, and vast beds are supposed to exist under the Wirral Peninsula, but at a considerable and not yet tested depth. Passing over the rocks of the Permian formation, which is to be seen in the Stockport district, we pass to the Triassic formation, which here attains its chief British development, and is about 3000 feet in thickness and includes the keuper and bunter beds. It is at Alderley Edge, where in early days copper ore was worked, but for various reasons, chiefly commercial, it has practically ceased. The lower keuper sandstones are quarried in various parts of the county, and the beds are often traversed by sun cracks and footprints of what is said to be a remarkable reptile, the Labyrinthodon, a trace of which was to be seen in Bowdon forty or fifty years ago, and had been originally found in the neighbourhood of Lymm, probably Millington.

The salt beds of Cheshire demand more than a passing notice, for it is on the production of this valuable commodity that the commercial prosperity of Northwich and district for many miles round depends. There, salt beds are found as far south as Nantwich, and westwards at Lymm, the latter part being of quite recent discovery and working. Farther north, at Dunham Massey, there is what may be termed a portion of the same bed, and attempts to create another Northwich in that district proved futile. To trace the original formation of these beds we are led to believe that the Triassic rocks were deposited in great inland salt lakes, the water being so concentrated as to deposit their excess of salt in beds more or less thick.

Taking Northwich, which was known as Sallincae by the Romans, and by the Celtic name of Hellath Dhu, or the black salt town by Ancient Britons, as the main example in the salt field of Cheshire, we read that salt was dug out of the earth for a long period anterior thereto. How long before, we know not; even tradition gives us little or no clue. There have been prophecies of its ultimate fate, one notably by Nixon, the Cheshire prophet, reputed to be a clodhopper, or ploughboy, who was under the protection of the Cholmondeleys, and he predicted that ultimately water would cover the whole of the town. There is a widespread belief even to-day in the truth of these prophecies, especially in Over, which is in the vicinity of Nixon's birthplace. To cite only a few instances of their fulfilment. He prophesied that Ridley Pool would be sown and mown. That pool is one of the Cheshire meres which was drained by the abstraction of brine underneath, so that the large sheets of water, known as " Flashes " at Winsford, have resulted, and are gradually increasing in area as the years roll on. Another prophecy was that carriages, not drawn by horses, would run past Vale Royal, near Northwich. The main line of the railway from Liverpool to Crewe and London has been cut through the Delamere estate, and locomotives, which are certainly not horses, have helped to fulfil the prediction. He also wrote that men would fly in the air like birds, dive under the sea like fishes, and run like lightning on the ground. A good deal of this may have come true in the World War of the twentieth century, but we do not agree with him when he says, " Lincoln was, London is, but York shall be, the greatest city of the three ! "

Subsidences have been numerous in the past fifty years. Macaulay is a famous historian, but in many cases he is hopelessly out in his facts. He " read " rapidly, but did not digest them. For instance, he says " the first bed of rock salt had been discovered in Cheshire not long (?) after the Restoration, but does not appear to have been worked until much later. The salt which was obtained by a rough process from the brine pits was held in no high estimation. The pans in which the manufacture was carried on exhaled a sulphuric stench ; and when the separation was complete the substance which was left was scarcely fit to be used with food." To this he adds the interesting and laughable information : " Physicians attributed the scorbutic and pulmonary complaints which were common among the English, to this unwholesome condiment. It was, therefore, seldom used by the upper and middle classes, and there was a regular and considerable importation from France." Seeing that salt was a staple product in Cheshire in the days of the Ancient Britons as well as the Romans, from whom we derive the word " salary," thereby indicating the value they attached to the product, and is to-day a staple of immense value, we may safely leave the verdict to a discriminating and more enlightened posterity.

A most remarkable, if not the most remarkable subsidence on record, took place at Northwich on Monday, 6th December 1880. About six o'clock on the morning of that day, a rumbling noise was heard in a district on the outskirts of Northwich, known by the name of Dunkirk, which is completely honeycombed with abandoned salt mines. Immediately, the ground seemed to be heaving as if from an earthquake, and the lakelets in the neighbourhood varying from nearly half an acre to nearly two acres in area, and thirty to forty feet in depth, commenced to boil and bubble all over, the water being forced up violently some feet above the surface. The whole area of these lakelets was in a furious state of commotion, and the noise of the bubbling water could be heard three hundred yards away. All round, for a space of two thousand feet in diameter, at every weak point in the ground, air and foul gas were being expelled ; and where in its course the gas met with water, it forced it up in jets, usually accompanied with mud and sand. For a space of at least one-fourth of the circumference of the largest lakelet, called Ashton's Old Rock Pit Hole, which covered nearly two acres, there were at intervals regular mud geysers, spouting intermittently to a height of about twelve feet. In one space of about thirty yards in extent, there were at least twenty of these playing at one time. The more violent ebullitions subsided after three or four hours ; though in some cases the bubbling and gurgling mud craters continued in action for two days and the ebullition in the various pits continued on a smaller scale for three days. The whole of this bubbling and boiling was evidently caused by the air that filled the old mines being violently driven out by the inrush of descending water and earth. The whole surface of the Weaver and the top of the Brook was lowered fully a foot, over one hundred and sixty acres, in about four hours, and if we add to this the whole of the water of the Wincham Brook for twelve hours, we shall find that not less than six hundred thousand tons of water rushed below. Many hundreds of tons of rock salt that had been brought to the surface, as well as the tramways, wagons, tubs, tools, and all materials were totally lost, and the mine as a mine, totally destroyed.

But the ultimate fate of Northwich was seriously predicted by one De Rance, a modern geologist of high standing, at a Government inquiry at Northwich thirty or forty years ago, held to inquire into the amount of compensation to be paid to property owners in the area affected, which was of wide extent, by salt proprietors who were draining the district of its life's blood, so to speak, by the abstraction of brine. This witness stated that owing to the flooding with water of the old salt workings and the pumping of liquid therefrom, the huge pillars of rock salt which were slowly but surely being dissolved and causing these subsidences, Northwich would be suddenly covered by one vast lake as certainly as the waters cover the sea. " How long will that be ? " asked one salt boiler of another—they were both elderly men. " As long as the old cow milks," came the reply. This is probably an allusion to an old Cheshire saying that the more you milk a cow properly the more milk she gives. The " old cow," however, is still yielding the precious " milk " abundantly, quite as much and more than she did a century ago. Nixon's prophecy, or that by De Rance, has not come to pass so far. Old inhabitants have asserted that the salt area of Cheshire is, in parts, of immense thickness, and this is geologically proved to be true, so

A modern Northwich Subsidence

photo HDavies

photo Northwich Shop Damaged by Subsidence *H. Davies*

that a constant source of brine is derived from underground springs, which flow in certain stated directions, and that the supply to be derived therefrom is practically inexhaustible. And there we may safely leave it.

Before quitting the geological aspect we should like to refer to another matter more immediately connected with the Bowdon district. The meres of Cheshire are characteristic of the county, and, it is surmised, were formed after the sea had disappeared in the course of ages. One large inland lake existed formerly, bounded by Delamere Forest and the adjacent high lands on the east by Alderley Edge, and the elevated banks extending to Bowdon in that dim past when

> The sun's eye had a lightless glaze,
> And the earth with age was wan.

There is an old tradition that Rostherne Mere was bottomless, but soundings have proved it to be $105\frac{1}{2}$ feet deep in its deepest part, and its surface area 115 statute acres. Rostherne Mere has locally laid a foundation for the pleasing legend of the imaginary mermaid that finds her way, so tradition says, by some underground passage from the sea. She rises on Easter morn from the water, seated on a bell which has rolled into the Mere by supernatural agency, sedately combing her flowing locks:—

> Her song dies out, and the waves roll on,
> The sunbeams rest where the metal shone,
> The bell has sunk with a sad refrain,
> The Naiad bindeth her locks again ;
> With a mocking laugh she waves adieu,
> Then dives, mayhap, to the deeper blue,
> For a purple mist enshrouds her fate,
> And the Mere rolls drear and desolate.

There are no smelts caught in any part of the Mersey. T. A. Coward states that there does not appear to be any record of the introduction of the fish, though it was found in the Mere early in the eighteenth century, say, 1740. Sprats were taken annually for ten days before Easter, and are not to be distinguished in any way from sea sprats in colour, size, or taste. A remarkable circumstance is this, that though there is a rivulet running through the Mere into the Mersey, and although there are several weirs between the Mere and the river, yet no sprats have ever been caught or seen between those two places. Therefore the question arises, how could they get out of the river into the Mere or lake ? If they do come from thence it must be by means of a flood, and even then the fact remains that those fish must reject two or three other rivers that run into the Mersey and the Birkin, which are joined by the rivulet that runs through the Mere before they reach the Mersey. There is a similar instance in favour of this opinion, there being two rivers in Cheshire, the Weaver and the Dane, which meet at Northwich, yet salmon, when they came out of the sea, entered the Dane, but have never been known to visit the Weaver.

An opinion has been expressed that sprats entered the Mere through the Bollin, Birkin, and Blackburn's Brook. Rostherne Mere is generally supposed to be in a hollow caused by subsidences over salt deposits, and it being doubtful that sea fish could live permanently in fresh water it has been suggested that the water at the bottom of the Mere is salt, and that this salt is being continually dissolved from the broken deposits and drawn off a very dilute solution. Until chemistry solves the question it is impossible to decide the point.

The remains of early man appear to be scarce. Of Paleolithic or older Stone Age, no traces have been discovered, but there are instances of stone or flint tools, or Neolithic, or the newer Stone Age, which came to a close in Britain about 2000 years B.C. A Neolithic celt or stone axe was found at Tranmere, which had part of its wooden handle remaining. The greater part of the wood had perished, but enough remained to show that the handle had passed in a slightly diagonal direction towards the upper end of the stone. An old British axe was found on one occasion in the moat at Tabley, with a large flint handle ground into an edge, which would, no doubt, have been used as a battle-axe by some prehistoric warrior. Another perforated axe, made of grit and $7\frac{1}{2}$ inches long, was found at Siddington, near Macclesfield. A quoit-shaped instrument, 6 inches in diameter, from the drift 20 feet below the surface, was taken at Stalybridge, and a similar ring was found in the gravel near Macclesfield in 1860. A hammer stone or maul, probably used in the working of its copper mines, was found at Alderley Edge, and a stone axe at Weston Point. These indications of habitation of a remote antiquity are confirmed by the discovery of ancient barrows or tumuli in various parts of the county, evidently burial places of British chieftains.

Allusion has already been made to the far-reaching geological fact mentioned by Tennyson in one of his poems on the world's evolution. Ever since literature had a beginning, says Dr H. Smith Williams, there have been masters who have grasped eagerly after all the scientific knowledge of their time. Shakespeare may be taken as a prominent illustration. Dante knew the depths of rudimentary fourteenth century science based largely on Ptolemaic astronomy, in the "Divine Comedy"; and the sixteenth century science, which Milton knew so well, entered into "Paradise Lost," but the science which transcends the bounds of unaided human senses, which reaches out into the infinities of space, and down into the infinitesimal regions of the microcosm, revealing a universe of suns and a universe of atoms; the science which explains the origin of worlds of sentient beings, of Man himself; the science which brings Man's intellect under the sway of scale and measure, and makes his tendencies, emotions, customs, beliefs, superstitions even, the object of calm, unimpassioned investigation—this science is new, even of our century, even of our own generation. Some day, perhaps, another Milton, learned in later science, may give us a new epic depicting the evolution of organic forms in true sequence, and the slow, tortuous struggles of man toward a paradise which he has not yet gained.

> So careful of the type ? But no,
> From scarpéd cliff and quarried stone
> She cries, " A thousand types are gone ;
> I care for nothing—all shall go."

CHAPTER II.

The genesis of Cheshire history—Sir Peter Leycester's illustrious work, " Beginnings of Things "—Pen picture of a dreary landscape—Enter Caesar's legions—Chester's mythical origin—Ancient British burial places—Chester a Roman colony—Advent of Agricola and prosperity—Roman civilisation in Britain—Roman roads and remains in Cheshire—Chester a pleasant place of residence then—Roman religious observances—The " Rows " and their patrons—Cestrians, " bloated monopolists "—Roman roads from Chester to Wirral and Hilbre Island—Monks and " superstitious fools "—Decay of Roman power—Exit Caesar's legions—Cheshire invaded by Northumbrians—King Egbert's trip on the Dee—Ethelfrida rebuilds Chester—Chester Castle, its dungeons and Torture Chamber—Outcome of Howard's visit to Chester—King Canute and Knutsford, etc.

THE records of the Bucklow Hundred and its antiquities, by Sir Peter Leycester, form the basis of all Cheshire history. Sir Peter began to search into " the beginning of things " by telling a humorous story of a renowned Welshman, David-ap-Jenkyn-ap-Rhys, who compiled his family pedigree. One of his successors had possession of that famous and probably mythical sword, of which it was written that—

> When it had slain a Cheshire man
> 'Twould toast a Cheshire cheese.

When Rhys had dealt with his predecessors for some centuries, he interpolated the remark, " About this time Adam was born." Having told this story, Sir Peter pursues his theme, dealing with the Deluge, the confusion of tongues, the Babylonish captivity, the death of Julius Caesar, until we find ourselves standing, as it were, in front of Chester Castle in this year of Grace, at liberty to adorn another tale in the Annals of County Palatine and point to the prospect

> Where queenly Britain to the Hibernian sea
> Her side presents. Here Cheshire displays its pleasant fields ;
> Cheshire, a starry crown set full of noble men,
> As when a field grows proud with countless flowers.

But we should look in vain in those far off days for undulating scenery dotted with pleasant pastures made picturesque by billowy vegetation and Magpie timbered homesteads so familiar to Cheshire, alternated with homely villages with their rustic surroundings, with towers and spires of village churches emphasised by " the free fair homes of England," and the market towns and other adjuncts of manufacturing and commercial enterprise. On the contrary, we should have looked down upon a waste of stunted trees and scrub, of heather and sand, of patches of greenery which probably afforded a precarious subsistence for northern reindeer and for the ancient Britons whom we first

SIR PETER LEYCESTER,
First Cheshire Historian

EARL EGERTON OF TATTON

find inhabiting a kingdom called Mercia, stretching from north to south in a westerly direction, and it is said that from this kingdom the Mersey derives its name. It was the ancient Britons, probably the Cornavii, who were found by the Romans, and who were afterwards driven out of their native country by the invading Saxons and Englishmen to find a refuge, some in the fastnesses of Wales, others in Cornwall, and some as far north as Scotland where the Celtic language is spoken to this day.

Thus by " jumping o'er time and turning the accomplishment of years into an hour-glass," we find invading Romans dividing Britain into two great provinces. Cheshire became a part of Britannia Secundus, and on a further division into smaller provinces it became a part of Flavia Caesariensis. From the Caestre Sceyre of the Romans it is an easy transition to Chestershire or Cheshire. The county, which gives its name to the ancient and picturesque city of Chester with its time-worn walls, whose beginnings are lost in the mists of antiquity, is bounded on the north by the Mersey, which divides it from Lancashire, and by a small portion of Yorkshire; on the east by Derbyshire, and here the Rivers Etherow and Goyt form the boundary; south-east by Staffordshire; on the south by Shropshire; north-west by Denbighshire and on the west by Flintshire and the sea. Its area is 110,489 square miles, say 707,078 acres.

During the period which would elapse, as described in the preceding chapter, and the peopling of the country by the ancient Britons, there were conspicuous changes in the appearance of both landscape and seascape. Its desolate aspect would have changed. The sandy desert and stunted trees would have given place on the south and east over a tract of country eastward and southwards to forests and grass covering thousands of square miles of land, including the great Cheshire plain; and north and west we should look over the wide estuary of the River Dee, with the gloomy Welsh hills forming an appropriate and striking background. Further eastwards would be dense forests in which probably the Druids, whose doings were only known by oral tradition, carried out their mysterious rites. Probably this has not lost anything by continuous repetition and tales of victims immolated to appease an offended god, victims taken in tribal wars, or children and maidens bearing some relation to the sacrifice to the Moloch of scripture may be regarded as fanciful or unfounded as the reader may choose. Cannibalism in connection therewith was also said to prevail, but of this there is no actual proof.

Certain it is that 2500 years ago, roughly 500 years before the arrival of the Romans, there would in such a favourable position be a number of people forming a community who had probably emigrated from the East, chiefly the Mediterranean sea-board. Here also there would be rough fortifications. A Roman general described the place as a collection of huts within a mound or *vallum*, which commanded a strong position on the banks of the Dee, and this would be the nucleus of the settlement. A visitor from the Greek colony of Marseilles states there were sheep and cattle and wheat in the country, evidencing pastoral and agricultural progress, and allusion is made to the variable climate and the manufacture of an intoxicant by the natives out of corn and honey

Here we are still in the region of myth and speculation. " Leon Gawer, a mighty strong gyant," is said by Higden, a monk of St Werburgh, who died in 1363, to have laid the foundations of the city, and " built many caves and dungeons, but no goodly building, proper or pleasant." King Lear, the titular head of Shakespeare's melancholy tragedy, " a Briton fine and valiant," it is asserted, " enriched Chester by pleasant buildings which was named Guer Leir by him."

The Celtic imagination, too, has made Chester the Neomagus founded by Magus, son of Samothes, son of Japheth, son of Noah, many years after the Flood. It is also stated that a giant named Leon Vaur (probably Leon Gawer), a conqueror of the Picts, built a city here, which was afterwards beautified by two British princes, Caerleid and Carleir. The chronicler of this remarkable statement says they are "raw antiquaries" who credit it, and we are therefore compelled to fall back on more reliable records.

History is, as already noted, to a large extent, a reflex of the past throwing a shining light on the present. Hence we find in Cheshire, barrows or tumuli, burial places of the ancient Britons, marked on the Ordnance Survey maps, but they were not common to this country alone. They were extensively used by the Greeks, Romans, and Scandinavians, and some of these tumuli, as at Marathon, were very large, and the higher they were the greater must have been the esteem in which the deceased was held by his fellows. In Dunham New Park is a mound called Beech Mount, marked by a cluster of noble trees, which is referred to in " Britannia Romana " in 1732 by Horsley in discussing the controversial theme of the site of the Roman station, Condate. He states that urns and other remains were found in Dunham Park, and part of the Roman Road was in the middle of a field directly leading from Manchester to Chester, probably Watling Street. Thus is recorded an important fact. It is in this road that the Romans have left a mark of their greatness when all appearances of ancient Saxon power had been completely effaced. The urns speak to us of Rome in her palmy days, but the mounds tell a story which extends beyond. Imagination pictures a somewhat rugged country studded with the kraals or mud dwellings of the aboriginal inhabitants. Near the great high road would be the dwelling of the hardy chieftain. At his death, guided by those aesthetic tastes instinct even in savage nations, the nearest spot on which Nature had greatly lavished her beauties would be selected for his burial place, and at what would then be the head of a mossy dell would his remains be laid. There would be the long procession of bearded warriors and slaves, headed by weirdly robed priests, who, amidst moanings and lamentations, would perform with mysterious and perhaps ghastly rites, the last offices for the dead. The huge tumulus would be raised, with nothing but its height to remind the people that buried greatness there reposed in its last long sleep, with no image or legendary scroll to record for the information of succeeding generations the names and deeds of the mighty dead; their very remembrance would in time be blotted out. But the chieftain would have a grand burial place, not perhaps graced with the virtues of consecration, except in the sense in which Nature reflects Nature's deity. There we may leave him in Nature's Presence Chamber itself, standing out like the refreshing greenery of a desert oasis in the forest primeval, where—

> The murmuring pines and the hemlocks
> Bearded with moss, in garments green,
> Stand like Druids of old, with voices sad and prophetic;
> Stand like harpers hoar, with beards that rest on their bosoms.

The invasion of Britain was not determined upon by Julius Caesar without due observation and preparation. He was only too well acquainted, by reports received by him in Gaul, of the stubborn nature of the ancient British. His famous legions, however, quickly effected their subjugation, the circumstances attending which are matters of history. Chester then became for a long period a flourishing Roman Colony. Ostorious Scapula was the Legate of the Emperor Claudius, and to him is the foundation of Chester really ascribed, being the country looking on the sea, towards the coast of Ireland. In A.D. 58-59 we find Suetonius Paulinus, another Imperial Legate, representing the infamous Nero, who, according to history, was an amateur fiddler who made an exhibition of his skill while Rome was in flames. Nero, it is written, had Christians sewn in the skins of wild animals, and then roasted slowly to death, while Antoninus Pius (what a horrible travesty on a good name!) had them "scourged until their veins and sinews were laid bare; many were dismembered and torn asunder by wild horses." Agricola finally established Roman dominion in these islands. He governed during the reigns of Vespasian, Titus, and Domitian, A.D. 78-85.

Under his beneficent rule the country flourished, and he no doubt was the projector of those famous roads which are a marvel and subject of speculation in the present day. There was even an approach to commercial practice, as pigs of lead bearing the names of Vespasian and other Roman Emperors have been found, evidently produced in the neighbourhood of Chester, while the roads enabled the salt from Northwich to be transported to all parts of the kingdom.

Of documentary evidence there is very little. All is fragmentary and isolated and hidden, except where casual excavation or intermittent though, to some extent, systematic exploration has taken place. Speaking roughly, for two and a half centuries, say from A.D. 400 to A.D. 650, we know little, although considerable light has been thrown upon it by modern research. The Roman civilisation of Britain was of a high character. When they conquered the country they introduced their language, their arts, their literature, their system of agriculture, for Cheshire cheese later became an article of commerce and was used for the consumption of the Roman army. Their roads have remained ever since the great arterial lines of communication, and are to-day followed by the main lines of railway radiating from London. We can picture Chester as a pleasant place of residence in Roman times. We can compare it in some respects to Silchester (Galleva) near Reading, especially in the extent and thickness of its walls. Evidences are found there, such as rings, personal ornaments, and even safety pins, showing that the citizens led a refined and often luxurious life. One historian goes so far as to say that Chester then boasted a fire engine. Throughout Roman Britain the same high degree of civilisation is everywhere manifest. We find in many places in Cheshire reminders of this important fact. For instance, at Hale Barns, near Altrincham, which is well off the direct Roman road to Mancunium, or Manchester, there was discovered on digging the foundation for the Manor House sixty or seventy years ago, a tessellated pavement and other Roman remains. On the tithe map for the township of Hale is a field termed Vallum Field. There is very little doubt that if further excavations were made there would be uncovered the remains possibly of a large Roman villa, if not those of a Roman station. The configuration of the ground favours this supposition. Watkin, in his monumental work on Roman Cheshire, deals fully with all branches of this interesting subject.

There is much of this ancient record rich with the spoils of Time yet to unroll. The homes and villas of the Roman residents in Chester, we are told, were surrounded by beautiful gardens, groves, and fish ponds, picture galleries, and libraries within elaborate settings of gorgeously decorated rooms, rich hangings, luxurious baths or hypocausts replete and beautified with all that wealth could suggest or artists achieve. Near the centre of the city was to be found the stately Praetorium where the law was administered—the Forum, the common hall, showing the greatness and importance of the city. Here would be found all phases of human life—the arrivals and departures of the units of the Roman legions, a human touch in the arrivals of new citizens from Rome and the Continent; also school play, processions, feast days, etc. The religion of the Romans was "the unknown God," but we cannot find that there was a circus as at Rome with victims devoured by wild beasts in the arena. We can recall in imagination the visits of the Roman matrons, probably accompanied by their children, to the shops in the novel and inimitable " Rows " to patronise the Roman predecessors of the Browns and the Bollands. There, as now, only different in character and consonant with the times, they would find their needs supplied by ancient purveyors in the way of rich clothes, velvets, silks, hoods of a primitive character, fitted with novel clasps, rare manuscripts, books, missals, novel footwear, gums, spices, and delicate perfumes—indeed, all the wealth of the Orient, Rome, and other Continental cities—enough to make even we luxurious moderns green with envy at their apparent good fortune.

Chester was indeed then a pleasant place of residence, for doubtless in the groves or on fair Deva's banks would be found shady retreats realising Wordsworth's idea of those fair scenes for childhood's opening bloom, gilding life also for sportive youth who strayed therein as well, for manhood to enjoy his strength, and where the aged could pass away in ease and comfort. In striking contrast to all this grandeur we are told that slaves were trafficked in by the inhabitants. Possibly it was the evil of slavery that made political freedom and constitutional government in Rome impossible. As in Athens in earlier times, it fostered a spirit of selfishness and sensuality, of lawlessness and insolence which is not consistent with political equality, political justice, and political moderation. In this respect Great Britain may be looked upon in the present century as an example and a model worthy of imitation to the rest of the nations of the earth.

The "Rows" have been described as a unique feature of Chester's architecture. They are more—they are a national asset and a local glory. To descend to the prosaic, they may be described as rows of shops one over the other. But there is nothing like them in any other part of the world. Every Cestrian in his way, therefore, can regard himself as "a bloated monopolist" —a monopoly of which he may well be proud. While the idea of these "Rows" is attributable to the Romans, there is also a little doubt that at the hands of mediaeval builders and their successors they were worked out in times when "plague, pestilence, and famine," and inroads by the Welsh permitted of peaceful intervals. It is also stated that they would furnish a convenient means of street defence. They are confined within a certain area covered by Upper Bridge Street, as far as Whitefriars on the one hand, and Pepper (or Piper) Street on the other. Watergate Street, Eastgate Street, and Northgate Street also have a full share. They date back to 1278, when Chester was devastated by fire, but the earliest reference in the city records is 1331. There are three rows noted—Ironmongers Row in Northgate Street, Baxter Row and Cooks Row in Eastgate Street. There was a tendency, as is found in the present day, of trades developing in certain centres. Hence in Watergate Street were the fleshers or flesheners in Butchers Row, with the fishmongers as near and very appropriate neighbours. The mercers were located in Upper Bridge Street, near by Pepper Alley Row; Shoemakers Row, and, suggestively enough, Brokenshin Row, where citizens would doubtless be

B

taught by painful experience to walk warily. These are, in the present day, an object of much interest to tourists.

The Roman roads of Cheshire form a network over the county. Probably they in their turn followed to some extent the lines of their Celtic predecessors, for, as already pointed out, there are many evidences of their having inhabited it from the very earliest times to the coming of the Roman cohorts. The work of the conquerors was, however, more substantial and enduring. The Romans were great road makers, just as their successors, the modern British, are great railroad builders. Taking Chester or Deva as a starting point we will now proceed to trace their ramifications.

The most important was, in all probability, the road to Manchester or Mancunium. This ran through Northwich where there was a junction with that from Wilderspool, and on to Dunham Massey, to a point still known as Street Head, to the ford of the street (Stretford) direct to Manchester. There was a branch road from Northwich to Kinderton (Condate), and from the last named station a direct road to Stockport. From Stockport again ran a road eastward to Melandra Castle on the borders of Yorkshire. In the same district another communicated with Buxton. Returning to Chester, a road ran through Malpas, Burton, Beeston, and Bunbury to Nantwich, while another, starting from near Boughton, also reached Nantwich *via* Beeston Castle. To the southeast this road continued to Chesterton, Staffordshire. At Farndon are Roman remains, as also at Holt, a short distance away. Cart-loads of broken pottery, tiles, and drain pipes have been found, many of which bear the stamp of the XX Legion, with its badge of the wild boar. Roman tiles and portions of a hypocaust have been found at Crewe Hill. Farndon was on the road between Chester and Wroxeter, and it has been suggested that the site of Holt may have been occupied by kilns for the manufacture of tiles and pipes. Mr Thompson Watkins in his " Roman Cheshire " favours the idea that Holt or Farndon, and not Bangor-is-y-Coed, may have been the site of the Roman Boviam, as they are nine English and ten Roman miles from Chester, whereas Bangor is at least fifteen miles from that city. Although not very clearly defined on the map, there was an important Britanno Roman settlement in the peninsula of Wirral, where at the present day are to be found the remains of a submerged forest near Leasowe. Near this spot at Hoylake (originally Hyelake), as also Hilbre Island, were found various antiquities belonging to the Roman and Saxon periods. It is further notable that from Meols, William III. embarked his army in 1690 to try conclusions with James II., which ended so disastrously for the last named at the Battle of the Boyne.

Hilbre Island was, according to Hollinshed, the goal of " a set of superstitious fools on pilgrimage to our lady of Hilbery, by whose offerings the monks were cherished and maintained." Bradshaw, the monk, gives an account in his life of St Werburgh of the miraculous intervention of that saint on behalf of the then Earl of Chester. The Earl was on a pilgrimage to the well of St Winefred near by, when he was attacked by a strong party of Welsh and took shelter in Basingwerk Abbey. This place was very insecure in the face of such bloodthirsty foes, and praying for the intercession of St Werburgh, the saint promptly threw up sand banks which separated the waters The constable of Halton arrived in the nick of time and, assisted by his troops, achieved a providential rescue. It is asserted that this gave a widespread celebrity to the island from which the monks reaped no small advantage from "the credulous fools" aforesaid.

Roman civilisation in Britain rested mainly on city life, and in Britain, as elsewhere, the city was thoroughly Roman. The bulk of the population scattered over the country, however, seem to have clung to their old laws and language, and to have retained a semblance of the allegiance to their native chiefs. For centuries the Roman sword secured order and peace, and with peace and order came a wide and rapid prosperity But evils which sapped the strength of the Roman empire told at last on the province of Britain. Wealth and population declined under a crushing system of taxation, under restrictions which fettered industry, under a despotism which crushed out all local independence. And with decay within came danger from without. To defend Italy against the Goths, Rome in the opening of the fifth century withdrew her legions from Britain and left her to struggle unaided against a crowd of enemies.

With the incoming of the Saxons and Danes there was marked another epoch in our "rough island story." She became a victim to the Picts and Scots. For nearly half a century the Britons fought against these invaders, internal differences, tribal fighting in Wales and West Cheshire, brought warriors from Jutland in A.D. 449, with Hengist and Horsa at their head, and struck a note which made the history of Englishmen in this land. With this notable landing English history begins.

Meantime, Cheshire had become an object of attention on the part of the Danes, who landed on the western portion of the Wirral Peninsula. But the most dangerous enemy to Cheshire came from the north. In A.D. 607 Chester was captured and destroyed by Ethelfrid, King of Northumberland. He came to avenge the quarrel of St Augustine, the first Archbishop of Canterbury, to whose metropolitan jurisdiction the British monks and bishops refused to submit. Ethelfrid, in his turn, was defeated by several British princes, and in 613 Cadwan was elected King of Wales by an assembly of the Britons at Chester.

In A.D. 830 Cheshire was finally wrested from the ancient Britons, and we have the historic event of King Egbert being rowed on the Dee by eight tributary kings or chieftains—Kenneth III. of Scotland, Malcome of Cumberland, Macon of the Isle of Man, James of Galloway, Howell of North Wales,

Owen of South Wales, and two joint rulers, Speth of South Wales, and Inkel of Cumberland. He afterwards held a court at Chester and received the homage of his tributary kings " from Berwick unto Kent." The Danes, however, became troublesome, and in 894 took possession of Chester.

They, however, met with considerable opposition from King Alfred's forces, and were compelled to take refuge in Wales, where it is traditional history that they mingled with the natives, and became part and parcel of a British tribe, then inhabiting that part of the country. Of Ethelfrida or Ethelfleda, daughter of King Alfred, and Queen of Mercia, it is recorded that she was by her power " terrible to men," and although she was " by nature a queen, courage made her a king." She rebuilt the walls of Chester in 907, and adorned them with turrets. She did more—she repaired, enlarged, and beautified the city, and various authorities have attributed to her the building of Chester Castle, although probably its foundations may have been originally laid and some buildings erected in the time of the Romans.

Ethelfrida, after her husband's death, built a town or fortress at Eadelburg or Eddisbury (" happy town," according to Camden), in the forest of Delamere, and another at Runcorn. The high ground within the enclosure of what is known as the " old pale " is said to have been the site of Ethelfrida's city at Eddisbury. On the summit of the hill are evidences of extensive earthworks and fortifications, surrounded by a dry ditch and embracing a considerable area. The castle at Runcorn was built on land projecting into the river opposite Runcorn Gap. This commanded the passage from the kingdom of Mercia into that of Northumberland. Castle Rock is supposed to have been the site of the castle, of which no vestiges remain. It probably stood on a mound of earth near by, and appears to have been defended by a ditch of from twelve to sixteen feet in width.

Earthworks were thrown up by her, whilst the line of the ditch that belonged to the mound on which the flag tower stood may still be discerned. The late Mr E. W. Cox, who made a minute examination of the modern buildings on the west side of the court, satisfied himself that the lower story of the flag tower still existed enclosed within modern work, and was the only evidence of Norman masonry having been erected on the site.

A portion of the mediaeval work is preserved in the Julian tower besides the walls on the south and west. The tower is of three storeys, each room being vaulted in stone, the centre one having been a chapel, and it was in this chapel that James II. heard Mass on the 27th August 1687, before he departed from the city in great dudgeon at the reception he had met with at the hands of a section of the citizens. In the lower court was a noble hall, where, it is said, Hugh Lupus held his court, and adjoining was the exchequer and parliament house of the Earls of Chester.

In or near this part were the torture chamber, cells or dungeons, which were built in Saxon style with loopholes and gratings. At the main entrance was a high wall with a heavy oak and iron door bristling with nails, and of immense thickness, the whole having a forbidding and desolate appearance. Once inside, the poor wretch who was in charge of the sheriff or his deputy, could certainly abandon all hope of seeing the light of day again unless powerful interest was brought to bear in his favour. There was a hive of cells, narrow and contracted, and scarcely allowing of the poor prisoner stretching at length upon the damp and noisome ground. Of ventilation there was very little and the mortality amongst the prisoners was extremely great. Infection was frequently communicated to the inhabitants of the city outside with lamentable results. An inner room, generally on a level with the foundation, was the torture chamber, in which was a fireplace for heating the implements used. It was awful for prisoners to descend into these unknown depths. There was no loophole or lamp. The prisoner was always sent there by the sheriff, a person of high consideration, always an esquire, and often a knight. The sheriff appears to have performed the duties now discharged by His Majesty's judges. He had the right of summary trial of prisoners, and could either order their release or sentence them to death. This was the gaol delivery, a duty now performed by the Judge of Assize. He presented Bills of Indictment to the Grand Jury, then, as now, composed of twenty-four gentlemen of the county. These returned a true bill (*billa vera*), if no true bill (*ignoramus*).

In the last named case the sheriff had the privilege of tearing up the Bill. In these modern days it is cut with a pair of scissors by the foreman of the Grand Jury. The sheriff was accompanied by vergers, the coroners were part of the sheriff's cortege, and the clerks of the market as escort, and with gentlemen of the county and their servants in gorgeous liveries made up a handsome suite. He embodied, according to one authority, the life of justice, of law, and of the country. These customs are abolished, though we get an idea of it now from the ceremonial entry at the Assizes of the judges, accompanied by the sheriff, his retinue of javelin men, and other officials.

All the prisons in England at this early time had their chambers of torture. Norman legislation has been described as "a tamed tiger with a velvet paw," but the claws are still there in the form of what can be done under the penal code. Many an English judge " has stuck lovingly to an antiquated atrocity so long as it had a Saxon or Norman derivation." In 1867 an Irish fenian was sentenced to be hanged, drawn, and quartered. Still, past history soberly asserts that torture was never practised in England. Matthew of Westminster says, " Saxon law was very clement and kind, did not punish criminals by death, but limited itself to cutting off the nose and scooping out the eyes." This, and other forms of torture, prevailed in Chester for some centuries. Yet it was not called torture. It was putting a man to what was dignified by the classic term of "*Peine forte et dure*" (As much as a man could stand and sometimes more).

There were various forms. It was at Nuremburg, the cradle of the Hohenzollerns, that the greatest and most terrible instruments of torture were to be found. The most fiendish ingenuity was displayed in their construction so that they should inflict the greatest amount of suffering. Neither age nor youth was spared its horrors or its shame. Torture was allowed in Bavaria and Hanover and some of the smaller German states until the end of the eighteenth century. Torture in England was common at one time, and the last instance recorded under a " torture warrant " was in 1640. The "*Peine forte et dure*" entailed fearful and agonising torture on the victim. If he refused to plead he was laid flat on his back, with his arms and legs drawn as far asunder as possible by ropes. On his breast and stomach was placed a plate of iron, on which reposed five or six large stones. There was, however, some preparation before this could be done. The man must have refused to answer any questions, notwithstanding chains, shackles, fetters, and irons. This process occupied three days. On the first day he was given nothing to eat or drink. On the second day they gave drink, but nothing to eat. At three different times and in three different glasses they forced open his mouth and poured a pint of water (taken from the common sewer of the prison) down his throat. If after this he refused to answer, he was left to die. We gladly draw a veil over this revolting record, merely giving it as one of many forms of punishment such as men being flogged, flayed, hanged, burned, and roasted to death, etc. There are instruments proving this still preserved at Chester. Cheshire had thus more than one martyr.

In 1788 the Castle was the prison for debtors and felons, and its condition shocked even John Howard, the philanthropist. They were much of the same description as those noted above, no change having apparently been made for centuries. No difference was made between convicted and unconvicted prisoners, and it was no uncommon thing for males and females to be herded together. Amongst the instruments of torture, in addition to those noted above, there were used the thumbscrew and what was sarcastically described as a necklet. The last named instrument was made to fit round the neck and the inner part was fitted with sharp pointed iron studs. It is a pleasant task to record that Howard's efforts were the cause of the abolition of this terrible state of things.

Knutsford or " Cnutsford," early in the eleventh century, is supposed to have received its name from the fact of King Canute, or Cnut, as his name was anciently written, having crossed a ford in the neighbourhood with his army against the Prince of Cumberland and the King of Scotland. Green, in his " History of Knutsford," points out that it is no mere piece of imagination to suppose that tradition only hands down a historical truth, and that Knutsford is really the ford of Canute the King. Domesday Book gives it the name of Cunetesford. Canute, when he reigned over England, committed the government of this part of Mercia to certain men, upon whom he conferred the title of " Earls of Chester." During the closing years of the Anglo-Saxon period three of these ruled under that title—Leofric, the son of Leofwin ; Algar, the son of Leofric ; and Edwin, the son of Edgar. Canute is said to have waded through slaughter to a throne, as many other semi-barbarous monarchs did in those ages. He employed himself as a kind of spiritual fire insurance in his old age in exercises of piety, built churches, endowed monasteries, and undertook a pilgrimage to Rome, where he was present at the Coronation of the German Emperor Conrad, but with an eye to the " main chance," in exchange for the strict payment of Peter's pence and other ecclesiastical dues, he obtained an abatement of the large sums exacted from the Archbishops for those ornamental, but little needed, head coverings, called " palls," and some privileges for English pilgrims when they visited Rome. He was also the hero of a sloppy little fable which credits him with teaching his courtiers a lesson when he ordered the incoming tide not to wet his royal feet. His death occurred in 1035, which event opened up the Norman period of English history.

CHAPTER III.

Feudalism and the Divine Right of Kings—The first Anglo-Saxon King—Relations between Lords of the Soil and their Vassals—Effects of the Feudal System—Land, produce, and prices—The Conqueror's descent — The Norman Earls — Hugh Lupus, Randle Blundeville, and others— Cheshire's first Parliament—Charters granted for trading by Earls and Barons—The first House of Commons—Earl John's unfortunate marriage—Edward, first Royal Prince of Wales and Earl of Chester—The Conquest of Wales and death of Llewellyn.

WITH the advent of the Conqueror, feudalism in this country attained its full development. It had existed in a military form under the Danish régime, and its nucleus originated in the nations of Scandinavia. With the World War of 1914-18, the last of the feudal idea, as developed in the German confederation, comes to an end. With it also comes an end to the theory of the "Right divine of kings" and Kaisers, which the English nation, three centuries ago under the aegis of a Christian Bismarck, named Oliver Cromwell, effectually "squelched." This Cromwell, the son of a Huntingdon brewer, attached his name to treaties as Protector of England above that of the King of France, and founded the maritime domination of this country on the sure lines of victory and commerce. He cleared out the Dutch and Spanish navies, and enabled England to enter into the sea coasts of the world. She has since ruled the seas, thereby commanding the world. It is said that Cromwell's Regiment of Ironsides figured in the fears of Europe against an army. He wished and succeeded in making England as respected as was the Republic of Rome. Yet in the rebound of the Restoration, gibbets had been provided for the Regicides (long before dead), and the term "traitor" had been written in the register of the church where Bradshaw was baptised; other times, other manners. Thus there was laid the foundation of a democracy which is being developed in full in the twentieth century.

At the time of the Saxon subjugation of England, British names generally gave place to Anglo-Saxon ones, and it was under this régime we get a settled or regular monarchical government. Ella of Sussex was the first to assume the title of cyning or king, but this was elective throughout the whole of the period, and there was no rule of hereditary succession. Hence we get two principal classes—eorls (earls) and ceorls (churls)—gentle and simple, nobles and yeomen. Out of this state of things sprang national councils (witenagemote, or assembly of witans or wisemen), division of the land, shires, hundreds, tythings, really securities for the peace; guilds, etc. The blood bond gave its first form to English justice, as it gave their forms to English Society and English warfare. All classes fought side by side on the soil. The woodland and pasture land of an English village was open and undivided, just as in the Norman period the inhabitants or burgesses had the right of turning their swine or cattle out to feed on the land or forest up to the " hay " or hedge of land belonging to the lord of the district. This method of sharing in the common land marked the difference between freeman and the unfree man or laet, the tiller of the land which another owned. The laet tilled the ground he held. He had house and home of his own, and as time went on he came to be recognised as a member of the nation, summoned to the folkmoot, all owed equal right at law, and was called, like the freeman, to the " hosting " or gathering of the tribe. He had no rights, however, against the lord of the soil, and he could not leave land or lord at his will, but was bound to render due service in tillage or in fight. So long, however, as these services were done the land was his own.

The township or village, small as it was, was the primary and perfect type of English life, domestic, social, and political. All that England has developed into since lay in these little commonwealths drawn together for war or mutual defence. The meetings of the wisemen, the witenagemote, also formed the council of war, and thence the ealdormen (chiefs) brought the men of the village to the field. The force was made up of levies from the various districts of the tribes, the larger of which probably owed their names of hundreds to the hundred warriors each originally sent. The form passed away with the lapse of time, but there are remnants to be found in Cheshire to this day of the old Parliament, presided over by Hugh Lupus, which derived authority and power from the Conqueror, as a County Palatine. This, in due course, was abolished, and its power became centred in the Crown, and Cheshire had the privilege of representation in the Commons House of Parliament. From this radiated again local government in councils, county and local, but the court-leets, now only carried on in a few townships in a formal manner, had in those far-off centuries the administration of local affairs under a charter granted by the feudal lord, all of which will be dealt with in this and subsequent pages.

" Under the feudal system," says Froude, " men were held together by oaths, free acknowledgments, and reciprocal obligations entered into by all ranks high and low, binding servants to their masters, as well as nobles to their kings ; and in the beautiful roll of the old language in which the oaths were sworn we cannot choose but see that in changing to modern practices that we have lost something in exchanging those ties for the harsher connecting links of mutual self interest." The ceremony at which the vassal acknowledged his feudal dependance was called homage—a man (homo) became the man or servant of his lord. This was accompanied by an oath of fealty on the part of the vassal and investiture on the part of the lord, which was the conveying of possession of the fief by some pledge or token. He had to do personal service in the army, and could not free himself from his fief and service by merely renouncing them. There were two kinds of homage, liege and simple, and the liege man took the oath of fealty on his knees without sword and spurs, with his hands placed between those of his lord. In simple homage he did this standing, girt with sword, and with his hands at liberty. Thus, in the case of fealty, the statute said: "He shall hold his right hand 'upon' the book and shall say: 'Hear you, my lord, that I shall be to you both faithful and true, and shall owe my faith to you for the land that I hold, and lawfully shall do such customs and services as my duty is to you, at the times assigned. So help me God and all His saints.'"

"The villein, when he shall do fealty to his lord, shall hold his right hand 'over' the book, and shall say: 'Hear you, my lord, that I from this day forth unto you shall be true and faithful, and shall owe you fealty for the land I hold of you in villeinage; and that no evil or damage shall I see concerning you, but I will defend and warn you to my power. So help me God and all His saints.'"

A burgess seems to have been the oldest voter known in England, and it is recorded that they made their elections—that is, of members to serve in parliament in the time of Henry VIII. The poll was originally taken in a very different fashion to that now in vogue. The meaning of the word polling is "a counting of heads." From this we derive the word polled, "cut even at the edge." There is a picturesque account in the Book of Numbers and other chapters of the counting or polling of the tribes. Absolom, the chief of the conspirators and contemnor of good counsels, was much praised for his beauty; "from the crown of his head to the sole of his feet there was no blemish in him." And when he polled his head at every year's end, he weighed the hair cut off at two hundred shekels after the king's weight. Another injunction was that the priests should only poll, not shave, their heads.

Although the feudal system has been railed at as having been productive of many evils in connection with land tenure in modern times, many learned historians are unanimous that, on the whole, it worked well in the age in which it was first evolved. For instance, the overlord residing in his country seat, usually a fortified mansion or castle, lost in course of time in a great measure his acquaintance with the reigning prince or king, and added every day new force to his authority over the vassals of his barony. They received from him education in all military enterprises; they enjoyed his hospitality and life in his great hall; their ample leisure made them perpetual protectors of his person and partakers of his sports and amusements; their ambition was generally satisfied by figuring in his train, his displeasure exposed them to contempt and ignominy, and they felt every hour the necessity of his protection, both in differences with other vassals, but in what was more material, the daily inroads and injuries of neighbouring barons. There was then, no doubt, a state of subjection and serfdom, from which the rise of cities and the progress of commerce was in later ages destined to free them.

But it was truly patriarchal, and no doubt inspired Macaulay's lines apropos of Roman civilisation when he wrote that

> "None were for a party,
> But all were for the State;
> The rich man loved the poor
> And the poor man loved the great."

In the distribution of the produce of the land, again, it is on record that "men dealt fairly and justly with each other," and in the material condition of the bulk of the people, which in later times gave rise to a sturdy, high-hearted race, sound in body and fierce in spirit, and furnished with thews and sinews which, under the stimulus of "great shins of beef," their common diet, were the wonder of the age. "What comyn folk in all this world," says a state paper in 1515, "may compare with the comyns of England in riches, freedom, liberty, welfare, and all prosperity? What comyn folk is so mighty, so strong in the felde as the comyns of England?" This was written in the early days of Henry VIII., and there are numerous expressions in the time of Elizabeth and her successors to confirm the fact that bread, beef, and beer (genuine home brewed) was the staple food, with rare exceptions, of the English people, before tea and slops became the prevailing fashion. In proof of this, the state of the working classes of the period is to be found by comparison of their wages with the price of food. Wheat averaged 6s. 8d. per quarter, except in times of war and failure of the crops. Beef and pork were ½d. per lb.; mutton, ¾d. Strong beer, such as that which in these days costs around 2s. to 2s. 6d. per gallon, cost 1d. per gallon; table beer less than a ½d. The best pig or goose in the country could be bought for 4d., a chicken for a 1d., and a hen for 2d. In 1302 the Earl's cook at Chester Castle was paid 2d. per day, and the gardener 3d per day. A pig could be bought for 3s. 4d., an ox for 6s., and the rent of an acre of land was 8d. per year. In 1379 a bushel of wheat sold in Chester for 6d., a gallon of claret for 4d., a fat goose for 2d., and a fat pig for 1d. In 1414 wheat sold at 4s. per quarter, and in 1437 at 7s., which was very dear, and caused "great suffering among the poor." In the time of Edward VI. an Act of Parliament was enacted that "Forasmuch as of late, divers sellers of victuals, not contented with moderate and reasonable gain . . . have conspired and covenanted together to sell their victuals at unreasonable prices—butchers, brewers, bakers . . . costermongers, or fruiterers; first offence, £10 fine or twenty days' imprisonment, and bread and water for his sustenance; second offence, £20 and the pillory; third offence, £40 or the pillory and ears cut off." Need we wonder that with such profuse abundance the English owed the great physical power they possessed, coupled as it was with the soldier's training, in which every man was bred from childhood.

Few people are acquainted with the descent of the Conqueror, whose advent in this country had such momentous and far-reaching consequences. His great ancestor was one Anfrid or Amfrid, a Dane, and Hugh Lupus, the first Earl of Chester, was a grandson of Richard, son of Anfrid. Earl Hugh was given by the Conqueror "the county of Cheshire." This was made sure to him by charter, as well as to his successors, by "the sword of Dignity, to call parliaments at his will, to order his subjects after true justice, as a prepotent Prince, and statutes to devise." In fact, his mere word was absolute law.

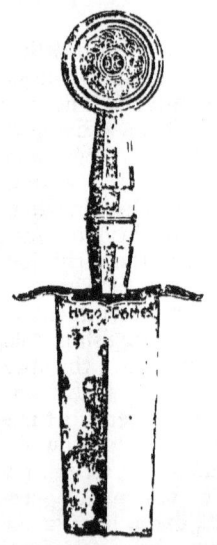

The sword of Hugh Lupus is inscribed "Hugo Comes Cestriae" (Hugh, Earl of Chester). It is double edged, tapers to a point, and is nearly four feet in length, the width of the blade near the handle being two inches. The handle is gilt, elaborately inlaid with mother-of-pearl, and adorned with scrolls of flowers and leaves. The guard, which is wanting, is given on the authority of Dr Gower, and is represented as being beautifully inlaid with mother-of-pearl, each segment presenting a different design of very tasteful and well-proportioned outlines.

Hugh Lupus' Sword.   Hugh Lupus' Guard.

It is recorded in Domesday Book that there was originally twelve hundreds, including Chester, in the county. These were reduced to seven at a later date. The city of Chester was made a distinct county, except the Castle, by Henry VII. in 1506. New hundreds, including Wirral, Eddisbury, Maxfield (Macclesfield) were formed out of the others, Bucklow and one or two of the old hundreds remaining.

Speed describes Cheshire as "the seedplott of gentilitie," and Camden as a "most surpassing nursery of ancient gentry above any other county in England," and Leycester regarded Bucklow Hundred as "the prime border of that nursery."

It is generally supposed that Hugh Lupus, who had for his crest a wolf's head, which was also that of the XX. Legion, was the first Earl of Chester.

This is not so. Sometime prior thereto, in 1070, William the Conqueror conferred it upon Gherbod, a nobleman of Flanders, for military assistance rendered in the country, but he, falling into the hands of his enemies, underwent a long and tedious imprisonment. In Saxon times the title of Earl of Chester, as noted in a previous chapter, applied not only to this county but to the kingdom of Mercia. Hugh Lupus, however, was a person of note amongst the Norman nobility, and as an expert soldier was placed near Wales, then part of unconquered Britain, " the better to restrain their bold invasions." He was nicknamed by the Welshmen and other descendants of the Ancient Britons, " Hugh the fat," or gross, and was described by an old historian as being " very prodigal, daily wasting his estate and delighting more in Falconers

Hugh Lupus' Crest.

and Huntsmen than in tillers of the land or Heaven's orators (prayers) and ministers." He was also given to " gluttoning, whereby in time he grew so fat that he could scarcely crawl." That he was a lover of worldly pleasure and " similar pomp " there is no doubt, but he would nowadays be regarded as a thorough sportsman. He was a terror to the Welsh by reason of his cruelty and bloodshed, and no doubt salved his conscience by having in his train clerks (priests) and soldiers who were " men of great honour." His confessor was Anselm, afterwards Archbishop of Canterbury. As time went on he became, it is said, a great devotee of religion, and three days before his death, " with sickness hanging heavy upon him," he caused himself " to be shorn a Monk in the Abbey of St Werburgh." He could well afford to be prodigal with his wealth, as he was an extensive landed proprietor in " twenty of the fairest counties of England," and he also possessed forty-eight towns, chiefly market towns, including all in Cheshire. It is further asserted that he had several illegitimate sons and daughters who were " almost swept away by sundry misfortunes."

We prefer, however, to take more authentic records. Hugh Lupus married Ermantrude, daughter of the Earl of Bevois, in France, and had a son, Richard, who succeeded. There was some doubt about another son, Ottiwell, and a daughter, Gevas, both of whom he acknowledged, and to whom he bequeathed certain lands which some contemporary historians contend legitimatised them. Richard married Maud, daughter of Stephen of Blois, and Gevas married one Geoffrey Riddell.

It is recorded that King Henry, the reigning monarch, after receiving the homage of the Barons of Normandy, set sail from Barfleur, leaving his son, Prince William, behind. He, in turn, was to have sailed by the " White Swan," but was detained, and the interval was spent by the captain, Thomas Fitzstephens, in a debauch of drink, and in their anxiety to overtake the King's ship he drove the vessel on a rock and she foundered immediately. William was put in the longboat and had got clear of the ship when, hearing the cries of his natural sister, the Countess of Perche, he ordered the seamen to row back, in the hope of saving her ; but the numbers who crowded in sank the boat, and the Prince with his retinue perished. Richard, son and heir of Hugh Lupus, had attached himself to the Court of Henry, and he and his Countess, his brother Ottiwell, his sister Gevas, and his brother-in-law Riddell, including above 140 young noblemen of the principal families of England and Normandy, were lost on this tragic occasion.

Henry I. died in 1135 from eating too plentifully of lampreys, a food which always agreed " better with his palate than his constitution." A humorist has suggested that as he was surnamed Beauclerc that he devoted too much time to study, and that he really expired from " lamp-rays," or too much burning of the midnight oil !

In King's Vale Royal is a plate representing Hugh Lupus, holding a court, attended by his barons, and the Abbots of Chester and Combermere. These Abbots were summoned to the parliament for the county palatine, in the same way as other ecclesiastics, in the reign of the early kings of England, to the royal court. These barons were appointed for eminent services and superior knowledge of war. They were : Nigel, the Earl's cousin, Baron of Halton, High Constable and Marshall of Cheshire ; Robert, or Eustace Crewe, Baron of Monte Alto, or Montalt (Hawarden and Mold), High Steward of Cheshire ; William, Baron of Wich Maltberg or Malbank (Nantwich) ; Robert Fitzhugh, Baron of Malpas ; Robert de Vernon, Baron of Shipbrooke ; Hamon or Hamo de Massie, Baron of Dunham Massie ; Gilbert Venables, Baron of Kinderton, whose heirs survived in direct line until 1679 ; Nicholas, Baron of Stockport ; and Robert, Baron of Rhuddlan.

Hugh and other Norman Earls of Chester had their chamberlains, barons of exchequer, sheriffs, and other officers similar to the officers of the Crown at Westminster. The barons were also invested with wide and far-reaching powers. They had their own courts of pleas, suits, and plaints so dear to the legal mind, excepting the powers reserved especially by the Earl and his descendants. They had power of life and death over their servants, retainers, and the inhabitants generally. The last person to be tried for murder in the court of Sir Thomas Venables, Baron of Kinderton, was Hugh Stringer, who was executed in 1503. In return the barons were bound to attend on the Earl in time of war, especially when he went to fight the Welsh, and to find for each knight's fee, one horse harnessed and two unharnessed within the divisions of Cheshire, and their knights and free tenants were to be furnished with breast-plates and haubergeons, and to defend their respective fees in person.

Richard, the eldest son of Hugh Lupus, was succeeded by Ranulph de Meschines, his cousin, whose aunt was sister of Hugh Lupus.

Of the Norman Earls of Chester, pride of place is given to Randle III., surnamed Blundeville, who took an active part in the affairs of the county, especially Chester, and he gave three charters about 1202 to the city, which was a port in the true sense of the word, vessels then being able to anchor under its walls, and the citizens carried on an extensive trade with Ireland. The citizens had powers of merchant guilds or guilds mercatory (societies for free trading), as in the time of his ancestors, and any one disturbing or preventing them were subjected to the then heavy penalty of £10. They were given the privilege of holding courts to settle disputes, and strangers were forbidden to bring merchandise to the city or buy or sell except through the citizens, excepting only at fairs held annually in June and September. John Scot, Earl of Chester, in his day confirmed these charters, although in the matter of supplies of food and merchandise to his household he appears to have reserved a preference for himself and his justiciaries.

Randle III. was one of the spirited gentry who refused to pay tithes or imposts to the Pope of Rome. He expelled the Pope's officers from the county palatine. This was in striking contrast to the conduct of the rest of the people in this country, as also Scotland and Ireland, who paid the dues and probably looked as pleasant as possible under the operation. Probably the Earl was influenced by the fact that papal aggression at this period reached a high pitch, and that under the feeble rule of Henry III. preference had been given to foreigners over those of native birth. He further asserted his independence by refusing, in 1232, to accede to the demand from Henry III. for money at a critical period in the country's history. The barons of England were in direct conflict with the king, and the country was riven by civil war. There was a powerful combination by them against an illegal administration. That good came out of evil is manifest in that the barons in this reign extorted from the Crown the great charter which laid the foundations of the English constitution. Many stormy episodes accompanied by bloodshed followed. The powerful Simon Montfort, Earl of Leicester, in 1265, laid the foundation of what may be justly regarded as our present House of Commons, the mother of parliaments. He ordered returns to be made of two knights from each shire, and, what was more remarkable, two representatives from each boro, inhabitants of which had previously been regarded as too "mean" to take part in the councils of the nation.

At the marriage of Henry III. to Queen Eleanor, the above-named John, the Scot, last and eighth Earl of Chester, carried the sword of St Edward before the King, in token that he was the Earl Palatine, and "had the power by right to restrain the King if he should do (anything) amiss." His constable (nicknamed Hell Fire Lacy) attended him and "beat the people back with a rod or staff" when "they pressed disorderly upon him." Scot died shortly afterwards at the Abbey of Darnhall. He had no issue, and under the pretence of preventing the earldom being divided amongst distaffs, as his sisters were rather sneeringly termed, the king seized the domain.

For a long period before the death of the aforesaid John Scot, Llewellyn, a fiery Welsh prince, with an equally fiery daughter named Helena, had been exceedingly troublesome to the English living in Cheshire and on the Welsh borders. In order, as he thought, to secure peace the Earl married Helena. She turned out to be " wild and turbulent," and is said to have poisoned him, with the result mentioned above so far as the earldom was concerned. Edward I. in 1283 finally subdued the Welsh. The nobility submitted to the laws of England, sheriffs and ministers of justice were established in the principality, and though it was long before national antipathies were blotted out and a thorough union established, yet this important conquest, which had required eight hundred years to mature, was fully effected, and the young heir, Edward, born at Carnarvon, became Prince of Wales, a title which has been borne by the eldest son of the kings of England since that time.

Some years afterwards, when this Royal Earl, son of Edward I., made his first visit to Chester in that capacity, he received the homage of his nobles, officers, and military tenants, as also of the Bishop and clergy. He also granted a charter confirming and enlarging the privileges of the citizens, but strictly guarding the royal feudal rights. Under this charter the government of the city became settled for more than a century. In later years, Edward, the Black Prince, personally confirmed this, and preceding charters in addition, giving the citizens plenary powers over the tolls, dues, and customs on imports on the Dee between Chester and Arnold's Eye (Hoylake). The borders of the city were also considerably extended at a cost to the citizens of 500 marks, or about £337, paid to the Prince in four annual instalments. There were other charters giving exceptional privileges as to trade, especially with Ireland, characteristic of the reign of the first Edward and subsequent reigns, which could not fail to be of great benefit and advantage to the citizens of the capital of the county.

CHAPTER IV.

Whence came Christianity to Cheshire?—Paul, "the Apostle to the Gentiles"—Prehistoric Irish Literature, a striking curse—The Christian Church and Ireland—Welsh Saints and Augustine—Werburgh and Plegmnnd, two Cheshire Saints—Miracles wrought at the Shrine of St Werburgh—The fame of St Plegmund—The foundation of St John's Church—Abbots and their servants—Morality at a low ebb—Suppression of religious houses—Its effect in Cheshire—Easily obtained indulgences—Origin of Chester Cathedral—Its restoration in modern times—Dean Howson's memorable work—Public and private gifts—The martyrdom of Marsh at Chester—Church feuds at Rostherne—Queen Mary's messenger and the pack of cards—An alleged "humorous incident"—The old Consistory Court.

WHENCE came Christianity to Cheshire? Answers to the question vary considerably, and have been the subject of much controversy in the past, and may give rise to much more in the future. The early religion of the Ancient Britons was Druidism, and following the Roman invasion for at least two centuries Cheshire, with the rest of the country, was under the spell of paganism, or such religion as the Romans permitted. There was probably considerable traffic overseas with various parts of Europe, especially Rome, and some historians have gone so far as to assert that St Paul, "the apostle to the Gentiles," actually preached at Chester. For this they assume a warranty from the Epistles to the Corinthians, where he speaks of having been shipwrecked on three occasions, and having suffered greatly in his journeyings, entailing hunger, cold, nakedness, and other forms of suffering.

We tread on firmer ground, however, when we cast our eyes across the waters to the sister Isle. Ireland, in the century before Christ, had a literature in which figures heroic warriors, law givers, and statesmen. One chapter of pre-Christian Irish literature relates to the death of the children of Usnach, and is taken from the King Conor Macnessa cycle, first century B.C. It relates that King Conor goes to a banquet in the house of Feilimid, his storyteller. During the festivity, Deirdre, the daughter of Feilimid, is born. Cathbad, the druid, foretells her future beauty and the destruction it will bring upon Ulster and on kings and nobles. Thereupon the nobles demand the death of the infant, but the King orders her "to be shut up in a strong tower until she grows old enough to become his wife."

A charming love story is deduced from the above. Deirdre saw and loved Naisi, the son of Usnach. So they departed into another country, taking with them "three times fifty men of might, three times fifty women, three times fifty greyhounds, and three times fifty attendants." Naisi took Deirdre to be his wife, and they fled to Alba (Scotland). Here Deirdre suspects they will be the victims of foul play, and she and her husband set sail with all his retainers for Ireland. Dierdre, on leaving, sings a song of farewell to Alba and her green shealing on the shores of Glen Etive. A terrible battle is fought against King

Conor, in which Naisi especially distinguishes himself, and " till the sands of the sea, the dewdrops on the meadows, the leaves of the forest, or the stars of heaven be counted, it is not possible to tell the number of hands and heads, and lopped limbs of heroes that there lay bare and red at the hands of Naisi and his brothers on that plain." Deirdre sings the funeral song over sons of Usnach—

> " Woe is me ! by fraud and wrong,
> Traitors false and tyrants strong,
> Fell Clan Usnach bought and sold
> For Barach's feast and Conor's gold ;
> Woe to Emain, roof and wall ;
> Woe to Red Branch, hearth and hall ;
> Tenfold woe and black dishonour
> To the foul and false Clan Conor ;
> Dig the grave both wide and deep,
> Sick I am and fain would sleep.
> Dig the grave and make it ready,
> Lay me on my true love's body."

So saying, she flung herself into the grave and expired.

There are also episodes from the Tain Bo Cauilone, of cattle spoil of Coolney, the chief epic of ancient Ireland, also Cuchullin's wooing of Eimer. Hers were " the gift of beauty of person, the gift of voice, gift of music, the gift of embroidery and of all needlework, the gift of wisdom, and the gift of virtuous chastity." In it is described the fight of Cuchullin and Ferdiah at the ford, when he is threatened by the Bardic curse " which withers and dishonours heroes," and afterwards Cuchullin is treacherously slain, and the great hero of the Gael falls. " Thereat the sun darkened, and the earth trembled, and a wail of agony from immortal mouths shrilled across the land, and a pale panic smote the hosts of Meav, when with a crash fell the pillar of heroism, and the flame of the warlike valor of Erin was extinguished."

One can well imagine in face of the above that a Christian church was founded in Ireland in or near the fifth century, by St Patrick, and that he and his associates spread the light of the gospel in England and Scotland and other European countries. Indeed, it is asserted, that such was the fame St Patrick's missionary efforts had acquired that he was an honoured guest of the Great Charlemagne. It is on record that Christianity had been introduced into England in the sixth century, and it would appear that many religious houses were to be found in or near Chester, notably the monastery of Bangor or Banchor, which flourished with learned men at the coming of Augustine. Saints David, Asaph, and Padern all flourished after the Saxons had occupied England, and the sixth century saw not only the foundation of Welsh bishoprics, but also of the great Welsh monasteries, which were the especial glory of the church in Wales. But "the British Christians liked not the haughty ways of Augustine and his new-fangled customs," and at a council refused subjection. It would appear that a large number of monks attended this council, and because they did not rise from their seats on his entry into the place of meeting he waxed wroth, and said that "if they would not preach the way of life to the English they should at their hands undergo the vengeance."

When Cheshire was overrun by King Ethelfrid the Britons were defeated. Chester was captured and 1200 monks of Bangor were slaughtered. Bede, who had Roman leanings, saw in this slaughter the execution of the divine judgment and a fulfilment of Augustine's prophecy, but Ethelfrid's triumph was of short duration. The Welsh princes marched with an army on Chester, drove out the Northumbrian King with great slaughter, and elected Cadwan, King of Wales, at Chester.

Doubts have been expressed as to the number of monks slain, but it appears that they were grouped in communities so that the report is not to be wondered at.

Cheshire boasts two Saints, Werburgh and Plegmund. "The holy lyfe and history of Saynte Werburgh, very fruteful for all christen people to rede," was the work of Henry Bradshaw, a monk, who died in 1513. St Werburgh, whose descent was royal on both sides, was born in 650, and Penda, King of Mercia, whose ancestor was Woden, and a pagan at that, had descendants who earned the title of saints from their father's side. Wulfhere and his queen lived at Stone in Staffordshire, and here she was educated in a religious atmosphere, and she was described as a minister of the abbey over which she presided.

> "Piteous and merciful and full of charity
> To the poor people in their necessity.
> . . . . .
> She never commanded systers to do anything
> But it was filled in her own doing."

A truly saintly character, which her life and actions fully deserved. She is said to have died about the year 699. Her remains were, in 875, to prevent their desecration by the pagan Danes, removed to Chester, where her shrine was erected in the mother church of St Peter and St Paul. This was possibly near the site of the present Cathedral, which, in its turn, is said to have been built on a Roman temple dedicated to Apollo. Ethelfrida, daughter of King Alfred, built a separate minster to St Werburgh, joining it to the east end of an older church. This was rebuilt by Leofric, a pre-Norman Earl of Chester, and gave place to the Norman church of Hugh Lupus. Throughout the changes the name of St Werburgh was associated with the dedication of the church, and miracles were supposed to have happened at her shrine when barbaric nations, such as the Welsh, threatened to destroy the city. In 1180 it was said that a great fire which threatened to destroy Chester was subdued when the holy shrine was borne through the streets by the monks. No trace remains of the earlier structures, but the fifteenth century one has, in recent years, been placed at the west end of the Lady Chapel of the Cathedral as being probably near the spot where it originally stood. At the foundation of the See, and up till 1870, says Archdeacon Barber, the lower portion formed the base of the Bishop's throne, the crown being lowered so as to form the balustrade in front of the Bishop's seat. In this adaptation certain stones were removed, and were built up in the wall which enclosed the staircase which led from the Bishop's study directly into the Cathedral. In removing this staircase in 1885, these stones were discovered, and have again been placed on the shrine, which is thus restored to its original proportions. The shrine was adorned with canopied niches, in which were sculptured figures bearing their names on the scrolls, representing the kings and saints of the Mercian kingdom.

St Plegmund is said to have exercised a wide and beneficent influence on Church and State, both in his own day and succeeding generations. Like St Werburgh, he was a native of Mercia. His birthplace and parentage are unknown, but his name is preserved in the parish of Plemstall, or Plegmundstall. Here he established himself as a hermit, in solitude amid fens and marshes, far from the inroads of the Danes. The fame of his learning caused him to be called to the Court of King Alfred, where he found other learned men of the time, and was associated with the monarch in the promotion of learning and the interests of the nation. Plegmund was consecrated Archbishop of Canterbury by Pope Formosus at Rome about 890, but as some doubt and discredit was thrown upon the actions of this pontiff he made a second visit to the Eternal City, and was reconsecrated by Pope Stephen, thus "submitting to a rite of more than questionable propriety." In conjunction with the King (Alfred) he published the pastoral care of Gregory the Great, a copy of which was sent to every English bishop. There was a preface by the King himself, in which he acknowledged what he had learned of Plegmund, "my Archbishop, and of Asser, my bishop, and of Grimbald, my presbyter, and of John, my presbyter." The late Mr Thomas Hughes, F.S.A., has delightfully pictured the laying of the foundation of St John's, Chester. "First there were Ethelred and Ethelfrida, the joint founders; near them might stand their Royal ward, Athelstane, the Etheling heir to his father's throne. Prominent among the group would be Plegmund, the Archbishop of Canterbury, a native of Mercia, and but a few years before a modest recluse at the hermitage in that island home at Chester." He died in 914, and his memory is preserved in St Plegmund's well.

We need not enter into definitions of abbeys, priories, preceptories, etc., except, perhaps, to notice the immense power wielded by the abbots during the early period under review. In connection with St Werburgh's Abbey, they were frequently called upon to exercise judicial functions and take evidence in secular law suits in addition to performing their religious duties. They also appear to have claimed powers equal with those of the barons, as mentioned in their charters. That the abbots or their servants, on many occasions, adhered to what they thought were their legal rights, is evidenced by the complaint to the Archbishop of York, just before the Reformation, of Marjery Clarke, his "poor Bedewoman," who was a tenant at will of John, " late Abbot of St Werburgh." She stated that she, her late husband, William, and five children had been ejected from their home in the depth of winter, and had taken refuge for three weeks in the Parish Church, until they were turned out by the vicar at the instigation of the abbot. This expression goes to show that parish churches were then used for housing the homeless poor, just as they were used by coroners for holding inquests. It was further alleged by Marjery that the farm stock, furniture, and household goods were thrown into a pond of water and destroyed, and that in consequence her husband was seized with illness and " shortly departed this world." It appeared that in the meantime the abbot had resigned, but she asserted that his successor refused to compensate her unless ordered by the king to do so. She does not appear to have fared well, for she could not, owing to lack of means, pursue the matter against "a great Lord of such honour and dignity."

Prior to this, in 1458, there is record of a " composition " being made between the abbot and the parishioners of St Oswald's for their new church. In a land dispute which followed the Reformation, Alderman Wm. Goodman deposed that he was "seised of a pasture adjoining Pynchewer Heys in the county of the said cytye, under lease from the late abbot and convent of Chester, which premises your majesty (Henry VIII.) has since given to the dean and chapter of the cathedral church in Chester," and that " riotous persons to the number of three hundred, in one great rout assembled, cut down the quykwood thorns and other trees growing there for the defence of the pastures, putting in danger of destruction great quantities of whete and other graynes growing nere unto the said pasture." This is interesting as showing how easy was the transition of national property from one governing body to another.

The monks of Vale Royal enjoyed under the grant of the reigning king many great privileges, including the right of "advowry" or probation of criminals, and the power of life and death within the manors of Darnhall, Over, and Weaverham. Disputes with tenants were frequent, and in one case offenders who took up arms made submission to the abbot with ropes round their necks, and ten forfeited their goods and chattels. In a subsequent insurrection the ringleaders were thrown into prison. In their turn, the abbots and certain monks were ordered to be seized by sergeants of the peace for encouraging banditti which infested the county, but " they sat tight," remaining in their own desmesne, and the precept was returned to the effect that they could not be seized without infringing the rights of Holy Mother Church. There were other disturbances in the county in which their servants mutilated the debtors, one poor fellow having one of his ears cut off. On the credit side it should be stated that one, John Buckley, the thirteenth Abbot, distinguished himself by bravely leading the tenantry of the Abbey, 300 in number, at Flodden Field. At the Reformation Thomas Leigh, Esq., was selected for the inspection of religious houses in Cheshire, and he gave striking reports on the immorality prevailing in the district. The education of the poor, he said, was neglected (" the good and godly instruction of the rude and poor people "), " certyn of the knights and gentlemen and most comonly all, lyvyth so incontinently havynge ther co'cubynes (concubines) openly in their houses with v. or vi. of their chyldren, putting from them their wyfes that all the countrey thereat be not a lettill offynded and taketh evill example."

Sir Peter Leycester has the following " note " regarding the granting of indulgences in mediaeval times : " Sir John Seyvill, knight, brother of the hospital of St John of Jerusalem, and procurer of the pardon of indulgence of the Castle of St Peter (by virtue of the indulgence of Pope Alexander V., granted to those who put their helping hand to the fortification of the said castle, that they should choose themselves a confessor) now granteth to Hugh de Toft and Alice his wife, because of their charity and aid towards the said castle, full liberty by the Pope's authority, to choose themselves a Confessor ; whereunto the seal of the Indulgence of the said castle is affixed, dated 1412, and on the back of the said deed is written in Latin, ' The Lord Jesus Christ who hath given his disciples power of binding and loosing, absolve thee ; and I by the Apostolic authority of St Paul, and the whole mother church, by the help of both which and the Pope's Indulgence do absolve thee from all sins, of which by contrition thou hast confessed, or hereafter shall confess, and I grant thee full remission of all thy sins, that thou mayest have eternal life for ever. Amen.' And if it happens that thou recover not this present infirmity, I reserve it for thee even in the very point of death."

In the reign of Henry VIII. came the great conflict with the Pope, accompanied by the excommunication of the monarch by the Roman pontiff. The suppression of religious houses above a certain value followed, by which in Cheshire, in common with the rest of the kingdom, vast revenues, movables, money, and jewels were " alienated." Great discontent and distress led to open rebellion, and further exactions and destruction by this rapacious monarch. Out of the revenues he afterwards founded six new bishoprics, including Chester, and deans and prebendaries reigned in place of abbot and monks. Tenants at will under the Abbot of St Werburgh, afterwards held lands of the Dean and Chapter, which had been given to them by the king.

St Werburgh's Abbey is preserved in the present Cathedral, which is legally named "the Cathedral Church of the Blessed Virgin Mary in Chester," and likewise the Cathedral Church of the diocese. The dissolution of the monasteries thus gave to Chester the ancient church of the monks, which, with adjacent buildings and varying styles of architecture, is full of interest to all classes. The Norman edifice is attributed to Archbishop Anselm, to whom reference has been previously made. The ancient buildings passed through the ordeal of fire, and they were left in ruins. In the work of renovation and additions in succeeding years following their foundation, the abbots must be credited with a large share, assisted by the barons, prominent amongst whom was Randle Blundeville. The Parish Church of St Oswald was a part of the south transept of the Cathedral, and was occupied by the parishioners until 1880, when it was once more thrown into the main building, and the partition which had separated it was removed. The restoration of the interior, some years ago, was effected as a memorial to Hugh Lupus, first Duke of Westminster. The dukedom was conferred by Queen Victoria—a fitting reward for years of devoted labour in the service of Cheshire and the nation at large. The choir stalls, with their beautiful and elegant woodwork, including quaint and richly carved misereres and the delicate tabernacle work with which they are crowned, are well preserved. In the Lady Chapel is preserved another treasure in the shrine of St Werburgh, which took the place of an earlier fourteenth century structure. It is adorned with forty figures, richly gilded, representing ancestors or relatives of St Werburgh.

A part of the Abbot's Chapel, including the wine cellar and the room above, now form the baptistry, and in it is a beautiful fifth century font, of Italian origin, which was given by the late Earl Egerton of Tatton, in 1885. This font came from a ruined church in Romagna, but it was not known whence it came to Venice. It is rectangular in shape and cut out of white marble. The gates of the north and south choir aisles, given by the first Duke of Westminster, are French, of the date 1558. Another gift of the Duke, a unique work of the seventeenth century, is a narwhal tusk, seven feet six inches in length, carved by a Flemish hand. The leading subject is the Incarnation of our Lord, passing on to the exaltation of the Cross. A Jesse tree occupies about three feet, and above this is seated the Blessed Virgin with the Holy Child. Higher up is the Cross, with the figure of our Saviour, whose countenance is full of compassion. Behind this is a representation of the Crucifixion, including a figure of St Michael the Archangel thrusting down Lucifer with a cross. Above this come figures of St Peter and St Paul, the four Evangelists, etc. This curious and beautiful piece of carved ivory is supposed to have belonged to some Franciscan church.

An exquisite and richly carved oak reredos was placed in the former Parish Church of St Oswald, and was the gift of Mr and Mrs T. Brocklebank of Rosecote, Heswall, in memory of Mary Adeline, and Margaret Elsie Royds, and Mary Petrina Brocklebank, their children, " who caused this reredos to be made when the altar was reinstated on its ancient site in the year of our Redemption 1906." A reredos, strictly speaking, is the wall at the back of the altar or holy table in churches. In Spanish churches the reredos is often the most decorative feature, generally as wide as the nave, and reaching to the vaulting of the roof. There is a reredos somewhat resembling these at Christchurch, Hampshire, and there are other richly decorated and carved examples in other churches and cathedrals, of which the above in St Oswald's is a notable example.

In the centre is the figure of St Oswald, and on either side two scenes from his life, flanked by angels in canopied niches, holding scrolls on which is inscribed " Alleluia." The Saint holds in his right hand the wooden cross; his left hand rests upon the sword which is girt to his side, and the crown on his head betokens his kingly origin. The first incident in the battle of " Heaven's Field " is represented in carving on the left or north side, where Oswald was victorious over Cadwallon and the Welsh army. The carving on the south side represents St Oswald's death at the hands of Penda, King of Mercia.

The altar cross in this part of the Cathedral contains, in the quarterfoil endings of the arms, the evangelistic symbols in silver, and bearing at the back the following inscription : " Remember O Lord our God, thy servants Thomas and Arthur Randall Flintt, who out of this life passed to Thee, Sepr. 12, 1887 ; Sepr. 27, 1903." There are two chairs on the north side, which are from Florence, and are exact copies of Savonarola's chair in that city.

The lectern was the gift of Miss Eliza Potts, of Chester, and the Bishop's throne was mainly contributed to by the clergy of the diocese. The beautiful ornamentation of the ceiling and walls of the Lady Chapel was executed in the time of Dean Anson, at the expense of Mrs Hamilton of Hoole House, in memory of her family. The window of the south transept was erected in 1887, by the late Earl Egerton of Tatton, as a memorial to his father, the first Baron Egerton of Tatton, and there are numerous memorials of officers and members of the Cheshire Regiment and the Earl of Chester's Imperial Yeomanry.

A notice of the restoration of Chester Cathedral in 1868 would be incomplete without a reference to the work of the Very Rev. John Saul Howson, who held office as Dean from 1867 to the time of his death in 1885. The work of restoration was on an extensive scale, and the sum of £90,000 was contributed, principally by churchmen, and augmented by members of other denominations, who regarded Chester Cathedral as one in which they had more than a passing interest

Unrest in the kingdom during the later years of Henry VIII. found an echo in church disputes at Rostherne, or Rowesthorne, which had been held for thirty years by John Lancaster, Prior of Lande, Leicestershire. " Sir

George Bothe of Donham, Randall Bruerton (Brereton), and other dyvers mysruled persons," it is said, desired a lease of it, to which Lancaster would never agree. According to his story they so threatened him with violence that " he secretly departed from Purley parsonage to his monasterys." " At the time William Hardwyche (Hardwick) was the parson and Rychard Leghe, esqr., Randall Antrobus, priest, Randall Venables, John Shuttylworthe, Henry Glayve (Gleave), Roger Bratchegurdyll (Bracegirdle), by command of William Venables, Esq.," came violently to Rostherne Church, " pulled the vicar out of his stall, and installed Randall Antrobus in his place, who remained, having no auctoritie (authority) so to do," and to empower this there were about two hundred persons armed for the most part " with staves," probably bludgeons.

Snede, another priest, who had evidently been sent by the Prior of Lande to assert his authority, denied that Venables had any right to interfere, and tried to bribe the parishioners by a promise that he would forgive them all their tithes in arrears to the Prior if they would aid him. Very few of the congregation made any movement, and Richard Legh stood up and invited them " to speke masters." They then replied that they " wold assist him " but whether it was Snede or Venables, it is difficult to say. The dispute seems to have proceeded, and apparently came to a head in Passion week. There, at the high altar, stood Snede's retainers, with " swordes, buklers, and daggers, and did receive the tithes and ' houselyng money ' for use of their master, and would not allow anyone to pay tithes to the prior's proctor." In the fourth week in Lent one Nicolas Skeylhorne (Skelhorn), a blacksmith, pulled the lock off the chancel door with swords, etc., though it is difficult to say how he accomplished this feat with a sword. Snede or Sneyd declared that the tithes belonged to the Prior of Lande, and he would not allow Hardwick, the vicar, to say Mass. We find that at this time the vicar was twenty-seven years of age, and that William Heighfield, who collected the tithes of the parish for over sixteen years, stated they amounted " to £17, within ten shillings more or less."

The advowson and parsonage of Routhesthorne, for so the name is once more spelt, were claimed by Wm. Venables through one of his ancestors of the same name, as appendant to the manor of Kinderton, and that he was heir, having held the glebe, and that he presented Raufe Sneyd, who was lawfully instituted and admitted by the Archdeacon's authority. We do not know the outcome of this little quarrel, but there is every probability that Venables held possession, especially in view of the Legh and Booth interest, which was all-powerful in the parish.

Bishop Bird, D.D., was a descendant of an ancient Cheshire family, and was the first Bishop of Chester appointed by Henry VIII. in 1541, and on the accession of Queen Mary he tried to accommodate himself to the new order of things by observing the changes which were introduced. He was deposed from his position, and for a few brief months—months full of cruelty and zeal n the promotion of Popery it is recorded—George Cotes, his successor in 1554, held sway. By his authority the pious George Marsh was burnt to death at Chester for alleged heresy. Marsh was born at Dean in Lancashire, and brought up as a farmer. On the death of his youthful wife he entered the University of Cambridge, and became curate to the " holy martyr," Lawrence Saunders, of Langton, in Leicestershire. He afterwards laboured in his native county as curate to William Rothwell, vicar of Dean. When Queen Mary came to the throne and re-established the Roman Catholic religion, he refused to conform, and openly preached against the doctrines of Romanism. He resolved to stand firm, even unto death, for Christ and conscience sake. In one of his addresses to his congregation, whom he calls the faithful professors of Langton, he writes : " Wherefore, my beloved in Christ, let us, on whom the ends of the world are come, take diligent heed unto ourselves that now in these last and perilous times we withhold not the truth in unrighteousness, believing, doing, or speaking anything against our knowledge and conscience, or without faith. For if we do, for whatsoever cause it be, it is a wilful and obstinate infidelity, and a sin unto death ; and, as our Saviour Christ saith, If ye believe not ye shall die in your sins." Being urged by his friends to "flee" the country, in order to escape threatened imprisonment and persecution, he answered : " My life, mother, children, brethren, sisters, and friends, with other delights of life, are as dear and sweet unto me as unto any other man, and I would loathe to lose them as another would, if I might hold them with a good conscience and without the ignominy of Christ ; and seeing I cannot do that, my trust is that God will strengthen me with His Holy Spirit to lose them all for His sake ; for I take myself for a sheep appointed to be slain, patiently to suffer what cross soever it shall please my merciful Father to lay on me." He was imprisoned in Lancaster Castle. Bishop Cotes sent for the gaoler, and rebuked him because he suffered Marsh to fare so well, and ordered to have him more " straitly kept and dieted " ; but, said Marsh, " If his lordship were tabled but one week with me, I do not think he would judge our fare but slender enough."

The poor prisoner was soon afterwards removed to Chester Castle, and the Bishop sent for him and conversed with him. He also sent his chaplain and schoolmaster to him, in order to convert him. Transubstantiation was the theme of their argument, but Marsh was firm against it. Bribes and threats alike failed to move him ; and in a few weeks he was brought before the Bishop and his colleagues, in Our Lady's Chapel in Chester Cathedral, to take oath upon the charges made against him, and to receive sentence of death. The chancellor " stopt " the Bishop twice while reading the sentence, and, with the people, appealed to Marsh to recant. He answered : " I would as fain live as you, if in so doing I should not denie my master Christ, and again he should denie me before his Father in heaven." Having read the sentence, the Bishop said : " Now will I no more pray for thee than I will for a dog," and Marsh answered that he would, notwithstanding, pray for his lordship. The officers carried him to his dark prison in the North Gate, where he was very closely kept " till his death." "Some of the citizens who loved him for the gospel's sake would in the evening, at a hole in the wall of the city opening into his dungeon, ask him how he did. He would answer them cheerfully that he did quite well, and thanked God most highly that he would vouchsafe of his mercy to appoint him to be a witness of His truth, and to suffer for the same, wherein he did most rejoice. Once or twice he had money cast in at the same hole, for which he gave thanks to God and used for his necessity."

The day for his martyrdom having arrived, the sheriffs (Amry and Cowper) led him out to Spital Boughton, within the liberties of the city. After the exhibition of a conditional pardon by the vice-chamberlain (Mr Vawdrey), and the refusal of it by Marsh, " he began to speak to the people, showing the cause of his death and exhorting them to stick to Christ." Whereupon one of the sheriffs (Amry probably) said : " George Marsh, we must have no sermonising now," to whom he replied, " I cry you no mercy," and " kneeling down, made his prayers, and then was chained to the post, having a number of faggots under him, and a thing like a firkin filled with pitch and tar over his head. The fire being unskilfully made, and the wind driving it to and fro, he suffered great torment, but yet endured it most patiently." The people, headed by Sheriff Cowper, " pressed forward to attempt a rescue, but were driven back by the other sheriff." When Marsh had been a long time tormented in the fire without moving, they supposed he had been dead ; but suddenly he spread his arms saying, " Father of heaven, have mercy upon me," and so " yielded his spirit into the hands of the Lord." Many of the people said openly he was a martyr and " died marvellously patiently and godly," whereupon the bishop preached a sermon in the Cathedral, affirming that " Marsh was a heretic, burnt like a heretic, and was now a firebrand in hell." The ashes of the martyr were privately interred in the burial ground of the Chapel of St Giles, in Spital Boughton. The sheriff, Cowper, in consequence of the zeal he had shown to save Marsh, was obliged at once to " flee " over Holt Bridge into Wales. He was outlawed, and had his estates seized by the Government. He remained " privately " (the Cheshire term is " hudlance ") in Carnarvonshire until the death of Queen Mary. It is interesting to note that a lineal descendant of Marsh lived in Chester fifty or sixty years ago, and suggested that famous motto, " Defence not Defiance."

Cotes was succeeded by Cuthbert Scot. He was a great politician in his day, and, being opposed to the reformed religion and disaffected towards Queen Elizabeth, he was imprisoned in the Fleet. He escaped to Louvain, where he died about the year 1560. It was during his bishopric that Dr Cole passed through Chester with a commission for the persecution of the Irish Protestants, and met with a somewhat extraordinary "interruption." The commissioner stayed at the "Blue Posts" in Bridge Street, where he was visited by the Mayor, to whom, in the course of conversation, Dr Cole communicated his errand by taking a leather box out of his bag, and saying in a tone of exultation, "Here is what will lash the heretics in Ireland." This exclamation accidentally reached the ear of the landlady of the house, who had a brother in Dublin. Whilst the Mayor was complimenting his worship downstairs, the landlady, prompted by an affectionate fear for the safety of her brother, opened the box, took out the commission, and placed in lieu of it a pack of cards with the knave of clubs uppermost. This the doctor carefully packed up, and the deception was not discovered until his arrival before the Privy Council in Dublin. The doctor was sent back for a second commission, but before he could return Queen Mary had passed away. Queen Elizabeth, her successor, rewarded the woman, whose name was Elizabeth Edmonds, with a pension of £40 a year during her life. This alleged humorous incident has no basis in fact, although all Cheshire historians, from Ormerod to Hemingway, place it on record as such. There is no mention in any English or Irish State document of Dr Coles' mission. Further, there is no record of a grant from Queen Elizabeth to Mrs Edmonds.

The old Consistory Court, before which Marsh was cited, is an appendage to the ecclesiastical institutions of the diocese of a most quaint and interesting character. It gives specimens of every style of architecture, except, indeed, the Saxon. There is Norman work in the remains of St Anselm's Church and buildings, exquisite examples of early English in the Lady Chapel and Chapter House, decorated and perpendicular, of every period in the choir, nave, and great south transept, and the Jacobean in the Consistory Court and other minor details. The Consistory Court is the Bishop's court, in which the principle is that he is surrounded by representatives of the clergy of his diocese, who act as his council. When the Abbey Church became the Cathedral of the new See, it would seem that the Lady Chapel was used as the Consistory Court. There is an old world appearance about the court, with its fittings put up nearly three centuries ago. There is a square enclosure, surrounded by a partition of oak some four feet high, with entrance doors at each corner. On the west side is a raised seat for the chancellor, and the judgment seat is flanked by another seat. Above this is an elongated oak canopy with a carved cornice and Jacobean panelling supporting it. There is a curious seat fixed on the top of the oak partition which surrounds the enclosure—a most uncomfortable looking piece of furniture, probably where the defendant or prisoner was seated—or it might have been used for the examination of witnesses. At any rate, it is extremely interesting as one of the oldest Consistory Courts in England, in which the fittings and arrangements were in vogue nearly three hundred years ago.

CHAPTER V.

Foundation of Nonconformity laid in England—Elizabeth, the strength and support of the Church—"A scrap of paper" in the olden times—Chester Nonconformity—"Nonconforming Churchmen"—Matthew Henry and Chester—Prynne's adventures in Cheshire—How his entertainers were dealt with—Brian Walton, "a weak backed Bishop"—Puritans in the Church of England—Sermons then "like motley the only wear"—The sailing of the "Mayflower" —The Pilgrim Fathers at New Plymouth—Petition of Right and Declaration of American Independence—Adam Martindale's checkered life at Rostherne—Nonconformity at Bowden —Lord Delamere's kindly attitude—Marriages before Magistrates—Burying in linen—Fear of Popish Ascendancy—Evangelical interment and the Unitarians—The Cheshire Congregational Union—A religious scandal at Dukinfield—Quarrelsome Quakers—Wesley and his work — The oldest Sunday School in Cheshire—Stockport Sunday School—Resignation of Bishop Jayne and appointment of Dr Paget—Centenary of Primitive Methodism in Cheshire.

IT was in the reign of Elizabeth, in 1550, that the keynote of Puritanism was struck by Bishop Hooper, and the foundations of Nonconformity were laid. He would even have gone farther than Cranmer in his objection to rites and ceremonies. The exiles who had found refuge in Switzerland and neighbouring countries returned, and the bishops and ministers who had been ejected under the Marian régime found their places occupied by Romish priests, who went on celebrating Mass as usual. A strong current had set in against Romanism in Edward VI.'s reign, and many churches were disfigured in consequence. The first prayer book of Edward VI. was imposed by an Act of Uniformity in 1549, with the object of checking the Anabaptists and converting the Papists. The second service book, more Protestant than the first, was published in 1552, and the forty-two articles, afterwards reduced to thirty-nine, agreed to by the bishop and other learned men in the Synod of London, were set forth by royal authority in 1553. There was a strong undercurrent of popular opinion which supported the reformers, and Elizabeth appears to have been desirous of bringing about a union of Romanists and Protestants by the service book which met the sacramental views of the former, and the articles which satisfied the latter. There appear to have been many clerical vicars of Bray about this period. Altar candles were used, vestments were worn, and even Mass was celebrated by many clergymen, but the chief claim to the support of the people was Elizabeth's refusal to accept the jurisdiction of the Pope, or any other foreign prince or potentate in this realm of England. She was regarded, not only as the head, but the strength and support of the church in this land, and Whitney, the Cheshire poet, in one of his "Emblems," expresses this view. The device is an obelisk or spire, with ivy twined round and clinging to it, with the motto underneath, "Te stante, virebo," and the following explanatory lines—

> A mighty Spyre, whose toppe dothe pierce the skie,
> An iuie (ivy) greene imbraceth rounde about
> And while it standes, the same doth bloome on highe
> But when it shrinkes, the iuie standes in dowt ;
>> The piller great, our gratious Princes is :
>> The braunche, the churche whoe speakes unto hir this :
>
> I, that of late with stormes was almoste spent,
> And brused sore with Tirants' bluddie bloes,
> Whom fire, and sworde, with persecution rent,
> And now sett free and ouerlooke my foes,
>> And whiles thow raignst, oh most renowned Queene,
>> By thie supporte my blossome shall bee greene.

The Puritans for several years at the opening of the reign of Elizabeth refused to perform popish ceremonies and to wear vestments, and their abolition was only lost in convocation by a single vote. Thus began the prolonged struggle between Puritanism and Episcopacy. In both Lancashire and Cheshire many learned ministers refused to conform, and paid the penalty by suffering ejectment from their livings.

Carlyle in his virile English writes : " It is stern business this killing of a king. Charles I. refused to *understand*. His word did not represent his thought. A man of this kind is not a man you can bargain with. You must get out of that man's way or put him out of yours. The Presbyterians in their despair were still for believing Charles, though found false and unbelievable again and again. For all our fighting, says Cromwell, we are to have a little bit of paper. No." Thus does history repeat itself. We, of this world-wide Empire were, in 1914, told by autocratic Germany, when we entered a war for the defence of treaties and the pledged word of nationalities, that we were only fighting for " a scrap of paper ! "

" Man grappling with man in fire-eyed rage—the infernal element in man called forth. This was the thing to be done. Cromwell did it. He had the eye to see (says Carlyle), the heart to dare, to advance from post to post, from victory to victory."

The Presbyterians and the Independents were at this time jealous of each other. It was a great struggle for supreme power or ascendancy, and for a time Congregationalism went under. The Restoration brought Episcopacy, and with it persecution, and united both bodies in one bond of suffering and opposition to established authority; but an attempt at union in 1691 failed. The prop of Presbyterianism in Cheshire was Sir George Booth.

The Puritans in Cheshire petitioned Parliament, declaring against Episcopacy, which was largely signed. To this the Royalists responded by a counter petition for the establishing of the Book of Common Prayer and the suppression of the Schismatiques. Cheshire became the cockpit of the two

CHESHIRE: ITS TRADITIONS AND HISTORY

factions. The Cheshire rising was quelled by Lambert's soldiers, who published a paper, famous at the time, entitled " Twenty-one Cheshire Queries." One of these was " whether the late insurrection in Cheshire was not like a hog shearing, where there is a great cry and little wool ? " " Whether he (Sir George), who penned the first declaration for a free parliament, was a Cavalier, a Jesuit, or a fifth monarchy man, and, whoever he was, whether he had never have barked than not have bitten ? " " Whether it would not have been prudently done if parliament, for the better undeceiving of posterity, to produce an Act to make void and of non-effect the old proverbial speech, Cheshire, chief of men ? " And much more criticism of Sir George and his Cheshire associates.

Chester Nonconformity has a long and interesting history. It is in this connection we come across the phrase " nonconforming churchmen." Curiously enough it has come down through the centuries. We found it recurring in a Cheshire town over half a century ago at a local vestry meeting, where a protest was made against the payment of what was deemed a form of church rate. Two or three well-to-do gentlemen offered, if it were made voluntary, to recompense the vicar out of their own pockets. They declared themselves " nonconforming churchmen," and proved the sincerity of their convictions by attending afternoon service at the parish church accompanied by their families. Since then politico-religious asperities have been smoothed materially, and such scenes as those above narrated have died out.

The celebrated Matthew Henry, a son of Philip Henry, ejected from Wybunbury, Flintshire (? Cheshire), was born in 1662, when so many ministers were driven from their cures. He was ordained in London in 1687, and in that year preached in Chester, where he was welcomed " with great joy and thankfulness " by the dissenters. It was then customary for them to attend their respective parish churches morning and afternoon. Dean Fog held this to be " schismatical," and they apparently separated from the church and held their own services. He appeared to have many influential friends. He produced his well-known Commentary, and was indefatigable in his Christian ministry. He removed to Hackney in 1712, and died suddenly when on a visit to Nantwich in 1714, in the fifty-third year of his age. He was buried at Trinity Church, Chester, his remains being followed to the grave by numerous dissenting ministers, eight conformist ministers, and by persons of note and distinction on all sides.

William Downham, D.D., one of Queen Elizabeth's chaplains, followed Scot as Bishop of Chester, and died in 1577; and in 1579 Wm. Chadderton was nominated to the See, and the same year accepted the Wardenship of Manchester, his native town, where he chiefly resided. Both these bishops were strongly against the puritanical clergy of the diocese, but Dr Bridgeman, who was consecrated in 1619, was even more so. He was also a pluralist, holding the rich living of Wigan. He was, however, a much greater persecutor of the Puritan than his predecessor. He appears to have feared the steps Archbishop Laud might have taken against him, for we find that when Chester citizens visited the Puritan Prynne, then on his way in custody to Carnarvon Castle, he had them cited before the High Commission at York. They were imprisoned and heavily fined, one £100, and another £300, besides costs, as also cost of expensive journeys to York, and they were forced to make a public recantation in the Cathedral. Calvin Bryan, or Bruen, was a bookseller in Chester, and Bishop Bridgeman, in inviting his Metropolitan at York to send warrants for the arrest of Prynne's entertainers, says that as soon as Dr Layton's book, " Zion's Plea," appeared, he took it from him, and " he being threatened and affrighted promised conformity in future." There was no other stationer in the city but Peter Ince, but the citizens appeared to get hold of Puritan issues as soon as they appeared, and, in Bridgeman's opinion, they were obtained through him. Peter Leigh, a Chester grocer, was amongst the sufferers who offered entertainment to Prynne. Prynne was active with his pen during his imprisonment, and in 1637 he was again brought up for pamphlets against prelacy.

If his persecutors had used whips before, they now used scorpions. He was sentenced to have the stumps of the ears he had previously lost cut out, was branded on both cheeks with the letters S. L., and to continue in prison at Carnarvon Castle. One of Prynne's aiders and abettors was John Brun or Bruen. The Brun, or Bruen, family was settled at Bruen Stapleford as early as 1230. In 1530 the name was given as Bryne and Bruyn. A famous Puritan member of the family was John Bruen, who in " the early days of his manhood lived a life of gaiety and dissipation." In 1587 his father died, leaving him, as it were, guardian to his twelve brothers and sisters, and charged with their bequests. This induced him to adopt a life of economy, and as a commencement the park of Bruen-Stapleford was cleared of its deer and " converted to a more profitable purpose " ; and the domestic arrangements of the family were on a rigid system of religious discipline. As the painted glass in his own chapel, and in the church at Tarvin, did not suit his religious prejudices, it was removed, and a great part of it broken. The hospitality and charity of Mr Bruen were unbounded. Mr Bruen had an old and faithful servant, named Robert Passfield, who, to retain in his memory the numerous sermons he heard, invented a " girdle of leather, long and large, which went twice about him." This he divided into several parts, allotting every book in the Bible to one of the divisions. For the chapters he had thongs for every division, and he divided the verses by similar means. By this help to his memory he was enabled to repeat to his master the purport of the sermons he heard, in a very accurate manner. Mr Bruen called it the " girdle of verity," and after Passfield's death hung it up in his study.

William Barlow, D.D., descended from the ancient family of the Barlows, of Barlow Hall, Lancashire, was born about 1564. He was brought up in the family of Bishop Cosin, whose life he wrote in 1598, and subsequently became Fellow of Trinity Hall, Cambridge, and Chaplain to Queen Elizabeth. In 1603 Dr Barlow was nominated by James I. one of the divines at the Hampton Court Conference, the substance of which controversy he afterwards published. On the death of the Earl of Essex he preached a sermon at St Paul's Cross, now very rare. On 13th December 1604 he was installed Dean of Manchester, and on 30th May in the following year he was consecrated at Lambeth, Bishop of Rochester. Having held that See, at that time the poorest in the kingdom, three years, he was translated to Lincoln and enthroned 1st September 1609. He acted as chairman of the Westminster Committee of Translators of the Bible, which was responsible for the Epistles. Bishop Barlow had the character of a learned and excellent preacher, and was in high esteem with King James and those in power about the Court. He died suddenly at his place at Buckden, 7th September 1613.

On the re-establishment of Episcopacy at the Restoration, Brian Walton, one of the authors of the famous Polyglott Bible, was appointed Bishop of Chester. He had published it in 1647 under the auspices of Cromwell, on account of his knowledge of Oriental tongues, and it is recorded that on its first issue he made due acknowledgment of this to Cromwell, but in a second edition he altered it and tendered his gratitude to Charles II. instead of the Protector. He died in 1661, and was succeeded by Dr Henry Ferne, who died five weeks after his consecration. His successor, George Hall, D.D., son of the pious Bishop Hall, of Norwich, was very severe on Nonconformists, owing to his father's sufferings. He committed Wm. Cook to the common gaol of Chester and harried Martindale out of his living at Rostherne.

The Puritans formed a great body within the Church of England, which seems to have agreed with Bishop Hall that it was better " to swallow a ceremony than to rend a church." They were too intent on reforming than to think of leaving it. The Puritan divines who held high positions either slighted or omitted the Liturgy in many parishes. At this period sermons, like " motley, were the only wear." The deep seated reverence for the scriptures had taken the place of older superstitions. There was a strong tendency to revert to the stern spirit of the Old Testament rather than to adopt the external forms of the New. Separatism sprang up, and separation from the church was promoted by persecution. Amidst all the wrangling and fighting issued the forlorn hope of Puritanism. From this, like a melancholy procession, arose the Pilgrim Fathers, those pioneers of New England, who made a way into the wilderness over the dead bodies of half their company when the " Mayflower " landed at Plymouth rock. But—

> Amidst the storm they sang,
>   And the stars heard and the sea ;
> And the sounding aisles of the dim woods rang
>   To the anthem of the free.
>
> The ocean eagle soared
>   From his nest by the white wave's foam ;
> And the rocking pines of the forest roared—
>   This was their welcome home !
>
> Aye ! call it holy ground,
>   The soil where first they trod,
> They have left unstained what there they found—
>   Freedom to worship God.

These Pilgrim Fathers were the vanguard of that greater body of Puritans, non-separatist religious reformers, amongst whom were some bearing Cheshire names still surviving in the States, who united in 1691 with the Plymouth Colony, and which merged into the larger one of Massachusetts.

No doubt the eccentricities of the adherents to the Puritan party caused the popular raillery of a not over-observant public in this country. The Puritans had little or no sense of humour. Their garb, the cut of their hair, their insistence on literally interpreting forms and abhorring ceremonies, compared with the strikingly picturesque clothing of the cavaliers, whose flowing curls and gaiety of manner, oaths, and ribald conversation had an attraction for those disposed to jeer and laugh at something uncommon. They objected especially to all forms of popular amusement as savouring of Satan and his devices. It was said that they objected to bull baiting, not so much for the pain it gave the bull, but for the pleasure it gave to the spectators. There is good ground for this statement in the fact recorded by Martindale, that he and his servants " whipt " down a maypole in the night at the village of Rostherne, so that the parishioners should not have the enjoyment connected with this old English pastime. They evidently made light of the truthful assertion of Dickens' humble showman, who told old Gradgrind that the people must and would have their amusements.

But all this was a featherweight compared with the influence of the responsible leaders of the movement. It was really heralded by the famous Petition of Right, full of judicious censure and warning to the first Charles by the Lords and Commons—the King who would not " understand," and who ultimately lost his head in consequence. Alongside this and in striking parallelism must be placed the majestic Declaration of Independence by the Congress of the United States to George III. of England, protesting against usurpations and abuses perpetuating absolute despotism, and formally taking upon themselves " all acts and things which Independent States might have the right to do." Every tyro in history knows the sequel.

And the steady stream of liberty has flowed on and broadened until our own times, when the free nations of the world have combined to fight and efface another and more deadly form of autocratic despotism (German), such as has never before been known in recorded history.

Martindale complained strongly of the treatment he received at the hands of Bishop Hall, who truckled to the patron of Rostherne (Peter Venables, a descendant of the Baron of Kinderton), " a gentleman of £5000 per annum, a huge benefactor, having given £500 towards the repairing of his Lordship's palace, and so great honourers of one another that the bishop offered his services to marry the patron's dear daughter and only beloved child, to Mr Fowler, alias Levison, and was accordingly sent for (and I question not nobly paid), for confirming them first and marrying them after."

Martindale's clerical life at Rostherne, or, as he wrote it, Rostherstone, was full of trouble from a section of his parishioners. Soon after his return from Chester, where he had to undergo a term of imprisonment for some breach of ecclesiastical law, they began to give him their unwelcome attentions. He defines them as " a rabble of prophane youths and some doting fools that took their part." The more he reproved them for their folly, the more they jeered at him. A gentleman who had come from Congleton to preach at Rostherne for a Sunday or two, heartily supported Martindale's views regarding the May Day festival " as a relic of the worship of the Strumpet Flora in Rome." When he saw the maypole he called them most opprobrious names, as " scumme, rabble, rife, rafe (riff-raff) of the parish." Martindale had his revenge, for in the night his wife, assisted by three serving maids, " whipt it down with a frame saw brest high." His opponents tried to repair the damaged pole by tying up a piece of wood to it, but it was " a crude, rough, and crooked ugly thing." Whether they had their dances round the substituted maypole is not recorded, but very probably they had.

According to Martindale, Sir Geo. Booth was a warm friend of the Presbyterians, both before and after he was ennobled as the first Lord Delamere. He had divine service in his own house, and was very kind to the ministers after the passing of the Act of Uniformity. Newcome, also an excluded minister under the Act, sheds a delightful sidelight on the religious atmosphere surrounding the family at Dunham. Newcome, who was an exemplary preacher at the Collegiate Church (now Manchester Cathedral) and subsequently at Cross Street Chapel, says : " 22nd August 1657, I went to Dunham and preached there the next day in the forenoon, and at the Chapel in the afternoon at Bowdon, on Heb. ii. 3, ' How shall we escape, if we neglect so great salvation,' and at this time had first knowledge of and acquaintance with the honourable person, Sir George Booth." Eaton and Martindale lived for a number of years at Dunham. Martindale read mathematics with Lord Delamere and his children, and instructed them therein. He also officiated at Dunham for fourteen years, and tells us that the then Bishop of Chester (Cartwright) " preached fiercely against Nonconformists at Bowdon, and as one that had a notable faculty of extracting salt water out of a pumice (stone), upon these words ' We are not ignorant of his devices ' (2 Cor. ii. 11), made even the most harmless practices of the Nonconformists, devices of satan soe farre as his Episcopall authoritie would authenticate such doctrine."

The religious controversies of that period (1662) were extremely bitter, the extent of which we have no conception in these days. There was no doubt a strong element of Nonconformity in Bowdon. Probably under the influence of Lord Delamere himself, the vicar of that day did not array himself in opposition, and whilst attending the Parish Church, as Lord Delamere himself did, also probably attended Martindale's ministrations at the Sunday evening services at Dunham Hall, where he was his lordship's chaplain.

Martindale heard from his friend Newcome that the King did not really wish to be so hard upon the Nonconformists, and that he would take it unkindly if they threw up their livings unforced. Accordingly, " on the following Sunday, no bells rang from Rostherne Church tower, but the church doors were open, and the music of the bells floated over lake and mere as usual. Outside the church there was no change. Inside there was a large congregation, but there was no man," says Martindale, " to break the bread of life to their hungry souls," so he officiated once more. He told his people " he came there in opposition to no man, but solely for the King's pleasure."

It turned out that the fact of there being no minister was a device of the then patron of the living, in order that he might be petitioned by the parishioners to procure one. Martindale's successor was the Rev. Benjamin Crosse, and it is on record that while he resided in the district Martindale attended divine service at Rostherne Parish Church. He acted as a schoolmaster, having as pupils sons of numerous gentry, but being driven from this source of livelihood through ecclesiastical threats to his patrons, he had to turn to some other means of support for himself and his family. At first he thought of medicine, but " being too conscientious," says one writer, " to kill his patients, he took to teaching mathematics," and found a great helper in Lord Delamere, who, on this and other occasions, proved his good friend. Further, he " profited greatly by Lord Delamere's kindness."

In 1653, during the Commonwealth period, there was a very stringent Act of Parliament passed requiring marriages to take place before a Justice of the Peace. The form usually adopted was the following :—

" Publication of banns of marriage was made in our parish church of Bowdon three several Lords days between John Yeates of Lime parish and Margaret Baxter of this parish, wh. days of publication were the 4th, the 11th and the 18th dayes of December in the year 1653, and were married the 23rd day of December within the same year before me, Peter Brookes, Esquire."

The following contains the first reference to a trade which was the staple one pursued in the district—" Publication of banns of marriage was made in our parish church of Bowdon three severall Lords days betwixt Wm. Tippinge, of Hale, woollin webster (woollen weaver), and Katheren Hall, of Ashley, both of this parish of Bowdon, wch. dayes of publication were the 22nd, 29th dayes of January, and the first day of February, and noe objection being made but that they might lawfully proceed in marriage: and were married by me, Thomas Standley (Stanley), of Alderley, Esquire, one of the Justices of Peace for this County, the 6th day of February 1653."

Proclamation was in some instances made, generally by the bellman, at the cross in the market-place. These proclamations usually read as follows:—

" Publication of banns was made in the Altrincham Market, within our parish of Bowdon, three severall market dayes betwixt Edward Woodall, of the parish of Ashton upon Mercey Bancke, and Anne Carrington, of this parish, which dayes of publication were the 15th, 22nd, and 29th dayes of August, in the year of our Lord God 1654, and were marryed the 16th day of September, in the year of our Lord God 1654, before Tho. Brereton, Esquire."

Some of the entries state that publication was made between the hours of eleven and two in the market-place, but this does not appear prior to the year 1656 to have been a popular method, as three-fourths of the proclamations were made in " our parish church." The majority of the marriages took place before Thomas Brereton, Esquire ; but it is interesting to note that on one or two occasions Colonel Henry Bradshaw, of Marple, brother to President Bradshaw, also officiated. In 1656 and 1657 the publications were, with few exceptions, made in the local market-place " at the close of the morning," or 12 o'clock. In 1658 they were made in solitary instances, but they are solemnised by the Vicar, James Watmough, " in the presence of numerous people." This elaborate style of entering marriages then ceases, except in the instances of the principal families of the district, when the details are given with some minuteness.

In the year 1667 an Act of Parliament was passed for the encouragement of the woollen and paper manufactures in the kingdom. It enacted that no corpse should be buried in " shirt, sheet, shroud, or shift," but in woollen, and an affidavit made within eight days of interment that the dead was not shrouded in linen. A penalty of £5 was incurred if the law was broken. These affidavits are regularly entered in the Bowdon Parish Registers, which is brought forward as an instance, as having been made, except in solitary instances which were at once notified to the churchwardens. No specific entry of the enforcement of the Act appears until June 1709, when there was—
" Alice, wife of Thomas Warburton, of Hale, buried in linnen contrary to Act of Parliament. He paid ye fine to ye churchwardens of Bowdon for ye use of ye poore." Not many years afterwards, the fine of £5 was enforced in the

case of—"Mary Leigh, widow, Bowdon, buried in linnen. £2, 10s. whereof went to the poor."

In 1728, Nicholas Waterhouse, of Bowdon, a dissenting teacher, "was buried in linnen," but there is no note made as to whether any fine was enforced. This famous Act was not repealed until 1814, and then not without some opposition.

There are many curious entries in parish registers about this period, but the following notices from a South Cheshire church would be difficult to surpass—

	£	s.	d.		£	s.	d.
1634. To Geo. Beeston for hanging the Mad Dog	0	2	6	1693. April 16, Paid then at the clerks being spent on the parson which preached on that day being a stranger	0	1	0
1638. To a preaching minister	0	3	4				
For burying the cobler of Holt	0	1	6				
For ringing the Coverfu	0	3	4	1718. Gave to a *Righting* master yt had lost ye *yeuce* of his Right Thumb	0	0	6
1641. Given to a Minister	0	2	0				
1048. Paid for killing Fox cubs	0	0	6				
1666. Drink for Ringers when we beat the Dutch	0	0	6	1750. Dinner and Drink when we walked the bounds	0	7	6
1670. Morning drafts for Slater and his men	0	1	0	1757. A bottle of wine for Mr Ruddal, bellfounder	0	2	0

In 1637 there is evidence of "a strike" of wardens at a church in Chester, when the following entry occurs : " Paid for ' not ' ringing (the bells) when the Bishop came to view the church, 00.03.04 (3s. 4d.)." Another reads, " Paid for a quart of sack and white wine an sugar."

The fear of Popish ascendency in England caused Parliament to pass the Test Act in 1673-4, which rendered the reception of the Sacrament according to the Established Church and the renouncing of the dogma of transubstantiation necessary conditions for government appointments. " In supporting this Act," according to the authors of Nonconformity in Cheshire, " the Nonconformists sacrificed their own rights for the sake of averting the common danger then threatening. Though the latitudinarian clergy, who were then called the Low Church party, wished to exempt the Nonconformists from the penal laws, the High Church or Court party preached passive obedience, and enforced these laws against them in their full vigour. . . . Eight thousand Nonconformists perished in prison during his (James II.) reign, their only crime being their dissent from the dominant establishment."

After the Revolution a Union of Presbyterian and Congregational ministers was formed in London in 1690, and the heads of an agreement drawn up under the Toleration Act were subscribed to by the dissenting ministers of those bodies at Macclesfield, in 1690-1, and the ministers of the Cheshire Association continued down to March 1745.

The Evangelical movement had taken root in England in the same year. The Unitarians, as they are termed nowadays, retained the chapels and endowments, being the old dissenters, and new places of worship began to be erected by the seceders from their ranks. Wesley and Whitefield were the leaders of the movement. One founded the Wesleyan denomination; the other, Calvinistic Methodism. Captain Scott became famous as the Cheshire Whitefield. He quitted the army, and was ordained to the office of Evangelist, and devoted his energies chiefly to this county. Several of the more modern churches of Evangelical Nonconformity at Chester, Nantwich, Congleton, Middlewich, Macclesfield, and Northwich were gathered and sustained by means of the energetic labours of this Christian soldier.

In 1786 an Association of Congregational Ministers and Churches in parts of Lancashire, Chester, and Derbyshire was formed, but for various reasons a Cheshire County Union was formed at Macclesfield in November 1806. This claims to be the successor and representative of the first Cheshire Association of 1653, and of the second Cheshire Association formed in 1691.

The old orthodox Presbyterianism is almost extinct in the county. Unitarians still cling to the name, but they reject doctrines which the old Presbyterians held as fundamental—the Trinity and the Divinity of Christ—and their present church government is congregational. The Cheshire Congregational Union resembles the second Association in doctrine as well as in descent, and is like the first (to use the words of Adam Martindale), "a voluntary association for mutual advice and the strengthening of one another."

Notwithstanding the chequered course of Nonconformity in Cheshire, there were periods of comparative quiet when the authorities ceased from troubling, and they enjoyed comparative rest. Some of the ministers were in extreme poverty. The father of the famous Matthew Henry was on one occasion reduced to his last threepence. Mr William Armitage, a native of Huddersfield, came to Queen Street Chapel, Chester, in 1772, and introduced a daring innovation in the shape of a Thursday evening lecture weekly. The announcement caused great curiosity, and an extraordinary event happened at the first meeting. "Some strollers were to exhibit 'a puppet' in a room adjacent. Many," he writes, "debated in their own minds whether the show or the sermon would afford them the greatest entertainment. As I was just come to town I was entirely new to them; several on this ground resolved to hear me, and reserve their visit to the puppet room for a future evening. It was happy for them that they came to this accession, for that very night the place and about two hundred persons were blown into the air by the explosion of gunpowder, which had taken fire in a room under that in which they were assembled. Forty were killed on the spot, and many others were most miserably scorched and mangled. Those who attended on me made an application of my text to themselves, 'If the Lord had intended to kill us He would have permitted us to go to the puppet show, but as He has spared us we will never go again.' Some of these have attended my ministry ever since, and I trust not without profit." In striking contrast was the treatment of people meeting in private houses. The doors were broken in, and the worshippers tried to save themselves as best they could. Some hid under beds, others took refuge in closets, or hid in corners or private places, but in all about sixty persons were secured and brought before the Mayor. Some were very influential citizens, and paid their money for a first conviction. Others were severely dealt with. One of the Nonconformist ministers, Dr Harrison, formerly attached to the Cathedral Church, was ejected under the Act of Uniformity. He settled in Dublin, and was a most successful preacher, attracting large congregations. A certain Lord Thomas had a high opinion of his abilities, and " often used to say that he would rather hear Dr Harrison say grace over an egg than hear the Bishop pray and preach." When he died the whole of Dublin put on mourning, and his funeral was largely attended by all sorts and conditions of people.

Geoffrey Whitney, who has often been referred to in these pages, was a native of Nantwich, and wrote " A Choice of Emblems and other Devises "—" a work adorned with varietie of matter, both pleasant and profitable. . . . Because therein by the office of the eye and eare, the minde may reape double delighte, throughe wholesome precepts shadowed with pleasant devises: both fit for the virtuous to their incouraging, and that of the wicked for their admoneshing and amendment." Whitney in his religious views, it is contended, was a " thorough Puritan." One of the emblems was an open Bible with the outstretched wings of the spirit above throwing light on its pages, and at the bottom was a picture, " the Devil and his imps pulling hard." The lines under this device expressed the characteristic idea of Puritanism in that day—

>Thoughe Sathan strive, with all his maine and mighte
>To hide the truthe and dimme the law divine ;
>Yet to his worde the Lord doth give such Lightes
>That to the East and West the same doth shine,
>And those that are so happie for to look ;
>Salvation finde, within that blessed booke.

Another piece relates to a virtuous wife, and is dedicated to his sister, M. D. Colley. It represents a " faire woman " standing on a tortoise, holding her tongue in one hand, and a large bunch of keys in the other—

>This represents the virtues of a wife,
>Her finger staies her tonge to runne at large,
>The modest looks doe shewe her honest life ;
>The Keys declare shee hathe a care and charge,
>Of husbands goodes ; let him goe where he please,
>The tortoise warnes at home to spend her daies.

Edward Burghall, the Puritanical Vicar of Acton, of which the town of Nantwich was but a chapel ease in 1662, was a versatile writer, and a diary he wrote is valuable on account of its details of the Siege of Nantwich. It is, however, somewhat astonishing to read that Burghall, "in common with other ministers in those days," was subject to annoyance from the Quakers. In March 1660 he writes: "Two Quakers came to disturb me in the public congregation. I so ordered my studies that the sermon was pat against them: they had liberty to speak and were answered; at last one of them denied the Scriptures to be the word of God, on which they were with shame turned out by the congregation. 9th June: Two Quakers came into my church with a lanthorne candle while I was preaching; their design was (as they confessed) to have lighted a sheet of paper, which they had, as a sign of God's anger burning against us." Burghall alludes to the Act of Uniformity, when "many ministers were outed everywhere that would not conform, and amongst the rest myself." His successor, Mr Kirkes, Chaplain at Woodhey, he says, "took possession of the church, November the 10th, the day before Martinmas, when all the tithe calves in Wrenbury and Acton were due to me (the substance of my means), and were wont to be gathered; yet I had but one half of the calves in Acton, he had all the rest, though I had taken the pains the whole year before. This year there were many strange prodigies. In January came forth a declaration from the king promising some liberty of conscience the next session of Parliament, but it came to nothing." Burghall did not long survive his ejectment. He fell into great poverty which was alleviated by the assistance of sympathising friends. He died in 1665.

There appears to have been some jealousy between the Congregationalists and Quakers at this period. George Fox, the Quaker, visited various parts of Cheshire, amongst them Dukinfield, where he made converts, including some of Rev. Samuel Eaton's congregation. "The professors (of religion?) were in a rage, all pleading for sin and imperfection, and could not endure to hear talk of perfection of a holy and similar life. Though they were chained in darkness and sin, which they pleaded for quenched the tender thing in them— the Lord's power was over all." To counteract the teaching of Fox, Eaton published a small treatise, entitled "The Quakers Confuted: being an answer to nineteen queries propounded by them and sent to the elders of the church at Dukinfield in Cheshire, in 1653," and related to some scandal between one Richard Waller and a maidservant. The couple evidently married afterwards, and as she happened to have been a member of Eaton's congregation, a service was held with a view "to settling and establishing her faith in Christ," telling her that she was very precious to them, "though your miscarriage for God hath been very great, etc." The Quakers indignantly refuted Eaton's words and his followers' insinuations, stating that they "found in the paper many slanderous speeches and false accusations against us, whom the world scornfully calls Quakers; we wrote some things to the paper and sent it back to the Church (as they call it) certain queries to be answered." The Quakers' reply was variegated with expressions such as—

"Oh Eaton thou lyar! Oh thou lyar, doth Satan transform himself into ministers of righteousness?
Here I charge thee in the presence of Christ to be a lyar, O thou dark sot."

Eaton came of an old Cheshire family, which left the Church of England and joined the Puritans. He went through many trials on this account. He was lodged in Newgate, where he held services with the approval of the governor. He escaped to Holland, and became founder of Newhaven Colony in Connecticut. Eaton returned to England, and preached at Chester and "at Knutsford, a great market town in the same county." At Dukinfield he became "a teacher" of the Church of God in that town, where he was under the patronage of the famous Colonel Dukinfield, one of the foremost Puritanical leaders in Cheshire. He died in January 1664.

A pleasant contrast to this exhibition of "Christian" quarrelling is to be found in the milder methods pursued by Wesley, who a century or so later visited Cheshire, and whose preaching was attended with such marvellous results as to lay on wide and deep foundations one of the most powerful religious denominations the world has seen in these later days Even here, we may say that we read in his famous journal particulars of a discussion he had on religious topics with a Cheshire Quaker, so that the combative element was not eliminated as we find is the case in 1914-19. We do not find much evidence of Whitefield's religious demonstrations in this county. He does not seem to have had the organising powers of Wesley, who was the social reformer and philanthropist, founding charity schools, orphan homes, and medical dispensaries, in addition to conducting many-sided religious activities.

It would appear to have been the custom at that time for persons to inscribe their autographs on window glass with a glazier's diamond. At several Cheshire farmhouses where Wesley was entertained, these panes of glass are highly treasured relics by the descendants of his entertainers. But this practice was not confined to autographs. On one occasion Dean Swift journeying to London, not receiving the attention he desired was his due from his clerical brethren in Chester, wrote on a pane of the hotel where he stayed, a couplet as follows : " Mouldering without and rotten within, this place and its clergy are both of a kin."

There is no doubt that Wesley roused the Church of England from its somnolency, real or imagined, to a sense of its duty to the people. It was a creature of slow growth, but it has since borne great fruit. But Wesley had his critics. One was the famous Horace Walpole, son of the Prime Minister of the period (1766), who has a sly dig at Wesley when he says, " he went to his chapel and heard an opera. They have boys and girls with charming voices that sing hymns in parts to Scotch ballad tunes, but indeed so long that one would think they were already in eternity and knew how much time they had before them." He describes the chapel as a neat one, with true Gothic windows, though he was not converted by them, as also the furnishings in which he discovers evidences of luxury—scarlet armchairs, etc., and a balcony " for elect ladies." There was also "a throne of the Apostle." " Wesley is a lean, elderly man, flesh coloured and hair neatly combed, but with a soupcon of curl at the ends; wondrous clean, but evidently an actor as Garrick. He spoke his sermon, but so fast and with so little accent that I am sure he has often uttered it, for it was like a lesson. There were parts and eloquence in it; but towards the end he exalted his voice and acted very ugly enthusiasm—decried learning, and told stories, like Latimer of the fool of his college, who said, ' I *thanks* God for everything.' Except a few from curiosity and some *honourable women* the congregation was very mean. There was a Scotch Countess of Buchan, who is carrying a pure rosy vulgar face to heaven, and who asked Miss Rich if that was the *author of the poets*, I believe she meant me (Walpole) and the noble authors." As has been written on many occasions, " comment on this amazing effusion is needless."

It was in 1771 that Raikes, the editor of a local newspaper, made his first experiment in the way of a Sunday school at Gloucester.

He was struck by the number of children playing in the street on Sundays and their wretched appearance, and he thought that by putting them to school this profanation of the Sabbath might be prevented. He engaged several women, evidently mistresses of dames' schools in the neighbourhood, and paid them for their labour. They had to instruct the children in reading and the catechism. His example was followed by other charitable persons, and in a few years Sunday schools were established in almost every part of Great Britain. In 1786 it was estimated that 250,000 children were receiving instruction in Sunday schools.

Two years after Raikes founded his Sunday school, Rev. Oswald Leicester set to work to initiate a similar effort in Altrincham. At that time there was no parish church in Altrincham. Bowdon was the supreme head over a large district, but even then there was the throbbings of a more intense effort, caused no doubt by the awakening of the Wesleyan movement. In this way the Rev. Oswald, who owned a Wesleyan father, but who, in some miraculous way, was diverted into the Church of England, came to the Curate of St George's Parish. He is described as being one of the Old School. He wore a three-cornered hat, *a la* the Vicar of Wakefield, square cut coat, knee breeches, and had silver buckles on his shoes, and rode a pony, on which he visited his future parishioners in Baguley, Timperley, and the surrounding district. Tradition has it that he commenced operations over a stable in what is now called New Street. Our Saviour Christ was laid in a manger at His birth, therefore there is nothing inappropriate in this. Simple and small beginnings have had large and abundant and blessed results. The Rev. Oswald was a pastor in the truest sense of the word. Altrincham at that day had not a street in it; it was simply a small village with a few houses clustered in the old market-place. There was, however, the upper town and the lower town. The boys of the upper town and the lower town used to assault each other. The grown-ups on the occasion of the now abolished Sanjam, or St James' fair, used to join issue on sundry questions of local interest, and sundry cracked heads were the result. At Bowdon there was bull-baiting. Cock-fighting was also indulged in at Easter, in a field close to the Downs. But famous as Bowdon and Altrincham were for bull-baiting and cock-fighting the lieges of the Georges' reign knew how to grow potatoes. Bowdon Downs potatoes commanded a high price, often 2s. per lb. in the market at Manchester. Oftentimes has a friendly blanket been taken from the domestic bed and laid over the budding "spuds" to counteract the effect of an unexpected frost. Those were not the days of Jerseys, or even the periodical eruption from the neighbourhood of Delamere Forest. Thus the seed was sown in receptive ground. The Rev. Oswald moved about like the pastor in "Hiawatha," a veritable father in the parish. He was a special favourite of the little folks, who used to pull his coat-tails with something like youthful vehemence, only to awaken a quiet and appreciative smile. He was an all-round popular man.

St George's, Altrincham, has been singularly fortunate in its ministers. One and all have taken an interest in its schools, day and Sunday alike. The generation is gone which remembers their anniversaries, in pre-organ times, when there was a local orchestra in which the double bass and the bassoon played a conspicuous part, and when friends and relations for miles round gathered together and contributed in no small measure to the Sunday and day school fund. Those were truly happy days. The school continues to flourish to the end, "that peace and happiness, truth and justice, religious and piety may be established amongst us for all generations."

The Tractarian movement in the Church of England was active about the middle of the last century. It was headed by Dr Pusey, and other eminent divines also gave added impulse, although while aiming at spreading High Church doctrines it was really directed to what would happen, and what would be the position of the Established Church under altered political conditions.

Keble had just warned his contemporaries of the perils to England which lay in the biblical and theological speculations of German professors. No one thought then that those speculations would have the result of demoralising the moral and righteous fibre of a great nation and causing that World War, the consequences of which will afflict humanity for untold generations. Cardinal Newman was one of the greatest masters of style in the English language, and the author of that soul uplifting hymn, "Lead Kindly Light."

As one reads his autobiography in the wonderful and striking " Apologia pro vita Sua," one cannot help thinking with regret the pang it must have caused him as well as the loss to the Church of England which his secession entailed.

For a long period the aftermath of the unrest caused was noticeable in the effort of extremists on both sides, one raising the bogy of the " scarlet lady " in any change or movement in ritual. The disuse of the Geneva gown, with which the preacher attired himself before the sermon when he was solemnly escorted to the vestry by the verger and back again, was only effected after considerable agitation against the change to the surplice. The verger, by the way, was a most important personage (in his own estimation). He was the orthodox successor of the parish beadle, who, in our childhood's days, headed the Sunday-school procession to the Parish Church. He was a striking personage. He wore a dove-coloured coat, knee breeches tied with ribbons, and had shoes on which the buckles shone brightly, especially on Sunday mornings. He also wore a large three-cornered hat, and with his silver tipped staff duly impressed us, not only by his majestic aloofness, but also with awe as the embodiment of Church and State.

For the verger we had no such feeling. He only wore a very ordinary stuff covering, and had no silver tip to a thin, unimpressive wand or stick. We youngsters most irreverently regarded him with contempt. We christened him the " dognoper," as being only fit to strike a stray dog and clear it out of the church on occasion. But there were occasions when he proved his usefulness. He kept a strict eye on boys who fell asleep during the service, and used his wand quietly but vigorously on the offenders. This generally occurred while the churchwardens paraded the township roads and visited the village public-houses to bring in the stray sheep of the flock, and although required by law to be closed during service the publicans conducted " business as usual." Sometimes they returned alone, and remained behind the outer curtain until their services were needed in making the collection. On other occasions it must be recorded in strict justice that they were the means of causing much secret drinking to be stopped when it reached the proportions of a public nuisance, as recorded in the books of many townships in Cheshire.

As we have given a sketch of the oldest Sunday school in Cheshire so we can now refer to what was claimed to be the largest in the world at Stockport. Its origin is traced as far back as 1784. It was founded by a few religiously active and benevolent men of different denominations, who lamented the prevalent ignorance of the town, and who overlooked the interest of party in the earnestness and comprehensiveness of their desire to promote the knowledge and happiness of their fellow-men. The schools were held at first in cottages, and then an empty factory was taken, and step by step the cause advanced, until the magnificent building was raised in which, in 1806, the first of the annual sermons which excite so much interest in the town was preached by the Rev. Richard Powell, Vicar of Wibsey, Yorkshire. Private subscriptions were from the first obtained from all sects and parties, and collections were made from time to time in the churches and dissenting places of worship in aid of the common and public interests of education. Although the selfishness of Sectarianism soon began to display itself, and the collections to which we referred were discontinued, yet the basis of the Sunday-school system remained firm and secure, and to the present day the school is recognised as a town's institution. The teachers belonged to all the denominations of Stockport, who, in the spirit of harmony, laboured together for the common object of giving sound Scriptural education to the rising generation. Church and chapel schools have been formed and multiplied, but the old institution continues as popular and useful as ever.

Returning to the succession of bishops we find a notable one in the Right Reverend Charles Jas. Blomfield, D.D., who was born in 1786, at Bury St Edmunds, where his father had a school. In October 1804 he went from the Bury Grammar School to Trinity College, Cambridge; was elected a scholar in the following year; gained Sir W. Browne's medal in that year, and again in 1805; and was elected Craven Scholar. In 1808 he graduated as third wrangler and first chancellor's medallist; in 1809 he was elected Fellow of his College. He proceeded to M.A. in 1811, and D.D. in 1820. He was ordained by the Bishop of Bristol, and served successively at Quarrington and Dunton in Lincolnshire; Tuddenham, Suffolk; St Botolph's, Bishopsgate, London; and as Archdeacon of Colchester in 1822. Nominated on the 8th, elected on the 9th, Queen's assent 11th, confirmed 19th, and on 20th June 1824 he was consecrated Bishop of Chester by Dr Harcourt, Archbishop of York. He was translated to the See of London in August 1828, where he died in 1857. His Lordship's reputation as a classical scholar, founded upon his editions of Æschylus and Callimachus, etc., was too well established to render it necessary to dwell upon the subject here. The list of his works and those relating to them occupy six pages in the British Museum catalogue.

Dr John Bird Sumner, Prebendary of Durham, was consecrated on 26th August 1828. In his life and writings he boldly accepted the facts of geology and treated them in relation to the Christian religion with such ability that he received the second Burnett prize of £400. Another great work was his "Evidences of Christianity, Derived from its Nature and Reception." No fewer then 233 new churches were consecrated by him. During his occupation of the See, the Diocese was twice divided, once in 1836, on the formation of the Diocese of Ripon, and again in 1847, when the Diocese of Manchester was formed. In 1848 Bishop Sumner was created Archbishop of Canterbury.

Dr John Graham became Bishop in 1848. He was succeeded by Dr William Jacobson in 1865. He resigned in 1884. Dr Jacobson was known

CHESHIRE: ITS TRADITIONS AND HISTORY

as a High Churchman, and was a nominee of Mr Gladstone. The bulk of the Cheshire churchpeople at that time looked askance at High Churchmen. Dr Jacobson was somewhat brusque in manner, and not of a popular type. He, however, ruled with great judgment, and the ecclesiastical calm of the diocese was not unduly ruffled. There was also a savour of politics in the appointment. Dr Jacobson was chairman of Mr Gladstone's committee at Oxford, when he renounced Toryism, and was defeated by Mr Gathorne Hardy, afterwards Lord Cranbrook. Dr Jacobson's appointment to the Chester Bishopric was the last piece of ecclesiastical patronage given out by Lord Palmerston before his death. In Dr Jacobson's tenure of office the Diocese of Liverpool was created, a most important departure, but one his Lordship handled with consummate tact and some amount of self-sacrifice. He was of a "solid" rather than the brilliant type, and he gave the closest attention to minor details. One instance of this came under our observation at a confirmation at Bowdon early in the seventies. He put the orthodox question—"Do ye here in the presence of God and of this congregation, renew the solemn promise and vow that was made in your name at your baptism, etc. ?" And every one should answer, "I do." The response from the candidates was almost inaudible. "A most inadequate answer indeed," his lordship remarked. He repeated the question, and this time the result was all that could be desired.

Bishop Stubbs, Regius Professor of Modern History at Oxford, succeeded Dr Jacobson in 1884, and was translated to Oxford in 1889. He was one of the foremost exponents of constitutional history of his day.

His successor, Dr Francis John Jayne, was the thirty-third Bishop of the Diocese, who was consecrated in the same year (1889). He was educated at Rugby and Wadham College, Oxford, and had a brilliant university career, being Hoy Greek Exhibitioner, first class Mods, Greats, Law and History, Fellow of Jesus College, 1868, Senior Hall and Houghton Greek Testament prizeman in 1870. He was curate of St Clements, Oxford, 1870–71 ; Tutor Keble College, 1871–79 ; Preacher at Whitehall, 1875–77 ; Principal of St David's College, Lampeter, 1879–81 ; Select Preacher, Oxford, 1884 ; and Vicar of Leeds in 1886, until his preferment to Chester in 1889.

At the outset he displayed wonderful business capacity. The periodical visitations in the diocese assumed a different aspect. Directions were given as to the preservation of the fabric of the churches and other details appertaining to the duties of churchwardens. He afterwards questioned each warden individually on insurance and the provision made for dilapidations, and whether all necessary repairs were duly carried out. In the early days many embarrassing positions arose. Wardens were evidently unaware of the legal aspect of their position, especially the extent of their responsibility in matters of detail, but later they carefully prepared their returns, and everything moved with the greatest smoothness. Bishop

Jayne was exceedingly popular in the northern portion of the diocese with the Nonconformists, where in certain circles there might have been some danger of friction, but his Lordship " glided over thin ice," with dexterous freedom, and had it been possible would have been entitled to the appellation conferred upon another distinguished Manchester prelate of being " the bishop of all denominations."

At Easter 1919 Bishop Jayne issued a farewell letter to the brethren of the clergy and laity of Chester, announcing his resignation to take effect on 1st May. He is the son of John Jayne, Esq., J.P., of Pont-y-Bailea, Breconshire, and was born on New Year's Day, 1845. Whilst at school he showed both mental and physical prowess. He carried off the gold medal of the school, and, according to report, had no superior as a football player. In social matters Dr Jayne's ideas were in favour of constructive legislation. Long ago he came into public prominence by his leadership of the movement for the establishment of the Gothenburg system of public-house management in this country. Mr Joseph Chamberlain was an advocate of that system, and as far back as 1879 a committee of the House of Lords reported that legal facilities should be given for the adoption of either the Gothenburg system or Mr Chamberlain's modification of it. The Bishop obtained the support of numerous influential people, and as a tentative measure of reform modified experiments were made. Public-House Trust Companies came into existence, and here and there, including Cheshire, some well-known inns became " Trust " houses, the principle of management being to encourage the sale of non-alcoholic refreshments. In view of the State control of the liquor traffic during the war, and the prominence of the question at the present time, it is interesting to contrast the Bishop's propaganda and its reconstructive proposals with the vindictive and destructive aims of others whose opinion is of less importance.

The retirement of Bishop Jayne caused deep regret amongst all classes of the community. Preaching in the Cathedral on 4th May 1919, the canon in residence, the Archdeacon of Chester (the Venerable W. L. Paige Cox, M.A., B.D.), referred to the fact that the Bishop had resigned his charge of the diocese owing to ill-health, and set out in eloquent terms his Lordship's devotion to his heavy and always exacting functions. It had been God's favour that they had had amongst them a Bishop of brilliant endowments, who had used his gifts so unreservedly and indefatigably on their behalf. " The results of such faithful service," said the preacher, " are incorporated into the church life of the diocese. If we cannot trace them all—and who can fully trace the effects of God's employment of human powers in the region of spiritual influence ?—they live and will last and call for our earnest thanksgivings to Him from Whom all good things do come. Our Bishop has now gone into retirement to spend the days that remain to him on earth, we all hope and pray, in bodily ease and tranquillity of mind and spirit. But he will be ' remembered ' by us in the sense in which the Apostle enforces that duty of reverence and gratitude. We shall cherish his fine example. We shall, while our working time lasts, try and serve the Master with the same self-forgetting earnestness as he. And we shall look forward to the time, when earth's tasks completed and its imperfections removed, we shall, Chief Pastor and people, take part together, by God's Mercy, in the ' inheritance incorruptible and undefiled, and that fadeth not away.' "

At the time of his appointment he was youngest bishop, but on his resignation he was the senior in episcopal service to all bishops, though only slightly senior to the Bishop of St Asaph. Referring to his Lordship's resignation, a Manchester newspaper wrote : " The See of Chester is now a light burden on an ecclesiastic, and, if it be compared with the See before the great north-western population, was adequately bishoped. But in the period when the Bishop of Chester had under his care the districts of Lancashire, even then very populous, the See was indeed a great one. One Bishop of Chester, Bishop Sparke, in 1810, could boast of having confirmed 8000 persons in one day at Manchester —a remarkable feat—and without that kind of assistance welcomed by another bishop of later times, who was not grateful for girls' hairpins. ' I confine myself to the lads,' he said, ' leaving the young porcupines to my suffragan.' There was another Bishop of Chester who actually included this great See with the incumbency of Bishopsgate in the City of London, and Bishopsgate then was a cure of ten thousand souls. At one time or another the Bishops of Chester have wielded ecclesiastical rule over all Cheshire, Lancashire and Westmoreland, over parts of Denbighshire, Flintshire, Cumberland, and Yorkshire ; even Chester diocese was once merely part of a much greater See, for Chester, Lichfield, and Coventry were once co-ordinated." He was regarded with the greatest affection by both clergy and laity, and two years before was the recipient of a touching address from them. He declined all offers of preferment, including the wealthy See of Durham.

Dr Jayne was succeeded by Dr Paget, Suffragan Bishop of Stepney, whose preferment to full Bishop followed thirteen years' service as a suffragan, first at Ipswich (1906-9) and then at Stepney. He is the third son of the late Sir James Paget, first baronet, the eminent surgeon, who was Sergeant-Surgeon to Queen Victoria, and surgeon to King Edward when Prince of Wales. His eldest brother is the second baronet, Sir John Rahen Paget, M.K.C., of Harewood Place, Middlesex, his younger brother being Mr Stephen Paget, the well-known London surgeon. Another brother was the Right Rev. Francis Paget, Bishop of Oxford, who died in 1911. It is an interesting coincidence that Dr Paget, like Dr Jayne, has associations with Leeds, famed as a nursery of bishops by reason of so many of its clergy attaining high preferment. Dr Paget in 1877 was curate of Leeds, and spent a year as lecturer at Leeds Clergy

E

School. Dr Paget came to Chester with ripe experience. He followed one who was held in affectionate regard by the whole of the diocese, and we can offer no better welcome to Dr Paget than the hope that he will succeed to that good will as well as to the episcopal office.

The new Bishop married, in 1892, Elma Katie, daughter of Sir Samuel Hoare, first baronet, and there are two sons of the union. Mrs Paget is well known for her interest in social questions, particularly in matters affecting women and children. The announcement of the appointment was received with much pleasure by the churchpeople of the diocese, and he will in future years, as he did in the dioceses of Norwich and London, win the same confidence and affection. His installation took place on the 24th of September 1919, with what was described as due ecclesiastical pomp, and, according to the local newspapers, it left a lasting impression on the mind by the singular dignity of form and ornate beauty of the music that so fittingly marked the celebration of a great and historic rite. There was a large attendance of surpliced clergy, as also the Mayor, members of the Corporation, and representatives of the law, etc. The Council of the Free Churches was represented by the Rev. A. Hills (President), the Rev. James Travis, the Rev. J. Ll. Jones, and G. F. Osborne. A noteworthy coincidence was that the Venerable Dean Darby performed the same ceremony in 1889 in connection with the enthronement of Bishop Jayne. He died on Wednesday, 5th November 1919, within fifteen days of attaining his eighty-eighth birthday. His funeral evoked a most impressive tribute of his worth and character from all classes of the community. After his installation, Bishop Paget took an early opportunity of visiting many important centres of the diocese and received a cordial welcome. His previous experience as Suffragan in the South, including a hearty manner and shrewd commonsense, stood him in good stead, and points to a maintenance in their fullest energy of those high traditions attaching to his sacred calling.

The Primitive Methodists of Chester and district celebrated their centenary on Whit Monday, 1919, at Great Saughall, which is regarded as the Mecca of Primitive Methodism so far as the Chester first circuit is concerned. Joshua Reynolds of Saughall, who certainly bore an historic name, first "missioned" Chester. Cheshire shares with Staffordshire the claim to being the cradle of Primitive Methodism, and Mow Cop, that "craggy eminence which runs north and south, and is in both counties, is the spot where in May 1807 the banner of Primitive Methodism was unfurled, and it is looked upon as the Mount Carmel of the Connexion." The Tunstall revival, of which the missioning of Cheshire was the first fruits, began with a camp meeting held on 23rd May 1818, at Wrinehill, and among the human instruments of that revival was Hugh Bourne, who engaged for itinerant evangelism James Crawfoot of Delamere Forest, one of the "Forest Methodists." "The

Cheshire Mission," as it came to be called, was begun in the spring of 1818, by John Wedgewood. It was in all probability the autumn of 1819 when John Wedgewood first visited the Chester district. His itinerary included Huxley, Burton Hall, Walk Mills, Stapleford, Churton, and Chester, and thence to Saughall, Stanney, Sutton, Two Mills, Neston, etc. The Rev. Thomas Brownsword soon after Reynolds visited Chester, conducted many successful services, and the Machine Bank, which he visited, became a regular centre of operations in the city. The first church met in the house of one Thomas Ellis, in Steven Street. He applied to the Bishop of Chester, and was granted permission to use the place for religious worship. Afterwards they met at King Street, and here the worshippers were "much disturbed by certain of the rowdy set"; and when an appeal was made to the city magistrates for protection, the reply was that the worshippers themselves ought to have stayed at home and not given an occasion for the disturbance of the peace. The first chapel in Boughton was built in 1823, and here again we have the same record of rowdyism, and in 1853 the Mayor of Chester was appealed to for police protection. Afterwards the George Street Chapel was built. In 1832 the Chester circuit reported 300 members; in 1919 the total membership of the six circuits, which was originally included in it, was 2090.

CHAPTER VI.

Martial Cheshire—The Crusaders—Legend of the Seven Sisters and the Baron of Dunham—The romantic aspect of chivalry—The early Civil Wars—Chester fined for its loyalty—Cheshire gentlemen beheaded—The deadly Wars of the Roses—Flodden Field—English " moderation and natural good humour "—King *versus* Parliament—The first bloodshed in the Civil Wars—Pitched battle at Tarporley—Reduction of Beeston Castle and other Fortresses—Sir Wm. Brereton repulsed at Chester—King Charles' hopes blighted at Rowton Heath—His departure from Chester—Siege and capture of Chester—Alleged vandalism by the victors—Damage to Chester Cathedral.

THE objective of the tenth century crusaders was in striking contrast to that of the allied armies who have fought in the East and West in the twentieth century. The early crusades have been stigmatised as " the most signal and durable monument of human folly that ever existed in any age or nation." Those of the later age, in the twentieth, on the other hand, have saved the world for freedom from a would-be dominant military autocracy. The tenth century monument was not an enduring one. The twentieth century achievement will leave its impress for good, it is hoped, for all time. The first crusaders, coming, as they did, when the Norman position in England was somewhat precarious, did not affect this country to the same extent as the rest of Continental Europe. They were not encouraged by King William, whose eyes were directed at the moment more to his own private interests than the freeing of the Holy Sepulchre from the grip of the infidel. Hence we find little reference to them in Cheshire beyond tradition.

It is on record, however, that Robert Grosvenor was one of the valiant ancestors of his house who accompanied Richard, Coeur de Lion in his expedition to Palestine in 1190. He was with him at Messina during the delays and difficulties which arose in Richard's quarrel with the Greek King Isaac, whom he dethroned, taking possession of the Island of Cyprus. At Limasol Richard was married, in May 1191, to Berengaria, daughter of Sancho IV., King of Navarre. After a brief honeymoon he set sail for Acre, and Richard Grosvenor was in his retinue. When this crusader king had, it is said, vindicated the Christian religion by hanging 2700 of his Turkish hostages outside the walls of Acre, he turned his steps in the direction of the Holy City, which was the scene in the twentieth century of another, but bloodless, victory by modern crusaders. Robert Grosvenor shared in the glories of the victory gained over Saladin at Jaffa, and very probably took part in the fruitless march to Jerusalem, as well as in the retreat to Ascalon when the perilous enterprise was abandoned.

Dotted over the country there are misty records of crusaders' cedars.

At Dunham Castle one is alleged to have been brought a sapling from the Holy Land by an old crusading baron, and that it died out with the last of the race. Probably, too, the fact of the last of these barons dying without leaving a lawful son to succeed him gave rise to the romantic legend of the Seven Sisters, in connection with the park at Dunham, where there is a clump of trees which is known by that name. Many people are acquainted with it, and, no doubt, lament the tragic end of the youthful heir, who was struck dead by lightning just as he was passing the Seven Sisters—

> And each fatal tree was stained with gore ;
> And so was the bloody earth ;
> And the same night saw his dreadful death
> That first beheld his birth.

And the legend closes—

> The seven sister trees may still be seen,
> Though the mortal ones are fled ;
> And none of that fated house was left,
> When the squire himself was dead.

Hamon, who was the fifth and last of his race in a direct line, also reminds us in a most striking manner of Longfellow's melodious poem, "The Norman Baron." We can well picture to ourselves the then stately Castle of Dunham. In his chamber on Christmas Eve lies the dying baron. The King of Terrors has already laid his relentless hand upon him, and the humble monk, seated by his bedside, recites the prayer and paternoster which shall usher the fast fleeting soul into eternity. Outside the tempest thunders and shakes the castle turret, but the sufferer is unmindful of it. Within its precincts serf and vassal are holding their Christmas festival. As their lays they chant the sound rises above that of the tempest, and the dying baron turns his weary head to listen to the carol, in which is heralded the birth of the manger-cradled stranger, Christ, who was born to set us free. In an instant the spirit of repentance appears. He thinks of the justice, long withheld, due to those under his iron rule, and they are by him freed again. As on the sacred missal he inscribes their freedom, death relaxes his iron features, and the monk repeats a deep amen.

> Many centuries have been numbered
> Since in death the baron slumbered
> By the convent's sculptured portal,
>   Mingling with the common dust :
>
> But the good deed, through the ages,
> Living in historic pages,
> Brighter grows and gleams immortal,
>   Unconsumed by moth or rust.

From the crusaders of the tenth century we derive the Knights Hospitallers, Knights of St John of Jerusalem, and other orders, which originated in Palestine, their aim being to succour and protect Christian pilgrims visiting the Holy Sepulchre. The organisation consisted of three grades—the fighting forces, the chaplains, whose duty it was to continue the religious traditions, and the serving brethren who performed menial work. The chief power was vested in the Grand Master, and certain knights who governed preceptories and commanderies. On the suppression of the Templars in 1312, the headquarters were situate in Rome, and the members are now in the service under the Geneva Convention. From these Hospitallers we get our modern hospitals, which many centuries ago were said to have been founded by Buddhist priests in India prior to the Christian era.

The early crusaders have also another redeeming feature in that they left to us the romantic aspects of chivalrous knighthood in their highest sense—to protect the distressed, to sustain right against might—and had its development in Arthurian and Charlemagne romances, and last, but not least, gave us those sweet songs of Tristan and Isolde, so dear to the hearts of the poet and student.

On 23rd July 1403 was fought the battle of Shrewsbury. Hume says:— "We shall scarcely find any battle in those ages where the shock was more terrible and more constant. Henry (IV.) exposed his person in the thickest of the fight; his gallant son, whose military achievements were afterwards so renowned, and who performed his noviciate in arms, signalised himself in his father's footsteps, and even a wound, which he received in the face with an arrow, would not oblige him to quit the field."

Percy (Hotspur) supported that fame which he had acquired in many a bloody combat; and Douglas, his ancient enemy and now his friend, still appeared his rival amid the horror and confusion of the day. But while the armies were contending in this furious manner, the death of Percy by an unknown hand decided the day, and the Royalists prevailed. Hotspur had the men of Cheshire principally on his side. In order to stir them to action he had had it twice proclaimed in Chester and in every market town in the country that the unfortunate Richard, who was supposed to have been assassinated three years before, was still alive, and was then at Chester Castle, where he might be seen by all such as should repair thither. Although they had been so forward in expressing their attachment to Henry a few years before, they now took part with Hotspur. The result was particularly disastrous to them. Upwards of 200 knights and esquires were slain, with a great number of their retainers. The Baron of Kinderton and Sir Richard Vernon fell into the hands of the King, and were beheaded. A few of the Cheshire knights and gentlemen appear to have adhered to the King, Sir John Calveley of Calveley and Sir John Massey of Puddington falling on his side. In the following year the King pardoned the citizens of Chester for the part they had taken in the rebellion, on payment of a fine of 500 marks.

On 23rd May 1455 was fought the battle of St Albans in which the Yorkists gained a victory over the Lancastrians. This was the first bloodshed in the civil wars of the period, which were not finished in less than a course of thirty years, and which was signalised by twelve pitched battles, which opened a scene of extraordinary fierceness and cruelty, and is computed to have cost the lives of eighty princes of the blood, and almost entirely annihilated the ancient nobility of England. Queen Margaret, the Amazonian Consort of Henry VI., who visited Chester in 1455, bestowed badges in the shape of silver swans on the Cheshire gentlemen who espoused her cause. Civil war on a large scale, however, did not ensue until 1460, and arose out of a petty quarrel between a member of Henry VI.'s retinue and a partisan of the Yorkist party. Students of history will be familiar with the many battles which ensued in the contest for succession between the Houses of York and Lancaster. The one in which the men of Cheshire appear to have been especially prominent was the battle of Blore Heath, Staffordshire, fought on 23rd September 1459. The feeling of the county, as in the differences of later years, appears to have been pretty equally divided, and amongst those slain were Sir Thomas Dutton, Sir John Done, Sir Hugh Venables, Sir Richard Molineux, Sir William Troutbeck, Sir John Legh, and Sir John Egerton. The poet Drayton represents the conflict as taking the form of a duel, in which one relative falls a sacrifice to the resentment of the other. The lines have been often quoted, but from their graphic style they will bear repetition—

> There Dutton, Dutton kills; a Done doth kill a Done;
> A Booth a Booth; and Leigh by Leigh is overthrown;
> A Venables against a Venables doth stand,
> A Troutbeck fighteth with a Troutbeck hand to hand;
> There Molineux doth make a Molineux to die,
> And Egerton the strength of Egerton doth try.
> O Cheshire, wert thou mad of thine own native gore,
> So much until this day thou never shedd'st before!
> Above two thousand men upon the earth were thrown,
> Of whom the greatest part were naturally thine own.

On the 9th September 1513 was gained the great and decisive victory over the Scots by the Earl of Surrey, at the fatal battle of Flodden, in which King James IV. of Scotland was slain and his army destroyed, and which is stated by Sir Walter Scott, in his "Tales of a Grandfather," to be "one of the most calamitous events in Scottish history." During the absence of Henry VIII., in the French war of the period, James, contrary to the advice of his more sagacious counsellors, and to gratify private enmity, led an army into England, and took several Border forts. He was met by the Earl of

Surrey, with an army collected mainly from war-like inhabitants of the northern counties, at a hill called Flodden. The position chosen by the Scottish King was a capital one, and no amount of wheedling or strategy on the part of the English general caused him for some time to vacate it. Surrey, becoming distressed for provisions, was obliged to resort to another mode of bringing the Scots to action. " He moved northward, sweeping round the hill of Flodden, keeping out of the reach of the Scottish artillery until, crossing the Till near Twisell Castle, he placed himself with his whole army betwixt James and his own kingdom. The King suffered him to make this flank movement without interruption, though it must have afforded repeated and advantageous opportunities for attack. But when he saw the English army interposed betwixt him and his dominions, he became alarmed lest he should be cut off from Scotland. In this apprehension he was confirmed by one Giles Musgrave, an Englishman, whose counsel he used upon the occasion, and who assured him that if he did not descend and fight with the English army, the Earl of Surrey would enter Scotland and lay waste the whole country. Stimulated by this apprehension, the King resolved to give the signal for the fatal battle. With this view, the Scots set fire to their huts, and the refuse and litter of their camp. The smoke spread along the side of the hill, and under its cover the army of King James descended the eminence, which is much less steep on the northern than the southern side, while the English advanced to meet them, both concealed from each other by the cloud of smoke. The Scots descended in four strong columns, all marching parallel to each other, having a reserve of the Lothian men commanded by Earl Bothwell. The English were also divided into four bodies, with a reserve of cavalry led by Dacre. The battle commenced at the hour of four in the afternoon. The first which encountered was the left wing of the Scots, commanded by the Earl of Huntly and Lord Home, which overpowered and threw into disorder the right wing of the English, under Sir Edmund Howard. Sir Edmund was beaten down, his standard taken, and he himself was in danger of instant death when he was relieved and extricated.

Thus went matters on the Scottish left. Upon the extreme right of James's army, a division of Highlanders, consisting of the clans of Mackenzie, MacLean, and others, commanded by the Earls of Lennox and Argyle, were so insufferably annoyed by the volleys of English arrows that they broke their ranks, rushed tumultuously down the hill, and, being attacked at once in flank and rear by Sir Edward Stanley with the men of Cheshire and Lancashire, were routed with great slaughter." Sir Walter Scott thus bears testimony to the bravery of Cheshire men in this decisive encounter, and local history notes that they were most actively engaged, and suffered greatly. The greatest part of the Macclesfield contingent, with their Mayor, Sir Edmund Savage, are stated to have been left dead on the field—

> Link'd in the serried phalanx tight,
> Groom fought like noble, squire like knight,
> As fearlessly and well;
> Till utter darkness closed her wing
> O'er their thin host and wounded king.
>
> Tradition, legend, tune, and song
> Shall many an age the wail prolong:
> Still from the sire the son shall hear
> Of the stern strife and carnage drear
> Of Flodden's fatal field,
> Where shiver'd was fair Scotland's spear
> And broken was her shield.

Charles the First erected his royal standard at Nottingham, 22nd August 1642, and the lengthy struggle between king and parliament began. Historians have expressed various opinions as to divisions which animated the people. The bulk of the nobility, dreading a total confusion of rank from the fury of the populace, sided with the King, whilst the city of London and most of the great corporations took the side of Parliament. Contrasting the manner in which the war was carried on in Scotland Sir Walter Scott says:—" Greatly to the honour of the English nation, owing perhaps to the natural generosity and the good humour of the people, or to the superior influence of civilisation—the civil war in that country, though contested with the utmost fury in the open field, was not marked by anything approaching the violent atrocities of the Irish, or the fierce and ruthless devastation exercised by the Scottish combatants. The days of deadly feud had been long passed if the English ever followed the savage custom, and the spirit of malice and hatred which it fostered had no existence in that country . . ." Having given this testimony to what is undoubtedly a grand characteristic of the English people, we now turn our attention to the course of the civil war in Cheshire.

At the commencement of the struggle both parties were naturally anxious to gain the advantage. Parliament ordered that the magazines of the several counties should be put into the hands of the lord lieutenants, and shortly afterwards the King issued his commissions of array, but their efforts to carry out his orders were strongly opposed in Cheshire by Sir Thomas Stanley and others. In an affray at Manchester on the 15th July, Richard Percival, a linen weaver or "webster," was slain, which was said to have been the first blood shed, and afterwards led to the impeachment of Lord Strange for high treason. The raising of the standard at Nottingham caused great disappointment, as Lord Strange had 20,000 men in readiness in Lancashire, and he purposed doing the same in Cheshire. The King paid a visit to Chester on the 23rd September, where he was presented by the Corporation with a purse of £200, and Prince Rupert with £100, afterwards returning to the south. On Michaelmas Day Lord Grandison, with a considerable body of horse, attacked Nantwich, which was held for Parliament, and which, being in fear of the royal army at Shrewsbury, was conditionally surrendered. In this affair Lord Cholmondeley and Sir Hugh Calveley were with Lord Grandison. Subsequently, a part of Lord Cholmondeley's troops were taken and disarmed at Northwich. On the 8th December an attempt was made to seize Macclesfield for the King by Colonel Legh of Adlington, but this was frustrated by Mr Mainwaring, who roused the county and "attacked them with great fury." Two soldiers were slain, and their leader fled. "Mr Manwaring" marched into Nantwich on 10th December.

At this time Chester was occupied for the King by Earl Rivers, and the adverse parties beginning "to be a good deal afraid of each other," several meetings took place at Bunbury, articles for "the pacification and settling the peace of the county" being drawn up. These articles, under certain conditions, provided for an absolute cessation of arms within the county, and were signed by Robert Kilmorrey and Orlando Bridgeman on the one side, and William Marbury and Henry Mainwaring on the other. These proceedings, however, did not please Parliament, who so far had had the advantage throughout the country generally, and after declaring the articles null and void, and as having been made without proper authority, sent down the celebrated Sir William Brereton to assume the offensive.

With his advent, on the 28th January 1643, active hostilities began. He attacked Sir Thomas Aston at Nantwich about four in the evening, and after a sharp conflict threw the Royalists into confusion by the unexpected explosion and flash of a small piece of cannon. "Sir William" discharged his drake, which wrought more terror than confusion, for the ground was very rough, but the enemy cried, "Let us fly for they have great ordnance." The headquarters of the Parliamentarians were fixed here—those of the Royalists at Chester. On 21st February, what was described in an old Parliamentarian pamphlet as "a pitched battle," was fought at Tarporley. It states: "We saluted one another with fire and lead. They played on us for the space of an hour with cannon and musket, yet we lost not a man. Only three were shot, scarce wounded, and a horse's hoof hit with a musket ball out of the cannon, which was a miraculous providence of God in the judgment of all men." In Chester the Royalists boasted that they had got "Sir William's (Brereton's) hat and feather, a great trophie," though upon examination it was found to belong to one of their own soldiers. The attempt made by Sir Thomas Aston to occupy Middlewich for the King ended in his total defeat by Sir William Brereton. This action was fought on the 13th March 1643, and up to the following November the forces in Chester and at Nantwich appear to have been engaged in several skirmishes. At the fight at

Middlewich a number took refuge in the church, and several of the Royalists were slain on the top of the steeple. " Their ordnance and much powder was taken, besides abundance of money." The Parliamentarians lost six men killed and ten wounded, while of the Royalists thirty were slain, and " they knew not how many wounded." A solemn thanksgiving was offered at Nantwich for " the glorious victories" which had crowned the Parliamentary arms. Indeed the Royalists seems to have got the worst of it in many places, but the turning point nearly came on the arrival at Chester of Lord Byron, with reinforcements from Ireland for the King. Beeston Castle, Doddington Castle, Crewe Hall, Dorford Hall, and Barthomley and Acton churches, all of which had been garrisoned for the Parliamentary army, were taken. Great cruelties were committed by the Royalists at Barthomley Church. It is stated that several of the inhabitants of the township had gone there for safety, but the Royalists soon got possession, and having set fire to the forms, rushes, mats, etc., the men who had retreated into the steeple were obliged to call for quarter. This was granted, but when they surrendered, they were stripped naked, and twelve murdered, three only being allowed to escape. This atrocious act formed one of the articles against Charles I. Acton Church, which had been converted into a prison, maintained a stout resistance, but Beeston Castle, almost impregnable, and accessible only on one side, surrendered without resistance to Captain Handford, who had arrived with the Irish reinforcements. This enterprising partisan, with only eight of his soldiers, availing himself of the night, contrived to mount the steep ascent, escalading the wall, and get possession of the upper ward before morning, and on the same day it was surrendered. The governor, Captain Steele, was afterwards shot at Nantwich for cowardice. Crewe Hall made a vigorous defence, but was obliged to capitulate on the 28th of December for want of victuals and ammunition. In the month of December 1643 Lord Byron defeated the whole of the Parliamentary forces under Sir Wm. Brereton, at Middlewich. Those who escaped fled to Nantwich. In consequence of this action Northwich fell into the hands of Lord Byron. Nantwich being the only garrison in Cheshire in possession of the Parliament, was besieged during the greater part of the month of January 1644.

The tide of battle ebbed and flowed. The Parliamentary forces generally had the advantage. There was a marked absence of the deadly sacrifice of human life which marked the great war of 1914-18. There were no weapons of precision or high explosives then. Gradually the Parliamentarians drew the net closer round the ill-fated capital of the County. Prince Rupert had been signally defeated at Stockport, and Sir William Brereton fulfilled the reputation he had acquired previously, by occupying the suburbs, and seizing the sword and mace left in the house of the Mayor of the City. Then followed the decisive battle of Rowton Heath, and although the City held out for four months longer, it was not to be wondered at that King Charles effected his escape on that occasion, not without personal danger, to Denbigh Castle.

In the month of December Colonel Booth, with the Lancashire forces, joined Sir William Brereton in his siege of Chester, when such dispositions were made " that the city was quite encompassed nor was ever any place more straitly beleaguered, so that this town and garrison were obliged to feed on horses, dogs, and cats ; notwithstanding this distress, they refused nine several summonses, nor did they answer the tenth till they had received undoubted assurance that there was no hope of any succour. No shot was fired after the 25th of December. A treaty was then set on foot, which was carried on for several weeks by commissioners on each side ; the result was that the city and castle were surrendered on the 3rd of February 1646, upon terms equally honourable to the besiegers and to the besieged. Sir William Brereton immediately took possession of the Castle with its ordnance and arms, the county-palatine seal, sword, and records ; pursuant to one of the articles of the treaty, two thousand stand of arms, and five hundred and twenty headpieces were brought into the Castle court ; the sword and mace were restored to the city, but contrary to the terms of the treaty, the Parliamentary army pulled down the high cross, defaced the choir of the cathedral, destroyed the organ, broke the painted glass in all the church windows, and demolished all the fonts." The Governor, Lord Byron, on its surrender, was " to march out with due attendance, and to have two coaches and four for his lady and other ladies and gentlemen in his suite, to take eighty of his books, and all his deeds and evidences and MSS.; all other noblemen and officers, according to their rank, to have a proportionate attendance, and to be allowed to take a limited sum of money ; the citizens to be secured in their persons, goods, and liberties ; no churches or any evidence or writings belonging to them to be injured ; the Castle, without any injury, to be delivered up to Sir William Brereton, with all the ordnance, arms, records, etc., also, the horses, arms, etc., not to be taken away from the garrison, but to be brought into the Castle court." On the rumour of some attempts being set on foot for restoring the King's power, the fortifications of Chester were put in complete repair. In the month of August 1648 Captain Oldham and Lieut. Ashton formed a plan for seizing the city and castle for the use of the King, but the design being discovered, they both suffered death.

CHAPTER VII.

Martial Cheshire (continued)—The splendid traditions and services of the Militia—Origin of the Earl of Chester's Yeomanry—Clerical contributions of man and horse—Defaulters dealt with—Yeomanry's work in civil disturbances—Volunteer enthusiasm in 1803—Its services in South Africa—Volunteers of the Georgian era—Old-time Reviews at Chester— Incentives to Patriotism—Cheshire's part in great movement of 1859—" Punch " and the Volunteer Movement—Growth in public favour—Nucleus of the Territorial Army.

THE traditions of the Militia extend back to the Fryd or the levy of freemen of the Anglo-Saxon kings, and unquestionably those traditions have redounded to its honour. It had followed the Great Alfred, fought at Maldon against the Danes, won distinction at the Battle of the Standard, and suffered with the rest of the English army at Bannockburn. In the words of a distinguished general, it was the militia which up to the legalisation of a standing army in 1689, may be said to have fought the battles of England and rendered possible the victories of the Peninsula and Waterloo. Yet it was, notwithstanding these great and unobtrusive services, regarded as the Cinderella of the Forces for a long period. No degrading epithet was too bad to apply to the Militia. For instance, during the Crimean War they were made the butt of public contempt in a piece of derisive doggerel, which informed the " brave boys " that the Russians were coming to invade England, but they had no need to worry, for after the old women had given them a poke (with their umbrellas?) " the Militia would give them their finishing stroke ! " While all this was going on, the Militia were garrisoning our outposts abroad and indirectly doing splendid service in releasing the regulars for their important work in the fighting line. We have outgrown all this. England is no longer an island. Even the Navy, which has been the salvation of the Empire, would probably have been powerless to prevent a landing on our shores in 1914 had the forces in France suffered defeat, and had not risen to the supreme occasion and secured the safety of " our far flung battle-line." The Militia originally, as will be seen, was a body of soldiers for home defence, but as the result of the Crimean War, the force was brought more directly under the control of the Crown, and the system of balloting for members was replaced by one of voluntary enlistment for a period of six years, while measures were taken to train the force in conjunction with regular troops.

For the earliest reference to the Earl of Chester's yeomanry cavalry we have to go back to the reign of the second Charles, when Cheshire provided troops of Light Horse, one for the Hundreds of Wirral, Bucklow, Macclesfield, Broxton, Nantwich, Northwich, and Eddisbury. There is scarcely a family of local historic note that was not connected with it.

In 1666 a list was published of the names of gentlemen charged to find horses, men, and arms, under the command of the Right Hon. Lieut.-Colonel Sir Philip Egerton, Kt., with the names of the soldiers. In Broxton the Lord Bishop of Chester "finds" one; Lord Cholmondeley, three; Sir Thomas Grosvenor, Lady "Talbott," Lady Calveley, heiress of Charles Whalley, the parsons of Malpas (there were two), the ministers of Warburton, Dodleston, Alford, and Dutton, the Dean and Chapter of Chester, one each; in other Hundreds, Mr Brereton, the Baron of Kinderton, Sir Thomas Wilbraham, Bart., and Sir Thomas Delves, Bart., three each. This mandate was signed by Lord Derby, R. Cholmondeley, J. Arderne, P. Leycester, and R. Brooke. Later we find a letter from the authorities to Sir Philip Egerton, referring to the number of absentees and defaulters at a general muster ordered at Middlewich in the same year. Some who had had notice to send horses and "ryders" had not sent one. The Lord-Lieutenant of the County accordingly authorised a general levy or fine, the same to be paid over to the treasurer of the Militia. This was in July 1666, and among those who paid sums of £5 each were Mr John Davies, Lady Calveley, the Prebends of Chester, and Sir Thomas Grosvenor. Those who had sent inferior animals were fined £3 each. Those who had neglected to send in arms with their men, "Rack, brest and pott," were mulcted in £1. Sir Robert Cotton of Combermere appealed successfully. In Bucklow Hundred, amongst the persons fined £5 each for neglecting to provide a charge of horse under George Warburton, Esq., were the Vicar of Budworth, the Vicar of "Runkorne," the parson of Mobberley, the Vicar of Rostherne, and the Vicar of Bowdon. The Hundreds to contribute one hundred men each were Bucklow, Macclesfield, Northwich, Nantwich, and Broxton. When the Prince of Orange landed in England in 1688, Thomas Latham of Hawthorn Hall, Wimslow, in conjunction with Mr Finney of Fulshaw, raised a troop of horse for the purpose of assisting the progress of the Revolution. They joined Lord Delamere's Regiment, which was sent to Ireland. At the end of the campaign it is recorded that the regiment returned to Cheshire, and there was great and general rejoicing thereat.

The Yeomanry was an irregular cavalry force raised among men willing to provide their own horses, and officered chiefly by county gentlemen. It is the oldest branch of our volunteer force, and was instituted in 1761. In November 1796 a meeting of the inhabitants of Cheshire was held at Northwich, convened by George Harry, fifth Earl of Stamford, and presided over by Peter Warburton, Esq., when it was resolved to form a regiment of Cheshire troops to be commanded by a colonel, a lieut.-colonel, one major, three captains, five lieutenants, and six cornets, to act as a corps of light cavalry. Colonel Sir John F. Leicester was the colonel on its being organised in 1797, and they formed the Cheshire Legion, and assisted the civil powers in various parts of the country to suppress disturbances or to protect private property.

CHESHIRE: ITS TRADITIONS AND HISTORY

A century ago what was known as Peterloo, when a political meeting was broken up by the military, contemporary accounts accused the Cheshire Yeomanry with having acted with disgusting brutality. There were six different bodies of troops employed on that occasion. Some 400 men of the Cheshire Yeomanry met at Sale in August 1818, and, riding to Manchester, took up their assigned station in St John Street, where they remained, dismounted, for over two hours. They were then led by a circuitous route to St Peter's Fields, where they drew up in Windmill Street, just behind the hustings, in excellent order. Immediately afterwards the 15th Hussars lined up in Mount Street and swept the crowded square, riding from Mount Street right across to Deansgate. They were, of course, sent in primarily to rescue the Manchester Yeomanry, who were hopelessly entangled in the crowd.

All the evidence we can find goes to show that during the sweep, which was over in ten minutes, the Cheshire Yeomanry remained drawn up. Captain Smyth, who led one of the troops, says that the Yeomanry stationed at the corners of the Square "opened out" to allow the fugitives to pass. A contemporary plan represents the Yeomanry as "cutting at the fugitives." Here we are met by one of the many contradictions which make the story of Peterloo such a difficult one to unravel.

All this happened on the Monday. It was not till half-past ten on the Wednesday morning that the Cheshire Yeomanry—having spent one night in patrolling the town and another "lying at their horses' heads in St Peter's Fields"—mounted and rode away home.

When the other yeomanry regiments were disbanded in 1802, three new troops were raised at Chester. Troops were also formed at Stockport and Norton, and Lord Grosvenor raised the Western Cheshire Volunteer Cavalry. In all fourteen troops with a strength of 750 men were formed. In 1803 the Prince of Wales granted permission for the regiment to use his crest as their badge, with the title of the Earl of Chester's Yeomanry. Infantry companies from Knutsford were incorporated with the yeomanry, the amalgamated force being known as the Earl of Chester's Legion. When the Prince of Wales came to the throne, it became the King's Chester Volunteer Legion, and subsequently, when the infantry portion was disbanded, it became the King's Regiment of Cheshire Yeomanry Cavalry.

For a long period, under Sir John Leicester's command, the Cheshire Yeomanry went for training to Seaforth, near Liverpool, but it soon became apparent that Chester was a more appropriate and convenient rendezvous, and that the spacious Roodee was the natural resort of the regiment. Here members with other companies from Altrincham, Bowdon, and other townships on the Stamford estate, met for drill, but for various reasons they ceased to attend some fifty or sixty years ago, and their places were filled from other districts.

The period of training was not altogether made up of hard work on the Roodee. The men had a thoroughly good time in the city in the evening after drill, every effort being put forth by the citizens generally to secure their enjoyment. They were good trenchermen always, and on several occasions paragraphs appeared in the local newspapers illustrative of the gastronomic powers of certain yeomen, who, after eating a leg of mutton, could face a large helping of plum pudding. We could never obtain any confirmation, official or otherwise, of this remarkable performance, but there is no doubt many could consume an enormous quantity of provisions before their appetites were satisfied. Neither could we obtain the exact truth of a legend that these gallant yeomen emulated their forefathers in Flanders in the use of bad language. Certainly there appeared in a Manchester journal of that period, some twenty years after Waterloo, the following lines indicative of that town probably, and might be also of general application—

> Oh that the Muse might call without offence
> The gallant soldier back to his good sense !
> His temporal field so cautious not to lose,
> So teachers quote of his eternal foes !
>
> Soldier ! So tender of thy Prince's fame,
> Why so profuse of a superior name ?
> For the king's sake the brunt of battle bear,
> But for the King of King's sake, do not Swear !

Whether or not this excellent advice was followed deponent sayeth not.

In 1897 the muster roll of the Earl of Chester's Yeomanry Cavalry gave the following list of officers :—Honorary Colonel, His Grace the Duke of Westminster ; Lieut.-Colonel, Commandant Piers Egerton Warburton ; Honorary Lieut.-Colonel, Major the Earl of Harrington ; Surgeon G. Harrison ; Veterinary Surgeon R. E. Edwards ; Bandmaster Joseph Clement ; Reg. Sergt.-Major G. Coope ; A. Tatton Troop, Captain the Hon. Alan de Tatton Egerton (Hon. Major) ; B. Troop, Captain H. A. Birley (Hon. Major) ; B. (Eaton) Squadron, C. Troop, Captain Lord A. Grosvenor ; H. Troop, Captain G. Wyndham ; C. Squadron, Arley and Bostock Troops—Captain O. M. Leigh, Arley Troop ; Captain France Hayhurst, Bostock Troop ; D. Squadron, Forest and Congleton Troops—Forest Troop, Captain J. Tomkinson (Hon. Major) ; Congleton Troop, Captain W. B. Brocklehurst.

In 1900, the period of the South African War, came the demand for the services of mounted riflemen, and the opportunity for the regiment to prove its mettle in the field. The volunteers from the regiment formed the 21st and 22nd Companies of the 2nd Battalion Imperial Yeomanry. The officers of the 21st Company were Major Lord A. Grosvenor, in command ; Lieuts. W. Rennie, H. C. Beaumont, R. Barbour, and the Hon. R. Grosvenor : and of the 22nd Company, Captain O. M. Leigh, in command, and Lieuts. Phillips, Massey, Reynolds, and Daniels. These two companies sailed on the 30th of January of the same year, and shortly after their arrival went with Lord Kitchener to Britstown, where they formed part of Settle's force. Their principal sphere of action was in Preiska and Appington, and they shared in the actions at Hoopstadt, Vryburgh, Gelegifpontein, and other places at which the column was engaged, Captain Rennie being mentioned in dispatches. The casualties of the two companies during their participation in the campaign were: of the 21st Company two killed in action, and four died from disease; and of the 22nd, two in action, and seven from disease. The companies returned home in June 1901.

In 1803, on a flood tide of patriotic enthusiasm, no fewer than 300,000 Englishmen enrolled themselves in different volunteer corps and associations. The star of the first Napoleon was in the ascendant. Like another potentate of modern times, but without a tithe of Bonaparte's genius, he aimed at European, if not world domination. A few years later this aim received its quietus at Waterloo. Cheshire then, as now, did its duty. The capital city, every town, every village, supplied its contingent of volunteers, as the local records show. In February 1804 the volunteers were inspected at Chester by General Cuyler. Colours were presented in March to the Chester Volunteers. On 18th May the Ashton Light Horse, the Wigan Rifle Corps, and St Helens Volunteers assembled for permanent duty at Chester, followed by the Warrington Volunteers in June. On 1st October the Chester Volunteers were reviewed by General Burton, after which they set off in fifty-six wagons through the city to Vicars Cross—then through Littleton and Christleton to Foregate Street, "with a view to ascertaining the facility with which they might be conveyed in case of invasion." On 5th October the volunteers were reviewed by the Duke of Gloucester and his son, Prince William, on the "Roodeye."

Candidates were everywhere invited to join for the defence of his glorious Majesty King George III. and the preservation of our happy constitution in Church and State. "All lads of true Cheshire blood willing to show their loyalty and spirit" were invited to repair to the Plough at Ashton-on-Mersey, or to Captain Moore at Sale Hall, Sale, "where they will receive high bounties and soldier-like entertainment." "Now for a stroke at the Mounseers, my boys. King George for ever! Huzza!—John Moore, Captain; Robert Say, Lieutenant." This is given as a specimen of the placards of the period. Colours were presented to the corps on 25th January 1804, by H.R.H. Prince William Frederick, Lieut.-General the Duke of Gloucester. The corps took part in the review of 6000 men on Sale Moor, by Major-General Bergen, General Benson, and Lieut.-Colonel Cuyler, 5th Dragoons. Captain Moore was in command of the Ashton-upon-Mersey and Sale Volunteers, and had the honour to attend upon H.R.H. the Duke of Gloucester. On the disbandment of the Volunteers after Waterloo, the thanks of the King for their services were conveyed to all ranks through the Lord-Lieutenant of the County (Earl of Stamford and Warrington).

But the year 1859 witnessed a tremendous upheaval, which brought into being the existing volunteer and territorial forces, which have proved of incalculable value in our own day. To the children of that period the country seemed to be on fire. Even the grown-ups had no clear conception that the name of " Bony-part " had been of service in frightening many of their predecessors to sleep when children, but that cry was again revived. Be that as it may, by the end of the year 1859, 180,000 men had joined the ranks of the volunteer force. When it is remembered that each member had at first to provide his own uniform, accoutrements, Enfield rifle, and ammunition, even to making his own bullets and cartridges, some idea can be formed of this worthy expression of the patriotism of a free people determined to uphold its rights and honour. The ill-fated Emperor Napoleon, whose hopes of a high imperialism were shattered in 1870, proved, notwithstanding many charges against him of a Machiavellian hostility, loyal to his friendship for England. The answer, however, to the grim threatenings of invasion were the volunteer force.

For a long time afterwards, when the occasion had passed, it did not bask in the sunshine of favour, either with the War Office or the general public. Even the genial Mr Punch on many occasions poked fun at it. In " Diversions of Drill " (1860) a company is pictured on parade. The paunch of one member, who is obviously out of condition, was exceedingly prominent, and the following dialogue ensues : " Captain — Dress back, No. 3, *do* dress back. Company, fours. As y'were. No. 3, Mr Buffles, how often am I to speak to you, sir ? Will you dress back, sir ? Further still, sir. You are not dressed exactly yet, sir, by a ——. Buffles (goaded to madness)—Bet yer five pounds I am—there." No doubt this and many similar stories had a substratum of truth, and many a choleric employer would give vent to his indignation, both publicly and privately, at being ordered about by his own clerk, as often happened, in those early days. But in course of time a tardy recognition of its inherent value was given by the military authorities.

In 1904 a royal commission, known as the Norfolk Commission, was appointed to inquire into the organisation, numbers, etc., of the Volunteer Forces, and to report what changes were required in order that they might be maintained in a condition of military efficiency and adequate strength. This was the germ of the Territorial army. The Commission reported that the volunteers were solely for the purpose of resisting a possible invasion of the country, and fell short of the condition involved in war and the battlefield, involving the defeat of the enemy. The Commission recommended that the

Force, amongst other things, should be organised in its war formation of brigades and divisions; that the financial system which threw the expense of administration on the commanding officers should be altered; that "the training of the Volunteer Force should be concentrated upon what is essential to its tasks in war. Corps told off for special duties in war should ensuring peace, practise those duties"; that "ranges and grounds of exercise for all corps should be provided for all corps at the expense of the State"; that "transport and equipment for mobilisation should be provided." The section which contains these recommendations, concludes with a grave and weighty estimate of the position held by the Volunteer Force in the opinion of the Commission: "The Volunteer Force has had a great effect in educating the people of Great Britain to think of the army as a national institution, and at the same time it has enlarged the ideas of the means and methods of military training. We deprecate any changes which would modify the spirit which this Force has cherished, or any fundamental change in its position, except as a part of some comprehensive measure which would replace both the Militia and Volunteer Forces by an organisation which, while giving greater military efficiency, and at least equal numbers, would also render permanent that sympathy between the nation and the army which, before the rise of the modern Volunteer Force, was undoubtedly defective."

Sir John Burgoyne, so far back as 1847, as did Lord Roberts in recent times, endeavoured to impress on the nation the loss of prestige it would suffer in case of defeat amongst the other European powers. The Volunteer Defence Movement of 1859 was in its infancy, and he contributed an article to the *Cornhill*, which Mr Walter Richards, an author of repute on this matter, held we were placed in by our then system of military service, " and will become more and more valuable in proportion as it shall conform itself gradually to such arrangements as will make our Volunteers efficient for acting with our regular forces. . . . The first and prevalent idea from which the volunteer system sprang was that of a levy *en masse*. . . . That our volunteers would be ready to devote their lives, as they are devoting their time and energies to the defence of their country against invasion, no one who appreciates the English character will doubt; but that such a heterogeneous body of men if opposed to a highly trained and disciplined force of veteran soldiers would be able to repel the attack of an enemy is now admitted to be a fallacy. . . . Volunteers to be efficient must form a component part of an army. Every part of an army in the field must be well in hand of the generals in command. . . . By this alone will they be really formidable, and by this alone will they acquire a confidence and steadiness which mere innate courage can never give. There is one class of volunteers the formation of which will be attended with unexceptionable advantages — and that is localised bodies on the coast for service near their own homes. These may be either artillery or infantry, or, better still, both combined." There is a prophetic ring in these words, which has been amply justified by the events of 1914-18.

The Territorial Army was composed of four factors or constituent parts at that period, viz. :—Fourteen mounted brigades, fourteen divisions, army troops, and troops for coast defence. Its functions have been described as being " to provide support and expansion to the Regular Army," and in that connection " to supply garrisons for naval and other fortresses, to repel raids, and, by voluntary agreement, to furnish units for the expansion of the Expeditionary Force." The establishment of this Territorial Army is put by an Army Order of March 1908 at a trifle over 314,000 of all ranks, and these are localised in Eastern, Northern, Scottish, Southern, and Western Commands, and the London district. As has been repeatedly emphasised, the informing principle of the organisation is completeness in component parts. Each mounted brigade consists of cavalry (yeomanry) ; a battery of Royal Horse Artillery, field ambulance, transport and supply column. The division comprises: infantry; field artillery—Howitzer brigade and heavy battery ; engineers— field companies and telegraph company ; a regiment of divisional cavalry ; transport and supply column ; field ambulances.

The " army troops," colloquially describable as " general utility " troops, are referred to as " battalions of infantry and other units not required to complete the division, and under the command of the General Officer Commanding the Territorial division."

The Cheshire Railway Battalion of the Royal Engineers was famous amongst Territorial corps as being the first to be raised from one commercial undertaking—The London and North-Western Railway Co. The contingents from the reservists of the battalion were attached to the 8th, 10th, and 31st Companies Royal Engineers, and shared to the full the arduous and invaluable labours performed by the engineer arm of the service, the work that chiefly fell to the representatives of the battalion being the duties of railway construction and repairs, engine driving, etc. They served at the actions of Belmont, Graspan, and Modder River. Lieut. Sidgwick was mentioned in dispatches, and received the D.S.O. Sapper Jones received the medal for distinguished conduct in the field. Colonel Cotton Jodrell, a former commanding officer, was, in June 1908, appointed Deputy Assistant Director of Territorial Forces.

The Cheshire Field Company, Royal Engineers, part of the Western Divisional Royal Engineers, represented the 1st Cheshire Royal Engineers (Volunteers), dating from 1859. It was a regiment of which the people of Crewe were exceedingly proud, and it is noteworthy that one of its members, Lieut. Chambers, who left in 1866, served under Garibaldi, the liberator of Italy. A presentation was made to him in the Market Square, in which this fact was specially referred to, and the writer of these lines had the pleasure of recording the event in the local press. A proposal of the War Office to incorporate the corps with the 2nd Welsh Field Company later on met with strong opposition in Cheshire, and, as it was pointed out that the proposed change would have a deterring effect on recruiting, the old county style was retained. Their work in South Africa, other than that of entrenching, etc., was principally in connection with the railway lines between Pretoria and the Portuguese border. The corps had to regret a few casualties from battle and disease, two men being killed at Burgersdorp, and one, Sapper Mitchell, being mentioned in one of Lord Kitchener's dispatches in 1902.

Prior to the formation of the Territorial Army the 4th Battalion Cheshire Regiment, the former 1st Volunteer Battalion, was raised at Birkenhead early in 1859; the 5th Battalion is composed of the 2nd (Earl of Chester's) and the 3rd—the former raised at Chester in 1859 and the latter at Knutsford in the following March; the 6th is the former 4th Battalion, raised at Stockport in March 1860; and the 7th was the old 5th Volunteer Battalion, raised at Congleton in September 1859. In connection with the 4th, the name of Colonel King was regarded with affection and veneration on the Mersey side, while the late Colonel Sir T. H. Marshall, who died some months ago, by his marvellous organising power brought the 3rd Cheshires to a high standard of efficiency. In May 1908 the Earl of Chester had the honour and satisfaction of being the first unit of the Territorial Army to provide a guard of honour on the occasion of the visit of His Majesty the King to Chester. The name of Lieut.-Colonel Shakerley, Bart, T.D., was also associated for a long period with the 7th Battalion Congleton, and that of Colonel J. D. Johnston, V.D., with that of the 6th Battalion. Sections of all these served with distinction in South Africa.

Chester, as we have read, held out of all English towns against the invincible Conqueror. And then, as one writer puts it, came the fierce border warfare with the Welsh, in the course of which Llewellyn took Chester and plundered it, and the Territorialists of the day, not to be behind him, followed the Lords of the Marches into Wales, and wrought well and fiercely like valiant warriors.

The Welsh Border Mounted Brigade Transport and Supply Column, raised in 1908, owed the nucleus of their force to the old 1st Cheshire Royal Engineers, dating from 1859, and in their previous existence served in South Africa as already noted. The Cheshire Brigade Company Army Service Corps formed part of the Welsh Divisional Transport and Supply Column, and the Welsh Border Mounted Brigade Field Ambulance represented the former Brigade Bearer Company, attached to the Cheshire Volunteer Infantry Brigade, dating from 1902. This corps became, under the Territorial Forces Act, a mounted unit, Lieut.-Colonel Sidebotham, V.D., being the Commanding Officer at that time

CHAPTER VIII.

The Cheshire Regiment—Its work on " India's coral strand "—Victories in Canada, Meeanee, etc. —Monument in Chester Cathedral—The " Cheerful Cheshires' " world-wide services—Their Work in Flanders, 1914-18—Return of conquering battalions—Chester *en fete*—Visit of the King and Queen—The story of the miniature colour—Its rescue and return to Chester—Many brave deeds—Admiral Beatty and Sir Douglas Haig receive the Freedom of the City—Easing the lot of the sick and disabled—Curious reappearance of a (reported) dead Cheshire man—" The bravest street in Cheshire "—Lest We Forget.

THE Cheshire Regiment, afterwards known as the 22nd, commenced a distinguished career in 1689, when it was raised at Chester by the Duke of Norfolk, for service in Ireland under King William III. The regiment sailed from Hoylake for Ireland, and took part in the capture of Carrickfergus in 1690, the victory of the Boyne (1690), being afterwards reviewed by the King, the Siege of Limerick (1691), and other actions of the campaign, including the battle of Aughrim in 1691. After serving in the Netherlands the regiment returned to Ireland. It was sent to Jamaica in 1702, and in 1726, after serving in the West Indies, proceeded to the Island of Minorca in the Mediterranean. In 1727 five hundred men took part in the lengthy siege of Gibraltar against the Spaniards. We now hear of them at the battle of Dettingen in 1743, when the King (George II.), being hotly pressed by the French cavalry, a detachment, of which the regiment formed a part, gathered round him under an oak tree and drove off the enemy. The King plucked a leaf and handed it to the Commander, desiring the regiment to wear it as a reminder of their gallant deed.

In 1756 the regiment embarked for North America, and in 1758 took part in the conquest of Canada from the French, and was present at the siege and capture of Louisberg, which name was one of the first to be emblazoned on its colours. The bravery of the men during the storming of the advanced batteries is described as being unparalleled. After the siege a regiment of Grenadier Companies from several regiments was formed, in which the 22nd participated. They were named the Louisberg Grenadiers. The grenadiers of a regiment were No. 1 Company, which was composed of the tallest men, after the fashion of the Guards of the modern times. The Louisberg Grenadiers were in the first line in the attack on the heights of Abraham at the siege of Quebec. It was their bravery and steadiness which defeated the French counter-attack and won the battle As is well known, General Wolfe was in command, and it was in the hour of victory that he fell and died in the arms of one of the grenadiers of the 22nd Cheshires on the 13th September 1759.

The regiment was at the reduction of Martinique in 1762, and in 1775 took part in the American War of Independence, and was present at Bunkers Hill, Quaker Hill, and other battles, where, as usual, they displayed great bravery. In 1782 George III. gave the regiment its present title, the 22nd or the Cheshire Regiment. For a period of about sixty years, up to 1840, it was engaged, with other regiments, on foreign service in various parts of Europe, Cape of Good Hope, East and West Indies, and Ireland. At Meeanee, Hyderabad, etc., in 1843, the regiment earned the names which have made it so famous in the British army, and which also appear on the scroll with the well-known acorn badge. Scinde is close to the North-West Frontier of India, and is inhabited by the Beluchees. On the 16th February 1843 Sir Charles Napier received information that a Beluchee force of 35,000 were entrenched at Meeanee, and decided to attack them with 1500 men, of whom the 22nd was the only British regiment. On the 17th, at 3 a.m., he commenced his march of ten miles through a sandy plain, and found them occupying the dry ditch of a watercourse, in strength. He advanced to attack, and, noticing a high wall with a gap in it, through which he feared the Beluchees would attack him in flank, he sent Captain Tew's Company of the 22nd—the Grenadiers—to hold the gap to the last, if necessary. The company held the gap and prevented a force of 6000 Beluchees getting through. Captain Tew and many of his men died at their posts, but the remainder held the gap until the battle was won. In the meantime the remainder of the force reached the Beluchee lines, when, after a desperate hand-to-hand fight, lasting four hours, the Beluchees, unable to hold out against the bravery of the English, turned and fled, leaving 8000 dead on the field, with all their guns, standards, and tents. On the 23rd the village of Dubba was attacked, and after a desperate struggle, in which the 22nd held the place of honour at the front, captured it. Then was discovered a feature which will ever reflect credit on the regiment. It was afterwards found that several men were trying to march who had been wounded at Meeanee, and concealed themselves in order "to do their bit" in the fight at Dubba. It should also be remembered that in many cases the men had to march and fight under a burning sun, and almost without water. On their return to Bombay they received an honour never before accorded to a regiment. The Governor and Commander-in-Chief received them, and the regiment was saluted as it marched to barracks.

The 2nd Battalion was raised in 1858, after the Crimea and Indian Mutiny, and in 1881 the regimental number, the 22nd, was discontinued, and the regiment was distinguished as the Cheshire Regiment. The old facings were pale buff. In 1887-88 the 2nd Battalion was on field service in Upper Burmah, and in 1888-89 the 1st Battalion took part in the Karen and Chin-Lushai expeditions. In January 1900 the 2nd and 4th Battalions embarked for South Africa, and these were followed by the 3rd Battalion in 1902. Later in the year the 2nd, 3rd, and 4th Battalions returned to England, the 2nd proceeding to Aldershot. In 1903 the 1st Battalion was stationed at Quetta, and left for Bombay in October. The 2nd Battalion at this period was still at Aldershot. On the 30th July 1904 a special service was held at Chester Cathedral, when the old colours of the 2nd Battalion were handed to the Dean and Chapter, and at the same time a monument, erected by the Cheshire Regiment to commemorate the memory of those who fell in South Africa during the Boer War, 1889-1902, was unveiled by Lord Roberts. The north window of stained glass in the east aisle was erected in memory of Major-General Pym, by officers of the regiment. The beautiful tablet referred to above is erected on the east wall, and there is also a smaller tablet placed, in 1904, on the west wall, by the Earl of Chester's Imperial Yeomanry, in memory of comrades who died in South Africa. In 1906 the 1st Battalion was stationed at Lichfield, and the 2nd Battalion at Wellington (Madras) and other stations.

Lieut.-Colonel Kellie writing of later events says: — "We find a British army, proportionately greater than that which won Meeanee, facing, with the old indomitable spirit of their race, proportionately greater odds. The march of time has brought many changes in the army. Vanished are the old numbers, with their glorious associations; gone the scarlet uniform which has figured on so many victorious fields; but the new names and the new colour have already gained a glory which the past can certainly equal, but can hardly excel—the rearguard of an army in an honourable retreat. Once again the successors of the men of Meeanee have taken the field. Drawn to-day, not from the green fields of Tipperary, but from the broad acres of Cheshire, they stand alone at death-grips with the foe, facing again overwhelming odds with the old pride of regiment, and in addition, jealous for the honour of their dear native country.

"At 1 p.m. the storm breaks. The brigade, about 3000 strong, is attacked by a whole German army corps. All through the sultry afternoon they fight doggedly and well, until at length about 4 p.m. the regiment is left unsupported and alone, facing this German army corps. The enemy's fire grows more and more intense, the sky is rent with shells, and the shrapnel lashes the fields like rain. Three officers have already met a glorious death—one was shot down after refusing to surrender—the gallant Colonel has been severely wounded, and is now in the hands of the foe. Still, with obstinate courage the fast diminishing remnants fight on. Slowly and sullenly they retire from position to position, their well-known marksmanship, carefully taught in peace, laying many a foeman low. In one part of the field four officers (all that are left in that area) lead desperate charges against the oncoming foe, until three out of the four are wounded and incapacitated from further action.

"Then the kindly night falls. On the morrow the remnant of the brave old battalion, some 300 strong, pass their Commander-in-Chief outside St Quentin. He addresses their Commander in these few kindly words:

CHESHIRE: ITS TRADITIONS AND HISTORY

'Although your regiment suffered so heavily at Mons, the march discipline is splendid; the men are marching as if on a ceremonial parade at Aldershot.'"

Sir Charles Napier, when presenting Colours to the 1st Battalion the Cheshire Regiment, a few years after Meeanee, concluded his speech with these words: "And may the ancient city of Chester, begirt with her old walls, exult in the glory of her own brave regiment. May she not exult now?"

The month of April 1919 will be noteworthy in years to come as being the month in which the little remnants of the 1st and 2nd Battalions of the 22nd Regiment returned to England after taking a glorious part in the greatest of all wars. The two battalions have not been together in the United Kingdom since the late sixties or early seventies of the last century, when it is stated that by a curious coincidence one battalion was route marching under Ash Bridge at Aldershot at the exact moment when a train bearing the other battalion passed over the bridge. The home-coming of the 1st Battalion, on 25th April, was made the occasion of a splendid reception by the citizens. The streets were gay with flags and bunting, and a large crowd gathered at the Chester General Railway Station. Major M. F. Clarke, D.S.O., commanding the Regimental Depot, Chester Castle, who commanded the 1st Battalion in France, and Captain H. C. V. M. Freeman, Depot Adjutant, officially met the cadre, consisting of thirty-six men, under the command of Captain Sproule, M.C., at the General Station. The battalion band, under Bandmaster A. E. Noble, on the arrival of the train struck up the "Middy March," and a stirring scene was witnessed as the troops, in full equipment, began to detrain, many of them being greeted by relatives and old friends. Oak leaves and acorn wreaths, brought from the depôt, were placed on the colours, which were carried by Captain J. Oakley (king's colour), and Captain Whiteman (regimental colour). The redoubtable Corporal "Todger" Jones, V.C., D.C.M., of Runcorn, famous for his daring deeds during the war, was with the escort.

The progress of the cadre, headed by the band, through the principal streets of Chester to the Town Hall was witnessed by thousands of spectators, who greeted the men with cheers, waving handkerchiefs and miniature flags. The heroic representatives of the county regiment had a remarkable ovation on reaching the Town Hall Square. The guard of honour from the Castle, under the command of Captain Matterson, who was taken prisoner at Mons, included about thirty-two of the original members of the battalion. The miniature battalion flag, which was lost at Mons on the retirement from there in 1914, and recovered under remarkable circumstances, was carried on the march from the station by Corporal "Todger" Jones.

On arriving at the Town Hall they were received by the Mayor (Sir John Frost), the Sheriff (Alderman Williamson), the High Sheriff of Cheshire (Sir Kenneth Crossley), Sir Owen Phillips (member for the Parliamentary Division of Chester), the Countess Grosvenor, Lady Ursula Grosvenor, Lord and

Lady Arthur Grosvenor, Major Sir Philip Grey-Egerton, Bart., Lieut.-Colonel J. Meadows Frost, and Colonel Kellie, formerly of the 1st Battalion. The headquarters of the Western Command was represented by Lieut.-Colonel Phillips, D.S.O., Lieut.-Colonel Griffiths (Indian Cavalry), Remount Department, Major Beazley, M.C., Major Torr, D.S.O., M.C., and Captain the Hon. Charles Harris.

Addresses of welcome, coupled with high appreciation of the gallant deeds of the regiment, were given by the Mayor, Sir Owen Philips, M.P., the High Sheriff (Sir Kenneth Crossley), and Lord Arthur Grosvenor. Captain Sproule stated that since August 1914, 567 officers and at least 9000 men had served with the battalion. Some were still in the armies of occupation, others had been demobilised, and a great number had been left behind. On the day they had been longing for for years, the day of their welcome home, they must remember the brave men they had left asleep under the ground in the little part of England over the water.

In the evening the officers and men were entertained to dinner by the Mayor of Chester. Captain Sproule, who responded to the toast of the Battalion, proposed in a brief but eloquent manner by Mr John Dodd, paid a high compliment to the Mayoress and the ladies of Chester for their kindness in sending comforts which had been found of great service at the front. "Todger" Jones, V.C., also responded in a characteristic speech in praise of the Cheshires.

The 1st Battalion has more than upheld the famous traditions of the 22nd Foot during the present war. The battalion, as is well known, left Londonderry at the outbreak of war, as part of the immortal 5th Division, and went into action on the first day of the 1914 retreat from Mons. To them fell the honour and hard task of protecting the left flank of the British army in the retreat. As Cheshire people so well know with pride, the county regiment covered themselves with glory, and were almost annihilated during the early days of that memorable struggle, as the published casualty lists showed. The remnant of the battalion did well in the historic fighting at Le Cateau, one of the most important phases of early hostilities. After receiving reinforcements, they took part in the first and second battles of Ypres. In 1916, during the battle of the Somme, the battalion was sent over against some of the most difficult of the enemy's positions, fighting at Delville Wood, Falfemont Farm, Morval, and Guillemont, and in the great spring offensive of 1917 they did well round Arras and Oppy Wood. Later in the year they shared in the Messines Ridge affair. Before going to Italy, just after the battle of Cambrai in the autumn of the same year, they had a strenuous time holding the line in the Ypres sector. Their stay in Italy terminated with the enemy's great attack on the Fifth Army in March of 1919, and they were hurried back to France to take part in the work of stemming the wave of the enemy's invasion. April found them in Nieppe Forest, where they did very good work.

The battalion earned a magnificent name in the final stages of the British advance, during which they attacked Achiet-le-Petit, Bengay, Beaucamp, Beaurain, and Pont-sen-Sambre. Throughout the advance the battalion, despite enormous casualties, never failed to reach their objective. The honours gained by the battalion are too numerous to mention.

The 1/15th Battalion was mobilised on 5th August 1914, and was equipped for active service at Cambridge on January 1915. It sailed for France in February 1915, landing at Le Havre on the 15th February. After two days at the base it proceeded to join the 5th Division at Bailleul, and became part of the 14th Brigade, then under the command of Brig.-General Maude, who afterwards became General Officer Commanding of the British troops in Mesopotamia. The battalion was in the line until the winter of 1915–16, when at the commencement of 1916 a reorganisation of divisions was made, and in February of that year the battalion was appointed Pioneer Battalion to the 56th London Territorial Force Division, under the command of General Sir Amyatt Hull, K.C.B., with whom they remained until the division was finally broken up in June 1919. During 1916 the battalion took part in the attack at Gommecourt on the 1st July, and later in the operations on the Somme, which resulted in the capture of Combles. During these latter operations tanks were used for the first time in the history of the war, the battalion having previously constructed trenches and other obstacles for demonstration, for showing the capabilities of the engines of warfare, which the division gave before the General Officer Commanding-in-Chief and other Allied Generals at St Riguier. On leaving the Somme the battalion moved to Laventie, where it remained until March 1917, where it was chiefly occupied on the intricate system of drainage and repair of front line trenches in that sector. It then proceeded to Arras and made preparations for the first battle, in which the division played a very conspicuous and successful part. The battalion remained in this sector till July, and then proceeded with the 56th Division to take part in the operations in front of Ypres, particularly round Polygon Wood. On leaving Ypres it took over Laguincourt sector in front of Cambrai, and later took part in the surprise attack on Cambrai and the subsequent German counter-attack, where the division formed the left hinge of the British line and withstood, with the utmost gallantry, the continued heavy attacks of the enemy.

From here the division moved to Vimy Ridge sector, when the battalion had its headquarters at St Catherine. It afterwards took part in strenuous fighting.

The battalion on arrival in France was under the command of Lieut.-Colonel J. E. G. Groves, C.M.G., T.D., who remained with them until February 1918, when the command was taken over by Lieut.-Colonel W. A. V. Churton, D.S.O., T.D. The battalion has gained one C.M.G., one D.S.O., eleven M.C.'s.

three D.C.M.'s, thirty-two M.M.'s one Croix de St George, one Belgian Croix de Guerre, and ten M.S.M.'s. The battalion won, in 1916-17, 1918-19, the Divisional Association Football Cups presented by General Sir A. Hull.

The cadre of the 5th Battalion Cheshire Regiment, the Earl of Chester's and the City's Own, composed of men principally from the city and surrounding district, arrived at Chester on 13th June 1919. Again was the city beflagged, and again was the same hearty welcome accorded to the representatives of the 5th. The cadre was composed of thirty-six Warrant Officers, N.C.O.'s and men, under the command of Lieut.-Colonel W. A. V. Churton, D.S.O., a household name in the city. The other officers were:—Captain and Adjutant G. Fell Milner, Captain and Q.M. W. C. Cunningham (9th Royal Scots, Attached), and thirty-six other ranks, of whom the following came out of the original battalion : Lieut.-Colonel Churton, D.S.O., T.D. ; R.Q.M.S. T. Whitehead, M.S.M. ; C.Q.M.S. C. G. Hewitt, M.M. ; Sergeants F. Moss, G. Cruickshank, T. Burkill, and W. Jackson ; Lance-Corporals T. Starkey, F. Moran, and P. Loftus ; and Privates C. Daniels, S. Oldfield, and J. Beard.

The returning soldiers were officially received and welcomed at the station by Colonel Thompson, C.B., secretary of the Cheshire Territorial Force Association, and Captain E. D. Dickson, T.D. A party of officers and men who had served overseas with the battalion also attended to give the home-comers that very best of welcomes which comes from old comrades in arms. Among other officers on the arrival platform were Lieut.-Colonel A. G. Hamilton, O.B.E., R.A.M.C. ; Majors Ashton, M.C., T.D., N. D. Ellington, M.C., Timmins, and A. J. Musgrave ; Captains H. L. Churton, Oscar Johnson, Cowap, M.C., and R. E. Miller ; Lieuts. Frater, Spicer, Wyman, Arthur Birch, and Armstrong. The old comrades party was under the command of Colonel T. J. Smith. Sergeant Mellor, O.B.E., chief clerk, Territorial Force Association, was with the band of old comrades. The Town Hall Square was crowded, and a special guard from the Castle Depot was on parade, under the command of Captain Matterson and Lieut. A. Squires, M.C. Major Jackson had charge of the arrangements, and Majors Clarke, D.S.O., and N. R. Freeman, M.C., also attended. Lieut.-Colonel Churton received a cordial welcome from the Mayor (Sir John Frost), with whom was Lady Frost, the Sheriff, the Town Clerk (Mr J. H. Dickson), several members of the aldermanic bench, Colonel Thompson, Colonel Kellie, Mr E. Peter Jones, etc.

The visit of the King and Queen to Chester Castle took place on 14th May 1919, in perfect weather. Punctually at 12.30 their Majesties arrived, and were received with a royal salute on taking their places on the dais. His Majesty decorated several officers and six N.C.O.'s and men with medals, commencing with the bestowal of the D.S.O. on His Grace the Duke of Westminster. Amongst others decorated were:—Major Marshall F. Clarke, D.S.O.; Sergeant S. Harvey, D.C.M.; Private J Whitely and Private

J. Hewson, M.M. Sergeant Martin, Worcester Regiment, also received the D.C.M. Amongst those presented to their Majesties were Lieut.-Colonel R. J. Cooke (commanding the depôt), and Mrs Cooke. We may here introduce the story of how Private Thomas Alfred Jones, Cheshire Regiment, won the Victoria Cross for most conspicuous bravery. He was with his company consolidating the defences in front of a village, and, noticing an enemy sniper at 200 yards distance, he went out, and, though one bullet went through his helmet and another through his coat, he returned the sniper's fire and killed him. He then saw two more of the enemy firing at him, although displaying the white flag. Both of these he also shot. On reaching the enemy trench he found several occupied dug-outs, and, single-handed, disarmed 102 of the enemy, including three or four officers, and marched them back to our lines through a heavy barrage. He had been warned of the misuse of the white flag but insisted on going out after the enemy.

Another member who also shed honour on the "Cheerful Cheshires" was Second Lieut. Hugh Colvin, who was awarded the Victoria Cross for most conspicuous bravery in attack. When all the officers of his company except himself—and all but one in the leading company—had become casualties, and losses were heavy, he assumed command of both companies, and led them forward under heavy machine-gun fire with great dash and success. He saw the battalion on his right held up by machine-gun fire, and led a platoon to their assistance. Second Lieut. Colvin then went on with only two men to a dug-out. Leaving the men on top, he entered it alone and brought up fourteen prisoners. He then proceeded with his two men to another dug-out, which had been holding up the attack by rifle and machine-gun fire and bombs. This he reached, and, killing or making prisoners of the crew, captured the machine-gun. Being then attacked from another dug-out by fifteen of the enemy under an officer, one of his men was killed and the other wounded. Seizing a rifle, he shot five of the enemy, and using another as a shield he forced most of the survivors to surrender. This officer cleared several other dug-outs alone or with one man, taking about fifty prisoners in all. Later he consolidated his position with great skill, and personally wired his front under heavy close-range sniping in broad daylight, when all others had failed to do so. The complete success of the attack in this part of the line was mainly due to Second Lieut. Colvin's leadership and courage.

Another V.C., of whom Cheshire people may be proud, as he had his home for five years at Sale, was Lance-Corporal Onions, 1st Devons, a native of Bilston, Staffs. Through some slight breach of military discipline he was deprived of his rank as second lieutenant, but he was determined to "make good," and at once volunteered as a private in the Devonshire Regiment, and on arrival at the Devons' training depot he asked to be sent to France immediately. After firing a musketry course he was given embarkation leave, and on his return pleaded to be allowed to take the place of a man who was going overseas next day. The adjutant agreed, and on 17th April 1917 he went to the Devons in France. A month later he found himself in a hospital at home. As soon as he was well again he pleaded to be sent back to France, and in March 1918 he was again with the 1st Devons. He was promoted lance-corporal, and on 22nd August, south of Achiet-le-Petit, his chance came. In company with another man he was sent out to re-establish communication with a battalion on the right. In an old trench he saw a large force of Germans approaching. He placed his comrade on his exposed flank and opened rapid fire. They inflicted heavy losses on the Germans, and some threw up their hands. Corporal Onions called on them to surrender. No fewer than 200 Germans gave up, Onions and his companion marching them back to headquarters. For this he received the Victoria Cross, but regretted that he was not restored to his former rank as officer. When demobilised in March last he gave up all hope of reinstatement, but since then his case has been considered by the Army Council, and he was gazetted second lieutenant as an act of grace in recognition of his valuable services. He was wounded several times on the day he won the Victoria Cross. In February 1919 he received at a Sale public gathering a cheque for £180, a gold watch, and a gold brooch for his wife—presented by the local council.

On the day of the signing of the Armistice, 11th November 1918, there were great rejoicings throughout Cheshire, in common with the rest of the country. The capital of the county, good old Chester, excelled itself. There was a great display of bunting, and joy bells rang out from every church tower. As it was appropriately and feelingly put by " H. F. K.", after four long, weary years of waiting, victory had come at last, and an erstwhile arrogant foe had, with due humility, signed the historic armistice which marked his downfall from among the great nations of the world, the triumph of the Allied cause, and this dear old England of ours, in spite of many reverses, many muddles, and infinite sorrows, emerging from the awful struggle triumphant as of old. This is what it means to the general public, stunned though it may be by the dramatic suddenness of the foe's collapse, and hardly realising as yet that on all fronts the din of years'-old strife had died down suddenly, and let us hope for ever, into that almost uncanny silence which points to the dawn of perpetual peace. He pictures the delighted crowds parading the streets and the display of military strength, the music, and the cheering, with artistic literary touch. " The music dies down, and the main features of the four past tragic, glorious years flash before him like a dream which precedes the hour of waking —Mons, the old Contemptibles of the 1st Battalion covering themselves with glory in the great retreat; the 2nd Battalion brought hurriedly home from India in the grim winter of 1914 to take their place in Flanders in that struggle which astonished the world, so great were the odds against them, so

CHESHIRE: ITS TRADITIONS AND HISTORY

gallant the hearts which endured and won ; the battalions of Kitchener's Army raised in the mud, desolation, and discomfort of Salisbury Plain, to win the undying renown in Gallipoli and Mesopotamia, and together with the Old Mother Battalion in Flanders and France ; the old badge of the regiment carried to victory in Italy, Palestine, and Macedonia—hardly a quarter of the globe where the oak leaf has not shown the way to glory ; and in the last few splendid months, when the tide on the Western Front has turned to triumph, the Old Mother and her bantlings, both Service and Territorial, going forward in the great and glorious advance of 1918, to avenge those who fell in the equally glorious retreat of 1914, and eventually to fly the flag of our Empire on the farther bank of the Rhine."

The story of how the miniature colour, belonging to the 1st Battalion, was retrieved, after having been for four years safely hidden away in Belgium, is as follows :—In 1911 the ladies of the regiment were asked by Lieut.-Colonel Kellie, then commanding the 1st Battalion, to embroider the regimental colour in miniature, a quarter of the size of the original. This was done and presented in Belfast on Meeanee Day, 17th February 1912, to the best shooting company of that year. The colour was competed for each summer, and was hung in the barrack room of the company holding it, which was called the Colour Company, and formed the escort for the colours for that year.

In 1914 the miniature colour was held by "B" Company, who took it with them to France with the Expeditionary Force. In the action of 24th August the colour was carried by Drummer Baker, who hid it in the roof of a house, and afterwards died of wounds. Riley, while in hospital in the Convent of the Holy Family in Audregnies, knowing that the colour was likely to be found by the Germans, tried to fetch it from the place where it was hidden, but was prevented by his wounds. He confided the circumstances to a nun, and drew a rough map to show her the hiding-place. The nun fetched the colour to Riley the next day hidden under her dress.

Riley, on passing through a Belgian village called Audregnies, dashed into a barn and hid the trophy under the eaves, behind some straw. On arriving at the convent he explained to the Sister where it was, and asked her to take care of it. She informed the priest, who, accompanied by the schoolmaster, went to find it, at the risk of their lives, and carried the colour to the church, where they hid it behind the choir stalls. The three principal Belgians concerned —the Curé, M. C. Sardou ; the Communal Secretary, M. G. Dupont ; and M. Alphonse Ballee—were each presented with a silver rose bowl, suitably engraved with the name of the recipient and the circumstances of the presentation. Accompanying the rose bowl was an illuminated letter of thanks on parchment with a representation of the colours on the top.

Shortly after the Armistice was signed the 15th Battalion (the well-known Bantams) were demobilised at Ripon, and the colour party proceeded to

Birkenhead on 1st May. They were received by the Mayor, Mr Alfred Bigland, M.P. (the founder of the 15th and 16th Cheshires, the original Bigland's Bantams), and many of the old officers of the battalion and numerous ladies and friends.

The Mayor gave them a warm welcome and recounted the history of the battalion from its earliest days, and gave particulars of the honours won by the battalion. The colour was presented to the Mayor, and the 15th Battalion of the Cheshire Regiment passed into the world of the future, with " its identity preserved." The battalion had been through some exceedingly " stirring " times and seen a lot of fighting. It has been mentioned by name in dispatches—a great honour, and added its share of fresh honours to the glorious traditions and honours of the old 22nd Regiment of Foot.

The 1/7th Battalion took part in the memorable landing at Suvla Bay, and on the evacuation of the Gallipoli peninsula proceeded to Egypt. After a short spell in the Western Desert it was moved to the Suez Canal defences, and later took part in the advance across the Sinai Desert, and after the hard fighting at Gaza and Beersheba was one of the first battalions of General Allenby's victorious army to enter Jerusalem. Being transferred to the Western Front in June 1918, it was soon hard at work, and won great credit whilst working with the French army under General Mangin in the operations which were considered to mark the turning point of the war. Rejoining General Plumer's army it took a prominent part in the final advance, which led up to the Armistice.

The honours include three D.S.O.'s and Bar, one D.S.O., and twenty M.C.'s, besides innumerable D.C.M.'s and M.M.'s, and foreign decorations (French and Belgian).

In a special order of the day General Sir G. F. Milne, K.C.M.G., D.S.O., Commanding-in-Chief, British Salonica Force, 28th February 1919, said the 12th Battalion Cheshire Regiment was "a marvellous battalion, which had shown the finest courage, enthusiasm, and endurance.

The Croix de Guerre presented to this battalion is now in the custody of the Officer Commanding the Depot, Chester.

The 2nd Battalion cadre, after a hazardous and varied career during its service abroad, arrived home in June. They were welcomed at the station by Major R. G. Bagley, Lieut. and Adjutant Taylor, and Lieuts. Horsley and Stead. Notwithstanding their long stay in malaria-infected regions in Maecdonia, they looked remarkably fit and well.

The admission of Sir David Beatty to the Freedom of the Ancient City of Chester was carried out with all the pomp and ceremony befitting such an important occasion. This notable event took place on the 31st March 1919, at a special meeting of the Town Council, and in the presence of a crowded gathering of influential citizens and distinguished visitors. Alderman D. L.

EARL BEATTY.

COUNTESS BEATTY and VISCOUNT BORODALE

Hewitt, in the absence through ill-health of Alderman W. H. Churton, the Father of the Council, proposed the formal resolution that Admiral Beatty be admitted to the honorary freedom of the City. Proceeding he said, "The honour we are about to confer upon Admiral Beatty is the honour of the freedom of the ancient and loyal city of Chester, no mean city, with a history dating back to the first century when the Roman general, Victor Valerius, with his 20th Legion, pitched his camp on the banks of the Deva ' Antiquity's pride we have on our side,' and an honourable and glorious history of service rendered, and of deeds performed to the State, of an embellished record of unswerving loyalty to the throne. And we remember with pride that kings have honoured our ancient city by accepting and using the title of Earl of Chester. There is an interesting feature belonging to the Mayoralty of the city which I now mention. It is that, by an ancient charter, the Mayor of the city was Admiral of the Dee, with a jurisdiction extending from Hilbre Island, as far as the tide flows, and the emblem of his office was an old silver oar, still preserved as a symbol of the Mayor's maritime office. Admiral Beatty was a fighting naval strategist, and as commander of that vast and mighty fleet of warships which, by its unceasing vigil, its untiring devotion, and undaunted heroism, secured for us the necessaries of life, the blessings of freedom, safeguarded our army and its supplies, and kept our land unpolluted by the foot of a devastating and barbaric foe. In honouring Admiral Beatty we honour the men of the Fleet, and we render homage to those officers and men who sleep their last sleep in the great cemetery of the world, the inviolate, the eternal sea—those men who place honour and duty first, to whom the honour of the flag was more precious than life itself, that flag which goes the world around and waves in every breeze, and wherever it goes the world over is the emblem of freedom. We are apt to think of all the men who manned the Fleet as a separate part of our national life, trained for war in peace time. But in this last great war a large proportion of the crews of the warships were composed of just ordinary men—men from the workshop, men from behind the counter, men from the desk, men from the ordinary avocations of life, and men from the plough. But these men early imbibed the traditions of the Navy, and early learnt the rules of the service as given by the poet—·

> Steady to hand in times of squalls
> Stand to the last-by him that falls ;
> And answer clearly the voice that calls,
>   ' Aye, aye ! Sir.'

" In this connection we remember with pride the ship which bears the name of this ancient city. We remember the heroism of the boy, Jack Cornwell, V.C. The battle of the Dogger Bank and the battle of Jutland will for ever be associated with the name of Beatty, be a proud tradition of the senior service, and I can imagine future generations adapting the poet and saying : ' Oh, England was England, and the mighty brood she bore, when Beatty came swooping from the Nore.' We remember that he was captain in the Navy at the age of twenty-nine, that he was a rear-admiral at so early an age that they had to pass a special order in council so that he might take the duties of that high office and assume the responsibilities attached to it. The Admiral had the honour of receiving the German navy when it came as a whipped dog from its kennel at the call of its master. And his signal, ' The German flag will be hauled down at sunset to-day and will not be flown again without permission,' deserves to be set up at the Peace Conference for delegates there to read, learn, and inwardly digest.

" Gentlemen of the Council, by your vote to-day Admiral Beatty's name will be added to the list of eminent men who have loved and served our ancient city. It will also be added to the names of those persons of distinction who, like the late Lord Roberts, rendered eminent service to the nation, and when coupled with the names of Sir Douglas Haig and the Right Hon. David Lloyd George, will for ever remain a pleasing possession of this ancient and honourable city."

The eloquent address of Alderman Hewitt, of which the above is a summary, was endorsed by Councillor W. Carr, the senior member of the Council present, and also by the Mayor, Sir John Frost, who asked the acceptance by the City's newest Freeman of the illuminated scroll bearing the resolution and the honour, together with a piece of Georgian silver plate. He coincided with everything said by the mover and seconder of the resolution as to the gratitude and admiration they felt for the splendid part he, and those under his command, had taken in the Great War. " The honour of the freedom of this ancient city," he added, " is not conferred lightly, but on our part we recognise in the acceptance of it, have conferred an honour upon us."

Sir David, before signing the Honorary Freeman's Roll, took the freeman's declaration, which he repeated after the Town Clerk. It ran :—" I do declare that I will be faithful, profitable, and true to the King of Great Britain, and to the commonalty of the City of Chester, and duly the franchise of Chester maintain, and be not assenting, nor abetting, to any confederacy or conspiracy against the city or my neighbours."

The ceremony of making Sir David a member of the Most Ancient and Worshipful Company of Bakers was inaugurated by Mr R. G. Gerrard, acting Chairman of the City Guilds. Mr C. J. Parry, Clerk of the Bakers' Company, administered the oath, and presented the Admiral with a certificate of membership.

Sir David Beatty said he felt proud to be an honorary freeman of that ancient city. " In accepting this great honour," he added, " I do so as Commander-in-Chief of the Grand Fleet ; it is as a token of your appreciation of their services that I am so proud to accept the honour to-day. If anything could add to my pride in this matter it is with that fact that my earliest associations are crowded into the hunting-fields of Cheshire. I accept this great honour, I said, as the head man, as the Commander-in-Chief of the Grand Fleet, and they know that, in my doing so, they also are being honoured. I regret that I have not representatives in the matter of ships, or in the matter of officers and men to support me to-day, but still, the fact that they are not here does not remove the knowledge from them that they are associated with me in this great honour which this great city is conferring upon me." (Applause.) He dwelt on the splendid work done by the Cheshire Regiment during the war, and the prominent and gallant part played by the battleship *Chester* in worthily upholding the traditions of the ancient city The very fact they had conferred the great honour they had done upon him and his fleet indicated quite clearly that Chester realised to the full the real value and meaning of having a fleet which was worthy of that great command of the sea which was passed down to us by those heroic souls of the Elizabethan era, who wrested it for us, and imposed upon the country the maintenance of the British Navy in sufficient strength to meet the requirements of the nation in its duty " of cherishing merchandise and preserving command of the sea."

On the same occasion Sir George Carter, K.B.E., presented the city with an oil-painting by Mr Alfred Burgess, R.I., of H.M.S. *Chester*, the gift of Messrs Cammell, Laird, & Co., and in doing so alluded to the fact that both the *Chester* and the *Birkenhead* were built at the far-famed Merseyside shipbuilding yard.

Early in July Sir Douglas Haig, General Officer Commanding of the British Army in France, received the Freedom of the City, and the great soldier's reception was distinguished by the same whole-hearted enthusiasm which was manifested when Admiral Beatty was similarly honoured. He was also admitted to the Honorary Freedom of the Ancient and Worshipful Company of Joiners, Carvers, and Turners. The Mayor and Mayoress will have a permanent memorial of their illustrious guest, as in the course of the afternoon Sir Douglas planted a young oak tree, presented by the King of the Belgians, in the grounds of their residence at Upton Manor.

An Earldom was conferred on Sir David Beatty and Sir Douglas Haig in recognition of their invaluable services to the country.

A memento of the grand part played by the Red Cross and the Order of St John of Jerusalem will be found in the memorial banner placed, in July 1919, on the south-east pier of the tower in Chester Cathedral. It was subscribed for by all branches in the county, and was the subject of a service of thanksgiving at which assembled a large and representative congregation. It was of a beautiful and elaborate design. On the front the emblems of the two orders, the Order of St John and the British Red Cross Society, occupy the central position, and below them on a scroll are their respective mottoes in Latin—" Into the arms of Charity," and " For the benefit of humanity." On the background is stencilled in rose colour a design of the Tudor rose, the Scotch thistle, and the Irish shamrock growing from the Welsh leek. The Tree of Life springs with its oak leaves, and across from the centre of the lower border (of hospital blue) and on the branches hang ninety-eight regimental badges, representing the regiments of those sick and wounded soldiers who were patients in the eighty-six voluntary and auxiliary hospitals in Cheshire. At each corner are shields with the arms of England, Scotland, Ireland, and Wales in their heraldic colours. In the centre of the border, surmounting the banner, is the silver dove—the emblem of peace—with an olive branch in her mouth, surrounded with the laurel wreath of victory, and the golden rays of the Holy Spirit shedding glory over the whole. The dove and badges were worked in gold and silver tinsel by disabled soldiers and sailors. Inscribed on the back of the banner are the eighty-six auxiliary hospitals in Cheshire.

At a subsequent meeting in the Music Hall, presided over by Her Grace Katherine, Duchess of Westminster, who retired, and was succeeded by Lady Cholmondeley, some interesting facts were given. Sir Arthur Stanley, who gave a spirited address, referred at length to Cheshire's wonderful war work. Cheshire could certainly look back with pride and satisfaction upon the part they had played in the Great World War. For its size and population, Cheshire had more hospitals than any other county. Mr H. J. Brydon (County Director) filled in some interesting figures to complete the picture. At the time of the signing of the Armistice the county branch had 80 hospitals, 75,000 patients, 88 women's detachments, 18 men's detachments, and 4 transport detachments, with a total personnel of 6000. The workers connected with the clothing and comforts had turned out 2,000,000 garments of various kinds. The 100 ambulances and 250 cars of the transport had made up, to the end of February, 320,000 journeys, and had travelled about 1,500,000 miles. The expenditure of over £2,000,000 of public money had been supervised at the cost of a little over one-third of a penny in the pound. Perhaps his greatest pleasure was that they had raised £95,000 for " Our Day " and the work abroad. Thanks were voted to all who had taken part in the work, and there were many interesting presentations of a personal character. The most touching was the handing of a picture to the Duchess of Westminster, of her son, Lord Hugh Grosvenor, who had fallen in the war, together with a sum of £200, which she handed over as a contribution to the County Memorial scheme which the Red Cross and St John hoped to establish as a training or working colony for discharged men and others suffering from tuberculosis.

In September 1919, Chester welcomed home the heroes of the city who had nobly done their part in securing victory. Men of the Army and Navy took part, and no efforts were spared to give them a right royal welcome home. The Citizens' Committee was presided over by the Mayor. The streets were gay with bunting, but not only the "Rows," but the streets were thickly lined with spectators. The task of providing for 3386 men was a heavy one, but the feat was carried out without a hitch or mishap of any kind. The parade through the streets was an inspiring sight, which will long be remembered by those who witnessed it. The men were loudly cheered along the line of route ; the disabled occupied motor cars and ambulances, and they were received with even greater cheers than the other participants in the procession. The parade was formed under the command of Colonel Bretherton, V.D., late Commanding Officer of the 4th Cheshire Regiment, who, during the war, commanded the 5th Service Battalion Cheshire Regiment, and subsequently the 1st Battalion of the Manchesters in India. He was assisted by Lieut.-Colonel Bonnalie, T.D. (Royal Field Artillery, Territorial Force), Lieut.-Colonel C. E. Bromley, T.D. (5th Reserve Battalion Cheshire Regiment), and Major F. M. Clarke, D.S.O. (Cheshire Regiment). The bands of the 1st and 2nd Cheshires played the procession through the streets. The men who served with the various naval and army units followed in detachments, marshalled in official order of precedence, under the following officers: Royal Navy and Royal Marines, Lieut. H. G. Hinks, R.N.R. ; Cavalry and Yeomanry, Captain P. A. Mules ; Cheshire Brigade, R.F.A., Lieut.-Colonel J. Meadows Frost, D.S.O. ; Royal Engineers, Major H. L. Smith, M.C. ; the Cheshire Regiment, Major W. A. V. Churton, D.S.O., T.D. ; Foot Guards and Infantry of the Line, Lieut.-Colonel W. E. Brown, D.S.O., M.C. (the Welsh Regiment) ; Machine Gun Corps, Tank Corps, and Labour Corps, Lieut. T. S. Williams (Tank Corps) ; R.A.S.C., Captain R. G. Cockrill ; W.B.M.B.F.A., R.A.M.C., Lieut.-Colonel A. G. Hamilton, O.B.E. ; R.A.M.C., R.A.O.C., A.P.C., etc., Lieut.-Colonel J. H. Peyton, D.S.O. (R.A.M.C.) ; Royal Air Force, Captain T. M. Dutton ; disabled (in conveyance), Lieut. Astbury (Northumberland Fusiliers). The pavements, balcony, and spaces of the Town Hall were densely crowded with people, and all points of vantage were taken up when the procession wheeled from St Werburgh's Street into the Square. A Cenotaph, after the London model, was erected on the pavement adjacent to the west side of the King's School, and was duly saluted. It was simply decorated with a wreath of classic Greek victor's laurel with bow of red, white, and blue, a floral cross appearing above, and the words, "To Our Glorious Dead," below. The base of the shaft was a mass of beautiful wreaths tastefully arranged by loving hands. Flags of the Allies were displayed on the façade of the Town Hall. The Union Jack was flying from the flagstaff in the Square and on the top of the King's School, whilst in Northgate Street, the Cross, Bridge Street, and Grosvenor Road, flags were numerous, and the whole scene was of an inspiring character. Tributes were received from the following :—The Mayor and Mayoress, Cheshire Regiment, oak leaves (per

Major W. A. Vere Churton); the Hon. Mrs H. N. Gladstone, officers and members of the Chester City Division of the B.R.C.S., members of the staff of the Northgate House County Offices, Comrades of the War Club, Chester Y.M.C.A. (red triangle of roses), Chester United Football Club, Parkgate Hospital, Catholic and Associate Members of St Francis' Catholic Club, Colonel and Mrs Sheriff Roberts (in memory of their three sons). Many of the wreaths bore pathetic inscriptions, and the occasion was obviously affecting to those who brought them. " In remembrance of my dear master, Colonel Logan," was written on one card. There were three wreaths in memory of Fred Travers Vernon. At the Castle the salute was taken by Lieut.-General Sir T. D'Oyley Snow, K.C.B., K.C.M.G., G.O.C. Amongst others present were the Mayor, Alderman Sir J. M. Frost, the Countess Grosvenor, Lieut.-Colonel Dawes (Royal Air Force), Colonel W. Bromley Davenport, C.M.G., C.B.E., D.S.O., Colonel Thompson, C.B., Colonel Hayter, Captain Dickson, Captain H. G. Freeman, Captain Matterson, Mr T. G. Frost, Mr John Jones, Mr C. P. Cockrill, Mr J. Wynne Foulkes, etc.

Sports of a varied character took place in the evening on the Roodee, the prizes being presented by the Countess, her Ladyship being accorded a hearty vote of thanks for her gracious services. It is stated on good authority that never in the annals of the city had such a large company sat down as was the case at the dinner which followed the sports. The whole of the market was completely filled with long tables, and all the large rooms at the Town Hall were requisitioned as dining-rooms, including the Assembly Room, the Council Chamber, the Magistrates Room, the Education Offices, etc. His Worship the Mayor took the Chair, and thanked all those present for their attendance, everything connected with the meeting having been an unqualified success. He remarked that many of those present had been on various fronts during the last four or five years. Only last week he had the privilege of seeing the battlefields of France and Belgium, which they all knew much better than he. He saw the dug-outs in which many of them had lived in. As he passed through the battlefields his heart bled when he saw miles of country growing nothing but thistles and weeds. The Labour Battalions, assisted by Japanese, Chinese, and Africans, were now clearing up. Such was the aftermath of war! Now he could appreciate all the more what they had gone through. He thanked them again for accepting the hospitality of the citizens; the citizens were proud of them, and he hoped they had done a little towards recompensing them. (Applause.)

General Sir T. D'Oyley Snow, in a brief speech, referred to the excellent spirit of comradeship which had prevailed at the front. They were all pals out there, and they all palled together. The men deserved the welcome they were getting, as half the people in England did not realise the awful time they had undergone in the trenches. After dinner, smoking concerts were held in the Assembly Rooms and the Market Hall to the satisfaction of every one concerned.

CHESHIRE: ITS TRADITIONS AND HISTORY 103

On the 5th of September 1919 the 2nd Battalion the Cheshire Regiment, raised sixty-one years ago, bade farewell to their old quarters at Oswestry, and new colours were there consecrated. General Anderson, whose father raised this battalion at Preston, and was for the last fifteen years of his life full Colonel, was present on the occasion. Thirty years before, the old colours were presented, and they had seen lustre added by the battalion to the history of the regiment. On parade were officers and men who served in the South African War, 1899–1902, and helped to gain the first 2nd Battalion honours on those colours. Reference was also made by General Anderson to the services of the battalion in France and Salonica. The new colours were hung on the walls of the Cathedral.

Other memorials were erected in the Cathedral to the officers and men of the Cheshire (Earl of Chester's Yeomanry), who lost their lives during the war, 1914–18. Another memorial to all the battalions in the County Regiment took the form of the completion of the existing memorial Chapel by the erection of a reredos. About 10,000 names of those who had made the supreme sacrifice were inscribed in an appropriately bound vellum leaved volume, kept on a desk in the Chapel for permanent reference.

All the cadres of the battalions at depots in other parts of the county were accorded official welcomes, and their record of service showed that, in conjunction with their other comrades, they had worthily upheld the traditions and honour of the regiment of which they were such splendid units.

Soon after the outbreak of the war the sick and wounded came streaming back, and of these a large number were Cheshire men. All classes of the community vied with each other in their several degrees in easing their tragic lot. Castle, mansion, hall, even cottages in some cases were surrendered by their owners, and handed over for the duration of the war. At the end of 1916, Sir John Leigh, Bart., of Beech Lawn, Altrincham, equipped Townfield House, a fine old country mansion in Altrincham, as a hospital for the accommodation of 100 wounded officers, and, apart from the ordinary Government allowance, maintained it at his own cost. When the hospital was no longer required, in May 1919, Sir John handed it over to the Ministry of Pensions for the accommodation of shell-shock patients, and undertook to pay the charges over and above the amount granted by the Government. In June 1918 Sir John Leigh made his father's former residence at Woodbourne, Brooklands, into a hospital for shell-shock cases, at a cost of several thousand pounds. The hospital, which is known as the John Leigh Memorial Hospital, was given to the Ministry of Pensions by Sir John in memory of his father. The entire cost, outside the Government grant, is borne by the donor. The hospital was opened in June 1918 by H.R.H. The Duke of Connaught. It is a substantial stone building, in beautiful surroundings, and accommodates some seventy or eighty patients, whose disability is due to shell shock, one of the worst of the many forms of disease occasioned by the wickedness of the war. Here the men are taught habits of self-reliance, and, where possible, suitable trades, and it has been productive of great benefit in a direction not originally provided for by the State. Sir John further contributed the princely sum of £50,000 to the King's Fund of £3,000,000 for giving the returned soldier an opportunity of starting again in life and recovering his former position in society. In all these ameliorative movements, Sir John found an active helpmeet in Lady Leigh, whose devoted labours will ever be remembered by those who came under her gracious sway. Sir John Leigh, D.S.O., gave to Altrincham a public park, which he purchased from the Earl of Stamford for £7000. This noble gift gave great pleasure, and at a large gathering in the park a resolution of thanks was passed to Sir John for his public spirit and generosity.

On a sunny Saturday afternoon in April 1919, Altrincham, one of the old market-towns of Cheshire, with a feudal charter granted in 1296, was *en fête* on the occasion of the unveiling of a memorial, which undoubtedly entitled Chapel Street, in that town, to the designation of "the bravest street in the County Palatine." The memorial took the form of a roll of honour, on which were inscribed the names of 161 heroes out of a street of 60 houses, who responded to the call of king and country during the war. It had been the outcome of subscriptions of the inhabitants of the town, who were proud of their record, and the handsomely framed scroll is affixed on the kerb adjoining All Saints' Church, which stands at the entrance to Chapel Street from Regent Road. Of the 161 of the original residents, 30 gave their lives for their country. About 70 men from Chapel Street took part in a procession through the principal thoroughfares. Prior to the unveiling ceremony they were joined by Lord Stamford, Lord of the Manor, and public representatives. Amongst those present were Sir Arthur Haworth, Bart., Sir John Leigh, Bart., Mr G. F. Turner (Chairman of the District Council), Mr G. Faulkner Armitage (Mayor), wearing his robes and chain of office, nearly the whole of the members and officials of the District Council, several of the burgesses, the constables of the Court Leet (Messrs J. Brown and C. F. Redford), bearing the official staves, besides many others identified actively with the public life of the town. The Members' Committee, who were also present, comprised Messrs J. Butler and C. Nickson (marshals), T. Furness, J. Ratchford, J. W. Davies, D. Hennerley, J. Norton, J. Rowan, P. de Courcy, and T. Corfield.

At the outset of the proceedings Lord Stamford read a telegram addressed to Mr Turner, in which Lord Stamfordham, at the command of the King, conveyed His Majesty's thanks to the inhabitants of Altrincham for their loyal assurances to which the message gave expression. "The King congratulated them, and especially those living in Chapel Street, that out of its 60 houses 161 men served in the war, 30 of whom had made the supreme sacrifice. His

The Bravest Street in Chesire - Chapel Street, Altrincham

An Old Time Bull Bating

Majesty is proud to think that a roll of honour has been subscribed for, and will be unveiled as a record of the patriotism and fighting spirit so prominently displayed by the people of Altrincham."

Addresses were delivered by Lord Stamford, who had only come of age the year before and who takes a deep interest in the welfare of the district, Sir Arthur Haworth, and the Mayor of Altrincham. The unveiling took place amid a scene of great enthusiasm, and it will be long before it fades away from the memory of those who were privileged to witness it.

A remarkable incident in connection with the war was the reappearance of a Liverpool man named John Moore, a private in the 1st Cheshires, who was posted as "missing, believed killed," and was charged at Chester Castle Petty Sessions for an offence under the motoring law. He was recognised by several old comrades, who had not seen him after the first day's fighting at Mons in August 1914. He happened to be a stretcher-bearer that day, and one of the cases he carried was C.S.M. Francis of "C" Company. The Germans came on, and he was driven into their lines, but never taken prisoner. He "dodged about" and disguised himself, and eventually got back to the British lines. He was taken on the strength of the Worcesters, and afterwards transferred to the Royal Irish Regiment. It can easily be imagined that he was not severely dealt with by the magistrates, whilst he received great honour at the hands of his old comrades at the depôt. The rejoicings on the conclusion of Peace were general in Cheshire, and will long be remembered in the County Palatine.

LEST WE FORGET.
The Effort.

Raised by the British Empire for service on land	. . . .	8,654,467
Navy 450,000	Merchant Service . .	200,000

The Sacrifice.

Killed, missing, and prisoners 1,042,006	Money spent . .	£9,000,000,000
Wounded 2,074,910	Tonnage lost . .	. 9,031,000

Whilst many rolls of honour and war memorials were dealt with locally, in Chester a Memorial Roll containing the names of 697 citizens—officers, N.C.O.'s, and men—was presented to the City by Sir John Meadows Frost. and will occupy a conspicuous position in the Town Hall. A beautiful design for its reception was drawn up by Mr P. H. Lockwood, the well-known City architect. Unfortunately, it is difficult, indeed impossible, to obtain the number of Cheshire men who laid down their lives in this supreme contest for civilisation, but it is certainly, in killed and wounded, upwards of 30,300.

CHAPTER IX.

Chester's Fair in the days of King John—Cheshire minstrels pay homage to their Chieftain—A call to battle—Earl Blundeville besieged in Rhuddlan—" Rags and tatters " to the rescue—Wedding and wassail at Chester Castle—Tournament and joust at Gawsworth—Whitsun plays and their players—The entertaining play of St George and the Dragon—Soulers and their songs—Marlers and merriment—Bull-baiting in Cheshire—Cock-fighting, ancient and modern—The last recorded cock-fight in Cheshire.

CHESTER fair had been an honoured institution from time immemorial, but in 1216, during the earldom of Randle Blundeville, a notable event occurred in its annals. The historic fair was in full swing. The whole place, according to an old scribe, was ringing with noise of harps, fiddles, bagpipes, rotes, and rebecks. There was a Nebuchadnezzar-like ring in that there was the sound of flute, sackbut, psaltery, dulcimer, with a stormy accompaniment of human bellowing, shouting, and laughter. All the adjuncts of a fair, ancient and modern, were there — jugglers, tight-rope dancers, and others, but it was also attended by merchants and pedlars, with products from all parts of the earth. There was cloth, velvets, silks, and furs of all kinds. There were vendors of boxes of curiously-wrought wood for the storing of rare manuscripts. Others exhibited books and missals, in magnificent velvet covers, also rich boots and shoes, with enormously long toes, some twisted like serpents, some curled up so as to resemble a ram's horn, some imitated the peaked fool's cap, and one pair had double points with a hook at the end of each. In booths adjoining were displayed drinking cups of all shapes and sizes, and glassware, then rare and valuable. In another place were gums and spices, and other articles useful to the apothecary. In yet another were delicate perfumes and cosmetics, palm oil and ambergris, frankincense and attar of roses, and an immense variety of other things, just as if the world from

Courtyard, Chester Castle, *circa* 1215.

CHESHIRE: ITS TRADITIONS AND HISTORY

China to Peru had been raked of its treasures and a clean sweep made of the whole.

In striking contrast, near by, were booths and tents for the refreshment or entertainment of the populace, where feasting and revelry were unknown at other times of the year. To sum up, there were—

> Beggars and vagabonds, blind, lame, and sturdy,
> Minstrels and singers with their various airs,
> The pipe, the tabor, and the hurdy-gurdy,
> Jugglers and mountebanks with apes and bears,
> Continued from the first until the fourteenth day
> An uproar like ten thousand Smithfield fairs.
> There were wild beasts and foreign birds and creatures,
> And Jews and foreigners with foreign features.
> All sorts of people there were seen together,
> All sorts of characters, all sorts of dresses;
> The fool with fox's tail and peacock's feather,
> Pilgrims and penitents, and grave burgesses;
> The country people with their coats of leather,
> Vintners and victuallers with cans and messes;
> Grooms, archers, varlets, falconers, and yeomen;
> Damsels and waiting maids and waiting women—
> The vulgar, unenlightened conversation
> Of minstrels, menials, and courtesans and boors
> (Although appropriate to their meaner station)
> Would certainly revolt a taste like yours;
> Therefore, I shall omit the calculation
> Of all the curses, oaths, and cuts and stabs
> Occasioned by their dice and drink and drabs.

There was also another auxiliary to the fair in the Court of Pied Poudré, or "Dusty Foot," which dealt out justice swift and strong in case of dispute arising between buyer and seller outside. It had summary powers in that "he who draws a sword in strife within the limits of Chester fair, or strikes an officer of the Pied Poudré Court, forfeits his left hand without appeal."

Presently a procession is seen wending its way slowly through the streets. It is that of the Cheshire minstrels, who are singing a stirring song to the accompaniment of fiddles and other instruments. There is a round dozen of initiates in its ranks, in long snow-white capes, headed by the banner of the leader, Sir Roger Dutton. Arriving at the High Cross, the ceremony begins by the presentation by the minstrels to Sir Roger Dutton of four flagons of

A Heated Discussion.

wine and a lance, every minstrel also paying the sum of fourpence halfpenny for the privilege of exercising his craft in the city and county. The Lord of Dutton was usually joined on the occasion by many gentry, who rode on horseback. The procession afterwards moved to St John's Church, where the musicians played several pieces of "serious musick on their knees," after which prayers were intoned. The heir and the Lord of Dutton were especially prayed for. The procession returned to the hostelry adjoining the Court, where there was "joyous" entertainment. A jury of licensed musicians was empanelled, who gave their verdicts and made presentments, and the newly joined minstrels took the following characteristic oath—" You are hereby required to behave yourself well and lively, as a licensed minstrel of this court ought to do, during the time you are licensed to play upon any instrument of musick or minstrelsy, within the said county and city of Chester, and you shall inform the lord of this court, or his steward, a deputy for the time being, if you know of any person that shall play upon any instrument of musick for gain or reward, within the city of Chester, not having first obtained and had his or their license so to do. So help you, God."

"Rags and Tatters" to the Rescue.
Cheshire Minstrels en route to Rhuddlau.

But amidst all this riot and revelry came a rude interruption. A mounted messenger arrived from Rhuddlan (or Rothelan) Castle to say that the Earl of Chester was closely besieged by the warlike Welsh. The constable of the Castle (Hugh de Lacy) could not leave the fair, even had he had the men at his disposal. The garrison was depleted owing to the absence of many of its members in the service of the king in other counties. It is alleged that Sir Roger had had his fortune told in the fair by a gipsy, who stated he would win a victory with "rags and tatters," and that

He soon should reign over fiddles and beer;
And every Dutton should have his mutton.

CHESHIRE: ITS TRADITIONS AND HISTORY

He would also ultimately marry the lady of his choice, " though she be much given to jealousy." This lady was Mary only daughter, of de Lacy, the constable of Chester Castle. Much is, of course, left to the reader's imagination in this connection, but it is certain that Sir Roger made a stirring appeal to his " merrie men all," and there was a motley gathering, stiffened by a small number of men-at-arms from the Castle. Soon they were singing—

Roger Dutton's going to fight
   In his doublet and his hose—
Who is wrong and who is right,
   No one cares and no one knows.

Follow me, my merrie men all,
   We are going to do great things ;
If we meet the devil and all,
   We will make him find his wings.

Roger Dutton leads the fight,
   The bold fiddlers and their crew ;
If he meets the Welsh to-night,
   He will give the devil his due.

Roger Dutton's won the fight
   In his doublet and his hose—
Who was wrong and who was right,
   Lady Mary cares and knows.

The Welsh Routed.

    By this remarkable victory, Dutton of Dutton and his heirs " for ever and a day after had the control of all ' letchers ' of Cheshire," which remained with their descendants until 1756, when the court fell into disuse. Great as this privilege was thought to be, it would no doubt be made all the more so by the fact that six days afterwards the great hall of Chester Castle was one blaze of light. All the lords and ladies and gentry of the county were assembled when Sir Roger and Lady Mary were made one, and, to use the old formula, " lived happy ever after."

    Of the tournament or joust a few lines may be written. In Cheshire this sport anciently took place at Gawsworth, near Stockport. " Impartial taste," says Gibbon, " must prefer a Gothic tournament to the Olympic games of classic antiquity. Instead of the naked spectacles, which corrupted the manners of the Greeks, the pompous decorations of the lists was crowned with the presence of chaste and high born beauty, from whose hands the Conqueror received the prize of dexterity and courage. The skill and strength that were exerted in boxing bear a distant and doubtful relation to the merit of a soldier; but the tournament, as invented in France, and eagerly adopted both in the East and the West, presented a lively image of the business of the field. The single combat, the general skirmish, the defence of a pass or castle, were rehearsed as in actual service; and the contest, both in real and mimic war, was decided by the superior management of horse and lance." They reached their full perfection in France in the ninth and tenth centuries. They were introduced into England soon after the Norman conquest. Jousts differed from tournaments in being single contests between two knights, while tournaments were performed between two parties of cavaliers. Jousts were of two sorts—the *joûte à l'outrance*, or mortal combats between two knights of different nations; and the *joûte à plaisance*, or joust of peace, which often took place after a tournament, but at times and places specially appointed for the purpose. This was not by any means a sport indulged in by the common herd. Certain qualifications of birth were required for admission to the tourney, and their respective hostels or tents were assigned by the king-at-arms and heralds. The place of combat was the lists, a large, open space surrounded by ropes or a railing. Galleries were erected round the lists for the spectators, among whom were seated the ladies, the supreme judges of the tournaments. After the sports the prizes were delivered to the successful knights by the Queen of Beauty, who had been chosen by the ladies. On the second day there was often a tournament for the esquires, and on the third a melée of knights and esquires in the lists. The era of "villainous saltpetre," however, changed the art of war, and tournaments went out of fashion.

The celebration of the ancient customs of the county centred chiefly at Chester, and flourished from an early period. The "Midsummer show" is said to have been held long before Hugh Lupus possessed the city, and was composed "of processions of different companies, attended by divers pageants and devices." Among the Harleian MSS. is an agreement between a Mayor of Chester and two artists, for the annual painting of the "City's four giants, one unicorn, one dromedary, one luce, one camel, one asse, one dragon, six hobby horses, and sixteen naked boys."

Whitsun plays were the work of Randle Higden, a monk of Chester, who translated the Bible into several parts and plays, so that the common people might learn the same by their playing and also by their action. These were acted by the city companies. "Noe and his shippe" was a very prominent feature. Early English calendars quite confidently assert that 17th March was the date on which Noah entered the Ark, and add that he came out again on 29th April. But mediaeval legend was even more intimate in its knowledge of Noah's family affairs. For some reason or other his wife was often represented in mystery plays as a typical shrew. When Noah tells her that the world is to be destroyed by a flood she is made to sneer at him for his credulity and abuse him as a habitual bearer of bad news, and quite a pretty quarrel is depicted between them, with a fight in which poor Noah is bested and runs away to get on building his Ark. When that vessel is ready she refuses to be cooped up in such a thing. In one play she finally jumps in when the flood is rising fast; in another she flatly refuses unless her " gossips " are invited too, and a tavern scene follows, she and her friends drinking and gibing at Noah, until her three sons drag her into the Ark, where she instantly picks a quarrel with Noah. It is a curious thing that mediaeval opinion should have decided, on no evidence, that Mrs Noah was so unpleasant a character, but the belief was certainly traditional. Chaucer, in his " Canterbury Tales," takes it for gospel, and makes Nicholas say Noah must have wished " that she had had a ship hireself alone."

There was also " The Fall of Lucifer," by the Tanners ; " The Creation," by the Drapers ; " The Deluge," by the Dyers ; " Abraham, Melchisedek and Lot," by the Barbers ; " Moses, Balak, and Balaam," by the Cappers ; " The Salutation and the Nativity," by the Wrights (carpenters) ; " The Shepherds Feeding the Flocks by Night," by the Painters and Glaziers ; " The Three Kings," by the Vintners ; " The Oblation of the Three Kings," by the Mercers ; " The Killing of the Holy Innocents," by the Goldsmiths ; " The Temptation," by the Butchers ; " The Purification," by the Blacksmiths ; " The Blind Men and Lazarus," by the Glovers ; " Jesus and the Lepers," by the Cowesarys ; " Christ's Passion," by the Bowyers, Fletchers, and Ironmongers ; " Descent into Hell," by the Cooks and Innkeepers ; " Resurrection," by the Skinners ; " Ascension," by the Taylors ; " The Election of St Matthias," " Sending of the Holy Ghost," etc., by the Fishmongers ; " Anti-Christ," by the Clothiers ; and " The Day of Judgment," by the Websters (weavers).

The entertaining play or pastime of St George and the Dragon flourished at this period, and was performed annually at Eastertide. Its observance appears to have practically died out. Four " soulers " formerly preceded the characters, at the head of which was St George. He entered, with a hobby horse girded round his waist, with which he cut most laughable antics. Following him was Slasher, a Moor, called the Prince of Paradine ; a so-called Doctor ; Hector, a very prominent fire-eater indeed ; and Devil Doubt, in ragged garments, wearing an antiquated silk hat, considerably concertina'd, and carrying a broom over his shoulder. After a series of gory combats, from which St George emerges victorious, Devil Doubt appears with his broom, and in default of largess from the spectators threatens " to sweep them to the grave."

The song of the "soulers" was formerly heard on All Souls' Eve, and parties made up of both sexes visited farmhouses and the principal mansions in the parish. They sang, " Soul, soul, for a soul cake, pray you, good mistress, a soul cake." This form of address resembles a practice in some parts of York shire which formerly prevailed. It was known as " Collop Monday," and boys called at houses and said, " Pray, dame, a collop." The " collop " was generally a slice of bacon, but in the absence of the collop a few coppers took its place.

The observance of " souling " is referred to Catholic times, and is probably a remnant of the old custom of praying for the souls of the dead, or even to the times of the Jewish prophets, when women made cakes for the worship of the Queen of Heaven. The sacred " bun," or holy bread, of the Egyptians, made of honey and fine flour, offered in heathen temples, has probably some reference to it. In Shropshire it was the practice to set upon a board a high heap of soul cakes, lying one upon another like the picture of the shew bread in the old Bibles. They were about the " bigness " of twopenny cakes, and every visitant took one. There is an old rhyme or saying—" A soule cake, a soule cake, have mercy on all Christian soules for a soule cake." The following is the " souler's " song—

> You gentlemen of England, I would have you to draw near,
> To these few lines which we have wrote, and you soon shall hear
> Sweet melody of music all on this evening clear,
> For we are come a-souling for apples and strong beer.
> Step down into your cellar, and see what you can find,
> If your barrels are not empty, I hope you will prove kind,
> We'll come no more a-souling, until another year.
> Cold winter it is coming on, dark, dirty, wet and cold,
> To try your good nature this night we do make bold,
> This night we do make bold, with your apples and strong beer ;
> We will come no more a-souling until another year.
>
> All houses that we've been at, we have had both meat and drink,
> So now we're dry with travelling, and hope you'll on us think ;
> I hope you'll on us think, with your apples and strong beer.
> God bless the master of this house, and the mistress also,
> And all the little children that round the table go,
> Likewise young men and maidens, your cattle and your store,
> And all that lies within your gates, I wish you ten times more ;
> I wish you ten times more with your apples and strong beer,
> For we'll come no more a-souling until another year.

Also

> Soul Day, Soul Day, Saul,
> One for Peter, two for Paul,
> Three for Him who made us all.
> An apple or pear, a plum or a cherry,
> Any good thing that will make us merry.
> And put your hand into your pocket and pull out your keys,
> Go down into the cellar, bring up what you please,

A glass of your wine, or a cup of your beer,
And we'll never come souling till this time next year.
We are a pack of merry boys all in a mind,
We have come a-souling for what we can find.
    Soul, Soul, sole my shoe,
If you have no apples, money will do.
Up with your kettle, and down with your pan,
Give us an answer, and let us be gone.

In some parts of England the " souling " customs have nuts connected with them, and All Souls' Eve is then named Nut Crack Night. Nuts were thrown into the fire by sweethearts and their swains, to learn something of the course of true love by the way in which nuts burn or burst. This last custom is beautifully described by Gay in his " Spell "—

> Two hazel nuts I threw into the flame,
> And to each nut I gave a sweetheart's name;
> This with the loudest bounce me sore amaz'd,
> That in a flame of brightest colour blaz'd;
> As blaz'd the nuts so may thy passion grow,
> For 'twas thy nut that did so brightly glow.

The pips of the apple are used for the same purpose. They are silently placed in a row on a bar of the fire grate, and a name is given to each pip, and as the pips hiss, or spit or burst, or lie quiet, so may the tempers be ascertained of the persons whom the pips typify.

While on this subject we will mention just another most strange piece of divination on All Souls' Eve, recorded by Brand (vol. i. p. 386); it is to know whether a woman will have the man she wishes. The receipt is like one from some old cookery book, and needs only the addition—" First catch your swain and then truss him. Get two lemon-peels, wear them all day, one in each pocket; at night rub the four posts of the bedstead with them; if she is to succeed, the person will appear in her sleep and present her with a couple of lemons; if not, there is no hope."

The Solomons of our enlightened century doubtless will lift up their hands and exclaim, " What exceedingly silly customs these are!" And silly in truth they would be, did they not tend innocently to lighten the cares that press upon young hearts, and to give them at least some moments of merriment. In this respect they are not simply harmless, they inspire a cheerful spirit, and that, we are assured, " maketh a continual feast."

> Yes, let the proud disdain
> The simple pleasures of the lowly train
> To me more dear, congenial to my heart,
> One native charm, than all the gloss of art.   *Goldsmith.*

The ceremonies of the marlers were almost peculiar to Cheshire, where, as the numerous pits in the fields by the roadside testify, the practice once so extensively prevailed of spreading marl as a top dressing for land. In the western hundreds of the county, and in Bucklow among the rest, the marlers used to elect a lord of the pit, demand money from the neighbouring landowners, whom they saw passing near the pit, and proclaimed their acquisitions both daily and at the end of the week. " Previous to this proclamation, and subsequent to it they form a ring, joining their hands and inclining their heads towards the centre, shouting repeatedly, and finishing with a lengthened cadence. The words vary between the shouts, but are to this effect—Oyez, oyez, oyez! Mr of —— has been with us to-day, and given my lord and his men part of a hundred pounds"—but if the donation be more than sixpence, they say, "has given my lord and his men part of a thousand pounds." The ceremony was repeated at the village alehouse, where they spent their acquisitions on Saturdays; and the sound of the last prolonged shout, as it died gradually away, could be heard for miles on a still summer's evening.

In Chester, from 1599 to 1754, the mayor and corporation for a long period attended the bull-baiting in their official robes, and the bellman opened the proceedings with the formula: " Oyez, oyez, oyez, if any man stand within twenty yards of the bull ring, let him take what comes." Ultimately the force of public opinion caused a cessation of this practice, and although bull-baiting continued for a long period it had not official cognisance, and it was abolished early in the last century.

Bull-baiting also took place at the village wakes, which were held in early and late autumn in various parts of Cheshire. The animal was usually a " circuit goer," trained for the purpose. All the bull dogs of the district, great, heavy, rather sluggish creatures, were brought to take part in the "sport." The bull was tied to the stake by a rope of a certain length, and it was so trained that it placed its forehead close to the ground and thereby kept a watchful eye on the attacking party. When they attacked on the hind flanks he often sent them flying yards away with his hoofs; while, when they attempted to seize his nose, he used his horns with considerable effect. It was always heavy odds against the bull, for he was apt, after a prolonged combat, to become exhausted, and he was eventually brought bellowing in pain to his knees.

Bear-baiting also prevailed in Cheshire, but not to the same extent. It is reputed that Congleton was a great centre of this pastime, and that the town authorities once sold the Church Bible to buy a bear! In some towns the ring, where the baiting took place, was called the bear croft. It was at one time a fashionable resort, and was said to have been patronised by "Good Queen Bess" and her attendant courtiers.

There was more actual cruelty in connection with cock-fighting than bull-baiting. The game cock's troubles commenced when it was a full blown cockerel, and it was "dubbed." Its comb was then nearly grown, and this was cut off close to the head and seared with a red hot iron, which prevented the comb being seized and torn by an adversary. To dress a cock for the

Game Cocks—Clipped, Dubbed, and Spurred, ready for Battle.

pit attained the dignity of a fine art in those days. With a pair of scissors the tail feathers were cut off, as also those by the head and shoulders and neck. This was so much less for the enemy's beak. The cock's wings were then extended, and each feather cut one after the other to a point, and thus the wings were furnished with darts. Then its claws were scraped with a penknife, its nails sharpened and fitted with spurs of sharp steel. Thus it became often a redoubtable champion, and it is said the trimmer would remark that this was the way to make a cock an eagle, and a bird of the poultry yard a bird of the mountains. The newspapers of the seventeenth and eighteenth centuries bristled with advertisements of mains of cocks between the gentlemen of Cheshire and Lancashire, often lasting a week, and betting was fast and furious. On 2nd June 1752 ended a great cock-fight in the Riding School, Salford, between the gentlemen of Lancashire and the gentlemen of Cheshire. The former won by several battles.

In or about 1860 cock-fighting in Cheshire may be said to have received its quietus. Owing to strong expressions of public feeling a case was heard at a local petty sessions, at the instance of the Royal Society for the Prevention of Cruelty to Animals. The defendants numbered twenty-six in all, and included magistrates, army officers, farmers, merchants, publicans, a London dog fancier, and others. An Oldham weaver and the dog fancier were charged with causing to be "cruelly abused and tortured" certain cocks, and the others with aiding and encouraging and assisting. Certain police officers saw upwards of two hundred people assembled in the orchard of a farm-house, and witnessed fifteen cock-fights during the day. There was a ring about five yards by five. It was formed of chairs, tree roots, etc. After the ring was formed, two cocks were brought out in bags. Scales and weights were produced, and the cocks having had their legs tied together and a cloth thrown over them, were put into the scales and weighed. After that the ring was cleared, and the handlers held the birds about a yard from each other, and let them peck each other two or three times on the head. They then placed them on the grass. Each bird was armed with a spur of silver, or some other bright metal. They fought for about a quarter of an hour, and one cock then lay down and held up his head as if he were blind. He got up again and was killed. The birds bled most profusely in the fights which took place. After the second battle one of the cocks had his neck pulled out. An inspector and a constable entered the ring and protested against the fight proceeding. The "sport," however, went on. Some of the cocks had only a few feathers on their backs. One Smith gave the Irish party credit for the way their birds had fought, and one of them replied, if they had brought the cocks over a day or two sooner, the English cocks would have been beaten. There were fourteen fights altogether and a "banker." The Irish party got seven, and the others got seven. Betting went on freely, one gentleman offering to bet £50 to sixpence on one of the cocks. It was arranged that the defendants should plead guilty to one information, on condition that the other three were withdrawn, and a heavy penalty was not pressed for. On behalf of two of the defendants it was urged that they happened to be in the neighbourhood, and hearing of the fight went out of mere curiosity to see it. At the close the principal defendants were fined £5 and costs;

eight others, £2, 10s. each and costs. The money was, in each case, paid immediately.

Cock-fighting in the time of Hogarth was designated " a royal sport," and he propounded a query for the consideration of the clergy after his picture of the cock ring at that period. " Might it not," he says, " have a tendency to check that barbarous spirit which has more frequently its source in an early acquired habit arising from the prevalence of example, than in natural depravity, if every divine in Great Britain were to preach at least one sermon every twelve months on our universal insensibility to the suffering of the brute creation—

> " Wilt thou draw near the nature of the Gods ?
> Draw near them then in being merciful,
> Sweet mercy is Nobility's true badge."

CHAPTER X.

Cheshire sports and pastimes—The Bishop Blaize Festival—A singular handbill—Archery and its associations—Cheshire dances: Morris dance, Plough dance, etc.—Village sports, broadsword and singlestick—Bowling, ancient and modern—Quoits, cricket, Chester Races, football, " lifting "—Ducking stools for scolds—The village stocks—Beating the bounds—Wakes revelry —May day festivals, Arley and Knutsford—The Knutsford processions and their members—The town basking in the sunshine of Royalty—Origin of the " Royal " May Day Festival—After the War, 1919.

THE festival of Bishop Blaize, the patron saint of the craft of Woolcombers, was celebrated universally a century ago in Cheshire. St Blaize, or Blaisius, was a bishop of Sebaste in Armenia, and suffered martyrdom in A.D. 316. His chief virtue, so far as woolcombers are concerned, appears to have been that his name could charm away sore throats. The procession connected with the festival was headed by a band, and, surrounded by guards in a wonderful get up of fleeces and wool slivers, or strands, which did duty as stoles, were a king and queen, Jason and the Princess Medea. The principal figure, however, was the bishop himself, holding a pastoral crook and attended by his chaplain. Following were shepherds and shepherdesses, countrymen clothed in bright green, and woolcombers wearing old-fashioned flowing wigs of combed wool. At some convenient point a piece, written for the occasion, was recited, to the following effect—

> Hail to the day whose kind auspicious rays,
> Deigned first to smile on famous Bishop Blaize.
> To the great author of our combing trade
> This day's devoted and due honours paid
> To him whose fame Britain's isle resounds—
> To him whose goodness to the poor abounds.
> Long shall his name in British annals shine,
> And grateful ages offer at his shrine.
> By this, our trade, are thousands daily fed,
> By it supplied with means to earn their bread.
> In various forms our trade its work imparts ;
> In different methods and by different arts
> Prevents from starving, indigents distressed,
> As combers, spinners, weavers, and the rest.
> We boast no gems, nor costly garments vain,
> Borrowed from India or the coast of Spain ;
> Our native soil with wool our trade supplies,
> While foreign countries envy us the prize.
> No foreign broil our common good annoys,
> Our country's product all our art employs ;

> Our fleecy flocks abound in every vale,
> Our bleating lambs proclaim the joyful tale.
> So let not Spain with us attempt to vie,
> Nor India's wealth pretend to soar so high ;
> Nor Jason pride him in his Colchian spoil,
> By hardship gain'd and enterprising toil ;
> Since Britons all with ease attain the prize,
> And every hill resounds with golden cries.
> To celebrate our founder's great renown,
> Our shepherd and our shepherdess we crown ;
> For England's commerce, and for George's sway
> Each loyal subject give a loud Huzza.

Bishop Blaize is remembered by few, although public-houses named after him were sometimes found in villages in the northern counties. Machinery superseded hand-combing, and has long had the best of the race.

The following is a literal copy of a handbill issued about 1820, which relates to " diversions " at Northwich at that period—

> There Will Be a Bull Batted (baited) At The Bowling
> (Green ?) In Liftwich & Wee Shall Try Him On
> Saturday Night Between 4 & 5 O'clock To
> Practise & Try The Bull. There Will Be A
> Brass Coller For Every Dog & He That Brings
> The Best Dog Shall Receive A Good Dinner and 1
> Quart of Beer. There Will Be A Capte Goose
> To Be Rode For Precisely At One O'clock
> & The Horseman That Carries The Gooses Head
> Away Shall Receive The Prise. Likewise a
> Race For a Capte Hat & A Smok Race For A New
> Shift All To Be On Monday & Tuesday.
> There Will Be A Pig Race At One O'clock &
> Other Diversions Wich Will Satisfy The Inspectors
> & The Best Dog or Bich Shall Receive The
> Coller pin, or Not.

Archery is a very ancient method of warfare, practised probably in the Stone Age, and for centuries it formed a part of the English method of waging war. Cheshire had a company of famous bowmen at Flodden, but there are numerous records of the excellent work of this branch of infantry on many occasions, notably in the Wars of the Roses. Arrowhead making was a recognised branch of industry in Chester in the time of Henry VIII., but remains of Neolithic arrowheads and bows are numerous. The Egyptians, Scythians, the Romans, and other nations of antiquity used the bow extensively. The Saxons used it for subduing the ancient Britons, to whom it was a strange and wonderful instrument, and spread terror in their ranks. The words "shaft," "bow," and "arrow" are all of Saxon origin, and the Saxon "boga" survives both in Welsh and English.

The use of the English long bow was encouraged by the different kings of England from the time of Edward the First, and rendered signal service at Poictiers and Agincourt. The archery laws enacted that all able-bodied males, especially yeomen, should practise with the bow on Sundays and holidays from childhood. Butts were set up at Chester and other castles, and in every village. In the reign of Henry VIII. the use of cross bows and hand guns was forbidden, as it interfered with the practice of archery, and all archers above the age of twenty-four were commended not to shoot with their light-flight arrows at a distance under 220 yards, the effective range of the old archery. But as firearms came into general use, commencing with the seventeenth century, the war bow and shaft fell quickly into disuse. It was customary for the two sheriffs of Chester to shoot with bow and arrows on Easter Monday, for a breakfast at which calf's head and bacon was the principal dish, after which the company went to the commercial hall of the city, where "the mayor, alderman and gentlemen and the reste take part together of the saide breakfast in loveing manner. This is yearly done, it being a commendable exercise, a good recreation and a loveing assemblye." In March 1670 the sheriffs were fined £10 for not keeping the calf's head feast.

It was a Cheshire pastime carried on within the past fifty years, chiefly amongst the gentry, and the scene on the lawn in front of many an ancient mansion, in which both ladies and gentlemen took part, was exceedingly pretty in summer-time. The ladies, for the most part, were attired in white, wore green sashes, with beautifully designed arrow sheave cases, by their sides. Some of the gentlemen on gala occasions wore suits of Lincoln green. The muse of the famous Squire Warburton of Arley, in his hunting songs, etc., illuminated archery in the highest degree—how the graceful forms that take aim at sixty paces, and those stout and stalwart who drive the bolt home at one hundred gather in the poet's picture. They stand before us in full contrast of womanly gentleness and manly power, and yet blend harmoniously. The laws of "forestrie," severe though they were in the olden times, have lost their terrors; and they who once would have forfeited life and limb for pursuing unlicensed the archer's mystery upon a deer, now are invited freely to use their skill in the noble rivalry of shooting with the bow.

> Come, every stranger, every guest draw nigh;
> No peril waits you save from beauty's eye.
> As the minstrel calls on the archer
> To hit that golden centre, where love and friendship dwell.

Cockpit at Lymm Hall.   Arley Green.

Drawing, Miss G. W. Ridgeway   photo, C. E. Arderu

photo   Morris Dance   *C.E. Arden*

photo   Lymm Stocks   *C. E. Arden*

We fancy he has just risen from good old Latimer's Sermon, in which, from the pulpit before Edward VI., he enforced the practice of archery. "It is," said the Venerable Bishop, "a godly art, a wholesome kind of exercise, and much commended in physic." It will be remembered that it had the approval of Galen—

> All honour to the long bow, which merry men of yore,
> With hound and horn at early morn in greenwood forest bore.

There were various dances practised in Cheshire in addition to those mentioned in other parts of this work. The morris dance, revived of late years and in growing popularity, is said to have been introduced by John O'Gaunt, "Time-honoured Lancaster," on his return from Spain during the time of Edward III. Antiquaries have differed as to whether the morris dance originated among the Moors or came from Scotland, as association with the sword would suggest; but Handel—no mean judge—considered the morris dance to be characteristically English, as the minuet is French, and the saraband Spanish. We imagine Handel to be correct. It was popular early in the last century in the north of England. It was not general in Lancashire or Cheshire, as evidenced by the fact that for some years dancers from the Derbyshire borders figured prominently in the May Day processions at Knutsford and danced through the streets. They were attired in white starched shirts, black velvet knee breeches, white stockings and black buckled shoes. They carried short rods, which they waved as they danced. These were tied with ribbons and bells, and thus imparted an additional air of gaiety to the scene.

The garland dance must have been very pretty. The musicians struck up. Several couples stood opposite to each other. Ropes of flowers and wreaths were then distributed to the dancers. The ropes of flowers occasionally got entangled and brought somebody to the ground, or knocked off a hat or bonnet, but the effect of the dancing was uncommonly good. Instead of hands across, the ends of the garlands were taken, and when going down the middle the lads not infrequently twined the ropes round their partners' waists, or held them above their heads.

The plough dance must have been a rough exhibition, and has been thus described:—A dozen young men enter, clad in clean, white, woollen shirts, ornamented with ribands, tied with roses on the sleeves and breast, and with caps decked with tinsel on their heads and tin swords by their sides. These mummers are yoked to a plough, likewise decked with ribands, which they dragged into the middle of the room. They were attended by an old woman with a tall, sugar loaf hat, and an immense nose and chin, like those of mother goose in the pantomime. The old beldame supported her apparently tottering limbs with a crutch-handled staff, with which she dealt out blows right and left, hitting the toes of the spectators and poking their ribs. By the side of "Old

Bessie" was an equally grotesque figure, clothed in a dress partly composed of a cow's hide and partly of the skins of various animals, with a long dangling tail behind, and a fox skin cap with lappets on the head. This was the fool. Over his shoulders he carried a ploughman's whip, with which he urged on his team, and a cow's horn served him for a bugle, from which he produced unearthly sounds. "The musicians strike up a lively tune and the dance begins, the mummers first forming two lines, then advancing towards each other, rattling their swords together in mimic warfare; advancing again and placing all their points upon the plough, forming a rose, next a 'square' rose; then bounding over each other's heads, laying down their swords, joining hands and dancing round 'Old Bessie' and the fool, who are frolicing funnily by themselves."

There were at village sports often a bout of broadsword and singlestick. The broadsword differs from fencing with the foil in that the weapon employed is intended to cut as well as to thrust. For practice a stout, straight stick is used, called a singlestick, having a cowhide and basket handle to protect the knuckles. The positions and movements of the combatants are very similar to those seen in fencing with the foil. There are seven cuts with seven corresponding guards, and three thrusts, and it very much resembles a target placed opposite a pupil with its centre in a line with the centre of his breast. The cuts cross the whole circle through the centre.

The quarter staff, once a favourite weapon with the English for hand-to-hand encounters, and still sometimes used in athletic exercises, is a stout pole of heavy wood, about six and a half feet long, often bound with iron at both ends. It is grasped in the middle and end (hence, apparently, the name quarter-staff), and the attack is made by giving it a rapid, circular motion, which brings the loaded ends on the adversary at unexpected points. The combatants are protected from the effects of the blows by thick leather helmets and thick leather coats. It is very seldom seen nowadays, though on rare occasions it is seen at country sports.

Bowling is still a very popular game in Cheshire, but nowadays unattended by the terrible incidents referred to in the following chapter dealing with the days of "Bluff King Hal," when a brutal murder was committed at Brereton. In England the game is played on what is termed a "Crown" green—that is, there is an imperceptible rise from the outer edge until it reaches the centre. In Scotland the green is level, and the bowling is in alleys. The "woods," as the bowls are called, are of various weights, and their trend is regulated by the finger or thumb bias, which is indicated by the number of pips in each wood. There is a smaller wood, called a "jack," at which the larger woods are sent, the nearest in each round constituting the score. There are two handed games, in which two players compete; others in which four or even six are seen, but in matches, two players is the maximum, and in cases of difference an outside player or spectator is called in to measure the distance between the bowl and the jack, an operation calling for the greatest nicety and steadiness of vision. Of late years the game has been regulated by means of county associations. Cheshire formerly played in conjunction with Lancashire, but some years ago Cheshire seceded owing to the progress of the game in popular estimation, and formed a separate body. The Cheshire and Lancashire Associations are apparently really the only ones which matter, and the friendly rivalry existing is very keen. For some years Cheshire, although with a much smaller margin of players, was the champion county, but Lancashire has since joined issue and come off victorious, though the fortunes of each have swayed from side to side with varying circumstances.

Quoits has long been a popular English game, especially amongst the middle classes. The quoit is a direct descendant of the Roman discus, a ring of iron or stone, from six to ten inches in diameter. It is thrown as an exercise of strength or skill, and as it is generally played in the open air, it is an exceedingly healthy and muscle-developing pastime. The beautiful figure of Myron's Discobolus, or quoit thrower, which existed in marble in the fifth century before Christ, is familiar to many. The modern quoit is an iron ring, averaging six pounds in weight, flattish in shape, and convex on the upper side, so as to form sufficient edge for the quoit to stick in the ground when falling. The ring is about two and a half inches broad and nine inches in diameter, with a hollow dint on the outer rim for the forefinger or the thumb. Two hobs or pins are placed in the ground, generally nineteen yards apart, and the players usually number two, but occasionally four, and endeavour to cause the quoit to light on the hob or pin, or as near it as possible. When it catches and lights on the ring it is called a ringer, and counts two, and the nearest quoit one, as in bowls or curling. It is a very popular amusement on shipboard, but in that case the quoits are made of rope rounds. Seeing that this was a game in Roman times it is not surprising that it was played in Norman times. It is related that Hugh de Lacy, Constable of Chester Castle, frequently took a hand in the game with his retainers. Allan, the harper at the Castle, was wishful to marry one of the maids he was in love with, and surprises the old constable with his strength and skill. Time after time he caught the quoit on the ring of metal. His sweetheart happening to pass, the old man exclaimed "that if he would do that again three times in succession, he should marry her and have a farm in soccage (practically free from rent) with her." The maid, it is said, blushed like a rose, and as he did it again and again, amid the cheers of the onlookers, the constable confirmed his offer. The wedding took place, according to tradition, in due course.

Cheshire has not figured conspicuously in county cricket, although the former head of the Lancashire team was a resident for many years within its borders. The reason, so far as the northern part is concerned, is not far to seek. Lancashire, ever on the alert to introduce new blood in the shape of promising " youngsters," spreads out an attractive net, and they are speedily captured. For many years the gentlemen of Cheshire played some capital matches, but since the war popular interest in the game, so far as a Cheshire county team is concerned, has practically died out.

Chester races are a great event in the racing world. They had a rather humble origin, in that three silver bells were run for on the Roodee, and this custom probably gave rise to the proverb, " to bear the bell." About the year 1623 Robert Amerie, who was Sheriff of Chester city in 1608, at his own cost caused three silver cups of good value to be made, the which silver cups were upon St George's Day for ever to be run for on the Roodee at Chester. He also appears to have had a considerable hand in seeing that Randle Higden's Whitsun plays should be duly performed in his native city, and it was looked upon as a thing honourable to Mr Amerie that he should have identified himself so thoroughly with the sports and pastimes of his day, and in his praise the following verse was sung—

> Amor is love, and courage is his name,
> That did begin this pompe and pryncely game,
> The charge is great to him that all began,
> Who now is satisfied to see all so well done.

In connection therewith he, conjointly with Richard Davies, wrote the following work, which has since been reprinted in the Chetham Society's series of publications, " Chester's Triumph in Honour of her Prince, as it was performed upon St George's Day, 1610, in the aforesaid citie." Afterwards the cups above mentioned were sold and more money was added, with the result that " one faire sylver cuppe " was provided, which was to become the property of the winner for ever. Chester Cup day is an attraction to sportsmen from many counties, and is probably a reminder of the ancient days when it was a one day event. Formerly the meeting was open free to all comers, but since 1802, when the Roodee was closed, it has become a gate money meeting. The worth of the prizes now total around £2500, and with the cup is, or was, awarded a bumping Cheshire cheese. Our illustration shows the horse (Tom Pepper) being led in after winning the historic cup in May 1919.

Football in Cheshire had, it is stated a somewhat gruesome origin. In one of the numerous battles which took place between the Danes and the English, one of the former was taken prisoner. He was decapitated, and the head was kicked through the streets to the delight of the lookers-on. We prefer, however, to take the version which says that centuries ago the game was played on the Roodee by an unlimited number of players. The shoemakers of Chester were bound by their charter to provide " a ball of leather," of the value of 3s. 4d., and, as in other parts of the country, it was kicked through the streets by the citizens. In 1564 football was played on the Dee, which was frozen over in that year, and it is said to have been played under similar conditions on other occasions. Modern football, however, is a direct descendant of the ancient Roman game of harpastum, in which the object of the players on each side was to seize the ball and carry it by some means or other across a line marked on the ground in the rear of their opponents. In some cases the pastime was forbidden in England, especially in the streets, but, notwithstanding this, it was very popular with the lower classes. It has had chequered fortunes, but in the middle of the last century the game was taken up by public schools, and two sorts of football arose, one championed by Rugby, which allowed of the ball being carried ; the other at Cambridge, which was the dribbling game. Then arose Rugby, or " rugger " ; the other, Association, or " soccer." Both games are too well known to need description.

The records of the Royal Chester Rowing Club, although not so ancient as the races, are full of interest, many of its members having distinguished themselves at various regattas in all parts of the country, and have won numerous laurels which will, doubtless, be added to as time goes on.

" Lifting " was an ancient usage performed on Easter Monday and Tuesday. In the year 1290 King Edward I. paid a sum of money to the ladies of the bedchamber and maids of honour for having at Easter taken their " sovereign lord, the King," prisoner in his very bed, and complied with the universal practice of giving him " a heaving or lifting "—*i.e.*, a raising up symbolically towards heaven. The custom is said not to have been a decorous one, and " honoured more in the breach than the observance."

The ducking stool for the " cure " of scolds, as also the brank or scold's bridle, and the whipping post were at one time indispensable institutions. Women who were given to brawling were soused in stercore or stinking water until almost suffocated. Some poet says the first dip did not always quieten the poor creature operated upon.

> Down in the deep the stool descends,
> But here, at first, we miss our ends ;
> She mounts again and rages more
> Than ever vixen did before.
> If so, my friend, pray let her take
> A second turn into the lake ;
> And rather than your patience lose,
> Thrice and again repeat the dose.
> No brawling wives, no furious wenches,
> No fire so hot, but water quenches.

The stocks, made famous in " Hudibras," were to be seen near every parish church in the county, and sixty years ago and even less, culprits were exposed to the gaze of the parishioners for some hours, until they had purged their offence.

In a field near the Firs, at Bowdon, races were held at wakes time, in which women took an active part. A common prize was a smock or shift, and in a programme of Bowdon Wakes, published in the early part of the last century, there occurred the following :—" The same day a race for a good Holland smock by ladies of all ages, the second best to have a handsome satin ribbon. No lady will be allowed to strip any further than the smock before starting."

" Beating the bounds " was a custom observed in Cheshire for many generations. When villages grew into towns many difficulties were placed in the way, owing to the blotting out of ancient landmarks and boundary lines being covered by fences and buildings. Generally beaters were armed with long switches with which they smote the ground. If there was a beadle of the parish, he often headed the procession. At a later period the overseer officiated. In the course of time comical situations arose. A vicarage was built on a field covering the boundary line between two townships. The difficulty was met by the party entering the front door and making its exit by the back. On one occasion they partook of excellent fare provided by the hospitable vicar. In another case, a canal intersected two townships, and boats were commandeered to overcome the difficulty of " beating the bounds." In some instances hedges were broken through, high walls were climbed, and garden beds, sometimes laid out and radiant with lovely flowers, were devastated in face of their indignant owners. In the north, as at Morpeth, " riding the bounds " prevailed, the authorities and public taking part, being mounted on horseback.

Wakes, or village feasts or festivals, furnished the occasion for the annual holiday in every parish in the county. They were held on the eve of the feast of the patron saint of the church, and were of a more religious nature than obtains at the present day. Now they are entirely devoted to pleasure, but in some places the members of clubs and friendly societies form processions and attend church, which may be a lingering remnant of the religious aspect of the wakes. In former times, too, rushes were borne to church, hence the rush-bearing at Lymm, and in some counties adjacent to Cheshire. The beams of the church were formerly hung with garlands in honour of young women of the parish reputed to have died virgins, and the pillars were decorated with white paper cut and twisted to resemble knots and roses, in honour of these memorials of chastity.

The celebrating of May Day with processions and dancing round the maypole is not as common in Cheshire as formerly. Once upon a time every village had its maypole, and while the reign of Puritanism cut off many of the people's enjoyments in this direction, the revival of these festivities has been received with every expression of popular approval and sympathy. "May Day," says an old writer, "is one of the festivals set apart for the special purpose of keeping in remembrance one of the happiest anniversaries of festivity known to our forefathers. After divine service in the Chapel at nine o'clock in the morning, the children and congregation assembled on the green (always kept in the nicest order) and decorated the maypole, which is then raised amidst the joyous shouts of the assembled throng. The Queen of May then marches in procession round the green, the act, so to speak, of dedicating the ground on which her festival is about to be held; her Majesty of Flowers then takes her station at the pole, when the violin throws out its best, stirring sounds, and the villagers trip in merrily round the bonnie May Queen." It was a pleasant sight to see "Squire" Warburton of Arley, as he was affectionately termed by his neighbours and tenantry, when, accompanied by members of his family, he made his appearance on the village green, and the young heir selected as partner a farmer's daughter to open the dancing, which was vigorously carried on during the afternoon, varied by "kiss in the ring," and other innocent games. The children were feasted, and amid scenes of good-humoured merriment, May Day at Arley passed away to be remembered may-hap in after years as a pleasant milestone passed on the rough journey of life.

After its discontinuance at Arley, where, by the way, this branch of the Warburtons has been seated for centuries, and whose heir, Piers Warburton, was killed in the 1914–18 war, the venue was transferred to Knutsford in 1864. Knutsford was, a couple of centuries ago, in Rostherne parish, where one of its vicars (Martindale), prominent in other chapters, was a great opponent of May Day rejoicings, which he stigmatised as a "profanation." He was not alone in this, as is shown in a publication by a brother cleric in 1660, who fulminated on the downfall of May games. He described the trial of "Flora, of the City of Rome, in the County of Babylon," and the indictment runs: "That, contrary to the peace of our Sovereign Lord, his crown and dignity, she had brought in a crowd of practical fanatics—viz., morrice dancers, maskers, mummers, maypole stealers, health drinkers, together with a rascalian route of fiddlers, etc." Justice is called for against the turbulent malefactor, and poor Flora is condemned. Yet, even in Cheapside itself, the rude rabble has set up the ensign of profaners, and he assures us—

> There's not a knave in all the town,
> Nor swearing courtier, nor base clown,
> Nor dancing lob, nor mincing quean,
> Nor popish clerk, be't priest or dean,
> That will give thee a friendly look
> If thou a Maypole canst not brook.

We had the pleasure of witnessing those early spectacles at Knutsford on more than one occasion. They were greatly contracted editions of those which take place in the present day. The characters were few in number, and brightness of colour and gay dresses were not very prominent. A most striking figure was " the Cheshire champion," very much akin to the Black Knight of Ashton-under-Lyne, whom he very much resembled in the way of armour, helmet, etc., and his " mount " was of the cart-horse breed. The May Queen was selected from the parish church school, and the procession was marshalled in the roadway known as Adam's Hill. " Her Majesty " was much more plainly attired than her gorgeously clad successors of later years.

The garnishing of the streets, called " sanding," is only practised at Knutsford in this county, so far as our observation goes. It arose through a desire on the part of the townspeople to announce that a wedding was taking place in their midst, and they spread sand in various shapes, such as true lovers knots, hearts, and posies, etc., in front of the bride's house. In course of time the custom spread and included other houses. The strewing of flowers before the bride and bridegroom was also commonly observed, and the maidens

> All prepared and ready stand,
> With fans and posies in their hands.

The custom of " sanding " is thus described in a song of the period—

> Then the lads and the lasses their Tun dishes handing,
> Before all the doors for a wedding were sanding;
> I ask'd Nan to wed, and she answered with ease—
> " You may sand for my wedding as soon as you please."

May Day became included in its observance. Gradually the festival grew from a village to a town's function. The vicar and the townspeople generally took an active interest. There was a band provided, and numerous features were added to the procession. There was a short service in the Parish Church in the afternoon, which was discontinued as the function lengthened out in attractiveness and importance. On one or two occasions so great was the people's interest that the vicar's son assumed the role of weather prophet, and at some distance from the town sent bulletins hourly indicating the probability of fine weather. There was great excitement as they were posted outside Siddeley's stationer's shop opposite the Royal George Hotel. The prophecies on several occasions were very correct.

Knutsford is said to have been the scene of one of Knut's or Canute's victories. It is more than probable, however, that when Canute paid his traditional royal visit to this centre and metropolis of the Bucklow Hundred, which gave the title to Leycester's famous history, that he had not the reception which was accorded to Queen Victoria, then Princess Victoria, who passed through the town in pre-railway days. Her mother, the Duchess of Kent,

Leading in Chester Cup Winner (Tom Pepper) May 1919

Daily Sketch photo

Photo   Crowning of the Knutsford May Queen 1919.   H. Davies

gave the title "Royal George" to the hotel, and the townspeople displayed before the royal visitors some of the town's attractions in the way of "sanding" the streets in various pretty designs.

On the occasion of the visit of the Prince and Princess of Wales to open the magnificent Jubilee Exhibition at Manchester in 1887, the royal party were the guests of Earl Egerton at Tatton. Thousands assembled in the streets and accorded a right royal welcome. The decorations were also of a striking and appropriate character. Two triumphal arches were erected in Princess Street and Tatton Street. The other streets were gay with flags, banners, and streamers, and the free use of evergreens added to the general effect. Several of the designs were very original, and many of the displays exceedingly pretty. Everywhere the note of welcome seemed to be sounded. The triumphal arches were relieved by mottoes, flags, and evergreens. On the arch in Princess Street there was the motto, "Welcome to the Prince and Princess," on one side, and on the other, the striking words "Loyalty and Honour." A little farther on was the motto, "Ten thousand times welcome," stretched across the street. On the arch in Tatton Street, in blue letters on white ground, were the words "Ich Dien," and on the other side, "Welcome Prince and Princess."

Next day a pretty scene was enacted by royal request. It was no less than a modified representation of the May Day festivities, which had only a few days before been celebrated on the historic heath. On an extemporised throne, in front of the Town Hall, radiant in mimic dignity, surrounded by the members of her court, was the youthful "Queen of May." On each side were "her Majesty's" sceptre-bearer, crown bearer, and the royal falconer. Grouped around were the royal "Beef-eaters," and various characters, including Britannia, who was a striking figure in the picture. Near by was John Bull, in blue cut-away coat, top boots, and old fashioned hat, true to type. To keep him company was Robin Hood, that "forester" good as ever drew bow in the "merrie greenwood," supported by his faithful attendant, "little John." Representations of the seasons, spring, summer, autumn, and winter, appropriately costumed, kept them company. There were jolly tars waving Union Jacks, Italian girls, etc. But we missed the stalwart Cheshire champion already alluded to. Like the champion of England at the monarch's coronation, there is no need for him in these days. The Prince and Princess of Wales, accompanied by many noblemen and ladies in attendance, on arriving, viewed the scene with the deepest interest, the Prince acknowledging the cheering of the surrounding crowd, which the May Queen's courtiers justly joined in, by raising his hat. The writer proceeds: "Then the youthful May Queen rises from her throne, and with dainty steps treads the carpeted platform to the royal carriage, and with almost bewitching dignity, but with becoming modesty, presents a bouquet to the Princess of Wales, who receives it with a smile, and cheer after cheer breaks forth from the youthful court around, which is taken up by the children of larger growth in the road beyond. The young lady is to be crowned Queen of the May, by the request of the Princess, and the ceremony is performed with due solemnity, the Princess again kindly acknowledging this imitation of royalty with a pleasing smile. The Prince then intimated to the Chairman of the Reception Committee, an old and respected resident of Knutsford (the late Mr Wm. Nicholls) that in future the event would be known as the 'Royal May Day Festival,' an announcement which evoked round after round of cheering."

After an interval of some years, owing to the war, the celebration was revived on a colossal scale in 1919. The ancient town, bathed as it was in brilliant sunshine, on Saturday, the 3rd May, with its decorations and artistic sandings, never looked gayer, and the ceremony of crowning " the May Queen " was duly performed, as shown in our illustration, amidst cheers of the assembled multitude drawn from all parts of the County and Lancashire.

CHAPTER XI.

Cheshire in the days of "bluff King Hal"—Good and bad points of the Star Chamber—Local names, habits, and customs—"Orators and their piteous compleyntes"—Murder at a bowling match—the Law of Sanctuary—Other murders—Affrays and abductions—Matrimonial and social differences in the olden times—Defiance of the King's letters "to proceed to the Warres"—Bolde lady of Cheshire—A Dukinfield land dispute—How bailiffs executed warrants and their dangers—How a Chapel of Ease to Stockport was built—Seizure of the Manor of Timperley—The disputes of the Dutton family—Curious customs as to heirship—Abduction of an infant heir—"Executed" for a breach of ecclesiastical law—The Holford family; its differences, matrimonial and otherwise—A battle royal at Northenden, accompanied by an alarm bell—Rough and ready way of carrying out the law.

THE records of the Court of Star Chamber, especially in the reign of Henry VIII., shed an interesting sidelight on the inner life of Cheshire people extending over centuries in our rough island story. A popularly accepted view is that this chamber was an offshoot of the reign of the Stuart kings. It was certainly at that period it attained execration and notoriety on the part of the nation by extortions and unjust imposts, especially by Charles I. and James I., until its abolition in 1641, the first-named monarch "losing" his head in the process—in more senses than one.

Still, the Court of Star Chamber, say, under the Tudors, had some good points to recommend it, particularly from a kingly standpoint. In the reigning king's hands it was regarded as an invaluable instrument for holding the barons and officials in check. Beside the development of the House of Peers as the highest Court of Judicature in this realm, the development of the Great Council had long been going on. The customary powers of this Council arose from need of a court too powerful and independent to be in danger of being intimidated or bribed by influence or wealth—able to penalise gross miscarriage of justice fraudulently procured, and to take in hand cases with which the ordinary courts would have had great difficulty in dealing. It was in its procedure analogous to that of the powerful ecclesiastical courts of the time. Under Henry VII., we are told, its functions "were exercised at least mainly in the cause of justice. They were used to the public satisfaction as well as to the strengthening of the king's own hands."

So far as cases arising in Cheshire are concerned, there is ample proof of this in the cases themselves. There appeared to be every facility afforded to both sides for an impartial hearing. There is also much valuable matter in the study of local names, manners, customs, language, and habits, social and otherwise, of the Cheshire people. Murders, assaults, violent seizures of land and buildings were common. Rights of tenants and use of common lands had some doughty champions, and there were occasionally battles royal between clergy and laity for possession of emoluments and rights in connection with places of worship in the county. Invariably the petitions were addressed direct to the king, that "most dradde (dread) soveragne lorde," by his " poore subject and daily orator "—or " oratour," as it is sometimes given. Here we have the origin of the close of a parliamentary form—" And your petitioners will ever pray, etc." These orators were " suppliants " or " beseechers " for the King's decision, through the legal advisers, in their favour. Some of them "lamentably compleyned" of the alleged injustice they had suffered ; others " compleyned most piteously," to the " knyges Grace Highnes," etc. In a few cases appeal was made " to the most reverend father in God, Lord Thomas, Cardynall Archebechoppe of York and Chauncellor of England," or to " the most reverent Fader in God, Tomas, Lord Cardynall Lagate a latere, Archebishop of York and Chauncelor of Englonde," one and the same person, though the name is spelt differently in both cases.

Over three centuries ago the game of bowls was regarded in Cheshire, as well as in other parts of England, as a quiet and healthful pastime. By some of the Star Chamber officials it was variously spelled " bollis " and " bowllys." It does not, however, readily lend itself to the crime of murder. Yet it is directly responsible for one which came under the notice of the court. It was in connection with a petition to the king, " your good and gracious heyhnes," by Alice Swetnam, who stated that her husband, Laurence Swettenham, paid a visit to Brereton "on the Monday next after the Feest of St Oswald, the King, in God's peas (peace) and King Henry's." There he met John Cotton of Cotton, gentleman, and Harry Cotton, his brother. They, in their " myschevous and malycous mynde persuaded, or of purpose prepense, exorted and labored Laurence to play at bollis." The poor fellow, " thynkyng noo harme ner ill to any person, accompanied them to a bolling ale " (bowling alley) at Brereton Green. At the sixth cast, when Laurence should have delivered his wood, John Cotton, in the presence of " associates and adherentes," began a quarrel by saying that Laurence " stode amyss "—in other words, was taking mean advantage of him. Laurence " replyed that he would not quarrel with him but would leave the place," when a man named John Breddon, or Briddon, struck Laurence from the back with a bill, exposing the brains and splitting his head open. He died within less than a quarter of " a owre without speaking a word." Some of the onlookers, " well disposed subjects of the king," endeavoured to seize the "mertherrers," but Cotton's adherents rescued them. Most of them appeared to have returned home ; but John Briddon, who struck the fatal blow, and his wife took " seintwarie " (sanctuary) at Knoll in Warwickshire. On the petition of Swettenham's wife or widow, who is " the poor oratrice," the Sheriff of Cheshire and Sir William Brereton took Briddon's statement. We then find that the affair occurred at Brereton Wakes. There was a large number of persons present, some of whom played at " bowllys " and Cotton and Swetnam having words, Briddon struck the latter as alleged. After that Briddon seems to have wandered about the country. He was " bold " in his sanctuary, feeling probably that his skin was safe, and he apparently regarded his examination with indifference. The commissioners regarded the murder as committed of malice prepense, in " a most heynous manner." They were of opinion that " if he were examined outside and good pollicie used," he might say something. His wife would not, like a sensible woman, say anything. Briddon, however, went so far as to admit that he went to Newport in Shropshire and told Thomas Bulkley of Eyton, Cheshire, of the murder, and Bulkley said " he was sorry to hear of the matter."

George Baryngton, or Beryngton, yeoman, who was alleged to be one of those who took part in the disturbance, examined before Sir Thomas Lovell and Sir Henry Marney and other " kinges lernyd counsell," said that Swettenham was murdered, but he was not privy to his death, and that he was daring enough to abide his trial before a jury. He was in " Rauf Sladen's " house at Brereton all the afternoon " dawncying," at the time of the murder, and he went with such of the company as had " dawnced " with him to take the murderers, who fled, and he then went home to his father's house. John Thorley attended " Masse " at Congleton in the morning and went to Brereton in the afternoon, when they were about to bury Swettenham. Two years afterwards there was an examination of Sir William Brereton by the " Lord Cardynell " upon the matter connected with the murder, and he said he had retained Benyngton, or Beryngton, and Roger Dale, yeoman of the King's guard, in his service and had maintained them. Bills of indictment were put in at Chester Assizes by Laurence Swettenham's father, but owing to influence brought to bear by friends of the accused, the jury would not find true bills against the murderers owing " to their near relationship to Sir William Brereton and others of the same class."

Swettenham, the father, continued to pursue the matter against Sir William Brereton, John Fitton, and Thomas Bulkeley, Esquires, for " meyntening and comforting John Cotton and others," indicted for " murderying " the said Laurence, thus showing that some progress had been made in bringing the murderers to justice. Henry Cotton, one of them, when imprisoned after arrest at Congleton, was taken out of prison by William Brereton, clerk, Vicar of Wereham (Weaverham), without lawful authority, and by him taken from " alehouse to alehouse " of the said town, and Henry tarried there five days, " Sir William Brereton being then and yet Mayor of the said town." Seeing that the authorities there on one occasion sold the Parish Bible to buy a bear, such a condition of things in Congleton is not to be wondered at. Brydon, or Briddon, the real murderer, had been in the meantime allowed to escape. The proceedings no doubt dragged on for some years, as we find Sir William Brereton being made the object of certain allegations by William Swettenham, the father, that he had offered John Thorley, who married Laurence Swettenham's widow, the sum of 40s. " for amends," and that " Thorley took the money, but whether for his own use or the use of the said Alice he knew not." So ended this gruesome tragedy so far as these records are concerned.

Randall (Randulph) Davenport, gentleman, of Wirral, was murdered in a fray by " a great no. (number) of evyll doers," when he was returning from Chester market, and Richard Houghe was alleged to be the murderer. An inquest was held by the coroner of the " Hundred of Wirrehall," but owing to local influences Houghe was protected, it is alleged, by perjured witnesses, whose intention was to save Houghe's lands from confiscation, which were of the yearly value of 20 marks or above. The coroner put " lyght persons as were servants and frendes to the murderer and his kynsmen " on the jury. He also locked William Clayton, one of the King's sergeants, out of the church where the inquest was held, and brought in a " Byll " which was not a true record of the verdict. Although an attempt was afterwards made to have the verdict reviewed, the coroner held that he only had jurisdiction over his court— a right claimed to the present day. We hear nothing more of the matter. A similar state of things prevailed in connection with an inquest when Robert Drake was slain at Baddeley (Badeley) in connection with the seizure of certain ground at the instigation of Thomas Starkey, Esquire, and others. John, son of this Thomas, warned the jurymen to stick to their verdict first given, or they would undo (ruin) his father, as also his cousin, Honkyn Maynwaring. It was added that Robert Woodwart (Woodward?) and David Grey, the murderers, might have been taken at Wrenbury Church on a Good Friday but for Starkey's interference.

Of a different complexion was a complaint of Richard Daune (Done) in regard to a murder charge against Sir Piers Dutton, who at the time of the murder and a good time after was " in strait keeping " at Chester Castle, on a charge of causing or inciting Rauf (Ralph) Dutton (probably a near relation of his) to do the deed. Although Piers was, so he declared, " heavy and sorry in his mind in consequence," he kept no fewer than 120 persons, probably retainers, in his house, and also apparently sent them careering over the countryside, so that Richard and his friends were afraid to leave their homes and go to market. On the other hand the " innocent " Richard must not have been quite so frightened as he pretended to be, for when Piers went to answer a writ at Chester Castle, Richard, with the help of 140 persons, assembled in the city, bent on slaying him, and in this enterprise he had the active assistance of his brother William, who was " a great captain and offender in the said riot." William was afterwards an outlaw. And here again we are left in a state of uncertainty as to any punishment which was administered.

Murders and affrays must have been very common at this period, and other members of the house of Dutton were implicated, for we read that Sir John Dutton, "prest," a near kinsman of Sir Piers Dutton, was implicated along with him in the murder of Thomas Huchyns (Hutchins), in that he conveyed the murderers from Cheshire to Oxfordshire, and then back to Cheshire, and gave them large sums of money. They were hidden away in places unknown, owing to a dread of being brought under the lash of the law, and apparently escaped the consequences of their crime.

In September 1518 Ottiwell Booth was stabbed to the heart in Stockport Market, where he was engaged in selling corn and produce, by Robert Ponall, or Pownall. Before he did so Pownall " toke the same Ottiwell by the bosom, and saying, ' Ah horeson, art thou here to-day ? ' took out his dagger and stikked him." A large number of people were about at the time, including " Alexander Hunt, prest, William Bradburne, gent., Richard Damport (Davenport), gent.," and amongst those who helped Robert Pownall to escape into Lancashire were " Thomas Byrche, prest, Sir Geffry Bradeles prest," and others. When they got to a place called Soldersgate, beyond Lancashire Bridge, Olyver Elcock (Alcock) aided Pownall to get away. Ralph Marsland seized Pownall and was rewarded with a blow on the head by Nicholas Brixshawe (Brookshaw) with a hedging bill, and he fell on his knees. Bradburne also struck at Marsland, but the blow was warded off by Piers Stanley. Brookshaw then told Pownall " to goo his way for Booth was killed." Pownall ran away, followed by the crowd, who wished to apprehend him, but Bradburne and others " sett their bakkes against the gate " and threatened his pursuers with death. No constable appears to have been at hand at the time. Thus does history repeat itself. Who, in these modern days, has not heard complaint as to the police being out of the way when wanted? Evidently Pownall made good his escape.

But surely the climax was reached when John Jenyns, a household servant of the Abbot of Combermere Abbey, stabbed one Dan Ottiwell to the heart with " a dagger, and slew him out of hand." His body was laid upon a bed in his clothes, and Dan Edmond, a monk, and certain servants of the Abbot, requested Thomas Hammond, the Prior of the Abbey, to have Jenyns arrested, but he refused, remarking that " this Abbey is already in an evyll name for usying of mysrule." He said he would have the murder kept secret as, if it was openly known, the abbey would be "undone" (ruined), and he swore those present to secrecy " on a book." Thomas Tounde, yeoman, afterwards arrested Jenyns, and lodged him in Chester Castle, but he was not indicted, and it is evident he did not get his deserts.

Assaults on practically all occasions were accompanied by violence, and appropriation of property consequent thereon, legal and illegal, are also numerous. James Bostock was at Mylton, " in goddes peace and the king's " when he passed " Hugh Calvely, esquyer, and other evill disposed malefactors " armed " with staves, swords, bucklers, daggers, and other weapons, as well defensive as invasive," who set upon Barton, who was on horseback, and stole his horse and refused to " redeliver or go to the sterred (Star) chamber."

Matrimonial differences were in evidence in those far back days. In 1542 Sir Richard Brereton of Tatton, Knight, informed the king that Dame Brereton, his wife, being " blynde "—though why the circumstances called for this statement is not apparent on the face of it—had, contrary to " the law of God and her bounden duty," as also had her son, the heir to the property, named Richard, after his father, aided and abetted her in this course of conduct, and that she had not " repared " herself to her said husband. The King had requested the lady and her son to return to the father, but they had disregarded this command and seized corn in the barns, " and driven Sir Richard's men off the land, from the plowes and from their labours." They even set their retainers to assault his chaplain and a keeper, whom they " grevously " wounded. A pathetic note is struck in that Sir Richard afterwards became blind, but this did not prevent them taking by force the produce of certain demesne lands at Worsley, County Lancaster. Sir Richard was, with his servants, engaged in thrashing corn, and his wife and son threatened to " kylle and slee " (the old Cheshire pronunciation of the word " slay ") any one who went near. Sir Alexander Ratcleve and Sir William Laylond, local justices, interfered, but without avail, and the wife and son remained in possession of the field, and apparently the victorious party.

Actions to recover possession of property were common, and incidentally we come across tenure by military service. Thomas Brereton, who asserted he owned a house and water mill at Wettenhall, near Over, let the premises to one Thomas Johnson, as tenant at will at a yearly rental of 28s. 8d. The king addressed "gracious letters" to Roger Brereton, Esquire, ordering him to furnish a contingent of men to be ready " at one houres warnyng " to attend the Duke of Norfolk to proceed to the " warres in Scotland." Thomas, the friend and kinsman of Roger, and also " a petye capten," ordered his tenants, of whom Johnson was one, to the number of one hundred, to meet at Cobler's Cross, but Johnson openly refused to go " to warre and do the kynge service," although the others were quite content to do so. It was an example which came near to shipwrecking the expedition. He therefore gave Johnson notice to leave and " avoyde " the premises, but Thomas refused. He held them with a strong hand, " kepyng the dores and windows fast shutt," and added to his other iniquities by fishing in the mill-pond and converting the proceeds to " his own use."

Johnson's answer was, that he did not hold the premises under Brereton, but from a man named Manley, and as he had spent 20 marks on the repair of the cottage, and £40 on the mill and the dams, it would mean his ruin (undoing) were he to give them up. Brereton had never any authority to compel him to do military service, and he denied having taken fish " in the manner and form as in the bill alleged."

In a petition addressed to the Archbishop of York, Henry Brodbent (Broadbent) of Duckenfield, brought an action against John "Dokynfeld," Esquire, alleging that he would give him a lease of land held by Edmund Leez if he would marry Elsabeth, daughter of Edmund. He accordingly married Elsabeth, and on the death of Edmund entered into occupation, and gave Sir John a "heryett" (heriot) according to custom, and remained on the land. Then servants of John "Dukynfeld" put in an appearance, armed with swords, etc., and finding Broadbent's wife and a servant " plowing and erying " (ploughing and harrowing), ordered them to desist and leave the premises, or they would " kutte the armez besyde their bodyes, and other fereful words." They turned out his wife and seven small children, evidently the orthodox quiverful, judging from the wording of the petition. Not content with this, the owner on Tuesday " in passyon weke sent a number of men, tenants and lovers of the same Dokynfeld," who commenced ploughing and cultivating the garden. Elizabeth Bordebent (Broadbent's sister) ordered them off the premises, but so far from complying they "drew her, bareheaded, backward over a stile, and so took her to the Hall of Dokynfeld, and threatened to put her in the stocks." Thereupon she fell to the ground " in a swonde," and no wonder. They further took Broadbent's wife, who had a child " soking " (sucking) at her breast. They threatened the poor creature with " a stay " in Chester Castle, and as Broadbent was in fear of his life he claimed protection for his wife and small children (number not stated), etc.

The answer of " John Dokenfeld, Esquyer," was that " on the death of Leez he (Broadbent) should only reap the next crop and then vacate the property. Possession was taken on an Exchequer Warrant from Chester Castle, by " the King's bailye of Maxwoodefeld " (Macclesfield) hundred.

In consequence of opposition by the Broadbent clan, the " bailye " had to safeguard himself by employing a number of men to retake possession. Dokynfeld denied he made any such covenant as alleged by Broadbent, and he paid no heriot for himself, but only one cow with a young sucking calf, according to custom of the manor after the death of Leez.

Other disputes occurred at Mottram Andrew (Mottram St Andrew), Wistaston, and Monks Coppenhall or Crewe, in which we find local names variously spelt. Brindley became Brundley and Bryndeley; Barthomley, Bartmuley; Over, Ouuer; Crewe, Cru; Nantwich, Namptwiche; etc. Those interested in the derivation of names might trace Whittakers to Whiteacres. There were lawsuits relating to the manor of Codyngton, and Cheadle or Chedull, land at Mouldsworth, the right to cut turf and dry it, a very valuable privilege in many parts of the country, and was necessary for fuel to maintain the house fires or " fyarbote " of the inhabitants.

It was then a common custom, as it is to this day, for an assistant to accompany a bailiff, though in some cases he was roughly handled, and had to escape as best he could from an infuriated crowd. Another custom from time out of mind in Cheshire was that the heir of any person who died should have the choice of one kind of thing (the best), chattels, plate, and other things, that were in the house at the time of his decease, and this custom was the cause of numerous lawsuits. Notices to quit were also served in the orthodox manner, only instead of the modern phrase to " quit and deliver up peaceable possession," they were called upon " to leave and avoyde " the property. Attempts to enclose common lands were frequent, and it would appear that one claimant, who set to work to make the enclosure, drove off the cattle of the inhabitants, employing a number of men in the process, and, on one occasion, it is recorded that after driving off the cattle " great mastyff dogs " were employed to keep them out. Some opposition was raised to the action of Sir Peter Legh, who had, with the consent of freeholders and other inhabitants of " Distley and Walley " (Disley and Whaley) entered upon parcels of waste land and built " a Chapell in honour of God and our Ladye, five miles away from the Parish Church (Stockport ?), with lodgings, and made gardens for the ease and profit of the priests who should minister therein, and for other divers considerations concerning the weal of the said chapel." Sir Peter's action was subsequently approved by the authorities.

Chancery cases occasionally found their way into the Star Chamber proceedings. In one notable case the Booths of Dunham were concerned, where not only had the Manor of Timperley been taken, as alleged, by force from one Hamon Arderne, by John Legh of Baguley, but had caused Dame Elizabeth Booth, daughter of Sir John Warburton of Arley, to be introduced with others as a co-defendant. The petition was addressed to Sir Thomas Audley, Knight, Lord Chancellor of England, and was brought by William Ardern, " gentylman," showing that his father Hamon was possessed in fee and " just tytle of ten messuages, four score acres of lande, twenty acres of meadow, fiftye acres of pasture, four acres of wood, a hundred acres of turberye, with the appurtenannces." Then we find that Anne Arderne, " Elyzabeth Booth, wydow," and " Rychard Leghe, gentyllman," entered into three messuages and one close, called " the new folde." These defendants and divers other " ryotous " persons unknown " in ryotous maner arreyde, that is to say, with swardes, buellers, daggers, staves, and other wepyns invasyve again your pece mst drad soveraign Lord (Henry VIII.) in the moneth of Maye in this present XXXVth yere of your moost noble rayne, entrid into iij messuages," and had wrongfully taken the profits therefrom, so that if the petitioner should attempt to enforce his rights " there were lyk to insue danger and brech of the Kynge's peace, and so shall be without remedy therefor unless your graccious ayde be unto him shewed in this behalf."

Answers were filed by the defendants, who begged to be discharged, with their reasonable costs and charges. Anne Arderne was but an infant, Elizabeth Booth an "agett" woman of sixty years and over, and the said Richard being "seklye" and aged. It was asserted further by Richard "Leigh" of Baguley, Esquire, and Sir Edward Vawderey, priest, and two of the household servants of the said Richard Leigh, and also one John Nelde (Nield) that they carried no other weapons than such as they usually "were" (wear). Also, that the said Richard Leigh, being appointed by the King's Justice of Chester, to be her "gardien," "dyd giffe her counsell to enter into the premissis and into her inheritannces."

The Manor of Timperley, at this period owned by William Arderne, was "ten messuages, four score acres of land, twenty acres of meadow, fiftye acres of pasture, four acres of wood, a hundred acres of Turbary, with th' appurtenances," and the appurtenances referred to included Timperley Moss. In the course of the litigation Dame Elizabeth Booth died, and the case was continued by William Arderne, and George Booth, Esquire, became a defendant, along with one George Chatterton, gent., and others. The latter case showed that Arderne had dug turves or turf on the manor, which was a source of profit, and having been dried "ys and alwaye hath byn a usuell fuell for fyre" in those parts. The right to cut turf was then a valuable part of an estate. Edward Ryle of Timperley, Richard Hardy, "housbondman," Robert Vauderey, another husbandman, and others, under the direction of "George Boyth, esquyer," assaulted divers men, as well as women, and put them in such fear that they fled to save their lives and they were "fayne to flye and departe the sayde landes." The assailants removed in the night such turves as they required to the "grett hurte and losses of your sayd orator." Hamon Arderne, his father, was "a blynde man of th' age of four score yeres," who also "ys fled and departyd from Tymperley to the Cyte of London, where he led a poore lyve to his great hevynes," and that owing to the influence of the Booths in that city he had not the means or the ability to attain his remedy at law.

Answers to the bill of "compleynt" (complaint) were filed by George Bouthe, Chatterton, and Ryle, who all said that they did not know that the ground wherein the said turves were got was the "proper grounde and soille" of the said William Arderne, as stated in the bill, and they denied the charges of violence and assault. The suit appears to have been continued by Arderne, and accordingly "Edward Waren and Richard Legh" were directed to summon the defendants before them, and their answers were taken at Dunham Massey, 18th October, in the thirtieth year of the reign of Henry VIII. (1538). They declared the matter ought to be determined at common law in the County of Chester. They further alleged that the plaintiff's father sold three messuages in Timperley, with lands thereto, belonging to Robert Hondeford, gent., and James Barlowe, which descended after their death to Humphrey Barlowe, son and heir of the said James, and the plaintiff (William Arderne), being the King's servant, of " his high and cruel mind," with force wrongfully entered into the turbary belonging to the said three messuages. Barlow's tenants came to George Bothe, Esquire, at Altrincham, and required him to send to the plaintiff to "surcease his wrongfull digging." He sent Parker, who took Chatterton and Vaudrey " as his witnesses." In accordance with a writ, 20th November 1538, directed to Sir William Brereton, Sir Peter Warburton, Robert Dukenfeld, and Thomas Dannecalf, Esquires, depositions were taken at Chester on 17th January 1538-39. William Davorne of Timperley, aged 53, Robert Cryshawe (Kershaw), aged 40, and Richard Huntt, aged 30, stated that plaintiff's father was " seised of the Manor of Tymperley until he made a gift thereof to his said son William, about three years past." For sixteen years he and his sons " have gotten turves upon Tymperley Moss without interruption " till the instance complained of "George Boythe " and his servants were not privy to the carrying away of the turves. On the other hand, William Gybbins of Timperley, aged 53, knew of no such gift made to William Arderne, and alleged that Hamnett was still possessed of the manor. He knew of no disturbance to the plaintiffs getting of turves. He was supported in this by Edward Raynescroft, or Ravenscroft, aged 22, and Richard Derbyshire, aged 10. In whose favour the matter ended is not recorded, but the case is a specimen of others which came before the Court on numerous occasions.

The Duttons were prominent in other disputes of a different character to those already recorded. Julyan (Julia ?) Dutton, widow of Sir Piers, set forth in a petition to the king that on the death of her husband she possessed in her own right goods and "cattal," " a gold cheyne, value £36 and above, one bason and ewer of sylver of the value of £18," in the chief mansion house, Dutton Hall. Immediately after the death of Sir Piers, his son Rauf (her stepson), accompanied by his relations "and others of evyll disposicion, in August 1545, accompanied by divers other riottous persons and perturbers of the peace," assembled in " a great rout and conventicle " at Dutton Hall. They were armed " with swords, buklers, bylles and long spiked staves," etc., and burst open doors and chests, and evidently carried off all they could lay their hands upon. She described Rauf as a very young man, greatly given to games and pastimes and excessive expenses, so that it was very likely he would soon make away with them. She said they had only left her " a gown and a kyrtle of very coarse black." The schedule of clothing sent in showed her to have been a lady of fashion, and quite in keeping with a lady of that noble house. There were numerous gowns of velvet and damask, elaborately trimmed, "kyrtles of black satin, camlet, scarlet petycotes, mantles, clokes, hoods, hose, bonnets, a negge of pearls and bedes of gold between, and a frontlet of gold, a plain bonnet with a negge of gold and goldsmith's work, etc., a coverying

of tawny velvet for a saddle, with harness and bosses belonging thereto "
—indeed, a goodly array of considerable value.

The answer of Rauf was that his father, Sir Piers, had given him the goods for divers great causes and considerations, including " all his goods and chattels movable and unmovable, quick and dead, personal and mixed." On the death of his father, he, assisted by his servant, Rauf Manning, "took from Dame Dutton in a peaceable manner, and detained the ewer and basin in part payment of the charges, amounting to £100, attending the funeral of his father, disbursed by him and assented to by Dame Julyan." The wearing apparel, he asserted, he had tendered to her several times and she refused to accept them, and they awaited the order of the court. There was no riot as alleged.

The Holford family also contributed their quota to the litigation of the period. Sir George Holford, Knight, died, leaving Dame Elizabeth Holford, his second wife—who well deserved the title King James II. bestowed upon her in later ages of "the bowlde ladye of Cheshire"—his " executrice." She commenced by exhibiting a bill of complaint before the Star Chamber against Sir John Holford, his son and heir, and George " Holforthe," Esquire, another son by the first wife, when an order was made by the Court that she should enjoy a dower as widow of Sir George until it could be proved she was not his lawful wife. The question of who was entitled to the movables was referred to Dr Lee, " one of the auditors of Causes in my Lord Legate's Grace high court of audience," and it was found through Dr Olyver, afterwards " Master of the perogative," that the proper goods and chattels of the said Sir George were to be delivered and restored to the said Elizabeth. Sir John and his brother, however, refused to deliver up the goods. It turned out, so they said, that the maiden name of Dame Elizabeth was Borroughs, and George stated to the Court that she had not exhibited any testimony to the Ordinary, although she had been " monished " so to do. He proceeds : Immediately after he had knowledge of the death of his father, " he repaired in peaceable wise to the manor of Hulford, where his father then lay dead, with two of his own servants and two other neighbours, which minded to go to the burial, with the intent to pray for his soul and see his burial; he did not bring with him 100 men armed." Before he and his brother, Sir John, came to the burial, the complainant, Elizabeth, "taking little heaviness for his father's death," had spoiled and conveyed away from the manor most part of the goods and substance of the said Sir George, whereupon this defendant himself " gently " required her to declare if she were his father's executrix, and how his father, being a man of worship reputed in the country, should be buried, advertising her it should be convenient to have him in some honest wise buried, because many of the country, both poor and rich, would repair to his burial. Nevertheless, she refused to put any cost towards the burial of the said Sir George, refusing to give a sheet to wind him in. She refused to publish any will, and the defendant sent with all speed to the Ordinary of the diocese, advertising him of the premises, and obtained from him letters of sequestration, ready to be showed, and letters of administration of the said goods for the funeral of his father. By authority thereof he threshed part of the corn in his father's barns and killed some of his cattle, and expended the same about the burial ; and of such goods as he could come by (being under £50) he made a true inventory. He never hindered the children of Sir George, viz. Arthur, aged 10, Michael, aged 9, and Peter, aged 3, from having meat and drink. The said Elizabeth " was never accoupled in lawful matrimony with the said Sir George after the lawes of holy chirche, for the which cause she is scyted and monyshed in the spirituall lawe upon just causes of divorce at the instance of the said Sir John." In this defendant's absence, his wife, Isabel Holford, was informed that part " of his goods were privily conveyed to the houses of Lawrence Coppok, Heugh Foster and George Burrows. She went to those houses, and caused such of his goods as she found there to be put into safe keeping, which lawful was for her to do."

Meantime matters had been further complicated by a second marriage. Dame Elizabeth was uxoriously disposed, and set her affections on " Anthonye Daubeney," a gentleman of the court of the reigning king, and the petition set forth that " a decree had been made in a suit depending betwene the complaynants and Sir John Holdeforde, knight, concerning the joynture of the seid Elizabeth, that Sir John shuld permytt them peacibly to occupy the lands, etc., expressed in a dede of feoffment produced to the court, under payne of £100, now of late the said Sir John hath caused dyvers tenants to deny payment of their rentes to the complainants, and hath pursued, in the said tenantes names, divers writs of replegiarum in the countie of Chester agaynst your suppliantes for taking distresses," etc.

Sir John denied this most strongly, stating he did not interfere at all with Elizabeth's jointure. Dame Elizabeth was dead, and we find Daubeney taking up the cudgels in his own behalf, and he retorted that " she had been driven to her death by the unkind dealings of Sir John Holford and his brother, as also to sue as well for the keeping of certain small children she had by the said Sir George as for her dower. Upon which suit she had a decree in the Star Chamber, 11th February, 20, Henry VIII., the late Lord Cardinall and others, then being present."

On the death of Elizabeth, " the bowlde ladye " aforesaid, Sir John Holford brought an action against Daubeney questioning the settlement Sir George had made upon his wife, Elizabeth. It appeared that by an indenture between " Sir George Holford, ' diseased,' and Rauf Brereton, a marriage was arranged between Brereton's daughter, Margere, and heire-apparaunt of Rauf. Sir George agreed to convey to Willyam Bromley, Bartylmew Brereton, Robert Holford, and other trustees, all his estates 'in co. Chester or ellswhere in England' to provide rents of 20 marks yearly for the said young couple, and a provision of £13, 13s. 4d. yearly out of lands in ' Lostoke Gralham ' for his wife, Dame Isabell, if she survived him, or £20 for any future wife he should marry." " On 6th June following the said Sir George and Geffrey Mylington conveyed to the said trustees the manors of Holfford, Netherpeover and Plumley, to hold to the uses in the said indenture expressed."

A remarkable case (undated), headed " the ' peculiar ' (privilege or right) of the Manor of Clifton," appears in the records of the Star Chamber, which incidentally reflects the extraordinary powers exercised by the ecclesiastical officials of the time. It was the outcome of interrogatories administered on behalf of John Wheteley. Answer was made by Edmund Strethy, Clerk, Commissary to the Bishop of Chester, who testified that he had held the office for eight years and never " knew or herde " that any tenants and inhabitants in Clifton had at any " tyme their testamentes and last wylles provyd at the Court holden within the said manor before the steward. In his day one, Grimdiche (Grimsditch), bayliffe of the manor, refused to prove a will before him." For his contumacy therein the answer proceeds, " this deponent did execute him, and upon his absolution he provyd the same testament before this deponent." There appears to have been some precedent for this assumed right, but against this was set the fact that the testament of one, John Derby, and other tenants in the manor, was proved before Mr Stokesley, his predecessor, in the regular way. Thomas Segge, apparitor to the Commissary of Chester, testified that "he had known dyvers such testaments provyd before the steward since Mr Hercy had been Lord thereof, but for twenty years he had never had any such knowledge of any such practice," which showed that it was an innovation which could not be recognised or permitted by the regular court at Chester.

It must not be inferred from the above that Grimsditch was beheaded. The word " execute " is a common one in connection with wills, and no doubt after making confession of his willingness to submit to the legal authorities, the will, and not the man, was accordingly " executed."

There is only one case we can find recorded of the abduction of an infant heir. Elizabeth Whykstede (Wickstead), widow, " petously complayned " that John Maynwaring, the elder, and Thomas Morall, and six other armed men broke into her house at Wickstead, within the " pales " of Chester, and finding her and her ten children in their beds, carried off her son, Hugh Whyskstede, aged nine, to Sheffield Castle, where he was placed in the charge of George, Earl of Shrewsbury, and no doubt taken good care of during his minority. We get a glimpse of the terms under which he held his land from the Earl. It consisted of forty acres in Wickstead and two adjoining townships, and it was by knight's service at a rent of one penny. No further particulars are given.

Poaching, especially in Macclesfield forest, was common, the game killed being chiefly deer. Many of the poachers came from Staffordshire.

Stoppage and diversion of water courses was often resisted by the inhabitants, and with good cause; but more than usual friction appears to have arisen between Alexander Barlow of Barlow Hall, Chorlton Cum Hardy, and Robert Tatton of Withenshawe, as to the right of repair of the Weir at Barlow, and the grinding of his corn at the mill on the banks of the Mersey, of which he alleged he was the owner. Early in January (year not stated) a number of men went to the " weyre " (Weir) and pulled up a part, and after digging " a great trench," or ditch, furnished and stored the trench with a great number of stones, and built a house, evidently for the purpose of preventing any further repairs by Barlow. Observing the damage which had been done, he sent a number of his servants to repair the weir " in a peaceable and quiet manner." The record shows that they did not effect their object. The said Robert was accompanied by thirty " other riottous persons, and by his commandment of the said Roberte, in forcyble maner strongly and unlawfully harnisshed, with jacks and salletes, and also havinge divers and outragious weapons, defensive and invasyue, that is to say, swordes and bucklers, speares, billes and diuers ither unlawfull weapons, the said Roberte, havinge a polleaxe in his handes, did leade and conducte the said riottous persons after the maner of warre in the most rebellious maner, assembled unto the said weyre in the said county of Chester, and then and theare in like riottous maner with force and armes againste your grace's peace, crowne and dignity, the said Robert caused by estymacion CC (200) riottous persons or thear aboutes to your said orator unknowen to be well harnisshed and placyd inbusshementes and certen hedherowes dyches and groves neare adioyninge to the said weyre to be in redynes to ayde the said Roberte and his said companye, if neade required. And further he did cause a bell to be rounge alaroum, by reason of which warninge given thear was most rebellyously assembled of your Graces subgectes above the number of 700 persons in the favour and ayde of the said Roberte Tatton, and they did assaulte, wounde, and cruelly entreate the saide labourers or servantes then aboute to repayre the weyre, to wit, one with a speare in the arme, and another on the legge with a stone, who escaped away onlyve with great difficultie; and these rebellyous routtes continued the most part of the said daye. And the said Robert, not thus contentyd, doth yet continually with great force keepe wache and warde at the said weyre, to the perillous example of lyke offendors," etc.

There are many cases on record from Lancashire which bear a strong family likeness to those noted above, but the above instance is sufficient to show the rough and ready way in which the law was administered in the days of " bluff King Hal."

CHAPTER XII.

Cheshire's first Parliament — Representation at Westminster — The Stuart régime and local members — The Civil Wars — Sir William Brereton's mysterious funeral — Sir George Booth's first appearance in Parliament — Sweeping reforms — A thrice married Mayor and his notable quiverful — The Pensionary Parliament — Chester recorder's attempted bribery — The first Knight of Wynnstay — An age of startling happenings — The foundation of the National debt — Bribery and corruption rampant — The Bill of Exclusion passed — Lord Rochester's epitaph on Charles II. — The first Parliament of James II. — End of the great struggle for absolute power — Public lotteries opened — Queen Anne's connection with Cheshire — The first Parliament after the Union — Whigs and Tories — Parliaments of two Georges — Cheshire loyal to the Whig interest — An interesting Parliament — The first census of the Kingdom — Hotly contested and dearly bought elections — Joyous junketing — The Grosvenor interest triumphant.

THE first parliament in Cheshire was that of Hugh Lupus, the first Earl of Chester, under the Norman William.¹ It was held in the large hall of Chester Castle, and was attended by his barons, already enumerated, and abbots from the various monasteries in the County Palatine. We have seen in previous chapters how the House of Commons was evolved from the political unrest of the period. In 1259 a new form of government was instituted at Chester, in a mayor and two sheriffs, and this has persisted with one slight interval until the present day. In 1541 the inhabitants of the County and City of Chester represented to the king that although they were bound by acts and statutes of the high court of parliament, they had never been represented by their knights and burgesses in that court, having had a parliament of their own. They therefore petitioned for the privilege of electing two knights for the County, and two burgesses for the City. This was granted by an Act passed in the last year of the reign of Henry VIII.

In 1547 Cheshire, for the first time, was represented in the national parliament, Thomas Holcroft of Vale Royal being elected in November of that year. In March 1553 Sir Thomas was returned in conjunction with Sir Thomas Venables of Kinderton. For the City of Chester, Richard Sneyd, gent., and Rafe Mainwaring, Alderman, were the representatives. During the reign of Mary, which included the phantom sovereignty of Lady Jane Grey, John Crewe of Crewe, Sir Thomas Holcroft, and Edward Fytton of Gawsworth, Esquire, represented Cheshire, and Richard Sneyd and Thomas Massey, gent., Chester City. In the first year of Mary's reign Sir Henry Delves of Doddington, Knight, and Richard Wilbraham of Woodhey, Esquire, were members for Cheshire, and Richard Sneyd and Wm. Aldersey, gent., for Chester City. Three parliaments assembled in the joint reigns of Philip and Mary, from 1554 to 1558. Cheshire was represented at various times by Sir Richard

K

Cotton, Knight, Richard Wilbraham, Richard Hough of Leighton, and James Done of Utkinton; and Chester City by Richard Sneyd, Thomas Massey, Thomas Gerrard, and Sir Lawrence Smith. There were ten parliaments during the reign of "Good Queen Bess," and the representatives for Cheshire were:—William Brereton of Brereton, Esquire, Sir Rafe Leycester of Toft, Sir Thomas Venables of Kinderton, William Massaye of Podington, Thomas Calveley of Lea, William Booth of Dunham, Thomas Egerton, Solicitor-General, Hugh Cholmondeley of Cholmondeley, Sir George Beeston of Beeston, Thomas Stanley of Alderley, John Savage of Rock Savage, Thomas Holcroft of Vale Royal, John Done of Utkinton, Sir William Beeston of Beeston, and Mr Peter Legh of Lyme. Chester City: Sir Thomas Venables, William Alescher, William Gerard, John Yeworth, William Glasier, Richard Birkenhead, Richard Bavand (Alderman), Peter Warburton, Gilbert Gerard, William Brooke, Hugh Glasier, and Thomas Gamull.

The first parliament of James I. met in April 1603, when Sir Thomas Holcroft of Vale Royal, and Sir Roger Aston, Knight, represented Cheshire; and Thomas Lawton (Recorder), and Hugh Glasier, Chester City. Glasier was said to have been succeeded by one Kenrick ap Evans. This election was somewhat doubtful, and John Bingley, merchant, is officially returned as having been elected by the burgesses. In the twelfth year of James' reign, William Brereton of Brereton represented Cheshire; and Edward Whitby (Recorder) and John Bingley, aforesaid, Chester City. In 1621 the Cheshire members were Sir Wm. Brereton of Brereton, and Sir Richard Grosvenor of Eaton, and Edward Whitby and John Ratcliff (Alderman), Chester City. At the fourth and last parliament of James I., Cheshire was represented by William Booth of Dunham Massey, William Brereton of Ashley, Esquire, and Chester City by Edward Whitby and John Savage, Esquire.

In the first parliament of Charles I. Sir Robert Cholmondeley and Sir Anthony St John represented Cheshire, Chester City returning its previous representatives, Whitby and Savage. In the disputes between king and parliament which followed, Sir Richard Grosvenor of Eaton, Bart., and Peter Daniel of Tabley were returned for Cheshire; and Edward Whitby and William Samuel, for Chester City. Sir Richard Grosvenor was the first of his race, who had for many generations taken little part in public affairs, to take his share in county matters. He sat in that parliament which witnessed the fall of Lord Bacon and which voted the king a small subsidy. In the third parliament of Charles I., notable as that in which Cromwell was returned for Huntingdon, and in which he ruffled the usual course of the Assembly by denouncing the Bishop of Winchester for encouraging the preaching of "flat Popery at Paul's Cross, and bestowing preferment on ecclesiastics for proclaiming Arminian doctrines and the divine right of kings." Against this class was the Puritan, of which Cromwell was the chief corner stone. Sir Richard took part in the debate on the Puritan side most ably. On the writ for the levying of "ship money" being issued, Sir Richard definitely ranged himself with the Puritan party, and gave earnest of his sincerity by becoming surety for his brother-in-law, Peter Daniel of Tabley, a staunch parliamentarian, who had represented Cheshire in 1625. A number of lawsuits were brought against Daniel, which he contested as a Cheshireman would under similar conditions. He was outlawed in 1633, in connection with thirty-four actions, when he applied for a writ of certiorari to remove them. He was committed to the Fleet, despite the "protection" of the King's Council. These legal difficulties in this disturbed reign necessitated his withdrawal from public life, and he died on 14th September 1695 and was buried at Eccleston. His son, who bore the same name, succeeded him as Baronet. He was a strong Royalist, and both he and his son Roger were punished during the Commonwealth by the sequestration of their estates.

In the succeeding parliament appears the name of Oliver Cromwell. Sir William Brereton of Brereton was prominent in the stirring events of that age. Sir William, who was twenty-four years old, had been made a baronet the year before by King Charles, and the members for Chester were Whitby and Ratcliffe. Sir William Brereton married for his first wife, Susanna, daughter of Sir George Booth of Dunham Massey, and secondly, Cicely, daughter of Sir William Skeffington of Fisherwick, Leicestershire. He was in his youthful days of "a sober and religious turn of mind," but later on became one of the most distinguished military commanders of the age. In what is called the "Short Parliament," in the fifteenth year of the reign of Charles I., Cheshire was represented by Sir William Brereton and Sir Thomas Aston, and Chester by Sir Thomas Smith, Knight, Sir Robert Brerewood, Knight and Alderman. Charles then summoned his fifth and last parliament, in which figured Bradshaw, "the Regicide," and others. At this time Sir William Brereton of Handforth and Peter Venables of Kinderton were members for the County; and Sir Thomas Smith, Knight and Alderman, and Francis Gamull, Alderman, for the City of Chester. It is recorded that at this period Sir George Booth of Dunham Massey "displaced" one of the members for the County. This was probably caused by the action of Cromwell in making it illegal for any member of either House to hold a Commission in the Army, on which Brereton gave up his seat. He was then made Commander-in-Chief of the Parliamentary forces in Cheshire, Staffordshire, and Shropshire, Seneschal and Forester of Macclesfield Forest, and Seneschal of the Hundred—Sir Thomas Fairfax, the Yorkshire General, being appointed Commander-in-Chief in place of the Earl of Essex. In 1645 Sir George Booth was elected Knight of the Shire in place of Sir William Brereton; and in 1646 the representatives of the City, Sir Thomas Smith and Francis Gamull, were disqualified owing to their Royalist proclivities, and in the election which took place in December

1646 they were succeeded by William Edwards, Alderman, and John Ratcliff, Recorder. This Sir William Brereton died at Croydon, in the palace formerly belonging to the notorious Laud. Beyond the bare entry recording his death in the Cheadle Parish Register, the place of his interment is apparently unknown. A weird story was current in the district for nearly two centuries, that the body was brought from London to Cheadle. There had been heavy rains and the streams and rivers were in flood. When they reached a ford, probably on the Mersey, the coffin was torn from the hands of the attendants, and with its lifeless occupant was washed away and never seen again.

The "Long Parliament" of Cromwell was elected in 1656. In July that year there came the little or Barebones (Barbones) Parliament. No burgesses, except from London, and in some cases, one for the county, were summoned. Chester was represented during the "usurpation," by Robert Duckenfield of Dukinfield, Esquire, and Henry Birkenhead of Backford, Esquire. This parliament consisted on a reformed basis of 164 constituencies, by whom 400 members were elected for three years. Small boroughs were disfranchised more unsparingly than in 1832, and the number of county members greatly increased. The elective franchise was placed on such a footing that every man of substance, whether possessed of freehold estate or not, had a vote for the county.

In September 1654 the Protector opened his first parliament. Cheshire was represented by John Bradshaw, Sergeant-at-Law, Chief Justice of Chester, and Sir George Booth of Dunham Massey, Bart., Henry Brooke of Norton, Esquire, and John Crewe of Utkinton, Esquire. In the reign of Charles II., 16th September 1656 to 4th February 1658, the County was represented by Sir Charles Booth of Dunham Massey, Bart., Thomas Marbury of Marbury, Esquire, Richard Legh of Lyme, Esquire, and Peter Brooke of Mere, Esquire; Chester by Edward Bradshaw, Esquire, who was Mayor in 1647. He was thrice married, firstly to the daughter of Bishop Downham, by whom he had no issue; but by two other wives he had a huge quiverful in the shape of nineteen olive branches. In 1649 John Bradshaw was returned in conjunction with Richard Legh, and Chester was represented by Jonathan Ridge and John Griffith, Alderman. The events of this stirring period have been fully dealt with in previous chapters. In 1660 Sir George Booth and Thomas Mainwaring of Over Peover, Esquire, were representatives for the County; and John Radclyffe (Redclyffe or Ratcliffe), Recorder, and William Ince, Esquire, for Chester. Peter Ince was Mayor, 1642-43.

New writs were issued for the Convention Parliament of twelfth, Charles II., which met in May 1661 and continued until 1679. William, Lord Brereton of Leighlin and Peter Venables of Kinderton represented Cheshire; and Sir Thomas Smith and John Radcliffe, Esquire, Chester City. Says one writer: " This Parliament was keen after the loaves and fishes, and was known as the

Pensionary Parliament, and sat much longer than the so-called Long Parliament, much longer, in fact, than any English Parliament but one—for eighteen years." The successor to Lord Brereton, elected in 1664, was Sir Fulke Lucy, a son of Sir Thomas Lucy of Charlecote, Warwickshire, who married into the family of Davenport of Henbury. In 1669 Peter Venables was succeeded by Thomas Cholmondeley, Vale Royal, and Smith and Radcliffe were returned for the City. In 1672-73 an intermediate election took place for Chester, the candidates being Colonel Robert Werden and William Williams, Recorder of the City. It appears to have been conducted with some acrimony, and it was alleged that Williams, in order to secure his election by "hook or by crook," promised in case he was chosen to discharge a debt of £40 the City owed to the king; to lend to the Corporation £300, " free of interest for seven years gratis"; to serve them without salary; and " to spend his estate among them." This wholesale attempt at bribery was followed up by every effort on behalf of Williams. The polling lasted three days, and Werden was elected by a majority of five votes. Later, on the death of Sir Thomas Smith, who had represented the City for a number of years, Williams had his pertinacity rewarded by being elected to fill the vacancy. Williams, as will be seen, took a considerable interest in the affairs of the City. During his recordership he was elected Speaker of the House of Commons, and afterwards became Sir William Williams and the first Baron of Wynnstay. He was Solicitor-General in the reign of Charles II. He conducted the prosecution of the seven Bishops, causing a strong outburst of public resentment. Macaulay, writing of this prosecution, says: " Williams and his friend, Bishop Cartwright (of Chester), retired amid a storm of hisses and insults. For his violence he was universally hated, but the king rewarded him with a baronetcy." A little later his " unblushing forehead and voluble tongue" helped to hound James from the throne, and in six years more he represented the Crown before the four judges, who had been sent down to deal with the men who had been engaged in the " Manchester Plot." The result was acquittal, and once more Williams retired amid " the hisses and execrations of the populace."

After the election which took place in the thirty-first year of Charles II., parliament lasted from March to July 1679. Henry Booth, afterwards second Lord Delamere of Dunham Massey, and Sir Philip Egerton of Oulton were elected for the County; and Sir William Williams, Bart., and Sir Thomas Grosvenor, Bart., for the City. This brief parliament distinguished itself by passing the famous Bill of Exclusion, which assured the Protestant succession to the Crown, and the Habeas Corpus Act. On the dissolution of this parliament a proclamation was issued to meet in October at Westminster. Henry Booth was re-elected, his co-member being Sir Robert Cotton of Combermere, Bart.; and Chester returned the same members as before.

On the death of Charles II. in 1685, Lord Rochester, who made his mark as a poet, but whose effusions were generally of a licentious character, suggested the following epitaph for the dead monarch :—

> "Here lies our Sovereign Lord the King,
> Whose word no man relies on,
> Who never said a foolish thing,
> And never did a wise one."

The first parliament called by James II. met in May 1685, and was dissolved in July 1687, Cheshire being represented by Sir Philip Egerton, Knight, and Thomas Cholmondeley of Vale Royal, Esquire; Chester—Sir Thomas Grosvenor, Bart., and Colonel Robert Werden. This was the year of the Monmouth "Invasion" and other startling happenings. The prorogation took place in November 1685, and was immediately followed by the trial of four Whig leaders of eminence—Hampden (the grandson of the opponent of ship-money), Lord Delamere, Lord Gerard, and Lord Brandon (son of the Earl of Macclesfield). But the spirit of the country was not to be trifled with, and this was emphasised by the trial of the seven Bishops, who refused to read the Declaration of Indulgence in their churches. In the hope of appeasing the people James issued a proclamation convoking a fresh parliament to meet early in the year, but this not having the desired effect, he destroyed the writs and fled to France. The representatives of Cheshire at this time were Sir Robert Cotton of Combermere, Bart., and John Mainwaring of Over Peover, Esquire; Chester—Roger Whitley and George Mainwaring, Esquires. Thus ended the great struggle between king and people for absolute power, which had obtained from the reign of King John to the Accession of William and Mary. James believed in the efficacy of "touching" for the King's Evil, and is said on one occasion to have "touched" no fewer than 800 persons in Chester Cathedral.

After the Coronation of William and Mary writs were issued in 1689 for parliament to meet at Westminster on 20th March 1690. This parliament was dissolved in 1695, and up to 1701 Cheshire was practically represented by the same members. It was in the election for 1701 that bribery and intimidation were practised on a most shameless and extensive scale, the Whigs, it is alleged, carrying their candidates through their "moneyed interest." This reign was brought to an abrupt close by the accident to King William on 8th March 1702, in his fifty-second year. Public lotteries were first opened by this government, from which period till 1824 no session passed without a Lottery Bill being introduced. State lotteries were abolished in October 1826.

The National Debt at the commencement of William's reign was £664,263, which was left as a "legacy" to the country by Charles II. To this William added £17,730,439, which involved an additional annual charge of £1,271,017. From that date (1685) to the end of the reign of George II., during the whole of which time a succession of continental wars had been carried on, it is calculated that no less than 1,920,000 Englishmen had been slain in battle, and the debt had cost up to that time in principal and interest more than £3,500,000,000.

When Anne succeeded to the throne in 1702 she was in her thirty-eighth year. She was the second daughter of James II., by Anne Hyde, daughter of Edward Hyde, Earl of Clarendon, and born, it is said, at Norbury, near Stockport, the old family residence of the Hydes of Hyde and Norbury. Queen Anne was crowned 23rd April 1702, and on 25th May following she prorogued parliament. Meanwhile a fierce battle was taking place in the Scottish parliament on the subject of the union of the two nations. The Queen met her new parliament, 25th October, which turned out to be so completely Tory as to carry all before it. From Cheshire the representatives were :—Sir George Warburton of Arley, Bart., Sir Roger Mostyn of Beeston, Bart.; Chester—Sir Henry Bunbury, Bart., Peter Shakerley, Esquire. The Hon. Langham Booth and John Crewe Offley of Crewe, Esquire, with Bunbury and Shakerley, were the Cheshire representatives in Queen Anne's next parliament, and in this, as in the preceding parliament, party feeling ran high. In this parliament was introduced the Act of Union, which enacted that from 1st May 1707, the two kingdoms of England and Scotland should be for ever united under the name, Great Britain, and that the whole island should be represented by sixteen peers and forty-five commoners.

In the first parliament of Great Britain, which met on 23rd October 1707, it became a question whether it should be deemed a new parliament or not. The new parliament assembled 16th November, and proved " to be much in favour of the Whigs." The Cheshire representatives were again :—The Hon. Langham Booth and John Crewe Offley of Crewe, Esquire; Chester, Sir Henry Bunbury, Bart., and Peter Shakerley, Esquire. In the parliament of 1710 Sir George Warburton of Arley, Bart., and Charles Cholmondeley of Vale Royal, Esquire, represented Cheshire; and Sir Henry Bunbury, Bart., and Peter Shakerley, Esquire, the City. The elections for the new parliament were being " carried on with all the fire and zeal of the two parties. The Tories boasted of their successful efforts to stem the tide of expenditure for the war, to staunch the flow of blood, and restore all the blessings of peace." The Whigs, on the contrary, made the most of their opposition to the Treaty of Commerce with France, which they represented as designed to sacrifice our trade by the insane regard then shown to that country, and declared their zeal for the Protestant succession. Nevertheless, the country sent up a powerful majority, who were growing more and more favourable to the return of the Catholic Pretender, the Chevalier St George. Never, indeed, had the chances of his restoration appeared so great. In this, Anne's last parliament, the Cheshire representatives were :—Sir George Warburton of Arley, Bart., Charles Cholmondeley of Vale Royal, Esquire; Chester—Sir Henry Bunbury, Bart., and Peter Shakerley,

Esquire. After the death of Queen Anne so prompt and energetic were the arrangements adopted for securing the Protestant succession, that the friends of the Pretender were entirely thrown off their guard ; and before they could recover from their consternation at the suddenness of her death and the fall of Bolingbroke, Prince George of Hanover had landed in England, and had been acknowledged by most Continental princes. His first care, to dissolve parliament, coincided entirely with the views of the Ministry. From Cheshire were returned:—Sir George Warburton of Arley, Bart., and Hon. Langham Booth ; Chester—Sir Henry Bunbury, Bart., and Sir Richard Grosvenor, Bart. The Septennial Act was strenuously opposed by the Tories and the Ultra-Liberals in both Houses of Parliament, but it was finally carried in the Lords by a majority of 96 to 61, and in the Commons by 264 to 121, 7th May 1716.

In the new parliament the Cheshire representatives were :—Charles Cholmondeley of Vale Royal, Esquire, and John Crewe, Esquire; Chester—Sir Henry Bunbury, Bart., Sir Richard Grosvenor, Bart. The Cheshire election for this parliament took place 4th April 1722, when three candidates presented themselves, the third being the Hon. Langham Booth, who had sat in the last parliament for the county. In the early days of this parliament one of the chief members of the Government, and one intimately connected with the County of Chester, came in for a large share of public attention in the person of Thomas Parker, Earl of Macclesfield. He had a distinguished career, but abused his office, and was found guilty of fraud in 1725, and heavily fined and imprisoned in the Tower.

In the new parliament of George II., after his accession in 1728, Charles Cholmondeley of Vale Royal, Esquire, and Sir Robert Salusbury Cotton of Combermere, Bart., represented the County ; and Sir Richard Grosvenor, Bart., and Thomas Grosvenor, Esquire, Chester—the first time the city had been represented by two members of the Grosvenor family, both being sons of Sir Thomas Grosvenor, who represented the City during the reigns of Charles II., James II., and William III.

On the death of Sir Richard in June 1731, he was succeeded by his younger brother Robert. Hugh Warburton of Winnington, Esquire, came out as a candidate, but he retired, and Richard Manley of Lache, near Chester, was nominated, but was unable to overthrow the Grosvenor interest. On the death of Sir Thomas, Sir Charles Bunbury, Bart., filled the vacancy. In the new parliament Cheshire remained true to the Whig interest, and in 1735 Cholmondeley, Crewe, Grosvenor, and Bunbury represented the County and City until 1747, when Sir Philip Henry Warburton was returned. The Whig interest continued to predominate, and in 1754 we find the name of Samuel Egerton, Esquire, appearing in conjunction with the Cholmondeleys and the Grosvenors.

During this parliament there were two by-elections, when Thomas Cholmondeley succeeded Charles, and Sir Robert Grosvenor, Thomas Grosvenor, Esquire. George II. died in October 1760, having been created Prince of Wales and Earl of Chester on the death of his father in 1751. On 31st March the House of Commons was dissolved, and Sir Robert Grosvenor, the senior Member for the City, was created Lord Grosvenor. The General Election took place, and, as in former years, bribery was rampant. On the election for Chester something like £30,000 was spent. A new party, the " King's Friends," took an active part in the contest. Their professed object was to liberate the sovereign from " Whig thraldom." The movement started on non-party lines, and being backed by unlimited funds, the Whigs found their influence shaken and began to tremble for their supremacy. It was not removed, for Egerton and Cholmondeley were returned for the County; but the Grosvenor interest carried the day in the City. A more popular candidate than Roger Barnston (T.) could not have been found, but he only received thirty-eight votes.

At the time (1768) this parliament was dissolved politics in this country were in a state of flux, and the outcome of the unrest over a long series of years produced the drastic change of 1832, followed after much agitation by the Reform Act of 1867, based on occupancy and the payment of rates, direct and indirect, the crowning point being reached by the admission of women to the Parliamentary Suffrage in 1918, this privilege being first exercised by them in December of the same year. In 1768 Thomas Grosvenor and Richard Bootle Wilbraham were " elected members for the ancient City without opposition. Immediately afterwards they were carried through the principal streets, attended by great numbers of Freemen, etc., with loud acclamations," and then adjourned to Mr Leech's, the " Plume of Feathers," in Bridge Street, where " sumptuous and elegant entertainment was provided," and at which a numerous company of gentlemen attended. The day concluded " with ringing of bells and every demonstration of joy, and a considerable sum of money was spent amongst the Freemen on the occasion." There was no change in the representation until February 1780, when Sir Robert Salusbury Cotton, Bart., was returned in place of Samuel Egerton of Tatton, Esquire, and in 1790 Robert Grosvenor (Viscount Belgrave) was elected in conjunction with Thomas Grosvenor, as member for Chester, the latter being succeeded by his fourth son, General Thomas Grosvenor.

In 1801 the first census in this country was taken, when it was found that England and Wales contained nine millions of people, Cheshire, by estimation, numbering 107,000, and in 1750, 131,600. In 1802 the representatives of the County were :—Thomas Cholmondeley of Vale Royal, Esquire, and William Egerton of Tatton, Esquire ; and for Chester—Thomas Grosvenor, Esquire, and Robert Grosvenor (Viscount Belgrave), who became Earl of Grosvenor on the death of his father, and was succeeded by Richard

Drax Grosvenor. William Egerton, dying in 1806, was succeeded by Davies Davenport, Esquire. In 1807 John Egerton of Oulton was returned, along with the previous member for Chester, in succession to Richard Drax Grosvenor. In the General Election of 1812, the representatives for Cheshire were:—Wilbraham Egerton of Tatton, Esquire, and Davies Davenport of Capesthorne, Esquire ; and for Chester—Thomas Grosvenor and John Egerton, Esquires. The other candidates were Sir Richard Brooke, Bart., of Norton, and Edward V. Townshend, and the contest cost the Grosvenors £30,000, and the Egertons (of Oulton or West Cheshire) £15,000. Almost every inn and tavern, it is related, was thrown open for entertainment of all comers, with, in many cases, unlimited orders for free supplies of meat and drink of all kinds. As this occurred during the holiday of the great Michaelmas Fair, the result was disorder, riots, and drunkenness. In 1819 the Egertons were completely ousted from the representation of the City of Chester, and notwithstanding that every subsequent election was "hotly contested and dearly bought," they never succeeded in regaining their previous position.

As illustrating the keenness with which these contests were waged at this period, it is on record that one of the Grosvenor family, on returning from the city, was intercepted by a number of his opponent's supporters. They stopped the horses, cut the traces, and threw the carriage bodily over Handbridge into the Dee. The occupant of the vehicle was, luckily, rescued by his supporters, and by them "smuggled" into the "Bear and Billet" Inn, near the Bridge Gate.

CHAPTER XIII.

Parliamentary Cheshire (continued) : Trade depression and disorganisation—Chester " the Golden City "—Beginnings of commercial greatness—Manchester and Liverpool Railway opened—Agitation for Parliamentary reform—A luxurious election—County Divisions formed—Macclesfield and the Brocklehursts—The course of popular representation—The 1868 contest—Cheshire record—Altrincham, Northwich, and other Divisions—Stockport Elections since the Reform Bill—Some humorous features—Pocket Boroughs—Origin of the caucus—Abolition of the Hustings—Strong party feeling—Ballot and heckling—Elections of 1868 and 1918 contrasted—Notices of Cheshire Members of Parliament.

STUDENTS of history will be fully acquainted with the stirring events which attended the opening year of the reign of George IV. As a result of trade depression and disorganisation, bank failures occurred at Macclesfield, Nantwich, and Congleton, bringing down with them many families which had stood high in the commercial world. We find in 1830 Wilbraham Egerton of Tatton, Esq., and E. Davies Davenport of Capesthorne, Esq., returned for the County. Chester City was the scene of another fierce struggle between the Grosvenors and the Egertons of Oulton. The contest commenced on the 9th of June and closed on the 22nd, resulting in Lord Belgrave and the Hon. Robert Grosvenor being elected by small majorities over their Tory opponents, General C. B. Egerton and Mr E. V. Townshend, the figures being 830, 760, 743, and 661. The expenses incurred by the Grosvenor party were estimated at £20,000, and those of the other side, £10,000, giving Chester the right to be called the "golden city." The last parliament of George IV. was dissolved in July 1830, and to the first of William IV. the Hon. Richard Grosvenor and Sir Philip de Malpas Egerton were returned unopposed for the County; and Richard, Viscount Belgrave, and the Hon. Robert Grosvenor for Chester City. In August of the same year a meeting for the nomination of candidates for the County was held at Northwich, the hustings being erected near the Parish Church.

Hustings is a word of old English derivation, literally a house or assembly held by king, earl, or other leader of distinction, and distinct from the "ping" (general assembly) or "folkmoot," alluded to in previous chapters. In London, in early Saxon times, there was a hustings court at which elections were conducted, and where deeds were registered and pleas heard. Previous to 1872 it resolved itself into a temporary platform for the nomination of candidates for parliament. In boroughs the hustings were erected in the market-place, and in counties in front of the buildings where the county business was transacted. At any rate, this was the custom in Cheshire. An unpopular candidate had frequently to beat a hasty retreat from the hustings. We have also heard mention of "a second rate hustings orator," and we have also the assertion of

Lord Morley that "a National candidate has not a chance against a local candidate." On a show of hands, at the above election, Wilbraham Egerton of Tatton, Esq., and Richard, Viscount Belgrave, were duly elected. This year was memorable for the opening of the Manchester and Liverpool Railway.

The Hon. Robert Grosvenor had accepted the office of Comptroller of the Household, but omitted to subscribe the oaths on taking his seat after re-election; his election became void, and he incurred a penalty of £500 for every day he sat in the House. He was relieved from pecuniary liability by the passing by parliament of a Bill of Indemnity.

In the year 1831 there was much industrial and other unrest in the county. Amongst others "Orator Hunt" visited Stockport and delivered a "violent" speech against the Ministerial Measure of Reform.

There was no contest for the County in 1831. The election opened at the Shire Hall, but as it could not accommodate the large number of spectators— about 10,000—an adjournment was made to the Castle Yard, where Lord Belgrave and Mr George Wilbraham of Delamere House were elected. After returning thanks they were placed in two "splendid" chairs, and conveyed in triumph to the Royal Hotel, where dinner was provided for the Sheriff, members, and friends. About 2000 dinners were provided for the freeholders at the different hotels and inns in the city, a bottle of wine being allowed for each man. For Chester, Lord Robert Grosvenor and Foster Cunliffe Offley, Esq., were returned. All these members supported the Reform Bill of 1832, the passage of which was punctuated with riots in all parts of the kingdom, the king himself being mobbed in London. Amongst the first batch of peers to be created to secure its passage were Robert, Earl Grosvenor, who was made Marquess of Westminster, and Sir Edward Price Lloyd, Bart., Flint, Baron Mostyn of Mostyn, etc. By this Act fifty-six boroughs in England were disfranchised, thirty were reduced to one member, twenty-two boroughs sent two members, including Stockport and Macclesfield, and other striking changes took place. On the death of Mr Offley in 1832, two candidates were put forward for the City—Mr John Finchett Maddock, Town Clerk and Under Sheriff, and Mr Edward Davies Davenport of Calveley Hall. There was strong objection to Mr Maddock on account of his official position, but he was returned. He had the support of many Tories, who declined to vote for such "a rank radical" as Mr Davenport.

Under the Reform Act the County was formed into two divisions— the northern and the southern. The northern division included the whole of the Hundreds of Macclesfield and Bucklow; the southern the whole of the Hundreds of Broxton, Eddisbury, Nantwich, Northwich, and Wirral, together with the City of Chester. The courts for the election of Knights of the Shire were held at Knutsford for the northern division, and at Chester for the southern division. The polling places were—Northern: Knutsford, Stockport, Macclesfield, and Runcorn ; Southern : Chester, Nantwich, Northwich, Sandbach, and Birkenhead.

The great Reform Act admitted the middle classes to power, and under its provisions the House of Commons began to represent more widely the true interests and popular sentiment of the nation. The principle of popular representation was enlarged by the Reform Act of 1867, by which the balance of power was transferred to the small shopkeeper class, who were now endowed for the first time with the franchise. A further extension of the principle took place in consequence of the Act of 1884-85, the effect of which was to enfranchise the working classes and to transform the House of Commons into a strong, powerful, and purely democratic assembly.

Although many important events transpired from a national point of view after the passing of this great Act, the parliamentary history of Cheshire was tame to a degree. The Grosvenors, the Cholmondeleys, and the Stanleys influenced the representation, if they did not monopolise it, for a number of years.

In 1859 William Tatton Egerton, Esq., was made a peer of the realm, and he was succeeded by his son, the Hon. Wilbraham Egerton of Rostherne Manor, who was returned at successive elections until the death of Lord Egerton of Tatton. This year the representatives of the southern division were Sir Philip Egerton and Mr John Tollemache, afterwards Lord Tollemache of Peckforton. There was no change in 1865.

The year 1868 brought about Gladstone's famous campaign for the disestablishment of the Church in Ireland. He was then sixty-one years of age, but years seemed to have no effect on this versatile statesman. He was insistent in season and out of season. He was fiercest in his denunciation of "an alien Church in Ireland," which culminated in one of the most sensational and hotly contested general elections ever known in the annals of our history.

The nomination of parliamentary candidates is now a simple and peaceful matter. What it was like before the Ballot Act of 1872 abolished open-air nominations may be gathered from the debate which preceded the passing of that Act. One member declared he had spent as much money hiring prize-fighters to protect him on nomination day as any man in the House, and one of the most efficient was "a gentleman who was always clothed as a clergyman of the Church of England, but who was really an ex-champion of England, Bendigo by name." Even at this time pocket boroughs had not ceased from troubling. These were generally the heritage of some aristocratic son-in-law of a wealthy peer. In the early days those who were fortunate enough to turn them to good account were in the possession of from £4000 to £5000 per annum.

Although the ballot was an institution in the days of Greece and Rome, and attended apparently with good results, there were strong objections urged against its adoption in this country. It was long regarded as a privilege of the free and upright Englishman that he should give his vote openly in favour of the man he thought best fitted to represent him in parliament as by show of hands in the old hustings days. There was, above all, it was argued, something underhand about it. Gone were the days when the votes recorded were published hourly amid exultation of the "Blues" on the one hand, and depression amongst the "Yellows" on the other, or *vice versa* The country was " going to the dogs " when this could not be done. It was certainly the cause of more free fights and rowdyism than in these days of glorious uncertainty caused by delayed declaration of the poll. The ballot was the fourth point urged by the Chartists. For generations it formed the subject of contention between the two great parties in the land, until in 1872 an Act was passed by the Liberal Government that at Parliamentary and Municipal Elections, except for the Universities, the ballot should be employed. It has worked well, and in spite of the fulminations of extreme politicians, coupled with the terrible probable curse to the British constitution if it were adopted, " nobody seemed a penny the worse."

In Scotland " heckling " is a common practice, which has developed of late years in England. A Cheshire lawyer, hailing from Runcorn, and who afterwards held important ministerial rank, had a capital way of dealing with this class of interruption. His *modus operandi* was as follows : the customary sheaf of questions would be handed up, which he would scan in a most leisurely fashion. Generally a candidate would read each question aloud, and then reply to it—a tedious process, which evoked interruption and often adverse comment. The candidate referred to above would answer them in this fashion, without reading the question : " No. 1, ' No '; No. 2, ' Yes, I would be disposed to support that.' " and so on, and finished the roll before his spellbound audience could recover its breath. The rule that questions should be written was a salutary one and had the effect of limiting the time occupied in conducting an election meeting.

Great difficulties had to be overcome, but these gradually disappeared under an enlarged franchise. Still there was a plentiful crop of " carpet baggers." Where they came from was " wropt in mystery." In many parts of the country they were successfully foisted on the constituencies, but they found no resting place in Cheshire. Those were the days of the caucus. This word is a corruption of " caulkers' meeting," which was the title given to the meetings of an association of men connected with the ships at Boston (Mass.), who were very active in getting up opposition to England just previous to the American War of Independence. Several citizens were killed in a disturbance with the soldiers, and a meeting was held in the " caulk house to concert measures for redress." America has given us some quaint slang—for instance, the word " buncombe," denoting false sentiment, absurd ideas. It arose out of a speech by a North Carolina Senator, named Buncombe, whose name is thus for ever written on the scroll of fame in this connection.

Cheshire seemed in those rousing days to be divided into two hostile camps, each intent on ousting the other from power. Mid-Cheshire especially was the storm centre of conflicting interests, and was enveloped in " election dust " arising from hustings combats. All elections were keenly contested. Both sides flung out their old battle cries, claiming that " Codlin " and not " Short " was the true friend of the " Free and Independent electors of the enlightened constituencies," whose votes they made such magnificent efforts to obtain.

The contest in the Mid-Cheshire Division was memorable for bringing to the front a young Whig politician of great promise in the person of the Hon. John Leicester Warren, the only son of Lord de Tabley, in the Liberal interest. Frantic appeals were made at this period to " the Tory vassals " to cast off " chains and slavery." Amongst the gentlemen thus appealed to was the Rev. Henry Green, Unitarian minister at Knutsford. He bluntly told his would-be mentors that he had freedom enough. He lived under his own vine and fig tree, none daring to make him afraid. He was friends with his neighbours. They did not oppress him, and he was content. The climax was reached, however, when at the close of a peroration at the hustings Mr Warren invited the " down-trodden men " of Cheshire to " Awake, arise, or be for ever fallen ! " To couple them and their fortunes with Lucifer's was regarded as somewhat unfortunate ; but the farmers were as insensible to the beauties of Milton as to the arguments of Mr Warren and voted solid for Mr George Cornwall Legh and the Hon. Wilbraham Egerton (afterwards Earl Egerton of Tatton). At a bye-election of 1873 the Liberals were again unsuccessful. The late Colonel Egerton Leigh was pitted against Mr G. W. Latham, who took politics very seriously. Colonel Leigh looked upon an election without fun as " beef without mustard," and was endowed with pregnant wit. " Do you believe in the secrecy of the ballot ? " asked a fierce interrogator one night. Very pat came the reply, " I believe in the sneakrecy of the ballot," and Mr Interrogator sank to rise no more, overwhelmed by the roar of laughter which followed. Mr Latham also told the Cheshire magnates many distasteful truths which did not tend to increase his popularity. On the polling day Colonel Leigh secured the handsome majority of 1390 over his opponent. There was no contest in 1874, and the supposed " down-trodden " farmers were left severely alone. Cheshire did not then waver much in its old political faith. In 1884 and 1885 Mr Piers Egerton Warburton and the Hon. Alan de Tatton Egerton were returned, and on the formation of the Knutsford division the last named gentleman scored an easy victory. He was succeeded by Mr J. A. King (L.) and Sir Alan Sykes (C.), the present member.

Since 1832, when the first Reform Act was passed, no parliamentary return relating to Macclesfield has appeared which has not shown a Brocklehurst as one of its members—always on the Liberal side. John Ryle, banker, an honoured name in Macclesfield, headed the poll on the first occasion, John Brocklehurst coming second on the list. For six years he stood at the head of the poll, being run closely by Edward Christopher Egerton for three years, until 1859 when Egerton headed the poll by two votes! In the Conservative debâcle of 1868, Wm. Coare Brocklehurst headed the poll, with David Chadwick as a fellow member—the Conservative William Meriton Eaton, coming a close third with a small minority of 188 votes, thus evidencing the keenness of the contest. Both Brocklehurst and Chadwick were returned in 1874 and 1880. In the last named year, after a searching inquiry by a Royal Commission, the borough was disfranchised. The two election agents were sentenced to terms of imprisonment for countenancing " bribery and corruption," and some thousands of voters were struck off the register. Macclesfield division was merged in the Macclesfield division of the County, under the Redistribution of Seats Act in 1885.

Stockport, like Macclesfield, was one of those populous boroughs brought into existence in 1832. The name of Marsland at Stockport was one to conjure with. The first was a Liberal, and it is not surprising that there should be another Marsland (a major), who represented the opposite side in politics, being run in the Conservative interest. We find the honoured name of Lloyd —John Horatio to wit—running in double harness with Thomas Marsland as a Liberal. Elections then occupied several days. Great excitement prevailed at this election, and in the ebullition of so-called popular feeling there was a great deal of rowdyism and window smashing. On the second day, as the result of a coalition between the committees of Thomas Marsland and Lloyd, these gentlemen were returned. Since then Stockport has never taken its elections sadly, and some seventy years ago one man was killed in a street fight.

In the summer of 1837 Richard Cobden, the apostle of Free Trade, ventured his fortunes in the stormy realm of politics, but failed to score a triumph, and the Borough was represented by the two Marslands, Liberal and Conservative. Four years afterwards, in June 1841, Liberalism scored heavily, the Conservative Marsland being at the bottom of the poll, with 218 fewer votes than his Liberal namesake. Cobden came a good second, being only 26 votes behind his fellow member. In 1847, however, he headed the poll with 642 votes, his companion being a Conservative, James Heald, who stood high in the estimation of the inhabitants. At this election, John West, who was courageous enough to contest this borough as a Chartist—and he had evidently supporters equally so—received 14 votes! Cobden was brought forward at this time for the West Riding of Yorkshire, and being duly elected for the important and widespread constituency, he resigned Stockport and sat for the former. The vacancy was secured by another Liberal, James Kershaw, who beat his

Conservative opponent, Major Marsland, by 23 votes. In 1864, on Alderman Kershaw's death, Sir Edwin Watkin, a rising railway magnate, was elected to fill the vacancy, and in 1865 he again headed the poll by a fair majority.

At the General Election of 1868, which followed an extension of the franchise, a Conservative, Major William Tipping, who had taken a prominent part in the political affairs of the borough, headed the poll. Sir Edward Watkin was also returned on this occasion.

From this period Stockport entered on an enlarged political career. Liberalism was in the ascendant in 1885, when a surprise came in the return of two Conservatives—Mr Louis John Jennings, and that sturdy political veteran, Major Tipping, who always warned his hearers never " to get flabby," an old-fashioned phrase surely, but pregnant with good advice. Mr Jennings, a pleasant spoken, unassuming gentleman, an Anglo-American journalist, was sent from London to support the Conservative cause. This very fact apparently caused him to be held cheap by his opponents. His opening address in public did not possess any particular feature. There was no display of rhetorical fireworks. But as the contest developed and party feeling waxed warmer, he displayed qualities unsuspected by friend and foe alike.

The prime plank in his platform was the pensions scandal, which had been often brought before Parliament, but had received scant shrift from a hidebound official autocracy. He declared publicly that the system must go, and that pensions should not be continued from generation to generation. This secured a sympathetic hearing from many Liberals, who were of the same way of thinking, but towards the close he shone conspicuously at his meetings in which he had the support, amongst others, of Lord Randolph Churchill, who, by asserting at the outset that " of the making of speeches there was no end," secured the cordial hearing of an audience at one time showing, probably through overcrowding at the back of the hall, a somewhat hostile temper. But the climax came towards the close when Mr Jennings roused his hearers to fever heat on the subject of the defence of the Empire and its unity, and Mrs Jennings evoked a perfect tornado of cheering when she draped her husband in a Union Jack! From that time the Stockport election was regarded by the Conservatives, " as good as won." His certainty of victory reflected itself in a considerable degree on his fellow candidate, Major Tipping, and falsified to a great extent the assertion that an outsider " had no chance against a local candidate."

In 1892 honours were divided between Sir Joseph Leigh and Mr Jennings, the other candidates, Liberal and Conservative alike, being left in the cold. Messrs Leigh and Jennings were again returned in 1895. The whirligig of time showed the Conservatives again in the ascendant in the return of Messrs Whiteley and Melville. Sir Joseph Leigh and Mr J. Roskill were the defeated candidates.

In 1900 Sir Joseph Leigh (C.) and Mr B. V. Melville (L.) were returned ; Messrs Green (L.) and Hillier (C.) falling " with their backs to the field and their face to the foe." In 1906 and for some years afterwards comparative peace reigned, Mr G. J. Wardle, the Labour candidate, and Mr J. Duckworth being returned by a very substantial majority over Mr H. Barnston and the Hon. H. O'Neill, the Unionist candidates. With the unopposed return of Mr G. J. Wardle, Labour, and Mr Spenser Leigh Hughes, Coalition Liberal candidate in 1918, there came an end to the political history of the Borough of Stockport for the time being.

For a long period in Chester the election of corporate officers was carried on, with rare exceptions, on a political basis, both in municipal and parliamentary matters, not forgetting an ignoble part played by what was known as the " Kitchen Corporation," which had its own mayors and sheriffs, and often influenced the legitimate election of the citizens to the City Council. For a comparatively long period there was little change, and it is remarkable that from the passing of the Reform Bill until 1868, no Conservative represented Chester in parliament.

In 1865 the rising hope of the house of Hawarden, Mr Herbert Gladstone, now Lord Gladstone, was returned. At one election meeting, held at a later period, he scored heavily by terming a certain section of his opponents "nincompoops." This word tickled the audience immensely, and gave rise to much amusement in the city. It was at the 1868 election that Mr Henry Cecil Raikes, grandson of Chancellor Raikes, and a barrister on the Cheshire circuit, fought and won what, judging from previous contests, appeared to be a "forlorn hope," and came within 56 votes of Earl Grosvenor, who polled 2275 against the 2219 of Mr Raikes. He had been an unsuccessful candidate three years before, and was now the recipient of many congratulations on his victory from all parts of the country

In the following year Earl Grosvenor assumed the title of Marquess of Westminster on the death of his father, and as the Hon. Norman L'Aigle Grosvenor did not offer himself, Mr Raikes was returned at the head of the poll. The Right Hon. John G. Dodson, the Government nominee, came second, while a worthy and esteemed citizen, Sir Thomas Gibbons Frost, who had been knighted on the occasion of the visit of the Prince of Wales to open the new Town Hall a few years before, was a close third to Mr Dodson. The election which took place in 1880 will be long remembered in Chester. By the older generation of citizens then living the contest was likened to a revival of the ante-Reform contests. A petition was presented against the return of the successful candidates, which was heard before Mr Justice Lush and Mr Justice Manisty. After a hearing extending over five days, the members were unseated, and the report stated that there was reason to believe that " corrupt practices extensively prevailed." An inquiry into this matter lasting several weeks followed, and 700 or 800 voters were disfranchised for seven years for "treating" and other illegal practices. Chester remained unrepresented in parliament until January 1886. Under the Representation of the People Act, 1885, the city became a one member constituency. In 1886 Dr B. W. Foster, a well-known politician at that time, was returned, defeating Mr Robert Armstrong Yerburgh by a small majority. On the introduction of the Home Rule Bill, or, as it was termed, "the Better Government of Ireland Bill," when the Liberal Government resigned, Mr Yerburgh was returned. In 1872 he defeated Baron Halkett, and in 1895 was returned unopposed. In 1900 he gained a substantial majority over his Liberal opponent, Mr H. Idris, but in 1906 Mr A. Mond was elected by 47 votes over Mr Yerburgh. In the first parliament of George V., 1910, Mr Yerburgh regained the seat, and at the bye-election in February 1916, Sir Owen C. Phillips, K.C.M.G., was returned unopposed. In 1918 Sir Owen contested the seat as a Coalition Unionist, being returned by a majority of 5050 over his Liberal opponent, and 7244 over the Labour champion.

In 1885 Crewe became a division of itself. So far as Crewe itself was concerned there had been for many years an almost overwhelming preponderance of Liberalism, and naturally there was the utmost interest manifested not only in Cheshire but the country generally in the contest. A resident in the district, and a thorough going Liberal of the then modern school, was brought forward in the person of Mr G. W. Latham, who had contested Mid-Cheshire previously. Apart from his public services as a magistrate and Vice-Chairman of Quarter Sessions, Chairman of the District Highway Board, and founder of a Reformatory on his estate at Bradwall, he deserved well of the community. Many of the meetings he had addressed in Mid-Cheshire were often stormiest of the stormy, but at Crewe his reception was cordial in the extreme. His opponent, Mr O. L. Stephen, fought pluckily, but the Liberal element was too strong, and Mr Latham received what was regarded as a fitting reward of lengthy political service in being returned to parliament by a fair majority. He was again returned in 1885–86.

In 1892 Mr M'Laren (L.) was returned, and he scored yet another victory in 1894. In 1895 there was an unexpected and, for such a constituency, a remarkable turn-round, in the return of the Hon. A. R. Ward (C.), who was victorious by 550 votes. On Mr Ward's retirement there was another contest for the seat in the first parliament of King Edward VII., in 1900, when Mr J. Tomkinson, a representative Liberal and member of a county family which for years had been identified with the banking interests of the county, and which had survived the terrible crisis of 1832, was brought forward. He had a majority of 1199 over his Conservative opponent, Mr J. E. Reiss. Crewe remained faithful to the Liberal cause up to 1910, when, as a result of a bye-election in December, Mr E. Y. Craig (U.) was returned to the second parliament of King George V., the previous election to the first parliament having taken place early in the same year. In 1918 Sir Joseph Davies won the seat as a Coalition Liberal by a majority over his Labour opponent of 2953.

Hyde formed part of the East Cheshire Division, and here in 1885 Mr Thomas Gair Ashton, a popular local manufacturer and a Liberal stalwart, defeated Colonel William John Legh, who had been returned previously for the East Cheshire Division in 1880. Mr Ashton retained his seat for the Liberal party in 1886, but in 1892 he gave pride of place to Mr J. W. Sidebotham, who, like his opponent, was a popular local man, and who, after holding the seat at the 1895 election, resigned and was succeeded by Mr E. Chapman, who defeated Mr J. F. L. Brunner in 1900. Mr C. D. Schwann, a well-known Manchester merchant, afterwards defeated Mr Chapman by 63 votes.

Stalybridge, prior to 1886, was given as a Lancashire constituency. That year brought out two strong local candidates, in Mr Tom Harrop Sidebottom and Mr William Summers, Mr Sidebottom being returned. He was again successful in the succeeding contests of 1892, 1894, and 1895. The march of events was very rapid. He was succeeded in 1900 by Mr (afterwards Sir) M. White Ridley, who was in turn defeated by a small majority, a strong local candidate in Mr J. F. Cheetham, who was a member of the first Cheshire County Council, being nominated in opposition, and whose public services were thought to be recognised when he was returned by a majority of 454 over his Unionist opponent. Mr J. Wood turned the tables again in 1910, when he defeated Mr A. H. Bright (L.), a descendant of John Bright, whom the *Times* deservedly characterised as the People's Tribune.

With two exceptions, in 1906 and 1910, Birkenhead has returned a Conservative since its formation in 1861, its first member being Mr John Laird, a time-honoured name in the constituency. Mr Laird was returned at every election up to 1874, and on his decease he was succeeded by Mr David M'Iver, a well-known Liverpool shipowner. The latest representatives, Mr A. Bigland and Lieut.-Colonel Grayson, were returned as Coalition Unionists by a huge majority over their Liberal and Labour opponents in 1918.

The Northwich Division was created at the partition of Mid-Cheshire. From the earliest times the towns of Northwich and Runcorn had possessed a strong savour of Liberalism, but this was to a great extent neutralised by the Conservative element in the country districts. Under old conditions, especially in the northern portion of Mid-Cheshire, it had been strong enough to maintain Conservative supremacy. Very few people would have undergone the ordeal, however, through which the candidates of that colour went through at Northwich on the day of election, when they made a tour of the constituency. It was distinctly hostile, although the result was in their favour. In 1880 Mr

John Tomlinson Brunner, a powerful local candidate, was run in the Liberal interest for the newly formed division, being opposed by Mr W. H. Verdin, the head of an old established firm of salt manufacturers, who championed the Conservative cause, and held, like his opponent, in the highest esteem.

At this election Mr Brunner was called a "foreigner" by his opponents. He aptly replied, " My father was Swiss, my mother was a Manx woman, and I was born at Liverpool." He was a son of the Rev. John Brunner, who came from Zurich, in Switzerland, and established a private school in Everton, where Mr Brunner, as he then was, was educated, along with many others who afterwards made a mark in the " Ships, colonies, and commerce " doctrine for which Liverpool was, and is, justly celebrated.

In the three bye-elections throughout the country in 1887, of which Northwich was one, Mr Brunner was opposed by Lord Henry Grosvenor, the House of Westminster having broken with the Liberal party on Home Rule. This election he described as the greatest fight he had ever had in the division. It created, in common with the boroughs of Burnley and Spalding, the greatest excitement in Great Britain, and the victory at Northwich was celebrated in Ireland by the lighting of numerous bonfires.

Another election in Northwich, which attracted national attention, was the contest in which Colonel North, "the Nitrate King," espoused the Conservative cause against Mr Brunner. Colonel North candidly told the electors he knew nothing of politics, but he was the owner of some splendid racehorses, which had carried his colours to victory in classic races, and this undoubtedly appealed to the sporting instincts of many of his opponents. He cut rather a poor figure upon the platform, and Sir John, who had the year before been created a Baronet for national and local services, maintained and increased his hold on the constituency, being returned by the substantial majority of 1792. Sir John fought several other contested elections, and was succeeded by his son, now Sir J. F. L. Brunner, Bart., on his retirement in 1910. The son, however, was defeated in 1918, by the Coalition Unionist, Lieut.-Commander H. Dewhurst, greatly to the surprise of local Liberals and of many of the opposite school of thought, who felt a deep sense of gratitude to a family which had so greatly contributed to the progress and welfare of the district.

Within the borders of the Altrincham Division is to be found a constituency which, for intelligence, education, and wealth is not equalled for its size in the United Kingdom. It formed a portion of the old North Cheshire and Mid-Cheshire Divisions. In the days of the old North Cheshire period, it was represented, and represented worthily, as contemporary records prove, by a scion of the House of Egerton of Tatton. Then followed, on a redistribution of seats, Mid-Cheshire, embracing a wide area, of which Runcorn was the western termination, Northwich the south, Sale the north, and on the easterly side the Staffordshire hills overlooked the colliery district of Odd Rode. Included in its borders were the important towns of Altrincham, Congleton, Middlewich, and Sandbach, all varied in commercial and agricultural interests, and cosmopolitan in their connections.

The formation of the Altrincham Division was followed by the General Election of 1885, and this introduced Mr John Brooks to the constituency. The contest was fraught with interesting issues. Both sides were virtually in the dark as to the voting tendencies of the electors, and it became necessary to select a man who, while able to give an eloquent account of his political faith, should at the same time have some influence in the County. Mr John Brooks, after an exceptionally brilliant University career, gave ample evidence of conspicuous talent, which might be devoted to promoting the welfare and prosperity of the Empire. The Liberals appeared to have tired of local champions and turned with yearning hearts to the Metropolis for a candidate. He turned up in the person of Mr I. S. Leadam, a barrister of more than ordinary ability.

Mr John Brooks won a conspicuous victory in that year, and his career seemed bright with promise. Then came a dark day in March 1886, bringing with it the grim but startling intelligence that his spirit had passed into the unknown. No man was more clearly sacrificed on the altar of public duty; and no man, apart from his politics, was more sincerely mourned by all classes in the constituency. The work he did remained after him. The foundations he laid were deep and sound, and rendered the labours of his successors in carrying on the political work comparatively easy. The eyes of the leaders of the party naturally turned to his uncle, Sir William Cunliffe Brooks, Bart., not only as the embodiment of an English gentleman, but as a model parliamentary representative, whose experience of Cheshire was extremely valuable. His address issued after his selection by the Conservative party contained generous testimony to the self-denying labours of his nephew. Sir William was returned at the General Election in July 1886, by a majority of 583, and retired in 1892.

After a period of comparative calm Mr Coningsby Ralph Disraeli, only son of Mr Ralph Disraeli, and nephew of the Right Hon. Benjamin Disraeli, Earl of Beaconsfield, was introduced to the constituency in 1892, and received a warm welcome from the Conservative and Unionist party. Mr Leadam again ran, for the third and last time, mainly on the Home Rule ticket. The fight was a strenuous one on both sides, but Mr Leadam was again defeated by 708 votes.

The year 1895 witnessed another General Election with Mr A. M. Latham, son of the first member for Crewe, and a barrister practising on the North Wales circuit, but his attitude on the Women's Suffrage question did not apparently please the ladies of the division, with the result that Mr Disrael was returned by an increased majority. The Liberals were not even then disheartened. Mr E. F. Alford, who had formerly a local connection with the division, was brought forward, with the same result, Mr Disraeli being returned by a majority of 1508.

The Liberals then cast about for a suitable local candidate, and their choice ultimately fell on Mr W. J. Crossley, who had taken a prominent part in public and philanthropic work in Altrincham and Manchester. The Free Trade question bulked largely before the public, even overshadowing for the moment that of Home Rule. This caused some disunion in the Conservative ranks, and Mr Crossley was returned by a majority of 2691, to the delight of the Liberal party, who found that their persistent efforts to win in this important constituency had at last met with a triumphant result. Mr Crossley was created a Baronet, but he was not permitted undisturbed possession of the seat, and was again opposed in 1910, when he defeated Viscount Bury, a grandson of Earl Egerton of Tatton, by a majority of 901. Political events moved rapidly, and in a few months Sir William had his "Waterloo," being defeated by a narrow majority by Mr J. R. Kebtey Fletcher, head of a Liverpool provision house. Major G. C. Hamilton, the present member, defeated the Hon. L. U. Kay Shuttleworth, eldest son of Lord Shuttleworth, who subsequently met a glorious death on the bloodstained soil of France during the war. Major Hamilton was again returned by a large majority at the General Election of 1918.

The newly formed division of Wallasey, which included a portion of Wirral, was won by the Coalition Unionist (Dr Macdonald) during the war.

The General Election of December 1918, the first one-day polling in the United Kingdom, was characterised by an almost entire absence of excitement, the rarity of the display of party colours, the lack of vehicles for the conveyance of voters. The enfranchisement of women added an element of "glorious uncertainty" in the results, and they took full advantage, certainly in Cheshire, of their newly born privilege. The Coalition party, made up of Unionists, Liberals, and a small number, ten in all, of the National Democratic party, who were returned, totalled 484; and the non-Coalition party, composed of Labour (59), Unionists (48), Sinn Feiners (73), Liberals (26), and the remainder (16) made up of National party, Irish Nationalists, Independents, etc., totalled 222. The Coalitionists swept the board and scored the most overwhelming triumph ever recorded in Britain's political annals. The Coalition majority was 262, and Mr Lloyd George's triumph over the pacifists was complete. The oldest voter on the register was "Granny" Lambert, of Edmonton aged 105, who had never heard of Mr Lloyd George and did not know who he was. She was too tired to walk to the poll. On the other hand, a boy four years old, and a girl of nine voted in the neighbourhood of London.

CHESHIRE: ITS TRADITIONS AND HISTORY

BRIEF NOTICES OF CHESHIRE MEMBERS.

Altrincham.—Major C. George C. Hamilton, J.P., Coalition Unionist; son of the Ven. Archdeacon George Hans Hamilton, D.D., and Lady Louisa Hamilton; born 1877; educated at Aysgarth and Charterhouse; married Eleanor C. Simon of Didsbury; engineer. He represented Altrincham from May 1913; J.P., Cheshire; Major, Queen's Westminster Rifles; Director of Enrolment, National Service, 1917; Controller of Contracts Claims, Ministry of Munitions, 1918; Parliamentary Private Secretary to the Ministry of Pensions, 1919 (unpaid).

Birkenhead.—Mr Alfred Bigland sat as Unionist for Birkenhead from December 1910. He raised the Birkenhead Bantam Battalions of the Cheshire Regiment. He was appointed Controller of the Oils and Fats Branch of the Ministry of Munitions, and undertook a mission to the United States in connection with food supply and distribution.

Lieut.-Colonel H. M. Grayson is head of Messrs H. & C. Grayson, Limited, shipbuilders. He was appointed Director of Ship Repairs under the British Board of Admiralty, and after having organised the ship-repairing yards in the United Kingdom, was charged with similar work in Allied countries and the British Dominions.

Knutsford.—Sir Alan Sykes, member of an old Stockport family, was elected as a Unionist in 1910. He was formerly Lieut.-Colonel commanding the 6th Battalion Cheshire Regiment.

Chester.—Sir Owen Philips, G.C.M.G., is brother to Lord St Davids, and Chairman of the Royal Mail Steam Packet Co., and other companies. He became Unionist member for Chester in 1916, having sat for Pembroke and Haverford West. He has rendered public service in many capacities. He was Chairman of the Unionist Committee on enemy influence, which issued several important reports. In Parliament he rendered signal service to National Shipping interests.

Crewe.—Sir Joseph Davies was adopted as prospective Liberal candidate for Crewe in 1913. He rendered assistance to the Government in various ways during the war, and in recognition of his services he was made a K.O.B.E. In January last he took part in an important British Labour Mission.

Eddisbury.—The name of Barnston has been known for a long period in Cheshire, where the family has been located for centuries. Its members have rendered many valuable public services. Major Barnston has seen active service in France, and was previously a captain in the Cheshire Yeomanry. He was returned unopposed. He was also the first to receive from the people of the township of Farndon a memento of his services overseas in the war in the shape of a gold pendant with monogram bearing the inscription "Farndon's Thanks, 1914-1918."

Macclesfield.—John Remer was the son of the late John Sutton Remer; born 1883, at Waterloo, near Liverpool, and educated privately; married, 1912, Beatrice Humphreys Crummack; timber merchant and sawmill proprietor; President, North Wales Timber Merchants' Association; Director of John Remer & Co., Ltd., Liverpool, 1 Lombard Court, E.C. 3, and "Elmhurst," Blundellsands, Liverpool. He was returned as Coalition Unionist for Macclesfield.

Northwich.—Lieut.-Commander Harry Dewhurst is one of the firm of Messrs Dewhurst, Cotton Spinners and Manufacturers. He was a member of the Cheshire Hunt. He served during the War as remount officer in England and France. Later he acted as King's Messenger to the Admiralty, with the rank of Lieut.-Commander.

Stockport.—Mr Spenser L. Hughes has represented the Stockport constituency since 1910. He was educated at Woodhouse Grove School, near Leeds, and as a journalist has been connected with several London newspapers.

Mr George James Wardle, the second member for Stockport, entered the service of the Midland Railway Company as a clerk at fifteen years of age, and in 1898 was appointed editor of the *Railway Review*. He has represented Stockport since 1906, and was Parliamentary Secretary to the Board of Trade. Both he and Mr Spenser Leigh Hughes were returned unopposed in 1918.

Stalybridge and Hyde.—Sir John Wood, born in 1857, was created first Baronet in 1918, and is the only son of Sir John Hill Wood of Whitfield, Derbyshire. He was called to the Bar of the Inner Temple in 1880. He is a D.L., and J.P. for Herefordshire, Derbyshire, and Suffolk, and was High Sheriff of Herefordshire in 1900. He was Lieut.-Colonel and Honorary Colonel of the former 4th Battalion Cheshire Regiment, V.D., Commandant of the 5th Cheshire Volunteer Regiment. He has been a member for Stalybridge since 1910.

Wallasey.—Dr Bouverie F. P. Macdonald, well-known medical practitioner. During the war he worked on seventy-one committees, including the Wirral Recruiting Committee, Local National Relief Fund, Committee of Soldiers', Sailors' and Firemen's Association, and Advisory Committee.

Full figures of the results in the various Cheshire Divisions will be found in the Appendix to this work, which are given in the list commencing with the year 1832.

CHAPTER XIV.

Local Government is old as the hills (almost)—Court Leets and view of Frank Pledge—Jurisdiction of Court Leets—Two Welshmen hanged—Market lookers and ale tasters—Penalties against brewers and bakers—Charters of Incorporation of Boroughs—Origin of the Poor Law—Some of its humorous features—Overseers and their duties—Formation of Poor Law Unions—Lighting, Watching, and other Acts—County Councils, a social revolution—Urban and Rural District Councils and their functions—Constitution of the Cheshire County Council—First election on party lines—Mr Gladstone's approval—Polling for the first Council in 1889—Small Conservative majority—Incidents at the first Council meeting—Election of Aldermen—Presentation of portrait to Mr Duncan Graham—Election of Mr George Dixon to the Chair—His subsequent services—The present composition and scope of County Council work, etc.

LOCAL government is as old as the hills—almost. From the dawn of civilisation, when a coherent community was formed, efforts are apparent in the way of self-government. This was the germ of mighty consequences to follow, the effect of which was unknown to those strugglers for a higher form of life and living. A famous historian of the last century says, with truth, that change has become the law of our present condition, that it is identified with energy and moral health; to cease to change is to lose place in the great race; and to pass away from off the earth with the same convictions which we found when we entered it, is to have missed the best object for which we now seem to exist. We find this principle reflected in English history. The township or village was the primary and perfect type of English life, domestic, social, and political. In remote times when population was small and scattered, the moot hill, or sacred tree, was the meeting place of the inhabitants, and as it changed with their increasing knowledge, and changes indicated above, we get the witenagemot or meeting of wise men (witans), the gathering of ealdormen as representing the people. Out of this, under the Normans, we evolve our parliament or parliamentum. It is in this most interesting phase of our history that we have the Court Leet. The leet was originally spelt "laet," and he was above the condition of a slave. He was represented in the witenagemot by the lord whose land he tilled, and to whom he owed suit and service. These courts were common in Cheshire, as at Macclesfield, Stockport, Congleton, etc., but they have almost fallen into desuetude, though the old custom of meeting, styled "A Court Leet and View of Frank Pledge and Court Baron," is carried on in the County. The most important, that at Halton, near Runcorn, is undoubtedly the oldest, its records dating back to 1347, though it is believed that they go back about 660 years. It had formerly a wide jurisdiction, embracing most of the northerly part of Cheshire, and portions of Lancashire, including Widnes and Farnworth. In 1655 a man was fined by the Court for suffering his wife "to fight and draw blood." In

1380 William Harper was brought from Chester and hanged for murder. In 1474 two Welshmen were hanged for housebreaking at Keckwich, and there are also instances where men were hanged in chains for murder near the place where the crime was committed. There were also a variety of other matters with which the court dealt.

Next in importance, and still carrying out some of its ancient functions, is the Court Leet at Altrincham, which elects a mayor, burgesses, and various officials, such as constables, ale tasters, dog muzzlers, etc.

Fifty or sixty years ago there were leather sealers, who saw that the leather was of a good quality and properly cured; market lookers with weights and scales tested the weight of butter, and saw to it that the farmers' wives gave the "long pound" (eighteen ounces) in those halcyon days. There were common lookers, who saw that the commons were properly used by the burgesses for pasturing their cattle, and who took care that the privilege was not abused.

It was at Samjam (St James) Fair that the mayor and corporation blossomed forth in full pomp of power and glory. Having elected the officers, they proceeded to settle the affairs of the locality with efficiency and dispatch. The ancient proclamation, which was read, commanded all persons resorting to the fair to abstain from assaults and affrays, under the then heavy penalty of five pounds, coupled with a term of imprisonment. It was forbidden to bear unlawful weapons—that is to say, bow, bill-axe, gun, or spear. Further, all persons offering any article for sale above the value of $4\frac{1}{2}$d. had to pay toll to the lord of the manor, or dire consequences would ensue. Having laid down the law in this respect, the mayor, with the assistance of his officers, opened the Court of Pied Poudre, or Court of Dusty Feet, to deal swift justice in cases arising within the liberties of the fair.

The constable then made presentments. One brewer, who had not brewed good wholesome ale and beer, was presented and fined 20s. An alehouse keeper in the borough, who had sold a pot of ale which was not "a full quart," was fined 10s. Another beerhouse keeper, having allowed a townsman to sit for six hours drinking with a stranger, when the limit was one hour, was also fined 10s. The town's baker was charged with giving short weight in bread. He had also so neglected his business that "the inhabitants had not had their puddings, pyes, and other eatables out of the oven at six o'clock in the evening." Further, "he had not made good, wholesome bread for man's bodie, of sweet corn and not corrupted." For giving short weight he was sentenced to be immersed in stercore, otherwise stinking water (probably the village horse-pond), and for the second offence was fined 10s.

But the great punishment was reserved for the forestaller. He was "a man who was not suffered to dwell in any town. He sought his own evil gain, oppressing the poor and deceiving the rich. He goes to meet corn, fish, herrings, or other articles for sale, as they are being brought by land or water, carries them off, and contrives that they shall be sold at a dearer rate. He deceives merchant strangers bringing merchandise to the fair, by offering to sell their wares for them, and telling them that they might be dearer sold than the merchants expected; and so, by craft and subtlety, he deceives his town and country."

Engrossing consists of buying goods in large quantities so as to be able to control the market; forestalling was buying before goods reached the public market; regrating, buying cheap to sell dear. All these things were grave social offences in the Middle Ages, when it was necessary to safeguard the interests of the consumer by insisting on a just price as between buyer and seller. For the first offence the goods were confiscated, and on the third offence he was fined and imprisoned. This judgment applied to all manner of forestallers, and likewise included those who had given them "counsel, help or favour." We cannot find any reference to the regrater pest. Probably he was classed with the forestaller, and dealt with accordingly. These offences were legally abolished in this country in 1844.

We notice, however, as in Altrincham, many other beneficial activities in which the court was engaged. Most of the officers can be traced at work for two or three centuries back, all except ale-tasters. Two townsmen were fined twelvepence for neglecting to sweep their chimneys. An alderman (ex-mayor) of the town was fined on two occasions, 6s. 8d. and 10s. respectively, for not carrying out orders to "mussel" his dog. A lodging-house keeper was fined 10s. for entertaining vagrants contrary to Act of Parliament; and there are many orders for persons "to scour, ditch, slance, breast, and cleanse their ditches, and to fall (fell) brush, fence, and back-beat their hedges."

And if officers did not attend efficiently to their duties they were "pained" (fined). The well-looker, for instance, was fined 3s. 4d. for neglecting to see that the town's well was properly cleaned, and the dog muzzlers twelvepence each for not attending to their duties. In many other places we find numbers of people fined for selling ale or beer contrary to the statute "in that case made and provided"; for breaking the Assize of bread—that is, selling it contrary to legal regulations, or making spice bread, which was flavoured with nutmeg or cinnamon, and putting butter into cakes. The only difference in these days is that lard or margarine is substituted for butter, and in the manufacturing districts goes by the name of fat bread or fatty cake, generally with currants added. There were "affairors," who "affaired or assessed the amercements of fines levied." They also regulated the fines on delinquents, reducing them when they considered them to be too high or severe. These "affairors" were evidently the predecessors of our modern appraisers or valuers.

But as freedom broadened down, self-government assumed a most important aspect. Townships were granted Royal Charters of Incorporation and became boroughs, and thus distinguished from the old feudal boroughs, such as we have already instanced. Branching out from all these was the Poor Law. Until 1601 the relief of the poor was left to private benevolence, and this year is generally assumed to be the beginning of the English Poor Law. It provided for a general assessment in place of voluntary contributions. The Act appears to have worked fairly well so long as the administration was confined to the overseers elected in each parish. The overseers had to see that its poor had their wants supplied, and a compulsory poor rate was levied for that purpose. Relief was to be given in the workhouse, where work was to be found for the poor of the parish. Workhouses became so numerous as to give rise to considerable abuse. The system of out-door relief also led to oppressive poor rates. In 1822, under a body called a Select Vestry, the administration of the Poor Law progressed another stage. In some cases there appeared to be undue haste to reduce relief to such an extent as to make no call on the ratepayers. In some instances a hope was expressed that the " sentiments of honest independence, by which the poor of this country were once characterised, will gradually arise amongst them, and that their own exertion, aided by the occasional advice and assistance of their richer neighbours, will always remain their surest support in distress and sickness." Businesses were established in the hope that they would be a source of profit to the ratepayers, but so far from this being the case, the poor rate rose to several shillings in the pound to make good the loss. This was the age of Bumbledom, so cleverly satirised by Dickens. At one establishment where weaving was carried on, the overseers reported to the Select Vestry that " the governess of the workhouse has fled, taking her clothes with her, that her husband does not know where she has gone, or whether she means to return." As a matter of fact she did not return, and her husband was discharged.

Turning to the system of outdoor relief, there was the same want of economical administration displayed. The system of " piecing out " was rampant—that is, where a man did not earn sufficient to maintain his wife and family his rent was paid. To such an extent did it prevail at one time that it became a question of compounding with the landlords in a body. The overseers were also given to helping an unwanted member of the community to migrate to another district, and he or she (for there were members of both sexes to deal with) were provided with funds, in the hope that that would be the last heard of them in their native township. The law of settlement was not then in operation, and this plan did not work well. Often the overseers had to go considerable distances to extricate many of the migrants from " durance vile " and bring them home again. In one case " a donation of £3 was made to a man " to enable him to liberate himself " from some difficulty under which it appears to this meeting he is at present labouring." A lady was presented with a " petticoat " against the approach of winter. Another woman was guilty of the unheard of extravagance in asking for two " shifts," which the Scotch term "sarks." Most of the applications for out-relief were for help in the time of sickness. One man got a new spade; a violin was ordered for a lame boy to enable him to earn a living. One person received £1. 5s. towards his wife's coffin. A more sensible application of the funds of the township was the purchase of a loom. Handloom weaving at this period was a staple industry in most counties. Weavers were termed websters. Those who turned out a certain cloth or fabric were woollen websters or silk websters, as the case might be. Simple " musical " instruments such as accordeons, concertinas, flutes, and tin whistles were often provided. On the terrible evils of apprenticeship we need not dwell here.

The Amending Act, passed in 1834, put an end to a great extent to this appalling system. Two or more neighbouring parishes were permitted to form a union, and Guardians of the Poor were appointed to conduct its business, manage the workhouse, hear and adjudicate on applications for relief, fix the sum to be raised by the parish or the union, and the business of the overseer was devoted to levying and collecting for the purpose by means of the Poor Rate. They also had the preparation of the valuation lists of property, and the voters and jury lists. The office of overseer was a compulsory one, but the difficulty was got over by a salaried assistant overseer, where the work was sufficient to justify the appointment.

Although there has been a campaign initiated for the abolition of Boards of Guardians, of late years there has been a disposition on the part of the legislature to attach to them other even more important duties in rural areas. The Public Health Act of 1875, with various subsidiary statutes, forms the basis of the present Sanitary Law. Unions are divided into rural and urban sanitary districts for administrative purposes. Urban powers are given to towns, and in rural districts the Guardians act as a sanitary authority with medical officers, inspectors, and other officials, and provide isolation and other hospitals.

The Lighting and Watching Act of 1833 enabled a vestry to provide lamps, which at that period were lighted with oil, and " Charlies," as the watchmen were called, formed the butt of practical jokes by the " bloods " of that day. The Highway Acts also divided rural districts into highway districts, and these were controlled by Highway Boards, consisting of Justices of the Peace and highway wardens, and well did they perform their duties, until automatically dissolved by the County Council. They effected a great improvement in local highways. The great highways or turnpike roads were vested in trustees, and these again were abolished in 1878, and now constitute the main roads of the county.

The weak point about local government for a long period was weakness in administering the numerous Acts passed. This was in the hands of persons not responsible in many cases to the ratepayers. The whole system was revolutionised by the Local Government Act of 1888, which has been attended with such beneficial results.

The Local Government Act, which came into operation on 1st April 1892, further revolutionised the system of County administration. Previous to the passing of this Act the government of counties was entrusted to the magistrates, who had discharged those duties from 1327 down to the reign of Edward VII. By the provisions of the Act, the City of Chester, in common with Stockport, Birkenhead, and others, was constituted a county borough. In other directions the Urban Councils simply took over the powers formerly enjoyed by the old Local Boards, with one important exception, that the chairman for the time being was an *ex-officio* magistrate, and took his seat on the bench as an equal to the best in the land. Consequently, the chairmanship of an Urban District Council is a coveted distinction. The same qualification does not apply to Rural District Councils, and thus, as one humourist has remarked, "Hodge's wings are considerably clipped." Parish Councils were created, by the Act of 1894, for every rural parish having a population of 300 or upwards at the census of 1891. They may also be created by the County Council in smaller parishes, and a like order may group two or more parishes under one Parish Council. Except where an adoptive Act is in force a Parish Council cannot expend more than the produce of a sixpenny rate, or without the consent of the parish meeting more than the proceeds of a threepenny rate.

The County of Chester is governed by a County Council, consisting of nineteen aldermen and fifty-six councillors. The Chairman of the Council, by virtue of his office, is a Justice of the Peace for the County; the police of the County are under the control of a Standing Joint Committee of the Quarter Sessions and the County Council. The Coroners of the County are elected by the County Council and the Clerk of the Peace, appointed by such Joint Committee, and may be removed by them. The Clerk of the Peace of the County is also Clerk of the County Council. The administration of the County, which would, if this Act had not been passed, have been transacted by the Justices, is now transacted by the County Council.

All the elections for the first Cheshire County Council, in January 1889, were fought politically or on party lines. In many divisions, however, this was not strictly adhered to, many well-known Conservatives supporting the Liberal candidates. Political leaders were at variance on this point, Lord Rosebery asserting that it would be worse than criminal if the electors allowed party politics to creep in and influence their vote. On the other hand, Mr Gladstone wrote from Naples to the Honorary Secretary of the Rossendale Division of the Liberal party, stating that he thought Sir George Trevelyan had rightly shown that the political element should have a place in County Council contests as it had in municipal elections.

The polling took place on 30th January 1889. There were 48 representatives of the County Divisions; 14 were elected by Municipal Boroughs, and the Council was empowered to elect 19 aldermen. The Borough of Macclesfield had 4 members; Crewe, Stalybridge, and Hyde, 3 each; Congleton, 1. Twenty-two members were returned unopposed, of which 12 were Conservatives, 9 Liberals, and 1 Liberal-Unionist. Although many were Conservative in politics, they were described as Independents in the newspaper results. In the Sandbach Division, Mr Edwin Foden (L.) was returned by a majority of two votes over his Independent opponent, the Rev. J. R. Armitstead. Lord Egerton of Tatton, afterwards first Earl, scored an easy victory in the Knutsford Division, being returned by a majority of 453 over his tenant farmer opponent. The same remark applies to Davenport and Church Hulme, where Colonel France Hayhurst scored 530 votes to 312 recorded for his opponent, another tenant farmer, who stood in the Liberal interest. Macclesfield elected two Conservatives and one Liberal. Great interest was centred in the election in Bredbury Division, where two influential residents were pitted against each other, in Mr James Leigh (C.) and Mr Samuel Buckley (L.), the first-named gentleman being returned. Chester Castle Division returned a Conservative, and Tattenhall, Frodsham, and Malpas returned Liberals.

A serious accident, though fortunately not involving loss of human life, occurred at Winsford, where Mr John Brunner, as he then was, had sent a valuable horse and dog-cart to assist Mr Holland, the farmers' candidate. In a collision which occurred between Mr Brunner's turnout and another, also assisting Mr Holland, the shaft entered the breast of Mr Brunner's horse, killing it on the spot. The Conservative candidate, Captain Turner, was returned by a substantial majority. Wallasey and Seacombe returned Conservatives; Liscard was Liberal, as also Tarporley, where Mr Roger Bate, the strongest farmers' candidate who could have been secured to contest a division, was returned. Audlem also returned Mr Joseph Beckett, another farmer possessing great influence in the division, though his majority was rather a narrow one. In Mottram it is reported that the contest aroused great interest, and crowds awaited the issue, which resulted in a Liberal victory. Dukinfield, Daresbury, and Lymm returned Liberals, and Worleston a Conservative. The full returns showed that 27 Conservatives and 25 Liberals, 1 Liberal-Unionist, and 4 members whose political complexion was not stated, had been elected.

The first provisional meeting was held in February 1889, and dealt with preliminary matters as required by the Local Government Act, before taking over the administrative work of the county. Not one of the fifty-six members was absent. Like the war horse of Scripture, "they sniffed the battle afar," and girded up their loins for the coming fray. The meeting was held in the Grand Jury Room at Chester Castle, and although twelve noon was the hour fixed for the opening of the proceedings, members began to assemble early in the forenoon, and the interval was usefully employed in making the necessary statutory declaration of their acceptance of office.

Precisely at noon, Mr Roberts, Deputy Clerk of the Peace, asked them to elect a chairman. Lord Egerton was proposed by Mr J. Coutts Antrobus, and seconded by Mr Duncan Graham. Mr Joseph Beckett suggested that they should have an opportunity of voting for an alternative chairman, and proposed Mr Duncan Graham. Dr Hodgson, Crewe, seconded. He pointed out that the proposition that the aldermen should consist of an equal number of each political party of the Council had been met with a direct negative. This was met with cries of "No," and Dr Hodgson replied, that a meeting had been held to discuss the matter. He suggested that the name of Mr Duncan Graham would probably be accepted as indicative of a greater spirit of fairness in a solution of the difficulty. He objected to a chairman acting in a dual capacity, as Lord Egerton would do, as Chairman of the Court of Quarter Sessions.

Mr Duncan Graham asked the meeting to make the election of Lord Egerton unanimous, and pointed out that his Lordship would only be elected perhaps for a couple of meetings. The amendment on being put, received the votes of twenty-four members; for Lord Egerton twenty-eight voted. He was, therefore, declared duly elected. His Lordship, on taking the chair, briefly returned thanks for the confidence the Council had reposed in him in making him their Chairman. He hoped that as he had been chairman of many bodies, that his conduct and impartiality would not be impugned on that occasion.

By this time the atmosphere had become somewhat electric. The first symptoms of coming trouble arose on the election of aldermen. Circulars had been sent out by both political parties, each giving a list of names, and it was pointed out by the Chairman that no business could be transacted that day except what appeared on the agenda. This ruling gave rise to slight uproar, which was met by cries of "Chair," Mr Joseph Lewis remarking that the Chairman was shirking the question. Mr Lewis resumed his seat, sarcastically remarking, "That is impartiality," which was met by Mr Ralph Bates with the word "Impertinence."

The names of the councillors were next called over by the Deputy Clerk of the Peace. Dr Hodgson again referred to the proposal sent by the Liberal to the Conservative councillors at a meeting held that morning, when the Chairman pointed out that the agenda provided for the election of nineteen County aldermen. He suggested that by arrangement they should have an interval to think over the best course to adopt. He for one deprecated the strong party feeling shown. He had always advocated that the best men of all political parties should be elected. He trusted that the future deliberations of the Council would be conducted with absolute freedom from party feeling.

Mr Duncan Graham said it was no use ignoring the fact that party feeling had been displayed. Ultimately an adjournment was arranged, and as a result of repeated conferences the two political parties agreed to the following list of aldermen:—James Smith, New Brighton, merchant; Thomas Rigby, Sutton Weaver, miller; James Tomkinson, Tarporley, banker; Henry Nield, Northwich, gentleman; Thomas Collier, Alderley Edge, merchant; Samuel Hodgkinson, Marple, cotton manufacturer; David Basil Hewitt, M.D., Northwich, Director of Alkali Co.; Thomas Beeley, Dukinfield, engineer; Wm. Armitage, Altrincham, merchant; Alexander Bedell, Wilmslow, manufacturer; the Duke of Westminster, Eaton Hall, peer; Fred W. Webb, Crewe, engineer; Christopher Kay, Davenham, gentleman; Ralph Bates, Stalybridge, gentleman; Joseph Verdin, Northwich, salt manufacturer; Edward Greenall, Grappenhall, gentleman; Thomas H. Sykes, Cheadle, gentleman; Robert O. Horton, Tattenhall, gentleman; the Hon. Wilbraham Tollemache, Tarporley, gentleman. Of the above, eight were Conservatives, seven Liberals, and four Liberal-Unionists.

Mr Duncan Graham was unanimously elected Chairman at a subsequent meeting of the Council. His conduct of the duties of the office met with great acceptance from all parties and shades of politics, and his resignation, although he did not retire from the Council, was received with great regret. To commemorate his successful occupancy of the Chair, his portrait in oils was subscribed for by the members, and it was unveiled in the presence of a crowded attendance of members and a number of the general public, by the Duke of Westminster. His Grace, in his opening remarks, said: "I have had the honour, and I must add the great pleasure, of being deputed by the Portrait Committee, which consists of the Vice-Chairman and Vice-Chairmen of Committees of our Council—I can hardly say to present, the portrait of our Chairman to himself—but to order its unveiling. We attach so much importance and value to it that we mean to keep it in our own sight, or in that of those of us who have the prospect of a somewhat prolonged Council life—or our successors—and we may well congratulate ourselves and the county upon the acquisition of the admirable likeness of a very noble character." The portrait was unveiled amid the hearty acclamation of the spectators. A facsimile of the address in the handwriting of his Grace appears on facing page.

The vacancy caused by Mr Graham's resignation was filled at a meeting of the Council, held on 9th March 1893. Mr Graham expressed to the members his very warm thanks for the uniform kindness and consideration which had been extended to him during the four years he had had the honour of occupying the Chair. Colonel Dixon (now Sir George Dixon, Bart.) was nominated for the office of Chairman by Colonel Coutts Antrobus, seconded by Colonel France Hayhurst. Dr Hewitt nominated and Mr Eddowes seconded Mr Charles Lister, who was recommended for his experience as Registrar of the

I have had the honour and I must add great pleasure of being deputed by the Portrait Committee — the committee of the Vice Chairman and Chairmen of Committees of the Council — I can hardly say to present the Portrait of our Chairman to himself — but to order its unveiling — we attach so much importance & value to it that we mean to keep it in our own right, or in that of those who have the prospect of a somewhat prolonged County life — or of our successors — and we may well congratulate ourselves & the county upon the acquisition of an admirable likeness of a very noble character. —

Facsimile of MS., Duke of Westminster's Speech, Cheshire County Council.

Manchester County Court, and as second judge at the Court of Quarter Sessions. On a division, Colonel Dixon was elected by forty-one votes to twenty-nine, and on taking the Chair he thanked the members for putting him in the proud position of Chairman of the Council of his native county. He felt regret at the loss of such an able and popular Chairman as Mr Graham, who had left them all a bright and noble example to follow. Mr Jos. Beckett, who moved Mr Graham's election four years previously, proposed a hearty vote of thanks to him on his retirement, this being seconded by Mr H. Neville, supported by Mr Speakman, and carried by acclamation. Mr Duncan Graham, who met with prolonged applause on rising to reply, expressed his sincere thanks for this further demonstration of the goodwill of the Council.

Mr T. W. Killick, on being elected Vice-Chairman, named two traits of Mr Graham's chairmanship—dispatch of business and perfect impartiality—and promised to emulate him in these respects. In a circular letter issued to the aldermen and members of the Council, on 16th February, Mr Duncan Graham explained that he resigned the Chairmanship because the discharge of the duties devolving on him, in such a manner as alone would be satisfactory to himself, entailed greater demands on his time than he could conveniently respond to with due regard to the claims of other and previously existing arrangements. He hoped to continue to represent his division as an ordinary member of the Council.

There are in all thirty-nine committees, including boards, trusts, etc., dealing with the general work arising in the County. The General Purposes, the Executive Committee under the Diseases of Animals Act, 1894, Public Health and Housing Committee, and Local Pensions Committee consist of fifty-four members, many of which are co-opted, and are experienced in, or qualified to represent agriculture, mining, engineering, textile or other industries, Technical, Secondary, Council and Voluntary Schools. There are also representative teachers from Elementary, Technical, or Secondary Schools, and there are two Professors from the University of Manchester and the University of Liverpool. The Finance Committee consists of thirty members; the Main Roads and Bridges Committee, of forty members; the Mental Deficiency Act (1913) Committee, of forty-eight members, including members who are co-opted from Crewe, Chester, and Macclesfield, and various unions in the County, Ashton-under-Lyne and Whitchurch; the Polling Districts Committee, thirty-six members, four from each of the nine Parliamentary divisions into which the County is divided. A most important committee is that dealing with Small Holdings and Allotments, consisting of thirty members of the Council, and ten co-opted members representing Rural District Councils. At a meeting of the County Council, held in August 1919, it was reported that correspondence had passed between the Committee and the Board of Agriculture, on the subject of the provision of small holdings for men resident in the City of

Chester, and it was resolved that, as the Committee must give preference to applicants for holdings for whom they were primarily and directly responsible, they were of the opinion, in the interests of those residents of county boroughs who require small holdings, that the councils of such boroughs should provide the same.

Mr W. M'Cracken (the Chairman), in moving the adoption of the minutes, remarked that they were working to provide the ex-service men with land. So far as Cheshire was concerned they stood well in relation to other counties. Up to 20th June 1919 the only county which had exceeded Cheshire in acreage bought was Somerset. The figures were:—Somerset, 3480 acres; Cheshire, 2729 acres. He thought the position would be altered if the value of the land was added. The value of the land in Cheshire was probably higher than in any other county. In the Runcorn area, 2356 acres had been bought; Tarvin, 247 acres; Bucklow, 233 acres; Congleton, 219 acres; Macclesfield, 312 acres; Nantwich, 37 acres; Wirral, 15 acres. Originally they had a number of civilian applicants, but they had to wait for the ex-service men. They had 566 ex-service men and 157 civilians, making a total of 723 applicants. The total area bought since last spring was 3419 acres. There was a pre-war area yet to be developed of 484 acres, making a total of 3903 acres. The total purchasing price, including the pre-war patches, was £182,279. They expected to cut up the land into 92 small holdings and 63 cottage holdings. The estimate of the land required to meet the ex-service men's requirements was 8100 acres, and 3000 acres for civilian applicants. There were 11,000 acres still required. The approximate area of the land for which they were now negotiating was over 5000 acres.

The Weaver Navigation Trust consists of thirty-eight members. Of these eighteen represent the County Council, and six gentlemen have been appointed by the Council in place of existing trustees resigned or deceased. Four life trustees represent the existing trustees, with fourteen other gentlemen representative of the various trades connected with the navigation of the Weaver. The Cheshire Joint Sanatorium Committee has fourteen representatives from the County Council, four Birkenhead representatives, one Chester, three Stockport, two Wallasey, and six Stoke-on-Trent. The Local Committee for the County, under the Naval and Military War Pensions Act, numbers sixteen from the County Council, six on the nomination of the Soldiers' and Sailors' Families Association, three on the nomination of the Soldiers and Sailors Help Society, one nominated by the Crewe Trades Council, two by the Lancashire and Cheshire Federation of Trades and Labour Councils, one by the National and General Workers' Union, one by the Macclesfield Trades Council, one by the Lancashire and Cheshire Miners' Federation, one lady representing widows, and two discharged soldiers' representatives. Other committees deal with asylums, weights and measures, county insurance, live stock, fisheries, waterways, territorial forces, drainage, and other administrative work. The County Licensing Committee consists of thirty-nine members, two from each Petty Sessional Division, and one each for the Boroughs of Congleton, Crewe, Hyde, and Stalybridge.

In addition to the facts recorded regarding Poor Law Administration, we may point out that the Right Hon. C. Addison (Minister of Health) had spoken with no uncertain voice as to its future. He writes: " It is well known that nowadays ill-health and infirmity are the principal reasons which compel men and women to resort to the Poor Law. The Government feel that a new spirit and new methods should be introduced in place of an obsolete system, and they propose that in the future those who are in need of medical assistance should be entitled to receive treatment, not after, but before their sickness reduces them to destitution. This change will be brought about as part of the general transfer of the functions of the Boards of Guardians to other authorities, which the Government are pledged to carry out. All the services relating to the care and treatment of the sick and infirm, which are now administered as part of the Poor Law system, will no longer form part of that system, but will be made a part of the general health services of the community; and the Bill, which is needed for this purpose, will be introduced by the Government as soon as possible."

So far as the Maternity and Child Welfare Committee is concerned it can truly be said to have justified its existence. It numbers sixteen members, of which Mr Charles Wilson is Chairman, Rev. Canon J. Grant Bird, Deputy Chairman, with the Chairman and Vice-Chairman of the Council *ex officio*. The other members are: Rev. J. R. Armitstead, Frank Barlow, Rev. W. Bidlake, T. Raffles Bulley, C. E. Davenport, Rev. J. W. Fortnum, Wm. Parker, J. Somerville, Lady Forbes Adam (Audlem), Mrs L. A. Boston (Runcorn), Mrs A. M. Rankine (Hoylake), Mrs A. Summers (Stalybridge). Mrs Summers, O.B.E., had the honour of being the first lady magistrate to preside over a Bench in 1919 in the capacity of Lady Mayor of that borough. The advent of the ladies on public bodies has been attended with very beneficial results, especially Boards of Guardians. This is very noticeable, especially in connection with females, where tactful treatment and sympathy were indispensable. In the case of the committee above referred to, their activities took many courses, particularly in the National Baby Competitions. This made a direct appeal to mothers in regard to the care of their little ones, which cannot fail to react on the physical welfare of the children generally.

The elections for the County Council in March 1919 left the balance of parties unchanged. Both political parties endeavoured to avoid contests on this occasion, and where they occurred it was entirely due to local causes. In the majority of cases the contests were forced by the Cheshire Farmers' Union. At the outset this union issued a list of seventeen probable candidates, these including several who were already members of the Council. When the nominations closed it was found that ten Farmers' Union representatives had been returned without a contest. Twelve seats were the subject of contests, two of them being in the boroughs of Crewe and Macclesfield, where, of course, the agricultural consideration did not count to any extent. In the ten rural constituencies, ten farmers' nominees stood, and of these three were successful. This gave the Farmers' Union thirteen representatives on the Council. The Council was the poorer as the result of the election, by the loss of Colonel H. Cornwall Legh, who did not go to the poll at Knutsford; of Colonel Verdin, who retired owing to ill-health, on the nomination day, at Church Coppenhall; and of Colonel Greg, whose seat at Alderley was contested and won in his absence on active service by Mr J. O. Garner, Secretary of the Farmers' Union.

Whether the election represented the true feeling of the constituents is doubtful, but we leave the returns to speak for themselves, especially in view of the poor polls. Alderley Division—J. O. Garner (Cheshire Farmers' Union), 795; *Colonel Alexander Greg, 138. Total electorate, 3750. Bollington— J. E. Marsland, 443; J. Hall Brooks, 290. Total electorate, 3528. Malpas— William Parker, 502; J. N. Joyce (Farmers' Union), 428. Total electorate, 3484. Middlewich—*J. W. Fortnum, 860; O. Barker Whitehead, 708. Total electorate, 2686. Neston—*E. Peter Jones, 1346; Robert Jones (Farmers' Union), 346. Total electorate, 7733. Sale—James M'Donald, 563; William Plant, 442. Total electorate, 6598. Sutton—*T. Clayton Toler, 992; T. William Wood (Farmers' Union), 646. Total electorate, 3259. Tarporley— *C. E. Parton, 1009; Samuel Bratt, 524. Total electorate, 2865. Weaverham—William Hough (Farmers' Union), 606; *William Bancroft, 562. Total electorate, 4039. West Kirby—*Charles M'Iver, 879; A. S. Gaskell (Farmers' Union), 518. Total electorate, 9030. Crewe (North Ward)—J. H. Kettell, 340; *C. H. Pedley, 302. Total electorate, 4410. Macclesfield (No. 1)—William Brocklehurst, 459; W. H. Braid, 414. (The asterisk denotes retiring members.)

At the first meeting of the newly-elected Council, held at Chester on 15th March 1919, Colonel Dixon was again unanimously elected Chairman. He remarked that he was glad that the agricultural interest was so well represented on the Council. Eight of the nine retiring aldermen were re-elected. These were Sir J. Emmott Barlow, Mr W. B. Brocklehurst, Mr T. Raffles Bulley, Mr T. H. Gordon, Dr Hodgson, Mr W. M'Cracken, Mr G. Wall, and Mr H. E. Wilbraham. The Chairman expressed regret that one of the retiring aldermen, Mr J. W. Sidebotham of Merlewood, Bowdon, had resigned in consequence of ill-health. The new aldermen elected were Mr Coard C. Pain of Bebington and Mr John Morley, Sale.

It was with a deep feeling of gratification that the Council and the inhabitants of Cheshire, including the tenantry of the Astle Hall estate, heard that a baronetcy had been conferred upon Colonel Dixon in the New Year's Honours List. " It would be a difficult task to point to any gentleman throughout the county," says one authority, " who has laboured so diligently and at the same time so unostentatiously, for the welfare and betterment of Cheshire as the recipient of the honour. As chairman of the county's administrative body since 1893, he has had numerous opportunities of displaying his interest in the affairs of this important part of the country, and during the long period he has filled the chair he has never failed to give evidence of the keen appreciation of that fact." He was elected a member of the Council at the first election in 1889. Four years later he succeeded the late Mr Duncan Graham as chairman, and has been re-elected on each successive occasion, which in itself is a cogent proof of the fact that old and new members alike recognised his diligent attention to the duties appertaining to his post. In fact, there has not been a more regular attendant at the Council meetings or the many Committees of which he is a member. He was elected Alderman in February 1900 and a Deputy Lieutenant of the County in December 1901. He had previously filled the office of High Sheriff of Cheshire. So far back as 1874 he was placed upon the Commission of the Peace for the County, but it is in connection with the work of the County Council that the County learned to admire the great good that the master of Astle Hall was able to accomplish for Cheshire generally. As an old volunteer he took an active interest in that movement, and it was in a large measure due to his efforts that the volunteer force in Cheshire held such a prominent place in the history of the force in the country. He was Commandant of the Cheshire Volunteers during the war, and his comrades associated with him in that movement in the County heard with pride of the new distinction His Majesty conferred upon him.

CHAPTER XV.

The House of Dunham—The foundation of the Family—Death of the first Sir Robert Booth—" A faire chappelle at Bowdon "—An echo of Charlemagne—Gifts to Warrington and Birkenhead Priory—A greeting from Jane Seymour—A Booth knighted by Queen Elizabeth—Gifts by Dame Elizabeth Booth—" The beautiful seat of Dunham "—Purchase of the town of Warrington—Birth of Sir George Booth, first Lord Delamere—A pillar of Puritanism—Futile efforts to preserve peace in the County—Fuller's views on the restoration—" The Cheshire rising " under Sir George Booth—Summary of notable events taken from State Papers—His defeat and capture at Winnington—Lady Booth's efforts to secure his release from the Tower—The Literary History of the Period—The Restoration and Sir George's rewards—His improvements at Dunham—Death and burial at Bowdon.

THE Booths, an important Lancashire family, acquired a position at Dunham Massey, Cheshire, in the reign of Henry V. The name is derived from the Anglo-Saxon word Both, a seat, or chief mansion house, more usually a village. In the year 1402, Richard de Venables, heir to the estate of Le Bolyn, was drowned accidentally in the river Bollin, and by this event his two sisters Alice and Dulcia, or Douce, became co-heiresses. These lands were held in trust until Dulcia came of age. She was married to Robert del Bothe, or Booth, a younger son of Sir John del Bothe, Barton, near Manchester, " the Monday after the invention of the Holy Cross," in the tenth year of the reign of Henry IV. (1409), at which time she was only nine years of age. Twelve years afterwards the whole of the manors and estates were divided, Styal and Dean Row, and the mills on the river Bollin, with other lands in the County, principally in West Cheshire, falling to her share. Robert challenged his right to a portion of the land in this manor, which he contended ought to descend to him as one of the heirs by marriage through the Fittons and Venables from the last Baron of Dunham. Once having put his hand to the plough he did not look back, and ultimately it was agreed in the year 1433 between the holders of the barony, viz., Sir Thomas Stanley and William Chauntrell, sergeant-at-law, that one half of the lands, rents, and services in Dunham, Hale, and Altrincham should be given him. Thus, in brief, was laid the foundation of a family which is generally agreed to have been one of the most distinguished and influential in Cheshire.

This Sir Robert had a goodly number of sons and daughters, amongst them John Booth, afterwards Bishop of Exeter, and Warden of Manchester College. He and his eldest son, William, were made Sheriffs of Cheshire for both their lives in the year 1443 ; and Leycester remarks that this is all the more noteworthy as being the first patent for life which he could meet with in the County.

Sir Robert, the year of whose death is involved in some obscurity, was succeeded by his son William, who, in the year 1442, married Matilda, daughter of John Dutton of Dutton, Esq., and had issue, George, son and heir, and also other sons and daughters. He died on 6th April 1477, leaving certain lands in trust to provide a chaplain to pray for the health of his soul and that of his ancestors and descendants, in a Chantry Chapel which he desired to be built in Bowdon Church for that purpose; this was afterwards built, and was said from its spaciousness "to be a faire Chappelle." In his inquisition post mortem, or inquest after death, which was taken at "Knottesford," before Thomas Wolton, Escheator, and a local jury, it is stated that he died seised of certain lands, and that he had conceded to him lands in Altrincham, etc. His wife, Matilda, married for her second husband, Sir William Brereton, Knight.

George Booth, Esq., was 32 years of age when he was declared his father's heir. He married Catherine, daughter and heiress of Robert de Montfort, lord of Bescote, Staffordshire. It has been stated that his illustrious father-in-law was descended from Charlemagne, Emperor of the Romans, and David, King of Scotland, and that he was heir by his great grandmother to the ancient family of Clinton of Colchester. By this marriage large estates were brought to the family. By her he had issue, two sons and three daughters. He died the Sunday before the Annunciation of the Blessed Virgin Mary, 25th March 1484. In his will he desired that his body should be buried "in the new Chapel of St Mary of Bawdon." Katherine, who survived her husband, remarried. She died on the 7th December 1498.

At the time of his father's death, William, the next heir, was 10 years of age. On attaining his majority in 1494, the necessary proof of age was made. In about four years afterwards he was knighted. He was twice married, his first wife being Margaret, daughter and co-heiress of Sir Thomas Ashton of Ashton-under-Lyne; by her he had two sons, the heir being named George. The manor of Ashton-under-Lyne and other large inheritances in Lancashire passed by this marriage into the Booth family. His second wife was Ellen, the daughter of Sir John Montgomery of Throwley, Staffordshire, and by her he had issue seven sons and daughters. In one of the windows of Wilmslow Church there was formerly heraldic stained glass, representing Sir William Booth wearing a tabard of arms, and kneeling with six sons behind him, and his wife Ellen, also kneeling, with five daughters behind her. There was an inscription in Latin, desiring prayers for the souls of Sir William, and Ellen his wife, and for the souls of their children, who caused a window to be made in the year 1526.

The inquest after death, taken at Altrincham, before Sir Ralph Egerton, Knight, 30th November 1519, recites the lands he was possessed of, and that he died the Wednesday before the Feast of St Martin the Bishop (11th November), last past (1519), and that George Bothe was son and next heir, and of the age of 29 years.

George, the fifth owner of Dunham, married Elizabeth, daughter of Sir Thomas Boteler or Butler, of Bewsey, the scene of a tragedy, the remembrance of which is preserved by tradition, when a Butler was ruthlessly murdered by a relative. By her he was blessed with several " olive branches "; and one of his daughters, Ellen, was married to John Carrington of Carrington, Esq., and another, Dorothy, to Robert Tatton of Wythenshawe, Esq. He died on the 25th October 1531, his eldest son, George, being then 15 years of age. In his will he states—

" I, George Bothe, of Donnham Massie, Esquire, etc., bequeath my body to be buried in Jhesus Chappell at Bowdon churche, among myn ancestors. Alsoe, I give to ye prior of Birkenhed my best horse to praye for me; also at Birkenhed aforesayd ten shillings to say a trentall of masses for my soule; also I give to ye prior and ye freires at Warington ten shillings to say a trentall of masses for my soule. Item to ye same prior of Warington towards ye gildying of our Ladie iij^s. iiij^d. (3s. 4d.). Also I will that my best gown of velvet and my best dublet shall be made in two vestiments, and ye one of ye sayd vestements to be given to ye said chappell of Jhesus at Bowdon church, and ye other vestement to remene in ye chappell of Donnham for ever. Also I give unto George Bothe, my son and heire apparent, my cheine of gold and my signet of gold as heire lomes.

" Also it is my will that my chaplen, Sir John Percivall, or some other discrete prist, shall say masse, praye, and do devyn service for my soule and myn ancestors and all Xten (Christian) souls by ye space of vij (7) yeres nexte after my decese, and he to have for his salarie yerely iij^{li}. xiij^s. iiij^d. (£3, 13s. 4d.) And whereas I by my dede indented berying date ye xviijth day of Julie ye xxiij yere of Kyng Henre ye viijth have infeoffed my brother in law John Massie of Podington esquire, John Carryngton of Carryngton esquire, William Meyre of Meyre esquire, Richard Legh of High Legh esquire, etc., in my manor of Dunham Massie and in all my messuages, lands, tenements, rents and services in Dunham Massie, Stayley, Bolyn, Deyn Roe, Stiall and Wilmeslowe, in trust, etc., as by the same dede indented more plenly doth appear.

" Also I bequeth for ye makyng of ye side ile of ye Church of Bowdon at such time as it shall be taken down five marks of money."

His son George, who succeeded him, also contracted an early marriage, having at the age of 16 espoused Elizabeth, daughter of Sir Edmund Trafford of Trafford, Lancashire, by whom he had issue, William, son and heir, and three daughters. He was one of the gentlemen who received a letter from the Queen (Jane Seymour) dispersing the joyful news through the kingdom of the birth of Edward VI. in 1537.

The letter was in these words :—
"By the Quene.

"Trusty and wel-biloved, we grete youe well. And for asmuche as by the inestimable goodness and grace of Almighty God, we be delivered and brought in childbed of a Prince, conceyved in most lawful matrimonie between my Lord the King's Majestye and us, doubting not but that for the love and affection which ye beare unto us, and to the commyn wealth (commonwealth) of this realme, the knowledge thereof shuld be joyeous and glad tydings unto youe, we have thought good to certiffie to you of the same. To thintent (the intent) ye might not only rendre unto God condigne thanks and praise for soo gret a benefit, but also pray for the long continuance and preservation of the same here in this lief, to the honor of God, joye and pleasor of my lord the king, and us, and the universall weale, quiet and tranquillyty of this hole realm. Gevyn under our signet, at my Lord's manor of Hampton cort, the xii day of October (1537).

To our trusty and welbiloved
George Both, Esq."

He died in 1543, aged 28 years. His widow, Elizabeth, survived him and was twice remarried, firstly, to James Done of Utkinton, and, secondly, to Thomas Fitton of Siddington. George appears to have made Wilmslow his place of residence, and in his will he desired to be buried there. His raised altar tomb, bearing his arms and initials, with those of his wife, remained in the Booth Chapel for a long period, but was destroyed at the restoration of the church in 1863.

His son and heir, William Booth, Esq., was but three years of age on succeeding to his father's ample estates in 1546, and was ward to Henry VIII. He married Elizabeth, daughter of Sir John Warburton of Arley, and had a family of seven sons and six daughters. One of his sons, Robert, distinguished himself as a soldier in Holland. In 1571 he was made Sheriff of Chester, and seven years afterwards had the honour of knighthood conferred upon him by the virgin Queen. He died on the 28th November 1579, and was buried at Bowdon on 8th December following, so that he does not appear to have long survived the honours bestowed upon him. His will is a most interesting one. He bequeaths to his wife "the chain of gold," which he last brought with him from London, weighing about xxx^{li}., another small chain, a carcanet of gold, one pair of bracelets of gold, two suits of borders of gold, one single border of gold, one tablet of gold, with all the rings she was accustomed to wear, and certain small buttons of gold, enamelled black and white, three little gilt bowls, with his third salt cellar, and all the husbandry stuff at Stayley Hall. To his son George (his heir) he leaves all the rest of his plate (reserving one dozen of spoons " of the worser sort," which he gave to his wife), his best chain of gold with his signet, and all his apparel, with all his gold buttons except those before given to his wife. " To William Duncalf, my cast of ffawcons (falcons), my baie trotting nagge and my setting spaniells." To his well-beloved mother " my sealinge ring, usuallie wore on my little finger " ; to his brother-in-law, Davenport, all his hounds ; to his cousins, William Tatton, George Brereton (Ashley), and Edmund Joddrell, all his fighting cocks and hens ; to his sisters Davenport, Chauntrell, and Done, each a gold ring ; and to his brother-in-law, Mr John Done, " his best baie nagge and his pied horse," then at Stayley Hall ; to his daughter-in-law, Jane Bothe (married to his son George, then a minor), a black ambling nag that was Mr Carrington's, and also a gold brooch ; to his brother-in-law, Mr Peter Warburton, his best gray nag that he himself was accustomed to ride upon, and also his lute ; to his brother-in-law, Mr George Warburton, a young coal-black nag ; to Mr Vicar, of Rochdale, iiij^{li}. ; to William Leigh, his long black cloak ; to George Holme, his best pair of virginalls, etc.

His wife, Dame Elizabeth, survived him for the long period of forty-nine years, and appears to have distinguished herself by her widely diffused charity. In 1620 she granted to the Mayor and citizens of Chester the sum of £400 upon trust for ever, the interest of which at five per cent. per annum is to be annually paid out by them in certain sums, £5 of which is handed over to the overseers of Bowdon parish, amongst others, to be expended in weekly instalments in purchasing loaves of bread to be distributed weekly, on every Sunday, for ever, immediately after morning prayer in the Parish Church, to twenty-four poor aged people. It is divided over several parishes, and the distribution continues to be made in another form.

George Booth, the second surviving son of the preceding, lived in those critical times when the Protestantism of this country first rested on a firm foundation ; when, as one writer has eloquently put it, Englishmen performed those brilliant and glorious naval exploits, especially the destruction of the Spanish Armada, which are unsurpassed in our naval annals ; when the majesty of English prose was formed by the hand of Hooker ; when the harmony of English verse flowed from the lips of Spenser ; when the drama, the surest proof of advanced civilisation, had its first beginnings, and was perfected by the immortal genius of Shakespeare ; while Bacon opened up a new method of philosophy, whose practical fruits we may be said even now to gather. Born on 20th October 1566, Sir George was, on the death of his father, still a minor, and was made a ward of Queen Elizabeth. He was married in 1577 to Jane, daughter and heiress of John Carrington, he being 11 and his wife 15 years old at the time. She was an orphan, her father having died only the month previously. She died without issue, and he obtained, by suit, possession of the land of Carrington. His second wife was Catherine, daughter of

Sir Edmund Anderson, Chief Justice of the Common Pleas, and by her he had a large family. He was, like all Englishmen of the period, seized with the contagion of patriotism, and contributed liberally, as also did his mother, towards the armaments which were raised for the defence of the kingdom. He was Sheriff of Chester for the first time in 1597, and he is referred to by the gifted, but eccentric, Dr Dee, the then Warden of Manchester College, who records in his diary that he received a " viset " from Sir George, who had no doubt just been knighted by the Queen, and that " after some few words of discourse " he agreed to stand by the arbitrement of Mr Homfrey Damport or Davenport, " a Cownsaylor of Gray's Inne," concerning two or three tenements in his occupying in Dunham Massey. He also mentions a second " viset " he had from Sir George, who " sayed he wold yeld to me what he wold not yeld to the bisshop nor any other," thereby showing that the worthy doctor stood high in his estimation. Sir George was created a Baronet by patent bearing date 22nd May 1611, in the ninth year of the reign of James I., being the tenth person who was created a baronet after the institution of that order. To entitle him to this honour he was amply possessed of all material requisites. Webb, in his " Itinerary," speaks of the beautiful seat of Dunham, at that time " never more graced than in the present possessor, upon whom, and his most worthy son, William Booth, Esquire, the world hath deservedly set great love and affection, himself bearing a chief sway in the great commands of regiments in the country, and his son already giving proof of that wisdom and moderation in government which have adorned his ancestors before him."

Of the eldest son William, mentioned above, it becomes necessary to speak more at length, as his opening acts, conspicuous for great ability, gave promise of a brilliant future. It was by his efforts that the family acquired possession of Warrington. The instructions which he gave to his stewards on that occasion are remarkable, as being probably the last instance of an appeal being made on the old principle of feudal benevolence to the tenantry for pecuniary aid. The sum which was to be paid for Warrington to Thomas Ireland of Bewsey, Esq., was £7000, and in his instructions William wishes the tenantry to be called together, the amount to be paid signified to them, in order that by their assistance he and his father might be enabled to finish the purchase. It was an opportunity for the tenants to show their love, such as might never probably occur again, and the " desire " was for three years' rent, which, if they would give, neither he nor his father would require any more rents or gifts of them for their two lives. Failing this, " they might provoke him to ' sharpe courses.' " Other landlords in Cheshire and Lancashire, he reminded them, had recently demanded three years' rent only for spending money which had been readily granted, and from the fact of the purchase being rumoured about the country if the tenantry forsook them in this extremity it would cause much disgrace. The purchase was afterwards completed William did not live more than seven or eight years after this great event, but died on the 26th April 1636, in the lifetime of his father. He had married Vere, second daughter and co-heiress of Sir Thomas Egerton, eldest son of Lord Chancellor Egerton, and she bore him five sons and two daughters. Thomas, the eldest, died at Chester at the age of 12. Consequently, George Booth, the second son, succeeded to the baronetcy on the death of his grandfather, who attained the ripe age of 86, 24th October 1652.

At the period of the birth of Sir George Booth, in 1622, those aspirations for constitutional liberty inherent in a commercial nation were beginning to animate the mass of the people, and find vent in the House of Commons. Those aspirations, repressed for the nonce by an untoward display of regal prerogative, only burst out with greater violence at a subsequent period. It is not to be wondered at that the Booth family ranged themselves on the side of the people, and from this fact the grandfather of Sir George was looked upon as the chief corner stone of the Puritan or Presbyterian party in Cheshire. The word Puritan must not, however, be misunderstood. There were Puritans of various political complexions in those days, and ranked deservedly in the first grade were those who were in favour of maintaining the highest principles of civil liberty, apart from religious doctrine—not those sour, narrow-minded bigots, usually associated with the word, and which are popularly thought to be such in the present day. The part which the Booths of Dunham Massey were called upon to take was one fraught with danger and perplexity, but one which few have succeeded in carrying out with greater honour, and this at a time, too, when England had never before showed so many instances of courage, ability, and virtue.

In illustration of this, there appears the following quaint notice in Ricraft's "Worthies":—

"And next to this religious and faithful Lesley, is Sir George Booth, the leader of Cheshire, who, when the troubles first began, stood up for his country, exciting his tenants so to do, promising them that had leases of their lands from him that if any such did suffer in person or goods he would make them recompense, and if any had lease by life and should be slaine, the life of his wife, child, or friend, should be put in his stead, a brave religious resolution, which, if all the gentry that had adhered to the Parliament had done the like, the warres could never have lasted so long. But this religious brave Booth thought it not enough so to doe, but took a place of command himself, and was very active and courageous for the preservation of his country, did many gallant exploits which I hope hereafter to mention at large, and at present give him this character—free, brave, godly brave Booth, the flower of Cheshire."

When the signal of open discord and civil strife was given in August 1642, Sir George Booth and Sir William Brereton, who was described by his enemies "as a notable man at a thanksgiving dinner, having long teeth and a prodigious stomach," were the only two Cheshire gentlemen mentioned by name in the first order for arming the county and securing the magazines and equipments of the Royalists. The battle of Edgehill took place in October of the same year, and soon after a great Session or Assizes was held at Chester, where bills of indictment were preferred before the Judges against Sir George Booth and hundreds of others for high treason in taking up arms and adhering to Parliament in the war; but this indictment they would not see fit to appear in person to answer. In the following year (1643), that internal peace was necessary for the good of the country was greatly felt; and in July a meeting of the principal persons in the county was held at Bunbury. They appeared to be pretty equally divided between King and Parliament, and a treaty of pacification was then drawn up, which was signed by Sir George, on behalf of the Parliamentarians, and by Lord Kilmorey, Sir Harry Mainwaring and others, for the Royalists. This measure, however, appears to have been particularly distasteful to Parliament, who considered it of such importance as to immediately render it null and void, so far as they were concerned, by a special ordinance.

The year 1659 developed one of those crises which faces a nation at one time or another in its history. After Cromwell's death there was no cohesion amongst the numerous factions which had sprung up during the Commonwealth period. Bickerings followed, although there was a movement of fusion between the Church party and the Presbyterians. There was a secret longing on the part of the nation and the military leaders for a return to monarchy. Fuller, in his " Notable Men and Sayings of England," puts the matter in his own quaint way. Speaking of General Monck and his arrival in England, he says :—" Now the scales began to fall down from the eyes of the English nation (as from Saul when his sight was received), sensible that they were deluded, with pretenses of religion and liberty, into atheism and vassalage. They had learnt also from the soldiers (whom they so long had quartered) to cry out ' one and all,' each shire setting forth a remonstrance of their grievances, and refusing further payment of taxes. . . . The hinder (rump) part of the Parliament still sitting at Westminster plied him with many messages and addresses. He returned an answer, giving them hope . . . but he was an absolute riddle and no plowing with his heifer to expound him. . . . Immediately followed that turn of our times which all the world with wonder doth behold. . . . Christ on the Cross said to his beloved disciple, ' Behold thy mother,' and he said to her, ' Behold, thy son.' Thus was he pleased effectually to speak to the hearts of the English, ' Behold your Sovereign,' which inspirited them with loyalty and a longing desire of his presence; saying likewise to our gracious sovereign, ' Behold thy subjects ' . . . and now, blessed be God, both are met together to their mutual comfort."

But all this was not accomplished until a period of considerable excitement had been passed. The state papers contain an interesting outline of the various stirring events which should be carefully studied. News travelled slowly in those days, and in July 1659 the news of the Cheshire rising under Sir George Booth caused great excitement in Manchester, and following a sermon preached by the Rev. Henry Newcome at Stockport, it was announced that "the Quakers had risen and that the trained bands were to meet at Warrington." Five hundred men marched from Manchester when Sir George raised the cry for "a free Parliament." August 5th was observed as a day of humiliation in Manchester, as they were afraid of Lilburn marching on the town, but the record says that the imprisonment of "a bloody anabaptist" prevented him getting to know that the trained bands were absent. Although, as we have seen, the Cheshire rising failed, it showed the insecurity and unpopularity of the Government with the Presbyterians and Independents as well as Episcopalians.

Under date 5th August 1659, a paper runs : "We hear that the enemy has risen in several parts, but only abides in Cheshire and Lancashire with Sir George Booth at the head, and that Charles II. had been proclaimed King at Warrington. The Council at Whitehall sent Lambert against him with a large body of horse and foot, and urged that the utmost courage and resolution to withstand the enemy, whose every attempt had been frustrated." Amongst the orders in Parliament of 6th August 1659, appears the following note : "On calling in several Cheshire gentlemen and receiving from one a petition called 'The petition of some few of your Honour's faithful and suffering servants and containing the offer of an expedient for quelling the rising of our old enemies and apostalising friends in the County of Chester,' which was read. After they had withdrawn (it was) ordered that the Council of State consult and bring in a declaration according to the substance of the Petition, the debate to be held next Monday morning." We cannot find that the matter, whatever it was, was debated, nor that any declaration concerning it was ever published. Militia Commissioners were appointed for Cheshire, Lancashire, and other counties with great powers, as it was said that some "leading cavaliers and discontented Presbyterians were inclined to kingship," and that they had contrived a general insurrection in England "at the same instant on behalf of Charles Stuart. They had, however, acted more warily in Cheshire by drawing in Sir George Booth, Sir Thomas Middleton, Colonel Brooke, and others of repute, and by the help of some (Presbyterian) ministers and the treachery of two of the county troops whom they seduced to their party, they got together some thousand horse and foot, and persuading the magistrates at Chester, possessed themselves of the city where they now are." Another extract says : " You have heard how Sir George Booth, Thomas Middleton, and other rebels in Cheshire, appeared in arms and proclaimed King Charles at Warrington and Wrexham, and are themselves proclaimed rebels by Parliament. Lambert, however, had charge of the military operations, and the designs of the enemy had hitherto been frustrated by a gracious and all seeing God, save only at Chester, and there we have good hopes of reducing them to obedience." Further, "The revolt was then reduced to two counties, one of which was Cheshire, where Sir George Booth, a gentleman who has 200,000 livres rent (income) and lately bore arms for this very Parliament, is at the head of 10,000 or 20,000 men. He is a great Presbyterian and for politic reasons has not yet declared for the King, but for a Parliament freely chosen."

The union between the Presbyterians and the Royalists gave additional impetus to the cause in which Sir George had embarked. In July 1659 Sir George proceeded to Manchester, and, after holding a conference with the Presbyterians and the Cavaliers, returned to Warrington and fixed a rising for the 1st of August. Sir George also entered into correspondence with the Earl of Derby and Lord Kilmorey, and such of the gentry of Lancashire and Cheshire as desired to assist in the deliberations for restoring the monarchy were allowed to do so. These plans were, however, revealed to the prevailing powers, and the risings in other counties were suppressed. That of Sir George was only destined for a feeble continuance. A few of the followers in their jubilancy plundered some of the houses of the Cromwellians; but this action on their part was strongly condemned by Sir George. As showing the great affection still felt for him by many of his old acquaintances, one of those who had suffered from the exuberant handling of his followers, a relative of President Bradshaw, wrote, warning him that all the other counties in England were quiet but Cheshire. Still he persisted in his enterprise, notwithstanding that he complained that he had been falsely deserted by a large number of the " best in England " who had promised him assistance.

Pushing on to Chester, which city he took, though the Castle held out, he and his forces rendezvoused at Rowton Heath. An old tract of the period says that Sir George invited the gentry of those parts to meet him, when he declared " he was for a free parliament and *a single person*, which proved effectual with the malcontented party, and divers sparks appearing in this great flame." It appears they had above 3000 horse and foot, well mounted and armed, " with drums beating, and colours flying, and trumpets sounding "; and after they were drawn up on the Heath, Colonel Brooke and Colonel Blackburne divided the horse and foot into several bodies, " placing them in sundry warlike figures and postures, after which Sir George made a speech showing the grounds and reasons of their present engagements and undertakings."

This speech or declaration had great effect in rousing the drooping spirits of his party. Not being able to get possession of Chester Castle, he set off with a portion of his forces in the direction of York; but the rapid approach of Lambert from Ireland compelled him to return to his former position at

Chester, Clarendon remarking that Sir George went to meet him " with his natural impetuosity."

His misfortunes now appeared to be at their height. On the 19th August the decisive battle of Winnington was fought, resulting in the complete defeat of Sir George's troops and his own ultimate capture. The troops of the Royalists were quartered at Northwich, while Lambert's were at Weaverham. The two armies, on this eventful day, came into action amongst the enclosures at Hartford. The horse were unable to act, and the Royalists " retired uninjured from hedge to hedge, and passed the bridge without any other loss," says Lambert, " than that of reputation, and discouragement in meeting with those whom they found of equal courage, but engaged in a better (?) cause." The Royalists now endeavoured to secure the bridge, which would have given them a great advantage, seeing that at this point the river was unfordable, the bridge narrow, and flanked with a strong ditch at the far end, and a high hill which no horse could pass otherwise than along the side in a narrow path.

This coign of vantage was not long held by the flagging Royalists. " After three good volleys," says Lambert, " the horse, passing the bridge together with the foot, charged the horse of the Royalists, which advanced to cover the retreat." Sir George Booth's infantry retired in good order, following their colours up the hill, and protected by the gallantry of the cavalry. Lambert gives due praise and honour to the English valour of his adversaries, and states that within a quarter of a mile the Royalists halted to give battle, but were a second time routed, although disputing " the place very gallantly, both parties showing themselves like Englishmen." Such is the description of the battle of Winnington, taken from an old tract of the period ; and contemporary historians agree in describing it as very decisive. Sir George escaped with great difficulty, and, disguising himself as a gentlewoman, left the scene of action. He was, however, betrayed, having acted his part very badly, and was taken at Newport Pagnell, in Buckinghamshire, where he was riding on a pillion in the disguise mentioned. He was committed to the Tower.

Sweeping measures were taken by Parliament to prevent the spread of the so-called " rebellion," and as a precautionary measure the nobility and gentry who were favourable to the King were made prisoners. As it was bluntly put by a writer of the period, " the English nobility were strangely cowardly. The chief persons who declared themselves with Booth were the Earl of Derby, Lord Kilmorey, Colonel Ireland, Major John Middleton, and other private gentlemen."

But Lady Booth bestirred herself energetically on behalf of her imprisoned husband. She wrote to President Bradshaw, who replied that the best course for her husband to find favour was for both he and she to deal candidly with the Council by making a full discovery of the enemy's designs in which Sir George was lately engaged against Parliament. At the same time Lambert was desired to send Colonel John Booth (a relative of Sir George), Major Peter Brooke, Henry Brooke, and Major J. Egerton in safe custody to London.

As a result of Sir George Booth's examination, Bradshaw, Lord President of the Council, was empowered to sign warrants to apprehend the persons mentioned by him, with their papers, horses and arms, and to bring their persons in custody before the Council. As Lambert had suppressed the rising, or as peace was restored (State paper) " by God's blessing in the parts where Lord Lambert was concerned, he was summoned to attend before the Council, and they thought fit that Colonel John Booth and others already mentioned should be sent for examination, with their papers." Meantime the examination of Sir George was proceeded with. He ingenuously confessed to having treated with Morden, the King's agent, and to his wife having received a letter from the King. He discovered the whole design without mentioning the names of the others, and begged not to be pressed to do a thing which would wound his honour. Hitherto his confession had been voluntarily made, and his speeches showed that there had been a misunderstanding between them and the other chiefs (?) because he refused to proclaim the King, and that against his advice they drew near to the Parliamentary army and engaged in fighting; and that, before he arrived at the head of the troops, those who wished to attack Lambert had fled; that he tried to rally at Chester and then defend that town; that they refused to bear arms any longer for the cause, as they said " they had been abandoned by God." Parliament found out from him and other persons that many other persons of quality had promised to follow his example.

Early in September " the insurrections carried on on Charles Stuart's account were suppressed and peace everywhere restored. Sir George Booth and others were prisoners, and all the chief actors in the rebellion were submitting." The Government had ordered troops from Ireland, but Sir George Booth having been defeated, thus delayed King Charles and the Duke of York's passing to England. The intentions of the King were also very nebulous. Lady Booth " had sent a letter to Sir George Booth from C.R. (Charles II.) and other papers with the first examination of Sir George Booth."

Secretary Nicholas, writing to a correspondent at Brussels, said that " there was great fault in some in England for not rising as they promised to join Sir George Booth. The Presbyterians were so confident of prevailing that they refused many which would have joined them. His defeat was a great misfortune, and hopes were entertained that the King had heard of this defeat before he had had time to set off for England." John Tipping, servant to Sir George Booth, was examined before the Committee, who were to report to Parliament what should be done with him. The Committee for examination met in September 1659 to consider the case of Henry, Earl of Stamford, or any others charged with high treason or suspicion of it, and to procure and submit reports to Parliament, giving some idea of the intrigues going on at that time, that Sir George Booth " stood still so far and undiscovered as ever." The Earl of Stamford, Mr Jackson, and Mrs Kathrine Booth were accorded liberty to speak with Sir George in the Tower on his private affairs, in the presence of the Lieutenant of the Tower, and a similar privilege was accorded to Mrs Francis Booth.

Colonel Nathaniel Booth was at the end of September committed to the Comptor of Southwark for high treason in levying war against the King. Petitions of Frances and Kathrine Booth and Kathrine Jackson, relatives of Nathaniel Booth, were presented to the Committee. The literary history of the period from 1642 to 1690 teems with pamphlets and broadsides and works having for their theme current events and the maintenance of the Protestant religion. Sir George Booth was the subject of a large number, which are to be found in the British Museum, and we may also add the Chetham Library at Manchester, which may be recommended to students wishful to continue their researches into the events of this striking period of English history. Prominent amongst them is a declaration of Sir George " at the last general rendezvous near the City of Chester " (1659), and Sir George's letter " showing the reasons of his present engagement " (2nd August 1659). A conversation between Sir George Booth and Sir John Presbyter purports to be a dialogue between the two while Sir George was imprisoned in the Tower. Sir George expresses his great repentance at having been connected with parsons in any way and uses strong language concerning them. W. P(rynne), the Puritan, puts in a plea for Sir George and the Cheshire gentlemen, and in addition to those outlined in previous pages is an account of " a Bloudy Fight between the Parliament Forces and Sir George Booth's on Priest Moor, near Red Hill Castle, in the County of Salop."

The confinement of Sir George in the Tower was not of long duration. General Monck having declared for " a full and free Parliament " in which the nation would be thoroughly represented, the excluded members and Sir George were released from the sequestration under which they laboured. In 1660 the Long Parliament was dissolved, and what was called "the Convention Parliament," from its not being summoned by regal authority, consisting of Royalists and Presbyterians, assembled, together with " a legitimate House of Lords composed of hereditary Peers." This body was entirely favourable to a restoration of the Royal House. In his exile Charles sent his celebrated Declaration of Breda, in which he promised a free pardon to all (excepting those whom Parliament should name) who should return within forty days to their allegiance, a free Parliament, religious toleration, settlement by Parliament of all questions affecting estates whose ownership had been altered by the Civil War, all arrears of pay made to the army and taken into his service.

These terms were accepted, and from that date, 29th May 1660, dates the Restoration. This was the day on which he reached London, having landed at Dover four days previously. Although Charles did not actually come to the throne until 1660, the Judge of the High Court decided that his reign legally commenced 30th January 1649, the day of his father's execution. Honours were afterwards showered upon Sir George. In the same year the sum of £20,000 was on the point of being voted to him as a reward for his services and great sufferings, when he in his place in the House requested, with a high souled patriotism, which only those acquainted with the manners of the time can fully appreciate, that it should not be more than half that amount, which was accordingly granted by the Commons on 2nd August, and confirmed by the Lords the day following. As a reward from the Crown he was ennobled by the title of Baron Delamere of Dunham Massey, the patent bearing date 20th April 1661, and at the same time he had the liberty to propose six gentlemen to receive the honour of Knighthood, and two others for the dignity of Baronet.

During his eventful life, Sir George appears to have found ample time to devote to domestic matters. According to one old writer, he greatly improved the Manor house of Dunham Massey by building the north side thereof answerable to the opposite part, surrounded it with "a large outward court, with brick wall and a faire gate of stone," and made a domestic chapel on the south side of the house. It was "a large quadrangular pile, with gables within and without. The gables within the court were indented and scalloped, and large transome windows introduced. The exterior front appears to have been finished at a later period, with pilasters and ornaments in imitation of the Italian style of architecture, and large octagonal turrets were placed at the corners. It stood within gardens laid out in the stiff taste of the time, and surrounded by an ample moat, in one angle of which is drawn a large circular mound, with a summer house on the top of it, supposed to be the site of the Norman keep tower." The noble avenue of beeches was in its swaddling clothes, so to speak, being surrounded with large wooden guards, while the landscape is destitute of that sylvan beauty which is the admiration, and justly so, of modern times. He was twice married: firstly, to Catherine, the daughter of Theophilus Fiennes, Earl of Lincoln, who died in childbirth, leaving an only daughter, Vere Booth; and secondly, to Elizabeth, daughter of Henry Grey, Earl of Stamford, by whom he had seven sons and six daughters, and who died in 1690 at Oldfield Hall.

Sir George died on 10th August 1684, and was buried at Bowdon on the 9th September with great solemnity; on which occasion the Rev. F. Cawdrey, a Presbyterian minister, preached on the subject of salvation.

On a brass which was formerly fixed in a stone at the entrance to the family vault in the Stamford Chapel at Bowdon, was an inscription in Latin, of which the undernoted is a translation, and which will form a fitting record of such a notable career. It was not replaced at the restoration of the church.

"Under this monument are interred the remains of George, Lord Delamer (De la Mer), Baron of the ancient and noble House of Dunham Massey, who was distinguished by his piety, fidelity and affection to God, King and Country, and who in the sixty-second year of his age exchanged an earthly coronet for a celestial crown, died on the 10th day of August, in the year of our Salvation 1684. William Andrews, deploring the death of his most honourable Lord (in whose service he had continued for upwards of 30 years faithfully ministering and partaking in the loyalty which his master showed to his King) this monument to his ever blessed and happy memory has been erected, consecrated and preserved, and a hope added that when his life at the same time, with his official duty to that noble family came to an end, at the entrance to this tomb his ashes might rest, until the day when they might rise, together with those of his master, into the new and eternal life. Died 25th day of July 1685."

Clarendon describes Sir George as being of one of the "best fortunes and interests in Cheshire," but his deeds more than all entitle his memory to be held in veneration and esteem by his fellow countrymen.

CHAPTER XVI.

Lord Delamere's eventful life—The Stuart period reviewed—Lord Delamere's early days—His popularity—Advocacy of people's rights—His arrest and committal to the Tower on three occasions—Family life at Dunham—A terrible Christmas and New Year—Royalty jealous of Lord Delamere—Judge Jeffreys' hostility—Political leanings of the Jury of Peers—The historic "Tryall" for High Treason—Ancient formalities observed by the Court—Lord Delamere refuses as a Peer of the Realm to hold up his hand—A privilege of the Peerage—A formidable indictment—The Judge overrules objections—Evidence for and against—Some amusing witnesses —His Lordship's eloquent appeal and acquittal—Commission dissolved; Usher's wand broken —" God Save the King."

LOVE of country, coupled with personal piety of a rare and high degree, is the lesson to be learnt from the life of Henry, second Baron Delamere, first Earl of Warrington, born 1st February 1651, who succeeded to the peerage on the death of his father in 1684. Contemporary historians have done scant justice to his memory. Some pass him without notice. Even Macaulay, whose elaborate and brilliant record embrace a series of epoch-making periods in English history, stigmatises him as "a soured and disappointed Whig," but Bishop Burnett, in "A History of his own Time" (two bulky volumes), although generally adverse to Lord Delamere's policy, appears to deal fairly with his Lordship's movements in national affairs, notwithstanding what were styled certain "Reflections" on his public character. Ormerod, in his erudite "History of Cheshire," gives a fairly elaborate account of his family and connections, whilst Newcome, Martindale, and other non-conforming divines, whose writings throw a strong sidelight on his character from a religious standpoint, and from the view of a churchman of that period, evidenced a mind which was far too wide and broad and deep to be influenced by minor or petty considerations in religion and politics.

The story of the Stuart kings of England is one long record of struggles and turmoil between prince and people. In the outcome, the people, after going through throes of civil war, and an interregnum filled in with the powerful personality of Cromwell, triumphed, and laid the foundations of the liberties we now enjoy. Of one of these Stuart kings (Charles II.) it is said, "He never said a foolish thing and never did a wise one." Of another (James II.), "that he had a big head, a slobbering tongue, goggle eyes, a want of personal dignity, while he displayed coarse buffonery, pedantry, and contemptible cowardice in his dealings with men."

The principal features of the reign of the last of the Stuart kings (James II.) embraced on the part of the people a firm decision for the maintenance of the

The Rt. Honble Henry Booth Ld. De La Mer of Dunham
Massey in the County Pal. of Chester Ld. Lieutent. of the said
County One of the Lds of their Maties most honble Privy
Council &c One of the Lds Comrs of the Treasury &c

Wythenshawe Hall

C. E Arden   Lymm

Lymm Dell - A Picturesque Part of Cheshire

Protestant religion, sealed by the famous Declaration of Right, the proclamation of William III. and Mary as King and Queen of England, the infamies of Judge Jeffreys, the Monmouth Rebellion, and the historic Bloody Assize, where hundreds of people, chiefly in the West of England, were burnt at the stake, beheaded, hanged, or transported. A principle of bedrock importance to us in the present day, however, was the fixing of the authority of parliament to govern by and through the voice of the people, and the provision that no freeman should be obliged to " give any gift, loan, benevolence or tax " without common consent by Act of Parliament, which remains a fundamental law to this day. This period also sets forth in interesting fashion the habits and customs of the people of England at that period, sandwiched with such glimpses of court and national procedure as to make it a rounded whole. Whilst history has made us acquainted with prominent actors on the Stuart stage, principally court favourites and ladies of easy virtue, it is strangely silent regarding many Englishmen, Peers and Members of Parliament, who did a large amount of work publicly and privately in shaping the destinies of the nation during a trying and stormy period. One of the last mentioned was Lord Delamere of Dunham Massey, who was a thorn in the side of the two monarchs referred to above in whose reigns he lived. Singular to say, the Stuarts have provided us with most charming pictures of amusements, sports, pageants and costumes. It is on record that the costumes of the reign of the first Charles were the most elegant ever worn in our history. There was clothing distinguishing cavaliers, noblemen, gentry, farmers, tradesmen, peasants, youths and girls of the period, *et hoc genus homnes*, and it may be safely said that at this period a lord could not possibly be mistaken for a waiter, as has often happened in our day and generation.

The cavalier's costume, from the circumstance of its having been made the habit of the time in which Vandyke painted, became associated with his name, being frequently called the Vandyke dress. At the commencement of Charles's reign, however, the fashions of the older days of his father were retained, and there was scarcely a nation of Europe, except France, singular to say, that had not contributed its share to them. The cavalier dress consisted of a doublet of silk, satin, or velvet, with large loose sleeves slashed up the front, the collar covered by a falling band of the richest point lace with that peculiar edging called Vandyke. A short cloak was thrown carelessly over the shoulder; long breeches fringed or pointed met the tops of the wide boots, which were also trimmed with lace or lawn. A broad-leaved Flemish beaver hat with a rich hat band and plume of feathers was set on one side of the head, and a Spanish rapier hung from a magnificent baldrick or sword belt. The beard was worn very peaked with small upturned mustachios. A gentleman's dress of the period was of dark philliamot laced with silver. The suit was trimmed with scarlet taffeta ribbons, his stockings of white silk, and his shoes black with scarlet shoestrings, and garters; linen, laced with rich Flanders lace, and a black beaver buttoned on the left side was worn. Another costume was a long close vest of black cloth picked with white satin, a loose coat, black shoes and white stockings.

A condensed sketch leading up to the Restoration will be found illuminating and suggestive. In 1650 the Parliament in its fervour and hatred of monarchy drew up its declaration: " I promise to remain faithful to the Republic, without King, Sovereign or Lord." But many strange things happened under the Cromwell régime. It was remarkable for the exploits of an amateur soldier. He taught the Continent to tremble, and achieved the object of making the Republic as respected abroad as was the Republic of Rome. In signing treaties the Protector wrote his name above that of the King of France. The English Navy took possession of the sea coasts of the world and taught the once victorious Dutch to humbly salute the British flag. The equilibrium of the thrones in which the Stuarts formed a link had been overthrown. Charles II. had sent to his " longing " subjects, as we have seen in the previous chapter, the Declaration of Breda. " England had been in a dream. Charles II. was placed on the throne; Cromwell's remains hung on a gibbet."

In spite of the Restoration, the country was far from settled, for in one of his works Lord Delamere gives some advice to his sons, in which he recapitulates his father's and his own unfortunate experiences of imprisonment in the Tower. He proceeds, "And now in my thirty-seventh year, preceiving a boisterous storm to approach (anticipating the Revolution) by which I may be swept away in the common calamity, I conceive the best thing I can do for you is to advertise (warn) you of the rocks and precipices which by means of my troubles and sufferings I have discovered." A review of his lordship's works will be found in a subsequent chapter, which throws a sidelight on contemporary events. He had been elected a Member of Parliament for the County during his father's lifetime, 1678-81, and was appointed previously to the high office of Custos Rotulorum in 1673. He married Mary, daughter and sole heiress of Sir James Langham, Bart., of Cotters Brook, Northamptonshire. She died in 1690-91, leaving him with four sons and two daughters. He was distinguished at an early period of his career by his ardent advocacy of those liberties which were at that time overshadowed and threatened with extinction by the movements of the Papists. He was particularly anxious for the passing of the famous Bill of Exclusion, for which Lord Russell, on the morning of his execution, sent him a kindly message of respect and thanks.

He also made great exertions for securing the purity of parliaments, in instituting inquiries into the corruption of the judges, and in recommending the punishment of such as might be guilty. He was deposed in consequence from his public positions of trust in the reign of James II.

The intelligence of the second arrest of Lord Delamere in 1684 caused a great sensation in his family and in Bowdon parish. Newcome says, " They (his family) tremblingly await the issue of things. I look upon it as a strange thing, if possible to rescue Lord Delamere, whom I prayed for. Evidently thinking some miracle would happen, as God changed the nation to save his father in 1659, God can save him by reason of state." Again they heard of the granting of bail to Lord Delamere as a God given mercy, but he was soon " clapt up " again (in 1685)—in other words, committed to his old quarters in the Tower for the third time.

For seven weary weeks, Newcome continues, they at Dunham awaited the " tryall." There was a dull and anxious Christmas and the New Year dawned without hope, but there were great rejoicings when Lord Delamere was acquitted. " It was an unexpected mercy," Newcome adds, " after a period of prayer I honestly designed, and forwarded to his Lordship in London, a discourse of the use for God he would make of this unexpected happening, but his Lordship had evidently other pressing matters to attend to, and a reply was never sent."

The State records of this period fairly bristle with reports of intrigues, conspiracies, and rumours of risings about to materialise. In one plot it was alleged that Lord Delamere was engaged " after the manner of Judas," while others were " busy blowing the bellows of Rebellion." One, Evan Price, " a wandering person from Manchester," was singled out as an instrument who could be persuaded to give evidence against Lord Delamere, as, if Price refused, " they had already sufficient evidence to hang him." In another account of the transaction, Price is said to have been a bookseller, and he asserted that Sir Nicholas Mosley, a magistrate, had offered him £1000 to give evidence against those implicated in the conspiracy to overthrow the Government. Price, on refusing to do this, was committed to Lancaster Assizes, where the judges also tried to induce him to turn King's Evidence, and Mosley's offer was renewed by the High Sheriff. Mosley had stated, in an unguarded moment, that Lord Delamere was in the conspiracy along with others, and that Price had said so. Lord Delamere determined to wipe off this reproach, and promptly commenced an action for libel against Mosley. The matter was ended by a letter, presumably from the Court, ordering the judges to apologise for their illegal behaviour. Lord Delamere, however, insisted on the release of Price as well, which was accordingly ordered the following Lent Assizes.

Martindale also gives us a picture of family life at Dunham. At the end of September he was sent for to officiate as chaplain to his lordship. The employment appears to have been intermittent. The salary was £40 per annum, and four or five pounds more for teaching mathematics to members of Lord Delamere's family. " My employment there," he says, " besides accompanying my Lord abroad (that is, in walks and visits in the neighbourhood), was family duty twice a day, which before dinner was a short prayer, chapter, and more solemn prayer, and before supper the like, only a psalme or part of one after the chapter. When it was my Lord's wish that the Lord's Day or any of the King's days should be kept at home, I officiated, and when, on the Lord's Day we went to Bowdon (church) I catechised in the evening and expounded the Catechism in a doctrinall and practicall way, so it was as much pains for me and as profitable to the auditory as if I had preached a formal sermon." As already noted, the employment at Dunham Hall was intermittent, but for seven or eight years he attended at Dunham, usually from May, when Lord Delamere returned to his seat there, until October and November, when he took up his residence in the Capital. Lord Delamere's interest in small matters was as great as in the larger cares of his high estate, as evidenced by the fact that when Martindale's daughter was attacked with consumption, he sent from London a number of bottles of Daffy's Elixir, which, until comparatively recent times, was a popular specific and had a great vogue. The poor girl, however, succumbed to the fell disease.

Of Lord Delamere's friendship with the popular but unfortunate Duke of Monmouth, there cannot be two opinions. It was whole hearted and sincere, and he was, in consequence of his efforts in promoting the Bill excluding the Duke of York from the succession to the Throne, by no means a *persona grata* with King Charles II. Indeed his name was returned by the Court spies as one of the Cheshire gentlemen who attended Monmouth (at Dunham) in his memorable progress from Scotland to London in 1682. He met the Duke, in company with a large number of gentlemen of Cheshire, and right royally entertained him at Dunham, and it was one of the pieces of evidence brought forward at his famous trial—that he had intrigued with the Dutch to place Monmouth on the Throne in succession to Charles II.

The Duke, after the discovery of the Ryehouse Plot, " absconded " to Holland, where he remained until 1685. His " invasion " of England, as is well known, was shortlived and futile. He calculated on a rising in the west, and, according to information received, London was ready to revolt. It was further urged by his advisers that James was so intent upon the pomp and ceremony of his Coronation that for some time more important matters would not be thought of.

The jealousy of royalty concerning Lord Delamere and his movements, however, had been evidenced in 1684, when he was committed to the Tower. He was, however, in goodly company, having as associates Lord Brandon and Lord Gerard. They were liberated shortly afterwards without any charge having been made against them. Early in 1685, as already stated, he was arrested for the third time and again lodged in the Tower. This brought about a crisis. The House of Lords became restless under these conditions, and a petition was addressed to the King by the Lords praying that he should be brought to a speedy trial.

The jury which tried Lord Delamere was "packed" by his political opponents. They were selected by Judge Jeffreys, himself a Cheshire man, and a former Justice of Chester, to whom his Lordship had " on occasion " to administer some wholesome and unpleasant truths. In a speech in the House of Lords on the corruption of the Judges he thus referred to him—" The county for which I serve is Cheshire, which is a County Palatine, and we have two judges peculiarly assigned to us by His Majesty. Our Puisne Judge I have nothing to say against him, for he is a very honest man for aught I know. But I cannot be silent as to our Chief Judge, and I will name him, because what I have to say will appear more probable. His name is George Jeffries, who I must say behaved himself more like a Jack Pudding than with the gravity which beseems a Judge. He was mighty witty upon the prisoners at the Bar; he was very full of his joaks upon people that came up to give evidence, not suffering them to declose what they had to say in their own way and method, because they behaved themselves with more gravity than he; and indeed the people were strangely perplexed when they were to give in their evidence; but I do not insist upon this or upon the late hours he kept up and down our City (Chester). It's said he was every night drinking till two a clock, or beyond that time, and that he went to his chamber drunk, but this I have only by common fame, for I was not in his company; I bless God I am not a man of his principles or behaviour, but in the mornings he appeared with the symptoms of a man that over night had taken a large cup. His Lordship also complained of the Chief Justice in appointing Assizes when he pleased, of leaving many causes untried, and thus causing expense to the people and delay in executing justice."

Lord Churchill was foreman of the jury, and other Peers were : Laurence, Earl of Rochester ; Robert, Earl of Sunderland ; Henry, Duke of Norfolk ; John, Earl of Mulgrave ; Charles, Earl of Shrewsbury ; Theophilus, Earl of Huntingdon ; Daniel, Earl of Nottingham ; John, Earl of Coarsdale ; William, Earl of Craven ; and Vere Essex, Lord Cromwell, etc.

The historic trial took place in Westminster Hall on 14th January 1685, his Lordship only having completed his thirty-fourth year. It was conducted with all the pomp and circumstance of so high a Court, and the proceedings throughout were quaint and interesting. The Judge entered escorted by the Garter King-at-Arms, in picturesque garb, and the Gentleman Usher of the Black Rod. Following were the Attorney-General, Solicitor-General, Sergeant-at-Arms, and other officials of the court. We now proceed with a report of the trial taken from the official records :—

The Gentleman Usher made three obeisances and handed his wand to the Judge, who returned it to him to hold during the trial.

Sergeant-at-Arms—Oh yes, oh yes, my Lord the High Steward of England, his Grace, does steadfastly command all manner of persons to keep silence and to give ear to the King's Commissioner, to his Grace, my Lord High Steward of England, upon pain of imprisonment.

Clerk of the Court—Sergeant-at-Arms, make proclamation.

Sergeant-at-Arms—Oh yes, oh yes, the Lord High Steward doth strictly charge and command all manner of persons here present, except Peers, Privy Counsellors, and all reverend Judges now assistant, to be uncovered.

Thereupon the general public removed their hats and the noble prisoner was escorted before Jeffreys by the Lieutenant of the Tower.

The names, as already given, were called, but three peers who had been summoned did not answer. They were, James, Duke of Ormonde, Lord Steward of His Majesty's Household; Christopher, Duke of Abermarle; and Richard, Earl of Burlington. After being admonished to make, if guilty, a full confession of his heinous crime, he was asked to hold up his hand. This he refused, as a Peer of the Realm, to do, and the Judge remarked that it didn't matter.

A formidable indictment, which ran as follows, was read by the Clerk of the Court:—

Henry, Baron Delamere, thou standest indicted in the County Palatine of Chester by the name of Henry, Baron de la Mer of Mere, in the City and County of Chester, for that thou as a false traitor against the most illustrious and most excellent Prince James, the Second, by the Grace of God, of England, Scotland, France, and Ireland, King, thy natural Lord, not having the fear of God in thy heart, nor weighing the duty of thy allegiance, but being moved and seduced by the instigation of the devil, the cordial love and true duty and natural obedience, which a true and faithful subject of our Lord the King ought of right to bear love, did plot against the tranquillity of the kingdom. And did further disquiet and cause war and rebellion against our sovereign Lord the King within this kingdom of England, to stir up, move, and procure and subvert and change and devote him to death and destruction, and thus did maliciously, devilishly and traitorously, and with other false traitors to the Jurors unknown, did conspire, compass, to deprive and cast down and kill the same King, and that thou Henry, Baron Delamere as a false traitor there and then to wit, with other men unknown, did gather sums of money to attack and take the Castle of Chester, and all the Magazines in the same Castle aforesaid. And further, that thou didst thus excite, animate, and persuade against the duty of their allegiance and against the statute in that case made and provided. How sayest thou, Henry, Baron of Delamere, art thou guilty of this High Treason whereof thou standest indicted and hast now been arraigned, or not guilty?

Delamere—My Lord, I have a plea to offer to your Grace and my Lords, and it is in reference to the privilege and right of the Peers of England.

Judge—If you have any plea to offer it must be received by my Lords.

Attorney-General—My Lord, the prisoner, Henry, Lord de la Mer, stands indicted as you have heard, for conspiring the death of his Majesty the King, and in order thereunto did attempt to raise rebellion in this Kingdom. The County Palatine of Chester was one of the stages where Monmouth's rebellion was principally to be acted, and preparatory to it great riotous assemblies and tumultuous gatherings were set on foot by the conspirators, and that the late Duke of Monmouth did look upon Cheshire as one of his chief supports, and upon my Lord Delamere as his principal assistant there. One, Disney, since executed for high treason, met Lord Delamere at a coffee-house in London. Lord Delamere changed his name to Brown, and accompanied by only one servant, a thing which was much below a person of his quality to do, went off by byroads, and would not keep the high and common road, with great speed into Cheshire. It was a case for great suspicion that he should assume the name of a commoner and post out of town, especially when Parliament was sitting.

Judge—Call your witnesses, Mr Attorney.

Attorney-General—I call my Lord Howard of Escrick.

Lord Howard—As to the noble Lord at the bar I have nothing to say against him.

Judge—You are not called as a particular witness against Lord Delamere, but to speak of the conspiracy for an insurrection.

Howard—If so, then I am called upon to give evidence not against Lord Delamere, but myself. I am filled with shame and confusion for my guilt and cannot but always reflect upon it with sorrow and horror. It was at a time when great heats did arise upon the election contests in the City of London.

Attorney-General—Your Grace, my Lord Delamere seems to be faint with standing. If your Grace pleases may a chair be provided for my Lord to sit in?

The Judge—By all means let a chair be provided.

(Chair was produced and Lord Delamere seated himself.)

Howard—These elections produced heat which was above the common expression of discontent, but I know nothing of any particular treason. There were great murmurings in the mouths of all sorts of people and very angry and warm speeches, but nothing else, and as I thought the business was over for that time I went away to my own house.

Attorney-General—Before my Lord Howard goes I would ask him one question in general—whether he knew of any design of a rising in Cheshire?

Howard—No, my Lord, none at all.

Attorney-General—Lord Grey.

Lord Grey—My Lord, I am subpoened hither by both parties. I do not know anything that I can speak of my own knowledge against the prisoner, nor have I anything to say that will be for his advantage.

Attorney-General—Richard Goodenough.

Goodenough—A messenger was sent from Amsterdam by one Jones, from the Duke of Monmouth to Lord Delamere, to the effect that he had promised to draw his sword on behalf of the Duke, and he hoped he would not break his promise.

Judge—My Lord, will you ask him any questions?

Delamere—I never saw his face in my life that I know of.

The Judge—That is pretty strange—so famous an Under-Sheriff of London and Middlesex as he was.

Attorney-General—Call John Jones.

Jones—I was asked to deliver a message to a crop-haired or crop-eared merchant in London, and to acquaint my Lord Delamere that the Duke of Monmouth was coming to England.

The Judge—My Lord, do you ask him any questions?

Delamere—No, my Lord, I never saw his face before to my knowledge.

Attorney-General—Stephen Vaux. I must acquaint your Grace that this is an unwilling witness and we are forced to pump all out of him by questions.

Vaux—I tell the truth of all that I know.

Attorney-General—I ask you whether you went the best way in to Cheshire with my Lord Delamere?

Vaux—We made it our way. It is the freest from dust!

Attorney-General—I ask you a plain question. Is it the best way?

Vaux—Truly, my Lord, I don't know. It may be.

Attorney-General—Timothy Edlin.

Edlin—I never saw Lord Delamere before that day in my life. He said he was going into Cheshire to see a sick child. He went by the name of Brown.

Delamere—Did you ever know anybody else that went by the name of Brown besides me?

Edlin—There was a discourse of Mr Vermuydens going by the name of Brown. Brown is rather a common name now.

Attorney-General—Thomas Saxon.

Saxon—At the beginning of June last I was sent for to Mere, my Lord Delamere's house in Cheshire. I was told I was an honest useful man, and they hoped I should prove so. Lord Delamere had undertaken to raise 10,000 men in Cheshire by the 1st of June, but they could not raise the money. They gave me money to convey a message to the Duke of Monmouth to this effect.

Attorney General—When did you see my Lord Brandon?

Saxon—Upon the Monday in Easter week at Over in Cheshire. I drunk a glass of ale with him and smoked a pipe of tobacco, and we drank considerably. After we had drunk pretty smartly there was a discourse on the election of parliament men and the maintaining of certain English liberties.

Judge—From whom did you receive money?

Saxon—From my Lord Delamere.

Judge—Did you say this to anyone?

Saxon—To Storey. I lay with him in the same bed in prison in Newgate.

Judge—I don't know when thou comest to Newgate. It may be thou hast oftener been there more than once.

Saxon—I gave my first information immediately after I was brought to town, when I was removed from Dorchester gaol.

Judge—What were you to do?

Saxon—I was a tradesman in Middlewich and much acquainted with the ordinary sort of people.

Delamere—Who let you into the house? Was anybody else there?

Saxon—No, you were so wise you would not let anybody be so fortunate.

Delamere—I believe this man Saxon who has given evidence was known as Blackhead. He is a common informer, and he was entertained, I am told, in my own house after coming to place documents in a flowerpot in the hall, with a view to convicting me of treasonable practices.

Attorney-General—My Lord is now at liberty to make his own defence.

Judge—Then, my Lord, the time has come for you to make your defence. You have heard what has been evidenced against you, and my Lords, the Jury of your Peers, now expect to hear what you have to say for yourself.

Lord Delamere—I have a great deal to say, and I apply for an adjournment.

The Judge—Yes, if it can be done by law. My Lords the jury consider it.

Lord Churchill—Where a trial is by a Jury there the law is clear. The Jury once charged can never be discharged till they have given their verdict, and the reason of that is the fear of corruption and the tampering with a Jury. No man knows what may happen, for they are weak men and may be wrought upon by undue influences.

The Judge—I confess I would always be very tender of the privilege of the Peers, wherever I find them concerned, but this Court is convened and held by me. Though you are judges of the law of this Court, which is within my province, my business is to see the law observed.

Attorney-General—Will your Grace give direction to my Lord to proceed?

Judge—Yes: he must proceed, I think.

Lord Delamere—I will now proceed to address my Lords in my defence. I can with great comfort and satisfaction say that these crimes wherewith I am charged, are not only strangers to my thoughts, but also to what has been my constant principle and practice. There are also few who have more heartily conformed to the practices of the Church as by law established in this land, and I must urge that there is little or no evidence from a legal point of view, and that there is no sufficiency to warrant my being found guilty on the capital charge. The man Saxon, who is the principal witness, is looked upon as a great Goliath, whose evidence is brought forward to maintain this accusation. How could it be thought I should summon him to my house, a stranger, and give him strong and convincing proof that I was disloyal to the Crown, to whom I had sworn due allegiance? I desire to call Richard Hall to give an account of a letter forged by Saxon in the name of one, Richard Hildage.

Hall—I paid to Thomas Saxon, on account of Richard Hildage, the sum of £6 odd money owed to Hildage, and afterwards, when at Newcastle-under-Lyme, Hildage asked me for it, I sent to Saxon for it, but the money did not come.

Judge—Did you ever get the money?

Hall—No, my Lord.

Judge—Look you, my Lord Delamere, the objection carries a great deal of weight in it to prove him a very ill man indeed.

Cryer—Richard Shaw.

Richard Shaw—I owed Saxon a little money, and he forged a letter in William Preston's name.

Judge—Is Preston here?

Shaw—No, my Lord, but he told me he did not write the letter.

Judge—This is just the same thing again. We all know how easy a thing it is to hear a bailiff tell a lie.

Hall—He certainly told me.

o

Judge—All that is nothing. It is a difficulter matter to hear such fellows speak the truth than anything else I feel sure.

Cryer—Peter Hough.

Peter Hough—My Lord, Saxon had of me £6, 10s. in money, 10s. in work, and he gave me a bond. After he made it out I found it was only for £6.

Saxon—My Lord, I had £5, 10s. off him in money, and 10s. in work, and gave him a bond for it.

Judge—If it were for £7, and he made it out for £6, it shows there was an intention to cheat him of 20s.

Delamere—That shows what kind of man he is.

Cryer—Edward Wilkinson.

Edward Wilkinson—Saxon hired a horse from me at 1½d. per day, and he never came again, nor had I the satisfaction of my horse, but I lost the horse by the bargain, and my money too.

Judge—I perceive according to your dates that he rode into the rebellion with this horse, and he was a very knave for so doing, upon my conscience.

Cryer—William Wright.

William Wright—I have had transactions with Thomas Saxon, and I never knew him to perfect his word in anything.

Judge—Not make good his word? I suppose that is a Cheshire phrase?

Wright—Then I met him one night after evening prayer, and I said to him, Thomas Saxon, if I cared no more for keeping my word than thou dost, for to be sure if thy mouth opens thy tongue lies. And he turned away from me and would not answer me a word. He said if I did trouble him over the thing it would be worse for me, whereof all the town knows as well as I, and I cannot set him forth in words as bad as he is.

Delamere—My Lord, I have shown Saxon to be a man of no reputation in Cheshire. It is a most improbable story he has told, and he cannot be trusted out of Newgate, whence he comes to give evidence.

Lord Delamere called witnesses to prove that he was not at Mere at the time deposed to by witnesses for the prosecution.

Mr John Edmonds (sworn, said)—On the 5th of May my Lord Delamere did me the honour to come to my house, and he stayed there a little while and desired me to be a witness of his taking possession upon a lease of my Lord Bishop of Chester, and we went into the house which is next to mine, and there he took possession.

The Lord High Steward—Where is your house?

Mr Edmonds—At Boden, in Cheshire.

Mr Henry was called and sworn.

Lord Delamere—Pray, will you give his Grace and my Lords an account whether you were not an attorney and delivered me possession upon the lease of my Lord Bishop of Chester?

Mr Henry—My Lord, I was attorney by appointment, and the 5th May last I delivered possession to my Lord Delamere at one of the most remarkable places of the land that belonged to that lease of the Bishop.

Lord Delamere hoped that this was a satisfactory reason for his going down at the time, the Bishop being ill, and the lease worth £6000 or £7000. The next occasion he had to speak to was the 27th May. He said, "I had taken up the resolution before to go and see my child which was not well, but I had not taken my journey so soon nor with such privacy but that I had notice that there was a warrant out to apprehend me, and knowing the inconvenience of lying in prison I was very willing to keep as long out of custody as I could, and therefore I went out of the way and under a borrowed name."

At his Lordship's request his mother (the Dowager Lady Delamere), who sat by him at the bar during the trial, was examined. She said, in reply to questions, that this child of his was more than ordinarily "pretious" (precious) to him in regard it was born to him at the time " when he was an innocent honest man (as he was then a prisoner in the Tower for high treason) above two years ago, and she thought it had increased his affection to that child that God had given to him when he was in that affliction." While he was at Dunham, her daughter sent word that it had pleased God to visit his eldest son in London with a grievous distemper, and thereupon he made all the haste he could back (to Cheshire).

Witnesses were called to prove that persons said by Saxon to have been present on a given date were in London at the time, and, altogether, conclusive evidence was forthcoming to show that his testimony was not at all of a reliable character. Amongst these witnesses were two brothers of the noble prisoner. In the course of some further remarks he denied that he ever wrote or sent any message or had had any correspondence for three years past with the Duke of Monmouth. He pointed out circumstances in the evidence for the prosecution not borne out by facts, and concluded by reminding their Lordships that the eyes of the nation were upon their proceedings that day. "Your Lordships are now judging the cause of every man in England that shall happen to come under like circumstances with myself hereafter: for accordingly as you judge me now, just so will inferior courts be directed to give their judgments in like cases in time to come. Your Lordships know very well that blood once spilled can never be gathered up again, and therefore, unless the case be very clear against me, you will not, I am sure, hazard the shedding of my blood upon doubtful evidence. God Almighty is a God of mercy and equity. Our law, the law of England, is a law of equity and mercy, and both God and the law require from your Lordships tenderness in all cases of life and death; and if it should be indifferent or doubtful to your Lordships (which upon proofs that I have made I cannot believe it can be) whether I am innocent or guilty, both God and the law require you to acquit me. My Lords, I leave myself, my case, and the consequences of it with your Lordships, and I pray the All-wise, the Almighty God, to direct you in your determination."

The Jury retired to consider their verdict, and Lord Delamere was removed from the Court by the Lieutenant of the Tower. On their return the Judge said—

My Lords, are you agreed upon your verdict?

Lord Churchill—Yes.

Judge—How say you, my Lord Churchill, is Henry, Baron Delamere, guilty of the high treason whereof he stands indicted and hath been arraigned, or not guilty?

Lord Churchill (head uncovered and hand on breast)—Not Guilty, upon my honour.

Judge—Lord Lieutenant of the Tower, bring your prisoner to the Bar.

Lord Delamere was then brought in, and was thus addressed by the Judge—

My Lord Delamere, I am to acquaint you that my noble Lords, your Peers, have considered all the evidence that hath been given against you and for you, and have agreed upon their verdict, and by that verdict have unanimously declared that you are not guilty of the high treason whereof you have been indicted, and therefore I must discharge you of it.

Delamere—May it please your Grace, I shall pray to Almighty God that He will please give me the heart to be thankful to Him for His mercy, and my Lords for their justice, and I pray God deliver their Lordships and all honest men from ordinary and malicious lying and false testimony. I pray God to bless His Majesty, and long may he reign.

Judge—And I pray God to continue him to his loyal peers and all other of his loyal subjects.

Clerk to Crown—Sergeant-at-Arms, make Proclamation.

Sergeant-at-Arms—Oh yes, my Lord High Steward of England, his Grace straightly willeth and commandeth all manner of persons here present to depart hence in God's peace and the King's, for my Lord High Steward of England now dissolves this Commission. God save the King!

The Usher of the Black Rod then handed the Rod to the Judge, who holding it over his head, broke it in two. Thus closed one of the most memorable and momentous trials in English history.

CHAPTER XVII.

Lord Delamere's retirement to Dunham—His efforts in the Revolution of Cheshire—James's dismissal and dethronement—Honours showered upon Lord Delamere—Review of his Lordship's works—His advice to his children—Old-fashioned piety—Clerical opinion must not govern them—Warning against spies and informers—" Reason why King James ran away at Salisbury "—Charges to Grand Juries at Chester—Prerogative of Princes and Kings to declare War—People's veto on providing money—Government by good and bad Kings—Force of arms can only answer—Profanation of God's holy name by oaths and execrations—Some observations on the Prince of Orange's Declaration—Kings, Lords, and Commons—Union between Church and Dissent—Lord Delamere's work for the Revolution—Accession of William and Mary—The dismissal of King James—Lord Delamere's death—Memorials in Bowdon Church.

THE terrible strain which his Lordship had undergone in the course of his memorable " tryall " had made serious inroads on health and constitution, and undoubtedly had the effect of shortening his days. It is, therefore, no cause for wonder that he retired to his seat at Dunham Massey, and for a time abstained from taking part in public affairs. He wrote a number of tracts, all having a strong democratic flavour, and most of them strongly opposed to any extension of the prerogatives of royalty. An old volume, printed in 1694, contains his Lordship's collected works, including several speeches in Parliament and "occasional discourses."

In his Lordship's advice to his children, addressed to " My dear Sons," he gives us a pathetic touch of autobiography. Having lived, as already pointed out, "in an age where a few months has produced great revolutions and troubles, the mischievous effects of which having fallen heavy as well upon my own person as upon my family : for before I was nine years old, I saw my father a close prisoner in the Tower, seven months, for his loyalty to his King and country, and by little less than a miracle thence delivered ; and having but just past over my thirty-fourth year, for the next day (after having been a close prisoner in the Tower three times) I was tried for my life for adhering to the interest of my Country. And now in my thirty-seventh year, perceiving a boisterous storm (the Revolution) approaching, by which I may probably expect to be swept away in the common calamity, and consequently must leave you all very young ; I think it to be the best thing I can do for you, to advertise (warn) you of the rocks and precipices which by means of my trial and suffering I have discovered."

Here are a few sentences. " Be sure to begin and end the day with God." " Let not any business prevent you from spending some time in private devotion morning and evening." He does not advise hurry over these devotions " I have observed any morning that I have hurried over my devotions the day following has not been prosperous, and that thing which particularly occasioned me to such haste has met with ill success."

In the present day, when there seems to be a taint of atheism in our national blood, one almost envies this good man his loving trustfulness in the Almighty. " And now," he continues, " let me recommend to you the duty and affection which you owe to your country ; for next to God's glory, there is nothing that ought to be so dear to you as the common good : it is to be preferred to your life, estate, or family."

His Lordship gives some sledge-hammer blows at the looseness and immorality which prevailed in the courts of Charles the First and Charles the Second. " Though princes should be examples of piety," he says " as well as administerers of justice, yet there is so much looseness and disorder in their families, that a man who lives there must be well fortified with religion and morality, or he will be in great danger of losing his integrity." " For the several kings have taken upon them to govern by their wills, and this practice has prevailed for many successions and ages, yet this cannot give them a good title to their arbitrary rule."

His Lordship's further remarks on this subject range over a wide field. He points out from the above cause that differences and disputes too frequently arise between the king and the people, and advises the course the latter should pursue under such circumstances, especially impressing upon them not to let the opinions of the clergy govern them, " for none are blinder guides than they, and no one thing hath done more mischief in the nation than their politics." If his sons happen to be on the prevailing side, he advises them to use their advantage with moderation, but if they get the worst of it, they must not think any the worse of their cause ! If they happen to be brought to trial, he urges them to confess nothing, but argue against the insufficiency of what is " objected against them." He warns them against spies and informers, that they should only go abroad (from home) when they have real business to transact, and for recreation and neighbourly visits, " and those, too in as small numbers as may be." He gives directions for the " matching " of sons and daughters, and the best way of providing annuities for younger sons. In choosing a wife he also gives excellent advice. While a great fortune is welcome, he says, " yet the woman should be considered." He regards a woman of " middle birth " as a fortune in herself, and easily persuaded to a " competent way of living," and " verifies the true old adage, that you are not so much to regard what a wife brings as what she will save."

Of a very different complexion to the foregoing is a long article embodied in a letter to a friend, headed : " Reasons why King James ran away from Salisbury." It sheds a light on the history of the times not to be found in most modern text-books. He adds that the true and real reason why he ran away was " that he was acted (actuated) by fear more than anything else, from the first notice that he had of the Prince of Orange, his design, to the moment that he got into France; nothing but fear could make him neglect what is so expedient on such occasions. That is to clap up (imprison) every man of quality and interest that he suspects, but he was so far from laying hold of any man that he courted, and even humbled himself to those very people before whom heretofore he would not admit to his presence, and with so much abjectness made an offer of their franchises to the City of London and other Corporations."

"To have brought over so many Irish soldiers," Lord Delamere points out, "only bred distrust and divisions amongst his English adherents, and James was guilty of bad generalship in not detaching a sufficient number of men to meet the Prince of Orange on his landing in this country, thereby destroying his army or preventing reinforcements arriving, as would have made an end of the matter." The nation had been harassed so long in the two previous reigns that there was little of the old English spirit left in the people, " and most who declared for the Prince of Orange proceeded with so much caution that they showed more cunning than caution. King James's fear would not let him see where he had an advantage, and to save his life tho' at the price of his honour and three Kingdoms."

"So that if all were true that is reported of his former prowess, yet seems therein to have forct (forced) himself and acted a part, for it could not be the effect of courage and resolution: and upon the whole matter never did man (even Nero himself) show so much fear in any case as King James did in that matter." An additional incentive why King James should have stuck to his ground is that "he very well knew that Englishmen seldom turn their backs, and would go as far as their officers would lead them, while altho' the Prince had with him the greatest general in the world and a number of good officers and seasoned troops, yet the best officers could not make more than they were, nor put them in better condition." The declaration of the Prince of Orange for a "Free Parliament" had, however, the greatest effect in inducing James's army to lay down their arms, which appears to have been the great thing which "so astonished King James and put him to his wits' end." Moreover, the nation mistrusted King James, and vigour, courage, revenge, recovery of liberty, and despair made up too strong a composition for James's tender stomach, and turned his thoughts from fighting to contrive the best way to save his life, and this was the storm that drove him away from Salisbury. One is driven to wonder what would have happened to English liberty and English Protestantism had King James acted with the courage and resolution indicated by Lord Delamere. So much does this grow upon us that we are inclined to draw a veil over the subject.

Lord Delamere, when comparatively young, delivered charges to the Grand Jury at Chester Castle, and one easily sees how obnoxious he must have been to the two Charles's and James when he tells them plainly that "tho' it is the prerogative of princes and kings to declare war, it is for the people to say that they will provide the sinews thereof, that is, the money." He wrote an essay on government, good and bad kings, observations on the attainder of the Duke of Monmouth, made a speech in the House of Lords against bishops voting in case of blood, and gave a discourse showing who were the true "encouragers of Popery"—"Some reasons against the prosecution of the Dissenters upon penal laws." All these showed the deep interest he took in public affairs and the welfare of the nation generally. In one of his charges to the Grand Jury he says: "Every King of England holds his crown upon condition that he govern according to the known and approved laws of the land, and when he forsakes that good old way he ceases to be king and maladministration is a forfeiture of his crown. This was the opinion of our forefathers, for when the throne is vacant it naturally comes into hands of the people as by original right. No government can want power to help itself, but as we have seen in the case of the continental war, which sought to set aside the government of the English people by the people under the King, force of arms can alone answer force. Prayers and tears are our proper application to Almighty God, but signify little with an arbitrary Prince or Emperor. And since God has so wonderfully delivered us during the last (civil?) war, we could never answer if we did not do our parts, for if we perish through our neglect our blood lies at our own door, and we deserve the burial of an ass if we die like fools.

"And, therefore, Gentlemen, of the many things that are at this time under your care I would suggest for your consideration to suppress the profanation of the holy name of God by oaths and horrible execrations, and thus if you know of any that are common swearers or of any Petty Constables who have neglected to inform of their monthly meetings, you ought to present them. You ought also to present those who make light of the Sabbath by going to Church twice in a day, yet spend the remainder of it in sports and gaming, very frequently and too very commonly in an alehouse. The next thing you have to inquire of is the sin of drunkness, which is a sin of custom and not of Nature. What difference is there between a drunken man and a swine? Only this, that the brute has the better of him; for a swine follows that appetite which Nature has imbued him with, and when he is dead his carcase is worth the food he has eaten. But a drunkard forces himself beyond his appetite, and when he is dead is good for nothing. To suppress this swinish practice you ought to present all such alehouses as suffer people to drink in their houses at unseasonable hours, or harbour men suspected of evil fame, or that suffer any other disorder. I do not suspect you will be remiss on your parts, and therefore I will not trouble you further but dismiss you to your business, and I pray God to direct you in it."

In another charge to the Grand Jury at Chester he delivers himself at length of some observations " On the Prince of Orange's declaration before ascending the English throne." " If a Prince entertained a certain class of evil men as ministers, they were more than likely to make him a bad ruler, and they would not prove just and faithfull councilors to the people." Proceeding he says, " And here give me leave to say a word in my own vindication. I find I have been accused to be a Commonwealth's man, but if I were permitted to speak for myself, I would say ' that I like this constitution under King, Lords and Commons better than any other, and I defie any man to mention that thing which can give just occasion to think otherwise of me ; I am sure there is no man so hardy as to tell me to my face ; yet I say withall, that if through the Administration of those who are trusted with the Executive Power, or by other means, my liberty shall become precarious, I will then be for any other form of government under which my liberty and property may be made more secure, and until then I don't desire to change : and in this I think I am not much in the wrong."

Following are also potential aspects of his views on men and things : " There are a sort of people who will go ten or twelve miles to ' a three Pinny Doal ' (threepenny dole) that will refuse sixpence if offered them to go four or five miles, although they have scarcely rags to cover their nakedness. If you know of any such you ought to present them (to the Court), that they may be sent to a place where they'll be forced to work. . . . There are also a sort of people that spend high and live very plentifully, yet have no visible means of supporting that expense ; if you know of any such you ought to present them that an account may be taken of their way of living, which is very necessary at this time when ' clipping ' (shearing a small portion off a coin of the realm) and horse stealing are two such great trades."

Clipping of coins and horse stealing were formerly dealt with by the hangman, though one suspects that a little inquiry in the present day into the course of life indicated by Lord Delamere would not be amiss. We also find vagrants swarming in Cheshire, and constables not " seizing " them unless they were found pilfering, and " considering the law gave good encouragement for the apprehending of vagrants they were very backward in their duties." He therefore concludes " with this short word : that till vice and profaneness be supprest ; till there is more a face of religion, if not a sincere profession of the gospel ; till the Glory of God is more regarded ; till men be convinced that they cannot be true sons of the Church unless they be good Christians ; till the Government shall prefer men as well out of their honesty and upright conversations as for any other reasons, we must still expect to meet with difficulties and disappointments in our Affairs, if not to be overrun by an invasion or to be ruined by ourselves.'

Lord Delamere had not a good word to say for clerics. He was equally severe, if not more so, on lawyers, and says concerning the dispensing power that there was more to be feared from the twelve red coats (judges) in Westminster Hall than from 12,000 standing forces of army. He held Monarchy to be the best of Governments, "and the English above all others." He defended the Revolution which placed William and Mary on the throne, and was "persuaded that the Holy Scripture was never more wrested to serve a term than it was to maintain the Divine Right and absolute power of Kings as shown in previous reigns." He also advanced reasons for "an union between the Church and the Dissenters," and points out that there was no greater cause for general sorrow than "the rents and divisions" amongst Protestants. He suggested that as certain ceremonies were retained in the Church to bring in Papists, "why should we not have the same charity to lay them aside and bring in Protestant Dissenters. . . . It cannot but trouble any good man to see his brethren shut out of the Church, because he has not on such and such a suit of Cloaths, or will not bow to this or that post. . . . Every man's religion is to do justly, love mercy, and to walk humbly with God, to believe in our Lord Jesus Christ, and not to put our brethren out of the Church, for which God Almighty will not shut Heaven's gates against."

We now revert to the events which brought about the Revolution of 1688 and caused the return of Lord Delamere to public life. He felt that the deliverance of the nation must be worked by a miracle, and that as it would be presumption to expect the latter, he very wisely levied a force of his tenants to effect the former. He promised them that if they fell in the cause their leases should be renewed to their children, and he exhorted every one who had a good horse either to take the field or provide a substitute. He entered Manchester with fifty men armed and mounted, and with others soon afterwards joined the Prince of Orange and his forces.

There is no doubt, apart from the religious aspect of the question, that the accession to the throne of William and Mary gave a stimulus to social life and progress in the nation.

On the arrival of the Prince at Windsor, he despatched Lord Delamere, the Marquis of Halifax, and the Earl of Shrewsbury to London with a message to King James, commanding him to quit the Palace. His Majesty was in bed at the time of their arrival at midnight, but they were introduced to him by Lord Middleton, then Secretary of State. This event has been justly described "as a remarkable instance of the vicissitudes of fortune and of Divine retribution. Here was a subject (Lord Delamere) whom he had seen arraigned not three years before as a culprit at the Bar, now appearing with an order which virtually dethroned him. To his honour it is recorded that it made such an impression on the fallen sovereign that after his arrival in France he said that Lord Delamere, whom he had ill-used, had treated him with much more respect than the other two Lords to whom he had been kind and from whom he might better have expected it." Although Lord Delamere was one of the foremost in bringing about the Revolution it was singular that the accession to the throne of William and Mary evoked no popular demonstration in Manchester.

Lord Delamere now received the reward of his sacrifices and sufferings. He was made a Privy Councillor in 1689, which office he held for life. In the following April he was made Chancellor and Under Treasurer of the Exchequer, and subsequently Lord-Lieutenant and Custos Rotulorum of the County of Chester. In 1690 he was created Earl of Warrington, an acknowledgment of his peculiar services, and a pension of £2000 per annum was settled upon him, but this was only paid for the first half year, and the arrears are stated in a list of King William's debts drawn up by Queen Anne. Many minor honours were also conferred upon him, including the Mayoralty of the ancient City of Chester in 1691.

By some writers Lord Delamere has been accused of a too great leaning to Nonconformity, or, as he put it in one of his charges, " a Commonwealth's man"; but a proof of his wide range of thought is given by the testimony of the Rev. Richard Wroe, "Dr of Divinity and Warden of the Collegiate Church," whose advancement in the Church (of England) was due in no small degree to the countenance of Lord Delamere. His acknowledgments to that illustrious family Dr Wroe has placed on record in a sermon he preached at Bowdon, 6th April 1691, at the funeral of the excellent Countess of Warrington, to whose illness and death Newcome feelingly alludes. In the dedication Wroe writes: "That which I reckon myself most happy in is the opportunity I have hereby in acknowledging the obligations I have to the House of Dunham, and the respect I have always found from the obliging generosity which seems hereditary to your family, of which I shall always covet to be thought a true Honour," etc. Of the Earl—as Lord Delamere then was—Wroe says, "The part he acted on the (world's) stage was so eminent as would not allow him to be unknown and unobserved or pass off unregarded; and the scene of his life was attended with such variety as made his name so well known and his person so remarkable. He adorned the high station which he had merited, and guarded that honour which he had advanced his family to. His honour was the jewel which he most highly prized, and he could not be tempted to forfeit or prostitute it, and when combined with conscience was the real measure which renders a man truly great, honourable and noble."

The main cause of Lord Delamere's death, the preacher added, was a cold caught in the Great Hall of the Middle Temple, when in London on the argument of a case connected with the House of Lords, and this, added to an illness or "distemper" under which he was already suffering, brought about his death, "thus closing a career spent in pursuance of honour and justice and in vindicating the laws of God and his country."

Dr Wroe dwelt on his love of country as being remarkable throughout his life, and particularly in the trial for high treason, " when he defended himself to the great joy and satisfaction of his friends (but never by his enemies), and to the wonder, if not astonishment, of all who heard him, but to God he gave the glory."

The day of his acquittal, the 14th January, he solemnly marked with prayers and praises, and other offices of devotion to God. At the same time he clothed and fed twenty-seven poor people according to the number of Peers who composed the Jury who acquitted him, " that he might complete his own rejoicing and gratitude in the joy of seeing the feeding and refreshment of the poor and indigent. This was not the only occasion of his feeding the poor and necessitous, for those who went daily to his door were not sent empty away."

Prayer was offered " for the welfare of the yet tender but well promising hope of the same noble stock, the young Earl, coupled with the hope that he might find a pleasure in their affectionate hearts and thrive and grow up to the same maturity of worth and merit, and not only flourish in the love, but also excel the virtues of his progenitor, and transmit them to a lasting succession of his posterity."

Of the Countess, Wroe referred to her piety and said that " she had the Psalms by heart, than which there cannot be a higher strain of devotion and more Heavenly raptures for the soul to take its flight in. Besides these, she had some select portions of Scripture which she made her *Familiars* and endeared to her thoughts by daily meditations, having first writ them with her own hand in a book made and kept for that purpose, repeating them over every night, as she did also in her last sickness, and this among them this of my text which she had set a mark upon in the margin, with these words ' my funeral text,' ' wherefor He is also able to save them to the uttermost that come unto God by him, seeing he ever liveth to make intercession for them.' And I question not had a more lively impression on her mind of the comfortable import of it."

Truly, " the actions of the just smell sweet and blossom in the dust," and we acquire a deeper insight into Longfellow's lines when we realise that, so far as Lord Delamere is concerned—

> Lives of great men all remind us,
> We can make our lives sublime ;
> And, departing, leave behind us
> Footprints on the sands of Time.

The memorials in the Stamford Chapel at Bowdon Parish Church are worthy of more than passing inspection. The inscription to the memory of Henry, Lord Delamere pays tribute to his worth and work, and the monuments themselves are splendid specimens of the sculptor's art.

Burying Lane - Bowdon Church in Background

Warburton Old Church

Chester Railway Bridge Accident.

CHAPTER XVIII.

Plague, pestilence, and famine—The Black Death and its victims—Portents of the Great Plague of 1603—Precautions at Macclesfield and Congleton—Stockport attacked—Plague virulent at Malpas—Congleton suffers from civil war and pestilence—Little Bess, "a ministering angel"—Memorials in Macclesfield Forest—Cholera epidemics in the County—Smallpox—Cattle plague—Cheshire surnames, ancient and modern—A notable Cheshire will—Wythanshawe Hall and Cromwell—Highway robberies common—A famous Cheshire dwarf—A horned woman—A curious natural phenomenon—Cheshire "Gentlemen of the Road," Higgins, Dick Turpin—Extraordinary hoax at Chester—Levellers or Chartists at Dunham—Fatal accident on the Roodee Railway Viaduct—The Fenian Raid on Chester—Sandbach Crosses.

THE civilisation of Europe in the Middle Ages, and indeed far into the modern period, as is well known, was subject to awful visitations of disease, which are frequently referred to under the general name of "plague," and which had most important social, religious, and political consequences. The greatest authority on the subject, Hoecker, regards 1347-50 as the period of the "Black Death." "The plagues," he says, "which in the sequel often returned until the year 1385, we do not consider as belonging to the 'Great Mortality.' They were rather common pestilences, without inflammation of the lungs, such as in former times and in the centuries following were excited by the matter of contagion everywhere existing, and which on every favourable occasion gained ground anew, as is usually the case with this frightful disease." He estimates that the deaths in Europe from the "Black Death" were 25,000,000.

Chester did not escape the "sweating sickness" which broke out in 1507, when ninety-one householders died in three days, "and but for four of them widows." In 1517 the plague raged to such an extent in the city "that for want of trading the grass did grow a foot high at the Cross and other streets of the City." To add to the horrors of the time was a scarcity of provisions, corn selling in Chester at 16s. a bushel. In 1558 "few died, but many fled," evidently regarding discretion as the better part of valour. In 1574 the plague broke out anew "in Chester, but God of His mercy stayed His rod with the death of some few in the crofts." Of the visitation of 1603 we have this account :—

"The 22nd of August in the night time a wonderful exhalation of a fiery colour, likewise a canopy was seen over this city, and in September following the great plague began in Chester, in one Glover's house in St John's Lane." In the MSS. of Rogers it is added that "seven persons died in a short time out of this house, and that the plague kept increasing weekly until sixty died weekly. Michaelmas fair was not kept this year on account of the plague. The Court of Exchequer was removed to Tarvin, and the County Assizes were held at Nantwich. The infected persons were taken out of their houses and conveyed into houses and cabins built by the waterside, near unto the new tower, and were there relieved at the cost of the city. Nothing of importance passed because of the plague increasing amongst us, only the high cross was new gilt, to whom let it be memorable that liketh thereof; there died of the plague in this city, from Mr Glasier's time (mayor year previous) until 13th of October, 650; and other diseases, 61."

Macclesfield and Congleton also suffered. The authorities of the town and the county magistrates, Sir Urian Legh of Adlington, knight, Thomas Stanley of Alderley, and Randle Davenport of Henbury, Esquires, were very active to prevent its spreading, and in an MS. volume now preserved at Capesthorne, is an account of the precautions which were taken: "Watch and ward was taken at every common passage out of the towne and at cross lanes neare adjoyning ye towne to keepe in ye Townsmen." "A markett every Munday was kept in an open place 3 quarters of a Myle from ye Towne were weekly present to see ye towne and country kept asunder, and to see ye corpe, and other provision distributed which came from ye country either by tax or guift." "The justices had weekly notice which streets were infected, how many houses in each street, how many persons in each house and ye ability (the health) of ye parties." "The justices had every markett a bill (or list) of ye names of such as dyed the weeke before." A rate was levied throughout Macclesfield Hundred in aid of the town, and in the following year, 1604, one was levied throughout the county in aid of Macclesfield and Congleton, in which town the plague was even more severe. Under the date of 17th June 1604 there is an entry in the parish register of the death of "Dominick, a gentleman that died at Mrs Brereton's of Edge, of a plague of pestilence," and on the 22nd of the same month another entry of Thomas Plymley, a servant to Mrs Brereton, of the same malady. In this same year the plague continued still in Chester, increasing every week, for the weekly accounts were too tedious to repeat, tho' I could express it very near; but from the 14th of October to the 20th March 812 persons died." (Rogers' MSS.)

Towards the end of 1605 a very severe visitation of plague appears to have attacked Stockport, and the registers record that between the 9th of October 1605 and the 20th of March 812 persons died. "Madd Marye was buryed on the 9th October 1605, of the plague. Thomas, the reputed sonne of Thomas Rodes, of Stockport, suspected to dye of it, was buried 26th October 1605. James, sonne of James Williamson of Stockport, Alderman, dyed of plague, and was buried the 20th Julye 1606. Roger Orme of Stockport, dyed of the plague, buried 1st August 1606. John Oldham of Stockport, belman, dyed of the plague, buried 14th August 1606." In 1608 about fourteen persons died of the plague, which began at the Talbot in Chester, and there was a further mortality in 1610.

At Malpas, in 1625, the plague was very virulent, and the parish registers reveal a very pathetic and awful story. The entries begin with the death of Thomas Jefferie, servant, Thomas Dawson of Bradley, and Richard Dawson, his son, buried in the nights of the 10th and 13th August, after which also occurs the name of Ralph Dawson, also son of Thomas, who "came from London about the 25th of July last past, and being sick of the plague died in his father's howse and infected the said howse, and was buryed as reported, neare unto his father's howse." Then follow the burials of Thomas Dawson, sen., 15th August, at three o'clock after midnight; Elizabeth, his daughter, 20th August; and Annie his wife, the same day.

Richard Dawson, brother of the above-named Thomas Dawson, "being sicke of the plague and perceyveing he must dye at yt time, arose out of his bed, and made his grave, and caused his nefew, John Dawson, to caste straw into the grave, which was not far from the howse, and went and layed down in the said grave, and caused clothes to be layd uppon, and so dep'ted out of this world; this he did because he was a strong man and heavier than his said nefew and another wench were able to bury. He died about the XXIVth of August. Thus much was credibly tould he did in 1625. . . . John Dawson, sonne of the above named Thomas, came in unto his father when his father sent for him, being sicke and having layed him down in a dich, died in it the XXIXth day of August 1625, in the night. Rose Smyth, servant of the above-named Thomas Dawson, and the last of yt household, died of plague and was buried by William Cooke, the Vth daye of September, 1625, near to the saide howse."

Another entry shows that the plague continued its ravages to the middle of October 1625 :—" 9th Oct. : Mawde, the wyfe of Henry Clutton. Her husband and sister buried her. A child of Henry Clutton's, that died, as it is thought, of plague, buried XIIIIth daye of October, 1625. Its aunt and another wench buried it. *Nihil pro eccl'ia.*" (Without the rites of the Church.)

Cheshire appears to have escaped the visitation of 1630. Congleton between 1640 and 1642 suffered both from civil war and pestilence. Mr J. E Bailey has pointed out some interesting passages in the town accounts for those years. "The eye," he says, "dwells with most tenderness made to an active woman of diminutive stature, or it may be a young girl, named 'Little Bess,' who remained faithful to her duty of nursing the plague stricken when left to die. The money was given to Little Bess for wages and for purchasing necessaries for the sick or the dead. 'Paid Little Bess for keeping Mary Houlden's boy, 6s. 8d.' 'Paid to Little Bess her quarter's wages, 6s. 8d.' 'Bestowed upon Little Bess her mother in the time of sickness, 6d.' 'Bestowed to buy Little Bess's mother a winding sheet, 2s. 6d.' 'Paid to Little Bess for three days serving of the infected, 1s.' 'To Little Bess for one week's attendance to the cabins, 2s. 4d.'" The cabins were places to which the infected were removed. There are other payments to her at various times for balls of liquorice, white vinegar, candles, pitch, frankincense, etc. Evidence is afforded that her ministrations were subsequently extended to wounded soldiers. It is interesting to meet with one entry with her name, which was Elizabeth Smith, otherwise " Lancashire Bess." On the hills of the " Forest of Macclesfield " are some crosses said to have been used for the placing of provisions for those suffering, and near them are gravestones of some who are said to have died of the plague. In 1647 the Liverpool people were alarmed, and under the date of 12th June 1647, it was " ordered that strict wach shal be kept by the townesmen because of the rumour of sickness said to be begune at Warrington." On May 10th, 16th, and 18th, 1654, Wm. Gaskin, Thomas Gaskin, Ellen Gaskin, Thomas Gaskin, junr., and Ann Gaskin, of Tarvin, died of plague. There are no further notices of the spreading of the contagion. The Liverpool records again afford information of the presence of pestilence in Cheshire in 1665. On the 2nd of November a public meeting of the burgesses was convened by the Mayor (Mr Michael Tarleton), when it was resolved : " That upon consideration and apprehension of the spreading of the plague in divers neighbouring towns of Cheshire and of other parts, and the great concourse of people usually from those parts all the time the fairs kept in this town, it is generally voted, agreed, thought fit, and so ordered that the keeping of the fair on St Martin's day next (11th November), the eve, and other usual days after here accustomably kept, shall this present exigent of danger for this year be absolutely forborne and forbidden by open publication and notice thereof in the open market, and the next market day." Sir James Picton observes that "as we have no record of any attack of the plague, it is presumed that these precautionary measures proved effectual." A gravestone in the middle of a large field on the left-hand side of the road leading from Alderley Edge to Mobberley, and just before reaching the row of trees on Lindow Common, bears the letters E. S. and the date 1665. It is the only memento of the plague in the parish of Wilmslow. The following entry in the parish register explains it : " 1655. July. The 17th day was buried E—— Stonaw, at her own house, she being suspected to dye of plague, she but coming home the day before." In a note in a much later hand is added : " In a field near Smallwood House, now belonging to the Vicar of Knutsford. 1788."

The last outbreak of cholera to assume an epidemic form in Cheshire occurred at Winsford in 1865 and the early months of 1866, amongst a colony of foreigners brought over to this country to labour in saltworks in the district. It revealed a shocking state of things. The absence of sanitary measures was at the root of the evil. Evidently these poor exiles from their native land had been left to take care of themselves to a great extent. They appeared to have carried on the most elementary principles of sanitation, with the usual result— a harvest of misery and death, which aroused the local authorities and Government inspectors to take drastic steps to stamp out the disease. Insanitary surroundings which lay at the root of the matter were got rid of, and it quickly disappeared in consequence, and there has been no recurrence of this fell visitation. Smallpox, a century or two ago, was a highly contagious disease, and was said to have been the cause of one-tenth of the prevailing mortality in the seventeenth century. It is owing to Jenner's discovery of the protective power of vaccination that it is now a comparatively rare and mild disorder in civilised countries. Vaccination of children in infancy, now insisted upon by law of the land, renders a child practically immune for many years, and, it is held, tends greatly to modify any attack in adult life. We rarely see a face pitted by smallpox in these days, whereas eighty or ninety years ago evidences of this were quite common. In addition to vaccination we owe much to the spread of sanitary science that such spectacles are practically unknown in these days. Still slight outbreaks occur at times nowadays. There was one at Macclesfield in August 1919, but this was speedily subdued by isolation and ordinary medical treatment.

Influenza, an infectious epidemic disease, received its name from the Italians in 1741. It has reappeared in England on several occasions within the past thirty or forty years and has gone by other names, the best known of which was La Grippe, or Russian influenza. The latest and most widespread outbreak known in history was that of 1918, which prevailed over most parts of the globe, and baffled the resources of medical science to stay its progress. Rest and quiet appeared to be the best remedy, but it resulted in the death of thousands in the British Isles, while it is impossible to compute the mortality in other parts of the world. In this connection a few remarks may be admissible in regard to the outbreak in Cheshire, in 1865–66, of what was known as the cattle plague or rinderpest. How it was caused has never been properly explained. It was most insidious in its course. One day a fine herd would be grazing peacefully in the fields and next day it would be wiped out. It assumed curious forms. Sometimes in a shippon one animal would be left; in others alternate beasts would be taken; in others half would be taken. Various remedies were resorted to, such as isolating them in salt mines or steaming them in improvised hospitals, much after the manner of a Turkish bath. But all to no purpose. Wholesale slaughter was resorted to, followed by disinfection of cowsheds and shippons, which proved effective in the long run. The quickness with which the outbreak was subdued was only equalled by the rapidity with which the herds were replaced from other counties untouched by disease, and in a few years Cheshire resumed its position as a cheese-producing county.

Those fateful days when the cattle plague ravaged the herds of Cheshire were days which brought about an era of mutual trust and confidence between landowner and tenant, which had probably never existed to the same extent previously, good as those relations had always been, as many political agitators found to their cost in later years. Then, as in the days of the early English kings, were the Cheshire men averse to the stirring up of class strife. The landowners had shared their losses during a trying period and they did not forget it. Circumstances such as the world war of 1914-18, high death duties, and other modern conditions have brought about a silent revolution. Estates which have been in the hands of families for centuries have been sold at auction to the highest bidder. A large number, probably the bulk, have had facilities afforded which has encouraged them to purchase the homesteads and land, and so far as this is the case it makes for the betterment of the greatest and important of our national industries. The lesson of the past few years must not be forgotten too soon. We must continue to breed men, not mice, or persons akin to those timid rodents, and enlightened and up-to-date methods introduced which will enable us, in conjunction with our colonies, to bring about such a devoutly to be desired consummation. We have no wish to enter into any political aspect of the matter, but merely indicate the broad lines on which our world-wide supremacy may be maintained and extended.

A more agreeable study is to be found in the remarkable changes which have taken place in the course of time in the spelling of surnames. The most noteworthy in our Cheshire annals is that of Mainwaring of Peover. The celebrated antiquary Dugdale was employed in 1669, by Sir Thomas Mainwaring, to collect and copy out all the muniments of the family then existing ; and from these evidences contained in the Chartularium at Peover Hall there has been established 131 ways in which the name was written, each one verified by an autograph, or equally valid legal document :—

" Anno 1093. 7ᶠ Willi Rufi, Richard de Mesnilwaren."

" Anno ab incarnatione Domini MCXIX, regnante potentessimo Rege Henrico,"—" ego Rog. de Meinilgarin."

" Carta Edwardi fil priomgenit. Regis Henrici III. dnᵒ Thomae di Meynewarin."

" Acquietane' Willi de Maynwarying Rogᵒ fil' Rogi de Toft de XI Marcis sterling I. Edward I."

" Confirmaco dni Tho : de Menylgaring,"—" de Hugon de Bordeaux."

" Carta Willi de Maynwaring."   " MCCCI."

" An Endenture made between Hondekyn Maynwaring, Knygt, on yat one partie ; and Thomas Alkemontelowe, on yat oyr partie, XXI. Hen. VI."

" Carta Rog de Menewarynk."

" Carta Rog' i Knottesford et alior."   " Ranᵒ Maynwaryng Armᵒ fil' et her.   Johis Maynwaring Militas.   Dat XVIII. April, Aᵒ XVIII. Henr. VIII."

" A catalogue of the children of Sir Randle Mainwaringe, Kt., by Margaret his wife o' the times of their births as they are set down in a great Bible printed An MDLXXXIII." This Sir Randle Mainwaringe married on 4th September 1568.

CHESHIRE : ITS TRADITIONS AND HISTORY

There is also a paper at Peover Hall showing the name written in 394 different ways; its title is " The Name of the Mainwaring Spelt 131 different Ways in the ancient Deeds and the Evidences of Sir Thomas Mainwaring, late of Over Peover in the County Palatine of Chester, Baronet, who departed this life in the year of our Lord, 1689, as they were extracted by himself out of the said Deeds," etc. " To which are added 239 other variations, which may be made of the said name, making together the number of 394 Diversifyings thereof; the same being still capable of further variety of alterations, by adding the letter E for the termination after the letter G; as also by terminating the name with 'yng' instead of 'ing'; and likewise by omitting the letter G in the termination of the said name."

The following are some of the 131 variations extracted from Dugdale's Chartularium :—" 1° de Mesnilwaringe, 10° de Manilswaring, 20° Mainwaring, 30° Mainwaringhe, 40° de Meinewaren, 50° de Mesnilgarin, 60° Manwarring, 70° de Meynwaring, 80° Manwaring, 90° Maynwareing, 100° de Menewarynk, 110° de Meynwarin, 120° Mayngwaryyng, 125° Manwryng, 126° Mayneringe, 127° de Meynewaringe, 128° Manring, 129° Maynawring, 130° Meilanwarin, 131° de Meidenwarin."

There are surnames in the county to-day which were in existence centuries ago and still in common use. Adshead or Adshed (probably a woodcutter or carpenter), Alcraft, Alyn, Aprichard (Ap Richard), George Arrowehedmaker, Arrowsmith, Axton, Billingham (or Belyngham), Bird (Brydd, Bryde), Birkenhead (or Birkenhed, Byrchynhead, Byrkinhad), Bowyer, Bratchegurdyll (or Bracegirdle), Brawstaffe, Candelan, Clerk (Clercke, Clerke), Chorop (Thorpe), Cryshaw, Beswick (Bexwykes), Dickon, Daykon, Fidler (Fedelar, Fydler), Gaitschayle, Gaskell, (Gaitscayle, Gatscathe, Gatstall, Gayscaley), Glazier, Godbehere (Thomas), Goose, Hockerley (Hocurley, nr. Whaley), Geoffrey Horsekeeper, Jermyn (German), Leadbeater (Leydbyter), Lightfoot (or Lightfote), Maudlin, Massey, Nixon (Nickeson, Nyscon, Nyxon), Priket, Taylor (Taillior, Taiyler, Taylior, Taylour), Wodcoke (Woodcock), Woodward (Wodward, Woodewarde, Woodwarde, etc.), Whittaker (Whitacres, Whiteacres, Whyttakers,Wittakers,Wythacres), Scrivener (Scryvyner, Skrynener, Skynever).

Place-names in the same connection also furnish an interesting quest. Lower Aspals was in Wistaston ; Barthomley becomes Bartonley, Bartumley, Bartumly ; Biddulph, Bedull ; Bostock, the centre of Cheshire, Bostocke, Bostok, Bostoke ; Buxton, Buckstows ; Cheadle, Chedull ; Chester, Cestre, West Chester ; Combermere, Combermire ; Culcheth, Culchet, Culchethe ; Dalebridge, Dalebrige, Daleghbrige (in Butley) ; Dukinfield, Dukynfeld, Dockenfeld ; Lostock Gralam, Lostok, Lostoke Gralham ; Minshull, Mynchun, Mynshull ; Mouldsworth, Moldesworth, Moldisworth, Moldworthe ; Nantwich, Namptwiche, Nantwiche, Nathwiche ; Odd Rode, Odde Roode, Odred, Odrode, Roode and Rode ; our modern Peover still retains Pever as its rendering, phonetically and locally ; Sidebact, Sidebright, Sydebyght in Rishton ; Stockport, Stokporde, Stopford, Stoppcott ; Weaverham, Wereham ; Whaley, Walley, Wayley, Weeley, Wellay, Weyley, Wyley in Taxall ; Wistaston, Wistanston, Wisteston, Wystaston ; Wythenshawe, Withenshaw, Wethenshaw, Wythinshaw, Wythynshaw, Withensha, etc.

The Manor of Timperley was held at a very early period by a family assuming the local name, and amongst the charterers is Thomas Gerard of Riddings, gent., Riddings Hall having been purchased from the Vaudreys. Bank Hill (Bank Hall) and Riddings were both seats of the branches of the Vaudreys of Bowdon, and in 1567 Robert Vaudrey of Riddings made a lengthy will, in which he desires that his " bodie be chested decentlye, brought home and buryed at the Parishe Churche of Bowdon, in the Chappell, and placed where my parents do lye." " Item, to sixe of the poorest men of my ten'ntes wth-in the parishe of Bowdon, vj. white gownes, desirynge they'm heartfullye to praye for me, and to go afore my corps to the churche and buryall of the same. And to other vj. of the poorest of my ten'ntes wth-in the parishes of Northerden and Ashton-upon-M'see banck other vj. gownes of blacke cotton, desyrynge and hertfullye prayinge theym likewise to praye for me in comynge next after my corps to the Churche and buryall. . . ." The testator also disposes of his property and manors in Bowdon, Bollington, Hale, Ashley, Chester, etc., and to Margaret V. (Vaudrey, his daughter) " at suche tyme as she shall leave her dishonest and uncleane lyvynge for and durynge all such tyme after as she shall lyve honestlye V^{li} by yeare." There are bequests to his relatives and to poor kinsfolk friends, poor " maydes," poor men, poor children, and to the curates and clerks on certain feast days. He had a large number of Godchildren to every one of whom he left " iiij^d by estymation xxiiij^{li} viij^s." " I do bequeath and forgyve my disobedyent sonne Thom's all such and those sum'es of moneye wch he hath wrongfully recevved (embezzlement was not unknown in those times) and taken from me, and also the sum'e of C^{li} xvijsiiij^d wch he alsoe is indebted to me or such p'te thereof as shall remayne vulgived me at the tyme of my decease accordynge as by a bill of his hand appeareth willynge and com'andyne and upone my blessynge chargynge and requyrynge hym to use sobrietie, and to leave all evell and drynkynge companye and for to say o'r Lordes praier with such other praiers and thankes gevynge to God as he shall gyve his grace and put hym in mynd daylye uppon his knees everye mornynge humblye besekyne hym to have m'cye uppon all his creatures, and to gyve hym grace to lyve honestlye and iustlye in the world uppon my blessynge, also willynge hym to say the Articles of o'r fayth, the Crede, once everye week, and to be lovynge, kynde, and helpynge to his mother, brethren, and sister, exortynge her to repent her evell lyfe, and to lyve honestlye from henceforth, and also to be kynde and helpynge in his powre to all his poore cousens and friendes and to all the ten'ntes of the landes wch God hath lent me and I have left hym, and to take nothynge of theym nor of any of theym but only their due rente ande servyce, inasmuche as God hath sent hym the landes without labor, and they must labor and paye for theym, and to be satisfied wth the same wch is much better than was left me, and wuld have byn better to hym if he wuld have byn counselled or advysed by me or have shewed hym selfe obedient or lovynge toward me, for although I wuld not yet I rather desire to have hym dye affore me than to lyve to do hurt after me, wch God forbid, and uppon my blessynge I warn the said Thom's from, requryeynge hym to love areade and to serve God, to frequent to charitie," etc. For this he forgives him his " mysbehayvyor and tresspesses done to me, and gyve the my blessynge, besekynge God to do the same," etc. There are other legacies of personal effects, including more than " one bowe and a shoff of arrowes," and to Cousin William Barneston's two boys " iijs iiij^d to buy theym bookes." " To my sister Brock vj^s viij^d and a lambe." He appointed Ales, his wife, during her widowhood only, his sons, John and Richard Vaudrey, and the Rev. John Robinson, his executors.

Wythenshawe Hall stands about two and a half miles from Sale. Originally the structure was in the black and white style of Cheshire, and surrounded by a fortified wall and moat. It has numerous gables, which lend to it an air of great picturesqueness, and at various periods it has been the subject of many alterations and additions. The family has been singularly fortunate in retaining possession of the ancestral home. Webb, in his " Itinerary " (1614), states that " Wythenshawe, or Withanshaw, is a goodly Lordship and stately house, the mansion of Tattons, men of great worship and dignity. A race of them for a descent or two, through the variable inconstancy of all mortall happinesse, much eclipsed. And the heir of that house, though a gentleman of rare sufficiency and parts, answerable every way to the great worth of his ancestors, yet by troubles and encumbrances, whereunto greatest estates are oft subject, obscured : that he never yet shined in his own sphear ; and the chiefest hope now of raising the house remains in the Grandchild of his own loyns, a towardly child in minority."

Although Robert Tatton was married in 1628-29 to Anne, daughter of William Brereton of Ashley, Esq., a near relative of Brereton, one of the leaders on the Parliamentary side in the Civil War, this did not prevent him from warmly espousing the cause of King Charles. He suffered greatly in consequence, and Mr Earwaker, in his " East Cheshire," states there is preserved at Wythenshawe an " Inventory of all the Goods and Cattels of Robert Tatton, Esq., of Withenshaw, viewed and praysed the 2 June 19, Charles I., 1643," the total value being set down at £1649, 2s. 8d. Soon afterwards Wythenshawe was besieged by the Parliamentarian forces under Colonel Duckenfield, and for a year and a half it was defended by the owner. Amongst the defenders were—Edward Legh of Baguley, Esq., Mr Richard Vawdrey, Mr John Bretland and his man ; out of Baguley, William Hamnett, Robert Chapman and Nicholas his brother, Thomas Hill; also Robert Deane of Altrincham, Hugh Newton, Richard Grantham of Hale, Robert his son, and George Delahey of Timperley. Mr Thomas Gerrard of the Riddings, and Mr William Davenport of Baguley, are also mentioned. The house was taken on Sunday, 25th February, 1643-44, two pieces of heavy ordnance which were sent for from Manchester being brought against it. Had it not been for this, the besiegers might have had to beat a retreat. During this memorable and trying time one of the maid-servants is credited with a most daring act. Captain Adams was so bold that he ventured to sit on the outer wall. Being seen by the domestic in this exposed position, she asked for and was furnished with a musket, and so true was her aim that the officer was shot dead. However questionable this statement may be, there is no doubt Captain Adams met his death there. Six skeletons were found in the last century lying close together in the garden. They are supposed to have been the soldiers who fell under the fire of the garrison, and were buried as they lay. For his "Delinquencie," he had his estates sequestered by Parliament, and although it had been stated that he had been "damnified since theise troubles by the losse of his goodes, rentes, waste of his houses and tymber," £2500, and in other ways probably £2000 more, the resolution of a committee convened by the Parliament, inflicted a fine of £804, 10s. This was subsequently reduced to £707, 13s. 4d., a fine heavy enough in all conscience to appal the stoutest heart. Mr Tatton lived to see the Restoration of Charles II. "He died," says Mr Earwaker, "19th August, and was buried at Northenden, 24th August 1669; and it is somewhat strange that amongst the numerous monumental tablets to the various members of the Tatton family in Northenden Church, there is nothing to commemorate the life and character of one who suffered so much for his loyalty to his sovereign at a time and in a part of the country where loyalty was a crime and treason a virtue to be highly rewarded." However much we may question the accuracy of this sweeping statement, viewed in the light which history has unfolded, all will concur in the opinion that there is no record of the kind indicated to teach us a lesson of at least consistency and perseverance.

Numerous articles were removed from Wythenshawe after the siege, amongst them two bells, which appear to have confounded historians somewhat. By one it is stated that the old house bell was carried off, but afterwards restored by Charles II., with a small silver snuff-box, having the donor's initials and medallion upon it, as a mark of his esteem. Another has it that this bell remained with Colonel Duckenfield's successors until the 20th October 1807, when Sir Henry Duckenfield, their then representative, "gracefully restored this prize of war to the then representative of Withenshaw Hall, in which house it now hangs; and so a trophy snatched in a time of civil war was restored in a time of domestic peace, after a lapse of more than a century and a half." The inscription on this bell is—

"'Gloria in Excelsis Deo.'
MDCXLI."

Mr Earwaker states, however, that the chapel bell—which is evidently the one here referred to—after having been preserved at Duckenfield Lodge for over two hundred years, was recently presented by Mr Astley to Mr Tatton, and is now at Wythenshawe. Cromwell stayed at Wythenshawe Hall, and the room he slept in is still called "Oliver Cromwell's room." The bed, which is dated 1619, is of elegantly carved wood, the furniture and mirrors matching it and of the same age. "All's well that ends well."

Highway robberies were common in the county. On 30th April 1752 the Warrington stage coach was robbed at Stretton by a single highwayman, who took from the passengers, five in number, 25s. He was hotly pursued as far as Frodsham by the country people, and struck at several respectable people who met him on the road, "at whom he presented a pistol in each hand!" He rode into the fields, and getting into a bog quitted his horse, leaving his whip and riding coat behind. He escaped in the darkness of the night. Sometime afterwards a tradesman from London, travelling from Chester to Middlewich, was attacked by highwaymen in Delamere Forest and robbed of his watch, ten guineas and some silver. The gentleman desired them to return him one guinea to bear his charges, but they "returned him curses and said they wanted the money more than he," and galloped away "briskly" towards Chester.

A famous Cheshire dwarf was exhibited at Bartholomew fair in the year after the Great Fire. At the sign of the "Shoe and Slap," near the hospital gate at West Smithfield, was exhibited "a girl above sixteen years of age and not above eighteen inches long; having shed her teeth several times, and not a perfect bone in her body, only the head. Yet she hath all her senses to admiration and discourses, reads very well, sings and whistles in a way very pleasant to hear." Sixteen years after she was exhibited in Leeds, and according to Ralph Thoresby's Diary, although she had gained six inches in height, she was but six years older! "1683, June 12th.—Went to see a most wonderful woman, but about two feet long, though twenty-one years old. She was born at Bowdon Parish in Cheshire, near the Lord Delameres, and is said to have no bone in her body but the head, though I suppose a mistake."

At Great Saughall, near Chester, was the residence of Mrs Mary Davies, "the strange and wonderful old woman, that hath a pair of horns growing upon her head." She was remarkable for having an excrescence on her head, which, when she was sixty years of age, grew into horns; these after four years' growth were cast and renewed, which happened two or three times before her death. There is a portrait of her in the Ashmolean Museum at Oxford, where one of the horns is preserved. A few similar instances have occurred. In the University Library at Edinburgh is preserved a horn, cut from the head of Elizabeth Love, in the fifteenth year of her age. Mrs Allen, a woman who had a horn growing in her head, was exhibited in London in the year 1790.

The 20th July 1662 was a very stormy and tempestuous day in many parts of Lancashire and Cheshire. "On that day in the forest of Macclesfield there arose a great pillar of smoke, in height like a steeple, and judged twenty yards broad, which, making a most hideous noise, went along the ground six or seven miles, levelling all in the way, it threw down fences and stone walls, and carried the stones a great distance from their places, but happening upon moorish ground not inhabited it did less hurt. The terrible noise it made so frightened the cattle that they ran away and were thereby preserved; it passed over a cornfield and laid it as even with the ground as though it had been trodden by feet; it went through a wood, and tore up about one hundred trees by the roots; coming into a field full of cocks of hay ready to be carried in it swept all away, so that scarce a handful of it could afterwards be found, it only left a great tree in the middle of the field. From the forest of Macclesfield it went up by Taxall and thence to Whaley Bridge. It overthrew a house or two, yet the people in them received not much hurt, but the timber was carried away none knew whither, from whence it went up into the hills of Derbyshire and so vanished." This account was given by Mr Hurst, minister of Taxall.

A famous "gentleman of the road," a resident of Knutsford, was Edward Higgins, who, says the Rev. H. Green, was on visiting, as well as housebreaking, terms with the neighbouring gentry. He hunted with them during the morning, dined with them in the afternoon, and made himself familiar with their plate-chests by night. "The Squire's Tale," in *Household Words*, attributed to Mrs Gaskell, narrates some of his exploits. At Knutsford he appeared as a gentleman, keeping horses, and following the usual sports at that day of a man of independent fortune. He, too, kept a Black Bess, or some equally swift roadster, for on one occasion, when he had been pillaging a house near Bristol, the gallant mare brought him home in an incredibly short time. After many amazing adventures Higgins was convicted of housebreaking in Wales and executed at Carmarthen.

The scene of the exploits of another so-called "gentleman of the road," the notorious Dick Turpin, was in the Bowdon district. On one occasion the daring Dick had a narrow escape from paying the extreme penalty of the law for a robbery committed in New Bridge Hollow, and this escape was attributable, it is said, to the legendary speed of Black Bess. A lawyer was travelling from Altrincham to Chester, when he was attacked by Dick, in a lonely dell near Bowdon, and relieved of his cash. Turning the head of Black Bess, he put her to extreme speed, and on arriving at the "Kilton" at Hoo Green, he accosted the hostler with "Holloa! what o'clock is it, my cockolorum, eh?" With a view to receiving a speedy reply, he accompanied the question with a sharp blow on the shoulder, and, singular to say, he got the required answer. We use the word "singular," because a modern knight, "of more breeches than brains," would have replied with a torrent of well selected Billingsgate, and summoned him before a magistrate, with a view to having him fined. As it was, Dick calmly strolled on to the Green, where a number of county gentlemen were playing bowls, taking care, of course, to remark about the time. An investigation into the circumstances took place, and Dick found out the advantages to be derived from what Samuel Weller's "paternal parient" in "Pickwick," chose to call a "halibi." The groom was called, and as the difference between the time of the robbery and Dick's appearance in the inn yard was so small, only a few minutes, although the distance from the place was over three miles, the magistrates discharged him, under the impression that no horse could carry him in the time Black Bess did. Turpin appears to have gloried in the feat that he then accomplished, for it is made the subject of a song, which is given in "Rookwood."

In 1842 the Chartists, or "Levellers," paid a visit to Altrincham. In order to prevent a descent on Dunham Hall, the Earl of Stamford of that time ordered several barrels of beer, cheeses, and baskets of bread to be placed on the fringe of the park, near the present Green Walk gate, which good things the rioters eagerly consumed. In Stamford Street there was a ladies' boarding school. The mistress concealed all her valuables and the greatest part of her money, only keeping a few shillings at hand; she dressed herself in clothes which belonged to the cook, and when the rioters came to the school and demanded money, etc., she gave them the trifle she had by her, and pleaded that she had a very hard mistress, who gave her but scanty wages, and so escaped any further loss. The servants and several of the boarders had to turn out their pockets and contents of their boxes.

There is a singular grave at Hatherlow, of a dissenting clergyman, the Rev. R. Robinson, who was interred there about the year 1788. The grave is a brick building without roof, of about 15 feet square and 12 feet high, with a strong door in the centre of one side. The tradition is, that Mr Robinson left his property to his daughter as long as she continued to see him every day. To this end she caused a glass to be placed in the top of the coffin, so that anyone could see him who looked down. A line of trees was planted on each side of the path from the house, which is about 100 yards distant from the grave. The office of seeing her deceased parent daily is said to have been faithfully performed by Miss Robinson.

An extraordinary hoax was perpetrated at Chester about the time of Buonaparte's departure for St Helena. A respectably dressed man caused a number of handbills to be distributed through Chester, in which he informed the public that a great number of genteel families had embarked at Plymouth, and would certainly proceed with the British regiment appointed to accompany the ex-Emperor to St Helena. He added further that the island being dreadfully infested with rats, His Majesty's ministers had determined that it forthwith should be cleared of these noxious animals. To facilitate this important purpose he had been deputed to purchase as many cats and thriving kittens as could possibly be procured for money in a short space of time, and therefore he publicly offered in his handbills 16s. for every athletic full-grown Tom-cat, 10s. for every adult female puss, and half-a-crown for every vigorous thriving kitten that could swill milk, pursue a ball of thread, or fasten its young fangs on a dying mouse. On the evening of the third day after his advertisement had been distributed, the people of Chester were astonished by the irruption of a multitude of old women, boys and girls, all of whom carried on their shoulders either a bag or a basket, which appeared to contain some restless animal. Before night nearly 3000 cats were collected in Chester. Great uproar ensued, and next morning about 500 dead bodies were seen floating on the Dee, where they had been ignominiously thrown by the two-legged victors. The rest of the invading host, the victims of this cruel joke having evacuated the town, dispersed in the utmost confusion to their respective homes.

The Grosvenor Bridge, the second means of access to North Wales over the Dee, was formally opened by Queen Victoria (then Princess Victoria) in 1832. It was designed by Mr Thomas Harrison, whose work in the rebuilding of Chester Castle and the County Buildings at Knutsford stamp him as a man of genius and a master of craft. It consists of a single main arch with a span of 200 feet, which at the time the bridge was built was the greatest single span of any stone arch in the world. The story connected with its building is a remarkable one. That there could be a bridge which could hold together of a single span of that dimension was ridiculed by experts in bridge building, and difficulty was experienced in getting a contractor who would undertake the work. It was prophesied that the moment the supports were removed it would collapse. A young man was found, and as it was his first adventure of this kind, although he had undertaken some minor contracts, he put his whole heart into the work. The fabric arose in due course, and the time came when it was necessary to remove the scaffolding, including the supports of the bridge. One of the workmen volunteered to do the work, although it was felt there was a considerable element of uncertainty attending it. As he was a man with a family, the contractor said he would do it himself as he had no one dependent on him. The contractor knocked away the supports with a sledgehammer, and as we see the bridge is there to this day to testify to the substantialness of British bridge-building. It is a pretty story, but we narrate it as given by an old Cheshire man, and we hope it is true.

In May 1847 four persons were killed and nineteen injured by an accident on the viaduct crossing the Dee, an illustration of which is given in these pages. There is a field roadway shown crossing the railway on the Saltney side, and higher up is the tender where it was left after the accident. Just behind is the broken side of the bridge, one end of the girder resting against the pier, the remainder of the viaduct being shown stretching across the Roodee.

In February 1867 Chester had a reflex of the Fenian scare prevalent at the time by an organised attempt to seize the arms stored in the Castle. There was great excitement throughout the country caused by outrages perpetrated in various towns, traceable to Fenianism. In London the damage to Clerkenwell prison through an attempt to blow it up with gunpowder, resulting in loss of life, is still remembered. Every precaution was taken to prevent these outrages. Special constables were sworn in who took night and day duty in relays. In London and other Law Courts everybody passing in had to open his bag to the policeman on duty to show he was not carrying a concealed bomb. There were large movements of troops, and often at midnight Crewe Station presented a busy scene, the men being allowed to alight and spend an interval of leisure on the platform. As can be well understood, the excitement in Cheshire, Chester especially, was intense. In the early morning of the 11th February strangers began to arrive, large companies totalling 1000 to 1500, but in this, as in many instances, " when you wanted to roast an Irishman you found an Irishman ready to turn the spit." Some one had given information to the police at Liverpool and Birkenhead, and the affair quickly collapsed.

Probably the most astonishing "happening" after the war was the transformation of the County Gaol of Knutsford into a Theological College connected with candidates for ordination in the Church of England. It has been used as a county prison for some decades, and before the advent of the budding theologians had been occupied by German prisoners and "Conchies," or conscientious objectors, in turn. The main building is still used for county business and the trial of Cheshire prisoners from other centres. The gaol itself was called an "Ordination Test School," and thus served a higher object, it is to be hoped, in its highest sense.

Sandbach Crosses may indisputably be ranked amongst the finest monuments of antiquity, of this kind, now existing in the kingdom. They are of that description of crosses which have been supposed, in some instances, to have been erected shortly after the introduction of Christianity, on the places where it was first preached, and in others were erected, in the early Saxon period, over the graves of persons of distinction. The substructure consists of a platform of two steps, on which are placed sockets in which the crosses are fixed. The platform and the sockets are 5 feet 6 inches in height ; the present height of the greater cross is 16 feet 8 inches, and that of the smaller one 11 feet 11 inches, making the greatest present height from the ground 22 feet 2 inches.

According to Smith's "Vale Royal," these crosses were standing in the time of Elizabeth, and had, of course, been saved from the violence of the Reformation. Whether they were thrown down by the Puritans acting under the orders of Elizabeth against superstitious images, or during the civil disturbances of Charles I. does not appear, but it is certain they did not appear in a perfect state after this second period (1640-50). Towards the end of the seventeenth century the central part of the large cross and some parts of the other were carried by Sir John Crewe to Utkinton, and set up as an ornament in place of the figure of our Saviour on the Cross, which he considered to be a relic of Popery, being carefully covered with mortar. After the death of Sir John Crewe, these fragments were removed to the Rectory House, Tarporley, where Cole saw them and made drawings of them, remaining amongst his MSS. in the British Museum.

A brass plate on the pillar has the following inscription :—

> These Crosses
> Supposed to have been erected
> on the introduction of Christianity into this Island
> having been much mutilated,
> and in part broken down and carried away,
> were,
> by the liberality of Sir John Grey Egerton
> of Egerton and Oulton in this County, Baronet, in
> restoring those portions,
> which had been adornment to his grounds,
> and by the zeal of the inhabitants of Sandbach
> in collecting the scattered fragments,
> restored and re-erected
> as far as the imperfect state of the material would permit
> in the year of our Lord
> MDCCCXVI.

Palmer ascribes the erection of the cross to the year 653, when Penda returned a Christian convert from Northumbria to Mercia, attended, according to Bede, by four priests deputed to preach the Gospel throughout his dominions.

CHAPTER XIX.

Some Cheshire worthies—Lord Chancellor Egerton, instances of his wisdom · Sir George Beeston, a naval hero—Sir Hugh Calveley's doughty deeds—President Bradshaw, " Traytor and Regicide "—Nixon, the Cheshire prophet—Sir John Birkenhead's editorial labours—Sir Peter Leycester and other Cheshire historians—Banne, " a man of many parts "—Sir Thomas Ashton, a brave and loyal gentleman—Owen S. Brereton, a Liverpool Recorder—Arden, first Lord Alvanley—Bishop Heber and his career—Back, a distinguished explorer—The first Lord Brassey, a well-known yachtsman—Randolph Caldecutt, the caricaturist—Lord Birkenhead, his brilliant career—Its crowning consummation in the Lord Chancellorship—Other notable Cheshire men.

IT has been a standing complaint, principally on the part of old time writers, that Cheshire has not produced any man of great literary or artistic fame, such as Shakespeare, for instance. We had a narrow escape of distinction, however, when Milton married a Cheshire wife of the name of Minshull, a family of Nantwich origin, with whom he had some domestic differences on account of her ultra economical tendencies. While " pleading guilty, with extenuating circumstances " to this soft impeachment, we would point out that the " cheese county " has produced two Lord Chancellors of the realm—lawyers, if you like the term better—an Egerton, a scion of that illustrious family, and Sir F. E. Smith, who patriotically chose the name of his native town on his elevation to the peerage, and is known as Lord Birkenhead. There is another claim which cannot be disputed, in that we have produced a great warrior in Viscount Combermere, who is often mentioned in these pages. A great physician also may be claimed in Sir Henry Holland, a son of Knutsford's soil, a physician in ordinary to Queen Victoria, and whose recollections form a most interesting page in English social history. The latest addition to the list is a great Admiral, Sir David Beatty. These have a good right to be included in the long list of Cheshire worthies, such as Sir George Booth, first Lord Delamere, and his illustrious son, the second Lord, first Earl of Warrington, the Cheshire patriot, pietist, and statesman, *par excellence*, whose lives are set forth in the chapters devoted to an epitome of the House of Dunham.

An ancestor of the Egertons of Ridley and Tatton, Thomas Egerton, died Lord Chancellor of England. Hargreaves, in his " Authentick Evidences," attributed to the Earls of Bridgewater an ancestry derived from the kings of England and France, through Lady Frances Stanley, Countess of Bridgewater ; secondly, with some degree of heirship, to Edmond Plantagenet, Earl of Kent, second son of King Edward I. ; thirdly, with some portion of heirship to Edward III.'s son, John Plantagenet of Gaunt, Duke of Lancaster ; and fourthly, mixed with some degree of heirship to Henry III.'s son, Edmond Plantagenet, Earl of Lancaster, and his wife Blanche, Queen of Navarre, and daughter of Robert, Earl of Artois, brother of St Louis, King of France. The Cheshire descent, taken from a rare work by Francis Henry Egerton, an Earl of Bridgewater, whose will was set aside by a decision of the House of Lords, is as follows:—Robert Fitzhugh, Baron of Malpas, in the reign of William the Conqueror, dying without male issue, the Barony devolved on his only daughter, Letitia, who was married to Richard de Belward. Richard's son and heir married Beatrix, daughter of Hugh Keveliock, and sister of Ranulph, Earl of Chester. The sons of this marriage were David, Robert, and Richard. David was the common ancestor of the Egertons, and Robert of the several families of the Cholmondeleys. David, second son of Philip, was High Sheriff of Chester in the time of Edward I., and, possessing the Manor of Egerton, took, according to the custom of the age, the surname of Egerton from the place of his residence, which said estate and Manor of Egerton, situated to the south of the Broxborne hills in Cheshire, remains in the possession of the Egerton family to this day. "From that time to this," the noble owner remarks, "a space of more than five hundred years, has this great family discharged the highest offices in Church and State."

The Thomas Egerton above referred to was born about the year 1540. He was educated at Brasenose College, Oxford, and "trained to the highest celebrity and distinction." There is a tradition, as recorded by the aforesaid Francis Henry Egerton, Earl of Bridgewater, that one of the first public instances of Chancellor Egerton's shrewdness and ability in his profession, was shortly after he removed to Lincoln's Inn. He happened to be in Court when a cause was trying in which it appeared that three glaziers had vested a joint deposit of a sum of money in the custody of a woman who lived in Smithfield, upon the express condition that she was to account for it on their coming together to demand it. One of the glaziers, having persuaded her that he was commissioned to receive the money by his two partners, who were in the neighbourhood bargaining for some oxen, and only waiting for the money to conclude the purchase, prevailed upon her to entrust him with it, and he immediately absconded. The other two partners commenced a suit against the woman to recover the money.

The cause was brought on, and nothing now appeared to remain but that a verdict should be given in favour of the plaintiffs, when Mr Egerton stepped forward and begged leave to speak as *amicus curiæ*. Upon obtaining permission, he took care to establish the conditions upon which the defendant was entrusted with the money. These being readily allowed to be such as above stated, "Then," said he, "the defendant is ready to comply with the agreement. It is only the plaintiffs who can deservedly be charged with attempting to break it. Two of them have brought a suit against this woman to oblige her to pay them a sum of money, which, by agreement, she was to pay to those two and to the remaining partner jointly, coming together, to demand it. Where is he ? Why does he not appear ? Why do not the plaintiffs bring this partner along with them ? When they do this, and fulfil the agreement, on their part, she is ready to come up to the full extent of it on hers ; till then, I apprehend that she is, by law, to remain in quiet possession." Similar stories are related of Demosthenes, and of a Duke of Ossuna, Viceroy of Naples under Philip III. and IV. of Spain.

While Solicitor-General he represented his native county in Parliament in 1585, and he was raised to the high dignity of Lord Keeper of the Great Seal by Queen Elizabeth in 1596. In the discharge of this office, by command of her Majesty, he addressed the Parliament on the first day of its meeting, 24th October 1597. The speech is characteristic of the statesmen of that day, who comprehended the extensive movements that were going on among the nations of Europe, and who, while with a true conservatism maintained the great institutions of their country, were ever ready, by well-considered reforms, to remove abuses, and to bring the laws into conformity with the spirit and interests of society. Addressing the Parliament in the Queen's name, the Lord Keeper then said : " And whereas the number of the laws already made are very great—some also of them being obsolete and worn out of use—others, idle and vain, serving to no purpose ; some, again, over heavy and too severe for the offence ; others, too loose and slack for the faults they are to punish, and many of them so full of difficulties to be understood, and they cause many controversies ; you are therefore to enter into a due consideration of the said laws ; and where you find superfluity, to prune and cut off ; where defect, to supply ; and where ambiguity, to explain ; that they be not burthensome, but profitable to the Commonwealth ; which, being a service of importance, and very needful to be required, yet is nothing to be regarded, if due means be not had to withstand the malice and force of these professed enemies (the Spaniards), which work the destruction of the whole State." Warming up at the thought of the dangers which threatened the kingdom, he adds, " Wars heretofore were wont to be made either out of ambition to enlarge dominions or out of revenge to requite injuries ; but this against us is not so. In this the holy religion of God is sought to be rooted out, the whole realm to be subdued, and the precious life of her Excellent Majesty to be taken away; which hitherto, by the powerful hand and great goodness of the Almighty, has been preserved, maugre the Devil, the Pope, the Spanish Tyrant, and all the mischievous designs of her enemies."

One of the signatures to the treaty with the Dutch in 1598 is that of Thomas Egerton. To his custody Essex was committed on occasion of the disgrace into which that noble Earl fell with the Queen ; and in 1602, when the Bodleian Library was opened, the Lord Keeper was named one of the supervisors. He, too, was one of the three deputed by the Privy Council, in March 1603, to wait upon Queen Elizabeth, to know her royal will and pleasure upon the point of the succession to the throne. To this request she replied, in broken and interrupted accents, that "Her throne was a throne of kings, and that she had said she would not have any mean person succeed her." And the Secretary asking her what she meant by these words. "I will," said she, "that a king succeed me, and who should that be, but my nearest kinsman, the King of Scots?"

To this high station Thomas Egerton was raised by the special favour of Queen Elizabeth, and, as Camden expresses it, "with the mighty hopes and expectations of the country." The quaint, witty, and learned Fuller, in his "Worthies of England," says of them:—"Surely all Christendom afforded no person which carried more gravity in his countenance and behaviour than Sir Thomas Egerton, insomuch that many have gone to the chancery on purpose only to see his venerable garb (happy they who had no other business), and were highly pleased at so acceptable a spectacle. Yet was this outward case nothing in comparison of his inward abilities, quick wit, solid judgment, ready utterance." In the first year of King James, as Lord Keeper he was made Lord Chancellor, which is only another name for the same office; and Thursday, the 7th of November 1616, as Lord Ellesmere, he was created Viscount Brackley. It was an ordinary speech in his mouth to say, "frost and fraud both end in foul." His death happened in 1617. Sir John Davys, the Attorney-General, said of him that "he was the most excellent pattern of a most excellent Chancellor."

He was buried in Dodleston Church, where his first wife, Elizabeth, daughter of Thomas Ravenscroft, had been interred in 1588, and his son, Thomas, who died in 1599. The epitaph on the Lord Keeper is brief, but expressive—

> Anchora animæ, fides et spes in Christo—Orimur—
> Mormur.—Sequentor qui non præcesserint.

"The anchor of my soul, faith and hope in Christ—we appear,—
We disappear.—They will follow who have not gone before."

In 1601 died Sir George Beeston, aged 102 years, one of the illustrious commanders in the victory over the Spanish Armada. There was a monument to him in Bunbury Church, and from the inscription it appears he was 89 years old when he was knighted for his valour in that memorable engagement.

Sir Hugh Calveley—a celebrated warrior, who died in 1394, whose tomb ornaments the Church—was a younger son of Kenrick de Calveley of Calveley, in Bunbury. He served under King Edward III. in the French wars, but does not appear to have particularly distinguished himself before the Treaty of Bretigny, in 1360, when, with other disbanded officers, he became one of the leaders of a formidable, independent army of veterans, known by the name of "The Companions," who for a while committed great ravages in the provinces of France, and held themselves in readiness to join any warlike expedition in which their services were wanted. Being engaged to assist John de Montford in his claim to the Duchy of Brittany, they fought at the battle of Aurey, in 1364, under Sir John Chandos, and the fortune of the day was turned in favour of Montford by the bravery of Sir Hugh Calveley, who had the command of the rear-guard. During these wars Sir Hugh, Sir Robert Knolles, and twenty-eight companions in arms, engaged in romantic combat with thirty Bretons, whom they completely defeated. " The Companions " after this assisted in expelling Peter, the Cruel, from the throne of Spain, but the Black Prince having been induced to espouse the cause of the dethroned monarch, they ranged themselves under the banner of their prince, and the great victory of Nagara, which reinstated Peter on his throne again, is attributed by historians to the valiant prowess of Sir John Chandos and Sir Hugh Calveley. The first public situation which Sir Hugh Calveley held, was the government of Calais, to which he was appointed by King Edward III. in 1375. In 1377 he burnt twenty-six ships in the harbour of Bologne, and destroyed part of the town. About the same time he took the Castle of Marke, the same day on which it had been lost through negligence, and plundered the town of Estaples. The next year he and Sir Thomas Percy were made Admirals of England. In 1379, having conveyed the Duke of Brittany to St Malo, he drove off some French galleys with much bravery, and succeeded in safely landing everything belonging to the Duke and his household. In 1382, Sir Hugh was one of the commissioners empowered to treat with the Earl of Flanders. The next year he accompanied Henry Spencer, the warlike Bishop of Norfolk, in his expedition into Flanders. The Bishop, on his return, was blamed for his conduct, and some of his officers were sent to the Tower on suspicion of treachery, but we are told that Sir Hugh Calveley, " that ancient captaine," as Holinshed calls him, was retained by the Duke of Lancaster, who did him all honour, " by reason of his old approved valiancie." After this we hear nothing of his public services, but he continued in the Government of Guernsey until his death. He founded Bunbury College.

John, son of Henry Bradshaw of Marple, was baptised at Stockport on the 10th of December 1602. He was born at Wybersley Hall, a small building which appears to have been an appanage to that of Marple. Bradshaw relates in his will that he had his school education at Bunbury in Cheshire and Middleton in Lancashire ; and tradition adds that he was also for some time at Macclesfield, with the strange circumstance annexed to the tale that he wrote the following sentence on a stone in the churchyard there—

> My brother Harry must heir the land ;
> My brother Frank must be at his command ;
> While I, poor Jack, will do that
> That all the world shall wonder at.

Bradshaw served his clerkship with an attorney at Congleton, to which place he returned, after residing some time in Gray's Inn, and acted as councillor-at-law. The first time of his being employed in the affairs of Government seems to have been in the year 1644. In 1646 he was appointed one of the three Commissioners of the Great Seal for six months. In the February following, both Houses voted him the office of Chief Justice of Chester; and he was also

December: 1602
John the sonne of Henrye Bradshaw of Marple was baptized the: 10th traitor·

Bradshawe "Traitor"—from Stockport Register.

made one of the Judges for Wales. On the 3rd of January 1649, when the Lords had adjourned their house and it was found on their journal that they had rejected the ordinance for the trial of the King, the Commons voted the business to be performed by themselves alone, and chose Bradshaw and others for assistants. On the 10th the Commissioners appointed for the trial met, and elected Bradshaw (who was absent) as their President. His conduct in the High Court, which condemned the dethroned monarch to a violent death, has been so frequently related that we shall avoid entering into the detail, and only observe that the strong attachment to republican principles which appears to have actuated him on that occasion, animated him to the latest period of his existence; for when, on his death-bed, he was advised to examine himself about the matter of the King's death, he affirmed that if it were to do again "he would be the first man that should do it." On 14th February 1648 he was one of the thirty-eight persons whom the House had voted to compose a Council of State, and invested with extraordinary powers. In the March following, he was appointed Chief Justice of Wales, and in 1649 had £1000 voted to him by the Parliament. On the escape of Duke Hamilton and some other State prisoners, an Act was passed constituting a new Court of Justice, and Bradshaw was made President. This caused a very unexpected change in his affairs, for on the same day that Cromwell dissolved the Long Parliament—and by that means destroyed the Commonwealth—it occasioned him to lose the Protector's confidence; for, equally the opposer of unlimited power, whether

exercised by a king or an usurper, the Judge disdained to submit in silence to illegal authority. After expelling the members of the House, Cromwell went to break up the Council of State, and prefaced his design with these words:—
"If you gentlemen are met here as private persons, you shall not be disturbed; but if as a Council of State, this is no place for you, since you cannot but know what was done in the House this morning." To this Bradshaw boldly replied: "Sir, we have heard what you did at the House this morning, and before many hours all England will hear of it. But, sir, you are mistaken to think that Parliament is dissolved, for no power under heaven can dissolve them, but themselves." This speech completely alienated the Protector's affections from him, though at the same time it appears to have impressed him with respect, for, in a conference with Desborough, he observed that his work, after dissolving the Parliament, was not completed till he had also dissolved the Council of State, which " I did in spite of the objection of honest Bradshaw, the President." Before this the sum of £2000 per annum had been settled on him by the Parliament.

In the year 1654 Bradshaw was returned as representative for this county; and his behaviour was so inimical to Cromwell's designs that the latter exerted his authority to prevent his being a second time returned. He also required him to resign his commission as Chief Justice of Chester; but this he steadily refused, alleging that he held that place by a grant from Parliament, and whether he had carried himself with the integrity which his commission exacted from him, he was ready to submit to a trial by twelve Englishmen, to be chosen even by Cromwell himself. The firm adherence of Bradshaw to what he supposed were the principles of liberty, prevented his being any more employed in State affairs during the Protectorship; yet, after the death of Oliver, he was again returned for Cheshire to the Parliament that met in January 1658-59, and soon after appointed one of the Commissioners to hold the Broad Seal for five months, but was dispossessed of his high office by the army, who dissolved this Parliament—or Assembly as it was called—by force. After the Restoration, twenty-three persons who had acted as judges on the King were attainted, though in their graves. Bradshaw, who died in the year 1659, being among the number, his body was taken up, and on the 30th of January 1661, the day appointed for this act of retributive justice, as it was termed, was drawn on a sledge to Tyburn, where he, Cromwell, and Ireton were hanged on the several angles of the gallows, under which their mutilated trunks were afterwards buried, their heads having been first cut off and fixed on Westminster Hall. Bradshaw, in his will, made many charitable bequests, among which was the sum of £700 to purchase an annuity for maintaining a free school at Marple. The probate copy of his will was kept at Marple Hall, but the observance of its provisions was completely interrupted by the changes made in the destination of his property at the Restoration.

Henry Bradshaw, elder brother of the President, was a very prominent character during the rebellion. He signed the petition from the county for making Presbyterianism the established religion of the land. He was a magistrate, and had the command of the Macclesfield Hundred Militia. He sat on the trial of the Earl of Derby at Chester in 1652.

Robert Nixon, the Cheshire prophet (or William, as he is called in the Vale Royal MSS.), was born at Bridge-end House, in the township of Over, in Eddisbury Hundred. Daniel Lyson, in his history of the county, states that he was an illiterate ploughboy, his capacity scarcely exceeding that of an idiot, and that he seldom spoke except when he uttered his prophecies, which were taken down from his mouth by some of the bystanders. Many traditions relating to him are still current in the neighbourhood of the Vale Royal, Over and Winsford, where his story is implicitly believed. An anonymous author of the " Life of Robert Nixon, the Cheshire Prophet," places his birth in the reign of Edward IV., but Oldmixon's " Life " states that he lived in the reign of James I., and it is asserted in a letter annexed to the last-mentioned pamphlet, which has the signature of William Ewers and the date of 1714, that there was an old man named Woodman, then living at Coppenhall, who remembered Nixon, could describe his person, and had communicated many particulars of his life. If, according to Oldmixon, so extraordinary a person had lived at Vale Royal in the reign of James I., we might expect to find some mention of him in the parish register either at Over or Whitegate, both of which have been searched in vain, and it is almost incredible that he should not have been noticed by his contemporaries ; yet no mention is made of him either by Webb, in his " Itinerary " in 1622, or by the Randles Holme, father and son, who have recorded all the remarkable events of their times.

Many instances of the fulfilment of his trivial predictions are maintained in Cheshire, such as the meeting of the abbeys of Norton and Vale Royal in the building of Acton Bridge ; the removal of a mill to Luddington Hill by Sir John Crewe ; but by far the most important is, that an eagle should visit Vale Royal when an heir of that house was to be born. An eagle did come, remained near the house three days, and was seen by thousands of people. An eagle was kept caged at Vale Royal up to a recent period. It was certainly a tradition in the district that so long as a bird of this species was kept there the Delamere estate would never be without an heir. Oldmixon states the story on the authority of Lady Cowper, and of Patrick, Bishop of Ely, chaplain to Sir Walter St John, Mrs Cholmondeley's father. The same authority states that when this last event took place there was snow on the ground. Looking at the Cholmondeley pedigree, this may be found to accord with the birth of Charles, eldest son of Thomas Cholmondeley and Anne St John, his wife, on 12th January 1684-85, and he was born heir of Vale Royal, his last surviving brother by a previous marriage having died in 1679 ; but it must be remembered that Charles Cholmondeley died as late as 1756, and was only the grandfather of the present generation, and that this fulfilment of a prophecy said to have been looked to for generations by the county is not in two subsequent generations supported by the slightest memorandum, or even a single tradition preserved in a family it so much concerned.

Nixon is said to have attracted royal notice by the foretelling in Cheshire of the result of the battle of Bosworth on recovering from a sudden stupor with which he was seized whilst the battle was being fought in Leicestershire, and to have been sent to Court shortly afterwards, where he was starved to death through forgetfulness in a manner which he had himself predicted. This event is said to have happened at Hampton Court, where two places are pointed out by the person who showed the palace, each of which is said to have been the scene of his starvation. This part of the story will not bear the test of inquiry better than the others; there is no entry in the parish register of the burial of such a person in the reign of James I.

Sir John Birkenhead was born at Northwich in 1615, and was entered a servitor of Oriel College, Oxford, in 1632. During the Civil War, to Birkenhead was confided the editorship of *Mercurius Aulicus*, or the "Court Mercury," the vehicle of communication between the Court of Oxford and the rest of the kingdom. It was printed weekly in one quarto sheet, "and sometimes more," and was published from 1st January 1642 to the end of 1645, and afterwards occasionally. This Court journal was opposed by the Parliament in the *Mercurium Britannicus*, written by Marchmont Needham. Sir John excelled in satirical wit, and published a number of works in which this dangerous talent was not spared. At the Restoration he was knighted and made Master of Requests. He died in 1679.

Sir Peter Leycester, the antiquary and historian of the Hundred of Bucklow, was born in 1613, and was descended from a long line of knightly ancestors sprung, as he believed, from the ancient Earls of Leicester, but who for more than three hundred years had been settled at Nether Tabley. He was twelfth in lineal descent from Sir Nicholas Leycester. At the age of sixteen he was entered as a gentleman commoner at Brasenose College, Oxford, but did not take a degree. He brought from Oxford a taste for learning which he retained through life. In the year 1642 he embarked manfully in the royal cause. He suffered imprisonment at Chester Castle, and compounded for his estates on payment of the then huge sum of £788, 18s. 4d. It was about this period that he gave his attention to genealogical study, and spent two years in collecting materials for the "History of the Bucklow Hundred," referred to in our second chapter. He was created a Baronet at the Restoration, and in 1673 published his "Historical Antiquities" in two books, the first treating in general on "Great Britain and Ireland," and second, "Particular Remarks Concerning Cheshire," and a transcript concerning Cheshire copied from the original Doomsday record. He qualified as a Justice of the Peace after the Restoration, and was chairman for several years of the Cheshire Quarter Sessions. In 1666 Sir Peter altered the spelling of his name from Leycester to Leicester. He died 11th October 1678, and was buried in the family Chapel at Great Budworth. His wife survived him only a few weeks.

Although Sir Peter Leycester was in his day a great historian, no sketch of his life would be complete without reference to his controversy, the most notable of the seventeenth century, with Sir Thomas Mainwaring, as to the legitimacy of Amicia, a daughter of Hugh Cyveliock, Earl of Chester. No doubt Sir Peter noted the discrepancy in the table of descent, and with his desire for extreme accuracy he questioned whether she was born in wedlock, and over this there was great "ink-shed." It was a combat conducted by the heads of two knightly families of Leycester and Mainwaring. They buckled on their literary armour to do battle, but they were not, it is said, scholars and lawyers, but country gentlemen who had made antiquities their study "as an amusement." These knights appealed to the county, which watched their skill in the use of their weapons, applauded or condemned each tilt in the combat, and awaited with interest the final result. They awaited the publication of each pamphlet in the controversy much as the public of the present day welcome a popular magazine. Some made merry over it, though it is difficult to think why such a serious thing should provoke merriment. Briefly put, Sir Peter averred with much warmth that Amicia, from whom Sir Thomas Mainwaring was descended, was not the Earl's daughter by his wife Bertred. He defended his point strongly, but Sir Thomas did not abate one jot or tittle of his contention that she was legitimate, and in his last tract closing the series—for there were four volumes to be found at one time in the Mainwaring muniments concerning it—he reviews the whole subject temperately, without passion or prejudice, reminding one of a judge's summing up to the jury in a long and intricate case. On the conclusion of his "History of the Bucklow Hundred of Cheshire," Sir Peter wrote: "Thus have I, by God's assistance, run through Bucklow Hundred, according to such evidence and records as I have carefully collected concerning the same. If I had not met with some obstructions by some gentlemen, who, either from waywardness or jealousy, did refuse to let me have the perusal of their evidences, some things might possibly have been further discovered and illustrated. In the meantime I wish this may incite some more able hand to undertake the like for the reviving of those decayed monuments of antiquity in the other hundreds of this our county, which yet lie buried in the rubbish of devouring time."

Although Dr Ormerod was not a Cheshire man, he was, without doubt, the legitimate successor of Sir Peter Leycester, building on the foundation he had laid "wide and deep," and building a superstructure as perfect in its parts as it was possible at that day to achieve, leaving a monument of industry which has never been surpassed by any of his successors. George Ormerod was born in Manchester on the 20th of October 1785. He was educated at the King's School, Chester, and afterwards became a pupil of the Rev. Thomas Bancroft, ex-master of that school, at Bolton, Lancashire. He entered Brasenose College, Oxford, in 1803, and in 1807 received the honorary degree of M.A. In 1809 he was elected a Fellow of the Society of Antiquaries, and in 1819 a Fellow of the Royal Society. He was an authority on heraldry and topography, and possessed an excellent knowledge of the Semitic languages. He contributed many papers to different learned societies, and wrote for Smith's "Bible Dictionary"; but the work by which he is known best is "The History of the County Palatine and City of Chester," in three folio volumes, published in 1819.

We had the pleasure of the acquaintance, when resident in Chester, of Mr Thomas Hughes, F.S.A., whose "Stranger's Handbook to Chester" was read with great interest. His was a most engaging personality, and his genial manner won him "troops of friends." He was born at St Werburgh's Mount, Chester, on the 29th September 1826, and died on the 30th May 1890. He was educated at the King's School, Chester (1836–40), and afterwards became apprentice to Mr George Pritchard, the well-known bookseller. Early in life Hughes became an eager student of the history of his native city, and eventually acquired a widespread reputation as an antiquary. He was one of the founders of the "Chester Archæological Society" in 1849, honorary secretary of that institution from 1856 to 1887, and at the time of his death was one of its vice-presidents. He was a voluminous writer on his favourite subjects, many of his papers being enshrined in the published transactions of the Society, of which he was secretary. He also published an edition of "The Vale Royal of England" in 1842, which was dedicated to His Royal Highness the Prince of Wales. His "Stranger's Handbook to Chester" (1856), "Ancient Chester," (illustrated by local artists), are by no means the least valuable of his works. "The Cheshire Sheaf" is still continued in the columns of the *Chester Courant.* The last named forms an invaluable collection of local lore, the greater part of which was formerly by his own hand and the outcome of laborious research. He took a warm interest in the rebuilding of the King's School, and the endowment of its scholarships, and among the public offices he held was that of Governor of that foundation. He also served the office of Sheriff of that City in 1873–74, and was churchwarden of his parish church (St John's), in which a memorial brass has been placed to his memory. He was an indefatigable collector, and left behind him many books and engravings bearing upon the history of the City and the County Palatine.

Another important contribution to Cheshire bibliography is the monumental work on "East Cheshire," by the late J. P. Earwaker, who was a valued exponent of local history which enriched the columns of contemporary newspapers. There is, on similar lines, a " History of Stockport," a painstaking and carefully compiled record, by Dr Heginbotham, a native of that important district. Chester City has had in recent years Mr G. L. Fenwick, Chester's former Chief Constable, while the story of Chester, admirably told by the late James Williams, a conscientious and efficient official of the County Council administration, was given on popular lines. "The Memorials of Old Cheshire," by the Venerable Archdeacon Barber and the Rev. P. H. Ditchfield, do credit to their special spheres of archæological and ecclesiastical research. In special departments, " Cheshire Flora," by the late Lord de Tabley, " Reptiles and Amphibians," by Coward and Oldham, as also " Mammals and Birds," by the same authors, and " Fishes," by Johnstone, will furnish the student with admirable groundwork for further inquiry. From the above may be gathered some idea of the rich field open for the special study, locally, of the characteristics of places throughout the county.

Nathaniel Banne was a native of Cheshire and brought up to the church. He was for some time minister of Caldecot in Rutlandshire, but was ejected in 1662 for his Nonconformity, when he settled in Manchester as a physician, and became a noted person for skill in his profession. Martindale calls him " his dear friend," and Newcome frequently mentions him. On 4th April 1681, Easter Monday, he was chosen feoffee of the hospital of Manchester, and attended Newcome in his last illness. He had a large practice in Cheshire, and was the friend of several Nonconformists. He is said to have written some works for the Press, but it is not known whether any of them were ever published. He was the father of the Rev. N. Banne, the first rector of St Ann's Church, Manchester.

Sir Thomas Aston, Baronet, was a member of an ancient Cheshire family of that name, and " a brave loyal gentleman " attached to the cause of Charles I. In 1628 he was created a baronet, and in 1635 was High Sheriff of his native county. On the breaking out of the rebellion he raised a troop of horse for the king, but was defeated and wounded at Nantwich in 1642. Afterwards he was taken prisoner and carried to Stafford. Whilst there he tried to escape, but a soldier gave him a blow on the head, which, with other wounds, produced a fever, of which he died in 1643. Wood calls him " a stout and learned man." On page 5 of " A Remonstrance Against Presbytery," Sir Thomas gives a copy of " Certain Positions preached at St John's Church in Chester, by Mr Samuel Eaton, a minister lately returned from New England, upon Sunday, the third of January 1640 (1640–1), in the afternoon," and on page 6 he gives " Certain other Positions preached by the same man, at Knuttesford, a Great Market Town in the same County." He wrote and published " A Remonstrance against Presbitery Exhibited by divers of the Nobilitie, Gentrie, Ministers, and Inhabitants of the County Palatine of Chester, with the Motives of that Remonstrance. Together with a Short Survey of the Presbyterian Discipline, and a Brief Review of the Institution, Succession, and Jurisdiction of the Order of Bishops." Appended is a petition to the Parliament.

A memorial in Alderley Parish Church to the Rev. Edward Skepton rector, who died in 1630, had the following inscription :—

> Here lies below an aged sheepheard, clad in heavy clay,
> Those stubborne weedes which come not off unto the judgment day,
> Whilom he led and fed with welcome paine his careful sheepe,
> He did not feare the mountaines highest top, nor vallies deepe,
> That he might save from hurte his faithful flock which was his care,
> To make them strong he lost his strength, and fasted for their fare ;
> How they might feed, and grow, and prosper, he did daily tel,
> Then having shewed them how to feede, hee bade them all farewell.

Owen Salusbury Brereton, antiquary, was born in 1715. His father was Thomas Brereton, afterwards of Shotwick Park, Cheshire, who came into possession of that estate through marriage with Catherine, daughter of Mr Salusbury Lloyd. Owen Brereton (says Mr C. W. Sutton, M.A., in the "National Dictionary of Biography") was the son of a former marriage with a Trelawney, and added the name of Salusbury on succeeding to the estates in the Counties of Chester, Denbigh, and Flint, on his father's death, about the year 1756. He was admitted a scholar of Westminster School in 1729, and was elected to Trinity College, Cambridge, in 1734. He was called to the Bar in 1738, and in that year held the post of a Lottery Commissioner. He was also appointed Recorder of Liverpool, an office he retained till his death, a period of fifty-six years. When he proposed to resign in 1796 he was requested by the Corporation to retain his situation, and they appointed a deputy to relieve him of the pressure of its duties. He became a member of the Society of Arts in 1762, and was vice-president from 1765 to 1798, in which capacity he rendered great service to the society. He was also a member of the Royal Society and of the Society of Antiquaries (elected 1763), a bencher of Lincoln's Inn, treasurer of that body, and Keeper of the Black Book. He was Member of Parliament for Ilchester, in Somerset, from 1775 to 1780, and constable of Flint Castle, 1775. He died at his residence, at Windsor, 8th September 1798, in his eighty-fourth year, and was buried in St George's Chapel, Windsor, 22nd September.

Richard Pepper Arden, first Lord Alvanley, baptised at Stockport 20th June 1744, became a very distinguished man. The Admission Register (vol. i. p. 45) of the Manchester Grammar School says : " He was the second son of John Arden, of Harden Hall, Bredbury, and Underbank Hall, Stockport, and of Pepper Hall, Yorkshire." Richard Pepper Arden entered Manchester Grammar School with his elder brother, John, 20th June 1752. In 1763 he went to Trinity College, Cambridge, and soon distinguished himself by his public exercises. He commenced B.A. in 1766, and proceeded M.A. in 1769, his merits being further rewarded by an election to a Fellowship of his College. After a course of training at the Middle Temple and Lincoln's Inn, he commenced practice as a barrister at the Court of Chancery, and soon rose high in public estimation as a lawyer. He entered Parliament as member for Newton in 1782, and subsequently sat for the boroughs of Aldborough, Hastings, and Bath. We find him taking office as Solicitor-General in 1783, and in the following year he became Attorney-General and Chief Justice of Chester. In 1788 he succeeded Lord Kenyon as Master of the Rolls, receiving the honour of knighthood in June of the same year. On the resignation of Pitt in 1801, Sir R. P. Arden accepted office as Chief Justice of the Common Pleas under Mr Addington, and in May the same year he was created Baron Alvanley. He married Anne Dorothea, daughter of Richard Wilbraham, of Rode, Cheshire, and died 19th March 1804, aged 59. He left two sons, who in turn succeeded to the title, but with the last of them it became extinct. In the field of literature he has left but little to be remembered by, but if an opinion may be formed from some of the occasional verses with which he amused his friends, he was industriously represented, and for a long time believed, to be a very dull man, and could have retorted the keen shafts of the Rolliad with counter missives of equal brilliancy, point, and severity.

Dr Samuel Ogden, the famous sermon writer and a native of Manchester, had written three copies of verses on the accession of George III., the first in Latin, the second in English, and the third in Arabic. The epigram upon it, by Lord Alvanley, published in the Cambridge Verses of 1763, was as follows:—

> When Ogden his prosaic verse
>   In Latin numbers drest,
> The Roman language proved too weak
>   To stand the critic's test.
>
> In English verse he ventured next,
>   With rhyme for his defence;
> But, ah, rhyme only would not do,
>   They still expected sense.
>
> Enraged, the Doctor swore he'd place
>   On critic no reliance;
> Involved his thoughts in Arabic,
>   And bid them all defiance.

In the pleasure gardens of the old Hall at Gawsworth was buried the singular author of the play of "Hurlothrumbo." He was a dancing master, and contrived to be introduced as a table companion to the principal families in the neighbourhood. The gravestone has the following inscription:—

Under this stone rest the remains of Mr Samuel Johnson, afterwards ennobled with the grander title of Lord Flame, who after having been in his life distinct from other men, by the eccentricities of his genius, chose to retain the same character after his death, and was at his own desire buried here, May 5, 1773, aged 82.

> Stay thou whom chance directs or ease persuades
> To seek the quiet of these sylvan shades :
> Here, undisturbed, and hid from vulgar eyes,
> A wit, musician, poet, player, lies ;
> A dancing-master, too, in grace he shone
> And all the parts of op'ra were his own ;
> In Comedy well skill'd he drew Lord Flame,
> Acted the part, and gained himself the name ;
> Averse to strife, how oft he'd gravely say,
> These peaceful groves should shade his breathless clay,
> And when he rose again, laid here alone,
> No friend and he should quarrel for a bone ;
> Thinking that were some old lame gossip nigh,
> She possibly might take his leg or thigh.

Reginald Heber, afterwards Bishop of Calcutta, was born 21st April 1783, at the Higher Rectory, Malpas, of which his father was rector. He received his education principally under a private tutor, and in 1800 he removed to Oxford, where he was a Commoner at Brasenose College, and afterwards a Fellow of All Souls. It was at Oxford that he laid the foundation of his high fame. Besides being known for his general acquisitions in scholarship, he gained every distinction which the University had to bestow. He was also the successful competitor for an extraordinary prize that had been offered for an English poem, on the subject of Palestine. This poem is now of standard reputation, and certainly, for splendour of imagery and for poetical diction, it has deservedly placed its author—scarce twenty years old when it was written—in an elevated rank amid our English poets. After taking his degree, Heber left the University to engage in actual life. The living at Hodnet, was at his option, and this circumstance, coupled with his strong religious bias, determined him to devote himself to the church as his profession. But as he was still young for holy orders, he wished to employ two or three years in foreign travel, and the customary route upon the continent, then being shut up by war, he bent his steps towards Russia and the east of Europe. At length the time arrived when Heber was to devote himself seriously to the duties of his sacred profession in the humble office of a village pastor. There is, on his monument in Hodnet Church, a delightful testimony how, for fifteen years, he performed his pastoral duties " cheerfully and diligently, and with all his heart, and with all his soul, and with all his strength." And in this calm retreat, which the subsequent changes in his fortune seemed only the more to endear him, he would cheerfully have closed his days; but his reputation would not allow him to be buried in retirement. In 1822 he was elected preacher at Lincoln's Inn. This was an appointment peculiarly suited to him. With what credit he acquitted himself is well known, and it was generally believed that the highest honours awaited him at home, when he was called to another sphere of action, by his acceptation of the proffered bishopric of Calcutta.

Never, it is believed, did any man accept an office from a higher sense of duty. Once he declined the proposal; but his exalted piety considered it as a call from heaven, from which he might not shrink, and he resolutely determined to obey the summons. His career in India was short, but brilliant. It is not easy to conceive a situation of greater difficulty than awaited him there. He had to preside over a diocese much larger in extent than the whole of Europe, with his clergy scattered about at stations thousands of miles apart, and over a body of Christians living in the midst of a multitude of misbelievers—and those Christians, if such more than in mere name, accustomed to be a law to themselves in religious matters, yet to all these difficulties Bishop Heber resolutely addressed himself. He went forth strong and invincible; first, in his trust in God, and next, in that kindliness of disposition which almost disarmed opposition. His memorable exploit was his extraordinary visitation of his diocese: starting from Calcutta, he pursued the course of the Ganges almost to its source—visited the Himalaya Mountains—crossed the northern provinces of India—and, after visiting Bombay and the island of Ceylon, returned again to Calcutta. We may easily imagine what must have been the delight, to a mind ardent and poetical like Heber's, to have had the opportunity of visiting scenes so interesting and so novel; and we have the advantage of knowing the impression they made on his mind by the posthumous publication of his interesting journal. It was not long after the bishop's return from the visitation, of which we have been speaking, that he undertook another episcopal visitation, when the hand of death arrested him in his career of usefulness. On the 3rd of April 1826, at Trichinopoli, he was found drowned in a bath, owing, it was supposed, to the sudden transition to cold water after great exertion in confirming some native Christians. A deep and painful sensation was produced by his unexpected decease, both in India and at home, and in him the Christian civilisation of the East seemed to have lost its most zealous, most active, and most enlightened friend.

Sir George Back, a distinguished voyager and explorer in the Arctic regions, was born at Holly Vale, Stockport, in 1796. He entered the Navy at an early age, and accompanied Sir John Franklin on his Arctic voyages in 1818-19-23. In 1833 he undertook an overland journey in search of Captain Ross. On this occasion he descended Back River till he reached the Polar Sea, and then traced the coasts as far as Bathurst Inlet. The result of the journey was the publication of two volumes, respecting which the

View of Stockport, 1800.

Tatton Hall, 1797.

Athenæum of the day says : " Of all the voyages of discovery entered upon within our recollection, none engaged public attention so thoroughly as the expedition, the fruits of which are before us." In 1831 he was made captain, and in 1836 examined the coasts between Cape Turnagain and Regent Inlet. In 1838 he received the honour of knighthood, and was presented with the Geographical Society's medal.

Robert Brook Aspland, M.A., was the son of the Rev. Robert Aspland, a Unitarian minister at Newport, I.W., where he was born 19th January 1805. After being educated at a private school at Blackheath, he proceeded to the Glasgow University, where he took his degree in 1822, and afterwards studied theology at the Manchester College, York. His first call was to a congregation in Crook's Lane, Chester, in August 1826. From there, in 1833, he proceeded to Bristol, and from that town he came, in 1837, to Dukinfield. Here he remained for more than twenty years, till he removed, on account of his wife's health, to Hackney, to succeed his father, who had ministered there for forty years. He died somewhat suddenly on 21st June 1869, and was buried at Hackney. In 1845 he preached a sermon at Dukinfield on the occasion of the re-opening of the Old Chapel, which was subsequently published under the following title—" History of Old Nonconformity in Dukinfield : A Sermon preached on the afternoon of Sunday, 12th October 1845, when the Old Chapel was re-opened for Public Worship. With an Appendix."

Thomas Brassey, K.C.B., of the Grange, Bulkeley, Cheshire, first Lord Brassey, was born at Stafford in 1836, and was son of Thomas Brassey, the well-known contractor for public and railway works, who was a Cheshire man by birth, as the son was by inheritance. He was educated at Rugby and University College, Oxford, graduating in honours in the modern law and history school. He was elected M.P. for Devonport in 1865, and represented Hastings from 1868 to 1886, being appointed Civil Lord of the Admiralty in 1880, and Secretary to Admiralty in 1884. As a yachtsman Lord Brassey made many distant voyages. In 1876 he went round the world in the "Sunbeam." He was the first yachtsman who obtained a Board of Trade certificate for competency to navigate as master. At the General Election, 1886, Lord Brassey withdrew from Hastings, and offered himself as a Gladstonian Liberal for one of the divisions of Liverpool. He was defeated, and on the resignation of Mr Gladstone's Government he was raised to the peerage.

Cheshire produced no mean artist in Randolph Caldecott. Born at Chester in 1846, he was educated at King Henry VIII.'s School in the famous old city. Although he studied at no school of art or under any painter, he made his mark as an artist in humorous illustration. His fame became general in 1878 when he published one of his coloured picture-books. Their humour, especially in " The Mad Dog," was inimitable, and he appealed in this and his other books to the interest, almost universal in England, which is felt in animals and their humours. Another set of subjects he made his own was the hunting field, in which he proved a formidable rival to Leech, and, if possible, even more popular. He suffered for a long time from ill health, which brought on heart disease. Accompanied by his wife he left England for Florida, hoping for the best from a climate unequalled in the world. In that year a bad winter killed all the oranges. That winter also killed poor Caldecott!

Equally brilliant and honourable in the legal world, and a worthy successor of Lord Chancellor Egerton, was Frederick Edwin Smith, who was elevated to that high office in 1919. He was born at Birkenhead on the 12th July 1872, and was a son of the late Frederick Smith, Barrister-at-Law, Middle Temple, who was elected Mayor of Birkenhead, and who died exactly a month later—on 9th December. He was educated at Birkenhead School, where he quickly gave evidence of the possession of exceptional gifts. He passed to Wadham College, Oxford, where he had a brilliant scholastic career. He married, in 1901, Margaret Eleanor, second daughter of the late H. Furneaux, Fellow of Corpus Christi College, and their family consists of one son, Frederick William Furneaux, born 7th December 1907, and two daughters.

He was classical scholar of his college (Wadham), President of the Oxford Union, 1893; first class final Honorary, School of Jurisprudence, in 1894; Vinerian Law Scholar, 1895; Fellow and Lecturer of Merton College, Oxford, 1896; Lecturer, Oriel College, 1897; Oxford University Extension Lecturer in Modern History, 1898; Examiner in the Final Schools, Oxford, 1899-1900; Extension Lecturer in Modern History, Victoria University, 1900. His publications are :—" International Law," 4th edition, 1911; " Newfoundland "; articles in law, *Quarterly Review* and " Chambers' Encyclopædia "; " International Law in the Far East," 2nd edition, 1908; " The Licensing Bill," 1908; " Speeches, 1906-1909," 2nd edition; " The Destruction of Merchant Ships," 1917; " My American Visit, 1918," 2nd edition; and " The Indian Corps in France," 2nd edition.

He was Member of Parliament for the Walton Division of Liverpool from 1906 to 1908, when, under the Redistribution Bill, he fought and won West Derby. In 1908 he was made King's Counsel and Bencher of Gray's Inn, and Treasurer in 1917-18; and in 1915 he was appointed Solicitor-General, which carried with it a knighthood. In November of the same year he became Attorney-General with a seat in the Cabinet. He had been a Privy Councillor for some years. His Baronetcy was one of the New Year Honours in 1918. From the outset of his career, when he made his memorable maiden speech in the House of Commons, he was marked out as a force to be reckoned with in Parliament, and this, the record of his work, of which the foregoing is a summary, fully bears it out. As an officer (second lieutenant) of the Oxfordshire Hussars, Sir F. E. Smith went to France soon after the outbreak of war, and in September 1914 he was granted the temporary rank of Major, a year later being promoted to a temporary Lieutenant-Colonelcy. In 1915 he was among the officers of the General Headquarters Staff (to which he was attached) mentioned in dispatches.

The announcement of the Prime Minister's appointment of Sir Frederick to the highest legal position in the kingdom in January 1919, aroused the greatest interest on Mersey side, especially in Birkenhead, and was looked upon as the culmination of a brilliant career, both legal and political. At the age of 46, he is the youngest man who has ever been made Lord High Chancellor of England. On behalf of the town, the Mayor of Birkenhead (Mr D. Roger Rowlands) tendered sincere congratulations. The event, he said, was greeted with satisfaction and pride that one of the greatest of its sons had attained such high office. The Lord Chancellor afterwards visited the Mayor to ascertain from him, as chief citizen, whether the latter conceived that any objection would be raised by the community of the town in which he was born and received his early education to his assuming, on his accession to one of the proudest positions in the realm, the title of Lord Birkenhead. The Mayor had not the slightest hesitation in informing the Lord Chancellor that he was confident that it would be a great disappointment to the people of Birkenhead if he did not take that title and so perpetuate his close association with the town. The Lord Chancellor intimated that he was anxious to adopt that designation. Councillor Rowland replied that it was his firm belief it would be as Lord Birkenhead, one of the men of whom the town is most proud, the new Lord Chancellor would be known in the future.

Later, the Lord Chancellor paid a farewell visit to his former constituents in the West Derby Division, and was entertained at luncheon at the Liverpool Conservative Club, under the Presidency of Mr F. A. Goodwin, Chairman. His Lordship's health was proposed by the Chairman, and supported by Sir Archibald Salvidge and Sir Watson Rutherford. The Lord Chancellor dwelt on the arduous and responsible character of the duties he had undertaken, but he assured his hearers that if he had not believed that diligent application and zeal would enable him to discharge those duties with a reasonable measure of adequacy, he would never have undertaken them. In concluding his speech the Lord Chancellor said: " I am parting to-day, in one aspect of my life, from many old friends. The moment to me is one that I can never forget. The kindness which you have shown to me to-day will never leave my memory, but those who have been good enough to detect some upward progress in my career in the past in which, as an unknown boy, I came to seek my fortunes in Liverpool, will, I think, concede this, that if it be true that I have made progress, no step of that progress has ever estranged me from an old friend, however humble he might be. I am called now to a new position and to new responsibilities. No man who has ever cherished friendly feelings towards me will ever find that there will be any breach in our friendship, or that any coolness or estrangement will proceed from me."

One admirer says: "'A man who is at home in the world laughs and is gay.' No mere man is at home in the world—every boy is. In the Lord Chancellor the man rejuvenates himself in the boy and the boy energises the man for the man's task. Most of us fear the world and the world's opinion, but Lord Birkenhead 'laughs and is gay,' for he cares not what the world thinks so long as he is himself. Unconventional is a word that helps to describe him. He has done the unexpected and will continue to do it. Surround him with honours if you will, add office to office if you please—so long as F. E. the boy is not smothered Birkenhead people will be satisfied. It was Lord Birkenhead who signed the Roll of Freemen at Birkenhead ; it was the Lord Chancellor who was invited to accept the honour, but F. E. came, and it was he whom we welcomed and honoured. No matter how long he may live, he will die young, for the gods have given him the gift of perennial youth. And Lord Birkenhead cherishes the gift."

Lord Birkenhead was present as Lord Chancellor at the opening of the legal year in London in October 1919, and attended a special service at Westminster Abbey. His Lordship afterwards entertained about 250 judges and Counsel to breakfast at the House of Lords. The opening ceremony took place at the Law Courts. A procession, headed by the Lord Chancellor, marched through the Central Hall, and following him was the Lord Chief Justice (Lord Reading). There were also present, Lord Sterndale, President of the Probate and Divorce Division, and Lords Justice, in their black and golden robes, preceded the Judges of the King's Bench Division and Chancery Division in scarlet and ermine, and a great array of King's Counsel, wearing their full bottomed wigs, brought up the rear. There were two notable absentees —the Master of the Rolls, Sir J. C. Swinfen Eady, suffering from severe illness, and Mr Justice Darling, on duty on the Western Circuit. Business in the courts consisted chiefly of *ex-parte* applications, and the sittings were of brief duration.

There are many other Cheshire worthies who have made a name for themselves in long past history. Bishop Wilson, Sodor and Man, was born at Burton in Wirral in 1791, and it is said he built the Church anew in a then remote diocese. It was in vain that preferment to a wealthier see was offered. Like Bishop Jayne in our own day, he preferred to remain with his people whom he loved and by whom he was in turn beloved, and generations afterwards the fishermen of the island related how he taught their forefathers to sing those hymns invoking a blessing on their arduous vocation. Dr Hugh Bellot, Bishop of Bangor and Chester, was born at Astbury, and died in 1596. Bishop Rider was born at Carrington in 1562, and became Bishop of Killaloe in 1612. John Brownswerd, Master of Macclesfield Grammar School, was learned in the classics, and turned out many pupils who afterwards achieved renown. Randolph Crewe, a descendant of the Crewes of Crewe Hall, was born at Nantwich in 1588, and became Lord Chief Justice of England in 1624. Fuller said that he brought Cheshire into London "in the sprightliness and pleasantness of his structures." He was buried in the Crewe Chapel at Barthomley.

John Gerard was born at Nantwich in 1545, and afterwards practised as a surgeon in London. In 1596 he published a catalogue of the 1100 varieties of plants in his garden, and, in 1597, "The Herball or Generall Historie of Plantes." A large part of it was directly translated from a Dutch work, though much of it was original. A second edition of his principal work appeared in 1633, twenty-one years after his death.

Laurence Earnshaw, who has been described as "a mechanical genius more favoured by the endowments of mind than the gifts of fortune, was a native of Broadbottom, a hamlet near Mottram. He was early apprenticed to a tailor and afterwards to a clothier, but neither of these employments being congenial with his disposition, after serving both for eleven years, he placed himself for a short time with a clockmaker of Stockport. With the very little instruction he obtained from his desultory education, he became one of the most universal mechanists and artists that was ever known. He could have taken wool from the sheep's backs, manufactured it into cloth, and made every instrument necessary for the clipping, carding, spinning, reeling, weaving, fulling, dressing, and making it up for wear, with his own hands. He was an engraver, painter, gilder; he could stain glass and foil mirrors; was a blacksmith, whitesmith, coppersmith, gunsmith, bellfounder, and coffin maker; made and erected sun-dials; mended fiddles; repaired, tuned, made, played upon, and taught the harpsicord; made and mended organs and optical instruments; read and understood Euclid; and, in short, had a taste for all sorts of mechanics and most of the fine arts. Clockmaking and repairing was a very favourite employment to him, and he carried so far his theory and practice of clockwork as to be the inventor of a very curious astronomical and geographical machine, containing a terrestrial and celestial globe, to which different movements were given, representing the diurnal and annual motions of the earth, the position of the moon and stars, and various other phenomena, with the greatest correctness. All the complicated calculations, as well as the execution, of this ingenious work were performed by himself; and one of the machines, curiously ornamented, was sold to the Earl of Bute for £150. About the year 1753 he invented a machine to spin and reel cotton by one operation, which he showed to his neighbours, and then destroyed, through the generous apprehension that it might take bread from the mouths of the poor. This was previous to the later inventions by which cotton manufacture has been so much promoted. He was acquainted with that equally self-taught genius, the celebrated Brindley, born in the neighbouring county of Derby, and when

R

they occasionally met they would continue for many hours discoursing on the principles of science and their own respective modes of operation. His countenance was not peculiarly stamped with intelligence, but, on the contrary, might, at first view, be considered as indicative of stupidity, yet when animated by conversation his features beamed with the irradiations of intellect ; he conversed with fluency and clearly explained the objects of his discourse in the dialect and peculiar phrase of the county."

CHAPTER XX.

Cheshire characteristics, proverbs, and sayings—Building and furnishing houses—Check on Art in the Stuart times—The Duke of York's "little party"—Cheshire moods and manners—" Women friendly and loving "—Antiquity of County families—Fuller on Cheshire physicians—Farmers and folklore—Pigs and stormy weather—Horse shoes and whooping cough—Peculiarities of Cheshire dialect—Coats of Arms and public-house signs—Fuller on Cheshire cheese—The Spaniard cornered—" Not any more this time, thank you "—Qualifications of a Cheshire farmer's wife—Old-time teetotalism and its failings—Wetting the child's head—Giving him " what for "—As hard as a North toad—Pulling Lymm from Warburton—To grin like a Cheshire cat—Far fetched and dear bought—Parish lantern and parish water—St Peter's needle—Wheelbarrow farmers, etc.

WILLIAM of Malmsbury, who flourished about A.D. 1140, wrote that the County of Chester was scarce of corn, and especially of wheat, but plentiful in cattle and fish. Whereupon, one Ranulph, a monk, according to Camden, took up the cudgels, and says, that whatever this William may have dreamt, the county abounded in all kinds of victuals, was plenteous in all kinds of corn, flesh, and fish, and of " salmons," especially of the very best. It supplied trade with many commodities, and in the " confines " it had salt beds, mines and metals. Lucian, another monk, hints that their ideas of the laws of property were rather confused, especially when they " borrowed " other men's goods and forgot to return them !

Speed, quoting Lucian, the monk, who lived immediately after the Conquest, says of the inhabitants : " They are found to differ from the rest of the English, partly better and partly equal. In feasting they are friendlie ; at meat, cheerful ; in entertainment, liberall ; soone angry and soone pacified ; lauish (lavish) in words, impatient of servitude, mercifull to the afflicted, compassionate to the poor, kinde to their kindred, spary of labour, void of dissimulation, not greedy in eating, and far from indulging in dangerous practices."

Smith, in his " Treatise on Cheshire," about the year 1610, says : " In building and furniture of their houses, till of late years, they used the old manner of the Saxons. For they had their fire in the midst of the house, against a hob of clay, and their oxen under the same roof ; but within these forty years, it is altogether altered, so that they have builded chimnies, and furnished other parts of their houses accordingly."

From the reign of James I. to Queen Anne there were, it is said, few distinguishing characteristics in shapes or styles. Prior to the reign of Queen Elizabeth, household fitting was practically unknown. The Feudal System was responsible for the custom of lords and servants taking their meals together in one great hall, where the few benches and rough tables served their common needs, but with the collapse of the system came the introduction of " sitting rooms " and greater ease and comfort in domestic furniture.

Throughout the reigns of the Stuarts, with their various internal dissensions and civil war, Art received a check, and there was no development, with the result that for a century nearly all furniture was made of the same pattern. Chairs were scarce and costly, and only found in the most prosperous households. Pepys in his delightful way says, regarding a party he attended, he found the Duke and Duchess of York and ladies sitting on a carpet, playing at "I love my love with an 'A' because he is" so and so, "and I hate him with a 'B' because he is this or that." A bare board was used in Saxon times, and all the tables had ground bars, which were used as foot rests owing to the insanitary condition of the uneven and rush strewn floors.

"The people of the county," according to Smith, "are of a nature very gentle and courteous, ready to help and further one another; and that is chiefly to be seen in the harvest time, how careful are they of one another. In religion very zealous, howbeit somewhat addicted to superstition, which cometh through want of preaching. For the harvest is plenteous but the reapers are few. It is a thing to be lamented and redress to be wished, for in some places they have not a sermon in a whole year. Otherwise, they are of a stomach stout, bold and hardy; of stature tall and mighty; withal impatient of wrong, and ready to resist the enemy or stranger that shall invade their country; the very name whereof they cannot abide, and namely, of a Scot. So they have been always true, faithful and obedient to their superiors; insomuch that it cannot be said that they have at any time stirred up one spark of rebellion either against the King's Majesty or against their lord and Governor. Likewise be the women very friendly and loving, painful in labour, and in all other kinds of husbandry expert, fruitful in bearing children, after they be married, and sometimes before.

"Touching their housekeeping it is bountiful, and comparable with any other shire in the realm. And that is to be seen at their weddings and burials, but chiefly at their Wakes, which they yearly hold (although it be of late years well laid down); for this is to be understood, that they lay out seldom any money for any provisions but have it for their own, as beef, mutton, veal, pork, capons, hens, wildfowl, and fish. They bake their own bread and brew their own drink."

The writer of the foregoing may be said to be dealing with the beginnings of civilisation in Cheshire so far as it concerned the adherents of the great county families, for about 240 years ago the Rev. William Webb, M.A., who was, in 1615, Under Sheriff of Cheshire, wrote his "Itinerary," and gives a description of the houses occupied by the gentry, whose hospitality he no doubt enjoyed, and of whom and their surroundings he was induced to speak in the most eulogistic terms. He was then in the "Seedplot of Gentilitie," and it is remarkable that many ancient names are still to be found in Cheshire which "are taken from the language and circumstances of a people decidedly

Teutonic or Scandinavian"; and we arrive at the conclusion that the vast majority of the inhabitants possess an ancestry far anterior to the battle of Hastings, and belong to what the last Earl of Bridgewater describes as "the old, genuine, original, native families of England." We have had it shown to us by documents and otherwise that the same families, father and son, have tenanted the same farm for centuries, and probably had an antiquity as remote as that claimed for them by Lord Bridgewater. An old gentleman gravely argued of a place in North Cheshire, Carrington, that it was at one time a convict settlement, as only on such an assumption could the families have been settled there so long! We make a present of this to our Cheshire friends in that particular locality, famous for its apple orchards, merely throwing out an opinion for their guidance that the speaker evidently knew little of Cheshire, or the people connected with it. Certainly time has brought about many changes, but we are still inclined to believe from actual experience that history is only repeating itself, and that what held true of the seventeenth century may with equal truth be applied to the twentieth.

Fuller, in his "Worthies of England," when speaking of the physicians of Cheshire, says: "If this county has bred no writers in this faculty, the wonder is the less, if it be true what I have read that if any here (in Cheshire) be sick they make him a posset, and tie a kerchief on his head, and if that will not mend him, then God be merciful to him." He takes care to qualify this assertion by remarking that this only applied to common people, as the gentry "had the help (no doubt) of the learned in the profession." If the worthy Fuller had lived in these days he would have added that Cheshire had bred a famous physician in Sir Henry Holland (1788-1873), who was born at Knutsford in the first mentioned year. He became Physician to Caroline, Princess of Wales (1814), and was afterwards one of the physicians extraordinary to William IV. and Prince Albert, and one of the physicians in ordinary to Queen Victoria. He wrote "Travels in the Ionian Islands," 1815; "Medical Notes and Reflections," 1839; "Chapters on Mental Physiology," 1852; "Essays on Scientific and Other Subjects," 1862; and "Recollections of Past Life," 1872—the last named a highly interesting piece of biographical lore.

Farmers formerly had a great belief in superstitions, folklore, etc., and many ideas applied to domestic animals and plants which they held in veneration, and is not yet quite extinct. Bears are supposed to breed once in seven years. When breeding sows lost litters it was gravely remarked that "bears must be breeding this year." Sows when they farrowed were propitiated by a large slice of hot toast and lard to prevent them from eating their young. Pigs, it was held, should always be killed in a waxing or increasing moon, otherwise they would not weigh so well. When pigs run about and carry straw in their mouths it forebodes stormy weather, probably giving rise to the saying that "pigs can see the wind!"

There was also said to be a "master" in every herd of cows—a ring-leader in mischief—breaking through hedges when a turnip field happens to be handy. Milk given by a red cow was recommended by the doctor, and when all the cows in the herd were seen lying down in a field the weather was certain to be wet. A horse shoe nailed to a stable door kept out evil spirits, and a stripe on a donkey's shoulder, called a cross, was considered an infallible cure for whooping cough. A portion of the hair was sewn up in a piece of flannel and worn round the neck of the patient, or it might be chopped up very fine and eaten between bread and butter!

A hen which crowed like a cock was sure to bring bad luck, and should be killed at once, and an odd number of eggs should be put under a sitting hen. Bees should be "told" when the master of the house died, or they would desert their hives. They should never be bought, but begged or borrowed, or, if bought, should be paid for in gold, or exchanged for an equivalent—say, a sucking pig—or they would not be lucky. Clattering a frying pan or tin when bees swarmed was a common practice, and caused them to settle or "knit." The colour shown by frogs at various times of the day was supposed to indicate the weather, and it is even now a belief that hedgehogs suck a cow's teat and drink the milk. Horse beans grew the wrong way up in the pod in leap year. Parsley went nine times to the devil, and to insure a good growth should be sown on a Good Friday. Eschallots (shallots) should be planted on the shortest day and pulled on the longest. When yeast was mixed with dough, the goodwife made a cross with her finger to keep away witches, who would prevent the dough rising.

The study of local dialects is one of considerable interest. There does not appear to be any striking variation between North and South Cheshire, although it is not so pronounced in the North, where contact with manufacturing centres has caused a striking change in this direction. There is the same remarkable substitution of "e" for "a" in many cases. A plate is called a "pleete"; a crop of hay will be spoken of as a crop of "hee," and so on. The Rev. H. Green humorously puts it in this way: "A few years ago if a Knutsford beau or belle were asked to sing, the declining to do so was not infrequently in the words, 'Aw've got a cowd and lost my vice (voice), and connor,' and when John and Peter, just about the time of harvest, were sent into the cornfield with rattles, 'the two bys,' it was said, 'were in the kern, nyzing th' brids away'; and when a Sunday-school teacher asked a whole class of youngsters, 'What is a bird?' a little fellow, brighter than the rest, exclaimed, 'Hoo means a brid!' There was a hard striving and respectable woman who was renowned for the richness of her vernacular vocabulary and of her Cheshire brogue. 'Moy childer,' she said, 'are aw doosome;' and when a good lady was desirous of enlightening her mind as to some of the more difficult doctrines of theology, she told her, 'Au'm welly aukert at religion; yo con speak to moy William, he kno's aw about it.'"

Hulbert, in his "Cheshire Antiquities," gives a most amusing dialogue between a servant girl and her sweetheart, and in the late Colonel Egerton Leigh's lecture on "Cheshire Words, Proverbs, and Sayings," which is most excellent and amusing, we have the following: "'What have you got in your basket?' said a lady to a man whom she met. 'Nubbut a whisketful o' wick snigs,' was the reply, which meant he had got a basket full of live eels." How the natives pick up and adapt to their own use things with which these have no connection is evidenced by the fact that the Legh Arms Inn, Knutsford, is known as the "Snig and Skewer," or the "Sword and Serpent." "The Red Lion" in any place is sooner recognised by the toper as "Th' Rompin' Kitlin" (or Kitten), and to this day the "Barry Arms," at Grappenhall, is known as "The Dog and Dart." There is "The Eagle and Child," or "Derby Arms," at Alderley, and "The Jolly Thrasher" at Lymm and other places. No doubt there are many other instances which may be found in a work published many years ago by Fisher Unwin on "Public-house Signs."

We now come to the special consideration of Cheshire's pre-eminence in the production of cheese. Again Fuller says: "This county doth afford the best cheese, for quantity and quality, and yet the cows are not, as in other shires, housed in the winter (?) so that it may appear strange that the hardiest kine should produce the tenderest cheese. Some essayed in vain, to make the like in other places, though from thence they fetched both their kine and dairy-maids. It seems they should have 'fetched their ground too' (wherein surely is some occult excellency in this kind) or else so cheese will not be made. I have not the like commendation of the butter of this county, and perchance these two commodities are like stars of a different horizon, so that the elevation of the one tends to the depression of the other."

Cheshire cheese has always been a subject for pride, and justly so, to the agriculturists of the county, and probably many of our readers will be aware of the amusing poem of the Spaniard and the Cheshire cheese, given in Colonel Leigh's ballads and legends, where the Spaniard dilates at some length on the fact that in his country fruits are produced twice a year. The Cheshire man, not to be outdone, called for a Cheshire cheese, and effectually turned the tables on his opponent by declaring that in his country this fruit was produced not twice a year, but twice a day, and challenged him to produce anything of the kind in Spain. It is said that the richest and best cheese is made from the poorest land, but that the greatest quantity is made from the richest land. This is a point that will probably never be settled, as much depends upon the management in making, but it was almost an article of faith with the late Sir Harry Mainwaring (A.D. 1865) that the greater the quantity of reeds to be found in any land, the better would be the flavour of the cheese. On this, as on many other matters agricultural, when authorities differ, who shall decide?

THE CHESHIRE CHEESE.

> A Cheshire man went o'er to Spain,
>   To trade and merchandise,
> When he arrived across the Main
>   A Spaniard him espies.
>
> " Thou Cheshire man," quoth he, " look here,
>   These fruits and spices fine
> Our country yields these twice a year,
>   Thou hast not such in thine."
>
> The Cheshire man then sought the hold,
>   Thence brought a Cheshire cheese.
> " You Spanish dog, look here," saith he,
>   " You have not such as these.
>
> " Your land produces twice a year,
>   Spices and fruits you say,
> But such as in my hand I bear,
>   Our land yields twice a day."

There were some characteristics of Cheshire men in the past which do not seem so pronounced in the present day, except in the remote country districts. Of this county it was said, " Cheshire for men, Berkshire for dogs (pigs?), Bedfordshire for naked flesh, and Lincolnshire for bogs." " By waif, soe and theam you may know Cheshire men." They were tenacious of their legal rights and powerful in contending for them, as was instanced in many well recorded cases in the Court of Star Chamber. There were

> As many Leghs as fleas, Massies as asses,
> Crewes as crows, and Davenports as dogs' tails!

At one time it was as difficult to get a clearly expressed opinion out of a Cheshire man as it was to corkscrew the proverbial joke into a Scotsman. Instead of saying, " I think it is so and so," he usually said, " Well, as it seems to me as how it might be so and so." At club " feasts " and similar " dooments " common fifty years ago, on a diner being asked if he would have any more, instead of saying, " No, thank you," would reply, " Not any more this time, thank you." The nearest approach to direct reply was, " Are you Mr So-and-So ? " " Well, I reckon I am." They always " reckoned." To turn a narrow adlant (as the term " headland " in ploughing is termed) means that one has had a narrow escape from death or dire calamity. The idiom, " Bad luck top end," denotes that a man is rather deficient in intellect, or slow in grasping a proposition. " Tha's getten bad luck top eend (head) tha cumberlin."

It was a Cheshire farmer's ambition in those days,—far more than in these days of mixed farming and milk selling which has displaced, to some extent, cheese-making,—to be the owner of a large herd of dairy cows. In an old Cheshire May song we find the young daughter of the house addressed as follows :—

> Rise up, thou fair maid of this house, put on your gown of silk,
> For the summer springs so fresh, green and gay ;
> You are deserving of a man with forty cows to milk ;
> Drawing near is the merry month of May.

Another test of being a fit mate for a Cheshire farmer was her ability to lift the heavy lid of the oak chest in Peover Parish Church. A betrothed couple is said to "hing (or hang) i' th' bell ropes" from the third time of asking till the conclusion of the marriage ceremony. Anything which is one-sided or very uneven is said to be " all one side, like Parkgate," which any one acquainted with that once famous seaside resort and minor port will appreciate. When a couple of men resolved on a spell of teetotalism, they would set off to some wood a distance away and drive a nail into a tree, swearing at the same time that they " will drink no beer while *that* nail remains in *that* tree." After tiring of the vow they would set off some fine morning and *draw the nail* (pulling *that* nail out of *that* tree), after which they would, with a clear conscience, resume their former habit of beer drinking. " It's aisy howdin daan (long ' a ') th' latch when nobody poos (pulls) at th' string." This means that anything can be easily accomplished when there is no opposition ; but it is specially applicable to a woman who, never having had an offer of marriage, boasts about remaining single. This proverb has also reference to old doors, formerly very numerous in country districts, where the latch had a leather thong or string attached to it, so that the latch could be lifted from the outside by merely pulling the string. " The more the merrier," differs in Cheshire from that prevailing in other parts of England, and runs, " More and merrier, less and better fare like Meg o' Wood's merry meal." A " merry meal " is a junketing when a child is born.

On such occasions it is always customary for those in the house to have some gin and water or rum—and this is called " wettin' the choilt's yed " (wetting the child's head) ; and a parent would be considered rather shabby if he did not provide this kind of refreshment. Whilst on the subject of drinking, a person given to tippling is said to " Cock the little finger." When anything is especially difficult to obtain we say, " As well try to borrow a fiddle at a wakes." " Ugly enough to wean a foal," " As rugged as a foal,"

"As hoarse as a cuckoo," "As sulky as a bull," "As hard as a north toad," are all Cheshire colloquisms. Why a north toad should be harder than any other kind of toad we are unable to say. "Like stopping an oon (that is, an oven) wi' butter," is said to be an absolutely useless effort. The old brick oven has a flag called "th' oonstun" (*i.e.*, ovenstone), reared to the mouth to close it after the bread is put in to bake. The edges of this stone are plastered round with clay or mud to make the oven airtight. Obviously butter would be of no use for such a purpose. "He is allus backin' i' th' breechbant" is a Cheshire phrase in common use applied to a man who is never ready to go ahead. The breechband is a broad leather strap passing round the hindquarters of a horse, fastened to the shafts, against which he presses when backing a cart. "Lading and caling" (or teeming) is an idiom which means saving in little things. "Oo's a sore life on it for to mak' things do; oo's allus ladin' and calin'. The lanes where cottagers used to turn their cattle previously to the passing of the Highway Act, were often spoken of as "the long pasture." "Where do you keep your cows—you've no land?" The reply was, "Oh, I turns 'em into th' long pasture." To pull anything "Lymm from Warburton" is a very curious expression, meaning complete separation. The Church livings of Lymm and Warburton were formerly held in two medieties, but they were eventually separated, and the income of the rector of Lymm thereby reduced. The sayings relating to a Cheshire cat are well known, but the explanations given of them are extremely unsatisfactory. "To grin like a Cheshire cat" is probably the original one. Colonel Leigh gives the variants, "To grin like a Cheshire cat chewing gravel," and "To grin like a Cheshire cat eating cheese." Charles Lamb, in one of his letters to Manning, says, "I made a pun the other day and palmed it upon Holcroft, who grinned like a Cheshire cat." (Why do cats grin in Cheshire? Because it was once a County Palatine, and the cats cannot help laughing when they think of it, though I see no great joke in it.) The Cheshire cat may be an heraldic device. It is just possible that the arms of the Earls of Chester, namely, a wolf's head, may be the original Cheshire cat. The grin of a Cheshire cat, as depicted in "Alice in Wonderland," will perpetuate it so long as that charming book is read by the children of England. A round piece of wood is called a " mundle " about Middlewich, and is generally made of ash, used for stirring porridge, pig food, or cream which is put into a warm place to "starve" before being churned. In that neighbourhood the proverbial saying, "Have a little, give a little, let neighbour lick the mundle," illustrates the maxim, "Charity begins at home." The meaning is, if you only have a little, don't give much away—keep all the porridge for yourself— and only let others lick what remains on the "mundle" after stirring the porridge. Another common saying, when any one has demeaned himself to curry favour, is, "That's th' lad as licked the mundle." A person who is given to boasting is said to be "Big in the mouth." An old joiner said one day, " You may be sure a man as is big i' th' maith, has na mitch in him ; same as goin' dain i' th' cellar—if you hit th' empty barrels, they meken a din ; but if you hit the full uns, they howd'n their nize." " Empty barrels make the most noise " is also a Cheshire proverb applicable to empty-headed swaggerers. Another word sometimes heard is " sauce." When a maid has overstayed her hour of homecoming, say, at the village wakes, she often got a good scolding or " saucing " from her mistress. Another word which puzzled an English judge at the High Court hearing of a case some years ago was the word " call." This was an expression, " he called her for all he was worth." He did not " call " her in the same sense of wishing to be supplied with food, or to call her attention to some domestic matter, but it was a word of abuse and often insult.

The following proverbs and colloquial sayings come from Middlewich :—
" Far fetched and dear bought is good for ladies " ; " As whimsical as Dick's hat-band, that went nine times round, but too short to tie " ; " You are always in the field when you should be in the lane " ; " Go to bed and sleep for wit, and buy land when you have more money " ; " Quietness is best, as the fox said when it bit the cock's head off." " Best by yourself, like Lownds' tup," is a saying addressed to a quarrelsome person. Lownds was some local celebrity, whose ram was given to knocking people down. " Where there's least room there's always most thrutching (crowding)." " I'm sure th' owd lad has cast his club at him," is said of a mischievous boy. " Th' owd lad " is one of our Cheshire names for his satanic majesty. This is not the only instance where the devil is represented in Cheshire as carrying a club. In the play of " St George and the Dragon," which was performed generally at Easter, Beelzibub, who is one of the characters, says, on making his entrance—

> Here comes I, great Beelzibub,
> Up o' my shoother I carries a club.

" It runs i' th' blood, like wooden legs," is said of any family peculiarity. " As broad as narrow, like Paddy's plank," is synonymous with saying that anything is " much of a muchness "—and " much of a muchness " is peculiar to Cheshire. A stout person is said to be " Cheshire bred, beef down to the heels " ; a deceitful person, " As hollow as a shoe when the foot is out." " It's hard to get a stocking off a bare leg," was said apropos of a bankrupt whose assets were almost *nil*—as much as to say, you cannot get more from a man than he possesses. " Never no more " is an expression very frequently used to denote that the speaker never intends to have anything more to do with a person or thing ; that, having been " taken in," he is not to be caught again. " Next thowt "—*i.e.*, next thought—is an idiom used in Mobberley and the neighbourhood for " now I come to consider," or " now I come to recollect." " No durr "—*i.e.*, no door—is a very curious metaphor for any kind of failure ; it was used about Wilmslow. The expression appears to have its origin in a custom once very prevalent at Shrovetide in shooting for tea-kettles with bullets out of a common gun, with a door for a target. If the bullet missed the door altogether, the bystanders shouted out, "No durr." When any one absconds he is said to have "Run his country." The moon is often called the "parish lantern," and rain is spoken of as "parish water." "Patch and dautch" is an idiom meaning to strive hard. "Eh, missis, how oo'l patch and dautch an' oo'l powler for them childer." About Wilmslow the expression of "turning and towing" is equivalent to contriving, so as to make things fit. "To peck for one's self" is an idiom which means to gain one's own livelihood. A father complained one day how his grown-up son still lived upon him, and added, "It's toime he pecked for hisself; Oi peck for moisel'." There are two curious idioms used to describe the yellow, sickly appearance observed in young oats when they cease to draw nutrition from the seed and begin to feed from the soil. It is then said they are "pining for their mother," or that they are "being weaned"; and these expressions, strange to say, actually describe the physiological changes that are taking place in the plant. To "put the peg in" is an idiom which means to put a veto upon anything, or to cut off supplies. When a shopkeeper will trust no more he "puts the peg in." The origin of the expression is the method adopted to fasten an ordinary thumb latch which can be opened from the outside; or most likely it had its origin long before the thumb latches became common, when the latch was opened from the outside by means of a piece of string, or by a round hole cut through the door just under the latch through which the finger was inserted in order to raise the latch. In any case a latch could be effectually locked by simply putting a peg of wood above it in the "carry latch," or square staple, which fixes the latch in its place. To be undecided, or to shilly-shally, is expressed by the idiom, "Shaffling and haffling." "Oo's shafflin' and hafflin' and connor tell whether oo'll give up th' lond or not." "To put the shoulder out" is a curious idiom, meaning to take offence. "St Peter's needle" is a strange metaphor equivalent to serious misfortune. When a man became bankrupt and was sold up, he was described as having gone through "St Peter's needle." To "summer and winter," a person is to have known him sufficiently long to test his character or disposition under all circumstances. An extremely small matter, that which is next to nothing, is described as "a thing or nothing." "To-morrow comes never" means an indefinite time. "A wheelbarrow farmer" is a very small farmer. A very small farmer is one who only rents an acre or two of land. He is supposed to wheel his manure in barrow loads on to his land instead of carting it. "Uz wheelbarrow farmers pay more rent than big farmers, and we're obliged to grow twice as much on uz land," was a frequent complaint. They are very important members of the agricultural community, not only because they raise on their small holdings such produce as eggs, poultry, fruit, etc., which the "gradely" farmer thinks a little beneath his notice, but these small wheelbarrow farms have a great tendency to elevate not only the condition, but the character of the labourers who occupy them. " Wun up,"—literally, wound up—means "ready for action." Thus a countryman, being asked to sing, will excuse himself on the plea of not yet being " wun (wound) up," if he had had only one glass. After another glass or two he will have more confidence in himself, and will then consider himself sufficiently "wun up" to respond to the call. " Higgledy piggledy, Malpas shot," or " let every tub stand on its own bottom," is somewhat obscure. Lymm was at one time famous for its hay, and " a well got thing like Lymm hay " is expressive of the super excellence of that article. We hear little or nothing of it in these days.

" Wait until I catch him, I'll give him what for," was a saying frequently heard in Cheshire Session Courts before the Magistrates half a century ago. It cropped up very frequently in cases of assault, and gave ocular proof of the alleged offence, which was often accompanied with no small degree of violence on the part of the aggressor, supported by discoloured eyes and bloated features.

It seems strange reading in the present day that not seventy years ago warts were " charmed " away by the application and rubbing of raw meat on the part affected. The meat was afterwards secretly buried, and as it decayed the wart disappeared ! An infallible remedy for that dangerous and distressing disease, jaundice, was alleged to be found in the purchase of an ordinary pint mug in which a frog was caught, and both buried deep in the ground, but it was an indispensable condition of the "cure" that nobody must see the operation, otherwise it became of non-effect.

It would not be thought that the moon's changes at one time affected social amenities. It was an old custom at full moon for a farmer to take his wife or other members of the family and drive some miles to a neighbouring farmer's house for tea and supper, returning in the moonlight. If it was farmer Thorne's day to visit it would be termed " Thorne's moon " ; the next month it would be, say, farmer " Turmit's moon," and so on. Probably the attention to meteorology by all classes in those days gave rise to the saying, that when Bowdon wakes were held, winter was at Newbridge hollow. These wakes were held on the first Sunday after the 19th of September, but the observance may now be said to be confined to a well-known agricultural show, the largest one-day show in the kingdom, when the inhabitants of the district make merry to their hearts' content. In old masonic charters the meeting of the lodge was fixed for any day on or near full moon. As many of the members came long distances, this method of fixing it was very convenient. This practice is now discontinued, in new warrants the precise day of the month being mentioned.

CHAPTER XXI.

Ballads, traditions, and legends of Cheshire—Anthologies and their uses—Cheshire authors and their works—The young cavalier of Marple Hall—The love of Sir Robert Barton and Margery Legh—A ballad of Bramhall Hall—Sir Percy Legh and his lady—Colonel Egerton Leigh's striking personality—" When the daughter is stolen, shut the Pepper Gate "—Blessing the brine at Nantwich—" The Skeleton Hand," a terrible judgment—The wishing steps—" How a Spanish lady woo'd a Cheshire Knight"—The Minshull family and old Mab's curse—Milton's Cheshire wife—The old woman and the nuts—The death omen of the Breretons—Faint heart never won fair lady, a Dunham abduction—The dark lady of Gawsworth—Carrington fight, incident of a village festival—The barley "hump."

THE learned Dr Garnett, late curator of the British Museum, wrote an article some years ago on the value and use of anthologies. This is the old Greek idea of a gathering of flowers, much after the fashion of Montaigne, who, when complimented on his literary successes, modestly said that he had woven other men's flowers of literature into a beautiful nosegay for the gratification and enjoyment of future generations. Dr Garnett emphasised this idea when he pointed out that a modern newspaper turned out more literary matter in a day than all the scribes in Alexandria could have executed in a generation. For the general mass of authors, therefore, there only remained these alternatives—to be absorbed, to be excerpted, or to be virtually forgotten. This applies equally to modern times, just as much as it applied to the palmy days of Grecian literature.

Thus the writings of Leycester of Ormerod, and a number of others who have treated on Cheshire history and literature in later years, are in danger of being forgotten, but with this saving clause, that it is impossible to reproduce their ideas in the limited form embraced in this volume.

The two principal authors and compilers of " Ballads, Lays, and Legends of Cheshire," singular to say, bore the same surnames, Colonel Egerton Leigh of High Leigh, and Dr John Leigh of the Manor House, Hale, Altrincham, for many years Medical Officer of Health for Manchester. The last named was a kinsman of Eleanor Sophia Egerton, Lady Cunliffe, to whom his work was inscribed. These ballads were written during his visits to Lyme in the lifetime of the late Mr Legh, and at the suggestion of Mrs Legh appeared in a small volume, printed in 1861, entitled " Sir Percy Legh," and two of them were included in the " Ballads and Legends of Cheshire," collected by the late Colonel Egerton Leigh, and published in 1867. No doubt there is still a wide field for research in this direction. The ballad of " The Young Cavalier " is connected with Marple Hall. It is said that a daughter of Henry Bradshaw of

Marple, a brother of President Bradshaw, was engaged to a young Cavalier officer, with whose family the Bradshaws had long been intimate, and his fate gave rise to the ballad in question. It describes his journey through the countryside. "As he pricked his steed he trolled his song," and of his "ladie love the burden was," and "to her bower he quickly did him haste." In sooth, he was as gay a cavalier as "e'er delighted maiden's eye to see"—

> And up the road that led to Marple Hall,
> With gentle word he urged his jaded steed,
> Resolved to claim his wonted welcome there
> And gain the rest they both so much did need.

The dark shadow of civil war was over the land, but, notwithstanding, he received a hearty welcome, and on the massive table was spread ample store of good things, "venison, beef and wholesome bread, the goodly fare on which our fathers fed." In her heart the gentle Esther, the daughter of the house, loved the gallant youth and loved the cause in which he was engaged. She dreaded lest in evil hour her liege's arms would clash with her kindred's. After the meal she sang the songs he loved. They also sang "the songs of earlier days they both had loved, when brighter prospects beamed, and their voices through each other thrilled, their eyes with love's expressive fondness gleamed." But the horseman bore in his saddle-bags "portentous" looking documents in which her father and his friends were denounced, and the seizure of their persons commanded. This was discovered by the lady of the house, who deputed a manservant to be the cavalier's guide over the swollen stream. A tragedy followed. The girths of the horse had to be cut nearly through, and too late he found this to be the case. He was swept into stormy waters and "then a scream"—

> Wild, shrill, and agonised, came down the vale,
> As sank the helpless soldier 'neath the tide!
> So died he in his earliest manhood's prime—
> A shriek his requiem from his helpless bride.

She also died shortly after, and the burden of the ballad is that she haunts the spot, and "floating through the woods is heard to cry"—

> Of more than human sweetness rising high,
> In dulcet notes receding then away.

> And as the wind pursues his homeward track,
> The silver melody awakes his ear,
> With hastening steps he lists the syren's song,
> In wondering ravishment and trepid fear.

> And from the terrace of the ancient hall
> The weird-like music trembles through the air,
> Sad and mournful, yet divinely soft,
> As of a spirit in its last despair.

It may be added that a portrait on the staircase in Marple Hall was long shown as that of the unhappy lady. Another ballad was the subject of the loves of Sir Robert Barton and Margery Legh. She was the daughter of Sir Peter Legh, of Lyme and Haydock. Sir Peter was knighted in the thirty-sixth year of the reign of Henry VIII., for bravery at the siege of Leith.

A curious custom was formerly observed at Lyme of driving deer round the park about Midsummer, or rather earlier, collecting them in a body before the Hall and then making them swim the lake in front. The same custom was traditionally said to obtain at Towneley Hall, Lancashire, the seat of a collateral line of the Leghs in times long past. The ballad shows the maiden reclining on a moss-grown bank, declaring she would listen to no lover's tongue. Sir Robert wooes her and they are attacked by a herd of deer, Sir Robert being severely wounded by the antlered leader. They are rescued in the nick of time. He is carried to the hall.

> And long Sir Robert Barton lay,
> His life in jeopardie,
> And ever at his side was seen,
> The lovely Margaret Legh.
>
> Need we guess the sequel? The hours flew swiftly by,
> The Knight his suit still pressed,
> The maiden blushed and gently laid,
> Her head upon his breast.
>
> And the murm'ring whisper of summer leaves,
> Heard under the greenwood tree,
> Were the whispers of love, as it seemed to the ears,
> Of the Knight and his Margerie.

There is also a ballad of Bramhall Hall and a haunted chamber. A warrior returns from Spain and his return is awaited by the beauteous Alice; but on his way through Macclesfield Forest he is surrounded by a gang of highwaymen and slain. "And his frightened steed to Bramhall came riderless at dark." His body was afterwards found, and—

> They bore his corpse into the hall,
> And laid him in the place
> Where rested many a loyal knight,
> Of Bramhall's ancient race.

And long his hapless fate was told,
And many a saddened strain ;
And how his bride no tears had shed,
Yet never smiled again ;
And how within the lady's bower,
When sweeps the midnight gale,
Are heard the sounds of human woe,
And many a sob and wail ;
And rustling garments oft are heard,
And sounds that oft appal,
And still is told the hapless tale,
Of the Maid of Bramhall Hall.

The ballad of Sir Percy Legh is also told. In the park at Lyme, near the hall, is a beautiful conical hill, covered with trees, which has been called from time immemorial " The Knight's Low," and is supposed to have been the burial-place of one of the earlier knights of the family so long resident there. In another part of the estate, adjoining a stream which runs through the park, is a field, which was known within record as " The Lady's Grave," and also as " The Field of the White Lady." The ballad is founded on a tradition that at midnight " a muffled sound as of a distant funeral peal " is often borne on the wind, and that at this time a shadowy procession of mourners may be seen wending its way towards " The Knight's Low," bearing a coffin and pall, and followed by a lady arrayed in white, and apparently in deep distress. The main incidents of the ballad are founded on fact. Sir Piers or Percy Legh of Lyme, Knight Banneret, following his grandfather's example, engaged in his sovereign's Continental warfare, and dying at Paris " of honourable wounds received on the field of Agincourt," his body was brought to England to be interred. The verses describe the domestic side of life at Lyme, and after a brief spell of connubial bliss it is rudely interrupted by the call of the militant Henry to French soil—

Where many a gallant cavalcade,
From Cheshire plains might now appear ;
And many a proud and gallant Knight,
From Lancashire, with lance and spear.

Sir Piers is borne from the field, severely wounded, and—

They carried him to Paris town,
They carried him right carefully,
And there he felt his strength was gone,
And gently laid him down to die.

On hearing the sad news at Bramhall the poor lady lost her reason, and—

> They buried him within the Park,
> Which he had left so blithe and blee ;
> And followed in the mourners' track,
> All gaily dressed poor Agnes Legh.
>
> They heaped a mound upon his corpse—
> A mound whereon the fir trees grow,
> And many a wail is heard at night,
> Coming from the good Knight's Low.
>
> She rambled all the night forlorn,
> She rambled forth all drearilie,
> Till on the river's bank one morn
> Was found the corpse of Agnes Legh.
>
> They buried her where she was found—
> They buried her near the river's wave ;
> And ever since the land around
> Is known but as the Lady's Grave.

The legend attaching to Marple Hall is also set forth in those pages, and depicts the struggle between Cavalier and Roundhead, when the kingdom was rent with discord, and rebellion stalked through the land.

> And news was carried to and fro,
> Of Rupert and the King,
> Of what befell the Cavaliers
> Swift tidings they would bring—
> How that Lord Strange at Manchester
> Did threat the town to sack,
> When the people rose upon their foes,
> And beat his Lordship back ;
> And how at Stockport still the men
> Resolved to hold their own,
> And vowed to keep their arms until
> The king was overthrown.

Then followed the defeat of Charles by the strong, stern Cromwell. After Marston Moor and Naseby, the King was brought to trial.

> And though he made a proud defence,
> His foes yet willed it so,
> His head should from his shoulders fall,
> By ignominious blow.
> And he (Bradshaw) who did the doom pronounce,
> By which his head should fall,
> Came back at length a broken man,
> To die at Marple Hall.

> And in no grave his body lies—
> No tablet doth disclose
> That in the Sepulchre at last
> John Bradshaw found repose.

The ballads and legends connected with the County, compiled by the late Colonel Egerton Leigh, are more varied in number and many less serious than the effusions before noted. There is also a vein of humour in many of them that is absent from Dr Leigh's "Lays and Legends." Colonel Egerton Leigh's personality was a very striking one. He was above the average height, his features handsome, set off with a full, flowing beard which reached his breast. He remarked that this was given him to hide his blushes when complimented on his good looks by the fair sex! His work contains many humorous poems. "When the Daughter is stolen, shut the Pepper Gate"—in other words, "Lock the door when the horse is stolen"—this bears testimony to the elopement of the fair daughter of a Mayor of Chester with an enterprising swain, who carried her away on horseback. As he bears the lady off in triumph the irate father is excitedly giving orders and the gate is closed. It was customary some centuries ago, on Ascension Day, at Nantwich for the inhabitants to assemble in gala dress around an old salt biat or pit, which was dressed with rustic finery.

> Wreaths of varied hues we bring—flowers of the early spring.
> Hand in hand we form a ring, round old Biat pit to sing—
> God bless the brine.

"The Skeleton Hand" is an amusing production, and refers to an old crone who lived at Lim (Lymm), and who partook too freely of the "ruddy wine," with startling results to herself. She would persist in filling her pail with water from the old church spout, notwithstanding the warnings of her neighbours that something dreadful would happen through such blasphemous behaviour. There is a picture of a long skeleton arm and hand issuing from the rain-pipe. Her pail is seized and she gets a rough thwack on the head, which renders her senseless, and both pail and water disappear up the pipe. She told the neighbours, "in confidence," that it was a shaft of lightning that struck her, but the neighbours drew their own conclusions, and "never from that hour did she take her can to the old church tower."

"The wishing steps" on the walls at Chester are well known, and the lady who is single and who wishes to marry may have her wish gratified if she can ascend sixty or seventy steps and return without taking breath. Whether this legend has ever been fulfilled is not recorded. There is the well-known ballad of the "Miller of the Dee," and others of love and tragedy, country sports, etc., of which we have given specimens from Dr Leigh's book in other pages of this work.

HOW A SPANISH LADY WOO'D A CHESHIRE MAN.

Will you hear a Spanish Ladye,
How she woo'd a Cheshire Man ?
Garments gay and rich as may be
Decked with jewels she had on—
Of comely countenance and grace was she—
And by birth and parentage of high degree.

As his prisoner there he kept her,
In his hands her life did lie,
Cupid's bands did tie them faster—
By the liking of the eye :
In his courteous company was all her joy,
To favour him in anything she was not coy.

But at last there came commandment
For to set the ladies free—
With their jewels still adorned,
None to do them injurie.
Then said the lady mild, "Full of woe is me,
Oh, let me still sustain this captivity."

He.—Courteous Lady, leave this—
Here comes all that breeds the strife,
I in England have already
A sweet woman for my wife.
I will not falsify my vow for gold or gain,
Nor yet for all the fairest Dames that ever lived in Spain.

She.—Then farewell, my gallant Captain !
Farewell to my heart's content ;
Count not Spanish Ladies wanton,
Though to thee my love was bent,
Joy and true prosperitie go ever then with thee.

He.—The like fall ever to thy share, most fair Lady.

Sir Urian Legh of Adlington, the hero of the above ballad, was knighted by the Earl of Essex for his bravery at the siege of Cadiz. He was High Sheriff of Cheshire in 1613.

"Old Mab's Curse," relating to an ancient Cheshire family, had a curious fulfilment. The "curse" was denounced against the spendthrifts who should waste or sell their inheritance. Milton's third wife was a Minshull, and the family of a branch of it seems to have migrated to Manchester, where "Mynshull House," now hiding the Hanging Bridge in that city, is located. In the top left-hand corner at the entrance to a shop in Cateaton Street is the following inscription :—" Elizabeth Mynshull, born 1638, died 1728, niece of Thomas

Mynshull, was the third and best wife of John Milton, poet." This is evidently the copy of a previous inscription, and formerly adorned a building of prior date probably. Although allied to many of the best Lancashire and Cheshire families, and many " rich and broad acres " once claimed them for their masters, not a single yard in either county now belongs to it.

> Mabel's dole of pius fame,
> From Royale bleede they say shee kame ;
> Poor and needie folke's doe telle,
> The Mynshull's land noe one dare selle ;
> For " old Mab's curse " on hym wold lighte
> That ere sholde selle land, stone, or bighte ;
> His house shall come to povertee
> Until another Mab we see ;
> Centuries rounde thye globe shalle rolle
> Upon its axis on the pole,
> Ere Mynshull's House againe shall thryve,
> For selling Mab's lande, huts and style ;
> Such penance shall his sons long suffer,
> And thank the Virgin 'tis no rouffer,
> Blest be the son of all its race
> Who thus " Mab's dole " shall replace.

There is a legend connected with the very stones out of which the Cathedral at Chester is built. On a small manor, near Chester, the monks of St Werburgh are said to have quarried from the rocks there the stone necessary for the carrying out of the work. The steward of the estate had a daughter, Alice, " slight of figure and possessed of a pleasing face, just the girl who could tempt a man to sin, and who had just enough of the old Adam in her to lead her to wrong doing." " The lay brethren of the monastery had an overseer," a cleric of handsome person, whose dark visage showed his foreign descent. Her fall was brought about by him, and he slew his victim and buried her remains in a hole bordering the margin of a stream adjacent, near which grew a beech tree. In course of time this tree had to be cut down to make way for the foundation of a new house, and it was then that the remains of a human body—probably those of the murdered girl—were uncovered. For a long period visions of a cowled priest and a woman, so the story runs, had been seen standing under the tree. " One man on going to the spot saw them disappear. He heard three distinct sighs proceeding from the ground at his feet. Walking back to the house he saw a woman's form sinking into the stream a hundred yards away, and hurrying to the spot to save her, as he thought from drowning, he was surprised to find no traces of her." For a long period this legend was implicitly believed in by the residents of that district.

There is the story of an old woman who was, at her express desire, buried in a village churchyard with a bag of nuts under her head. The nuts she found to be uncomfortable, and she "turned in her coffin." The one side was as much plagued as the other had been, and she determined bodily to revisit "the pale glimpses of the moon" for a brief space, and to take the bag of nuts along with her. The nuts she cracked and ate, while she sat and shivered on her tombstone. She scattered the shells around, and, shaking the empty bag, folded it up for a pillow and resumed her place within the coffin. One solitary nut, however, remained uncracked and uncoffined. It fell out when the old woman shook her bag and she did not observe it. On the grave, however, the nut took root and grew into a vigorous hazel tree, which fruited annually and survived the storms of winter for many years!

The Venables of Kinderton were a noble Cheshire family in the days of Edward I., from which sprang many branches which settled in different parts of the county. Thomas Venables was a son of Sir William of that ilk, and cousin-german to the Conqueror. We have here a variant of that other story of the dragon of Malpas—that of Wantley, and other dragons which appear to have inhabited different parts of the country in mediæval times. According to an old chronicle, " yet chaunced a terrible dragon to remayne, and make his abode in ye Lordshippe of Moston in ye sayde countie of Chester, wheare he devouryred all suche p'sons as he laid hold on, which ye said Thomas Venable heringe tell of, consyderinge the pytyfull dystruction of the people, w'thowte recov'ie, who in followinge th' example of the valiante Romaines . . . dyd in his awne p'son valiantlie and courragiouslie set on the saide dragon, where firste he shotte hym throwe with an arrowe, and afterwards with other weapons manfullie slew hym, at which instant tyme the sayd dragon was devowringe of a childe."

Sir Richard Brereton of Malpas was one of the Breretons of Brereton, and there was in that township a pool, since drained, called Bagmere. Popular superstition gave to this pool the property of exhibiting supernatural tokens of the approaching decease of any chief of that ancient house. Drayton says :

> That black ominous mere,
> Accounted one of those that England's wonders make ;
> Of neighbours Blackmere name ; of strangers Brereton's lake ;
> Whose property seems far from reason's way to stand ;
> For, nea're before his death that's owner of the land,
> She sends up stocks of trees, that on the top doe float,
> By which the world her first did for a wonder note.

"The dark lady of Gawsworth," Mary Fitton, belonging to an old Cheshire family, was one of the Maids of Honour to Queen Elizabeth, and was said to have jilted Shakespeare, but modern research has shown this to be fiction and not fact. Besides, Mary's portraits show that she was not dark—that her hair was brown and her eyes grey. She is not, therefore, the person who had the glory of loving and deceiving Shakespeare, and of receiving, according to E. J. Herford, "his lyric disdain in a score of the greatest of English sonnets." "What then," he says, "becomes of Mary Fitton? And what of Gawsworth and its dark lady and Shakespeare's unhappy love? We fear there is no help. Romance, after its brief factitious lodgement among those black-and-white gables (of Gawsworth Hall), has taken flight like the cuckoo from a nest not built for it and where it was not bred. Gawsworth's moment of fabricated glory has faded; and the birthplace of Petrarch's Laura and of Dante's Beatrice needs no longer to fear to be rivalled or outdone in interest by the Cheshire manor-house, where Shakespeare's Mary Fitton saw light."

Besides the legends of the Crusader's cedar and the Seven Sister trees, referred to in earlier chapters, we have that of the abduction of a young heiress from Dunham Castle, where she was the ward of the then possessor of the district. There was the usual story of mutual passion with the stern refusal of the baron to permit of the visits of the young scion of a noble house, clandestine meetings and mutual vows, followed by a raid at Dunham, where the young lady is seized and carried away, and promptly married. One record says she was "removed" clad only in her nightdress, which we refuse to believe. The young hero of the exploit had to answer for his behaviour before the court of the Earl's dignity at Chester, where, no doubt, he duly purged his offence by suitable apologies.

Dragons were numerous in those days, not only in Cheshire, but in other parts of the country. "More, of More Hall, with nothing at all, he slew the Dragon of Wantley." We have already seen how a Baron of Kinderton did his part nobly in the same direction, and the Lord of Malpas also did his part in clearing one out of that part of the county. There is a moral, however, to the story. The dragon was looked upon as an oppressor and ravager, and took human form in inflicting injustice and torture on the peasantry and others who came under his yoke. The courageous individual who caused these evils to be abolished was the figurative St George of that age.

Carrington fight, or "feight," as it is termed, was one of the instances of the feuds which existed between the inhabitants of two neighbouring townships or districts. In the present instance, however, men came from Flixton in Lancashire, and the fight was unusually fierce. Finally, the Flixton men were routed and fled in confusion. It created a great sensation at the time, and was the subject of prolonged legal inquiry.

The barley "hump" was a small square piece of barley bread and was distributed at Dunham Hall to the children from the schools in Altrincham and Bowdon. They scampered over the Downs, but before the remnant arrived the stock had been exhausted and many went "empty away." It was a case of "first come, first served."

CHAPTER XXII.

King and Parliament—Cheshire and England's fate settled at Ashley Hall—Divided feeling in Cheshire—The gentry of Cheshire and their peculiarities—Their antiquity, hospitality, and loyalty—The memorable meeting at Ashley—Thomas Assheton and the gentlemen who took part—Their ancestry and position in the County—The Grosvenors, the Smith Barrys, the Cholmondeleys, etc.—The Egertons of Tatton—High Legh deeds—Cursing by " book, bell, and candle "—Weak digestions at High Legh—Rebel prisoners at Chester, who " died like rotten sheep "—The end of the Pretender—Tim Bobbin on the House of Stuart and that of Hanover—The Stuart supporters and their losses during the Commonwealth—Some curious occupations—Disregard of Pitt's counsels and its results.

IN August 1651 a remarkable event happened in Cheshire, which probably decided the fate of England at that period. It was at the deciding period of the Civil War between King and Parliament, just before Cromwell achieved " the crowning glory of Worcester." Lambert, Cromwell's greatest general, had marched from Warrington to Knutsford Heath. King Charles wisely declined battle with Lambert's powerful force of horse and dragoons, acting in open country highly favourable to them, which would have overwhelmed the Royalist army. In 1715, sixty-four years after this eventful period, not five miles from the same neighbourhood, another event, also fraught with grave consequences to the country, occurred at Ashley Hall, the seat of Thomas Assheton, Esq. The house of Brunswick was by no means seated firmly on the English throne. George I. possessed neither the dignity nor the tact which a monarch should possess. He was totally ignorant of English manners and knew little of the language, except to tell some of the noblemen that he " had come for their goots." The Rebellion of 1715 followed, and the standard of the Young Pretender was raised in Scotland. At this time party feeling in Cheshire ran high. The majority of the Cheshire squires were descendants of Cavalier families, and favoured " the King over the water." Others, of Whig or Nonconformist principles, upheld the Hanover succession. Some of the local gentry were in favour of joining the rebels ; others favoured the new form of constitutional government. It was a " happy thought " which induced Squire Assheton to invite his friends of different political shades to dinner, and, no doubt, over punch bowl and pipes afterwards, the burning question of the day would be discussed. Squire Assheton, it is said, gave his casting vote in favour of the reigning sovereign, and subsequent events bore testimony to the shrewdness of his judgment.

We are indebted to the late Earl Egerton of Tatton for an interesting contribution on the subject to the journal of the Chester and North Wales Historic Society in 1909. His lordship took a keen interest in county affairs, and, as a scholar, he had studied Cheshire history in all its details. Earl Egerton states that the gentry of Cheshire are said to be remarkable for four peculiarities—their number (which is greater than in any other county of the same size), their antiquity, their hospitality, and their loyalty.

From the time they formed a band round Richard II., who first called himself the " Prince of Chester," to that of the Civil Wars, they led numerous followers to the great battle-fields of Blore Heath, Bosworth, and Flodden. In the Civil Wars most of the old families took the side of the Cavaliers : the Tattons of Wythenshawe sustained a long siege in favour of the King. At the time of the Commonwealth the long list of those who " compounded " by heavy fines for the loss of their estates shows how many of the families in the county had taken part against the Parliament.

In 1715 their loyalty was sorely tried. The county was divided in feeling ; the Sovereign who had just ascended the throne was identified with Protestantism, while the old family of the Stuarts had but a feeble representative in a young man who was a Roman Catholic, and who had been brought up abroad. In the autumn of that year, Mr Forster, a gentleman of Northumberland, followed by the Earls of Derwentwater, Wintoun, Nithsdale, and Carnwath, and Lords Widdrington and Nairn, raised the standard of the Pretender, and led a small army into England, which reached Lancaster at the beginning of November. The leading gentlemen, who were in the habit of meeting for social purposes, were naturally led to talk over their future line of action. Some of them were descendants of those who had sacrificed their blood and treasure during the Civil Wars in defence of the Stuarts. They had to consider whether the old royal family had forfeited all claims to their affection and allegiance, or whether the king of a foreign race, who had just succeeded to the throne, had their sympathy as a Protestant and their respect as the guardian of the established order of things and the representative of constitutional government. They were accustomed to meet in turn, as members of a club, at each others' houses, and there is a tradition that they first met at Lyme Hall, but there are strong grounds for believing that they met finally to decide question at Ashley Hall. This was the residence of Mr Assheton, the governor of Chester Castle.

We do not know the names, says Earl Egerton, of those who voted for the Chevalier St George ; but after the failure of his hopes at Preston and Sheriffmuir they unanimously agreed to commemorate the fortunate decision by which they had saved the forfeiture of their estates—and perhaps their heads—and therefore to have portraits of those present painted, and hung on the walls of the room where they had met. They were taken in full length, and are dated 1720—the artist is unknown. They remained in the large room at Ashley Hall till 1860, when they were removed and placed in the upper panels of the staircase hall at Tatton.

Earl Egerton then reviews the personality and career of each gentleman present, commencing with the host. We find that—

THOMAS ASSHETON was born in 1678, the son of Thomas Assheton, and Lucy, the daughter of Thomas Legh of Adlington, who were married in 1670. He inherited the Ashley property from his grandfather, Ralph, who was the second son of Sir Richard Assheton of Middleton, in Lancashire, and married the sister of Thomas Brereton of Ashley, who died without issue in 1660. He married, about 1724, Harriet, daughter of the Right Honourable John Smith, Speaker of the House of Commons and Chancellor of the Exchequer; and after the death of Captain William Smith, took in addition the name of Smith. He died in 1759. His grandson, the late Thomas Assheton-Smith, sold his property in Ashley, in 1841, to the late Wilbraham Egerton, Esq., with the exception of this picture, which he left to his nephew, Mr Heneage, from whom it was purchased by the late Lord Egerton of Tatton. This branch of the family, which is now extinct in the male line, is represented by the Asshetons of Downham, Lancashire, being the twenty-ninth generation from the Conquest.

A great portion of the estates of this ancient family, the feudal lords of Ashton-under-Lyne, passed, by the marriage of the daughter of the last Thomas Assheton, to the Earl of Stamford and Warrington, and the manor and estates of Middleton, by the marriage of the daughter to the last Sir Ralph Assheton, to Lord Suffield.

Sir RICHARD GROSVENOR was the great-grandson of Sir Richard, first Baronet, and born in 1689; eldest surviving son of Sir Thomas, third Baronet and M.P.; was chosen one of the Members for the City of Chester in the first Parliament of George I., which met on 17th March 1714–15, and was returned at the two ensuing elections for the same city, of which he was also Mayor in 1715. At the Coronation of George II., in October 1727, he acted as Grand Cupbearer of England by presenting the first cup of wine to His Majesty to drink out of after he was crowned, and had the cup as his fee. He performed that service as Lord of the Manor of Wymondeley, in Hertfordshire, holding it of the Crown by tenure of Grand Sergeantry. He married first, in 1708, Jane, daughter of Sir Edward Wyndham, of Orchard Wyndham, in Somersetshire, and by her, who died in 1719, had one daughter, who died young; and second, in 1724, Diana, only daughter of Sir George Warburton of Arley, in Cheshire, who died 1729–30. By the latter marriage he had no issue, and died in 1732. He was succeeded by his brother and colleague in Parliament, Sir Thomas Grosvenor, Bart., whose nephew, Sir Richard Grosvenor, was created Baron Grosvenor, 1761, and Earl Grosvenor and Viscount Belgrave, 1784, and is represented by the Duke of Westminster.

Voltaire pronounced heraldry to be " the science of fools with long memories," but it may be added to the above account by Earl Egerton, that the Grosvenors have always prided themselves on their armorial insignia. Their claim was, in this instance, a shield bearing a diagonal bar, or cross-belt, of gold, upon a background of light blue (azure), and a bend'or was their exclusive property. Their right to this was disputed by the Scropes. The lawsuit commenced in 1375 or 1385, and lasted four years, involving commissions in Cheshire and Lancashire; witnesses included John o' Gaunt ("Time Honoured Lancaster"), Owen Glendower, Geoffrey Chaucer, the Duke of York, the King of Castile, abbots, earls, knights, and squires by the score. Witnesses had beheld, they said, the blazonry of the Grosvenors at Lincoln, amongst the Crusaders by the walls of Acre, in the Scottish wars of Edward II., at Crecy and other battles in the time of Edward III., at the tower of Brose, at the siege of Rochsirion in Poictou, in Guienne, at Viers in Normandy, at the battle of Poictiers, at the battle of Najara in Spain in 1367, and lastly, at the battle of Limoges in 1370 in the service of the Black Prince. Sir Robert Grosvenor refused to accept the verdict of the King, who gave him an alternative coat, and, according to Leycester, " he took unto him the coate of azure *une garbe d'Or*," scorning " to bear the other coate with a difference." Who does not remember the success of Bend Or, owned by the first Duke of Westminster, in the Derby of 1880 and other classic races?

JAMES, EARL OF BARRYMORE, was the fourth Earl, son of Richard, second Earl of Barrymore, and his third wife, Dorothy, daughter and heiress to John Ferrer, Esq., of Dromore, in the County Down, succeeded his half-brother Laurence, born in 1667. On his brother's death he sat in Parliament, 1703 ; in 1710-13 represented Stockbridge ; 1713, made Privy Councillor ; was member of the committee to prepare an address to His Majesty King George, 1715, to congratulate him on his happy accession ; and from 1714-47 sat for Wigan, till his death, which happened at Castle-Lyons, where a magnificent monument was erected in 1753.

This family is one of the most ancient in the United Kingdom. Their name is on the roll of Battle Abbey, among those who followed the Conqueror to England.

CHARLES HURLESTON of Newton was the son of Charles Hurleston of Picton, and Anne, daughter of Sir Geoffrey Shakerley. He was High Sheriff of Cheshire in 1727, and died in 1734. This family had been settled in Lancashire from the time of Edward III. He was the last of that line.

ALEXANDER RADCLYFF of Fox Denton, in Lancashire, was the son of Robert Radclyff, who married the widow of William Tatton of Wythenshawe, where he was born in 1677, and grandson of Sir John Radclyff of Ordsall Hall. This old seat of the Radclyffs is now the property of Lord Egerton of Tatton. He died at Newton Heath in 1735.

ROBERT CHOLMONDELEY of Holford was born about 1652; the son of Thomas Cholmondeley, who succeeded to the Holford property on the death of his father, Robert, Earl of Leinster. He married Frances, daughter of Edward Holland of Heaton and Denton, and died at Holford in 1722. He was descended from Sir Hugh Cholmondeley of Cholmondeley, who married Mary, daughter and heiress of Christopher Holford of Holford, who was called the "Bold Lady of Cheshire" by James I. The Cholmondeleys are descended from a common ancestor with the Egertons of Egerton and Oulton, William Belward, lord of a moiety of the Barony of Malpas, having taken the name of Cholmondeley from that part of the barony in the thirteenth century.

ROBERT WARREN was the son of Edward Warren and Dorothy, daughter and heiress of John Talbot of Samlesbury, in Lancashire, and grandson of John Warren, Judge of Chester, and one of the King's Counsel for the Welsh Marches. He was born in 1679, and died without issue, 1729.

HENRY LEGH, of High Legh, was born 1679 and died 1757. He was the son of Richard Legh and Mary, daughter of Thomas Legh of Adlington, Esq., married 1665, buried at Rostherne, 1700. He married Letitia, daughter of Sir Richard Brooke of Norton, Baronet. His great-uncle, George Legh, was slain on the side of King Charles, at Oswaldstrey.

The Ashley estate, at which the foregoing memorable meeting took place, passed by purchase at a later period into the hands of the Egertons of Tatton. At the time of the Conquest one, Randolph, held a portion of Tatton—Nigel, Baron of Halton, holding the remainder. A century afterwards it gave its name to one Alanus, who, according to the custom of the time, assumed the name of the township. It was afterwards held by a scion of the Masseys of Dunham, and passed into the hands of the family of Brereton. A member of this house, Richard Brereton of Tatton, settled all his estates on Sir Thomas Egerton, Lord Chancellor of England, from whom the Earls of Bridgewater are descended. They subsequently came to Hester, widow of William Tatton of Wythenshawe, who, assuming her maiden name vested them in her grandson, Lord Egerton. By a rapid process, devoid of lengthy pedigrees, bewildering dates, and redundant "authorities," but, nevertheless, of a truthful character, we are led by an almost natural sequence to consider the connection of the Egerton family with the county.

There are several branches, notably that of Oulton, more than one member of which has enriched the literature of our county by research and setting forth of antiquarian lore. But it is the family at Tatton to which we must revert. For a long period the heads of this noble house have identified themselves with county affairs. Their connection with it has been disinterested and alike honourable. Coming down to a recent and remarkable period, it may be noted that the grandfather of the late Earl Egerton of Tatton long refused a patent of nobility. He preferred to be known as "the richest commoner," and as such held special and undisputed sway. There are those who achieve greatness, and those who have it thrust upon them. It may in one sense be truly said that greatness was thrust upon Lord Egerton's ancestor, and when he took over his title of nobility he no doubt felt himself in a region not congenial to a man of active tastes and vigorous temperament. He, however, bore his "blushing honours" well, and in his sons, the late Earl Egerton and the Hon. Alan de Tatton Egerton (afterwards Lord Egerton), he has most worthy successors. The present writer has had many opportunities of noting the active interest which the first Baron Egerton took in the affairs of the county. He was an *ex-officio* guardian of the Altrincham Union, and as such exhibited a desire to further the public welfare, which we would well wish the modern race of *ex officii* to emulate. He was tall, spare and lithe in figure, somewhat stern under first impressions, but withal one of Nature's gentlemen. He was, too, a thorough business man, and no one could sit in his company without feeling that he had a man of the world to deal with. The late Earl Egerton inherited many of his late father's characteristics. Like him, he represented the county for many years in Parliament, and also took a deep interest in county affairs. He extended the area of his influence by assuming the Chairmanship of the Board of Directors of the Manchester Ship Canal, but first as an agriculturist of the first water—if a fluid term may be applied to anything but diamonds—he exercised a great influence in the past. His connection with the Royal Agricultural Society is well known. The mansion at Tatton also claims more than passing notice as being worthy of the traditions of a family whose interests are greatly intertwined with those of the County Palatine.

Many extensive additions have been made from time to time, not the least notable of which is a Japanese village brought over from that interesting land, containing quaint bridges and streams, and not the least striking of its characteristics, a real Shintoh temple.

Writing in 1886 the late J. P. Earwaker, author of "East Cheshire," etc., showed the wealth of antiquarian lore which lies hidden away in many an old Cheshire hall and mansion. He illustrates this by an interesting review of ancient Cheshire deeds, of which he had made a catalogue for Colonel Cornwall Legh. He says : " High Legh is in the parish of Rostherne, about five miles from Knutsford. It is very remarkable that in the thirteenth century the manor was held in moieties by two branches of the Legh family, whose descendants owned the two Halls, the East Hall and the West Hall, as they are called at the present day. The Leghs of the East Hall held one-half of the Manor of Legh, but the other moiety was sub-divided in the fourteenth century, the Leghs of the West Hall now owning one-fourth of the original manor of Legh, and Lord Egerton of Tatton the other fourth. As far as my researches go the two families of Legh do not appear to be descended from any common ancestor, or if this has been the case the ancestor has been so far back as not to be traceable. They have lived side by side for the last 600 years, and the only difference is that the members of one family spell their name Legh, and those of the other Leigh."

The earliest deed relating to the Legh family is like all early deeds, undated, but from the character of the handwriting, and the names of the witnesses, it may be put down to about the year 1230—689 years or more ago. It is a "quit claim to Adam da Legh (de Legh) of a bovate of land in the ville of Leye." The seal attached to the deed is still quite perfect.

After 1320 the deeds are regularly dated, and for the remainder of the century are fairly numerous, many of them being in Norman-French instead of Latin. There are some valuable deeds of settlement which supply many details in the true history of this old Cheshire family at that early period. The first deed in English is in 1406, and is a marriage settlement for John de Legh to marry Isabel, daughter of John de Polle or Poole. The next English deed is dated 1427. Latin continued to be the prevailing language until the end of that century. A document, dated 31st October 1442, is a commission and mandate from the Archdeacon of Chester, in Latin, addressed to all the chaplains and clergy within the archdeaconry, commanding them to admonish three times, and peremptorily, "all those sons of iniquity" who have cut and carried away trees and underwood of the Worshipful Thomas de Legh, of Northwood, in his woods, etc., at Northwood and Sworton; have fished his ponds and marl pits, and have carried off his timber from his houses at Knutsford, and have taken his household stuff and done him other injuries. And if these evildoers did not, within fifteen days of each monition, make full satisfaction and restitution, then they were to be openly and publicly excommunicated, and here follows the really interesting part of this deed—"With bells rung and candles lighted and extinguished, and the cross in the hands upraised" and all other legal solemnity. Any deed in which there is reference to the old mediæval practice of "cursing by bell, book, and candle," is of great rarity and much interest, as it has generally been believed that this form of cursing was as unknown in the Roman Catholic Church in mediæval times as it is unknown now.

In a curious notarial instrument, dated 1463, containing a record of a deed made in the chancel of St John's Church, Chester, there is mention of persons swearing upon the holy Evangelists and also upon the red book of St John, then placed upon the high altar there. This must have been a book that was evidently very highly valued, and of the sanctity of which there could be no possible doubt, as it would almost seem to occupy higher rank than the Evangelists.

In 1615 a licence was given by the Vicar of Rostherne, granting permission to George Legh of High Legh, and Elizabeth, his wife, to eat flesh upon certain days and times prohibited because of their ill-health and for what seems to us the very strange reason, " because their weake and feeble stomachs cannot in anie waye brooke or degeste fish soe well as flesh." About the year 1686, Richard Legh of High Legh, Esq., purchased from his nephew, Richard Legh of Swinehead (now pronounced Swinyerd or Swinyed), gentleman, the Swinehead estates, near High Legh.

There are many interesting documents amongst the miscellaneous deeds relating to various parts of Cheshire.

These High Legh deeds are by no means exceptional; many other landowners in Cheshire are in possession of deeds and documents, no doubt quite as important and as interesting as these, but their value is at present unknown, because they have never been properly examined and arranged. The Duke of Westminster set an excellent example by printing a calendar of the deeds of Eaton Hall, and in 1866 Mr Egerton Warburton printed a calendar of the deeds at Arley Hall; but these are the only two Cheshire collections, Mr Earwaker wrote, of which calendars have been made.

After the failure of the Pretender's so-called invasion, a large contingent of prisoners from Preston was incarcerated in Chester, and the following, amongst others, escaped—" William Sanderson of Highlee, Northumberland, a gentleman of many valuable and endearing qualities; John Talbot of Cartington, in Northumberland, a brave young gentleman (his father made himself famous for his courage at the siege of Buda, but was killed); Roger Salkeld of Cumberland, a papist, second son of Sir Richard Salkeld of Whitehall, in the said county."

In the Tenth Report of the Historical MSS. Commission there are some interesting letters written by Elizabeth, Lady Otway, at Chester, to Mr Benjamin Brown of Troutbeck. She says: " There are four hundred and fifty prisoners in the Castle. They all lie on the straw, the better and the worst alike. The King's allowance is a groat a day for each man for meat, but they are almost starved for want of some covering. . . . They die in droves like rotten sheep, and be four or five in a night throne into the castle ditch for their graves. The feavour and the sickness increaseth dayly, is begun to be spread much into the citty, and many guard soldiers is sick, it is thought by infection." The Young Pretender died in France.

John Collier (Tim Bobbin), a Lancashire schoolmaster, and the son of a poor curate, known to the public as the pioneer of works in the Lancashire dialect, to be, in the twentieth century, further popularised by Waugh, Brierley, and a number of others, has satirised the Stuarts and the House of Hanover in a poem full of stinging irony. He falls foul both of Charles II. and George I. He was also an extremely able artist, and most of his sketches bear a remarkable approach to Hogarth's genius.

In support of Collier's views it is noteworthy that as a result of the

Restoration a large number of petitions were lodged at Whitehall, several of them of a most curious character and based on personal services to the Stuarts and losses incurred thereby during the time of the Commonwealth. A Roger Penn petitioned for a place as " yeoman of the Guard," and this is only typical of many others at this particular period, and in support of his petition he stated that he had served the late King (Charles) throughout the (civil) wars, and his Majesty at Worcester, and " in Sir George Booth's business," and had lost his fortune thereby. Others petitioned for situations as " Groom in the Counting-house," " Sergeant of Carriages " (or Cart taker), " King's Coachman," " Master of the Toils," " Master of the Tents and Toils," " Controller of Tents and Revels," the last-named a particular and precious adjunct of the Stuart period. One petitioned for the position of " Bowyer, to keep the Magazine of Bows "; another to be reinstated as " Cockmaster "; another as " Surveyor of Hawks "; another as " Cormorant Keeper "—cormorants being used, under certain restraint, for providing fish for the royal table. Otter hunting also would appear to have been a kingly sport. Amongst those who asked for a restoration to the office of keeping the otters, was Richard Wood, he having held it since King James First came to England, until " the late wars," in which he served as a soldier. At the time of the petition he states he " was 95 years old, and had been compelled to retire to a dwelling at Walton " (on Thames). We do not find by later research how he fared, but no doubt some relief would be granted to him under such extreme conditions. Other petitions were of much greater importance. The survivors of old English families prayed to have their estates, which had been seized under the Commonwealth, restored. Very few of these petitions were granted. In fact it was impossible for Charles to comply with a tithe of them, for they were legion.

In some directions George I. gave grave offence to those who had supported the Accession of the House of Hanover by buying the loyalty of those who had fought for the " King over the water." The wise counsels of Pitt to make war upon Spain while her merchant fleet was on the high seas were disregarded, with the result that Spain, when in readiness, declared war upon us, notwithstanding the "soup meagre" which Collier asserts was doled out to us by France and other powers. Lord Bute, whose " wild Scotch instructions " are referred to in a poem, then head of the government, despite brilliant successes on land and sea, concluded the Peace of Paris, by which Collier asserts we were " bought and sold." It must be remembered, however, that he added, amongst other countries, Canada and the West Indies to our colonial possessions, and laid the foundation through the genius of Clive of our great Indian Empire, converting an association of traders into rulers of what afterwards became, and is, a large and magnificent dependency.

Photo Typical Cheshire Grange with Moat - High Legh *C. A. Arden*

Farmer Outwits Pitt - Evades the Horse Tax by riding his cow to Stockport Market

Photo　　　　　Eaton Hall, Chester　　　　　Phillipson & Golder

CHAPTER XXIII.

Early history of Provincial Grand Lodge—Antiquity of the Province of Cheshire—Randle Holme family—Provincial Grand Masters under the old Constitution—Formation of the United Grand Lodge—Memorial to Sir John Grey Egerton—Masonic ceremony at Delamere—" When George III. was King "—Provincial meeting at Chester in 1818—Unanimity Lodge, No. 89; Sir F. D. Astley, first Master—A Cheshire romance—" The old General "—Consecration of the Randle Holme Lodge—A notable installation—Notices of Stockport Lodges—Ladies and Freemasonry—The Chester Order of Hiccabites—Witchcraft and Masonry.

IT has long been a trite saying that Cheshire is as famous for its Freemasonry as its cheese. There are evidences of lodges having existed for some centuries in the county, and it is a tradition that the first operative lodge was founded in 845, when Ethelfrida is said to have built the Abbey of St Werburgh, which appears to have given employment to many generations of operative masons. There is, however, no written record extant of an operative lodge having existed in Chester at that early period, although, in 1322, the new water tower was built at the cost of the city by John Nelpstone, a freemason, who " conditioned to build the same by indenture, whereon is the heighth, bredth, and length, with the proportion of the same set down," and " he was to have for the building thereof, £100." There are also other references in the city annals which speak of work undertaken by Freemasons suggestive of guilds in Chester at that time as well as in other parts of England and the Continent which engaged " in the erection of stately and superb edifices," with which the Order is intimately associated.

The first Randle Holme was a member of an old Chester family of that name. He was at one time Mayor, but prior thereto he neglected to appear at the Coronation of Charles I. to receive a knighthood and was fined £10. The third Randle was his grandson, who, in 1688, issued an extraordinary book, " The Academy of Armory, or a Storehouse of Armory and Blazonry," which treated, says one critic, " on every subject under the sun save heraldic matters." Ormerod, rather erroneously, describes the book as " a strange jumble of natural history, mineralogy, and surgery, occasionally diversified by palmistry, hunting terms, cockpit laws, an essay on Time, and on men punished in hell." Those brethren who are curious on the subject may see a copy in the lodge room of the Randle Holme Lodge. Notwithstanding all this supposed eccentricity he was appointed deputy Norrey King at Arms, and became a distinguished member " of the Society called Freemasons." The joint literary labours of the various Randles in their relation to Chester and Cheshire filled 260 large volumes!

The lodge mentioned by Randle Holme III. as existing between 1650 and 1760 was purely speculative, and had probably worked for a long period, because, he says, " he honoured the fellowship of the Freemasons, because of its antiquitie." He gives the names of twenty-six brethren as members

Provincial Grand Lodge at Cheshunt

By the command of the Right Honble Lord Egerton of Tatton, Right Worshipfull Provincial Grand Master, a Special Provincial Grand Lodge was held at Chester Castle on Monday the 18th of April 1892 — for the purpose of laying the Corner Stone of the Randle Holmes Porch at the Church of St. Mary on the Hill, Chester.

The Ceremony and Muster was attended by the following

Provincial Officers

RW Sir Horatio Lloyd	VWDPGM	
"	James Salmon	PPGSW
"	John Clayton	PPTCW
"	Chas R Hodgson	PGChap.
"	Revd Thos Sturgeon	" "
"	J H Annett	PC Treas"

John Dennis	PPSB
J McLachanan	" SGW
S W Ramsden	" SD
Thos Cochrane	" " SGW
H A Sleir	" " DC
Thos E Young	" " SGW

Stone-Laying, Randle Holme Porch.

of the Chester Lodge in 1660. It is supposed that his father, Randle Holme II., was a Mason, as there are some Masonic emblems on the monument to his memory in the Church of St Mary on the Hill. The Freemasons of Cheshire commemorated this connection in modern times by rebuilding St Mary's Porch, the foundation stone of which was laid in 1892 by Earl Egerton of Tatton, Provincial Grand Master, with full Masonic honours.

His address to the assembled multitude is worth preserving as it runs in the majestic language of ancient usage :—" Men, women, and children here assembled to behold this Ceremony, Know all of you that we be lawful Masons, true and faithful to the laws of our country ; and established of old with peace and honour, in most countries, to do good to our Brethren, to erect magnificent structures, and to fear God, the Great Architect of the Universe. We have amongst us concealed from the eyes of all men, secrets which cannot be divulged, but these secrets are lawful and honourable, but not repugnant to the laws of God and Man. They were intrusted in peace and honour to Masons of antient times, and have been faithfully transmitted to us, and it is our duty and honour to convey them, unimpaired, to the latest posterity. Unless our craft were good, and our calling honourable, we should not have lasted so many centuries, nor should we have been honoured with the patronage of so many illustrious men in all ages, who have shown themselves ready to promote our interests, and to defend us against all our adversaries.

" We are assembled here to-day in the presence of you all, to assist in laying in antient form the Corner Stone of this Building, which we pray the Great Architect to prosper, for the promotion of Godliness, harmony, and brotherly love, until time shall be no more."

A phial containing newspapers and circulars was placed in a cavity of the stone. A brass plate was also laid over the cavity, with the inscription, " Provincial Grand Lodge, Cheshire.—This Corner Stone has been laid by the Right Hon. Lord Egerton of Tatton, P.G.M., Easter Monday, 18th of April 1892 " ; and the Corner Stone being placed above it, it was declared laid with the customary ceremonies and the singing of an ode, " Now thank we all our God." Brother W. Peers, W.M. of Chester Independence Lodge, proposed a vote of thanks on behalf of the building committee to the P.G.M., D.P.G.M., and the Provincial Grand Lodge of Cheshire for their attendance. Brother H. Taylor, F.S.A., S.W., Cestrian Lodge, Chester, in seconding, remarked there were five Randle Holmes, but the last having when young predeceased his father, there were only four of them known in history as heralds, antiquaries, and Freemasons. The first, second, and fourth filled the civic offices of sheriff and mayor. The second Randle Holme filled the office of sheriff the year that his father was mayor, namely in 1633, and in 1644 he himself was mayor during the celebrated siege of the city, and took an active part in its defence. The third Randle Holme being an officer of the Crown, did not take civic office, but as an author of distinction he was the most celebrated of that family of citizens. There was strong evidence that they were all Freemasons. They were also churchwardens of St Mary's, where they were baptised, and where their bones now rest. He had it on authority that there was no evidence on record of the appointment of a deputy King-at-Arms for life anywhere else in the kingdom, much less in a family holding that then very important office in those days. The above may be supplemented by the fact that the grandson of the last Randle, Holme Burrows by name, was mayor and sheriff of Chester, and Master of a time immemorial lodge in the city in 1673. Its successor after a long interval was the present Cestrian Lodge, No. 424, constituted in 1834. The vote was carried, and Lord Egerton of Tatton having returned thanks the proceedings concluded with the singing of the Masonic version of the National Anthem.

Chester was the first of provincial cities to come under the protection of Grand Lodge formed in London in 1715, and it is the first time in connection with Chester Masonry that the term Provincial Grand Master appears in its records. Lodges were not then known by numbers, but by the inn where the brethren met. Of the lodge meeting at the Sun Inn, Colonel Francis Columbine, the Provincial Grand Master, was W.M., Samuel Smith, D.P.G.M., Colonel Herbert Laurence and Captain Hugh Warburton, Wardens. The names of the members included an alderman, a lieutenant-colonel, captains, lieutenants, and a " cornett." They were all men of high social standing.

Freemasonry has suffered from the impress of the manners and customs of the ages through which it has passed, but its precepts and practices have always been, if properly carried out, for the betterment of mankind. It may have been scoffed at, but often those who " scoffed remained to pray," or, in other words, joined the fraternity. In the language of the Laureate of Masonry, Freemasonry triumphs :—

> Like as a rock on whom the angry sea
>   Dashes and charges with vehement roar,
> Repelling still in steadfast majesty—
>   Standing erect and noble as before.
>
> So is our Art on whom its foes would frown ;
>   It little recks the battle cry of men
> Who, knowing not its lustre and renown,
>   Can ne'er discern it with Masonic ken.
>
> It bids defiance to the selfish weak—
>   Surviving all their paltry scoffs and sneers,
> And casts its light on darkened ones who seek
>   To find its Virtues, known these thousand years.
> Unblemished yet and soaring heavenward still,
> For on it smiles, divine, Great God's all-perfect will.

An Old-Time Tyler.

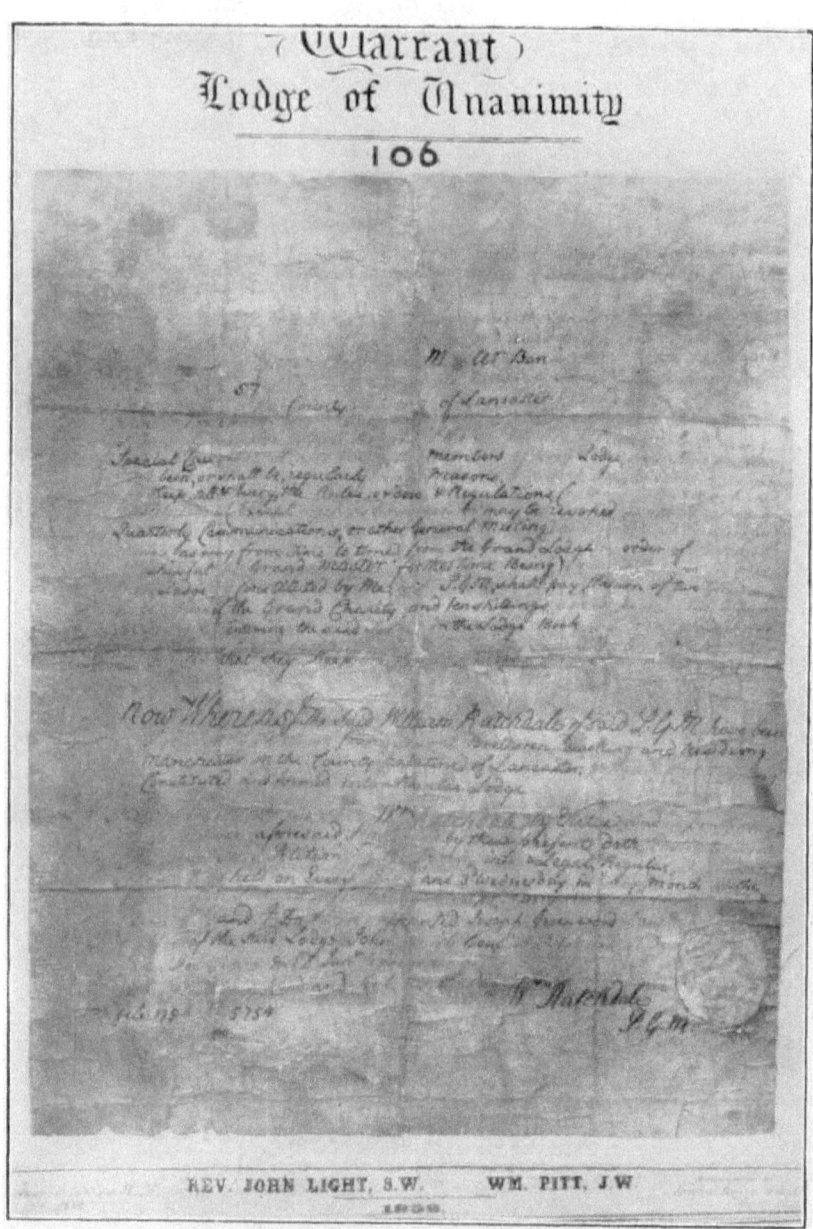

Ancient Warrant of Lodge of Unanimity, No 89, Dukinfield

CHESHIRE: ITS TRADITIONS AND HISTORY 293

There is a halo of romance surrounding the memory of Brother F. Dukinfield Astley, who was the last Provincial Grand Master of Lancashire, prior to its division into two provinces in the year 1826. Brother Astley was the first Master of the Unanimity Lodge, No. 89. It was constituted in Manchester in 1742, and was removed to Dukinfield (Cheshire), of which Brother F. D. Astley was Lord of the Manor, in 1807. He was the son of Mr John Astley, who came of an old Shropshire family, and was a painter by profession, and a man of fascinating address. Journeying through Knutsford in the latter part of the year 1789 or 1790, he attended one of the county balls, or "assemblies," famous even yet in that quaint old town, and gained unconsciously at the moment the heart of a young widow, Penelope, relict of Sir William Dukinfield Daniel, of Over Tabley. The tale of the marriage is that Astley was employed to paint Lady Daniel's portrait, and when it was finished the fair Penelope sportively asked him, if it was his choice, which he would prefer, the original or the picture. Gallantly enough, he answered that his preference would be decidedly placed on the original. By this marriage the whole of the Dukinfield estate, worth £5000 a year (at that time), passed into his hands.

The Lodge of Unanimity was constituted by the Provincial Grand Master of Lancashire, William Rachdale, in 1754, and is fortunate in having preserved all its minute books since that year. Its warrant is, therefore, at the time of writing, 166 years old, the oldest authentic English warrant known. Its meetings were held by the authority of James, Marquess of Carnarvon, afterwards Duke of Chandos, Grand Master of the Moderns (1754-56), and R.W.P.G.M. Rachdale signed the authority to make Masons, etc., usually done in those days when a lodge was constituted. Owing to the lapse of all the T.I. Lodges in Cheshire, No. 89 ranks as the senior lodge of the Province. The relics in its possession are also commensurate with its existence. It has, without doubt, the most interesting lodge room within its borders, reminding one somewhat of the historic meeting place of the York Lodge at York, which city may be truly regarded as the Mecca of Northern Masonry. The three magnificent chairs still used by the Master and Wardens are always objects of great interest to visitors. They are beautifully carved and adorned with appropriate Masonic emblems. The most striking objects in the Lodge are three large oil paintings representing the Virgin, Mary Magdalene, and St John the Evangelist, presented by Brother Francis Dukinfield Astley, first Master after its removal from Lancashire to Cheshire. A minute examination, however, rather throws doubt on the statement that they were also painted by him. The size and colouring are more suggestive of the Dutch school, and we would prefer to regard him as a gentleman of leisure and literary tendencies as evidenced by his efforts in this direction. A large cabinet within the entrance to the lodge room contains two Masonic jugs of portly dimensions and of great antiquity, the remainder being smaller and of more modern workmanship. Near by on a separate shelf is exhibited a huge punch bowl capable of holding sixteen gallons, which would probably be used on state occasions or in celebration of important public events. The jug to match the bowl is missing, but in the cabinet referred to are three dainty punch ladles, presented by Mrs Ann Young, wife of Brother William Young, and Mary Richardson, wife of Brother Richardson, 27th December 1802. The common gavel now used by the Worshipful Master bears the following inscription on a silver plate :— "The mallet after being used for laying the first stone of St John's Church in Manchester was left here as a memorial by Brother Powell, 1768." The perfect ashlar and its attachments also bears a plate to the effect that it was presented by Worshipful Brother Whitehead, Deputy Provincial Grand Master of this County (Lancashire), and the crane and block by the Worshipful Brother Nabb, 1769. In 1787 a mallet used at the laying of the first stone of the new gaol and penitentiary for the Hundred of Salford, by Thomas Butterworth Bayley, Esquire, was presented as a memorial by Brother Thomas Potter, together with two chisels and a silver trowel which was used by T. B. Bayley, Esquire, on the same occasion, and presented by Brother Haworth. In the centre of the Lodge, on the tessellated floor cloth, is a kind of semaphore-like stand, showing the four points of the compass, N. E. S. and W., flanked by the celestial and terrestrial globes, etc. Brother John Clayton, P.M., P.P.G.W., and A.G.D.C. (England), presented a number of portraits of its Worshipful Masters from 1875 to 1894, and from 1894 to the present time the various outgoing Masters have formed a pleasing continuation of the series. There is a couple of ram's horns, mounted on a miniature trolley, used as snuff boxes, as also a striking reproduction of a golden eagle. In an account under date 4th February 1754, jewels were provided for the incoming Secretary, amounting to £6, 17s.; painter for gilding the jewels, 8s.; wood jewels, 2s.; compasses, 6d.; cleaning and mending the sword, 3s.; aprons, carpet, and making sword, 10s. 6d.; candlesticks, painting, gilding, and brass work, and other things, totalling £19, 19s. 4d.

A special paragraph may be devoted to the Tyler of this Lodge, Brother Stafford, whose urbanity, old time courtesy, and strict adherence to Masonic forms and ceremonies endear him to its members. To visitors he appears to have grown with it and become one of its indispensable assets. In olden times the outer guard or tyler was stationed in the road to carry out the duties of his office. To protect him against the rigors of our climate he was attired in a heavy overcoat with tippets similar to those worn by stage drivers, save that he wore a cocked hat—*à la Wellington*. There must have been some reflex of this custom in the Unanimity as its Tyler when on duty wears a novel and striking headgear in the shape of a cap, which appears in the accounts of 1754 as having been purchased at a cost of 5s. It rather reminds

CHESHIRE: ITS TRADITIONS AND HISTORY

one of the plumes and trimmings of a North American Indian, and we venture to think that it is a unique survival of an older custom in Freemasonry.

Armstrong, in his work on Cheshire Freemasonry, says, " Under the rule of R.W. Brother Astley, the Lodge does not seem to have had a large membership, but that it was popular is amply evinced by the number of visitors who were entertained on Lodge nights. They frequently outnumbered the members by two and three to one."

The installation of Brother F. Dukinfield Astley took place at the Exchange Arms, Manchester, in 1814. There were present—The Right Worshipful F. D. Astley, Provincial G.M.; Daniel Lynch, D.P.G.M.; George Crossley, P.G.S.W.; Louis Magnus, P.G.J.W.; P. Longsden, P.G.T.; W. Charles Pidgeon, P.G.S.; and Roger Smith, P.G.S.B. The Master, Wardens, and Past Masters of nearly all the lodges in the county being present, a procession was formed in the usual order within the lodge, when " the grand and imposing ceremony " of installation took place, after which the Right Worshipful Grand Master appointed Brother Daniel Lynch, Esquire, of Manchester, to be his acting Deputy Provincial Grand Master, and he was forthwith installed " with like honours and ceremony as F. D. Astley, Esquire," after which the following brethren were duly installed as Provincial Grand Officers :—R. W. G. Crossley, P.G.S.W.; L. Magnus, P.G.J.W.; P. Longsden, P.G.T.; W. Chas. Pidgeon, P.G.S.; R. Smith, P.G.S.B. The brethren then walked in grand procession to St John's Church, where an impressive sermon was delivered by Brother the Reverend Robert Dallas, acting as Provincial Grand Chaplain, after which about eighty-two brethren sat down to dinner at the Exchange Room, " where they spent the evening in the greatest harmony."

Now comes a rather curious complication. At the laying of the foundation stone of Stockport Parish Church, in July 1813, Brother Astley is described in the minutes as, " F. D. Astley, Esquire, Provincial Grand Master of Freemasons for Lancashire, and also the Provincial Grand Master for Cheshire." By what authority Brother Astley acted in the last-named capacity does not appear on the face of the proceedings. According to the succession of Provincial Masters from 1717, Sir Robert Stapleton Cotton's name appears in 1785. Sir John Egerton's name next appears in the list as 1781, but this is manifestly an error, as he was not appointed until December 1809. Probably Brother Astley acted as Deputy Provincial Grand Master on the occasions referred to owing to the distance of Stockport from the capital of the Province, a distance now bridged by railroad communication. On the above occasion, the Scottish Forfar Militia Band, being all Masons, played during the procession.

The father of Brother Astley was, as we have seen, a painter. His son was, in turn, a poet. He wrote two or three volumes, small in their way, but replete with wit and humour, and a prose work on "Tree Planting in this Country." The Unanimity now meets at the Angel Hotel, in Dukinfield, but few people have any idea who the "Old General" was. In short, it was a fine old hunter!

> When Highflier took you o'er mountain and dale
> Did the courage and speed of Old General fail?
> He would lead you to water, but mark by the sign,
> He bids you leave water and leads you to wine.
>
> But it's time to propose, with loud cheering, a toast—
> May good fortune attend on the house of our host.
> And who would refuse a bumper of wine?
> To a sportsman's success with Old General's sign!

That he was capable of higher flights is illustrated by a hymn which he wrote to be sung on the Jubilee of George IV. The first verse reads:—

> Great Lord who builds the Throne of Kings,
> From whose high will flows all command—
> Under Thine own protecting wings
> Keep the loved sovereign of our land.

He composed other hymns in opposition to Voltaire's doctrines, and his translations from Bion, Theocritus, Anacreon, and Horace were eminently beautiful and well in accord with the spirit and feeling of the original. He was High Sheriff of Cheshire in 1806-7, at the age of twenty-five, an office which contemporary records state he carried out with something approaching feudal magnificence. To the great grief of the inhabitants of Dukinfield he expired suddenly at the house of a brother-in-law in Derbyshire, on the 23rd July 1825, at the age of forty-four. His funeral sermon was preached by the Rev. John Gaskell (a celebrated Unitarian Divine), and the title is, "The contemplation of death when aided by the assurance of immortality, conducive to human improvement and happiness." So mote it be.

The élite of the Masonic fraternity was present at the consecration of the Randle Holme Lodge, No. 3261, a Lodge which seeks to keep the name green in the Province of Cheshire. This notable event took place on Saturday, 7th December 1907, at the Girls' Institute, Port Sunlight. Those present were:—The Hon. Alan de Tatton Egerton, Vice-Lord Lieutenant of Cheshire, J.P., etc., Past Grand Warden of England, R.W. Provincial Grand Master; Fredk. Broadsmith, P.G.S.; Lieutenant-Colonel Hubert Cornwall Legh, P.G.S.W.; D. L. Hewitt, P.G.J.W.; George W. Haswell, P.G.D.C.; Rev. A. C. Evans, Provincial Grand Chaplain; Joseph Clarke, P.G.D. (acted as Consecrating Officers). Colonel C. S. Dean, P.G.S.D.; J. Morrison M'Leod, P.G.S.B. (Grand Officers). The Provincial Grand Officers were:—A. J.

Thompson (W.M. elect), W. H. Cooke, A. C. G. Wallace, J. F. Smith, S. Jones, E. V. Salaman, Edw. L. Bruce, Alfd. C. H. Davies, James Boughey, G. Hammond Danby, J. M'Leavy, Samuel Lee, Ronald Williams, Samuel Thompson, W. Arthur Pierce, W. Kelly, Clifford Collard, W. J. Doran, John Scott, E. J. Dugmore, Robert Harvey, Ernest Farrel, G. W. Makin, R. Sandham, Geo. F. Bird, J. R. Owen, Fredk. Smith, Richard Olive, Frank Pinder, Alexr. Saunders, Peter W. Smith, W. G. Cross, and Richard Parry. Officers of the Lodge and Master Masons :—W. H. Lever, Jno. Mellor, A. Hornby, J. H. Lawson, J. E. Ince, G. Doleman, J. Taylor-Davies, J. Walker, G. E. Lewis, J. T. Kerridge, J. M. English, G. M. Partridge, J. Rimmer, Wm. Toulouse, Geo. Swallow, W. J. Chester, Wm. Pryce, N. W. Dawson, Wm. Jones, Robert Goffin, R. Paterson, James Chipchase, E. B. Eastwood, E. Arthur, and W. Palmer.

The Worshipful Deputy Provincial Grand Master, Sir Horatio Lloyd, Kt., K.C., Past Grand Deacon of England, was unavoidably absent, which was a cause of much regret to the brethren present.

The Ceremony of Consecration was duly performed, Worshipful Brother A. J. Thompson being installed W.M. ; and the following Grand Officers were invested :—Worshipful Brothers Owen Jones, acting I.P.M. ; W. H. Cooke, S.W. ; J. F. Swift, J.W. ; A. C. G. Wallace, Treasurer ; Joseph Clarke, Secretary ; Ronald Williams, S.D. ; Jas. Wm. Shaw, J.D. ; J. Hamilton Jackson, Organist ; James Boughey, D.C. ; Richard Parry, I.G. ; Richard Olive, A.S. ; Frank Pinder, S.S. ; John R. Owen, S.S. ; and the following assistants :— W. Kelly, Peter W. Smith, Clifford Collard, Dr W. A. Pierce. Robert Sandham, and W. P. Pipe, and John Scott, Tyler. The following brethren were proposed as joining members :—James Morrison M'Leod, Secretary, Royal Masonic Institution for Boys, London ; Hubert Cornwall Legh, Esq., High Legh Hall, near Knutsford, P.G.S.W., W.M., Unity Lodge, No. 381; Peter Davenport, Sycamore Hill, Macclesfield, P.G.R., P.M., No. 295 ; John Morris, manufacturer, 20 Cable Road, Hoylake, P.P.G.T., P.M., Hilbre, No. 2375 ; Edmund V. Salaman, The Thorns, Bebington, P.M., Wm. Hesketh Lever Lodge, No. 2916 ; William Hesketh Lever, Soap Manufacturer, Thornton Manor, Thornton Hough, W.M. of the Wm. Hesketh Lever Lodge, No. 2916 ; and A. T. Harding, " Ashlea," Parkfield, New Ferry, P.M., Wm. Hesketh Lever Lodge, No. 2916. A byelaw was enacted that " Membership of the Lodge is restricted to Present and Past Provincial Grand Officers of the Province of Cheshire, and Past Provincial Grand Stewards," otherwise the number of brethren wishing to join would probably have rendered the Lodge somewhat unwieldly.

At the first regular meeting the joining members nominated at the Consecration were duly elected. At this meeting a very instructive and interesting feature was introduced in a lecture by Brother John T. Thorp, P.A.G.D.C. of England, Secretary of the Lodge of Research, Leicester, Member of the

Quatuor Coronati Lodge, No. 2076, London, F.R.H.S., F.R.S.L., etc., subject—" Freemasonry : Whence it came, what it once was, and how it became what it is now." The syllabus set forth how it originated in the East, how the Star of Masonry wended its way westward, just as the Star of Empire has done in subsequent ages, until it arrived in England, where it took the form of guilds, with their privileges and restrictions. Afterwards with their development in Masons and Masonry, we get the golden age of operative Masonry; the decline of which and the causes being duly traced. This in its turn gave place to Speculative or Philosophical Masonry, and through this we derive the continuity of English Masonry through five centuries. Worshipful Brother Thorp afterwards exhibited a number of Masonic relics which proved most interesting to the brethren, especially the work of Randle Holme III. entitled the " Academy of Armory and Blazonry," printed in the seventeenth century at Chester. To quote from the minutes, " after a hearty vote of thanks had been tendered to the lecturer," Worshipful Brother W. H. Lever referred to the book in question then in possession of the lecturer and " in his usual generous manner explained that it would be doubtless of interest if such a book were in the possession of the Lodge, and if such could be obtained, it was his intention to present one for the benefit of the brethren, an expression which met with the approval of all present."

The work was shortly afterwards presented to the Lodge by Brother W. H. Lever, and an appropriate casket of oak designed by Brother G. W. Haswell, P.P.D.C., together with a beautiful cushion, the handiwork of Mrs Haswell, on which it rests, placed therein. The oak from which the casket was made was, through the kindness of the Venerable Archdeacon Barber, brought from the Church of St Mary on the Hill, Chester, where the Holme family worshipped for generations. Thus the Lodge is in possession of a priceless relic, which will not only remind the brethren of a generous donor, but will serve also to impress on their memories a veneration for a famous past in Masonic annals.

Other presents have been made from time to time and the library enriched with various works on Masonry which will become increasingly valuable as years roll on. The lectures which have been given from time to time have also been of great interest, which leads to the reflection that it is greatly to be regretted that they could not be reproduced for the benefit of a wider audience. It is not generally known that in Manchester there has been in existence for ten years past an Association for Masonic Research which is becoming increasingly popular with the brethren in East Lancashire and Cheshire. At the headquarters which will ultimately be the projected Manchester Masonic Temple, lectures are delivered from time to time by distinguished visitors and members, and reproduced annually in a volume of transactions. There are " outings " to various places of interest. Just before the war a number of members journeyed to York, where they were entertained by the historic York Lodge. Their lodge room contains ancient furniture, warrants, ancient charges in rolls, one measuring fifteen feet in length of closely written parchment, and other interesting relics. The Association also a year or two ago paid a visit to the Capital of the Province of Cheshire, and had a cordial welcome from the Chester brethren. It has also a fine library accessible to members. The whole of this generous fare is provided for an annual subscription of five shillings ! There is no reason why a similar association should not be formed in Liverpool, which would be available for members resident on the banks of the Mersey. But we would add one word of warning. The Manchester Association has been fortunate in its officers, both past and present, especially in a splendid secretary, Brother C. P. Noar, whose work in that capacity is as unique as it is efficient.

The Installation of Brother Joseph Clarke, in December 1911, was rendered memorable by the attendance of many visiting brethren of distinction, including the Earl of Derby (Lord Mayor of Liverpool), Provincial Grand Master of East Lancashire ; the Mayors of Birkenhead, Wallasey, Bootle ; Sir Jos. Sykes Rymer, ex-Lord Mayor of York ; G. Potter Kirby, ex-Sheriff of York ; A. K. Barrow, W.M., York Lodge, No. 236 ; Samuel Weedham, S.W.; Wm. Johnson, J.W. ; H. L. Green, Secretary ; G. Y. Johnson, A. Secretary ; John Gresdale, I.G. ; J. W. Daniel, Steward ; and Past Masters O. G. Taylor, James W. Dow, W. R. Makin, and about thirty other brethren, including Fred. A. Gamage, Sheriff, and H. Craven, Town Clerk of York. The visit of so many brethren from the capital of Yorkshire was in response to an invitation given by Worshipful Brother Sir William Hesketh Lever, Bart. (now Lord Leverhulme). They arrived in Liverpool the evening before, and stayed at the North Western Hotel, were shown over Port Sunlight Works the next morning, and all entertained to luncheon at Port Sunlight, motoring to Thornton Heath, where by Dispensation the Installation took place, and returned to York by a special train from Bebington Station, at 9 p.m., reaching home shortly after midnight. All these arrangements were made and the expenses borne by Worshipful Brother Lever.

Succession of Masters :—1908, A. J. Thompson ; 1909, W. H. Lever, M.P., P.P.G.S.W. ; 1910, J. F. Swift, P.P.G.O. ; 1911, W. H. Cooke, P.P.G.D. ; 1912, Joseph Clarke, P.P.G.W. ; 1913, A. G. C. Wallace, P.P.G.R. ; 1914, J. Hamilton Jackson, P.P.G.O. ; 1915, Wm. Arthur Pierce, P.P.G.D. ; 1916, G. W. Makin ; 1917, Geo. F. Penny ; 1918, J. S. Warren.

Brother Sir Wm. Hesketh Lever was created Baron Leverhulme in 1917. He was initiated in the William Hesketh Lever Lodge, No. 2916, in 1902, and immediately took an active part in the work of the Province. He rendered yeoman service at the 111th Anniversary Festival of the Masonic Institution for Boys, presided over by Lord Egerton of Tatton, Provincial Grand Master, held at the Crystal Palace in 1909. There were 921 stewards present on that occasion, and Cheshire contributed £23,860 to the funds of the School, a record sum for so small a Province. He was a founder of several Lodges, notably the Lodge of King Solomon's Temple, Chester. He was invested as P.G.S.W. in 1918, and Junior Grand Warden of England in 1918. He is a Past Master of the Lodge which bears his name. He is Grand Scribe N. in the Royal Arch, and Senior Grand Warden in the Mark Degree. It goes without saying that his Lordship is a munificent supporter of Masonic charities. He was born at Bolton, Lancashire, in 1851, and took part in his father's business in that town, removing to Wigan in 1877. He afterwards commenced business in a small way at Warrington, and later purchased an estate in Cheshire, which he named Port Sunlight. Port Sunlight is a model village, with open spaces, and all adjuncts for recreation, as also spacious meeting halls for promoting the moral, social, and intellectual welfare of the employees at the works for which Port Sunlight is deservedly famous. He is the head of the firm of Lever Brothers, Ltd., which, with its associated firms and interests, possesses the colossal capital of one hundred million pounds. His interests are world wide. As one writer put it—"Lord Leverhulme is a hard headed man of business, but had he possessed no imagination (or vision), he might to this day have been selling soap in a little back street in Bolton." The same writer also points out that when he bought the Isle of Lewis many so-called business men thought he was a millionaire who wished to throw away his money, but predicted that before he had finished with the island he would be on the high road towards making hundreds of thousands out of it, and at the same time benefiting thousands of people. We raise our hats, metaphorically, to these wonderful Captains of Industry.

He is a Grand Officer of the Order of Leopold II., and a Fellow of the Royal Geographical Society. He was High Sheriff of Lancashire in 1917, worthily upholding its time-honoured associations, and his Mayoralty of his native town of Bolton was marked by the discharge of the duties of the office with his usual efficiency. His many gifts to that busy Lancashire borough, including a large park and recreation ground, will form a permanent monument more enduring than marble of his munificence. His Lordship spends a certain portion of his time in London, and has entertained Royalty at his residence at Hampstead. In 1919, Queen Alexandra acted as one of the sponsors on the occasion of the baptism of his grand-child, daughter of the Hon. William Hulme Lever.

The portrait of Lord Leverhulme in his regalia as Junior Grand Warden of England, is from a painting by Mr Hall Neale in the Collegium at Port Sunlight. The reproduction is from a photo by Mr Geo. J. Davies, New Ferry.

Many Cheshire Lodges of the Randle Holme and subsequent period seem to have died out. The oldest Chester Lodge now on the roll of Provincial

Photo   *Davies, Port-Sunlight*

Brother LORD LEVERHULME,

P. J. G. W. England.

Brother T. H. ANNETT,
Treasurer, Provincial Fund of Benevolence.

Grand Lodge is the Cestrian, No. 425, constituted in 1734. The Lodge of St John, No. 104, Stockport, is, with the exception of the Unanimity, No. 89, Dukinfield, the oldest in the Province. The other eighteenth century warrants in existence are Unity, No. 267, Macclesfield (1788); Unanimity, No. 287, Stockport (1792); the King's Friends, No. 293, Nantwich, and the Combermere Lodge of Unity, No. 295, Macclesfield (1793); and the Loyalty, No. 320, Mottram (1799). St John's Lodge, No. 104, is now the only one existing in the Province whose warrant was granted for the Antients or Atholl Masons. It sets forth that it was granted by the Grand Lodge " of the Most Antient and Honourable Fraternity of Free and Accepted Masons," according to the old Constitutions granted by His Royal Highness Prince Edwin at York, A.D. 926, and in the year of Masonry 4926.

The year 1806 marked a revival of Masonry in Stockport. Not only was St John's warrant revived in that year, but three other new lodges were constituted in the town, viz., Unity, Peace, and Concord suggestive of a friendly rivalry, or rather, which is more probable, that some brother of commanding influence saw a field for Masonry in the town and placed it on a comprehensive basis.

Unity, No. 321, is now held at Crewe, and it is regarded as a nursery or jumping off place for budding Provincials. Peace, No. 322, and the Concord, No. 323, are still held at Stockport. Lodge No. 104 has been migratory as to the place of meeting, including Mottram in Longdendale, Dob Cross, Saddleworth, Manchester Hill (Lancs.), and afterwards at various hostelries in Stockport proper. In its early days it had many vicissitudes. The members were in many cases cotton operatives receiving, when ill, sick relief, also aid in the way of funeral benefits. When the cotton trade was good the number increased, but when bad many " declared off." In 1829 the Papal Mandate was issued that Roman Catholics must give up their connection with Masonic Lodges, and many were obliged to resign. It is pleasant to record that the present prosperous state of St John's Lodge, No. 104, is principally owing to the interest which a few of the brethren connected with the Caledonian Lodge, No. 204, Manchester, also constituted by the Grand Lodge of the Antients, took in it several years ago. By their missionary zeal and efficient working they raised the membership from seven to nearly seventy. When compiling the centenary annals of the Caledonian Lodge we observed many entries in the minutes referring to paying visits and receiving visiting brethren from other Lodges, but we did not perceive any to St John's, No. 104. Probably this would be owing to members going on their own initiative to Stockport or having had local connections there.

The Centenary Banquet was on 13th November 1865, their warrant from Grand Lodge being dated October 1765. The Provincial Grand Master, Lord de Tabley, attended by Brother George Cornwall Legh, M.P., Past

Lodge of Unanimity No. 284.
Centenary Meeting
September 14th 1892.

Gaston T. Ashton. W.M.

Wyn at Salfortmorth
Thos Bantingdeer P.G.M.

Jno. Clayton P.P.G.S.N.

John Chadwick P.G. Sec. 1st Prov.G.Sec. &c.

Unanimity Lodge, Stockport—Autographs.

CHESHIRE: ITS TRADITIONS AND HISTORY

Grand Warden of England, and other Provincial Grand Officers of Cheshire and adjoining Provinces attended, and the proceedings were very successful. A Bible was presented by Brother Charles Wm. Provis. He also presented a valuable Jewel to the Lodge in commemoration of the event. Another Jewel, evidently a replica, suitably inscribed, was presented to Lord de Tabley by Brother W. H. Williams. W.M. Brother Provis was elected to succeed Brother Williams as Worshipful Master for the following year.

In 1866 Lord de Tabley held the first Provincial meeting after his installation in August 1865, at Stockport. Incidentally, it may be mentioned that a Past Master of St John's Lodge, Brother Wm. Booth, was Provincial Grand Director of Ceremonies on the Installation of Lord Egerton of Tatton at Chester in November 1886, and was publically complimented by the Earl of Lathom on the admirable manner in which the day's function had been conducted. Indeed throughout, it would be difficult to pass too high an encomium on Brother Booth's services to St John's Lodge, No. 104, in particular, and to Masonry in general during the last half century. In 1914 he was invested Past Assistant Grand Director of Ceremonies, England. He also received Honours as Past Grand Standard-Bearer in the Royal Arch and Grand Junior Deacon in the Mark Degrees. He was Chairman of the Benevolent Committee, 1912-1913.

About 1829 a period of depression set in which continued until 1862, and had it not been for the efforts of " the immortal seven," who by their meeting from time to time kept the warrant in force, this excellent Lodge would have ceased working and become extinct. They are often referred to at lodge meetings, and their names are worthy of permanent record. They were William and George M'Auley (apparently brothers), John Oldham, James Wood, John Perkin, Wm. Gee, and Richard Jones. Summary: Lodge constituted A.D. 1765 as No. 139, Antients; became No. 168 at the Union in 1813; No. 121 at the closing up of numbers in 1832; and No. 104 at the closing up in 1868.

The Cestrian Lodge, No. 425, is the premier lodge in the ancient capital of the Province. It has every claim, says Armstrong, to be regarded as the lineal descendant of the time immemorial " Royal Chester Lodge," whose furniture and effects came into its possession on its constitution in 1834, which was some four years before the old lodge was finally erased. That the T.I. constitution of the Royal Chester Lodge should have been allowed to lapse and a new warrant taken out to replace it, cannot but be a matter of regret, not only to those members of the Cestrian who are interested in the Masonic antiquities of the ancient city, but to every brother of our ancient Province. The application for a new warrant in 1834 was undoubtedly a mistake almost as grave as the payment for a new Constitution in 1739. In each case it had the effect of placing the most ancient of lodges on both occasions at the bottom of the Grand Lodge Roll. The Loyal British, Independence, and Royal Cheshire

Militia Lodges had been recently erased, but some of their members assisted in the founding of the Cestrian. In 1835 Mr John Jervis, M.P. for the city, joined the Lodge. He afterwards became Sir John Jervis, Bart., and Chief Justice of England. Another distinguished member was the son-in-law of Viscount Combermere, P.G.M., the Earl of Hillsborough, No. 6, London, who remained a member for thirty years. Amongst other distinguished initiates of the Lodge were Sir Watkin Williams Wynn, of Wynnstay; the Marquis of Devonshire; Lord Richard Grosvenor; Sir Robert Stapleton Cotton, grandson of Lord Combermere; Lord Arthur Hill; the Hon. Thos. Cholmondeley; Mr Talbot Clifton, M.P., Lytham Hall; Mr Richard Dymoke Vaughton, a relative of Sir Henry Dymoke, Champion of England, an office not then abolished; Henry Brougham Loch, afterwards Lord Loch; Aeneas J. M'Intyre, Q.C., etc.

An interesting event occurred in 1851 when Mr Horatio Lloyd, twenty-two, student in law, of the City of Chester, was proposed by Brother Dixon, P.M., as a candidate for Masonry. He was initiated on 10th December 1851, installed W.M. in 1854 in the presence of the P.G.M. Lord Combermere. He afterwards served as P.S.G.W., Recorder of Chester, 1866; County Court Judge, 1875; D.P.G.M., 1887; Knighted, 1890.

The Cestrian has at various times received numerous gifts of jewels, furniture, fittings, Masonic emblems, books, etc. But, above all, the Cestrian has received special mention from Provincial Grand Masters for its splendid efforts in the cause of charity, worthy of the best traditions of Masonry. Towards the end of 1900 Brother Armstrong informs us he was privileged to deliver a lecture on its glorious history, in which he endeavoured to set forth the unique position held by the Lodge in the Province of Cheshire, " not only on the possession of a practically complete set of minutes for the last 160 years, and of other documentary evidence, proving almost to a certainty a still prior existence of at least another century, but by its consistent and regular support of our great charities placing it in the very first place amongst Provincial Lodges." " The father of the Lodge," Sir Horatio Lloyd, entered upon his fiftieth year as a member on 11th December 1900, joining during the Mastership of Sir Watkin Williams Wynn, known far and wide as the " King " in Wales.

The Mersey Lodge, No. 477, Birkenhead, is the first and oldest Lodge on the Wirral Peninsula. It was opened by dispensation from Lord Combermere in April 1841, and it was constituted shortly afterwards by simply reading the Dispensation and the Warrant from the Grand Lodge. There seems to have been some difficulty concerning the appointment of officers, and at a Lodge of Emergency held in September, Brother Clark Rampling was " simply installed Master." He appointed Brother E. G. Willoughby, S.W., " a beautifully simple way of surmounting initial difficulties connected with the resignations of the W.M. and S.W. named in the warrant." In October 1841 the first to offer himself as a candidate was Mr Robert Harwood, the host of the

Market Inn, and to him belongs the honour of being the first Mason to be made in Birkenhead. Amongst the brethren who took an active interest in the welfare of the Lodge was the Hon. Henry Holbrook, the oldest Provincial Grand Officer in Cheshire, a member of the Thirty-third Degree, and afterwards Deputy Grand Master of British Columbia. Amongst the possessions of the Lodge is a portrait of the Hon. Mrs Aldworth, "the only Lady Freemason." Although the Mersey Lodge has had its ups and downs, like many old lodges, it is now one of the most prosperous in the Province, and holds a large number of votes for the Cheshire and Metropolitan Institutions.

We have often heard of Freemasons of the gentler sex, more or less mythical it must be observed, and an excerpt from the *Chester Chronicle* of 1802 records that Mrs Beaton, a native of Wales, died at Norwich in that year. She was commonly called "the Freemason," from the circumstance of having contrived to conceal herself one evening in the wainscoting of a lodge room, "where she learnt that secret, the knowledge of which thousands of her sex have in vain attempted to arrive at." She was a very singular woman and her secret died with her.

Bearing on this subject, the following advertisement appeared in the *Newcastle Courant* in 1770 :—

"This is to acquaint the public—That on Monday, the first inst., being the Lodge (or Monthly Meeting) night of the Free and Accepted Masons of the 22nd Regt., held at the Crown, the landlady of the house broke open a door (with a poker) that had not been opened for some years past, by which means she got into the adjacent room, made two holes through the wall, and by that stratagem discovered the secrets of Masonry; and she, knowing herself to be the first woman in the world that ever found out the secret, is willing to make it known to all her sex. So any lady who is desirous of knowing or learning the secrets of Freemasonry, by applying to that well learned woman (Mrs Bell that lived fifteen years in and about Newgate) may be instructed in all the secrets of Masonry." For the information of all whom it may concern, all efforts to trace the mythical Mrs Bell proved futile, and, therefore we prefer to take the Aldworth episode as the authorised version.

In Chester, in the year 1778, an ancient and honourable Order of Hiccabites advertised that a Chapter of the Order would be held at the Golden Talbot, at five o'clock in the evening, "when and where the Brothers and Sisters are requested to give their attendance. Ladies and gentlemen of capability and good character may then be admitted members.—By order of the Court."

A notice appeared in the paper a fortnight afterwards stating that "at a Ball and Supper given on Wednesday last by the Chapter of the most Ancient and Honourable Order of Hiccabites held at the Talbot, there were present a most numerous and brilliant assembly of the principal ladies and gentlemen of the place and neighbourhood ; many new members were admitted, and the evening was concluded with every mark of joy and festivity."

Some thirty years ago a Manchester newspaper published a remarkable leading article, which attracted great attention at the time, and is typical of the ignorance of the mass of people as to the non-intervention of our Order in denominationalism and politics. It serves, however, to point a moral even to-day :—" Withington and witchcraft do not seem to be more incongruous than the trio of assemblies represented by the last meeting of the Provincial Grand Lodge of Cheshire Freemasons, the gathering of the Catholic Truth Society at Hanley, and the International Anti-Masonic Congress which has this week been held at Trent in Austria. Nevertheless, they are all connected together with a thread of mingled fancy and fact, which may be said to envelop the sweet personality of Miss Diana Vaughan. The alleged revelations of Masonic devil-worship that that young lady has published to the world since her conversion to Roman Catholicism have received the imprimatur of several French bishops ; they have been earnestly debated and applauded by 400 Roman Catholic clergymen at Trent, and, as Cardinal Vaughan reminded us the other day, the Church of which he is an eminent dignitary is ' the same o'er all the world.' " It must, however, be rather difficult for English Roman Catholics to understand the feeling with which Freemasonry is regarded by a large and influential number of their co-religionists on the Continent. Such record of benevolent work as that published in connection with the Provincial Grand Lodge of Cheshire reads strangely beside the announcement that the Spanish Government has appointed a special commission to inquire whether Freemasonry should not be prohibited in Spain and all Freemasons in the Government service dismissed their posts.

At the Trent Congress Miss Diana Vaughan was described as an Englishwoman of gentle birth belonging to a family in which the worship of Satan (Freemasonry ?) had been hereditary for centuries. She states in her memoirs that she was " initiated at an early age into Freemasonry, and gradually rose to the Thirty-third Degree, from which she was promoted to be a member of an order called the Palladic, whose votaries worship Lucifer, the spirit of light and evil, in opposition to Adonai, the God of Judaism and Christianity." The remainder of the article contains reference to a personal interview she had with Lucifer, described as a beautiful young man, clad in golden mail and seated on a throne of diamonds, in the Palladist Holy of Holies somewhere in a Kentucky desert, and she appears to have been whisked from various centres much after the fashion of an old witch on her traditional broom. The world was divided into seventy-one Provinces, into which Palladic Masonry is alleged to be divided. Against No. 41 we read : " Province Triangulaire de Manchester (Angleterre) : Gd.-Maitre Provincial, John Yarker à Withington, avec gd-mait honoraire, qui est le Marquis de Londonderry." Brother Yarker, who was a great advocate of the higher degrees in Masonry, and wrote many learned treatises on the subject, promptly denied that he had ever heard of such a thing as Palladic Masonry until the report of it came over from France. "The vast majority of English Freemasons," concludes the article, "are certainly in the same position. Since the infamous perjury of Titus Oates, which cost the lives of many innocent Roman Catholics, there has been no such imposition on credulity as the farrago of abominable slander which has been seriously discussed by four hundred grave and reverend fathers at Trent."

CHAPTER XXIV.

Cheshire and the Grand Lodge of England—Attendance at Divine Service—A long interval—Sir John Egerton's interest in Masonry—King's Friends Lodge, Nantwich—Combermere Lodge of Union—The Moira Lodge—Benevolence, Marple—Congratulations to King George IV.—Appointment of Viscount Combermere as Provincial Grand Master—Beginning of an era of prosperity—Uniform working suggested—Appointment of Brother E. H. Griffiths as Provincial Grand Secretary—Fund of Benevolence—Cheshire Masonic Educational Institution for Children founded—Lord de Tabley, Provincial Grand Master—Tribute to the late Lord Combermere—Progress in the Province—The War of 1870—Assistance for sufferers.

IT is especially interesting to Cheshire Masons to know that under the Grand Lodge of England, revived in 1717, Cheshire was, in 1725, the first Province to derive its functions therefrom. North and South Wales comes next (1726); Bengal, India (1728); Shropshire (1731); and Lancashire (1734), etc. The first Provincial Grand Master of Cheshire was Colonel F. Columbine, who belonged to an old Derbyshire family. He was a relative of the Marburys of Marbury, and probably his connection with Cheshire arose owing to a Marbury having married Miss Columbine, a Derbyshire heiress, in 1683. Captain Hugh Warburton, who succeeded Colonel Columbine in 1727, was also one who took much interest in the craft. He was Provincial Grand Master of North Wales in 1726, and was a member of a now extinct branch of the ancient house of Warburton. For twenty-six years he ruled over the Province, when he was succeeded by John Page, Esq., in 1755, a descendant also of an ancient Cheshire family who resided for centuries at Erdshaw and Drakelow.

The first notice of attendance at church appears in the records during his term of office, in December 1758, when it is stated that the P.G.M., John Page, Esq., "acquaints ye different Lodges in Chester and he intends to have a procession next St John's day." He asks the Masters to recommend it to their members to come "decently and properly clothed" to attend him. The brethren accordingly attended divine service at St John's Church. This was the first occasion on which there was a procession to church. It survived in Cheshire up to within the last few years. There was, however, a Victory Thanksgiving at the Cathedral Church of the Diocese, on the occasion of the holding of the Annual Meeting of Provincial Grand Lodge at Chester in 1919. In 1771 we find J. Hugh Smith Barry, Esq., in office. He was the ancestor of the present holder of the Marbury estates, Lord Barrymore. Under what may be termed the old constitutions, the appointment of Sir Robert Stapleton Cotton was noteworthy as being the last. He was the father of the Right Hon. Lord Viscount Combermere, "the Cheshire hero" who later on filled Europe with admiration of his deeds of daring both in the Peninsula and on the burning plains of India. He also represented the County in Parliament from 1780 to 1796, and died in 1809.

It was on 27th December 1813 that the United Grand Lodge of England was formed, under H.R.H. the Duke of Sussex as Grand Master. Prior to this, brethren of the rival Grand Lodges were frequently distinguished from each other by the names of their respective Grand Masters. Thus the members of lodges under the "regular" or "Constitutional" Grand Lodge (1717), were known as "Prince of Wales" masons, or "moderns," while those under the jurisdiction of the Grand Lodge (1753) were styled "Atholl" masons or "ancients." Owing to unavoidable circumstances, no regular Provincial Grand Lodge had been held for some time, and accordingly, on 14th August 1816, one was called at the Feathers Inn, Chester, presided over by Sir John Grey Egerton, Bart., who then nominated his officers. The Festival of St John was held on the 27th December in the same year. Few families could boast of a more illustrious line of ancestry than the head of the House of Oulton. These Egertons originated from the marriage of William Belward with Mabilla, daughter and co-heir of Robert Fitz Hugh, the head of the powerful Barony of Malpas, in the reign of Henry I. The direct line terminated in David de Egerton, who left two sisters, co-heiresses, in the time of Edward II.; but the male heir was preserved in Urian, David's uncle, and continued in regular descent by the Egertons of Heaton, County Lancaster. Sir Phillip Egerton of Egerton and Oulton, County Chester, was created a Baronet in 1617. This Baronetcy passed to Sir Thomas Egerton, Earl of Wilton, on whose death it reverted to the above named Sir John Grey Egerton. A handsome cenotaph in Chester Cathedral marks his memory. It was erected by the voluntary offerings of the citizens of Chester, and the inscription is as follows :—

"Sacred to the memory of Sir John Grey Egerton, Baronet, of Oulton Park, in the County of Chester, Provincial Grand Master of the ancient Free and accepted Masons of the County Palatine of Chester, and one of the representatives of the City of Chester, in two successive parliaments. Born 11th July 1766, and died 25th May 1825. To record his many virtues exciting that admiration which he obtained from all, yet sought from none, his fellow citizens and friends truly attached to him when living, and deeply lamenting him when dead, have erected this monument desiring by their humble memorial of gratitude of affection to hold up for example manly uprightness, unswerving rectitude, unchanging friendship, zealous and incorruptible patriotism which ever mark the character and guided the conduct of their honourable and independent representative."

The foundation stone of Delamere Church was laid on 16th September 1816, with Masonic honours, and it is noteworthy as being the first ceremony of the kind carried out under the "New Constitutions." A Provincial Grand Lodge was held at the Globe Inn, Kelsall, at which there were present the

Provincial Grand Master, Sir John Grey Egerton, Bart., M.P.; Charles Hamilton, Esq., D.P.G.M.; Sir John Cotgreave, Kt. (Mayor of Chester), acting P.G.S.W.; Thomas Evans, acting P.G.J.W.; Wm. M. Henderson, P.G.J.W.; Wm. Ll. Wilbraham, acting as P.G.D.C.; Masters and Wardens of the Royal Chester Lodge, No. 80; Lodge of Independence, No. 482, Chester; Lodge of Trade and Navigation, No. 491, Northwich; Beneficent Lodge, No. 513, Macclesfield; Noah's Ark Lodge, No. 542, Middlewich; King's Friends Lodge, No. 553, Nantwich; Thomas Moulson, P.G.S.B., and Thomas Huxley, acting P.G.S. On arriving at the west end of the church the brethren formed in a semi-circle, and the stone having been duly laid by the Provincial Grand Master, corn, wine, and oil were poured upon it. A most eloquent oration was delivered by the acting Provincial Grand Chaplain, the Rev. Joseph Fish. The inscription on a brass plate let into the stone was as follows: "The foundation stone of this church was laid by the Right Worshipful Sir John Grey Egerton, Bart., Provincial Grand Master of the County of Chester, on the 3rd day of September, in the fifty-sixth year of the reign of King George III., A.D. 1816; A.L. 5816; attended by Sir John Cotgreave, Kt., Mayor of the City of Chester, the Provincial Grand Lodge, and the Lodges of the City and County. J. Gumery, Architect." The Right Worshipful Provincial Grand Master afterwards invited the brethren to Oulton, where "a most sumptuous and elegant repast, with costly wines, fruits, etc., in profusion, was laid before the guests," and "the numerous assemblage outside, numbering some hundreds, were treated with great kindness and liberality," and the chronicle concludes, "In short, there was not anything omitted that could at all contribute to the happiness of those present."

No meeting of Provincial Grand Lodge appears to have been held in 1817, but in the following year one was summoned at the Feathers Inn, Chester, and by adjournment, in the Grand Jury Room of the County, when the Master, Wardens, and Past Masters of the undermentioned Lodges attended:—The Royal Chester Lodge, No. 80; The Loyal British Lodge, No. 148; The Britannia Lodge, No. 168, Stockport; The Lodge of Independence, No. 482, Chester; The Lodge of Trade and Navigation, No. 491, Northwich; The Noah's Ark Lodge, No. 542, Middlewich; The Lodge of Unanimity, No. 543, Stockport; The King's Friends, No. 553, Nantwich; The Lodge of Loyalty, No. 603, Mottram; The Lodge of Peace, No. 607, Stockport; The Lodge of Concord, No. 608, Stockport; The Lodge of Benevolence, No. 640, Marple; The Lodge of Harmony, No. 705, Knutsford.

There was no answer from the Lodge of Unanimity, No. 136, Old General, Dukinfield; Beneficent Lodge, No. 513, Unicorn Inn, Macclesfield; Union Lodge, No. 555, Childers, Macclesfield; Lodge of Unity, No. 606, Unicorn Inn, Stockport.

Most of the lodges above named are now extinct. The Royal Chester,

No. 80, at one time figured prominently in the business of Provincial Grand Lodge, lodges in various parts of the Province having to be constituted under its banner for many years at Chester. The King's Friends Lodge was constituted at Nantwich in 1793, and, according to a paragraph in a Chester newspaper in 1795, the two local lodges, one meeting at the Crown Hotel, celebrate the Festival of St John by joining forces and marching in procession through the town. The Cotton family, of which Field-Marshal Viscount Combermere was afterwards the head, took a deep interest in the prosperity of the King's Friends Lodge. The whole of the jewels worn by its officers were the gift of the first Lord Combermere in 1799 and are of solid silver. In 1808 the members were all of the artisan class—joiners, gardeners, a locksmith, a haymaker (though whether he made this important article of commerce all the year round is open to doubt), a ropemaker, a cordwainer (shoemaker), a skinner (butcher), miller, etc. Up to the appointment of Lord Combermere as Provincial Grand Master in 1830, all Provincial Grand Lodge business had to be transacted at Chester. From that time all lodges were placed on an equal footing and had a share in Provincial representation. For many years this lodge was a favourite of Lord Combermere, as well as other members of his family who were members. It also furnished the Province with its first paid secretary, Brother E. H. Griffiths, who held the office for forty-seven years.

Combermere Lodge of Union, No. 295, Macclesfield, was constituted at Chester, as was then customary, in 1793, and had a more or less checkered career. In 1845 the Provincial Grand Lodge was held at Macclesfield, when Brother James Bland was W.M. He held office as Provincial Grand Treasurer from 1852 to 1873. Brother John Smith of Langley, P.G.S.D. in 1845 and P.G.R. in 1846, also receives due meed of praise for his services to this lodge in particular and Freemasonry in general. Brother Smith was Mayor of Maccles field in 1853. The Lodge celebrated its centenary festival in 1891, the oldest active P.M., Brother Thomas Lockitt — whose name is a watchword in Macclesfield Masonic circles—being in the chair. His name is perpetuated in the Thomas Lockitt Lodge. An excellent sketch of the rise and progress of the Combermere was compiled by Brother Robert Brown, P.M., a well-known local journalist and a founder of the Whiston Lodge, No. 3614.

The first meeting of the Lodge of Loyalty, No. 320, Mottram, was held by dispensation at Mottram in Longdendale, in June 1798, where it has since continued to meet. On 26th October 1898 the centenary festival was held, when there was a large attendance of Grand and Provincial Grand officers and brethren.

The Moira Lodge. No. 324, Stalybridge, was constituted in 1806, and was named after the acting Grand Master of England, Francis Rawdon Hastings, Earl of Moira. It received its centenary warrant in 1906.

The Lodge of Benevolence, No. 336, Marple, has a most interesting history.

It was constituted by dispensation in 1812, and was the last of the constitutions under the old regime before the union of the two Grand Lodges It has two warrants, one from Charles Hamilton, Esq., D.P.G.M. of Cheshire, and the second from the Earl of Moira. Amongst its relics are three splendid antique chairs, the silver jewels now worn by the officers, pillars, candlesticks and other furnishings originally the property of the Atholl Lodge, established at Stockport in 1759. The copper-plate from which the Lodge summons is struck has also, like the lodge, an interesting history. It was presented by Brother J. A. Newton, P.M. and Secretary, in February 1779. This plate was missing from 1880 to 1910, when, fortunately, it was recovered. The summons is beautifully and strikingly designed, and reflects credit on the producer.

On 26th June 1820 a Provincial Grand Lodge was held in the Grand Jury Room, Chester, and in addition to the above lodges, the Lodge of Industry, No. 718, Gee Cross, had been added to the roll of Grand Lodge. On this occasion it was resolved to present an address of congratulation to His Majesty King George IV., on his accession to the throne of these realms. The address set forth the delight which the brotherhood felt in knowing that " the King is our brother, that the monarch of England has patronised our order, and, aware of its internal philanthropic excellencies, has sheltered it from the ignorant by the fiat of his approbation." The brethren of this opulent county further assured His Majesty of their devotion to his royal person, and cordially united in hailing his accession to the throne—a significant circumstance in that the House of Brunswick was by no means so popular then as it has since become in its descendants. Hitherto, the members of Provincial Grand Lodge had not followed the laudable custom of attending Divine Service. After the transaction of business on this occasion they attended St John's Church, Chester, where an appropriate sermon was preached by the Rev. George Leigh, of the Noah's Ark Lodge, Middlewich. On returning from church an oration on the beauties of Masonry was delivered by Brother Lloyd Wilbraham, of the Loyal British Lodge, No. 148. So pleased were the brethren with Brother Leigh's sermon that there was a very unanimous request that he would allow it to be printed for the use of the brethren, with which request " he cheerfully complied." The Lodge of Industry, now No. 361, was afterwards removed to Hyde, and received its Centenary Warrant in March 1920.

On 21st October 1830 the Right Hon. Lord Viscount Combermere was appointed, by Patent from H.R.H. Prince Frederick Augustus, Grand Master of England, to the office of Provincial Grand Master, and his installation followed at the King's Friends Lodge, Nantwich.

Viscount Combermere was the eldest son of Sir Robert Salusbury Cotton, nd Frances Stapleton, his wife, and succeeded his father—himself a prominent Cheshire Mason and supporter of the King's Friends Lodge—as fifth Baronet, born November 1773, died February 1865. He was created Baron Combermere in 1814, then a Lieutenant-General, Governor and Commander-in-Chief in the Leeward Islands, K.G.C.B. of the Portuguese Order of the Tower and Sword, and of the Royal Hanovarian Guelphic Order, K.S.P., K.S.I., G.C.S.I., Commander-in-Chief in India, a Field-Marshal and Constable of the Tower of London, 1855, Colonel of the 1st Life Guards, and created Viscount Combermere of Bhurtpore, 1856.

From the date of his Lordship's installation, Freemasonry in Cheshire seems to have entered on a new era of prosperity. At the first Provincial Grand Lodge meeting held under his sway (12th September 1832), it was resolved that a local fund should be immediately established for charitable and other Masonic purposes, and a scale of fees was fixed to be paid by the various lodges in the Province. This was the forerunner of the Provincial Fund of Benevolence. At this meeting the Lodge of Love and Harmony at Over, which had assembled for some time past by virtue of a warrant granted by the Grand Lodge, was reconstituted by the R.W.P.G.M. as the " Combermere Lodge of Love and Harmony," and consecrated by Brother the Rev. Frederick Ford M.A., Rector of Lawton. A dispensation was issued in September for the Samaritan Lodge to meet alternately at Sandbach and Lawton, it being represented that several subscribing brethren resided at or near the last named village, which was at a considerable distance from Sandbach, and therefore inconvenient for them. In 1839 a notable event took place at the Provincial Grand Lodge meeting held at Northwich. There was a large attendance of visiting brethren, including the P.G.S.B. of England, G. P. Philipe, Esq., and a D.P.G.M. It was then resolved that bye-laws for the regulation of Provincial Grand Lodge be prepared and printed, an influential committee being appointed for that purpose, and also that a seal should be provided. The contributions received from certain lodges in 1833 were ordered to be repaid, so that all the lodges in the Province should be placed on an equal footing. It was also resolved that steps should be taken to procure the instructions of a brother skilled in the present system of working in the craft adopted by the Grand Lodge of England, to make a circuit of this Province to instruct all the lodges in the uniform system of working. There is no entry in the minutes of this resolution having been carried out. This was also the first occasion on which the Provincial Grand Lodge minutes were signed by the Provincial Grand Master. In March 1843 Lord Combermere visited Stockport, and a local newspaper stated that the town was " honoured with a scene which for magnificence and novelty was unparalleled in its history. The bells rang merry peals during the day, flags floated from the parish church and public buildings, and 500 brethren took part in a procession headed by Lord Combermere, P.G.M., and Provincial Grand Officers to the Parish Church. The dinner took place in the National School, and the tickets were 5s. each, ' covering malt liquor and dessert.' Amongst the decorations were the battles in which his Lordship had distinguished himself, such as Salamanca, Toulouse, Bhurtpore, Flanders, Oporto, Talavera, Torres Vedras, etc."

On 22nd March 1843 the first of the annual meetings of Provincial Grand Lodge, which have continued uninterruptedly to the present time, was held at Stockport. On this occasion Brother the Hon. Wellington Cotton, son of the Provincial Grand Master, was passed, the Lodge of Unity, No. 403, being adjourned to the National Schoolroom for that purpose. Brother Joseph John Moody, P.M. and P.P.G.D. of Lincolnshire, acted as Worshipful Master, assisted by the Worshipful Masters of the other Stockport lodges. The code of bye-laws was approved this year, and laws were also ordered to be prepared for a Fund of Benevolence. A sum of £40, 15s. 9d., lying in the Bank at Chester, was considered as forming part of this fund. On the 22nd August in this year the Provincial Grand Master and brethren assisted in the ceremony of fixing the keystone arch of the east window of the new church at Over. Thanks were voted to Brother Broady, Mayor of Over, for his kindness in granting the use of the Town Hall for holding the banquet, and for his active and zealous services on the occasion. For some time Brother R. B. Hinchliffe appears to have been acting as Grand Secretary of the Province, but it was now generally recognised that the duties were growing exceedingly onerous. It was at this lodge that Brother E. H. Griffiths of Nantwich, who held the office under three Provincial Grand Masters over a period of nearly fifty years, was appointed Provincial Grand Secretary, the sum of £10 per annum being voted him to cover the expenses of his office, " independent of his charges for postages, printing, paper, etc." It was unanimously decided that a fund be established having for its object apprenticing the sons and daughters of indigent brethren of the Province, and a committee was formed to arrange the matters and to obtain subscriptions.

Lord Combermere being abroad, the next Provincial Grand Lodge was held at the Royal Hotel, Chester, by his Lordship's dispensation to John Finchett Maddock, Esq. It is noticeable that at the Provincial Grand Lodge held at Chester in 1844, the Provincial Grand Superintendent of Works appears amongst the list of officers for the first time, Brother Henderson holding that office. Amongst the distinguished brethren present on that occasion were Sir Watkyn W. Wynn, Bart., M.P., Lord "Wemys" of Kilwinning Lodge, and Lieut. Walter Lawrence, P.M.W.S. of Rose Croix of Ireland. In 1845 Macclesfield was the place selected for the holding of the Provincial Grand Lodge. Several lodges were not represented, which caused the Provincial Grand Master to recommend that where numbers were too small to carry out the working of their own lodges efficiently they should join neighbouring lodges. Especially was this the case in connection with the Lodge of Virtue and Science, which had not met for some years.

The growing prosperity of the craft in Cheshire caused renewed interest to be taken in efficiently carrying on the work of Provincial Grand Lodge. Already the nucleus of a Fund of Benevolence had been formed, and from time to time the insignia of the lodge had been purchased. In 1848, as this fund now amounted to nearly £100, it was decided that a committee should be appointed to deal with it, and it was further resolved that all the lodges in the Province should unite in selecting one deserving brother annually for the benefits of the Royal Masonic Annuity Fund. Grants were made from the Fund of Benevolence accordingly, and it is also a very satisfactory feature that in 1850 the condition of Provincial Grand Lodge was most efficient, no lodges were in arrear, and the Fund of Benevolence, being too large to be deposited in a Savings Bank, it should be invested.

Dr Rayner of Stockport retired from the office of Treasurer in 1852. He stated that in 1844, when he took office, the Provincial Grand Lodge Fund was under £10, it was then upwards of £100. This amount was carried to the credit of the Fund of Benevolence, making the Fund £350, which was afterwards invested. Subsequently, it was proposed " and carried by acclamation that the best thanks of the Provincial Grand Lodge of Cheshire be presented to Brother Wm. Rayner, M.D., P.P.G.T., for the able and efficient services rendered by him to the Province for the past eight years." In 1856 Lord Combermere was prevented through illness from presiding over Provincial Grand Lodge at Egremont, but he was able to attend the year following at Stalybridge. The country was then convulsed with news of the fearful mutiny in India, and it is not to be wondered at that in Provincial Grand Lodge the hero of Bhurtpore, who only two years before had been made a Field-Marshal in the British Army, expressed himself in feeling terms at so many thousands of our countrymen and brethren being reduced to a fearful state of danger and destitution. He headed the fund, which was forthwith commenced with a donation of £50, and expressed his sanguine hope that this Province would be the first amongst the Provincial Grand Lodges of England in sending relief to their distressed fellow countrymen. A resolution was passed in Provincial Grand Lodge, in 1861, on the death of Brother Gibbs Crawford Antrobus, D.P.G.M., expressing their deep and sincere sorrow for the loss of one " whose amiability of manner and devoted attention to his Masonic duties had endeared him to every member of the Province." The following year at Sandbach Brother Bland stated that of the funds of Provincial Lodge, £800 were invested in three per cents. and the balance deposited in the Manchester and Liverpool Bank at Macclesfield. At this meeting also a most important project was introduced by Brother Willoughby in the scheme for the establishment of an Educational Institution for the children of distressed Masons in the Province on the basis of that in West Lancashire, which had been found to answer exceedingly well. It was explained that the scheme would not trench on the Fund of Benevolence, but rather assist it by undertaking to apprentice, as well as to educate, the children.

A Provincial Grand Lodge of Emergency followed at Crewe, and Brother Willoughby stated that he considered the establishment of such an institution would be "a lasting monument of the brotherly love and benevolence that should ever characterise the order." On the motion of Brother Lord de Tabley, Viscount Combermere was requested to act as President, and Lady Combermere as Lady Patroness of the institution. The Vice-Presidents nominated were the Hon. Colonel Cotton, R.W.D.P.G.M., Brothers Wm. Courtenay Cruttenden, P.G.S.W., and Captain Richard Cope, P.G.J.W.; Trustees, Brothers Colonel Cotton, Lord de Tabley, P.G.S.W., W. C. Cruttenden, P.G.S.W., H. A. Bennett, P.G.R., E. G. Willoughby, P.G.J.W., E. Samuelson, P.G.J.D., and J. Brattan, P.M. 701; Brother Moss, Treasurer, and Brothers J. P. Platt and H. Bulley, joint Honorary Secretaries. All the Worshipful Masters of the Province, together with the Secretaries and Treasurer, were appointed a working committee to carry out the functions of the institution, the place of meeting to be Birkenhead. The matter was taken up vigorously, and at the first Provincial Grand Lodge meeting held afterwards two elections were made. Brother Willoughby, the Chairman of the Committee, in his report issued in September 1864, complained, however, that apathy was shown by many lodges in the Province, although he thanked many individual brethren for their support, more especially the members of the Provincial Grand Lodge, for their cordial co-operation.

In 1864, at Dukinfield, it was decided that out of the balance in hand there should be invested in Birkenhead Dock bonds sufficient to make up the total investment of £1000. When the late Lord de Tabley assumed office as Provincial Grand Master early in 1865, almost his first duty was to call a Provincial Grand Lodge of Emergency at Crewe for the purpose of voting an address of condolence to the widow and family of their late beloved and lamented Provincial Grand Master, Field-Marshal the Viscount Combermere. Lord Combermere died at Combermere Abbey on the 21st February 1865, aged 91; but it is very remarkable that in the accounts which have appeared of his life there is little or no reference to his distinguished career as a Freemason. This venerated nobleman presided over the craft in the Province from 1830 to 1865, but we will allow the address presented to his family on his decease to throw a sidelight, so to speak, on its history. "The deeds which have rendered his name so conspicuous in the history of the nineteenth century," proceeds the address, "require no comment. The voice of a grateful nation will ever rank him foremost amongst the heroic band, the companions in arms of the illustrious Wellington, who so nobly struggled against the despotic power of Napoleon, and whose efforts were crowned by glorious victory, from which resulted a peace of forty years' duration. It is of that latter portion of his Lordship's long and useful career that they desire now to speak; and it is with heartfelt gratitude that they briefly recount his efforts for the promotion of those kindly principles dear to the heart of every Freemason. When Lord Combermere first accepted the office of Provincial Grand Master, Masonry in Cheshire was at a low ebb. The lodges were few in number, and its beneficial operation little known or appreciated; but his energetic, judicious, and benevolent efforts for its resuscitation were soon crowned with success. Wherever he appeared amongst his brethren, his kindly and courteous bearing, his sound and discreet advice gave an impetus to Masonry that has rarely, if ever, been equalled. New life was infused into every part of the Province, and men of all ranks rallied around him, anxious to assist in the extended diffusion of the pure principles on which the ancient, sacred, and Royal Order is founded. Under his Lordship's fostering care, Charity, which so pre-eminently distinguished Freemasonry, has assumed a tangible shape in the Province; and it is their earnest prayer that the example he has so worthily set, and the benefits conferred on the Craft through his Lordship's instrumentality may, for generations to come, serve as incitements to a noble emulation amongst his successors."

The installation of Lord de Tabley followed in due course. This event took place at the Assembly Room, Knutsford, adjacent to his Lordship's county seat at Tabley, on Tuesday, 1st August 1865, by the Right Hon. Earl de Grey and Ripon, D.G.M. of England, in the presence of a large assembly of other distinguished brethren, including Brothers Sedgewick, V.W.G.C.; I. L. Evans, V.W. President B. of G. Purposes; Sir Albert W. Woods, W.G.D.C.; Sir W. Watkin Wynn, Bart., R.W.P.G.M. of North Wales and Shropshire; Sir T. B. Hesketh, Bart., M.P., R.W.P.G.M. Designate of West Lancashire; T. H. Hall, R.W.P.G.M., Cambridgeshire; Colonel H. A. Bowyer, R.W.P.G.M., Oxfordshire; Captain Cope, W.G.S.B., and a full attendance of Provincial Grand Officers, Worshipful Masters, Past Masters, and Wardens of the lodges of this and adjoining Provinces. The ceremony of installation having been duly performed, Lord de Tabley assured them it would ever be his study to advance the interests of Freemasonry. The Provincial Grand Treasurer (Brother Bland) congratulated the brethren on the satisfactory state of the funds, and stated that a further sum of £700 had been invested since the last meeting of the Provincial Grand Lodge. Ten guineas were subsequently voted to the funds of the Royal Masonic Institution for Boys, and Provincial Grand Master invested his officers for the ensuing year.

At the next Provincial Grand Lodge meeting, held at Stockport, Lord de Tabley had to express his extreme satisfaction at the warm interest that had been displayed in the cause of Charity, he having, by the operation of the Fund of Benevolence Committee, subsequently confirmed by the Provincial Grand Lodge, been placed in the proud position of Vice-President of all the Great Masonic Charities—an honour not enjoyed by any other Provincial Grand Master. On 22nd August 1867 the foundation stone of St Thomas's Church

Hyde, was laid with Masonic honours by the Provincial Grand Master, Lord de Tabley, " in the presence of an immense assemblage of people." The handsome silver trowel used on the occasion was presented to the Provincial Grand Master through their Worshipful Master by the members of the Lodge of Industry, No. 361. It bore the following inscription : " Presented to Brother Lord de Tabley, R.W.P.G.M. of Cheshire, by Lodge Industry, No. 361, on the occasion of his laying the foundation stone of St Thomas's Church, Hyde, 22nd August 1867. John Burgess, W.M., Frank Wrigley, S.W., Beriah Cooper, J.W."

It is noteworthy that this is the first occasion on which the Provincial Grand Master Lord de Tabley signed the minutes after confirmation.

This year (1867) his Lordship consecrated three lodges, viz., the " Oakwood " at Romiley, the " Ashton " at Cheadle, and the " Clarendon " at Hyde, two of which, the " Oakwood " and the " Clarendon," still flourish. At the Provincial Grand Lodge, held at Chester, the Provincial Grand Master presented Brother James Bland, P.G.T., with a handsome gold watch and appendages as a small token of their recognition of his valuable services during the fourteen years he had held that office. The revised bye-laws of the Province were confirmed at Macclesfield in the following year (1868), and a sum of 25 guineas was voted as a contribution to the testimonial fund for celebrating the twenty-fifth year of the rule of Lord Zetland, M.W.G.M. A grant of 20 guineas was made to the Cheshire Educational Masonic Institution, whose prosperous position was now acknowledged, and Captain Cope, P.G.S.W., also gave 20 guineas, making the Senior Grand Warden of Cheshire a Vice-President of so useful an institution. An interesting speech was made on this occasion by Brother G. W. Latham, J.G.D. of England, who referred to the fact that at that time there was a party of surveyors and archæologists engaged in tracing the ancient buildings in Jerusalem, and in endeavouring to bring to light every vestige of that ancient city. This study was peculiarly interesting to Freemasons, because although some of them might doubt whether the earliest traditions of Masonry were absolutely and accurately true, the greatest sceptic among them could not hesitate to believe that their ceremonies and forms were all derived from the ancient Temple at Jerusalem. Everything, therefore, that was discovered in that capital, whether respecting the ancient ordinances or the particular shape and marks of the building, must be interesting to them as Masons. He, therefore, moved that a grant of 10 guineas be made to the Palestine Exploration Fund, and this being seconded by Brother Bland, P.G.T., was unanimously agreed to.

This year the Province had to lament the retirement of the Deputy Provincial Grand Master, Lord Combermere, son of the previous Provincial Grand Master, and he was succeeded by Brother George Cornwall Legh, M.P., P.G.S.W. Captain Cope was elected Chairman of the Fund of Benevolence.

In 1870 Provincial Grand Lodge was held at Congleton, when his Lordship referred to the satisfaction with which he found himself in that ancient borough, ancient and respectable in every way—a borough they looked up to with regard. He pointed to the progress made in the Province, and stated that when he first presided over them they had hardly a single vote for any of the Charities. They had now upwards of 500 votes and had paid to the different Charities during the past five years, from the funds of Provincial Grand Lodge, no less than £350, 10s., in addition to £184, 15s. for relief in individual cases. During the year a Masonic address was presented to Brother H.R.H. the Prince of Wales (Edward VII.)—an interesting event in any case, but peculiarly so in this case, as it was the first Masonic address received by His Royal Highness on the rank of Grand Master being conferred upon him. This year, it will be remembered, the terrible war between France and Germany raged for a comparatively brief period, but, though brief, it was waged with sanguinary effect on both sides. A fund was raised under the auspices of Her Majesty the Queen and H.R.H. the Prince of Wales, K.G., G.M., for aid to the sick and wounded, and as in many other instances, the Provincial Grand Lodge of Cheshire, as became its dignity and position, was the first to move in the matter. At an especial Provincial Grand Lodge of Emergency, held at Crewe, a grant of £50 was made. It might be said that the recipients of their Charity were foreigners and not Englishmen, but, added the Provincial Grand Master, "the cause of Charity is much larger than any nationality." He looked forward to the time when Masonry would so flourish that our craft might stretch forth its hand, not only to a Mason, but to every suffering creature. They had in the Bible one of the best known illustrations of Charity. They would all remember that it referred to one who was sick and wounded by the wayside, and that the one who gave him succour was not one of his own race, kindred, or even religion, but a foreigner and a heretic. It therefore well became the craft of England to endeavour to assist their suffering fellow-creatures by following so holy an example. In order to make the Provincial Grand Master a Vice-Patron of the Royal Masonic Institution for Boys and Girls, 100 guineas was voted from the funds for that purpose at Crewe in 1872.

CHAPTER XXV.

Provincial Grand Lodge History continued) : More votes for central Institutions—Gift to Chester Cathedral—Masonic progress in the Province—Death of Brother George Cornwall Legh, D.P.G.M. —Vote for Indian Famine Fund—Attempted assassination of Queen Victoria—Wirral Children's Hospital—Last Letters of Lord de Tabley—Death of a veteran Mason at Stockport—Interesting meeting at Altrincham—Cheshire Educational Institution—Resignation of Lord de Tabley—Installation of Lord Egerton of Tatton as P.G.M.—His duties during Jubilee Year—Resignation of Brother E. H. Griffiths—Jubilee appointments—Brother Newhouse, Provincial Secretary—Stockport Technical Schools—An enjoyable day at Tatton—Honours for Sir Horatio Lloyd—Cheshire Masonic Benevolent Institution inaugurated.

THE stream of Masonry seems to have flowed steadily and prosperously on. In 1874 Brother Bland, owing to ill-health, resigned the office of Provincial Grand Treasurer, which he had held for a quarter of a century, and was succeeded by Brother F. Jackson, whose services as a deputy had marked him out as specially fitted to discharge the duties with efficiency. A sum of 150 guineas was voted to the funds of the Royal Masonic Institution for Boys, constituting the Deputy Provincial Grand Master a Vice-Patron in perpetuity of that institution, and a sum of £100 was voted to the R.B. Institution for aged Freemasons and their Widows, having a similar object in view in connection with the institution. The valuable services of Brother J. P. Platt, as one of the founders of the Cheshire Educational Masonic Institution, as also active in the cause of Charity generally, were suitably recognised by the presentation to him of a gold chronometer, with appendages. The gift of a pulpit to Chester Cathedral forms a valuable item in indicating Masonic interest in our " stately and superb," as well as sacred, edifices. In September 1875 an important step was taken in making the influence of the Province felt more extensively in connection with the Royal Masonic Institution for Boys, when a sum of 500 guineas was granted for the purpose of aiding in the purchase of a perpetual presentation to that institution. The sum required was 1000 guineas, and after the matter had been considered by the Committee, a further amount of 500 guineas was granted from the Fund of Benevolence to complete the purchase. The presentation of the nomination was in the name of the Provincial Grand Master for the time being, the Chairman of the Fund of Benevolence, and the Provincial Grand Treasurer, power being reserved, on proper notice being given, to make any alteration that might seem expedient. The north-east corner stone of the Chancel of St Mary's Church, Newton Moor, was laid, 4th March 1876, by the Provincial Grand Master, Lord de Tabley. The Vicar of Newton (Brother the Rev. G. Jones) presented a silver trowel to the Provincial Grand Master as the gift of the teachers and scholars of St Mary's National and Hallbottom Sunday

Royal Masonic School for Boys, Bushey, Herts.

Brother WILLIAM BOOTH,
P.G A D. C, England.

schools. His Lordship, in accepting the trowel, expressed the great pleasure it gave him at being engaged in so interesting a ceremony. At the Provincial Grand Lodge meeting, held at Knutsford on the 20th September, his Lordship took occasion to review the progress made in the Province during his eleven years of office as Provincial Grand Master. At that time there were only twenty-six lodges, now thirty-nine. Also he said there was scarcely a vote for any of the noble charities which distinguished the order, but now, by the liberality of the Provincial Grand Lodge, he was Vice-Patron of the three great Institutions in London; the Deputy Provincial Grand Master occupied the same position; the Provincial Grand Senior Warden was in perpetuity a Vice-President of the Boys' School; and the Provincial Grand Junior Warden a Vice-President in perpetuity of the Boys' School, while there was scarcely a Master in the Province who was not a life governor of some of the Charities. The brethren had also presented a handsome pulpit to the Cathedral of Chester at a cost of £450, chiefly raised by individual subscriptions. The carvings on the pulpit represent the building of King Solomon's Temple, the preaching of St John the Baptist in the Wilderness, and the showing of the Heavenly City of the Apocalypse to St John the Evangelist. Lastly, from the funds of the Provincial Grand Lodge and from private subscriptions, they had purchased a perpetual presentation to the Boys' School in London.

In 1877 the brethren had to deplore the death of Brother Geo. Cornwall Legh, M.P., D.P.G.M. At the Provincial Grand Lodge held at Liscard, 20th September 1877, the sum of £100 was voted to the fund for the relief of the sufferers by famine in India; and at the same meeting Brother the Hon. Wilbraham Egerton, M.P., assumed the office of Deputy Provincial Grand Master. After a lapse of eighteen years Provincial Grand Lodge was held on the 12th September 1878, at Nantwich. At Runcorn, in 1880, the sum of 50 guineas was voted to the R.B.I. for aged Freemasons, and 50 guineas to the R.B.I. for Widows, thereby giving the Provincial Grand Master thirty votes at each election.

At the annual meeting of Provincial Grand Lodge at Macclesfield, 21st September 1881, the sum of 100 guineas was voted to the Royal Masonic School for Girls, and on the 21st March 1882 a special meeting was called at Crewe, when a resolution, expressive of horror and indignation felt by the brethren at the attempt on the life of Her Majesty the Queen Victoria, and their deep sense of gratitude at her happy escape under divine providence, was passed. An address embodying the sentiments of the brethren was duly drawn up, engrossed, and presented through the proper authority, the Queen returning thanks through Sir Henry Ponsonby.

An interesting event took place in the laying of the foundation stone of the Wirral Children's Hospital, with Masonic honours, in July 1882, by Lord de Tabley, P.G.M. The request came from the Mayor of Birkenhead (W. Laird,

Esq.), who represented the Building Committee, and a very beautiful trowel, provided by Alderman Roper at his own cost, was presented to Lord de Tabley by that gentleman. Afterwards thanks were accorded to Mr Clarke, architect, for his handsome present of mallet, level, square, and plumb rule, and to Brother Marquis for his present of a bearing altar for the volume of the Sacred Law, and five velvet cushions and wands for the use of the Provincial Grand Lodge. In this year the Provincial Grand Master, Lord de Tabley, was presented with his portrait by the brethren.

The condition of the Provincial Grand Master's health now began to give grave anxiety to the brethren. At the meeting of Provincial Grand Lodge held at Northwich on the 6th September 1882, the chair was occupied by Brother G. W. Latham, who in feeling terms alluded to the presentation of the portrait to Lord de Tabley and also to the touching nature of the ceremony. Much as the brethren desired it, they were never to see his Lordship in his place at their head again. There is also something touching in the letter his Lordship wrote to Brother the Right Hon. Lord Egerton of Tatton, D.P.G.M., dated Tabley House, Knutsford, 24th September 1882 :—

"My dear Brother Egerton,—It is with infinite reluctance that I am again compelled, by continued ill-health, to absent myself from Provincial Grand Lodge, and to call upon your kind assistance to preside over the brethren in my stead, but I know how ably you will do so, and how completely I can depend on the loyalty and affection of my brethren to support you, as my deputy, in the chair. Pray say to them how deeply I deplore not being able to take my place amongst them. Till lately I had hoped to have been able to do so, but my recovery is very slow. I trust it may please the Great Architect of the Universe to spare me 'yet a little while,' to continue my efforts for the good of the Craft and the Province which I have had such pride and pleasure in ruling. I know how brightly burns the flame of Freemasonry, and I most specially and deeply regret not being able to meet my brethren at Stalybridge."

This is, unfortunately, only a specimen of several letters, the reproduction of which might give to this brief sketch too mournful a cast; suffice it, that while events in the Province went smoothly and well, his Lordship, until called to the Grand Lodge above, watched them with a keenness which betokened the interest he had in a cause dear to his heart. Amongst the events of these later years was the opening of the Masonic Hall at Chester in 1883, the grant of 250 guineas to the Royal Masonic Institution for Boys, entitling the Province to 100 votes in perpetuity, and the presentation by Brother Robert Hunter, P.G.S.D., in the names of the three Stalybridge Lodges, of a handsomely bound Blackletter Bible, printed in the year 1620. The death of the oldest Freemason in the Province, Brother Cheetham of Stockport, at the age of ninety-eight years, took place this year (1883), and his remains were followed to the grave by a large number of his brethren, and interred with full Masonic honours.

The year 1884 will be memorable for the presentations which were made at the annual meeting at Altrincham on the 18th September. Brother S. von Sturmer, W.M. of the Stamford Lodge, No. 1045, in recognition of the great honour conferred by the Provincial Grand Lodge in selecting Altrincham as the place of meeting for that year, and being anxious to testify in some degree their sense of that honour, asked the acceptance of the brethren of two processional wardens' columns, which were accepted in a most courteous spirit by the Deputy Provincial Grand Master. Brother Marwood, P.G.S.W., in the names of the present and past Provincial Grand Officers, next presented Provincial Grand Lodge with a very handsome silver consecration service. He added that great praise was due to Brother H. Finch, P.G.D.C., for his zeal and labour in obtaining the necessary funds. The want of such a service had long been felt, and as the members of Provincial Grand Chapter had also subscribed towards the service, he trusted it might be at their disposal when required. And all good Masons will join in his concluding sentence, " that this consecration service might become curious from its antiquity in promoting the interests of Freemasonry, and he might also add, the honour and glory of the Great Architect of the Universe."

This year will also be memorable for the attack made upon Masonry from a leading quarter abroad. It is almost unnecessary to say that English Freemasonry is a very different sample to that which passes current for it in many continental countries ; but the admirable and conclusive way in which it was answered by the Provincial Grand Master, the Earl of Carnarvon, as to the religious objects and the law-abiding tenets of British Masonry, was universally adopted and approved by brethren and the vast majority of the outside public throughout the Empire.

Twenty years of the rule of Lord de Tabley as Provincial Grand Master had passed away in 1885, and at Birkenhead in that year, the Deputy Provincial Grand Master, Lord Egerton of Tatton, stated that during that period the Province had acquired 600 votes for the Boys' Institution, 400 for the Girls', 400 for the aged Freemasons', and 200 for the Widows'. Two of the Cheshire candidates had been this year elected on the London Charitable Institutions ; six boys were maintained at a cost of £45 each per annum, six girls at £40, and five widows at £32 each, so that the Province received from these Institutions a sum equivalent to nearly £1000 per annum. In addition to these benefits the Cheshire Educational Institution maintained twenty-eight children at a cost of £200 per annum, the interest from their investments producing an income of £222, and notwithstanding all this they were still fairly within their annual income. This year also marked the close of the five years' service of Brother Finch as Director of Ceremonies, and on the motion of Brother Beresford,

P.P.G.D., seconded by Brother F. K. Stevenson, P.P.G.S.B., a vote of thanks was passed by acclamation to him for the eminent services he had rendered in that capacity, and which subsequent events will show was as eminently deserved.

In September 1886 Lord de Tabley, owing to increasing inability to attend to the active duties of the office, placed his resignation as Provincial Grand Master of Cheshire in the hands of the Grand Master, H.R.H. the Prince of Wales. In November he caused the acceptance to be made public, and tendered his sincere and heartfelt thanks to the brethren for their loyal and affectionate support. During the twenty-one years of his rule, sixteen lodges had been added to the number existing in the Province; 1700 votes had been added to the number at the disposal of the Province—thus enabling it to carry the election of nearly every one of their candidates for the Masonic Charities; and the Cheshire Educational Masonic Institution had been formed for aiding the education and advancement in life of the children of poor and distressed Freemasons, whose capital was £5350. It was, therefore, with satisfaction and thankfulness that he could hand over his beloved Province to his successor, and, praying always for the unity, harmony, and prosperity, he, with heartfelt regret, bade them farewell. His Lordship (who died on the 19th October 1887) was succeeded by the Right Hon. the Lord Egerton of Tatton, under whose business-like and genial rule the Province, as will be seen by subsequent events, greatly flourished and more than maintained its splendid traditions.

There was something appropriate in the fact that the installation ceremony should take place in the spacious Town Hall of Chester, the capital of the Province, and this notable function was attended by a large number of brethren. It took place on the 15th April 1887, and the attendance of Grand Officers and Provincial Grand Officers from surrounding Provinces was the largest and most brilliant up to that time ever known in the history of the Province. The Right Hon. the Earl of Lathom, R.W.D.G.M. of England, represented the Grand Master, and acted as Installing Officer. He was supported, amongst others, by Earl Amherst, P.G.M. of Kent; Colonel Le Gendre Starkie, P.G.M. of East Lancashire; Sir Offley Wakeman, P.G.M. of Shropshire; the Hon. Sackville West, P.G.W. of England; the Rev. G. R. Portal, P.G.C. of England; Colonel Platt, D.P.G.M. of North Wales; His Honour Judge Horatio Lloyd; Rev. W. C. Spencer-Stanhope, P.G.C. of England; G. Sinclair, P.P.S.W. of West Lancashire; Rev. E. J. Reeve, I.G.C.L.; John Chadwick, P.G.S. of East Lancashire; W. Goodacre, G.S.B., etc.

The R.W.D.G.M. touched on the deep regret of the brethren at the resignation of Lord de Tabley, and, condoling with them upon his loss, heartily congratulated them upon having secured so able a successor as Lord Egerton of Tatton. The R.W.P.G.M. Designate was introduced by seven brethren of Lodges Stamford, No. 1045 (Altrincham), De Tabley, No. 941 (Knutsford),

Independence, No. 721 (Chester), Cestrian, No. 425 (Chester), Unity, No. 321 (Crewe), St John's, No. 104 (Stockport), Unanimity, No. 89 (Dukinfield).

The ceremony of installation having been gone through, the R.W.P.G.M. thanked the brethren for the hearty reception accorded to him on his appointment by His Royal Highness, the Most Worshipful Grand Master, as Provincial Grand Master of Cheshire. He assured them it would be his duty to follow in the footsteps of Lord de Tabley, to whom he paid a graceful tribute for the excellent work he had done during the past twenty-one years, and hoped the same record might be continued under his own rule. Subsequently, his Lordship invested Brother Sir Horatio Lloyd as Deputy Provincial Grand Master, and the other brethren then holding Provincial Grand Office were requested to continue their duties until the succeeding Provincial Grand Lodge at Crewe. The brethren attended Divine Service at the Cathedral, where an eloquent and appropriate sermon was preached by Brother the Rev. Canon Portal, P.G.C. of England, from 1 Kings vii. 15.

In October Provincial Grand Lodge was held at Crewe, and it may be considered remarkable as the first assumption of official duties by the Provincial Grand Master, and the Jubilee year of Queen Victoria. The Provincial Grand Master was, therefore, justified in referring to the pride which he, in common with all Freemasons, felt at the appreciation they had shown of the great services rendered to the nation by Her Majesty by most liberal contributions to Masonic Charities. No less a sum than £26,000 had been raised by English Freemasons for the benefit of those who were distressed and in want of pecuniary aid for the purposes of education and the relief of old age. His Lordship also expressed his gratification that the first meeting of Provincial Grand Lodge over which he had to preside as Grand Master should have been held at Crewe, the town in which a quarter of a century before he was initiated into Freemasonry. In conclusion, his Lordship proposed that a letter of condolence and sympathy should be addressed to Lady de Tabley in the loss she had sustained by the death of Lord de Tabley. The resolution was seconded by the Deputy Provincial Grand Master, and carried unanimously.

The presentation of a silver salver and a purse containing about £150 to the retiring Provincial Grand Secretary, Brother Edward H. Griffiths, followed. His Lordship thought it was almost unprecedented that during forty-seven years, and during the lives of three Provincial Grand Masters, the office should have been held for so long a period, and the duties should have been performed with such assiduity and courtesy by Brother Griffiths. As they would not find it likely to lead to a precedent he moved that he have a retiring pension of £50 granted to him. The proposition was seconded by Brother Lisle, and carried with the utmost unanimity. The venerable Secretary was visibly affected. He briefly returned thanks, particularly to Lord Egerton for his kind expressions. He added that he had served under three Grand Masters, and had never had the slightest unpleasantness with any of them. A pleasing feature also was the investing, by the Provincial Grand Master, of the following brethren, by special favour of H.R.H., the Grand Master, with Past Provincial rank to commemorate the Jubilee year of Her Majesty the Queen :—Brothers Joseph Slack and Wm. M. Lightfoot, as Past Provincial Grand Senior Deacons ; Brothers Samuel Jones and Wm. Johnson, as Past Provincial Grand Junior Deacons ; Brother John Blackhurst, as Provincial Grand Superintendent of Works ; Brothers Thomas Moore and Thomas A. Daniels, as Past Provincial Grand Sword Bearers ; Brothers George Moss and J. Kendrick, as Past Provincial Grand Standard Bearers ; and Brother Charles Booth, as Provincial Grand Pursuivant. On this occasion Brother Richard Newhouse was nominated to the office of Provincial Grand Secretary by his Lordship, and duly invested. Brother Newhouse, he said, was a Mason of long standing, and had had high honours conferred upon him, both in the Craft, Mark, and Royal Arch degrees. He was first Secretary of the Stamford Lodge, No. 1045, and on the occasion of his attaining twenty-one years' service in that capacity in 1887, he was presented with his portrait in oils. He had also discharged the duties of Provincial Grand Secretary of Mark Master Masons in Cheshire, was a Past Grand Deacon of the Mark Lodge of England, and Past Grand Sword Bearer, England.

The foundation stone of Stockport Technical School was laid on 8th September 1888, by Brother Polydore de Keyzer, G.S. of England, Lord Mayor of London, in the presence of a vast assemblage of people. His Lordship subscribed ten guineas to the funds of the Cheshire Educational Masonic Institution, and Mr Sedger, architect of the schools, presented to Provincial Grand Lodge a set of Ionic, Doric, and Corinthian lights. At the site, a beautifully illuminated address, on vellum, bound in garter blue morocco, and ornamented with Masonic emblems, was presented to the Right Hon. the Lord Mayor, by Brother Lieut.-Colonel Wilkinson, P.P.G.S.D., on behalf of the Freemasons of Stockport. The address in cordial terms welcomed his Lordship to Stockport, and spoke of the honour conferred upon the borough, at the invitation of the Mayor, to discharge that important duty of laying the corner-stone of a school for the technical instruction of the rising population of the town and district. Proceeding, the address stated: " Freemasonry has ever been identified with objects and institutions tending to promote the well-being, happiness, and prosperity of the community at large. Believing as we do, that the Stockport Technical School, commencing with such good and hopeful intentions, is eminently calculated to yield the most beneficent results, we feel sure that your Lordship and the members of the craft who have assisted you in this interesting ceremonial will always look back with pride and satisfaction on the work that your Lordship has this day so kindly inaugurated." The address was signed by William Gleave, W.M. 104, St John's ; George

M'Clelland, W.M. 287, Unanimity; David Higson, W.M. 322, Peace; and James Breen, W.M. 323, Concord, on behalf of the brethren of these Lodges.

In 1888 the annual meeting of Provincial Grand Lodge was held at Knutsford, the Provincial Grand Master, Lord Egerton of Tatton, presiding. His Lordship referred with pride to the fact that at the annual meeting in connection with the Royal Masonic School for Girls, the sum of £50,000, the largest ever known at such a gathering, had been subscribed by the Masons of England. After Divine Service at Knutsford Parish Church, where the sermon was preached by the Rev. W. Coleman Martin, P.G.C., the brethren spent a most enjoyable afternoon at Tatton, the ancestral seat of the Provincial Grand Master. The gardens and grounds were thrown open, and every provision made for the pleasure and comfort of the brethren, many of whom were accompanied by their wives. His Lordship, accompanied by Lady Egerton, went in and out amongst them, and in the evening a number congregated in front of the Hall, and on the proposition of Brother J. Beresford, P.P.G.J.D., a cordial vote of thanks was accorded to their noble host. Lord Egerton briefly replied, after which the brethren sang "Worthy Mason He." The National Anthem followed, and the brethren returned to their respective homes.

At the Provincial Meeting at Hyde in 1889, the Provincial Grand Master, while congratulating the brethren on the steady increase of Masonry in the Province, alluded to the removal by death of several of their oldest and most valued members, including Brother E. H. Griffiths, P.G.S. for nearly fifty years; Brother John Wood of Arden, P.G.S.W., a constant attender for thirty years; Brother James Arthur Birch, one of their best workers; Brother Fleming of Stockport, P.G. Tyler; and Brother Steward, a Mason for sixty years, and who had attended fifty Provincial Grand Lodges in succession. Subsequently a committee was appointed to revise the bye-laws of Provincial Grand Lodges. Brother Platt was thanked for his past services as Chairman in connection with the Fund of Benevolence. Brother Salmon was appointed in his place, and Brother Clayton, Deputy Chairman.

In 1890 Judge Sir Horatio Lloyd, V.W.D.P.G.M., received the congratulations of Provincial Grand Lodge on the honour of Knighthood, which it had pleased her Most Gracious Majesty to confer upon him. The revised bye-laws and regulations prepared by the committee appointed in September 1889 were adopted.

The annual meeting of Provincial Grand Lodge was held at the Mechanics' Institution, Stockport, on 17th September 1890, the Provincial Grand Master, Lord Egerton of Tatton, in the chair. The report of the Committee of the Provincial Fund of Benevolence was submitted, and showed that by an alteration on the bye-laws a Charity Committee could be elected, and by the admission of a member from each lodge, in addition to several *ex-officio* members, a greater interest in the Local Charities—that is to say, the Fund of Benevolence and the Cheshire Masonic Educational Institution—and also in the three great London Charities, would be stimulated. Afterwards, the Provincial Grand Officers were duly invested. Brother James Cookson, P.M., was unanimously elected Provincial Grand Treasurer, the selection, judging from the plaudits of the brethren, being a very popular one.

The most important event in the Province which had occurred for many years past was the inauguration festival of the Cheshire Masonic Benevolent Institution, which was celebrated at the Town Hall, Chester, in June 1893. As a result the sum of £3180 was invested. In 1895 the Provincial Grand Master congratulated the brethren at the annual meeting that the membership had risen to 2235, and that at the Boys' School Festival, over which he had presided, Cheshire had contributed the sum of £20,598. In 1896 the Festival of the Benevolent Charities realised £2200. A vote of congratulation was passed, by acclamation, to Queen Victoria on the celebration of her Diamond Jubilee.

In 1897 the Provincial Grand Master was presented with an illuminated address congratulating him on having been raised to the dignity of an Earl by Her Majesty the Queen, and in the year following, at the annual meeting at Altrincham, his Lordship said that the year had been a record in the history of Provincial Grand Lodge. There were now 52 lodges on the Roll, and 2466 members. He reported that he had attended the Centenary Festival of the Boys' School as a Steward, where the sum of £3000 was contributed by Cheshire. In August 1900, at Stockport, hearty appreciation was expressed by the members on the choice Her Majesty had made in the appointment of Earl Egerton as Lord-Lieutenant of the County, in succession to the late Duke of Westminster, K.G. They looked upon it as an acknowledgment of services freely and unstintingly given to the improvement of intellectual, social, moral, and material prosperity of the Country in general and the County of Chester in particular. Later on in the year, owing to increasing duties, notably in connection with the Manchester Ship Canal, his Lordship placed in the hands of the Grand Master, H.R.H. the Prince of Wales, his resignation as Provincial Grand Master of Cheshire, and in a letter addressed to the brethren, thanked them for the support he had received in discharging the duties of the office, and especially for the generous response they had made to the appeals in support of the Masonic Charities during the fourteen years he had had the honour of presiding over the Province. He had pleasure in handing over to his successor a Province in which Masonry was in a progressive and flourishing state. The loss to Masonry and to the Province, we may add, was severely felt, and keen regret was widespread at the event.

Chidlaw   *Chester*

Brother Alderman D. L. HEWITT,
P.A.G.D.C., England

LORD EGERTON OF TATTON,
Past Provincial Grand Master of Cheshire.

CHAPTER XXVI.

Installation of Hon. Alan de Tatton Egerton, M.P.—Progress in the Wirral Peninsula—Sympathy with the United States on President M'Kinley's assassination—Presentations to Brothers Newhouse and Annett—Centenary Festivals—Notable Meeting at Stockport—Resignation of Sir Horatio Lloyd—Installation of Lieut.-Colonel Legh—Dedication of Masonic Hall, Chester—Consecration of the Lodge of King Solomon's Temple—Festival of the three local Benevolent Institutions—Sympathy with Lord Kitchener's family—Memorable meeting at New Brighton—The 1918 meeting at Northwich—Brother Joseph Clarke, Provincial Grand Secretary—Brethren and their part in the Great War—Masonic Benevolence in 1918—The Earl of Chester (H.R.H. Prince of Wales) joins the Brotherhood—The late Brother Sir John Brunner—Memorable meeting at Chester in 1919—The Royal Arch and Mark Degrees in Cheshire—Succession of Provincial Grand Masters, 1901-19, and List of Provincial Grand Officers, etc.

THE installation of the Hon. Alan de Tatton Egerton, M.P., P.G.W. of England, as Right Worshipful Provincial Grand Master of Cheshire, took place at the Town Hall, Chester, in December 1900, in succession to his brother, the Right Hon. Earl Egerton of Tatton, who had been obliged to resign the office which he had held with such distinction for fourteen years, owing to the pressure of numerous public engagements. Every lodge in the Province was represented, and over 600 brethren were present. The Deputy Provincial Grand Master, His Honour Judge Sir Horatio Lloyd, opened Provincial Grand Lodge, and Brother E. Letchworth, Grand Secretary of England, acted as Installing Master, supported by numerous Grand and Provincial Grand Officers of this and neighbouring Provinces, to the number of 120.

A vote of thanks to his Worship, the Mayor of Chester, for the use of the Town Hall for the ceremony, was duly passed, and a collection was made in aid of the Masonic and Educational Institutions of Cheshire.

It was at the annual meeting at West Kirby, in September 1901, that the newly installed Provincial Grand Master delivered his first address to the brethren. He dwelt on the progress which Masonry was making in the Province, and especially in the Wirral Peninsula. There were fifty-five lodges in the Province and the membership was increasing, but he tempered his remarks with some excellent advice, warning the brethren as to the introduction of suitable candidates for initiation to the lodges. There had been a generous response to the appeal for the local benevolent institutions. A resolution of sympathy with the American people on the death of their President (Brother W. M'Kinley, assassinated 14th September 1901), who had done so much to increase the spirit of brotherhood existing between Great Britain and the American people, was passed. Especial meetings of the Provincial Grand Lodge were held in October and November for the purpose of laying the foundation stone of the new school of Christ Church, Stalybridge, and of St Mary's Parish Hall, Liscard. The Committee of Benevolence reported that at the Festival held at Knutsford in the previous year, in aid of the Cheshire Charitable Institutions, the total amount raised was £2052, 11s.

In 1902 at the Knutsford meeting the Rev. Dr C. C. Atkinson, P.P.G.C., presented for the use of Provincial Grand Lodge a gavel and stand made in Jerusalem from olive wood grown in King Solomon's garden. An illuminated address, in album form, was presented to his Honour Sir Horatio Lloyd, D.P.G.M., Kt., J.P., K.C., etc., tendering the congratulations of the meeting on his having completed his fiftieth year as a member of the fraternity, and wishing him long life and continued health and strength to discharge the high and important functions of the various public offices he so admirably filled. At his request the sum of £210, raised by the brethren for the purpose of presenting him with some token of affection and esteem, was devoted to the purchase of votes in the Royal Masonic Benevolent Institutions, resulting in an additional sixty votes for aged Masons and Widows. This thoughtful, kind, and generous act, the address added, would no doubt be a cause of thankfulness and blessing to the recipients in future years.

At Liscard in the following year a presentation was made to Brother Richard Newhouse, P.G.S.B. of England, P.G.S., of the sum of £460, in recognition of his valuable services to the Province. He was also heartily congratulated on having attained his jubilee of Freemasonry. Brother Newhouse in reply said he was thankful that his work as Provincial Grand Secretary had been appreciated. He believed he was the oldest Provincial Grand Secretary in England. He represented the oldest Province in the country, and probably in the world.

The Provincial Meeting of 1904 was held at Hyde. The Provincial Grand Master, in his address, said that the past year had been no less productive in good work than its predecessors. On this occasion Brother Thos. Henry Annett was presented with a Provincial Grand Treasurer's jewel and an illuminated address in recognition of his valuable services as Treasurer of the Cheshire Masonic Benevolent Institution, and as a mark of his untiring energy in the interests of the aged and necessitous. It is pleasing to add that Brother Annett's services have since been continued on their previous efficient basis, and he will, no doubt, live to see the good work, which has been so rudely interrupted by the World War (1914-18), resumed and brought to a triumphant climax in the near future.

It was shown in 1905 that great strides had been made in charitable work in the previous forty years. In 1865, when Lord de Tabley became Provincial Grand Master, the Province only held ten votes. In September 1885, when he resigned office, the Province held the following:—600 Boys votes, 400 Girls, 400 aged Freemasons, and 400 Widows. At that time (1905) votes numbered

2178 Boys votes, 1093 Girls, 1765 aged Freemasons, and 1117 Widows. In addition they had a perpetual presentation to the Boys' School, and two local institutions for the benefit of aged Freemasons and further education and maintenance of the orphan children of Freemasons.

The year 1906 witnessed the Centenary Festival of no fewer than five lodges in the Province—St John's, No. 104, Stockport; Lodge of Unity, No. 321, Crewe; Lodge of Peace, No. 322, Stockport; Lodge of Concord, No. 323, Stockport; and Moira, Stalybridge.

At the annual meeting at Birkenhead in 1907 there was a very large gathering of brethren, and the Provincial Grand Master congratulated the Charity Council of the Province on their successful work. The Province was fortunate in having such an indefatigable body of Masons of such eminence and experience on its Council. Having regard to the number of lodges which had celebrated their centenary in the preceding year, he suggested that each lodge in the Province should hold a festival on every twenty-fifth year of its existence in order to help forward the good work. In the following year (1908) the annual meeting was held at the Auditorium, Port Sunlight. The spacious edifice was placed at the disposal of the brethren by Brother W. Hesketh Lever, now Lord Leverhulme. Although the weather was very inclement, there was a large gathering of brethren, who highly appreciated the arrangements made for their convenience and comfort. This year the Centenary Festival of the Lodge of Benevolence, No. 336, Marple, was celebrated, and the laying of the foundation stone of the new Masonic Hall at Chester, by Lord Egerton of Tatton, P.G.M., was the cause of the assembling of a large number of Grand and Provincial Grand Officers and brethren, no fewer than seventy-three lodges in the Province being represented.

The annual meeting in 1909 at Stockport was presided over by the Provincial Grand Master, and the attendance was the largest known in the history of the Province. This ancient borough has been long famous for the hospitable welcome accorded to Provincial Grand Lodge, and the occasion was marked by the presentation of an address of welcome from the brethren of the Stockport district affirming their dutiful and loyal support to his Lordship on that occasion. They congratulated him on his accession to the Peerage, and pointed out that it was at Stockport that Earl Egerton of Tatton, whose death they sincerely lamented, resigned office in his favour, confident that he would maintain the best traditions of the House of Egerton, the interests of the Craft in the Province, and the welfare of the Masonic Order in Great Britain. A valedictory letter was received from the Deputy Provincial Grand Master, Sir Horatio Lloyd, asking his Lordship to convey to the brethren his sincere appreciation in the manner in which they had always received him when he came to Stockport. He was, he stated, appointed by the late Lord Combermere to the office of Deacon in the Province in the year 1866, made Senior

Warden by the late Lord de Tabley in 1887, advanced to the office of Deputy Provincial Grand Master by the late Earl Egerton in the same year. At the commencement of his career in Masonry the number of lodges in the Province was twenty. That number had now grown to seventy-four. Not only was this satisfactory in many respects, having added numerically to the list of lodges, but in a true Masonic spirit it had given additional power and influence to the position of the Provincial Grand Master which would be a source of just pride to his Lordship and a great support in all his undertakings. He urged them to let brotherly love and fraternal union be their watchwords, and he hoped every brother would do all in his power to promote unity of action, peace, and concord in his lodge. Sir Horatio concluded by expressing his strong feeling of attachment to Masonry and his earnest prayer that it might continue the beneficent course which it had so long and so beneficially occupied.

Lieut.-Colonel Hubert Cornwall Legh was then installed as Deputy Provincial Grand Master and saluted with Grand Honours in due form. Colonel Legh joined the Order in India, being initiated in Lodge Stuart in the Punjab in 1883. He was Junior Warden of Kyber Lodge, Province of the Punjab, in 1886, and Worshipful Master of the Unity Lodge, Crewe, in 1907. In the same year he was invested as Provincial Grand Senior Warden of Cheshire. He held high office in the Royal Arch and Mark Degrees. Colonel Legh had seen much active service. He was in the Afghan War in 1878-80, and took part under Sir Donald Stewart, in the capture of Kandahar, Khelet, and Ghilzai, the advance from Kandahar to Kabul, the actions of Ahmed Khel and Urzoo, and the capture of Ghuznee. Under Earl Roberts—then Sir Frederick Roberts —he was in the march from Kabul to Kandahar, and the actions at Kandahar on 31st August and 1st September 1880. He was in the Baluchistan Campaign of the same year, and holds the medal and special star for the Boer War of 1881, and for the Tel-el-Kebir Campaign in Egypt in 1882, being present at the capture of Cairo. He was a magistrate for Cheshire and Shropshire. His great-uncle, Mr George Cornwall Legh, M.P., was, for some time, Deputy Provincial Grand Master of Cheshire.

The Centenary Festival of the Lodge of Unity, No. 267, was celebrated at Macclesfield in September 1910, and a large gathering of brethren from all parts of the Province took part in the ceremony.

The dedication of the Freemasons Hall, Chester, took place on 8th January 1910, the ceremony being performed by the Deputy Provincial Grand Master (Colonel H. Cornwall Legh), who was attended by a numerous body of Grand and Provincial Grand Officers and brethren. Lodge of Independence, No. 721, and the Travellers Lodge, No. 2609, who were the promoters and founders, united in opening a Craft lodge, over which his Worship, the Mayor of Chester (Brother D. L. Hewitt), presided, the Senior and Junior Wardens' chairs being occupied by Brother Richardson and Brother W. MacLellan respectively. The

Centenary Souvenir, Lodge of Unity, No.321.

Birtles *Warrington*

LIEUT.-COLONEL CORNWALL LEGH,
Provincial Grand Master of Cheshire.

other officers of the lodge were the energetic Secretary, Brother H. Grant Bailey, Brother W. H. Davies (S.W. 2609), Brother R. Thomas (Organist 721), and Brother John Williamson (J.W. 721), I.G. The musical arrangements were admirably carried out by Brothers E. Robinson and R. Thomas.

The annual meeting of 1910 was held in September in the old Cheshire village of Lymm, on which occasion the Provincial Grand Master expressed the pleasure it gave him to meet so many brethren in that lovely corner of the county. King Edward VII. had passed away, and resolutions of condolence were voted to mark the sad event. Many old and valued members, including Brothers Lilley Ellis, George Ibeson, Thomas Lockitt, and William Booth were absent, being away for the benefit of their health. Amongst the honours conferred by Grand Lodge was that of Assistant Grand Director of Ceremonies of England on a veteran member, Brother James Cookson. Brother William James Nash had been elected Grand Treasurer of England, the first time Cheshire had been thus honoured. The brethren were urged by the Provincial Grand Master, in the words of one of the ancient charges, " to cultivate brotherly love, the foundation and copestone, the cement and glory of this ancient fraternity."

The Deputy Provincial Grand Master (Lieut.-Colonel Cornwall Legh) officiated at the foundation stone laying of the Wallasey Masonic Hall, Liscard, on 6th May 1911, and this was followed on the 13th of May by the laying of the foundation stone of the Birkenhead Masonic Hall, at which he also officiated. The principal business at the annual meeting at Chester was the passing of resolutions of congratulation to their Majesties, King George and Queen Mary on the occasion of their Coronation and enthronement, coupled with the prayer that they would be vouchsafed a long, happy, and prosperous reign, crowned with God's divine and choicest blessings. The members of the Provincial Grand Lodge had to mourn this year the loss by death of such worthy and distinguished brethren as Lilley Ellis, Thomas Lockitt, Sidney Croft, Alexander Saunders, and Joseph Whittaker, all stalwarts in Masonry, energetic in good work, and desirous of helping on the best interests of the glorious institution. At this meeting Sir Horatio Lloyd celebrated the sixtieth anniversary of his joining the Masonic body.

There were upwards of 500 brethren present at the annual meeting at Macclesfield in September 1912. Five new lodges were consecrated in the previous year.

At the annual meeting of the Provincial Grand Lodge held at Chester in September 1913, the Provincial Grand Master referred to the consecration of the Lodge of King Solomon's Temple, No. 3464, which appeared to be destined, he said, to become one of the most powerful and influential in the Province under the Grand Lodge of England. In wishing God-speed to this and seven other lodges consecrated in Cheshire, he hoped they might all be influential in disseminating the true principles of Masonry in the several districts in which they were situated, and united in binding each other in true friendship and fraternal union as Masons had done in all ages.

The warrant of King Solomon Temple, No. 3464, which is dated 19th August 1910, set forth the petition of Robert Freke Gould, P.G.D.; Albert Ephraim Coveney; Wm. Hesketh Lever; Albert James Thompson; Rev. George Gibson; Thomas Gabriel Lumley Smith; Henry John Pringle, D.G.M. of Jamaica; Alfred Elias Mitchell; Daniel Johannes Haarhoff, D.G.M. of South Africa (Central Division), and others, for consecration, the place of meeting being the Masonic Hall, Hunter Street, Chester, and appointing Brother Freke Gould, First Master, A. E. Coveney and Albert James Thompson, Senior and Junior Wardens respectively.

Brother E. G. PARKER,
W.M., King Solomon's Lodge.

Many distinguished names appear on the roll of members, headed by the Duke of Connaught, M.W.G.M.; the Earl of Derby; the Marquis of Zetland; Lord Egerton of Tatton; the Marquis of Tullibardine; King Christian XI., M.W.G.M. of Denmark; King Gustav, M.W.G.M. of Sweden; Theodore Roosevelt and Wm. Howard Taft (Presidents of the United States); the late Field-Marshal Lord Kitchener; the Earl of Dartmouth, P.G.M. of Staffordshire; the Lord Bishop of Chichester; Edward V. Paul, Past G.M., British Columbia; General T. J. Shrycock, M.W.G.M., Maryland, U.S.A.; Count Goblet D'Alviella, W.M. Past G.M. of Belgium; the Right Hon. Thomas Halsey, R.W.D.G.M. of England; Dr Donald A. Coles, Bishop of Jerusalem; the Right Hon. Lord Bolton, D.P.G.M., East and West Ridings, Yorks; the Very Rev. Arthur Purey Cust, Dean of York; R. G. Venables, D.P.G.M., Shropshire; Sir Joseph Sykes Rymer, Lord Mayor of York; Amand Singh, Burma. Altogether there were 224 members on the roll. The present Master of the Lodge of King Solomon's Temple is Brother Eustace G. Parker. He is one of the oldest Masons in the Province, having joined the Order in 1870. He holds Provincial rank in all degrees, including the Rose Croix. Several lodges under his fostering care have been kept going, and are now enjoying a well-deserved career of prosperity. He has served a stewardship in each of the Central Charities, being a Vice-President and Life Governor. He is Sub-Prior of Cheshire, etc., a member of the Council of the 31st Degree, and has been invited to join the 32nd. He will in due course reach the 33rd, which is the Supreme Council. The festival of the three local Benevolent Institutions was held in conjunction with the annual meeting of Provincial Grand Lodge at Knutsford in 1913, and proved a red-letter day in its history.

Additional interest was induced by the fact that the De Tabley Lodge, No. 941, named after Lord de Tabley, P.P.G.M., celebrated its jubilee on that occasion. As there was not accommodation in the Town Hall, many proceeded to Tatton Park, where, through the kindness of Lord Egerton, the grounds and gardens at the Hall were thrown open for their inspection, in which they experienced the utmost pleasure. Nearly 1000 brethren and friends sat down to a banquet in a spacious marquee in the afternoon, near the Knutsford entrance to the Park, and the after proceedings were enlivened with glees and songs rendered in excellent style by the members of the Manchester Cathedral Choir. Brother William Booth, in replying to the principal toast, as Chairman of the Charity Council of the Province, said the occasion was made unique by the number of brethren who brought their offerings in the sacred cause of charity. He traced the modest lines on which the Cheshire Educational Masonic Institution commenced its work in 1863 with two children on the books. Now, they had fifty children, clothed, maintained, and educated at a cost of £500 per annum, and an invested capital of £7000 sterling. The Committee of Benevolence, he added, had received great support from the late Earl Egerton, through whom other Benevolent Associations sprang into existence. Brother T. H. Annett, who also spoke, hoped that that day's festival would ultimately realise £10,000. Fine weather favoured the event, which was a magnificent success throughout.

At the Altrincham meeting in September 1914 there were over 700 brethren in attendance.

At Stalybridge, in 1916, Lieut.-Colonel Legh, D.P.G.M., presided. There was a large attendance, and special reference was made to the loss the Empire and Masonry had sustained by the death of Lord Kitchener, Past Grand Warden of England, and it was decided to send a letter of condolence to his family and relatives. Brother Sam. Thompson, Provincial Grand Tyler, retired through illness, his health having been seriously affected by the death of a fine son who had been killed at the front.

The annual meeting of the Provincial Grand Lodge at New Brighton Tower, on 18th September 1917, will rank as a landmark in the history of the Province. The brethren of the Wallasey Division entered with the utmost zest into the task of giving a hearty and hospitable welcome to the brethren from all parts of Cheshire, and their efforts were crowned with perfect success.

In the absence of the Right Worshipful Provincial Grand Master (the Right Hon. Lord Egerton of Tatton), P.G.W. of England, etc., which was a source of deep regret to the brethren, as also that of the Worshipful Deputy Provincial Grand Master (Lieut.-Colonel Hubert Cornwall Legh), who could not obtain leave of absence from the front, the throne was occupied by Worshipful Brother Colonel C. S. Dean, P.G.D. The Acting Deputy Provincial Grand Master was Worshipful Brother D. L. Hewitt, Past A.G.D.C.; the Senior and Junior Wardens' chairs were occupied by Worshipful Brother Thomas H. Annett, P.G.S.W., and Worshipful Brother Wm. Henry Pincombe, P.G.J.W., respectively.

The Acting Provincial Grand Master voiced the deep regret of all present that their beloved Right Worshipful Provincial Grand Master was unable to be amongst them. He also regretted to have to inform them of the absence of Lieut.-Colonel Cornwall Legh, who could not get leave of absence. He was doing his duty to his King and country. He wrote that he was very anxious to attend, but was unable to get away even for the short period required. He was sure it would be their pleasure, as it was his own, that their best thoughts and wishes might take the form of a message to be sent to the Right Worshipful Provincial Grand Master and the Worshipful Deputy Provincial Grand Master of all the good things they thought of them, and he asked if it was the wish of the brethren of the Province that such a message should be conveyed to both. There was an enthusiastic response on the part of the assembly. He added that the prosperity of the Province continued, and he hoped it would go on. He trusted they would make it their object that they should have quality and not merely numbers in their ranks.

It may be safely said that never was the annual meeting of Provincial Grand Lodge held under more depressing conditions than that at Northwich on 11th September 1918. The baleful influence of war appeared to overshadow the proceedings. Although numerous brethren assembled from the four corners of the Province, the meeting was robbed of much of its attractive influences by the absence, through continued ill-health, of the Provincial Grand Master, Lord Egerton of Tatton. Suffering under severe mental and physical strain, the Deputy Provincial Grand Master, Colonel Cornwall Legh, pluckily filled the breach. He had only just risen from a sick-bed, and was only partially recovered from the bursting of a blood vessel on the brain sustained while on duty at the front in France. Notwithstanding the war, brethren had nobly responded to the appeal on behalf of the local Benevolent Institutions, and had subscribed the handsome sum of £3216, in addition to which nearly £3000 had been forwarded to the Central Institutions in London. This record was exceedingly gratifying.

On the motion of Brother W. Booth, seconded by Brother D. L. Hewitt, it was unanimously and enthusiastically decided to send a message from the meeting to the Right Hon. Lord Egerton of Tatton, R.W.P.G.M., acknowledging his Lordship's valuable services to Freemasonry, coupled with a hope that he might be spared for many years to exercise a beneficial influence on the affairs of the Province over which he had ruled for eighteen years so wisely and well.

We regret to record that Brother Booth died at his residence in Stockport on 5th December 1919, full of years and honour. Provincial Grand Lodge and the Stockport Lodges were represented at his funeral, and there was a large gathering of the general public to pay a last tribute to departed worth.

The last meeting of Provincial Grand Lodge to be recorded in this volume took place at the Town Hall, Chester, on 19th November 1919. Owing to the much regretted resignation of the Right Worshipful Provincial Grand Master, Lord Egerton of Tatton, and the formalities attendant thereon, the usual gathering in September was postponed. This fact, however, did not appear to have prejudiced the attendance, as nearly 1000 brethren put in an appearance and manifested the utmost interest in the proceedings. The Chair was occupied by Lieut.-Colonel H. Cornwall Legh, P.G.M. Designate, supported by Alderman D. L. Hewitt, P.A.G.D.C. of England, as D.P.G.M., and Grand and Provincial Grand Officers and brethren who crowded the spacious hall.

The record of Masonic Benevolence, as disclosed by the reports, showed even a higher rate of progress than that of the previous year. The donations to the Cheshire Educational and Benevolent Institutions and the Royal Masonic Institutions totalled £9527, 9s. 6d. No wonder the Committee of Benevolence expressed their deep gratification and appreciation of the services rendered by such a large number of brethren and lodges. In connection with the Cheshire Masonic Benevolent Institution, the sum of £1000 had been invested in National War Bonds. During the year two brethren qualified as Vice-Patrons and one as Vice-President, and 195 brethren as Life Governors. For the Cheshire Educational Institution alone the donations from lodges and individual brethren reached the magnificent sum of £2055, 2s., an amount far in excess of that contributed in any ordinary year since its foundation. In this instance £2000 had been invested in National War Bonds. The total invested on its behalf was £13,151, 12s.

A service of praise and thanksgiving to Almighty God by the Provincial Grand Lodge of Freemasons in Cheshire for victory and for peace was afterwards held in Chester Cathedral. The preacher was Worshipful Brother the Rev. James Bourchier Sayer, M.A., P.P.G.C., Rural Dean of Birkenhead, Vicar of Oxton, and Hon. Canon of Chester; lectors—Worshipful Brother the Rev. Arthur George Sykes, M.A., P.G.C., Vicar of St John's, Over, and Worshipful Brother Rev. C. Hylton Stewart, M.A., P.P.G.C., Hon. Canon of Chester; organist—Professor Joseph C. Bridges, M.A., Mus. Doc., Organist of the Cathedral.

The installation of Lieut.-Colonel Legh as Provincial Grand Master of Cheshire took place at Chester Town Hall in December of the same year, when there was again a large attendance of brethren. The ceremony was most impressive and marked by a striking address by the Installing Officer, Lord

Ampthill, P.G.M. of England. Brother Cuthbert Leicester-Warren was invested as Deputy Provincial Grand Master. He is a lineal descendant of Sir Peter Leicester, or Leycester, as it was originally spelt—on whose work all Cheshire history is founded—and a grandson of the second Lord de Tabley, P.G.M. from 1865 to 1886, in which year he was succeeded by the late Earl Egerton of Tatton. He is the second son of the late Sir Baldwyn Leighton, Bart., M.P., who died in 1897. His mother was the Hon. Eleanor, third daughter of the second Lord de Tabley, who succeeded to the family estate on the death of her brother, the Hon. John Leicester Warren, the third and last Baron de Tabley, who died in 1895. He assumed by Royal Licence his present surname of Leicester-Warren in lieu of Leighton in 1899. He was initiated in the De Tabley Lodge, No. 941, in 1908; Provincial Grand Senior Warden in 1914, and Deputy Provincial Grand Master, 1919. He was formerly a Captain and Adjutant of the 16th Battalion London Regiment, and in 1901 qualified as a Justice of the Peace for the County of Chester.

The Earl of Chester (H.R.H. Prince of Wales) was initiated into the Household Brigade Lodge on the 2nd of May 1919, thus evidencing the intimate connection between the reigning House of Great Britain and Freemasonry, which has existed for nearly two centuries. In 1737 Frederick, Prince of Wales, father of George III., joined the Order, and since that year, with two exceptions, one of whom is King George V., nearly every prince of the royal blood has been a member of the Craft. It was exactly forty-five years since his grandfather, King Edward VII., was elected Grand Master in 1874. He was succeeded, on his accession to the Throne, by the present Grand Master, the Duke of Connaught.

A great loss to this Province in particular, and to Masonry in general, was caused by the death of Brother Sir John Tomlinson Brunner, in 1919. He was born at Everton, Liverpool, in 1842, and died suddenly at Chertsey, near London, from heart failure. He was initiated in the Sincerity Lodge, Northwich, some twenty-five years before, and the event was a very popular one with the members. He was the first Master of the John Brunner Lodge, No. 2799, Winsford, which was consecrated by Sir Horatio Lloyd, D.P.G.M., at the Brunner Guild Hall, Winsford, in 1900. The banquet on that occasion was served by Bollands, Chester, and was long remembered as being of a sumptuous and even princely character. In 1899 he was invested as Provincial Grand Senior Warden in the last year of the rule of the late Earl Egerton, G.M. of the Province. He was the head of Brunner, Mond, & Co., one of the largest alkali works in the world. He presented Northwich with a Public Library, Runcorn and Winsford with Guildhalls for the use of trades unions, friendly and other societies. He endowed Liverpool University with a Chair of Political Economy, was a benefactor to Witton Grammar School, and Vice-President of the Cheshire Football Association, etc. He was created Baronet in 1895, Privy

Saronie   *Birkenhead*

Brother JOSEPH CLARKE,
Provincial Grand Secretary.

Brother ALFRED INGHAM, P.M, etc

CHESHIRE : ITS TRADITIONS AND HISTORY

Councillor, 1906, LL.D. (Hon.) and Pro Chancellor of Liverpool University, 1909. He was succeeded by his son, Sir John Fowler Leece Brunner, formerly M.P. for the Northwich Division, County Councillor, 1882-95, and member of the Central Tribunal for Great Britain, 1917.

Brother Broadsmith, who had discharged the duties of Provincial Grand Secretary for some time prior to the death of Brother Richard Newhouse, died in July 1918. Brother Broadsmith had had a distinguished career in the Province, to which due testimony was forthcoming at the annual meeting of Provincial Grand Lodge at Northwich in 1918, as recorded in preceding pages. He was the author of the Masonic Book of Reference for Worshipful Masters, Directors of Ceremonies, Secretaries of Lodges, and brethren generally, issued in 1907. It enjoyed great vogue and had a world-wide circulation, especially in the United States. The Provincial Grand Master (Lord Egerton of Tatton) presented a bound copy to each lodge in the Province for the guidance of members.

At the Northwich meeting Brother Joseph Clarke, at the request of the Provincial Grand Master, undertook the duties of Provincial Grand Secretary until a successor was appointed. But there was no unnecessary delay. Brother Clarke had, in the meantime, shown such a grasp of the duties of the office, coupled with a long experience of Masonic procedure and the constitutions of the Order, that, acting in conjunction with his advisers, the Provincial Grand Master (Lord Egerton of Tatton) had no hesitation in conferring the position on Brother Clarke, the appointment dating from 2nd December 1918. Brother Clarke has had an active connection with the Craft and allied degrees for nearly forty years. He has been a member of no fewer than eight lodges ; he is a Past Master of the Dee Lodge, No. 1576, serving as Worshipful Master in 1889. He was a founder of the Lodge of King Solomon's Temple, No. 3464, also acting as Secretary at its consecration. He was installed as Worshipful Master of the Randle Holme Lodge, No. 3261, which was quite an event in Masonic annals of the Province. He is also a member of the London Boys' School Committee, in addition to having served on the Committee of the Cheshire Educational Institution and the Cheshire Masonic Benevolent Institution. He is Principal Z., etc., of Fidelity Chapter, No. 477, and a founder of the Broadsmith Chapter, No. 3261.

Since his appointment Brother Clarke has been paying a round of visits to the lodges, chapters, etc., in the Province, and has already made a most favourable impression on the brethren. His urbanity and readiness to impart Masonic information when his opinion has been invited will certainly confirm the acumen displayed at headquarters by his appointment, while all ranks will wish him health and strength as the executive officer of the Province to discharge the duties of his onerous position for years to come.

Brother Alfred Ingham, the author of this work, was initiated in the Earl of Chester Lodge, No. 1365, Lymm, in 1881; founder, 1886, De Tatton Lodge, No. 2144, Altrincham, and W.M., 1889; Provincial Grand Steward, 1888; founder, Cheshire Provincial Stewards Lodge, Sale, No. 3449; served Stewardship at 111th Anniversary Festival, Royal Masonic Institution for Boys, 1909; member, Royal Arch and Mark degrees. He is a Fellow of the Royal Historical Society, and has been actively engaged in journalism in Cheshire and Lancashire for over fifty years.

Many members of the Brotherhood have made the Supreme Sacrifice during the War, as is evidenced by the fact that no fewer than 200 boys, whose fathers died whilst on active service, have been admitted to the benefits of the Royal Masonic Institution for Boys, without ballot. Of 750 boys who have served their King and Country, 101 have laid down their lives. Many distinctions have been gained, including the C.M.G., D.S.O., 41 M.C.'s, and Medals, etc. The School at Bushey, Herts, is now full, 500 being educated there, while 383 younger boys are being educated outside, under the supervision of a number of brethren, who act as almoners.

War hospitals were equipped and maintained by the Craft at 237 Fulham Road, S.W., a first line hospital of 77 beds, and, with the approval of the Bishop of London, at Fulham Palace, where a hospital of 100 beds was commenced A Masonic Nursing Home was established at Cliff House, Caversham, near Reading, as a country annexe with 25 beds.

In connection with the Central Institutions and other branches of Charitable work, over a quarter of a million pounds sterling is raised annually. This is altogether apart from Provincial Benevolent Institutions, of which the record relating to Cheshire is embodied in preceding pages.

The oldest lodge in Cheshire to acquire a Centenary Warrant is Industry, No. 361, Hyde, which was constituted in 1820 at Gee Cross, and removed to Hyde about 1842. Following closely upon it was Fortitude, No. 461, which was constituted at Newton Moor in 1839 and removed to Hyde in 1852. Both these lodges have done useful work in the eastern part of the Province, as their votes in the Central and local Benevolent Institutions testify. The third lodge in Hyde, the Newton, No. 3024, was constituted as recently as 1904.

We now turn our attention from the Craft to Royal Arch and Mark Masonry in Cheshire. With reference to pre-united Grand Chapter Masonry in England and in Cheshire Brother Hughan states that "The Grand Chapter of 'Moderns' was formed in 1767, but the Degree of Royal Arch Masonry was worked in England, Ireland, and Scotland at least thirty years earlier, actual evidence existing back to 1743."

At the time of the union of the two Grand Chapters in 1817, and for many years afterwards, Royal Arch Masonry was at a low ebb in Cheshire, but notwithstanding this it is a matter for congratulation that all the seven Chapters then on the roll had sufficient energy to comply with the regulations laid down by the United Grand Chapter and have themselves formally attached to some lodge. Five out of the seven still flourish, though a majority of them at one time or another have been in abeyance for a considerable period.

The present Provincial Grand Chapter of Cheshire was constituted by Excellent Companion Henry Muggeridge, P.G.S.B. of England, who had been deputed to do so as Deputy for the Grand Z., the Earl of Zetland, K.G., on Tuesday, the 26th of October 1869, at the "De Tabley" Chapter Rooms, the George Hotel, Knutsford, in the presence of a large number of Companions of the Order, prominent amongst whom were:—the Right Hon. Lord de Tabley, Grand Superintendent Designate, E. J. M'Intyre, P.G.Sj., England, Richard Cope, H. and Wm. Bulley, E. G. Willoughby, S. W. Wilkinson, Thomas Lockitt (Z. 195), John Wood, Rev. F. Terry, J. Parry Platt, Jas. A. Birch, Jno. Twiss, Jos. Sillitoe, F. Jackson, Thos. Platt, etc.

Lord de Tabley's warrant of appointment as Grand Superintendent having been read, Companion Muggeridge then installed him according to ancient custom.

Companion W. W. B. Beach, M.P., Grand J. of England, who was deputed by the Most Excellent Grand Z., H.R.H. the Prince of Wales, installed the Hon. Alan de Tatton Egerton, M.P., as Grand Superintendent of Royal Arch Masons for the Province of Cheshire, on 29th November 1895.

List of Chapters in Cheshire:—No. 287, Stone of Friendship Ezel, Stockport, date of constitution, 1793; No. 295, Love and Friendship, Macclesfield, 1797; No. 320, Integrity, Mottram, 1807; No.322, Hope, Stockport, 1807; No. 323, Charity, Stockport, 1807; No. 361, Industry, Hyde, 1825; No. 89, Royal Cheshire, Dukinfield, 1839; No. 324, Reason, Stalybridge, 1844; No. 477, Fidelity, Birkenhead, 1845; No. 537, Zion, Birkenhead, 1864; No. 721, Grosvenor, Chester, 1864; No. 758, Bridgewater, Runcorn, 1867; No. 1045, Stamford, Altrincham, 1867; No. 941, De Tabley, Knutsford, 1868; No. 605, De Tabley, Birkenhead, 1869; No. 321, Faith, Crewe, 1872; No. 425, Cestrian, Chester, 1875; No. 533, Warren, Congleton, 1880; No. 428, Sincerity, Sale, 1884; No. 2433, Richard Newhouse, Birkenhead, 1897; No. 2132, Egerton of Tatton, Liscard, 1898; No. 3513, Palestine, Birkenhead; No. 3261, Broadsmith, Port Sunlight; No. 2799, John Brunner, Winsford; No. 1289, Temple, Birkenhead; No. 3653, Eminence, Birkenhead; No. 3731, Cheadle, at Cheadle; No. 3384, Doric, Marple; and No. 368, Samaritan, Sandbach.

The Provincial Grand Lodge of Mark Master Masons was constituted at Altrincham on 5th April 1873, as the Provincial Grand Lodge of Mark Master Masons of Cheshire and North Wales. A lodge of Mark Master Masons was first opened by Brother J. A. Birch, W.M. of the Stamford Lodge, No. 148, assisted by officers of the lodge. Right Worshipful Brother Romaine Callender, P.G.M.M.M. of Lancashire, and his officers were received and saluted with Grand and Royal honours. Brother John Chadwick, P.G.S. of Lancashire, read the Grand Mark Master's Dispensation, authorising Brother Callender to instal the Hon. Wilbraham Egerton, M.P., as Provincial Grand Mark Master of Cheshire and North Wales, which was carried out according to ancient usage. The P.G.M.M.M. nominated Brother the Rev. Chas. Wm. Stanhope as D.P.G.M.M.M., after which the P.G.M.M.M. nominated and invested the Provincial Grand Officers.

The reconstitution and consecration of the Ashton District Mark Lodge took place at a meeting of the Moveable Grand Lodge held at Dukinfield in February 1900. This was a very important landmark in the annals of Provincial Mark Masonry, as up to that time, and for upwards of a century, it had been popularly known as the Travelling Mark Lodge of Cheshire. At last Mark Masonry, so far as England and Wales and the Colonies were concerned, became one united whole. It was assigned a position on the roll commensurate with its great antiquity, and is designated the Ashton District Lodge, T.I. The Hon. Alan de Tatton Egerton in 1893 succeeded his brother, Lord Egerton of Tatton, as Provincial Grand Mark Master, and his installation took place at the Town Hall, Chester, on the 24th of June in that year. He continued to discharge the duties of the office with his customary zeal and urbanity until 1919, when, as Lord Egerton of Tatton, he resigned owing to ill-health and numerous engagements, added to in no small measure by the Great War. The regret felt at the step his Lordship was compelled to take was deeply felt by all ranks in the Province. He was succeeded by Lieut.-Colonel H. C. Legh, who was installed at Chester in September 1919, by Right Worshipful Brother R. Loveland Loveland, K.C., the venerable Deputy Provincial Grand Mark Master, assisted by Grand Officers. Brother Leicester Warren was appointed Deputy Provincial Grand Mark Master.

Succession of Grand Masters of Cheshire in the Grand Lodge and United Grand Lodge of England now existing, from 1717 to the present time.

Colonel Columbine, 1725; Captain Hugh Warburton, 1727; Captain Robert Newton, 1742; John Page, 1755; Hon. J. Smith Barry, 1771; Sir Robert Salusbury Cotton, M.P., 1785; Sir John Grey Egerton, M.P., 1810; Field-Marshal Stapleton Cotton, First Viscount Combermere, 1830; Lord de Tabley, 1865; Wilbraham, second Lord Egerton (afterwards Earl Egerton of Tatton), 1886; the Hon. Alan de Tatton Egerton, M.P. (third Lord Egerton of Tatton), 1900; Lieut.-Colonel Hubert Cornwall Legh, 1919.

Provincial Grand Officers, 1900-1919.

1900. *Chester.*—J. Fred May, Senior Warden; William Booth, Junior Warden; Revs. F. H. Mentha and J. B. Sayer, Chaplains; H. H. Royle,

CHESHIRE: ITS TRADITIONS AND HISTORY 343

Treasurer; Hy. Taylor, F.S.A., Registrar; W. Wood, Senior Deacon; B. C. Bradley and E. Taylor, Junior Deacons; H. Gordon Small, Director of Ceremonies; T. H. Davies, Deputy Director of Ceremonies; C. W. Phillips, J. T. Catlow, and Richard Parry, Assistant Directors of Ceremonies, J. W. Whiteley, Sword Bearer; A. Saunders and A. Frith, Standard Bearers; G. W. Bebbington, Organist; John Ferguson, Assistant Secretary; John Plant, Pursuivant; Wm. Clegg, Assistant Pursuivant; Sam. Thompson, Tyler; A. H. Whittaker, T. M. Draper, T. W. Atkinson, P. Lockwood, Dean Sutcliffe, and H. Coveney, Stewards.

1901. *West Kirby.*—James Cookson, Senior Warden; Dr T. W. A. Napier, Junior Warden; Revs. R. H. Pring and W. Hollowell, Chaplains; J. Morris, Treasurer; W. Shepherd, Registrar; W. Firth and Samuel Hall, Senior Deacons; R. L. Bourne and J. W. Leathley, Junior Deacons; T. A. Jackson, Superintendent of Works; J. Stanley Derbyshire, Director of Ceremonies; Ernest Hampson, Deputy Director of Ceremonies; Henry Newton, W. H. Jones, and W. O. Catlow, Assistant Directors of Ceremonies; John Smith, Sword Bearer; P. D. Hayes and W. Birch, Standard Bearers; Bridge Hopkinson, Organist; J. Ferguson, Assistant Secretary; F. Johnson, Pursuivant; J. C. Armitage, Assistant Pursuivant; J. Appleton, Henry Binns, Alfred Sharpe, George Austin, Frank Pinder, and William Severs, Stewards.

1902. *Knutsford.*—J. E. Raynor, Senior Warden; Dr Theo. Fennell, Junior Warden; Revs. Benj. Hayward Browne and Stuart Hall, Chaplains; George Leigh, Treasurer; John C. Wilson, Registrar; John Knott and George F. Willis, Senior Deacons; W. T. Thompstone and Edward Whitworth Armstrong, Junior Deacons; John Mayers, Superintendent of Works; John Lee, Director of Ceremonies; Geo. Wildgoose, Deputy Director of Ceremonies; W. S. Coppock, Geo. Grant, and Charles Dawson, Assistant Directors of Ceremonies; F. R. Oke and W. Sibell, Standard Bearers; Geo. H. Scott, Sword Bearer; James Shaw, Assistant Secretary; J. E. Lord, Organist; John Phillips, Pursuivant; J. W. Wrigley, Assistant Pursuivant; M. Agar, J. Kenyon, Albert H. Fray, J. T. Gresty, James George and George Henry Richards, Stewards. Past Rank—J. R. Simm, Geo. Howe, William Ramsden, and James T. Thompson, Senior Grand Wardens; Geo. F. Bird, Edward W Morrice, E. Percy Webb, and James A. Cookson, Senior Grand Deacons.

1903. *Liscard.*—Thomas Lockitt, Senior Warden; Fred J. Walmsley, Junior Warden; Revs. A. M. Hertzberg and W. M. Lutener, Chaplains; Robert Grundy, Treasurer; Tom Walton Foster, Registrar; Wm. Moody and Wm. Harrison, Senior Deacons; Jas. MacLeavy and Jas. Gregson, Junior Deacons; Fred Gregory, Superintendent of Works; John Lea, Director of Ceremonies; James Boughey, Deputy Director of Ceremonies; Giles W. Makin, Walter Young, and Wm. Johnson, Assistant Directors of Ceremonies; Wm. H. Davies, Sword Bearer; John Smith and Wm. Gleave, Standard

Bearers; John Ferguson, Assistant Secretary; Ernest Farnall, Organist; John Thomas, Pursuivant; J. A. Barlow, Assistant Pursuivant; John R. Owen, F. A. Ravenscroft, Albert Wrigley, W. H. Moore, John Taylor, and S. A. Williamson, Stewards.

1904. *Hyde.*—George Sillivan, Senior Warden; Alexander Rutherford, Junior Warden; Revs. Sandford Woods and Morris Jones, Chaplains; Alfred Firth, Treasurer; J. H. Pagen, Registrar; Robert Rear and H. H. Rigmarden, Senior Deacons; W. S. Clegg and John Hawker, Junior Deacons; John C. Clarke, Inspector of Works; J. T. C. Blackie, Director of Ceremonies; E. H. Thomas, J. E. Talbot, and John H. Ratcliff, Assistant Directors of Ceremonies; George Sykes, Sword Bearer; Edward Davies and W. H. Ross, Standard Bearers; Charles Needham, Assistant Secretary; Martin Middleton, Organist; Albert Yarwood, Pursuivant; E. Hamlet, Assistant Pursuivant; George Reid, Samuel Wilde, James W. Kemp, J. Gerrish, J. H. Hopwood, and J. F. Spedding, Stewards.

1905. *Alderley Edge*—Joseph B. Duckworth, Senior Warden; Arthur Lawley, Junior Warden; Rev. Dr C. C. Atkinson and Rev. L. C. A. Edgeworth, Chaplains; Wm. Severs, Treasurer; Francis S. Moores, Registrar; Joshua Preston and Herbert C. Howell, Senior Deacons; Julius Laurisch and P. V. Salaman, Junior Deacons; Samuel Lee, Superintendent of Works; John Lee, Director of Ceremonies; William Hall, Deputy Director of Ceremonies; Dr Laird Pearson, W. H. Jones, and Richard Johnson, Assistant Directors of Ceremonies; Albert J. Thompson and W. H. Moore, Sword Bearers; Wm. Hesketh Lever and Thomas Sherwin, Standard Bearers; James A. Dearden, Assistant Secretary; Geo. Barlow Cliffe, Organist; W. Wild, Pursuivant; F. Smith, Assistant Pursuivant; C. Brogden, H. F. Cunliffe, J. Harding, Ben Jones, J. Patteson, and O. Stott, Stewards.

1906. *Stalybridge.*—George Ibeson, Senior Warden; George Kershaw, Junior Warden; Revs. Dr C. C. Atkinson and Herbert Hampson, Chaplains; Robert Leach, Treasurer; T. A. Daniel, Registrar; W. Ackroyd, W. Slack, and R. Williams, Senior Deacons; R. Edwards, W. Welsby, and Geo. Spencer, Junior Deacons; H. Pemberton, Superintendent of Works; John Lee, Director of Ceremonies; Geo. W. Haswell, Deputy Director of Ceremonies; John Matthews, Thomas Turner, Anthony Evans, and Walter Bithell, Assistant Directors of Ceremonies; Geo. Marsden, Sword Bearer; Thomas Wilson and Wm. C. Moore, Standard Bearers; John Ferguson, Assistant Secretary; John E. Hardy, Organist; John Gould, Pursuivant; Horace Wm. Handley, Assistant Pursuivant; Robert Stanley, G. J. Whitney, Geo. J. Auburn, James H. Clayton, H. H. France, and Geo. Heathcote, Stewards.

1907. *Birkenhead.*—Colonel Hubert Cornwall Legh, Senior Warden; David Lythall Hewitt (J.P.), Junior Warden; Revs. Alexander Cockburn Evans and Joseph Chapman, Chaplains; Owen Jones, Treasurer; Peter Davenport (J.P.), Registrar; Alfred Webb, Joseph Clarke, and Alfred C. H. Davies, Senior Deacons; William Henry Cooke, John Albert Lord and Harry William Cook, Junior Deacons; Mark Warrington, Superintendent of Works; Geo. W. Haswell, Director of Ceremonies; Edward L. Bruce, Deputy Director of Ceremonies; William G. Cross, D. P. Morgan, Joseph Hulme, and William Hughes, Assistant Directors of Ceremonies; John Rudd, Sword Bearer; A. W. Boucher and R. H. Yeomans, Standard Bearers; Joseph H. Roberts, Assistant Secretary; James Hamilton Jackson, Organist; Thomas Moore, Pursuivant; Edwin Marshall, Assistant Pursuivant; William Kelly, Peter Smith, Dr Pierce, Robert Sandham, William Phillip Pipe, and Clifford Collard, Stewards.

1908. *Port Sunlight.*—William Hesketh Lever (M.P.), Senior Warden; John Lee, Junior Warden; Revs. W. T. Warburton and Samuel Gasking, Chaplains; Arthur Thomas Harding, Treasurer; George Proudman, Registrar; Thomas Eastwood, John E. Tomlinson, Albert Bloom, and Fred Jones, Senior Deacons; Charles James Hughes, R. Rowland Hughes, William Dykes, and W. C. Brewer, Junior Deacons; Chas. W. Bullock, Superintendent of Works; Edward L. Bruce, Director of Ceremonies; Wm. Mortimore, Deputy Director of Ceremonies; Wm. T. Haworth, James Sayer Warren, Joseph Andrew, and Fredk. A. Ravenscroft, Assistant Directors of Ceremonies; Robert S. Holland, Sword Bearer; Robert Stanley, Deputy Sword Bearer; Robert P. Stagg and Frank Eachus, Standard Bearers; Joseph Dutton, Organist; Patrick Joseph Walsh, Assistant Secretary; Robert Paterson, Pursuivant; Jabez Lightfoot, Assistant Pursuivant; H. Keays Bentley, J. H. Beynon, E. K. Mitting, G. F. Penney, W. S. Tafner, and Walter Baker, Stewards.

1909. *Stockport.*—Albert E. Coveney, Senior Warden; Richard C. Davies, Junior Warden; Revs. Alfred Henry Rhodes and Harold Norman Lowndes, Chaplains; Andrew Ellor, Treasurer; John Dodds, Registrar; Edwin Crewe, Jacob Winter, David Walmsley, and Edward Flamank, Senior Deacons; Samuel E. Williamson, Wm. Darby, William Taylor, and Joseph Slack, Junior Deacons; J. Taylor-Davies, Superintendent of Works; William Berry, Director of Ceremonies; John Smith Law, Deputy Director of Ceremonies; Fred E. Owens, Albert H. Taylor, John Henry Hopley, and Leicester Caldecutt, Assistant Directors of Ceremonies; Henry Branch, Sword Bearer; John Perry, Deputy Sword Bearer; John Chorton and Richard Oddie, Standard Bearers; Johannes Kokablas, Organist; Alfred Bowden Hale, Assistant Secretary; Charles Wm. Bradbury, Pursuivant; Albert Hurtig, Assistant Pursuivant; George E. Oppenheim, Joseph Briscoe, Isaac Adshead, Thos. Haslam, Frank Hyde Gaskell, and Joseph Brindley Walker, Stewards. Past Rank—Wilmot Eardley, Senior Warden; A. J. Thompson and Mark Oliver, Junior Wardens; J. Firth, Registrar.

1910. *Lymm.*—John Herbert Vernon, Senior Warden; Charles Kenworthy, Junior Warden; Revs. Clifton Wm. Thistlethwaite and Charles

Alfred Griffin, Chaplains ; William Kelsall, Treasurer ; Wm. J. R. Boler, Registrar ; Samuel John West, Lewis Buckley, Alfred Stott Cartwright, and Albert H Fray, Senior Deacons ; Robert Brown, Hermann Richard Romer, Richard Threlfall and Frank Coveney, Junior Deacons ; Sidney Croft, Superintendent of Works ; William Berry, Director of Ceremonies ; Walter Hulme Jones, Deputy Director of Ceremonies ; Clifford Collard, George Wm. Tinker, Thomas Dunham, Edward Wainwright, and Joseph Walker, Assistant Directors of Ceremonies ; Ralph Blackwell, Sword Bearer ; James Heaney, Deputy Sword Bearer ; Edward Johnson and Thomas Mayoh Johnson, Standard Bearers ; Edmund A. W. Wragge, Organist ; Joseph W. Lloyd, Assistant Secretary ; Elias Wild, Pursuivant ; David W. Pickering, Assistant Pursuivant ; John Royle Newton, Fred M'Krill, Thomas Rowlands, Albert E. Lord, Richard Edgell, and Edward J. Greenhalgh, Stewards.

1911. *Chester.*—Thomas Smith Deakin, Senior Warden ; Edward Webb, Junior Warden ; Revs. John Nankivell and W. H. Humphreys, Chaplains ; Philip Lockwood, Treasurer ; George F. Drinkwater, Registrar ; John H. Beynon, W. L. T. Eskrigge, Albert Wrigley and Edward C. Gaskill, Senior Deacons ; Edward Holt, George Wm. Doleman, James Taylor, and John Renshaw, Junior Deacons ; Fredk. R. Hughes, Superintendent of Works ; Clifford Collard, Director of Ceremonies ; Oswald Andrew, John A. Adey, Edgar Osborn, E. A. Ash, and Walter Ireland, Deputy Directors of Ceremonies ; Ernest Pritchard, Assistant Director of Ceremonies ; Chas. F. Poole, Sword Bearer ; Frank A. Lidbury, Deputy Sword Bearer ; James T. Kerridge and Charles Beadsworth, Standard Bearers ; Arthur Finney, Assistant Secretary ; Edward J. Greenhalgh, Organist ; George M'Loughlin ; G. Partridge, Pursuivant ; W. J. Pryce, Assistant Pursuivant ; A. T. Wright, H. Davies Cox, Edward Jones, James Kenyon, Chas. G. Haswell, and Alexander Adams, Stewards. Past Rank—Joseph Roby, J. H. Foster, and John Wagstaffe, Senior Wardens ; J. Sheriff Roberts and W. H. Davies, Junior Wardens ; Samuel J. Bruford, Peter D. Hayes, and George E. Oppenheim, Senior Deacons ; R. Olive, Thomas Eastwood, and A. Hornby, Junior Deacons ; John Croft, Pursuivant.

1912. *Macclesfield.*—Harry Beswick, Senior Warden ; Dr C. A. Bradley, Junior Warden ; Revs. C. R. Pembridge and Samuel G. Lloyd, Chaplains ; Thos. Wm. Sheldon, Treasurer ; Henry L. Ross, Registrar ; Johannes S. Buck, Wm. Pyke, Frank L. Pinder, and John Smith, Senior Deacons ; George Bellamy, Ralph Walker, James T. Boyd, and Thomas E. Foster, Junior Deacons ; Fredk. Richardson, Superintendent of Works ; William Berry, Director of Ceremonies ; Walter Baker, Henry C. Parry, Samuel Thornley, Alfred E. Walker, George F. Shaw, and Harry G. F. Dawson, Assistant Directors of Ceremonies ; Chris Campion, Sword Bearer ; Levi Todd, Deputy Sword Bearer ; Wm. G. Groves and Cecil Kidson, Standard Bearers ; John William

Jackson, Organist; Geo. J. Hufton, Assistant Secretary; E. S. Haighton and Fredk. A. Collier, Pursuivants; Fredk. R. Oldfield, James H. Hallowell, Fredk. May, Wm. Lund, Geo. Allen, and James Bate, Stewards. Brevet Rank—Owen Jones and Wm. Henry Cooke, Senior Wardens; Dr Wm. Arthur Pierce and Robert Aspden, Senior Deacons; John Wm. Lees, Geo. A. Eyre, F. W. Berisford, James Mobey, Junior Deacons; Charles Shaw and Albert Hurtig, Deputy Directors of Ceremonies; Charles Henry King and Wm. S. Tafner, Assistant Deputy Directors of Ceremonies.

1913. *Knutsford.*—W. H. Stott, Senior Warden; Dr H. Keays Bentley, Junior Warden; Revs. Francis L. Smithett and Archibald Ball, Chaplains; G. W. Bebbington, Treasurer; Thomas W. Potts, Registrar; Josh. Child, Assistant Secretary; Wm. R. Evans, Samuel Whitlow, George F. Adams, and George T. H. Lodge, Senior Deacons; George Hulse, Jeremiah Gerrish, Joseph O. Brandrith, and David T. Jackson, Junior Deacons; Wm. Levi Lockyer, Superintendent of Works; William Berry, Director of Ceremonies; George A. Sainsbury, Deputy Director of Ceremonies; David Morrison, Harry F. Cunliffe, Joseph Wilson, Isaac Wood, and Booth Taylor, Assistant Directors of Ceremonies; John Mansell Southern, Sword Bearer; William Higson, Deputy Sword Bearer; Thomas Audley and John L. Hulme, Standard Bearers; Richard T. W. Allen, Organist; Richard Edgell, Pursuivant; James Rosser, Assistant Pursuivant; Charles P. Sales, Dennis Goodman, Arthur Wm. Leving, John W. Venables, John Hill, and W. E. Horrocks, Stewards. Past Rank—Walter Newton and Samuel Wynne Jones, Senior Wardens; John Arnold, Wm Henry Jones, Richard Parry, and T. N. Richards, Junior Wardens; James Kenyon, John M'Lachlan, and Isaac Hinchliffe, Junior Deacons; Thomas W. Draper, Superintendent of Works; R. Butterworth, Organist.

1914. *Altrincham.*—Cuthbert Leicester Warren, Senior Warden; John Oldershaw, Junior Warden; Revs. Arthur Gascoigne Child and Geo. J. Lovett, Chaplains; Chas. Price, Treasurer; Chas. J. Blair, Registrar; Fredk. Woolridge, Wm. J. Chapman, W. J. S. English and R. Illingworth, Senior Deacons; Thomas Dutton Bayliff, C. S. R. Stephens, J. W. B. Harding and James Hodgkins, Junior Deacons; James Thos. Pott, Superintendent of Works; Wm. Henry Reilley, Deputy Director of Ceremonies; H. W. Treleaven, Simon J. L. Van Alten, Wm. Hamer, C. J. Meyer, and Edwin Hopley, Assistant Directors of Ceremonies; Thomas Power, Sword Bearer; W. C. Such, Deputy Sword Bearer; George Boulton and Joshua T. Birch, Standard Bearers; Harry Pearson, Assistant Secretary; Sam. L. Melville, Organist; Fred Southern, Pursuivant; James Chatterton, Assistant Pursuivant; Robert Colling, Geo. Edward Allwood, T. K. Bradshaw, Wm. Clarke, H. Loach, and Fredk. J. Mann Brown, Stewards. Brevet Rank—Geo. Leigh and Arthur T. Harding, Senior Wardens; Fredk.

Woolfall, Wm. J. Kerr, and John Ward Dale, Junior Wardens; Robert Wm. Shepherd, Thos. A. Edwards, and Geo. W. Thornton, Registrars; J. Millward Hughes, Geo. James Whitney, Thos. Ormerod, and Geo. Fredk. Penney, Senior Deacons; T. Wales and James Marchanton, Junior Deacons.

1915. *Birkenhead.*—George Harrison, Senior Warden; His Honour Judge Samuel Moss, Junior Warden; Revs. Walter Bidlake and Talbot M. M. Griffiths, Chaplains; Elsworth Greaves, Treasurer; Edgar T. S. Tadman, Registrar; Clifford Collard, Director of Ceremonies; John Hill Good, Wm. Whitby Lea, Daniel M'Laren, and Wm. Hulme, Senior Deacons; Robt. Wm. Hind, Benjamin Pownall, Hugh Lee Tatters, and Wm. Clarke Currie, Junior Deacons; Henry Grant Bailey, Superintendent of Works; John A. Heap, John Lavine, Joseph Shuttleworth, John Harper, Fredk. Vernon Harte, and Joseph Roditi, Assistant Directors of Ceremonies; John James Deane, Sword Bearer; Joseph Westwood, Deputy Sword Bearer; Richard Edgell and Wm. James Bluck, Standard Bearers; Fredk. Robert Wilson, Assistant Secretary; Edward Watson, Organist; B. Elvis Ross, Pursuivant; James Kenyon, Assistant Pursuivant; Maurice Gordon Jones, Wm. T. Bell, Wm. A. Robinson, Arthur Coles Perry, Wm. Matthew Haynes, and Wm. Heron Beck, Stewards. Past Rank—Harry Wm. Cooke and Geo. Proudman, Senior Wardens; Robt. C. Whitelegg, W. T. Thompstone, and John H. Laybourne, Junior Wardens; John Nicholson, Joseph Briscoe, and Arthur E. A. Jympson, Senior Deacons; Arthur H. Heap, Henry Bird Johnson, Wm. Lawson, and Richard Thomas Crosby, Junior Deacons; Alfred G. W. Provart and Jesse D. Ireland, Deputy Directors of Ceremonies.

1916. *Stalybridge.*—Thomas Henry Annett, Senior Warden; Wm. Henry Pincombe, Junior Warden; Revs. Arthur F. Aldis and John Ellis, Chaplains; Dr Geo. John Awburn, Treasurer; A. Marshall Higham, Registrar; Chas. Hewitson Nelson, Deputy Grand Registrar; Fredk. Woolfall, Director of Ceremonies; Wm. Dawson Booth, Reginald Ashley Larmouth, James Henry Howell, John M. Stuart Edwards, Senior Deacons; Samuel George Owens, Alfred Banton, Joshua West, and Dr Arthur Bicknell, Junior Deacons; Rev. Leonard T. W. Parr, Assistant Grand Chaplain; William Williams, Superintendent of Works; Richard England, Assistant Superintendent of Works; Fred Bird, Deputy Director of Ceremonies; Wm. Hargreaves, Geo. R. V. Pritchard, Isaiah Slater, Richard Timmis Turner, Edward Robinson, Deputy Directors of Ceremonies; Edwin H. Hewlett, Sword Bearer; Wm. Marsden, Deputy Sword Bearer; Sam. A. Rhodes, Assistant Sword Bearer; Humphrey Davies and H. Edward Howell, Standard Bearers; Wm. Armstrong, Assistant Secretary; J. Herbert England (Mus. Doc.), Organist; Robt. E. Goffin, Pursuivant; John Ramsden, Assistant Pursuivant; Richard Edgell, Tyler; Thornton Ousey, Robert W. Holland, Thos. Bovay Parry, Herbert Bates, Chas. B. Lowe, and Daniel Pogson, Stewards. Brevet Rank—James Thos.

Catlow and Thomas Dunham, Senior Wardens; Tom Simpson, J. Hamilton Jackson, and J. Fredk. Smith, Junior Wardens; John Lakin, Smith Garnett, James H. Clayton, Arthur Albert Cohoon, Senior Deacons; H. R. Boydell, M. C. Sunter, Dennis B. Seamon, Geo. Barlow, and Charles A. Toyn, Junior Deacons.

1917. *New Brighton.*—H. Channing Howell, Senior Warden; Wm. Slack, Junior Warden; Revs. James T. Vale and Samuel Gasking, Chaplains; William Henry Dean, Treasurer; Fred Thompson, Registrar; Percy J. Almond, Deputy Registrar; Frederick Woolfall, Director of Ceremonies; William Robinson, William Bates, Fred Newton and Charles Fredk. Read, Senior Deacons; William Edward Horrocks, Robert Rawlinson, Evan Williams, and Thomas William Sumners, Junior Deacons; Rev. David Catt, Assistant Chaplain; William Toulouse, Superintendent of Works; William John Reid, Assistant Superintendent of Works; Hugh Pemberton, John Crossley Pratt, Joseph Edward Cook, James Williamson, Joshua Garside, and Joseph Cooper, Assistant Directors of Ceremonies; Joseph Phillips, Sword Bearer; Walter Ernest Evans, Deputy Sword Bearer; Robert Hughes, Assistant Sword Bearer; James Benjamin Reynolds and Richard Clowes Done, Standard Bearers; David Roger Rowlands, Assistant Secretary; Harry J. Stephens, Organist; Charles Wilfred Statham, Pursuivant; James Pimlott, Assistant Pursuivant; John Henry Broomhead, Robert Charles Stephens, William Hayes, Thomas William Weale, A. E. Evans, and James Hodgson, Stewards. Brevet Rank—Vernon H. Henderson, Registrar; Edward F. Beddard, Walter Sutherst, John Cumming, and William Miles Bratt, Senior Deacons; Joseph E. Smith, Joseph K. M'Mahon, Thomas Lowry, Arthur Sharp, senr., H. S. Hayco, and Edward Jones, Junior Deacons; Edward Woodward, William Connor, and Squire Lord, Assistant Directors of Ceremonies. Bi-Centenary Promotions—Joseph O. Brandrith, William H. Moore, Senior Wardens; John Phillips, George W. Bebbington, A. C. G. Wallace, and Clifford Collard, Junior Wardens; Adolph Campbell Meyer, Deputy Registrar; Alfred J. Fishlock, Henry Branch, George Brooks, Bridge Hopkinson, W. G. Cronan, and James T. Kerridge, Senior Deacons; John Richard Owen, Junior Deacon.

1918. *Northwich.*—Edward Fredk. Beddard, Senior Warden; Walter Sutherst, Junior Warden; Revs. Samuel Gasking and Herbert Edward Stephens, Chaplains; Thomas Wilkinson, Treasurer; George Henry Hindley, Registrar; Charles Atkin, Deputy Registrar; Joseph Clarke, Secretary; Fredk. Woolfall, Director of Ceremonies; Frank Hyde Gaskell, Wm. Yowart Hodgson, Joseph Wainwright, and James Thomas Burns, Senior Deacons; Thomas H. Cookson, Daniel Pogson, William H. Dobbs, and Albert Mugelli, Junior Deacons; Rev. Wm. Robert-Jones, Assistant Chaplain; William Williams, Superintendent of Works; Wm. Henry Taylor, Assistant Superintendent of Works; James M'Lerie, John William Herringshaw, Thomas

Redfern, Joseph Heginbotham, Samuel Thompson, and Hugh Richard Thomas, Assistant Directors of Ceremonies; Captain William Oliver Davies, Sword Bearer; Arthur Cartwright, Deputy Sword Bearer; William Grayson, Assistant Sword Bearer; John H. Baird and John Williams, Standard Bearers; Henry Law, Assistant Secretary; James Watson, Organist; James Houghton Battley, Pursuivant; William Andrews, Assistant Pursuivant; Josiah Whate, Fredk. Richardson Yarwood, Christopher Thomas Eachus, Albert Ernest Littler, Edward Arthur Nickels, and Walter John Stanbridge, Stewards. Brevet Rank—Major James Wm. Shaw and Walter Conway, Senior Wardens; James George Frost, Ernest Pritchard, and J. W. Beaumont, Junior Wardens; William Sanders Garratt, Registrar; James Ratcliffe-Gaylard, M.D.; Thomas Irvine Overington, William Marquis Whitehead, and George Swallow, Senior Deacons; Henry B. Webb, Joseph Henry Wright, and James William Fairbrother, Junior Deacons; E. Sims-Hilditch, Organist.

1919. *Chester.*—Senior Warden: Fredk. Woolfall, No. 477, Mersey, Birkenhead. Junior Warden: John Williamson, No. 721, Independence, Chester. Chaplains: Rev. Arthur G. Sykes, No. 2799, John Brunner, Winsford; Rev. Milton P. Uttley, No. 428, Sincerity, Northwich. Treasurer: Albert L. Gardner, No. 2386, Clarence, Chester. Registrar: Richard Farmer, No. 321, Unity, Crewe. Deputy Registrar: Romeo H. Rideal, No. 3731, Cheadle. Secretary: Joseph Clarke, No. 1576, Dee, Parkgate. Director of Ceremonies: Alfred G. W. Provart, No. 3656, Stockport. Senior Deacons: Alfred Hulme, No. 322, Peace, Stockport; Frank Weston, No. 3294, Bohemian, Birkenhead; John Eades, No. 3382, Cornwall Legh, Sale; Charles Williamson, No. 3555, Timperley, Altrincham. Junior Deacons: James Herbert Lea, No. 533, Eaton, Congleton; Uriah Spencer, No. 830, Endeavour, Dukinfield; Thomas Ralph Garton, No. 2826, Birkenhead; John Gilbert Whyatt, No. 3749, Hale. Assistant Chaplain: Rev. John C. Magee, No. 2144, De Tatton, Altrincham. Superintendent of Works: William Williams, No. 2876, Birkenhead. Assistant Superintendent of Works, Andrew Boyd, No. 3513, Baron Egerton, Birkenhead. Deputy Director of Ceremonies: John James M'Quone, No. 3653, James Thompson, Birkenhead. Assistant Directors of Ceremonies: John Sherwin, No. 293, King's Friends, Nantwich; Harry L. Hutchinson, No. 721, Independence, Chester; Robert Martin, No. 1565, Earl of Chester, Lymm; Thomas Parr, No. 2690, West Kirby; Thomas Hugh Mason, No. 2876, Temperance, Birkenhead. Sword Bearer: Robert Rostron, No. 2368, Alan, Alderley Edge. Deputy Sword Bearer: Alexander Adams, No. 3449, Cheshire Provincial Stewards, Sale. Assistant Sword Bearer: James Joseph Mott, No. 2386, Clarence, Chester. Standard Bearers: John Joseph Yates, No. 3024, Newton, Hyde; F. H. Rogers, Assheton Egerton, Altrincham. Assistant Secretary: Henry Arthur Read, No. 3148, Edward VII., Altrincham Organist: John Williams, No. 2609, Travellers, Chester. Pursuivant: William

Russell, No. 3333, Friendship, Brooklands. Assistant Pursuivant: George Edgar Lewis, No. 2433, Minerva, Birkenhead. Stewards: Frank Findley, No. 3731, Cheadle; Wm. Singleton, No. 2609, Travellers, Chester; John Southard, No. 3447, Deva, Chester; Edward Woods, No. 3449, Provincial Stewards, Sale; Fred Caldwell, No. 3656, Stockport.

Peace Rank, 1919-20.—Senior Wardens: Sir John F. L. Brunner, No. 2799, John Brunner Lodge, Winsford; Oswald Andrew, No. 1406, Stamford and Warrington, Stalybridge; George E. Osborne, No. 3333, Friendship, Brooklands; Fredk. Richardson, No. 3447, Deva, Chester. Junior Wardens: Thos. H. Edward, No. 721, Independence, Chester; Dr William Arthur Pierce, No. 2496, Wirral, Birkenhead; John S. Derbyshire, No. 3148, Edward VII., Altrincham; Charles H. Nelson, St Hilary, Liscard. Registrar: Fredk. O'Connell, No. 3036, Wallasey, New Brighton. Senior Deacons: Thos. W. Johnson, No. 89, Unanimity, Dukinfield; Andrew Irving, No. 605, Combermere, Birkenhead; Oswald F. L. France, No. 1408, Stamford and Warrington, Stalybridge; John Taylor Milne, No. 2386, Chester; Robert Beattie, No. 2927, Coronation, Sale; Edward B. Eastwood, No. 2916, William Hesketh Lever, Collegium, Port Sunlight.

Past Rank, 1919-20.—Senior Wardens: Dr John Oldershaw, No. 3514, King George V., Liscard; William Slack, No. 323, Concord, Stockport; William Moody, No. 2144, De Tatton, Altrincham. Junior Wardens: Arthur Ernest Ash, No. 2132, Egerton, Liscard; Fredk. E. Owens, No. 2433, Minerva, Birkenhead; George James Whitney, No. 3449, Provincial Stewards, Sale; Hugh Pemberton, No. 3832, Ionic, Wallasey. Registrar: Alfred Barlow, No. 533, Eaton, Congleton. Senior Deacons: Harrop Marshall, No. 323, Concord, Stockport; John Brooke, No. 428, Sincerity, Northwich; Hubert J. Wild, No. 537, Zetland, Birkenhead; Joseph Peter Cox, No. 941, De Tabley, Knutsford; Wm. Morland Hocken, No. 3657, Bidston, Birkenhead; David Barker, No. 3671, Brooklands, Cheshire. Senior Deacon: Tom Martley, No. 3462, Oxton, Birkenhead

APPENDIX

BISHOPS OF MERCIA AND CHESTER, A.D. 656 TO A.D. 1919.

Bishops of Mercia—A.D. 656, Diuma; 658, Ceollach; 659, Trumhere; 661, Jarumnan.
Bishops of Lichfield—A.D. 669, Ceadda or Chad; 673, Winifrid; 675, Saxwulf. . . . 1503, Geoffrey Blythe; 1534, Rowland Lee.
Bishops of Chester (See of Chester founded 1541):—1541, John Bird, D.D., Oxon., deprived by Queen Mary 1554, buried at Great Dunmow, Essex, 1558. 1554, George Cotes, D.D., Oxon., died at Chester 1555. 1556, Cuthbert Scott, D.D., Camb., deprived, and died at Louvain 1565. 1561, William Downham, D.D., Oxon., died in November 1577, buried in Chester Cathedral. 1579, William Chaderton, D.D., Camb., translated to Lincoln 1595. 1595, Hugh Billet or Bellot, D.D., Camb., buried at Wrexham. 1597, Richard Vaughan, D.D., Camb., translated to London, 1604. 1605, George Lloyd, D.D., Camb., buried in Chester Cathedral. 1616, Thomas Morton, D.D., Camb., translated to Lichfield and Coventry, 1619. 1619, John Bridgman, D.D., Camb., held the See until Episcopacy was suspended by the Commonwealth; died about 1652, and was buried at Kinnersley, Shropshire. 1660, Brian Walton, D.D., Camb., died at London, buried in St Paul's Cathedral 1661. 1662, Henry Ferne, D.D., Camb., died at London before he took possession of the See. 1662, George Hall, D.D., Oxon., died at Wigan, and was buried in the Parish Church there 1668. 1668, John Wilkins, D.D., F.R.S., Camb., died at London, and was buried at St Lawrence Jewry. 1673, John Pearson, D.D., F.R.S., Camb., died at Chester, buried in the Cathedral. 1686, Thomas Cartwright, D.D., Oxon., died in Ireland, and was buried in Christ Church, Dublin, 1689. 1689, Nicholas Stratford, D.D., Oxon., died in 1707, and was buried in Chester Cathedral. 1708, Sir Wm. Dawes, Bart., D.D., Camb., translated to York. 1714, Francis Gastrell, D.D., Oxon., died 1725, buried in Christ Church, Oxford. 1726, Samuel Peploe, D.D., Oxon., died 1752, buried in Chester Cathedral. 1752, Edmund Keene, D.D., Camb., translated to Ely 1771. 1771, William Markham, D.C.L., Oxon., translated to York, 1777. 1777, Beilby Porteus, D.D., Camb., translated to London, 1787. 1788, William Cleaver, D.D., Oxon., translated to Bangor 1800. 1800, Henry Wm. Majendie, D.D., Camb., translated to Bangor 1809. 1810, Bowyer Edwd. Sparke, D.D., Camb., translated to Ely 1812. 1812, George Henry Law, D.D., Camb., translated to Bath and Wells, 1824. 1824, Charles J. Blomfield, D.D., Camb., translated to London 1828. 1828, John Bird Sumner, D.D., Camb., translated to Canterbury 1848. 1848, John Graham, D.D., Camb., died at Chester, 1865, buried in the Cemetery, Chester. 1865, William Jacobson, D.D., Oxon., died at Chester 1884, buried in the Cemetery, Chester. 1884, William Stubbs, D.D., LL.D., Oxon., translated to Oxford 1888. 1889, Francis John Jayne, D.D., Oxon. 1919, Henry Luke Paget, D.D., translated from Stepney Diocese of London.

CHESHIRE PARLIAMENTARY ELECTION RESULTS, 1832 to 1918.

1832. *North-East Cheshire*—Edward John Stanley; William Tatton Egerton. *South-West Cheshire*—Richard, Viscount Belgrave (Lord Grosvenor), 2410 votes; George Wilbraham, 2655. *Stockport*—Thomas Marsland (C.), 551; John Horatio Lloyd (L.), 444; Henry Marsland (L.), 431; Edward Davies Davenport (L.), 237. *Macclesfield*—John Ryle (C.), 443; John Brocklehurst (L.), 402; Thomas Grimsditch (C.), 186. *Chester*—Lord Grosvenor; John Jervis.
1835. *North Cheshire*—Edward John Stanley; William Tatton Egerton. *South Cheshire*—Sir Philip Egerton; Sir John Egerton. *Stockport*—Henry Marsland (L.), 582; Major Marsland (C.), 482; Edward Davies Davenport (L.), 361. *Macclesfield*—John Ryle (C.), 464; John Brocklehurst (L.), 424; Thomas Grimsditch (C.), 341.
1837. *North and South Cheshire*—No change. *Stockport*—Henry Marsland (L.), 467; Major Marsland (C.) 467; Richard Cobden (L.), 412. *Macclesfield*—John Brocklehurst (L.), 546; Thomas Grimsditch (C.), 471; Robert Hyde Greg (L.), 292.

CHESHIRE: ITS TRADITIONS AND HISTORY 353

1841. *North Cheshire*—Wm. Tatton Egerton; George Cornwall Legh. *South Cheshire*—John Tollemache; Sir Philip Egerton. *Stockport*—Henry Marsland (L.), 569; Richard Cobden (L.), 543; Major Marsland (C.), 351. *Macclesfield*—John Brocklehurst (L.), 534; Thomas Grimsditch (C.), 410; Samuel Stocks (L.), 327.

1847-57. The representation of *North and South Cheshire* remained unchanged. *Stockport*—Richard Cobden (L.), 642; James Heald (C.), 570; James Kershaw (L.), 537; John West (Chartist), 14. *Macclesfield*—John Brocklehurst (L.), 598; Thomas Grimsditch (C.), 428. By-Election—Mr Cobden elected to sit for the West Riding of Yorkshire, causing a vacancy at Stockport. Result: (elected) James Kershaw (L.), 545; Major Marsland (C.), 518.

1861. *Birkenhead*—John Laird (C.), 1643; Thomas Brassey, Junr. (L.), 1296. *Stockport*—Alderman James Kershaw (L.), 769; John Benj. Smith (C.), 641; Wm. Gibb (L.), 594. On the death of Alderman Kershaw, new writ, May 1864, Edward Wm. Watkin (afterwards Baronet). *North Cheshire*—Geo. Cornwall Legh (C.); Hon. Wilbraham Egerton (C.). *South Cheshire*—Sir Philip de M. G. Egerton, Bart. (C.); John Tollemache (C.). *Chester (City)*—Earl Grosvenor (L.), 1464; P. S. Humberston (L.), 1110; E. Gibbon Salusbury (C.), 708. *Macclesfield*—John Brocklehurst, Junr. (L.); Edward C. Egerton (C.).

1865. *North Cheshire*—Geo. Cornwall Legh (C.); Hon. Wilbraham Egerton (C.). *South Cheshire*—Sir Philip de M. G. Egerton, Bart. (C.); John Tollemache (C.). *Chester (City)*—Earl Grosvenor (L.), 1284; Wm. Henry Gladstone (L.), 860; William Fenton (C.), 565; Henry Cecil Raikes (C.), 533. *Macclesfield*—Edward C. Egerton (C.), 471; John Brocklehurst (L.), 469; David Chadwick (L.), 421. *Birkenhead*—John Laird (C.), 2108; Henry Mather Jackson (L.), 1073. *Stockport*—Edward Wm. Watkin (L.), 736; John Benj. Smith (L.), 664; William Tipping (C.), 601.

1868. *East Cheshire*—Edward Christopher Egerton (C.); Wm. John Legh (C.). On death of Mr Egerton, new writ, October 1869—Wm. Cunliffe Brooks (C.), 2908; Sir Edward Wm. Watkin (L.), 1815. *Mid Cheshire*—Hon. Wilbraham Egerton (C.), 3071; Geo. Cornwall Legh (C.), 3057; Hon. John Leicester Warren (L.), 2482. *West Cheshire*—Sir Philip de M. G. Egerton, Bart. (C.); John Tollemache (C.), returned unopposed. *Chester (City)*—Earl Grosvenor (L.), 2275; Henry Cecil Raikes (C.), 2219; E. G. Salusbury (L.), 1284; Richard Hoare (L.), 1031. On Earl Grosvenor becoming a Peer on the death of his father, new writ, December 1869, the Hon. Norman Grosvenor was returned. *Birkenhead*—John Laird (C.), 2935; Captain Sherard Osborn, R.N., C.B. (L.), 2056. *Macclesfield*—Wm. Coare Brocklehurst (L.), 2812; David Chadwick (L.), 2509; Wm. Meriton Eaton (C.), 2321. *Stockport*—William Tipping (C.), 2722; John Benj. Smith (L.), 2677; Sir Edward Wm. Watkin (L.), 2615; W. Ambrose (C.), 2497.

1874. *East Cheshire*—Wm. John Legh (C.); Wm. Cunliffe Brooks (C.), unopposed. *Mid-Cheshire*—Hon. Wilbraham Egerton (C.); Egerton Leigh (C.), unopposed. *West Cheshire*—Sir Philip de M. G. Egerton, Bart. (C.); Wilbraham F. T. Tollemache (C.), unopposed. *Chester (City)*—Henry Cecil Raikes (C.), 2356; Right Hon. John G. Dodson (L.), 2134; Sir Thos. Gibbons Frost (L.), 2125. *Birkenhead*—John Laird (C.), 2692; James Samuelson (L.), 1580. By-election, 24th November, David M'Iver (C.), 3421; Samuel Stitt (L.), 2474. *Macclesfield*—Wm. Coare Brocklehurst (L.), 3173; David Chadwick (L.), 2792; Wm. Meriton Eaton (C.), 2750; J. L. Croston (C.), 2250. *Stockport*—Chas. Henry Hopwood (L.), 3538; Fredk. Pennington (L.), 3538; Wm. Tipping (C.), 3406; Percy Mitford (C.), 3372.

1880. *East Cheshire*—Wm. Cunliffe Brooks (C.), 3424; Wm. John Legh (C.), 3310; Gibbon Bayley Worthington (L.), 2032; Thos. S. Bazley (L.), 1947. *Mid-Cheshire*—Hon. Wilbraham Egerton (C.), 3868; Piers Egerton-Warburton (C.), 3700; Geo. Wm. Latham (L.), 3374; Vernon Kirk Armitage (L.), 3247. On the Hon. W. Egerton becoming Lord Egerton, new writ, March 1883. Result of election: Hon. Alan de T. Egerton (C.), 4214; Geo. Wm. Latham (L.), 3592. *West Cheshire*—Sir Philip de M. G. Egerton, Bart. (C.), 4773; Hon. Wilbraham F. Tollemache (C.), 4637; Wm. Cornwallis West (L.), 4009; Charles Crompton (L.), 3785. *Chester (City)*—Right Honourable John G. Dodson (L.), 3204; Hon. Beilby Lawley (L.), 3147; Right Hon. Henry Cecil Raikes (C.), 2056; Thomas Myles Sandys (C.), 1961; F. W. Margarini (Ind.), 16. *Birkenhead*—David M'Iver (C.), 4025; A. J. Williams (L.), 3658. *Macclesfield*—Wm. Coare Brocklehurst (L.), 2946; David Chadwick (L.), 2744; Wm. Meriton Eaton (C.), 2678; T. C. Whitehouse (C.), 2188. *Stockport*—Chas. Henry Hopwood (L.), 4232; Fredk. Pennington (L.), 4103; Lieut.-Colonel Geo. Arthur Fernley (C.), 3873; Henry Bell (C.), 3685.

1881. *West Cheshire*—Henry J. Tollemache, *vice* Sir Philip de Malpas Grey Egerton, deceased. Writ issued April 1881.

z

1884. *Mid Cheshire*—The Hon. Alan de Tatton Egerton ; Piers Egerton-Warburton. *East Cheshire*—Wm. C. Brooks ; W. J. Legh. *West Cheshire*—The Hon. W. Tollemache ; Henry Jas. Tollemache. *Chester*—Writ suspended.
1885. *Cheshire (Wirral Division)*—Captain E. T. D. Cotton (C.), 4756 ; J. Tomkinson (L.), 3261. *Eddisbury Division*—H. J. Tollemache (C.), 4285 ; L. Irwell (L.), 4164. *Macclesfield Division*—Wm. Coare Brocklehurst (L.), 3311 ; W. C. Brooks (C.), 2846. *Crewe Division*—G. W. Latham (L.), 5089 ; O. L. Stephen (C.), 4281. *Northwich Division*—John Tomlinson Brunner (L.), 5023 ; W. H. Verdin (C.), 3995. *Altrincham Division*—John Brooks (C.), 4798 ; I. S. Leadam (L.), 4046. *Hyde Division*—Thos. Gair Ashton (L.), 4546 ; Colonel Wm. John Legh (C.), 3990. *Knutsford Division*—Hon. Alan de Tatton Egerton (C.), 4663 ; John Emmott Barlow (L.), 3419. *Chester*—Dr B. Foster (L.), 2740 ; R. A. Yerburgh (C.), 2440. *Birkenhead*—General Sir E. B. Hamley (C.), 5733 ; W. R. Kennedy (L.), 4560. *Stockport*—Louis J. Jennings (C.), 4855 ; W. Tipping (C.), 4498 ; C. H. Hopwood (L.), 4486 ; J. Leigh (L.), 4132.
1886. *Altrincham Division*—John Brooks (C.), 4798 ; I. S. Leadam (L.), 4046. By-election in March, *vice* John Brooks, died 8th March 1886, Sir W. C. Brooks (C.), 4508 ; I. S. Leadam, 3925. General election, July 1886, Sir W. C. Brooks returned unopposed. *Birkenhead*—Lieut.-General Sir E. B. Hamley (C.), 5733 ; W. R. Kennedy (L.), 4460. *Chester*—Dr B. W. Foster (L.), 2740 ; Robert A. Yerburgh (C.), 2440. *Crewe Division*—Geo. Wm. Latham (L.), 5089 ; Oscar Leslie Stephen (C.), 4281. *Eddisbury Division*—Henry James Tollemache (C.), 4285 ; Laurence Irwell (L.), 4164. *Hyde Division*—Thos. Gair Ashton (L.), 4546 ; Colonel Wm. John Legh (C.), 3990. *Knutsford Division*—Hon. Alan de T. Egerton (C.), 4663 ; J. E. Barlow (L.), 3419. *Macclesfield Division*—Wm. C. Brocklehurst (L.), 3311 ; Wm. Cunliffe Brooks (C.), 2846. *Northwich Division*—J. T. Brunner (L.), 5023 ; W. H. Verdin (C.), 3995. *Stalybridge* (before 1886 given as a Lancashire constituency)—Thos. H. Sidebottom (C.), 3169 ; William Summers (L.), 2950. *Stockport*—Louis John Jennings (C.), 4855 ; William Tipping (C.), 4498 ; Joseph Leigh (L.), 4486 ; C. H. Hopwood, Q.C. (L.), 4132. *Wirral Division*—Captain E. T. D. Cotton (C.), 4756 ; James Tomkinson (L.), 3261.
1892. *Wirral Division*—E. T. D. Cotton-Jodrell (C.), 5509 ; B. C. de Lisle (L.), 3051. *Eddisbury Division*—H. J. Tollemache (C.), 4578 ; J. Tomkinson (L.), 4042. *Macclesfield Division*—W. Bromley-Davenport (C.), 4332 ; J. C. M'Coan (L.), 3396. *Crewe Division*—W. S. B. M'Laren (L.), 5558 ; H. W. Chatterton (C.), 3990. *Northwich Division*—J. T. Brunner (L.), 5580 ; G. Whiteley (C.), 4325. *Altrincham Division* (By-election, July 1892)—C. R. Disraeli (C.), 5056 ; I. S. Leadam (L.), 4258. *Hyde Division*—J. W. Sidebotham (C.), 4525 ; T. G. Ashton (L.), 4220. *Knutsford Division*—Hon. A. de Tatton Egerton (C.), 4754 ; A. M. Latham (L.), 2792. *Chester*—R. A. Yerburgh (C.), 3148 ; Baron Halkett (L.), 2528. *Stalybridge*—Tom Harrop Sidebottom (C.), 3289 ; J. M. Wright (L.), 2943. *Stockport*—Joseph Leigh (L.), 5202 ; Louis J. Jennings (C.), 4986 ; Major M. Hume (L.), 4876 ; Hon. P. Bowes-Lyon (C.), 4681. *Birkenhead*—Viscount Bury (C.), 5760 ; W. H. Lever (L.), 5156.
1894. *Wirral Division*—E. T. D. Cotton-Jodrell (C.), 5599 ; B. C. de Lisle (L.), 3051. *Eddisbury Division*—H. J. Tollemache (C.), 4578 ; J. Tomkinson (L.), 4042. *Macclesfield Division*—W. Bromley-Davenport (C.), 4332 ; J. C. M'Coan (L.), 3396. *Crewe Division*—W. S. B. M'Laren (L.), 5558 ; H. W. Chatterton (C.), 3990. *Northwich Division*—J. T. Brunner (L.), 5580 ; G. Whiteley (C.), 4325. *Altrincham Division*—C. R. Disraeli (C.), 5056 ; I. S. Leadam (L.), 4258. *Hyde Division*—J. W. Sidebotham (C.), 4525 ; T. G. Ashton (L.), 4220. *Knutsford Division*—Hon. A. de Tatton Egerton (C.), 4754 ; A. M. Latham (L.), 2793. *Chester*—R. A. Yerburgh (C.), 3148 ; Baron Halkett (L.), 2528. *Stalybridge*—Tom Harrop Sidebottom (C.), 3289 ; J. M. Wright (L.), 2943. *Stockport*—Sir Joseph Leigh (L.), 5202 ; Major M. Hume (L.), 4876 ; Hon. P. Bowes-Lyon (C.), 4681. On the death of Mr Jennings, new writ, February 1893, George Whiteley (C.), 5264 ; Major M. A. Sharp-Hume (L.), 4799. *Birkenhead*—Viscount Bury (C.), 5760 ; W. H. Lever (L.), 5156. By-election, 17th October 1894. Result : Elliott Lees (C.), 6149 ; W. H. Lever (L.), 6043.
1895. *Wirral Division*—E. T. D. Cotton-Jodrell (C.), unopposed. *Eddisbury Division*—H. J. Tollemache (C.), 5176 ; R. Bate (L.), 3371. *Macclesfield Division*—W. Bromley-Davenport, unopposed. *Crewe Division*—Hon. R. A. Ward (C.), 5413 ; W. S. B. M'Laren (L.), 4863. *Northwich Division*—Sir J. T. Brunner, Bart. (L.), 5706 ; T. Ward (L.-U.), 4068. *Altrincham Division*—C. R. Disraeli (C.), 5264 ; A. M. Latham (L.), 3889. *Hyde Division*—J. W. Sidebotham (C.), 4735 ; G. W. Rhodes (L.), 3844 ; C. S. Christie (Lab.), 448. *Knutsford Division*—Hon. A. de Tatton Egerton (C.), unopposed. *Chester*—R. A. Yerburgh, unopposed. *Birkenhead*

CHESHIRE: ITS TRADITIONS AND HISTORY 355

—Elliott Lees (C.), 6178; W. H. Lever (L.), 5974. *Stalybridge*—Tom Harrop Sidebottom (C.), 3389; J. M. Wright (L.), 2757. *Stockport*—G. Whiteley (C.), 5410; B. V. Melville (C.), 5067; Sir Jos. Leigh (L.), 4933; J. Roskill (L.), 4562.

FIRST PARLIAMENT OF KING EDWARD VII.

1900. *Wirral Division*—J. Hoult (C.), 6084; W. H. Lever (L.), 5079. *Eddisbury Division*—H. J. Tollemache, unopposed. *Macclesfield Division*—W. Bromley-Davenport (C.), unopposed. *Crewe Division*—J. Tomkinson (L.), 6120; J. E. Reiss (C.), 4921. *Northwich Division*—Sir J. T. Brunner, Bart. (L.), 5377; C. L. Samson (C.), 4678. *Altrincham Division*—C. R. Disraeli (C.), 5685; E. F. Alford (L.), 4177. *Hyde Division*—E. Chapman (C.), 4774; J. F. Brunner (L.), 4195. *Knutsford Division*—Hon. A. de Tatton Egerton (C.), unopposed. *Chester*—R. A. Yerburgh (C.), 3303; H. Idris (L.), 2574. *Birkenhead*—Sir Elliott Lees (C.), unopposed. *Stalybridge*—M. White Ridley (C.), 3321; J. F. Cheetham (L.), 3240. *Stockport*—Sir J. Leigh (L.), 5666; B. V. Melville (C.), 5377; G. Green (L.), 5200; A. Hillier (C.), 5098.
1906. *Wirral Division*—W. H. Lever (L.), 8833; J. Hoult (U.), 7132. *Eddisbury Division*—Hon. A. L. Stanley (L.), 5315; Colonel E. T. D. Cotton-Jodrell (U.), 4192. *Macclesfield Division*—Colonel W. B. Brocklehurst (L.), 4251; W. Bromley-Davenport (U.), 3757. *Crewe Division*—J. Tomkinson (L.), 7805; J. H. Welsford (U.), 5297. *Northwich Division*—Sir J. T. Brunner, Bart. (L.), 6343; Colonel North (U.), 4551. *Altrincham Division*—W. J. Crossley (L.), 8358; C. R. Disraeli (U.), 5667. *Hyde Division*—C. D. Schwann (L.), 5545; E. Chapman (U.), 4482. *Knutsford Division*—A. J. King (L.), 5296; Hon. A. de Tatton Egerton (U.), 4596. *Chester*—A. Mond (L.), 3524; R. A. Yerburgh (U.), 3477. *Stalybridge*—J. F. Cheetham (L.), 3836; J. Travis Clegg (U.), 3382. *Stockport*—G. J. Wardle (Lab.), 7299; J. Duckworth (L.), 6544; H. Barnston (U.), 4591; Hon. H. O'Neill (U.), 4058. *Birkenhead*—H. Vivian (L.), 7074; Sir E. Lees (U.), 5271; J. A. Kensitt (Protestant), 2118.

FIRST PARLIAMENT OF KING GEORGE V., ELECTED 1910.

Birkenhead—H. Vivian (L.), 8120; A. Bigland (U.), 7976. *Eddisbury Division*—H. Barnston (U.), 5664; Hon. Arthur L. Stanley (L.), 4976. *Chester*—R. A. Yerburgh (U.), 3978; E. Paul (L.), 3776. *Hyde*—F. Neilson (L.), 4476; T. Eastham (U.), 4461; W. C. Anderson (Lab.), 2401. *Stalybridge*—J. Wood (U.), 3736; A. H. Bright (L.), 3679. *Knutsford*—A. J. Sykes (U.), 6199; A. J. King (L.), 5084. *Stockport*—G. J. Wardle (Lab.), 6682; S. L. Hughes (L.), 6645; G. C. Raine (U.), 5268; J. S. Rankin (U.), 5249. *Macclesfield*—Colonel W. B. Brocklehurst (L.), 4534; Lieut.-Colonel W. Bromley-Davenport (U.), 4384. *Altrincham*—Sir Wm. J. Crossley, Bart. (L.), 8709; Viscount Bury (U.), 7808. *Northwich*—J. F. L. Brunner (L.), 6661; C. Williams (U.), 5542. *Crewe* (By-election, 30th April 1910)—W. S. B. M'Laren (L.), 7639; J. H. Welsford (U.), 6041. *Wirral*—Gershom Stewart (U.), 10,309; E. P. Jones (L.), 8862.

SECOND PARLIAMENT OF KING GEORGE V., ELECTED 10th DECEMBER 1910, MET 31st JANUARY 1911.

Birkenhead (By-election)—A. Bigland (U.), 8394; H. H. Vivian (L.), 7249. *Altrincham*—J. R. Kebty Fletcher (U.), 8002; Sir W. J. Crossley, Bart. (L.), 7882. By-election, 28th May 1913—G. C. Hamilton (U.), 9409; the Hon. L. U. Kay Shuttleworth (L.), 8147. *Crewe*—W. S. B. M'Laren (L.), 7629; E. Y. Craig (U.), 5925. By-election, 26th July 1912—E. Y. Craig (U.), 6260; H. Murphy (L.), 5294; J. H. Holmes (Lab.), 2485. *Eddisbury*—H. Barnston (U.), 5312; Hon. Arthur L. Stanley (L.), 5023. *Hyde*—F. Neilson (L.), 5562; T. Smith (U.), 5268. *Stalybridge*—J. Wood (U.), 3807; A. H. Bright (L.), 3414. By-election, March 1916—T. O. Jacobson (Coalition), 4089; D. P. Davies (Independent), 3215. *Knutsford*—Colonel Sir A. J. Sykes, Bart. (U.), 6127; J. H. Whitworth (L.), 4658. *Macclesfield*—Colonel W. B. Brocklehurst (L.), 4410; B. Dent (U.), 4142. *Northwich*—J. F. L. Brunner (L.), 6071; J. de Knoop (U.), 5741. *Wirral*—G. L. Stewart (U.), 10,043; A. J. Ashton (L.), 7727. *Chester* (By-election, 29th February 1916)—Captain Sir Owen C. Phillips (U.), unopposed. *Stockport*—S. L. Hughes (L.), 6169; G. J. Wardle (Lab.), 6094; J. R. Lort Williams (U.), 5234; R. Campbell (U.), 5183.
1918. *Altrincham*—Major G. C. Hamilton (Coalition-Unionist), 20,421; A. Middleton (Lab.), 7685 (majority, 12,736). *Birkenhead* (*East*)—A. Bigland (Coalition-Unionist), 13,012; J. Finnigan (Lab.), 5399; H. Graham White (L.), 1787. *Birkenhead* (*West*)—Lieut.-Colonel H. M.

z 2

CHESHIRE: ITS TRADITIONS AND HISTORY

Grayson (Coalition-Unionist), 10,881 ; W. H. Egan (Lab.), 5673 ; H. C. Bickersteth (L.), 1753. *City of Chester*—Sir Owen C. Phillips (Coalition-Unionist), 10,043 ; Edward Paul (L.), 4993 ; Arthur Mason (Lab.), 2799. *Crewe*—Sir Joseph Davies (Coalition-Liberal), 13,392 ; J. T. Brownlie (Lab.), 10,439. *Eddisbury*—Major H. Barnston (Coalition-Unionist), unopposed. *Knutsford*—Colonel Sir A. J. Sykes (Coalition-Unionist), unopposed. *Macclesfield*—J. R. Remer (Coalition-Unionist), 14,277 ; —. Pimblott (Lab.), 10,253. *Northwich*—Lieut.-Commander H. Dewhurst (Coalition-Unionist), 15,444 ; J. F. L. Brunner (L.), 9723. *Stalybridge and Hyde*—Sir John Wood, Bart. (U.), 13,462 ; W. Fowden (Lab.), 6508 ; T. O. Jacobsen (L.), 6241. *Stockport*—S. L. Hughes (Coalition-Liberal) and G. J. Wardle (Lab.), unopposed. *Wallasey*—Dr B. F. P. Macdonald (Coalition-Unionist), 14,633 ; W. M. Citrine (Lab.), 4384 ; J. M. Hay (L.), 4055 ; T. D. Owen (Independent), 3407. *Wirral Division*—Gershom Stewart (Coalition-Unionist), unopposed.

POPULATION OF CHESHIRE—CENSUS 1911.

Population of Administrative County and County Boroughs, 954,779. Administrative County, 597,771 ; Urban Districts, 414,523 ; Rural Districts, 183,248. County Borough of Birkenhead, 130,794 ; Chester, 39,028. Stockport, Cheshire part, 76,682 ; Lancashire part, 31,858—total, 108,682. Borough of Wallasey, 78,504.

CONSTITUTION OF THE CHESHIRE COUNTY COUNCIL.

Representatives of County Electoral Divisions, 39. Representatives of Municipal Boroughs : Congleton, 1 ; Crewe, 4 ; Dukinfield, 2 ; Hyde, 3 ; Macclesfield, 4 ; Stalybridge, 3 = 17—total, 56. County Aldermen, 19. Total, 75. Quorum of Council, 19.

CHESHIRE COUNTY COUNCIL, 1919.

Chairman—Colonel Sir George Dixon, Bart.
Vice-Chairman—Wm. Hodgson, Esq., M.D.

County Aldermen (19)—Frank Barlow, Sir John Emmott Barlow, Bart., Rev. Canon James Grant Bird, Lieut.-Colonel Brocklehurst Brocklehurst, Thomas Raffles Bulley, Brigadier-General William Bromley Davenport, D.S.O., Chas. Edward Davenport, John Morley, Alfred Robert Norman, Coard Squarey Pain, Richard Taswell Richardson, Sir Joseph Verdin, Bart., George Wall, Hugh Edward Wilbraham, and John Wild.

County Councillors (56)—Representing the various Electoral Divisions—James Owen Garner, William Walton Baker, John James Whitley, William Huntley Goss, Simon Gleave, Coard Squarey Pain, James Edward Marsland, William Henry Carter, John Bateman, Peter Higson, William Haslam Cross, Thomas Gibbons Frost, Thomas Cooke Goodwin, Robert Shepherd, Rev. John Hornby Armitstead, John Norcross, John Clarkeson, Samuel Walker Gould, William Parker, James Thomas Pott, Rev. John William Fortnum, Harold Chapman, Richard Wright, Edward Peter Jones, Walter Sutherst, Andrew Thomas Smith, Robert Harold Posnett, James M'Donald, Francis Joseph Poole, Major Thomas Clayton Toler, Charles Edward Parton, Joseph Banks, John Arnold, William Hough, Charles MacIver, George Arthur Pedley, Theodore Crewdson, Reginald Grayson Barton, William Miles Bratt, Sir Walter Geoffrey Shakerley, Bart., Rev. Walter Bidlake, Charles Wilson, James Henry Kettell, Charles John Bowen Cooke, Herbert Bown, Joseph Cooke, George Frederick Drinkwater, Ammon Hirst Fawley, William Brocklehurst, John Somerville, Walter Brown, William Frost, Thomas Cook, Fred Thompson, James Storrs.

Clerk of the Council and Returning Officer at County Council Elections—Reginald Potts, Chester. Deputy Clerk of the Council and Clerk to Local Pensions Committee—Hubert Potts, Chester.

WEAVER NAVIGATION TRUST.

(Appointed under the Provisions of Weaver Navigation Act, 1895, in November 1916, for three years, Life Trustees excepted.)

Representing County Council—Robert Barbour, Theodore Crewdson, T. Gibbons Frost, J. A. R. Kay, Major Chas. MacIver, Wm. M'Cracken, A. R. Norman, Coard S. Pain, R. C. Parr, Francis J. Poole, R. H. Posnett, and C. Leicester Warren. Appointed by the Cheshire County Council in place of Existing Trustees resigned or deceased—Rev. J. H. Armitstead, Captain W. H. France-Hayhurst, Lieut.-Colonel H. C. Legh, Brigadier-General Arthur Hervey Talbot, Reginald Arthur Tatton, and R. N. H. Verdin. Representing Existing Trustees (Life Trustees)—Sir Philip Henry Brian Grey-Egerton, Bart., Sir Joseph Verdin, Bart., W. H. Verdin, and Major H. E. Wilbraham. Representing Traders—Harry Stewart Boddington, Roscoe Brunner, Frederick William Clark, George Henry Cox, Charles Ditchfield, Herman John Falk, Tom Walton Foster, J. H. Gold, G. W. Malcolm, Thomas Moore, Charles William Shirley, A. T. Smith, Charles Potter Walker, and John Isaac Watts. Representing Northwich—William J. Yarwood. Representing Winsford—R. G. Barton. Clerk to Trustees—E. S. Inman.

QUARTER SESSIONS OFFICIALS, ETC.

Lord Lieutenant and *Custos Rotulorum*—His Grace the Duke of Westminster, G.C.V.O., D.S.O. High Sheriff—Sir Kenneth Irwin Crossley, Bart. Chairman of Quarter Sessions—Sir Horatio Lloyd, Kt. Clerk of the Peace—Reginald Potts. Deputy Clerk of the Peace—Hubert Potts. Clerk of Indictments—William Parsons Reade.

CHESHIRE MAGISTRATES.

Altrincham—The Right Hon. the Earl of Stamford, Lord Colwyn, the Hon. John Edward Cross, Sir Arthur Adlington Haworth, Bart., George Faulkner Armitage, John Arnold, John Battersby, William Douglas Bullock, William Henry Carter, Alfred Charlton, Hugh Cumming Clanahan, John Clarke, Neville Clegg, John Coxon, Ernest Morland Crossfield, Samuel Davies, Gerard Powys Dewhurst, William Arthur Dewhurst, Frank Brookhouse Dunkerley, Edward Entwistle, Frederic Ernest Evans, Henry Edwin Gaddum, Edward Napier Galloway, William Gibbon, Alfred Golland, S. Walker Gould, Richard William Green, Colonel John Edward Grimble Groves, John Goodier Howarth, His Honour Judge Adam Spencer Hogg, Harry Holden, William Hughes, Admiral John Parry Jones-Parry, Major William Kenneth Kershaw, Thomas William Killick, Harry Vernon Kilvert, Nicholas Kilvert, Alexander Lawson, Lieut.-Colonel Hubert Cornwall Legh, James M'Donald, John Morley, John Alfred Morris, Matthew Shaw Newton, Harry Nuttall, M.P., Charles Price, Eustace George Parker, Richard B. Pettener, John Platt, George Rhodes, K.C., Robert Falkner Riddick, Thomas Joseph Ridgway, John Walter Robson, William Peter Rylands, Edward John Sidebotham, Joseph Watson Sidebotham (Chairman), Edwin Forsyth Stockton, William George Taylor, Alfred Tarbolton, Thomas Egerton Tatton, Thomas Foster Wainwright, Alfred Watkin, Gerald Whitwham, and Henry Hugo Worthington.

Broxton—Lord Arthur Hugh Grosvenor, Hugh Aldersey, George Barbour (Chairman), Robert Barbour, Harry Barnston, M.P., George Cooke, William Graham Crum, Francis Wolley Dod, Richard Fearnall, Colonel George Holdsworth, John Howard, William Jones, Evan Langley, Edward Richard Massey, Samuel Henry Sandbach, Thomas Murhall Lossford Vernon, Francis Alexander Wolryche, Frederick Wm. Wignall, and Lieut.-Colonel Hubert Malcolm Wilson.

Bucklow—The Right Hon. Lord Egerton of Tatton (Chairman), Sir Harry Stapleton Mainwaring, Bart., Sir Alfred Lassam Goodson, Hugh Arthur Birley, Frederick William Carver, George Comber, Joseph Peter Cox, Theodore Fennell, Major Collingwood George Clements Hamilton, M.P.,

George Leigh, Robert Charles Longridge, His Honour Judge Francis Hamilton Mellor, Frank Merriman, Henry Spurrier, Thomas Frederick Tattersall, and Cuthbert Leicester Warren.

Chester Castle—His Grace the Duke of Westminster, G.C.V.O., D.S.O., Sir John Meadows Frost, Kt., Sir Horatio Lloyd, Kt., Robert Beck, Henry Webster Boultbee, Percy Henry Guy Fielden, Henry Leslie Finney, Thomas Gibbons Frost, Rev. C. A. Griffin, Edward Peter Jones, Harry Beresford Jones, Edward Honoratus Lloyd, K.C., Colonel Wilford Neville Lloyd, M.V.O., John William Macfie, John Minshull, the Hon. Cecil Thomas Parker, His Honour Judge Albert Parsons, Richard Taswell Richardson (Chairman), Frederick Rigby, Thomas Arthur Rigby, Benjamin Chaffers Roberts, William Stockton, Colonel Richard Thompson, Alfred Osten Walker, Richard Pedley Walley, and William Williams.

Congleton—Colonel Sir Walter Geoffrey Shakerley, Bart., Crawfurd J. Antrobus, Charles Dennis Bradwell, George Percival Daintry, Colonel Robert Francis Gartside-Tipping, C.B., William Barton, Fred Jackson, Samuel Maskery, John Moir, George Herbert Shakerley-Ackers, Arthur John Solly, and Clement William Swetenham (Chairman).

Daresbury—Sir Gilbert Greenall, Bart., C.V.O., Edward Frankland Armstrong, Thomas Baxter, Joseph Taylor Baxter, Henry Charles Burder, Dr Harry Edward Bower, George Dakin, Lieut.-Colonel Brereton Fairclough, C.M.G., D.S.O., William Fletcher, Francis Aylmer Frost, Linnæus Greening, James Hepherd, Charles Jackson Holmes, Lieut.-Colonel Charles Lyon, Charles Marson, Frederick William Monks, Joseph Charlton Parr, Roger Charlton Parr, Robert Pierpoint, John Alfred Ransome, Henry Roberts, Lieut.-Colonel Henry Gordon Roberts, Hon. Brigadier-General Arthur Hervey Talbot (Chairman), and John James Whitley.

Dukinfield—Lord Ashton of Hyde, Sir George Wood Rhodes, Bart., Sir William Edward Garforth, Kt., Arthur Brook Aspland, James Avison, George John Awburn, James Bancroft, Charles Henry Booth, James Bottomley, Thomas Bradley, George Brownson, Harold Chapman, Joseph Cooke, John Edmund Gartside, Edward Gibson, William Grundy, Martin Luther Hall, Oliver Hibbert, Septimus C. Homer, Samuel Horsfield, Thomas Horsfield, John Ingham, Robert Innes, John Oliver Kerfoot, Joseph Wilfred Sylvanus Lawton, Wm. Clare Lees, James Grimshaw Lowe, George Robert Marshall, Colonel John Edward Mellor, William Morton, Samuel Mycock, Herbert Parkes, William Joseph Parkyn (Chairman), Thomas Perrin, James Pickup, John Henry Roberts, Allen Shaw, Colonel Albert Sidebottom, Colonel William Sidebottom, Daniel Stafford, James Storrs, William Underwood, Len Wadsworth, John Wagstaffe, Stanley Welch, and William Edward Wood.

Eddisbury—Lord Tollemache, Captain Hon. H. R. Baillie-Hamilton-Arden, the Hon. Marshall Brooks, Sir Philip Henry Brian Grey-Egerton, Bart., Sir John Fowler Leece Brunner, Bart., John Brotherton, Captain William Edward Burton, Joseph John Crosfield, Harry Dewhurst, M.P., James Edgar Dennis, Edward Wilbraham Dixon, William Gerrard, Edward Waldegrave Griffith, Theodore Drayton Grimke-Drayton, Walter Harrison, Captain William Higson, Rev. Canon W. O. M. Hughes, William Nelson Hutchings, Ernest Johnson, Geo. Holman Kent Kingdon, Nathan Large, Chas. Edward Linaker, John Bolton Littledale, Harry Percival Mortimer, John Murray, Walter Coleridge Richmond, George Crosland Taylor, James Taylor, Charles Threlfall, Chas. William Tomkinson, Major Hugh Edward Wilbraham (Chairman), Joseph Willett, Samuel Henry Woodhouse, Samuel Woodward, and Louis Slade Winsloe.

Middlewich—Charles Swain Agnew, Rev. John Hornby Armitstead, Arthur Beckett, William Boosey, Joseph Buckley, William Oswald Carver, Eustace Richardson Cox, George Dean, Captain William Hocken France-Hayhurst, George Garfit, William Harry Grindley, Edward Baker Harlock, Frank Abraham Haworth, John Arthur Rickards Kay, Lieut.-Colonel Charles Percy Lees, Egerton Leigh, Edward Howard Moss, and Oswald Barker Whitehead.

Nantwich—Lord Rotherham, the Hon. Richard Southwell George Stapleton Cotton, Sir Kenneth Irwin Crossley, Bart., John Baskervyle-Glegg, James Bayley, Edwin Reginald Bellyse, Ralph Brocklebank, Major Sir Henry John Delves Broughton, Bart., John Hastings Brown, Richard William Cartwright, Charles John Bowen Cooke, Charles Edward Davenport, William Joseph Dutton, John Emberton, Thos. Henry Hardy, Wilfred Harlock, Henry Hinde, William Hodgson, Albert Neilson Hornby, Major Robert Wilson Kearsley, William Walter Kellock, Arthur Knowles, Henry Knowles, William Lea, George Lewis, Charles Frederick Coryndon Luxmoor, William M'Cracken, Harold Broughton Newcombe, John Nunnerley, George Arthur Pedley, Bryan Davies Poole, Captain William Schroder, William Watson Corbet Stain, John Tayleur, Henry James Tollemache (Chairman), Charles Wilson, William Wright, Charles Ernest Young, and Lieut.-Colonel Richard Timmis Turner.

Northwich—Lord Barrymore, Sir Joseph Verdin, Bart., Alfred Ashton, Russell Allen, Joseph Oswald Brandrith, Henry Bratt, William Miles Bratt, George Henry Brock, Roscoe Brunner, Albert Henry Darwell, John William Deakin, Geo. Wm. Dunn Dutton, Ernest Stobart Inman, Oswald Mosley Leigh, Arthur Hornby Lewis, Cecil Francis Parr, Joseph Poole, Alfred Every Powles, Major Alexander Emil Jacques Reiss, Walter Sutherst, Alfred Jabez Thompson, George Vickers, and Thomas Wilkinson.

Prestbury—The Hon. Sir Arthur Lyulph Stanley, K.C.M.G., Colonel Sir George Dixon, Bart., Sir Harold Elverston, Kt., John Bancroft, Samuel Armitage Bennett, John Henry Birchenough, William Taylor Birchenough, Jabez Birtles, Henry Boddington, Lieut.-Colonel R. W. D. Phillips Brocklehurst, Lieut.-Colonel Wm. Brocklehurst Brocklehurst (Chairman), Hugh Cawley, William Chadwick, Theodore Crewdson, Brigadier-General William Bromley Davenport, D.S.O., Joseph George Frost, John Gardner, Andrew Archer Gillies, George Clementson Greenwell, Colonel Ernest William Greg, V.D., Henry Phillips Greg, Lieut.-Colonel Robert Alexander Greg, Herbert Seymour Hadwin, Edward Lascelles Hoyle, William Johnson, Arthur Masterton Robertson Legh, Colonel William Gorges Lowther, William Mewburn, Joshua Oldfield Nicholson, Robert Holland Owen, Francis Ratcliffe Robinson, William Smale, Charles Edward Thorneycroft, James Arnold Thompson, Wm. Ernest Thompson, William Sharp Waithman, Henry Wallworth, Harold Walter Whiston, James Whiteside, and Hercules Campbell Yates.

Runcorn—Sir Richard Marcus Brooke, Bart., Sir John Sutherland Harmood Banner, Kt., M.P., Sir Frederick Norman, Kt. (Chairman), Thomas Henry Annett, Francis Boston, William Carrol, William Edward Dudley, George Stevenson Frith, James Mason Frith, Ellis Gatley, Alfred Robert Norman, Robert Harold Posnett, James Pritchard, Andrew Thomas Smith, Samuel Taylor, Major Arthur Timmins, Thomas Dorning Timmins, and George Lloyd Wigg.

Sandbach—Chas. Dayman Braddon, Ernest Craig, William Young Craig, William Foden, William Huntley Goss, Edward Bela Joseph Harran, Edward Holland, Samuel Hollinshead, Henry Boston Massey, Thomas Frederick Owen, James Proudlove, Frank Rigby, Major John Fletcher Twemlow Royds (Chairman), Joseph Shaw, and George Wright.

Stockport—Lord Newton, Lieut.-Colonel Sir Alan John Sykes, Bart., M.P., Sir John Emmott Barlow, Bart., Ernest Bagshawe, Frank Barlow, John Bateman, Alfred Bell, Henry Bell (Chairman), William Bell, Ralph Blackwell, John Henry Bradshaw Isherwood, His Honour Judge Reginald Brown, K.C., William Edward Carrington, Alfred Rowland Clegg, Arthur Mann Cresswell, William Haslam Cross, Alfred Darbyshire, Thomas Davenport, Paul Etchells, J. W. Exley, J. E. Hall, John Alfred Hallam, William Norris Heald, Charles Heaps, Peter Higson, Walter Bright Hodgkinson, Henry Hollingdrake, Colonel John Goode Johnson, V.D., William Lees, William Bailey Leigh, William Marshall, Colonel Walter Mothersill, George Nelstrop, Alfred Pickles, Frank George Plant, Major James Edward Platt, Thomas Rowbotham, Robert Shepley Shepley, Arthur Henry Sykes, Major Thomas Clayton Toler, W. H. Tutton, John Wild, and Henry Wilson.

Winsford—Lord Delamere, William Bancroft, Reginald Grayson Barton, Edwin Hamlett, Joseph Pybus Jackson, Hector Leak, Harry Lockhead, Charles Massey, Thomas Massey, George Okell, James Arthur Reiss, John Rigby, Robert Unwin Stubbs, Archibald Stubbs, William Stubbs, Major James Aspinall Turner, Colonel Richard Norman Harrison Verdin, and William Henry Verdin (Chairman).

Wirral—Lord Leverhulme, the Hon. William Hulme Lever, Sir Thomas Royden, Bart., Sir William Bower Forwood, Kt., Alfred Ashby, John Barber, Charles Herbert Birchall, Ralph Eric Royds Brocklebank, Thomas Raffles Bulley, James Kennedy Catto, James Thomas Chester, Alfred Stephen Collard, Harold Coventry, Alexander Craigmile, William Clarke Currie, Stuart Deacon, John Robertson Dunn, William Paterson Evans, Colonel Thomas George Ewan, C.B., V.D., John Smith Ferguson, Frederick Woolven Flinn, Frederick Hynde Fox, Henry Neville Gladstone, G. Hastwell Grayson, Michael Tyson Graveson, Alexander Guthrie, Joseph Uttley Hodgson, Charles Edward Hope, William Hope, Samuel Mason Hutchinson, Thomas Hughes Jackson, John Joyce, Thomas Russell Lee, William M'Afee, Bouverie F. P. M'Donald, M.P., Charles Robert B. M'Gilchrist, Charles MacIver, Henry Mahler, Charles Henry Morton, Major David Andrew Shaw Nesbitt, John Oldershaw, Coard Squarey Pain, Walter Peel, Joseph Pemberton, Walter Ward Platt, Adam George Rankine, Samuel Sanday, Frank Sellars, Gershom Stewart, M.P., Roger Percy Sing, Edward Russell Taylor, William Calthrop Thorne, Thomas Tickle, Colonel Francis Gregory Walker, George Wall, William Charles White, and Wellington Archbold Williams.

CHESHIRE URBAN AND RURAL AUTHORITIES.

(*Explanation of Abbreviations*—P., Population in 1911; C.R.B., County rate basis; A.R.A., Assessable Value under Agricultural Rates Act.)

Municipal Boroughs—Congleton—P., 11,309; C.R.B., £37,024; A.R.A., £34,990. Crewe—P., 44,960; C.R.B., £172,844; A.R.A., £171,487. Dukinfield—P., 19,422; C.R.B., £78,760; A.R.A., 78,165. Hyde—P., 33,437; C.R.B., £142,866; A.R.A., £141,530. Macclesfield—P., 34,797; C.R.B., £120,175. Stalybridge—P., 26,513; C.R.B., £12,349; A.R.A., £122,489. Total—P., 170,438; C.R.B., £675,498; A.R.A., £6,677,056.

URBAN DISTRICT COUNCILS.

Alderley Edge, Alsager, Altrincham, Ashton-on-Mersey, Higher Bebington, Lower Bebington, Bollington, Bowdon, Bredbury and Romiley, Bromborough, Buglawton, Cheadle and Gatley, Compstall, Ellesmere Port and Whitby, Hale, Handforth, Hazel Grove and Bramhall, Hollingworth, Hoylake and West Kirby, Hoole, Knutsford, Lymm, Marple, Middlewich, Mottram, Nantwich, Neston and Parkgate, Northwich, Runcorn, Sandbach, Sale, Tarporley, Wilmslow, Winsford, Yeardsley-cum-Whaley.

Totals for Urban Authorities—Population in 1911, 414,526; County rate basis, £2,105,845; Assessable value under Agricultural Rates Act, 1896, £2,050,343; amount of 1d. in the £ on assessable value, £8543, 1s. 11d.

RURAL DISTRICT COUNCILS.

Bucklow, Chester, Congleton, Disley, Macclesfield, Malpas, Nantwich, Runcorn, Tarvin, Tintwistle, and Wirral.

Totals for Administrative County—Population in 1911, 597,771; County rate basis, £3,869,568; assessable value under Agricultural Rates Act, £3,486,785; amount of 1d. in the £ on assessable value, £14,528, 5s. 8d.

Totals for Rural Authorities—Population in 1911, 183,248; County rate basis, £1,763,723; assessable value under Agricultural Rates Act, £1,436,445; amount at 1d. in the £ on assessable value, £5985, 3s. 9d.

POOR LAW UNIONS AND NAMES OF CLERKS, 1919.

Ashton-under-Lyne—G. H. Partington, Ashton-under-Lyne. Birkenhead—S. R. Carter, Conway Street, Birkenhead. Bucklow—Geo. Leigh, Knutsford. Chester—G. S. N. Hull, Union Offices, 161 Foregate Street, Chester. Congleton—H. Ferrand, Sandbach. Hayfield—A. Walker, New Mills, near Stockport. Macclesfield—Frederick May, Macclesfield. Nantwich—H. G. Atkinson, Nantwich. Northwich—J. E. Fletcher, Northwich. Runcorn—Geo. F. Ashton, Runcorn. Stockport—Frederick Pidgeon, Union Offices, Stockport. Tarvin—H. Grant Bailey, Union Offices, Newgate Street, Chester. Whitchurch—A. Clayton, St Mary's Street, Whitchurch, Salop. Wirral—J. E. S. Ollive, 54 Hamilton Street, Birkenhead.

COUNCIL OF THE CITY OF CHESTER.

Mayor—Harry Faulkner Brown. Sheriff—A. S. Dutton. Aldermen—Sir John Meadows Frost, David Lythall Hewitt John Jones, Robert Lamb, John Williamson, William Henry Churton, Henry Dodd, Egerton Gilbert, William Vernon, and George Barlow. Councillors—William Arthur Vere Churton, Charles John Jones, Martin Gibbons, George Henry Dutton, Robert Townshend Wickham, Edward John Muspratt, Harry Faulkner Brown, H. D. D. Rogers, W. Conway, Alfred Simeon Dutton, E. Noel Humphreys, E. M. Sneyd-Kynnersley, Robert Matthewson, Charles Pritchard Cockrill, Alfred Hart Davies, Walter Welsby, William Henry Denson, John Sheriff Roberts, Allan H. Williams, Franklyn David Price, Arthur Wall, William Henry Griffith, Francis Holden Illingworth, W. A. Fitzgerald, Thomas Sharp Parry, W. H. Ebrey, William Carr, Harry Boulton Dutton, John Minns, and E. Green. Town Clerk—James Husband Dickson.

CHESHIRE: ITS TRADITIONS AND HISTORY

BIRKENHEAD BOROUGH MAGISTRATES.

Alderman J. H. M'Gaul (Mayor), David Roger Rowlands (ex-Mayor), A. H. Arkle, Alexander Mere Latham (Recorder), Edwin Arthur Beazley, G. H. Cox, Thomas Liddell Dodds, Peter W. Atkin, Thomas Sargent Floyd, M.D., Meadows Frost, James Gamlin, Alfred C. E. Harris, M.D., Jos. Heap, Thomas Hughes Jackson, B. Jones, J. W. P. Laird, Ed. G. Mason, William F. Miller, R. J. Russell, George P. Snape, Peter M'Mahon, E. Williams, Thomas S. Deakin, R. Owen Morris, M.D., H. Laird Pearson, M.D., Henry Bloor, E. T. Coston, J. H. Ziegler, L. C. Elmslie, Harold Bickersteth, A. Goodwin, William Jackson, Frederick Naylor, John Noble, M.D., Samuel Vaughan, A. W. Willmer, William Henry Adams, Charles Wesley Ashcroft, D. J. Clarke, William Henry Egan, Lieut.-Colonel M. C. Ellis, William Wallace Kelly, Thomas Taliesin Rees, Charles Wass, Godfrey Allan Solly, W. H. B. Yeo, E. Singleton, James Merritt, and James Morris. Clerk to the Justices—Edmund Spencer. Assistant Clerk—J. Woodend.

BIRKENHEAD TOWN COUNCIL.

Mayor—Alderman J. H. M'Gaul. Aldermen—H. Bloor, R. T. Curphey, J. Gamlin, E. G. Mason, A. H. Arkle, S. Vaughan, M. Byrne, F. Naylor, R. J. Russell, J. H. M'Gaul, A. Goodwin, T. S. Deakin, T. Shaw, and G. A. Solly. Councillors—J. W. P. Laird, C. J. Procter, A. H. Chalmers, J. Harrison, C. G. R. Stephens, H. Halsall, D. J. Clarke, J. Merritt, W. H. Major, H. Speed, Luke Lees, F. Tutty, J. W. Collin, H. B. Webb, John Platt, R. P. Fletcher, H. G. G. White, G. J. Jackson, C. E. Robinson, W. H. Egan, C. M'Vey, F. Tweedle, W. H. Adams, C. Nathan, James Platt, J. Coulthard, H. Triplett, J. Maddocks, W. H. Boston, F. Godsell, W. Harrie Bishop, J. Aspinall, W. H. B. Yeo, J. C. Paterson, Miss Laird, Mrs Hugh-Jones, Mrs Mercer, Miss Hickey, G. E. Banner, H. G. F. Dawson, D. R. Rowlands, and E. J. Hughes, Town Clerk.

CONGLETON BOROUGH MAGISTRATES.

The Mayor (Charles Dennis Bradwell), William Farrington, Samuel Maskery, William Lindsay Carson, George Pedley, Arthur John Solly, Harry Berisford, William Isaac Fern, James Thomas Lucas, George William Stubbs, William Taylor, Fred Jackson, and Henry Redfern. Clerk to the Magistrates—George Sproston.

CONGLETON CORPORATION.

Mayor—Charles Dennis Bradwell. Deputy Mayor—Councillor Fred Jackson. Aldermen—Charles Dennis Bradwell, Samuel Maskery, Arthur John Solly, Alfred Barlow, James Thomas Lucas, and George Pedley. Councillors—Henry Lawton, William Henry Cliffe, Massie Harper, William Henry Haddock, Frank William Pass, Dennis Walter Hill, John Hood, Clement Dale, William Isaac Fern, Frank Dale, Frederick Barton, Fred Jackson, Albert Bailey, William Taylor, Francis William Adams, William Jackson, Samuel Burgess, and Eli Mottershead. Town Clerk—E. A. Plant.

CREWE BOROUGH MAGISTRATES.

The Mayor (Harry Bullock), C. J. Bowen Cooke, J. Briggs, W. Hodgson, B. S. Bostock, John Jones, C. Wilson, F. Wooldridge, F. Manning, Joseph Jones, G. A. Pedley, G. Bates, J. R. Goulden, A. Jervis, T. Ormand, J. Williams, C. R. Wooldridge.

CREWE CORPORATION.

Mayor—Harry Bullock, Esq. Deputy Mayor, Alderman Alfred H. Badger. Aldermen—Alfred H. Badger, James Briggs, James Henry Kettell, C. R. Wooldridge, Charles Herbert Pedley, Abraham Jervis, Frederick Manning, and Edward Rainbow Hill. Councillors—William Micklewright, James Pemberton, Charles Alcock, George Parsons, Abraham Blount, David Henry Rawlings, John Hauldren, Joseph Seed, John R. Goulden, J. W. Jones, Albert E. Dutton, Samuel

Preece, John Booth, Ezra Nixon, John Smith, George Wilkinson, W. C. White, R. J. Mansfield, G. E. Dain, E. Yates, J. Shufflebottom, R. P. T. Darlington, William Worthy Cooke, and A. Hatton. Town Clerk and Registrar of Burial Board and Clerk to the Education Committee—Harold Stanley Kirkman Feltham.

DUKINFIELD CORPORATION.

Mayor—Alderman Herbert Bown. Deputy Mayor—Councillor Arthur Edward Grundy. Aldermen—James Avison, James Bancroft, Herbert Bown, George Dean, William Lee, and William Edward Wood. Councillors—Thomas Bradley, Israel Brooks, Arthur Edward Grundy, John Jackson, Francis Cheetham Webb, John Whitehead, Harry Bagot, William Dickenson, William H. Ashworth, Edward Gibson, David Chadwick Hill, Charles Holmes, Thomas Benson, Joseph Cooke, Walter Harrison, George Kaye, Frederic George Temple, and John William Underwood. Town Clerk—Ernest Barlow.

HYDE BOROUGH MAGISTRATES.

The Mayor, His Honour the Judge for Hyde County Court, Charles Bancroft, John Blackwell, James Booth, H. J. Cumberlidge, J. B. Davenport, A. M. Fletcher, Allan Harrison Hall, Samuel Horsfield, Luke Kenny, Walter Ingram Sherry, Daniel Stafford, Arthur Williamson, William Pope, Ebenezer Bury, John Turner Cartwright, Walter Gee, David Henry Shaw, and George Frederick Wild. Clerk—Thomas Brownson, B.A.

HYDE CORPORATION.

Mayor—Ebenezer Bury. Deputy Mayor, John Mirfin. Aldermen—Thomas Perrin, John Mirfin, Walter Ingram Sherry, Luke Kenny, Henry Goodier Turner, and Percy Hibbert. Councillors—Squire Fawley, Stanley Welch, Tom Cooper, Edward Bruton Charnley, Amos Winterbottom, Allen Shaw, George Spencer, Joseph Hibbert, William Ardern, George Goodfellow, Aaron Haughton, Clifford Ward Eastwood, Ebenezer Bury, Thomas Middleton, Annie Brooke, John Westbrook, Walter Fowden, and James Hibbert. Town Clerk—Thomas Brownson, B.A.

MACCLESFIELD BOROUGH MAGISTRATES.

The Mayor, Messrs John Somerville, W. B. Brocklehurst, W. T. Birchenough, Robert Proctor, J. O. Nicholson, His Honour Judge Reginald Browne, K.C., W. H. L. Cameron, Edwin Crewe, George Fountain, Walter Bowyer, Peter Davenport, G. H. Heath, William Smale, William Bates, Charles Augustus Bradley, Walter Brown, William Robert Brown, William Frost, Thomas William Sheldon, John Rathbone White, William Pimblott, Charles Averill, Joseph George Frost, John Webster, Joseph Whitmore, and the ex-Mayor for one year.

MACCLESFIELD TOWN COUNCIL.

Mayor—Councillor J. G. Frost, J.P. Aldermen—J. C. Bailey, C. A. Bradley, J.P., W. B. Brocklehurst, J.P., C.A., E. Crew, J.P., P. Davenport, J.P., E. Eaton, A. Frith, W. Frost, J.P., C.C., W. Harrison, G. Hood, J. R. Isherwood, and J. Whitmore. Councillors—J. Arnold, J. Barlow, W. H. Braid, W. R. Brown, J.P., E. R. Clark, J. D. Cooper, P. Cotterill, W. Day, N. Frost, J. Hampson, J. T. Harrison, A. W. Hewetson, R. L. Hidderley, V. Hope, F. W. Hulme, J. Hyde, W. H. Jackson, H. Massey, W. M. Maughan, J. Minshull, C. A. Newbald, J. Parker, W. Perkin, W. Pimblott, J.P., D. Sanders, W. H. Smith, A. Taylor, W. Thompson, G. Wardle, J. Webster, J.P., J. Wellings, J. R. White, J.P., W. S. Williamson, F. Wood, and E. A. W. Wragge.

STALYBRIDGE BOROUGH MAGISTRATES.

James Bottomley, Elias Wild, W. J. Hancock, W. Wadsworth, R. Needham, Joseph Schofield, R. Ridgway, J. B. Mason, E. C. M'Carthy, Robert Leach, J. Bradbury, William Hague,

CHESHIRE: ITS TRADITIONS AND HISTORY 363

Allwood Simpson, G. B. Howe, A. Bottomley, Thomas Cook, Robert Innes, John Booth, George Barrett, James Taylor, J. R. Norman, James Storrs, Harrop Mallalieu, J. A. Reekie, James G. Lowe, J. O. Kerfoot, John Ingham, and W. F. Kinder. Clerk—Fred Thompson, LL.B.

STALYBRIDGE CORPORATION.

Mayor—Mrs Ada J. Summers. Deputy Mayor, Alderman A. Simpson. Aldermen—James Bottomley, Abel Bottomley, William Frederick Kinder, Robert Wood, John Booth, Joshua Bradbury, Allwood Simpson, and Harrop Mallalieu. Councillors—Randal Ridgway, George Potts, Henry E. Towle, James Storrs, Robert H. Hartley, Bramley Buckley, William Herbert Rhodes, John Herbert Smith, Thomas Cook, William Hague, Philip Talbot, Mrs Ada J. Summer, James Grimshaw Lowe, Levi Wilson, Percy Lomax, James Wilson, Charles C. Britnor, John H. Hall, Tom Pagden, John Frederick Wood, George L. Flint, Thomas Buckley Williams, Arthur Hudson, and George Henry Tonge. Town Clerk—Frank H. Worsley.

STOCKPORT COUNTY BOROUGH MAGISTRATES.

C. Royle (Mayor), Edwin Rayner, William Edward Carrington, George Nelstrop, Louis Rivett, Robert Alexander Murray, William Lees, Francis R. Robinson, Thomas Lees Sutton, Peter Okell, Charles Edward Wilkinson, Giles Atherton, Alfred Ernest Ferns, James Horner, William Loose, Samuel Rigby, Edward Clarke, Richard Bettney Furnival, Hyde Marriott, William George Ward, Albert Bellamy, Thomas Rowbotham, Tom Cocker, William Henry Hollis, Robert Johnson, George Leigh, William Bateman, James Fernley, Joseph Bancroft Harrison, Samuel Frederick Perry, John Sowerbutts, John Bennett, Francis Connell, Thomas Edward Foster, Joseph Lloyd, Geoffry Christie-Miller, George Nixon, Thomas Tatton Sykes, John Barrodale, Joseph R. M. Brennan, Joseph Dean, Joshua Preston, Fred Rivett, George Travis, James Barnshaw, Henry Fildes, Richard T. Heys, William Johnston, George Padmore, Peter Peirce, Frederick William Plant, Samuel Ralphs, John Smith, William Astle, and Edwin F. Ward. Clerk to the Justices—Harry Newton.

STOCKPORT COUNTY BOROUGH COUNCIL.

Mayor—Alderman Charles Royle. Deputy Mayor—Councillor Thomas Rowbotham, J.P. Aldermen—Thomas Allcock, George Ball, Samuel Brewster, Arthur Briggs, John B. Chadwick, John W. Craig, James Fernley, J.P., Henry Green, William E. Hamnett, John T. Hopkins, William Lees, J.P., Ralph Morten, George Padmore, J.P., Charles Sharples, Henry G. Smeeth, Thomas T. Sykes, J.P., and James Welsh. Councillors—Alfred H. Barton, A. Walton-Smith, Edward Clarke, J.P., John Greenhalgh, Thomas W. Potts, O.B.E., Joseph Hough, Jacob Winter, John Butterworth, Samuel Lucas, William Thomas, Joseph Rogerson, William Hamlett, John Coupe, Charles Walmsley, Thomas Wilson, William A. Gould, Thomas E. Forster, J.P., James Brimelow, James Barlow, John Burgon, Francis Hennessy, Samuel H. Roberts, Thomas F. Tinsley, George H. Bennett, Robert A. Murray, J.P., Samuel Lees, Mary Jane Potts, Henry Patten, Frederick W. Plant, J.P., Elijah Lavender, Henry Barratt, John Barrodale, J.P., John T. Brocklehurst, William Merrison, Henry Bell, D.L., Fred Bowler, Ephraim E. Fogg, Thomas Rowbotham, J.P., William Slack, Henry A. Derwent, John R. Bell, James Barrett, James Harrison, Malcolm M. M'Gregor, William H. Hollis, J.P., Thomas Meredith, Charles F. Walker, John Brickell, William Morley, Alfred E. Ferns, J.P., Walter H. Brown, Robert Gregg, John W. Fitton, and John Williamson. Town Clerk—Robert Hyde. Assistant Town Clerk—Frank Knowles.

WALLASEY BOROUGH COUNCIL.

Mayor—Alderman Edward Geoffrey Parkinson, J.P. Aldermen—Thomas Valentine Burrows, Walter Eastwood, J.P., John Farley, John Oldershaw, M.D., J.P., Edwin Peace, Frank Fawcett Scott, Francis Storey, J.P., Benjamin Swanwick, J.P., Charles John Woodroffe. Councillors—John Airey, Thomas Samuel Ashmole, Walter James Bellis, J.P., George Alfred Burrows, William Canning, David Percy Charlesworth, Harris Louis Cohen, William H. M. Draper, Alfred Henry Evans, John Gourlay, Horace William Griffin, John William Holdsworth,

Francis Edward Howse, Joseph Hughes, Frederic Phelp Jones, John M'Millan, M.B., Albert John Mead, B.A., Charles Hewetson Nelson, F.S.A.A., J.P., David Andrew Shaw Neshitt, V.D., J.P., Charles Pearson, Augustine Quinn, Sidney Herbert Roberts, Arnold Albert Roden, Clarence Frederick Rymer, James Shaw, John Gladstone Storey, Harry Atchley Thomas, Peter Jones Tunnicliffe, James Urmson, and Albert Wrigley, B.A. Town Clerk—H. W. Cook.

THE MANCHESTER SHIP CANAL.

Opened by Queen Victoria, 21st May 1895. The entrance is at Eastham, 19 miles from the bar at the mouth of the Mersey, and it is 35 miles, passing through Cheshire until it reaches the large docks at Manchester and Salford. The total capital authorised in shares, loans, and debenture stock at the time of writing (December 1919) is £19,573,230.

Directors.—William C. Bacon, Chairman ; Alderman Tom Fox (the Right Hon. Lord Mayor of Manchester), Alderman William Kay, Deputy Chairman ; Sir F. Forbes Adam, Bart., C.I.E. ; Allan Hughes, J. D. Williams, Alfred Watkin, Sir William H. Vaudrey, Ernest Latimer (Managing Director), Sir C. T. Needham, W. E. Dudley, Donald Beith, Aldermen Plummer, Sir Charles Behrens, Sir T. Thornhill Shann, S. Dixon, T. Smethurst Bowes, and H. R. Box, and Councillors M. E. Mitchell and F. J. West. *Chief Officials*—Herbert M. Gibson, Chief Superintendent ; William Browning, Traffic Superintendent ; H. A. Reed, M.Inst.C.E., M.I.Mech.E., Chief Engineer ; F. T. Woolley, F.C.A., and W. H. Shaw, F.C.A., Auditors.

RAILWAYS IN CHESHIRE.

London and North-Western (formerly Grand Junction).—Crewe to Stafford and Birmingham, July 1837. Stockport *via* Liverpool, August 1842. Whitchurch *via* Nantwich, September 1858. Chester to Crewe, *via* Beeston Castle, September 1840. Chester to Birkenhead (through Wirral), September 1840. Chester to Frodsham and Warrington, December 1850. Flint to Holt, May and August 1848. Whitchurch *via* Malpas, October 1872. Stockport to Macclesfield, about 1845. Stockport to Buxton and Whaley, about 1858. Warrington to Altrincham, November 1853. Parkgate to Hoylake, July 1866. Neston to Hooton, October 1866. Hooton to Northwich, *via* Helsby, 1869. Sandbach, Middlewich, and Northwich, November 1867. Northwich to Sutton and Preston Brook, March 1870. Runcorn to Ditton, April 1869. Runcorn to Frodsham, 1873. Manchester to Wilmslow, *via* Styal, 1st May 1909.

Great Western.—Chester to Wrexham, October 1846. Nantwich to Market Drayton, *via* Audlem, October 1863. Also Upton, *via* Chester, Wrexham, Market Drayton, Nantwich, and Audlem later.

North Staffordshire Railway Co.—Crewe to Stoke, *via* Alsager, 9th October 1848. Congleton to Macclesfield, 18th June 1849. North Rode to Utoxeter, 13th July 1849. Sandbach to Lawton Junction, 21st January 1852.

Manchester, Sheffield, and Lincolnshire Railway Co. (now Great Central).—Godley to Manchester, 17th November 1841. Godley to Mottram, 10th December 1842. Mottram to Glossop, 24th December 1842. Macclesfield to Bollington and Marple, 2nd August 1869. Timperley Curve, 1st December 1879.

Manchester, Sheffield, and Lincolnshire Railway Co. (now Great Central jointly with the Midland Railway Co.).—Hyde Junction to Hyde, 1st March 1858. Hyde to Marple, 5th August 1862. Marple to New Mills, 1st July 1865. New Mills to Hayfield, 1st March 1868. Romily Junction and Bredbury, 1st April 1875. Romily Junction and Ashbury, 17th May 1875. Brinnington and Junction and Reddish, 1st August 1875.

Cheshire Lines Committee.—Altrincham to Knutsford, 12th May 1862. Knutsford to Northwich, 1st January 1863. Stockport to Woodley, 12th December 1863. Stockport to Timperley, 1st February 1866. Godley to Woodley, 1st February 1866. Northwich Salt Branches, 17th December 1867. Northwich to Helsby, 1869. Cuddington to Winsford, 1st June 1870. Altrincham (Skelton Junction) to Glazebrook, 1st March 1873. Mouldsworth to Chester, 2nd November 1874.

Hoylake and Birkenhead Co.—Birkenhead to Hoylake, *via* Bidston, 1870. Parkgate to New Brighton, *via* Heswell and Chester later.

INDEX.

(See also Chapter Headings.)

A

	PAGE
Abbey, St Werburgh's	18
Abbots and their powers	37
Abbot's Chapel, Cathedral	39
Abduction of young heir	143
Addison, Hon. C.	182
Aldermen, first County Council	178
Alford, E. F.	167
Altrincham—	
Court Leet	171
Elections	165, 166
Annett, T. H.	330, 335
Antrobus, Coutts	178
Antrobus, Gibbs Crawford	315
Appendix	352
Archery	119
Arden, R. P.	219
Armistice, Cheshire rejoicings	94
Armitage, G. Faulkner	105
Armitage, Rev. William	55
Ashley Hall	280
Ashton, Thomas Gair	164
Assheton, Thomas	280, 282
Aston, Sir Thomas	248

B

	PAGE
Bailiffs and infuriated crowd	138
Ballot Act, changes effected	157-158
Banns, publication during Commonwealth	52
Bantams disbanded	95
Barlow, Bishop	49
Barlow, Sir J. Emmott	183
Barons of Cheshire	30
Barrymore, James, Earl of	283
Bates, Ralph	177
Bear-baiting	120
Beating the Bounds	126
Beatty, Earl	96
Beckett, Joseph	177
Benevolence, Lodge, Marple	311, 331
Bigland, A.	164

	PAGE
Bird, Bishop	41, 62
Birkenhead—	
Borough Magistrates	361
Election	134
Town Council	361
Birkenhead, Lord	254
Bishops of Mercia and Chester, A.D. 656-1919	352
Blomfield, Bishop	62
Blundeville, Earl, rescue from Rhuddlan	108
Booth, Lady	195
Booth, Sir George	147, 191, 193
And Battle of Winnington	195
Created Lord Delamere	198
Booth, William	303, 335
Boroughs and Corporations (see Appendix)	
Bowdon Wakes	126
Bowls, murder at	132
Bowls, Cheshire Association	123
Bradshaw, Henry	270
Bradshaw, President	147, 148, 195, 241, 275
Brassey, Thos. (Lord Brassey)	253
Bravest street in Cheshire	104
Brereton, Owen Salusbury	249
Brereton, Sir Wm., his mysterious funeral	148
Parliamentary soldier	147
Part in Civil War	191
Bribery attempted by Chester Recorder	149
Bribery at Chester election	153
Bridgman, Bishop	47
Bright, A. H.	146
Broadsmith, Frederick	339
Broadsword and Quarter-staff	122
Brocklebank, T. and J.	39
Brocklehurst, W. B.	183
Brocklehursts and Macclesfield	160
Brooks, John	166
Brooks, Sir William	166
Brown, J.	105
Brown, Robert	311
Brunner, Sir J. F. L.	165
Brunner, Sir J. T.	165, 328
Bull-baiting	114
Bulley, T. Raffles	183
Burgesses, the oldest voters	26
Bury, Viscount	167

CHESHIRE: ITS TRADITIONS AND HISTORY

C

	PAGE
Carpet baggers	158
Carrington " Feight "	279
Caucus, origin of	158
Cestrian Lodge	292, 303
Cestrian Lodge, Mr Horatio Lloyd (*see also* Lloyd, Sir Horatio)	304
Chapman, E.	164
Chartists at Altrincham	233
Cheetham, J. F.	164

Cheshire—

And the Crusades	68
Cattle plague (Rinderpest)	225
Cheese	263
Christianity	33-34
Civil wars	70, 76
Coalfield	6
Cockfighting in	15, 117
Commons of England	27
Congregational Union	54
County Aldermen and Members	356
County Council Committee	180
County elections	191
Days of Bluff King Hal (*see* Chapter XI.)	
Dwarf	231
Educational Masonic Institution	328
First Parliament	145
Geological Features	5
Historians	247
Inroads of Picts and Scots	19
Magistrates	357, 359
Members, 1547-1830	145
Members, 1832-1918	157-169
New Parliamentary Divisions, 1831	156
Remains of early man	10
Roman occupation	13
Roman roads	18
Sacrifices in the War	105
Saints Werburgh and Plegmund	35
Salt beds	6
Sports and pastimes (*see* Chapter X.)	
Struggles for political supremacy	155
The Conqueror's descent	28
Thousand dinners provided at election	156
Urban and Rural Authorities	360
Worthies	238

Cheshire Regiment	40, 87
Civic welcome	89
Colours recovered	95
Memorials	103
V.C.'s	93

Chester—

	PAGE
Alleged humorous incident	44
And Provincial Grand Master	292
Capture and destruction	19
Castle and Ethelfrida	20
Castle torture chamber	20
Cathedral	35
City Council	360
Consistory Court	44
Cotes, Bishop	42
Early inhabitants	12
Elections in recent years	162
Extraordinary hoax	233
Fenian scare	235
First Royal Earl	32
Grosvenor Bridge story	234
King Egbert and tributary kings	19
Midsummer fair and plays	110
Mythical origin	14
Nonconformity	47
Outbreak of plague	220
Parliamentary representation accorded	145
Races	124
Railway Accident, Dee Viaduct	234
Roman residents	16
Rows	17
Rowing Club	125
" Sumptuous and elegant entertainment "	153
The " Golden City "	155
Cholmondeley, Robert	284
Clarke, Joseph	339
Cobden, Richard	160
Columbine, Colonel F.	308
Combermere Abbey, murder at	135
Combermere, Lady	316
Combermere, Lodge of Union	311
Combermere, Lord (*see* Viscount Combermere)	
Congleton	133, 223, 361
Cookson, James	328
Corfield, T.	105
Corporations and Boroughs (*see* Appendix)	
Cotton, Sir Robert Stapleton	308
Court leets	170
Craig, E. Y.	163

Crewe—

Borough Magistrates	361
Corporation	361
Parliamentary elections	163
Cromwell, Oliver	24
Crossley, Sir W. J.	167
Cursing by bell, book, and candle	286

	PAGE
D	
Danes and Chester	20
Davies, J. W.	105
Davies, Sir Joseph	164
Dean, Colonel C. S.	336
De Courcey	105
Deeds at High Legh	286
De Keyser, Lord Mayor of London	326
Delamere, Henry, Second Lord	200
De Tabley, Lord	303, 326
Disraeli, Coningsby Ralph	166
Divine Right of Kings	24
Dixon, Sir George	178, 183, 184
Dodson, Hon. John G.	162
Downham, Bishop	47
Druids and Druidism	13, 33
Duke of Westminster, First	39, 178
Dukinfield Corporation	312
Land seizure at	137
Dunham, House of (*see* Chapters XV., XVI., and XVII.)	
Dutton of Dutton	109
Dutton, Piers, in " strait " keeping at Chester Castle	134
Dutton, widow's difficulties at Dutton Hall	140
E	
Earl Egerton of Tatton	39, 40, 177, 280, 322-324
Earl of Stamford	196
Earls of Chester	19, 22, 23, 30, 31
Earth, man's appearance	2
Man's descent according to Darwin	3
Origin of	1
Earwaker, J. P.	247
Eaton, Rev. Samuel	57
Eddowes	178
Egerton, Hon. Alan	159, 329, 331, 336, 337
Egerton, Hon. Wilbraham	157, 159
Egerton, Lord Chancellor	237
Egerton, Wm. Tatton, created a Peer	157
Elections, first, in Great Britain	151
Election returns (1832-1918)	352
F	
Feudalism	24-25
Fitton, Mary, " the Dark Lady " of Gawsworth (*see* Chapter XXI.)	
Flintt, Thomas and Arthur	40
Football	124
Freemasonry in Cheshire	289

	PAGE
Freemason's Hall, Chester	332
Frost, Sir John	98
Furness, T.	105
G	
Garner, J. O.	183
Geology of Cheshire	5
Gladstone, Herbert	162
Gordon, T. H.	183
Graham, Bishop	6
Graham, Duncan	177-178
Grey, Colonel	183
Grey, Sir John Egerton	309
Griffiths, H.	314, 325
Grosvenor, Earl, First Marquess	156
Grosvenor, Sir Richard	146-282
Grosvenors, The	152, 283
H	
Haig, Sir Douglas	99
Halkett, Baron	163
Halton Court Leet	170
Hamilton, G. C.	167
Hamilton, Mrs	40
Haworth, Sir Arthur	105
Hayhurst, Colonel France	178
Heber, Bishop	251
Heckling at elections	158
" Hell Fire Lacy "	31
Hennerley, D.	105
Henry, Matthew	47
Hewitt, Alderman D. L.	98, 336, 337
Hewitt, Dr	178
Hiccabites, Order of	305
Highwaymen, Dick Turpin, etc.	232
Highway robberies	231
Hilbre Island	18
Hodgson, Dr	177, 183
Holbrook, Hon. H.	305
Holford family dispute	141
Horned woman of Cheshire	213
Howard, Prison philanthropist	22
Howson, Dean	40
Hughes, Spencer Leigh	162
Hughes, Thomas	217
Hugh Lupus	28
Human race, the cradle of	4
Hurleston, Charles	283
Hustings at Northwich	155
Hustings, scenes at	155
Hyde—	
Borough Magistrates	362
Corporation	362
Elections at	164

I

	PAGE
Indulgences easily procured	38
Industry, Lodge of	340
Ingham, Alfred J.	339
Irish First Century Literature	33

J

Jacobson, Bishop	62, 63
Jayne, Bishop	63, 64, 65
Jeffreys, Judge	205
Jennings, Louis J.	161
Johnson, Samuel (Lord Flame)	250

K

Kellie, Lieut.-Colonel	88
Killick, T. W.	180
King, Colonel	85
King, A. J., M.P.	151
King's Evil and James II.	150
King's Friends Lodge	311
Knutsford	22, 127, 130
County Gaol Ordination Test School	235
Royal Visit	129

L

Laird, John	164
Latham, A. M.	166
Latham, George W.	159, 318
Legh, Colonel W. J.	164
Legh, George Cornwall	159
Legh, H. Cornwall	183, 318, 332
Legh, Henry	284
Leicester, Rev. Oswald	60
Leicester, Sir John	77
Leicester-Warren, Cuthbert	338
Leicester-Warren, Hon. J.	159
Leigh, Colonel Egerton	263, 270, 275
Leigh, Dr John	270
Leigh, Sir John	103
Leigh, Sir Joseph	161
Leverhulme, Lord	299
Lewis, Joseph	177
Leycester, Sir Peter	12, 245
Lloyd, Horatio, law student	304
Lloyd, J. H., and Stockport	164
Lloyd, Sir Horatio	304
Local Government (see Chapter XIV.)	
Lockitt, Thomas	311
Lodge of King Solomon's Temple	333
Long Parliament	197

	PAGE
Lord Delamere (Henry Booth)	149, 150
Created Earl of Warrington	219
Family life at Dunham	203
Trial at Westminster	205, 212
(See also House of Dunham, Chapter XV.)	
Lord de Tabley	203
Lord Egerton of Tatton (see Earl Egerton, also Hon. Alan Egerton, Chapters X., XXII., and XXVI.)	
Lotteries abolished	150
Loyalty Lodge, Mottram	311

M

Macclesfield—	
Borough Magistrates	362
Town Council	362
Precautions against plague	222, 225
M'Cracken, W.	181
M'Donald, Dr	167
M'Iver, D., M.P.	164
M'Laren, W. S. B., M.P.	163
Mainwaring	137, 226, 246
Malpas, plague at	223
Manchester and Liverpool Railway opened	156
Manchester Ship Canal	364
Manorial privileges—a curious " execution "	143
Man's appearance on earth	3
Man's descent	3
Mark Masonry	341
Marriages before Magistrates	53
Marshall, Colonel T. H.	85
Marsh, Chester Martyr	42
Martial Chester (see Chapters VI., VII., and VIII.)	
Martindale, Adam	51, 52, 203
Masonic pulpit, Chester Cathedral	321
Matrimonial differences at Tatton	136
Matthew, Henry	47
May Day celebrations	126
Mersey Lodge	304
Moira Lodge	311
Mond, A., M.P.	163
Moore, John, missing " dead " man	105
Morley, Alderman John	183
Morley, Lord	156

N

National debt, origin of	150
Neville, T. H.	180
Newcome, Rev. Henry	193
Newhouse, R.	326, 330

	PAGE
Newman, Cardinal	60
Nicholls, William	130
Nickson, C.	105
Nixon, Robert, Cheshire Prophet	6, 244
Norman Earls of Chester	31
North, Colonel	165
Northwich—	
Fate of, prophesied	8
Parliamentary elections	164
Salt beds	5
Subsidences at	7
Norton	105

O

	PAGE
Ogden, Samuel	250
Ormerod, George	247, 270

P

	PAGE
Paget, Bishop	66
Parish registers, curious entries	54
Parliamentarians and Royalists	192
Parliament, Cheshire's First	145
Parliament of loaves and fishes	148
Peers, Cheshire gentlemen created	156
Peers, W.	291
Phillips, Sir Owen	163
Pilgrim Fathers	49
Plague, pestilence, and famine	221
Poor Law administration	173
Poor Law, Government forecast of future development of	182
Poor Law Unions	360
Population of Cheshire	356
Potts, Eliza	40
Primitive Methodism in Cheshire	66, 67
Prince of Wales and Masonry	338
Prince of Wales, First	32
Produce and prices	27
Proverbs and sayings	259
Provincial Grand Lodge of Cheshire	289
Facsimile of minute	291
Provincial Grand Officers (1900-1919)	342-351
Prynne and his persecutors	48
Puritanical eccentricities	49
Puritanism, Church of England	44
Keynote of	45

Q

	PAGE
Quakers v. Congregationalists	57
Quarter Sessions officials	357
Quoits, game of	123

R

	PAGE
Radclyffe, Alexander	283
Raikes, H. C.	162
Railways in Cheshire	364
Randle, Holme	289
Randle Holme Lodge	296
A notable installation	299
Ratchford, J.	105
Raynor, Dr	315
Red Cross Services	100
Redford, C. F.	105
Reiss, J. E.	163
Registers, curious entries	54
Restoration, The	198
Ridley, Sir M.	164
Roberts, Mr	177
Roman invasion of Britain	11
Roman roads	18
Rostherne, church disputes	40
Rostherne Mere, legend of	9
Sprats in	9
Rowan, J.	105
Rows, Chester	17
Royal Arch Masonry	340
Royal George, Knutsford	129
Royal Masonic School for Boys	340
Royal visit to Chester	92
Rural District Council	360
Rutter, J.	105

S

	PAGE
Sandbach Crosses	235
Saxon Subjugation of England	24
Schwann, C.	164
Scolds, ducking stool for	125
Scot, Bishop	43
Scot, John, last Earl of Chester	31
Shakerley, Colonel	85
Shuttleworth, L. U.	167
Sidebotham, Tom Harrop	164
Sidebotham, W. J.	164, 183
Sidebotham, Lieut.-Colonel	85
Slack, Joseph	326
Smith, F. E. (see also Birkenhead)	254
Soulers and their songs	111
St Paul and St Patrick	33
St Werburgh and miracles	36
Stalybridge—	
Borough Magistrates	362
Corporation	363
Stamford, Earl of	105
Star Chamber Records	131

	PAGE
Stockport—	
County Borough Council	363
County Borough Magistrates	363
Members for 160, 161, 162,	222
Sunday Schools	62
Technical School	326
Stocks at Lymm, etc.	125
Stuart Kings and people	200
Amusements and costumes	201
Stubbs, Bishop	63
Subsidences at Northwich	7
Succession of Provincial Grand Masters	342
Summers, William	164
Sunday Schools	59
Surnames, old Chester	226
Sykes, Sir Alan	159

T

Tatton (Wythenshawe)	144, 229, 281
Taylor, Henry, F.S.A.	291
Thompson, Sam	335
Tim Bobbin	287
Tipping, Major William	161
Tomkinson, J.	163
Torture Chamber, Chester Castle	21
Tournaments at Gawsworth	106
Trial of Lord Delamere	295
Turf, right to cut valuable	137
Turner, G. F.	105
Tyler, an old time	294

U

Unanimity Lodge, No. 89	293
Unity Lodge, No. 361	301
Urban District Councils	360

V

Vale Royal Monks	37
Vaudrey	228

	PAGE
Venables of Kinderton	278
Verdin, Colonel	183
V.C.'s	93
Viscount Combermere 304, 308, 312, 313,	314
Volunteer movement	81

W

Wakes festivals	164
Wall, G.	183
Wallasey Borough Council	363
Masonic Hall	333
Walton, Bishop Brian	49
War, Cheshire's sacrifice	105
Warburton	159
Warburton, Squire	120
Ward, Hon. A. R.	163
Wardle, G. J.	162
Warren, Robert	284
Warrington, purchase of	191
Watkin, Sir Edward	161
Weaver Navigation Trust	181, 357
Wesley's visits	58
Westminster, Duke of	177, 178
Whitney's Emblems	46
Wilbraham, H. E.	183
Wilkinson, Lieut.-Colonel	321
Winsford, cholera at	224
Wirral Children's Hospital	321
Peninsula, Danish invasion	19
Women and Masonry	305
Worship of God in the East	4
Wythenshawe	144, 229

Y

Yarker, John	306
Yeomanry, Cheshire	75, 80
Yerburgh, R. A.	163